McCORD MIDDLE S~
1500 HARE
COLUMBUS, (

D1466450

This BOOK IS THE PROPERTY OF

McCord Middle School
1500 Hard Road
Columbus, OH 45235
Phone (614) 833-3250

Book No. **105**

Teacher

ISSUED TO	Year	Condition

Pupils to whom this book is issued must not write on any page or mark any part of it in any way, consumable textbook accepted.

1. Teachers should see that the pupil's name is clearly written in ink in the spaces above in every book issued.

2. The following terms should be used in recording the condition of the book: New, Good, Fair, Poor, Bad.

105

HOLT SCIENCE & TECHNOLOGY

Inside the Restless Earth

HOLT, RINEHART AND WINSTON

A Harcourt Education Company

Orlando • **Austin** • New York • San Diego • Toronto • London

Acknowledgments

Contributing Authors

Kathleen Meehan Berry
Science Chairman
Canon-McMillan School District
Canonsburg, Pennsylvania

Robert H. Fronk, Ph.D.
Professor
Science and Mathematics Education Department
Florida Institute of Technology
Melbourne, Florida

Peter E. Malin, Ph.D.
Professor of Geology
Division of Earth and Ocean Sciences
Duke University
Durham, North Carolina

Inclusion Specialist

Karen Clay
Inclusion Specialist Consultant
Boston, Massachusetts

Safety Reviewer

Jack Gerlovich, Ph.D.
Associate Professor
School of Education
Drake University
Des Moines, Iowa

Academic Reviewers

Roger J. Cuffey, Ph.D.
Professor of Paleontology
Department of Geosciences
Pennsylvania State University
University Park, Pennsylvania

Turgay Ertekin, Ph.D.
Professor and Chairman of Petroleum and Natural Gas Engineering
Energy and Geo-Environmental Engineering
Pennsylvania State University
University Park, Pennsylvania

Richard N. Hey, Ph.D.
Professor of Geophysics
Department of Geophysics & Planetology
University of Hawaii at Manoa
Honolulu, Hawaii

Ken Hon, Ph.D.
Associate Professor of Volcanology
Geology Department
University of Hawaii at Hilo
Hilo, Hawaii

Susan Hough, Ph.D.
Scientist
United States Geological Survey (USGS)
Pasadena, California

Joel S. Leventhal, Ph.D.
Emeritus Scientist
U.S. Geological Survey
Lakewood, Colorado

Kenneth K. Peace
Manager of Transportation
WestArch Coal, Inc.
St. Louis, Missouri

Kenneth H. Rubin, Ph.D.
Associate Professor
Department of Geology & Geophysics
University of Hawaii at Manoa
Honolulu, Hawaii

Colin D. Sumrall, Ph.D.
Lecturer of Paleontology
Earth and Planetary Sciences
The University of Tennessee
Knoxville, Tennessee

Peter W. Weigand, Ph.D.
Professor Emeritus
Department of Geological Sciences
California State University
Northridge, California

Teacher Reviewers

Diedre S. Adams
Physical Science Instructor
Science Department
West Vigo Middle School
West Terre Haute, Indiana

Laura Buchanan
Science Teacher and Department Chairperson
Corkran Middle School
Glen Burnie, Maryland

Robin K. Clanton
Science Department Head
Berrien Middle School
Nashville, Georgia

Meredith Hanson
Science Teacher
Westside Middle School
Rocky Face, Georgia

James Kerr
Oklahoma Teacher of the Year 2002–2003
Oklahoma State Department of Education
Union Public Schools
Tulsa, Oklahoma

Laura Kitselman
Science Teacher and Coordinator
Loudoun Country Day School
Leesburg, Virginia

Copyright © 2005 by Holt, Rinehart and Winston

All rights reserved. No part of this publication may be reproduced or transmitted in any form or by any means, electronic or mechanical, including photocopy, recording, or any information storage and retrieval system, without permission in writing from the publisher.

Requests for permission to make copies of any part of the work should be mailed to the following address: Permissions Department, Holt, Rinehart and Winston, 10801 N. MoPac Expressway, Building 3, Austin, Texas 78759.

SciLINKS is a registered trademark owned and provided by the National Science Teachers Association. All rights reserved.

CNN is a registered trademark and **CNN STUDENT NEWS** is a trademark of Cable News Network LP, LLLP, an AOL Time Warner Company.

Current Science is a registered trademark of Weekly Reader Corporation.

Printed in the United States of America

ISBN 0-03-025542-2

2 3 4 5 6 7 048 08 07 06 05 04

Deborah L. Kronsteiner
Teacher
Science Department
Spring Grove Area Middle
School
Spring Grove, Pennsylvania

Jennifer L. Lamkie
Science Teacher
Thomas Jefferson Middle
School
Edison, New Jersey

Susan H. Robinson
Science Teacher
Oglethorpe County Middle
School
Lexington, Georgia

Marci L. Stadiem
Department Head
Science Department
Cascade Middle School,
Highline School District
Seattle, Washington

Lab Development

Kenneth E. Creese
Science Teacher
White Mountain Junior
High School
Rock Spring, Wyoming

Linda A. Culp
*Science Teacher and
Department Chair*
Thorndale High School
Thorndale, Texas

Bruce M. Jones
*Science Teacher and
Department Chair*
The Blake School
Minneapolis, Minnesota

Shannon Miller
Science and Math Teacher
Llano Junior High School
Llano, Texas

Robert Stephen Ricks
Special Services Teacher
Department of Classroom
Improvement
Alabama State Department
of Education
Montgomery, Alabama

James J. Secosky
Science Teacher
Bloomfield Central School
Bloomfield, New York

Lab Testing

Daniel Bugenhagen
*Science Teacher and
Department Chair*
Yutan Jr.–Sr. high
Yutan, Nebraska

C. John Graves
Science Teacher
Monforton Middle School
Bozeman, Montana

Janel Guse
*Science Teacher and
Department Chair*
West Central Middle School
Hartford, South Dakota

Norman Holcomb
Science Teacher
Marion Local Schools
Maria Stein, Ohio

David Jones
Science Teacher
Andrew Jackson Middle
School
Cross Lanes, West Virginia

Dwight Patton
Science Teacher
Carrol T. Welch Middle
School
Horizon City, Texas

Terry J. Rakes
Science Teacher
Elmwood Junior High
Rogers, Arkansas

Helen Schiller
Science Teacher
Northwood Middle School
Taylors, South Carolina

Gordon Zibelman
Science Teacher
Drexel Hill Middle School
Drexel Hill, Pennsylvania

Answer Checking

Catherine Podeszwa
Duluth, Minnesota

Feature Development

Katy Z. Allen
Hatim Belyamani
John A. Benner
David Bradford
Jennifer Childers
Mickey Coakley
Susan Feldkamp
Jane Gardner
Erik Hahn
Christopher Hess
Deena Kalai
Charlotte W. Luongo, MSc
Michael May
Persis Mehta, Ph.D.
Eileen Nehme, MPH
Catherine Podeszwa
Dennis Rathnaw
Daniel B. Sharp
John Stokes
April Smith West
Molly F. Wetterschneider

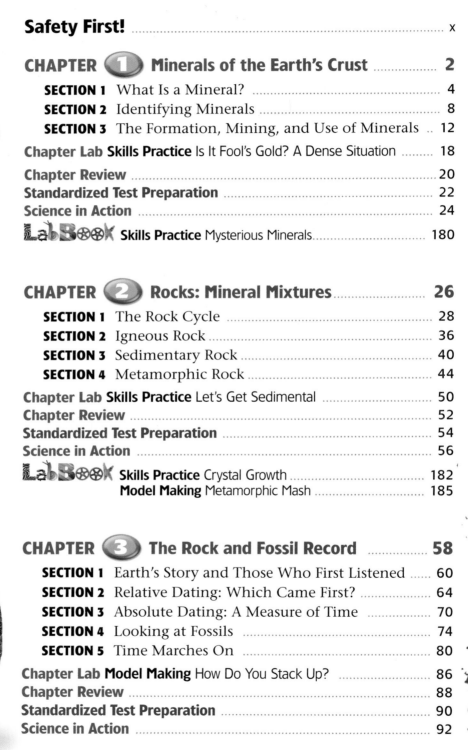

F Inside the Restless Earth

Labs and Activities

How to Use Your Textbook

Your Roadmap for Success with Holt Science and Technology

Reading Warm-Up

A Reading Warm-Up at the beginning of every section provides you with the section's objectives and key terms. The objectives tell you what you'll need to know after you finish reading the section.

Key terms are listed for each section. Learn the definitions of these terms because you will most likely be tested on them. Each key term is highlighted in the text and is defined at point of use and in the margin. You can also use the glossary to locate definitions quickly.

STUDY TIP Reread the objectives and the definitions to the key terms when studying for a test to be sure you know the material.

Get Organized

A Reading Strategy at the beginning of every section provides tips to help you organize and remember the information covered in the section. Keep a science notebook so that you are ready to take notes when your teacher reviews the material in class. Keep your assignments in this notebook so that you can review them when studying for the chapter test.

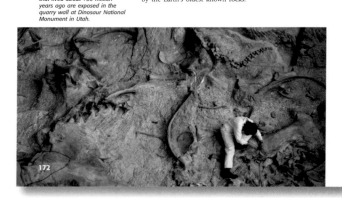

SECTION 5

Time Marches On

How old is the Earth? Well, if the Earth celebrated its birthday every million years, there would be 4,600 candles on its birthday cake! Humans have been around only long enough to light the last candle on the cake.

Try to think of the Earth's history in "fast-forward." If you could watch the Earth change from this perspective, you would see mountains rise up like wrinkles in fabric and quickly wear away. You would see life-forms appear and then go extinct. In this section, you will learn that geologists must "fast-forward" the Earth's history when they write or talk about it. You will also learn about some incredible events in the history of life on Earth.

Geologic Time

Shown in **Figure 1** is the rock wall at the Dinosaur Quarry Visitor Center in Dinosaur National Monument, Utah. Contained within this wall are approximately 1,500 fossil bones that have been excavated by paleontologists. These are the remains of dinosaurs that inhabited the area about 150 million years ago. Granted, 150 million years seems to be an incredibly long period of time. However, in terms of the Earth's history, 150 million years is little more than 3% of the time our planet has existed. It is a little less than 4% of the time represented by the Earth's oldest known rocks.

READING WARM-UP

Objectives
- Explain how geologic time is recorded in rock layers.
- Identify important dates on the geologic time scale.
- Explain how environmental changes resulted in the extinction of some species.

Terms to Learn
geologic time scale period
eon epoch
era extinction

READING STRATEGY

Brainstorming The key idea of this section is the geologic time scale. Brainstorm words and phrases related to the geologic time scale.

Figure 1 *Bones of dinosaurs that lived about 150 million years ago are exposed in the quarry wall at Dinosaur National Monument in Utah.*

Be Resourceful—Use the Web

Internet Connect boxes in your textbook take you to resources that you can use for science projects, reports, and research papers. Go to scilinks.org, and type in the SciLinks code to get information on a topic.

Visit go.hrw.com Find worksheets, **Current Science**® magazine articles online, and other materials that go with your textbook at **go.hrw.com**. Click on the textbook icon and the table of contents to see all of the resources for each chapter.

Figure 2 Well-preserved plant and animal fossils are common in the Green River formation. Clockwise from the upper right are a fossil leaf, a dragonfly, a fish, and a turtle.

The Rock Record and Geologic Time

One of the best places in North America to see the Earth's history recorded in rock layers is in Grand Canyon National Park. The Colorado River has cut the canyon nearly 2 km deep in some places. Over the course of 6 million years, the river has eroded countless layers of rock. These layers represent almost half, or nearly 2 billion years, of Earth's history.

Reading Check How much geologic time is represented by the rock layers in *Reading Checks*

The Fossil

Figure 2 shov formation. T Utah, and C were once p period of m common in the fine-grai delicate stru

The Cenozoic Era—The Age of Mammals

The Cenozoic era, as shown in **Figure 7**, began about 65 million years ago and continues to the present. This era is known as the *Age of Mammals.* During the Mesozoic era, mammals had to compete with dinosaurs and other animals for food and habitat. After the mass extinction at the end of the Mesozoic era, mammals flourished. Unique traits, such as regulating body temperature internally and bearing young that develop inside the mother, may have helped mammals survive the environmental changes that probably caused the extinction of the dinosaurs.

INTERNET ACTIVITY

Figure 7 Thousands of species of mammals evolved during the Cenozoic era. This scene shows species from the early Cenozoic era that are now extinct.

SECTION Review

Summary

- The geologic time scale divides Earth's 4.6 billion–year history into distinct intervals of time. Divisions of geologic time include eons, eras, periods, and epochs.
- The boundaries between geologic time intervals represent visible changes that have taken place on Earth.
- The rock and fossil record represents mainly the Phanerozoic eon, which is the eon in which we live.
- At certain times in Earth's history, the number of life-forms has increased or decreased dramatically.

Using Key Terms

1. Use each of the following terms in the same sentence: *era, period,* and *epoch.*

Understanding Key Ideas

2. The unit of geologic time that began 65 million years ago and continues to the present is the
   a. Holocene epoch.
   b. Cenozoic era.
   c. Phanerozoic eon.
   d. Quaternary period.

3. What are the major time intervals represented by the geologic time scale?

4. Explain how geologic time is recorded in rock layers.

5. What kinds of environmental changes cause mass extinctions?

Critical Thinking

6. **Making Inferences** What future event might mark the end of the Cenozoic era?

7. **Identifying Relationships** How might a decrease in competition between species lead to the sudden appearance of many new species?

Interpreting Graphics

8. Look at the illustration below. On the Earth-history clock shown, 1 h equals 383 million years, and 1 min equals 6.4 million years. In millions of years, how much more time is represented by the Proterozoic eon than by the Phanerozoic eon?

Phanerozoic eon   Hadean eon

Proterozoic eon   Archean eon

SCLINKS.

NSTA
Developed and maintained by the National Science Teachers Association

For a variety of links related to this chapter, go to www.scilinks.org
Topic: Geologic Time
SciLinks code: HSM0668

177

Use the Illustrations and Photos

Art shows complex ideas and processes. Learn to analyze the art so that you better understand the material you read in the text.

Tables and graphs display important information in an organized way to help you see relationships.

A picture is worth a thousand words. Look at the photographs to see relevant examples of science concepts that you are reading about.

Answer the Section Reviews

Section Reviews test your knowledge of the main points of the section. Critical Thinking items challenge you to think about the material in greater depth and to find connections that you infer from the text.

STUDY TIP When you can't answer a question, reread the section. The answer is usually there.

Do Your Homework

Your teacher may assign worksheets to help you understand and remember the material in the chapter.

STUDY TIP Don't try to answer the questions without reading the text and reviewing your class notes. A little preparation up front will make your homework assignments a lot easier. Answering the items in the Chapter Review will help prepare you for the chapter test.

Holt Online Learning

Visit Holt Online Learning
If your teacher gives you a special password to log onto the Holt Online Learning site, you'll find your complete textbook on the Web. In addition, you'll find some great learning tools and practice quizzes. You'll be able to see how well you know the material from your textbook.

CNN Student News™

Visit CNN Student News
You'll find up-to-date events in science at cnnstudentnews.com.

SAFETY FIRST!

Exploring, inventing, and investigating are essential to the study of science. However, these activities can also be dangerous. To make sure that your experiments and explorations are safe, you must be aware of a variety of safety guidelines. You have probably heard of the saying, "It is better to be safe than sorry." This is particularly true in a science classroom where experiments and explorations are being performed. Being uninformed and careless can result in serious injuries. Don't take chances with your own safety or with anyone else's.

The following pages describe important guidelines for staying safe in the science classroom. Your teacher may also have safety guidelines and tips that are specific to your classroom and laboratory. Take the time to be safe.

Safety Rules!

Start Out Right

Always get your teacher's permission before attempting any laboratory exploration. Read the procedures carefully, and pay particular attention to safety information and caution statements. If you are unsure about what a safety symbol means, look it up or ask your teacher. You cannot be too careful when it comes to safety. If an accident does occur, inform your teacher immediately regardless of how minor you think the accident is.

If you are instructed to note the odor of a substance, wave the fumes toward your nose with your hand. Never put your nose close to the source.

Safety Symbols

All of the experiments and investigations in this book and their related worksheets include important safety symbols to alert you to particular safety concerns. Become familiar with these symbols so that when you see them, you will know what they mean and what to do. It is important that you read this entire safety section to learn about specific dangers in the laboratory.

Eye protection

Clothing protection

Hand safety

Heating safety

Electric safety

Chemical safety

Animal safety

Sharp object

Plant safety

x

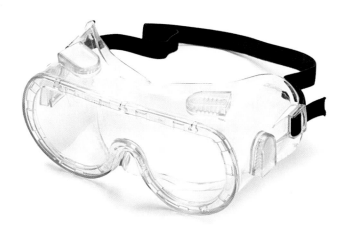

Eye Safety

Wear safety goggles when working around chemicals, acids, bases, or any type of flame or heating device. Wear safety goggles any time there is even the slightest chance that harm could come to your eyes. If any substance gets into your eyes, notify your teacher immediately and flush your eyes with running water for at least 15 minutes. Treat any unknown chemical as if it were a dangerous chemical. Never look directly into the sun. Doing so could cause permanent blindness.

Avoid wearing contact lenses in a laboratory situation. Even if you are wearing safety goggles, chemicals can get between the contact lenses and your eyes. If your doctor requires that you wear contact lenses instead of glasses, wear eye-cup safety goggles in the lab.

Safety Equipment

Know the locations of the nearest fire alarms and any other safety equipment, such as fire blankets and eyewash fountains, as identified by your teacher, and know the procedures for using the equipment.

Neatness

Keep your work area free of all unnecessary books and papers. Tie back long hair, and secure loose sleeves or other loose articles of clothing, such as ties and bows. Remove dangling jewelry. Don't wear open-toed shoes or sandals in the laboratory. Never eat, drink, or apply cosmetics in a laboratory setting. Food, drink, and cosmetics can easily become contaminated with dangerous materials.

Certain hair products (such as aerosol hair spray) are flammable and should not be worn while working near an open flame. Avoid wearing hair spray or hair gel on lab days.

Sharp/Pointed Objects

Use knives and other sharp instruments with extreme care. Never cut objects while holding them in your hands. Place objects on a suitable work surface for cutting.

Be extra careful when using any glassware. When adding a heavy object to a graduated cylinder, tilt the cylinder so that the object slides slowly to the bottom.

Heat

Wear safety goggles when using a heating device or a flame. Whenever possible, use an electric hot plate as a heat source instead of using an open flame. When heating materials in a test tube, always angle the test tube away from yourself and others. To avoid burns, wear heat-resistant gloves whenever instructed to do so.

Electricity

Be careful with electrical cords. When using a microscope with a lamp, do not place the cord where it could trip someone. Do not let cords hang over a table edge in a way that could cause equipment to fall if the cord is accidentally pulled. Do not use equipment with damaged cords. Be sure that your hands are dry and that the electrical equipment is in the "off" position before plugging it in. Turn off and unplug electrical equipment when you are finished.

Chemicals

Wear safety goggles when handling any potentially dangerous chemicals, acids, or bases. If a chemical is unknown, handle it as you would a dangerous chemical. Wear an apron and protective gloves when you work with acids or bases or whenever you are told to do so. If a spill gets on your skin or clothing, rinse it off immediately with water for at least 5 minutes while calling to your teacher.

Never mix chemicals unless your teacher tells you to do so. Never taste, touch, or smell chemicals unless you are specifically directed to do so. Before working with a flammable liquid or gas, check for the presence of any source of flame, spark, or heat.

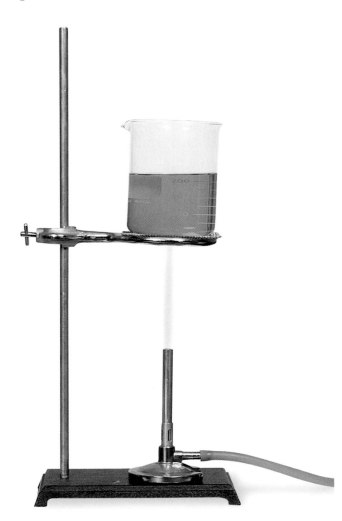

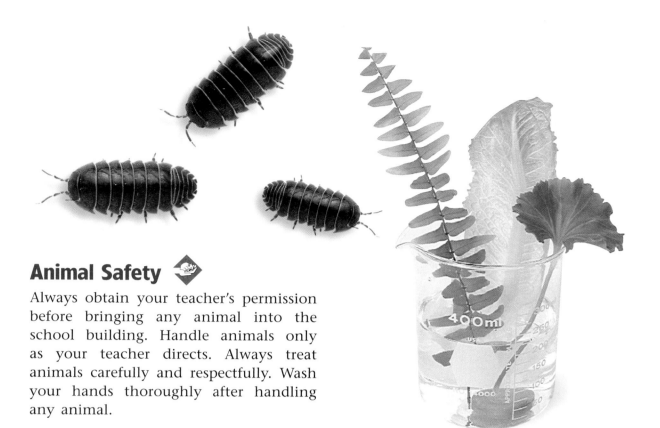

Animal Safety

Always obtain your teacher's permission before bringing any animal into the school building. Handle animals only as your teacher directs. Always treat animals carefully and respectfully. Wash your hands thoroughly after handling any animal.

Plant Safety

Do not eat any part of a plant or plant seed used in the laboratory. Wash your hands thoroughly after handling any part of a plant. When in nature, do not pick any wild plants unless your teacher instructs you to do so.

Glassware

Examine all glassware before use. Be sure that glassware is clean and free of chips and cracks. Report damaged glassware to your teacher. Glass containers used for heating should be made of heat-resistant glass.

Minerals of the Earth's Crust

About the PHOTO

Fluorescence is the ability that some minerals have to glow under ultraviolet light. The beauty of mineral fluorescence is well represented at the Sterling Hill Mine in Franklin, New Jersey. In this picture taken at the mine, minerals in the rock glow as brightly as if they had been freshly painted by an artist.

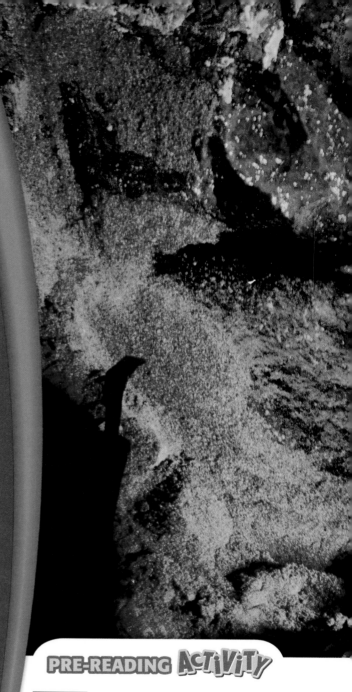

PRE-READING ACTIVITY

Graphic Organizer

Concept Map Before you read the chapter, create the graphic organizer entitled "Concept Map" described in the **Study Skills** section of the Appendix. As you read the chapter, fill in the concept map with details about minerals.

START-UP ACTIVITY

What Is Your Classroom Made Of?

One of the properties of minerals is that minerals are made from nonliving material. Complete the following activity to see if you can determine whether items in your classroom are made from living or nonliving materials.

Procedure

1. On a **sheet of paper,** make two columns. Label one column "Materials made from living things." Label the second column "Materials made from nonliving things."

2. Look around your classroom. Choose a variety of items to put on your list. Some items that you might select are your clothing, your desk, books, notebook paper, pencils, the classroom windows, doors, walls, the ceiling, and the floor.

3. With a partner, discuss each item that you have chosen. Decide into which column each item should be placed. Write down the reason for your decision.

Analysis

1. Are most of the items that you chose made of living or nonliving materials?

What Is a Mineral?

You may think that all minerals look like gems. But, in fact, most minerals look more like rocks. Does this mean that minerals are the same as rocks? Well, not really. So, what's the difference?

For one thing, rocks are made of minerals, but minerals are not made of rocks. A **mineral** is a naturally formed, inorganic solid that has a definite crystalline structure.

Mineral Structure

By answering the four questions in **Figure 1,** you can tell whether an object is a mineral. If you cannot answer "yes" to all four questions, you don't have a mineral. Three of the four questions may be easy to answer. The question about crystalline structure may be more difficult. To understand what crystalline structure is, you need to know a little about the elements that make up a mineral. **Elements** are pure substances that cannot be broken down into simpler substances by ordinary chemical means. All minerals contain one or more of the 92 naturally occurring elements.

READING WARM-UP

Objectives
- Describe the structure of minerals.
- Describe the two major groups of minerals.

Terms to Learn

mineral
element
compound
crystal
silicate mineral
nonsilicate mineral

READING STRATEGY

Paired Summarizing Read this section silently. In pairs, take turns summarizing the material. Stop to discuss ideas that seem confusing.

Is it nonliving material?
A mineral is inorganic, meaning it isn't made of living things.

Is it a solid?
Minerals can't be gases or liquids.

Does it have a crystalline structure?
Minerals are crystals, which have a repeating inner structure that is often reflected in the shape of the crystal. Minerals generally have the same chemical composition throughout.

Is it formed in nature?
Crystalline materials made by people aren't classified as minerals.

Figure 1 *The answers to these four questions will determine whether an object is a mineral.*

Atoms and Compounds

Each element is made of only one kind of atom. An *atom* is the smallest part of an element that has all the properties of that element. Like other substances, minerals are made up of atoms of one or more elements.

Most minerals are made of compounds of several different elements. A **compound** is a substance made of two or more elements that have been chemically joined, or bonded. Halite, NaCl, for example, is a compound of sodium, Na, and chlorine, Cl, as shown in **Figure 2.** A few minerals, such as gold and silver, are composed of only one element. A mineral that is composed of only one element is called a *native element.*

✔ **Reading Check** How does a compound differ from an element? (*See the Appendix for answers to Reading Checks.*)

Crystals

Solid, geometric forms of minerals produced by a repeating pattern of atoms that is present throughout the mineral are called **crystals.** A crystal's shape is determined by the arrangement of the atoms within the crystal. The arrangement of atoms in turn is determined by the kinds of atoms that make up the mineral. Each mineral has a definite crystalline structure. All minerals can be grouped into crystal classes according to the kinds of crystals they form. **Figure 3** shows how the atomic structure of gold gives rise to cubic crystals.

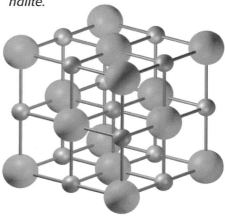

Figure 2 *When atoms of sodium (purple) and chlorine (green) join, they form a compound commonly known as rock salt, or the mineral halite.*

mineral a naturally formed, inorganic solid that has a definite crystalline structure

element a substance that cannot be separated or broken down into simpler substances by chemical means

compound a substance made up of atoms of two or more different elements joined by chemical bonds

crystal a solid whose atoms, ions, or molecules are arranged in a definite pattern

---

Figure 3 | **Composition of the Mineral Gold**

The mineral gold is composed of gold atoms arranged in a crystalline structure.

The atomic structure of gold

The crystal structure of gold

Crystals of the mineral gold

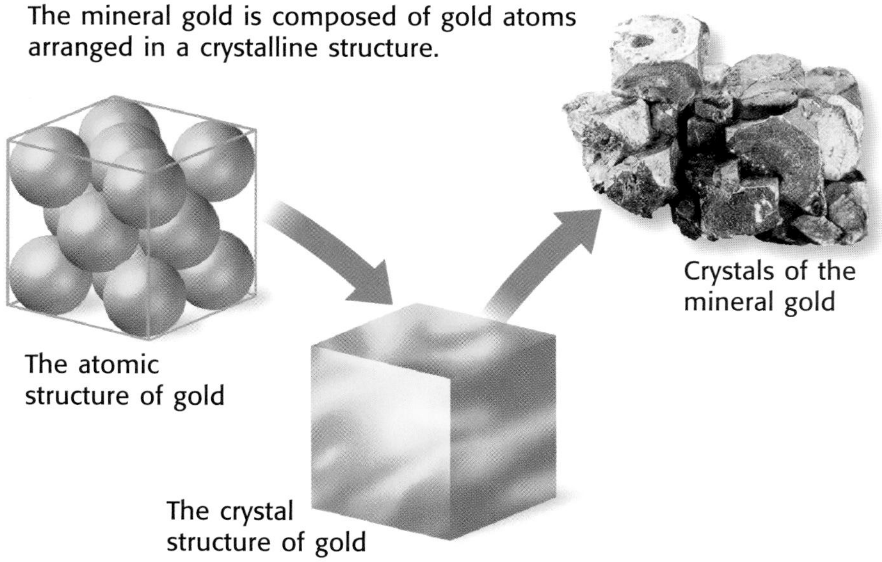

Two Groups of Minerals

The most common classification of minerals is based on chemical composition. Minerals are divided into two groups based on their chemical composition. These groups are the silicate minerals and the nonsilicate minerals.

Silicate Minerals

Silicon and oxygen are the two most common elements in the Earth's crust. Minerals that contain a combination of these two elements are called **silicate minerals.** Silicate minerals make up more than 90% of the Earth's crust. The rest of the Earth's crust is made up of nonsilicate minerals. Silicon and oxygen usually combine with other elements, such as aluminum, iron, magnesium, and potassium, to make up silicate minerals. Some of the more common silicate minerals are shown in **Figure 4.**

Nonsilicate Minerals

Minerals that do not contain a combination of the elements silicon and oxygen form a group called the **nonsilicate minerals.** Some of these minerals are made up of elements such as carbon, oxygen, fluorine, and sulfur. **Figure 5** on the following page shows the most important classes of nonsilicate minerals.

✓ **Reading Check** How do silicate minerals differ from nonsilicate minerals?

CONNECTION TO Biology

WRITING SKILL **Magnetite** The mineral magnetite has a special property—it is magnetic. Scientists have found that some animals' brains contain magnetite. And scientists have shown that certain fish can sense magnetic fields because of the magnetite in the brains of these fish. The magnetite gives the fish a sense of direction. Using the Internet or another source, research other animals that have magnetite in their brains. Summarize your findings in a short essay.

silicate mineral a mineral that contains a combination of silicon, oxygen, and one or more metals

nonsilicate mineral a mineral that does not contain compounds of silicon and oxygen

Figure 4 **Common Silicate Minerals**

Quartz is the basic building block of many rocks.

Feldspar minerals are the main component of most rocks on the Earth's surface.

Mica minerals separate easily into sheets when they break. Biotite is one of several kinds of mica.

Figure 5   Classes of Nonsilicate Minerals

Native elements are minerals that are composed of only one element. Some examples are copper, Cu, gold, Au, and silver, Ag. Native elements are used in communications and electronics equipment.

Copper

Oxides are compounds that form when an element, such as aluminum or iron, combines chemically with oxygen. Oxide minerals are used to make abrasives, aircraft parts, and paint.

Corundum

Carbonates are minerals that contain combinations of carbon and oxygen in their chemical structure. We use carbonate minerals in cement, building stones, and fireworks.

Calcite

Sulfates are minerals that contain sulfur and oxygen, SO_4. Sulfates are used in cosmetics, toothpaste, cement, and paint.

Gypsum

Halides are compounds that form when fluorine, chlorine, iodine, or bromine combine with sodium, potassium, or calcium. Halide minerals are used in the chemical industry and in detergents.

Fluorite

Sulfides are minerals that contain one or more elements, such as lead, iron, or nickel, combined with sulfur. Sulfide minerals are used to make batteries, medicines, and electronic parts.

Galena

SECTION Review

Summary

- A mineral is a naturally formed, inorganic solid that has a definite crystalline structure.
- Minerals may be either elements or compounds.
- Mineral crystals are solid, geometric forms that are produced by a repeating pattern of atoms.
- Minerals are classified as either silicate minerals or nonsilicate minerals based on the elements of which they are composed.

Using Key Terms

1. In your own words, write a definition for each of the following terms: *element*, *compound*, and *mineral*.

Understanding Key Ideas

2. Which of the following minerals is a nonsilicate mineral?
   a. mica
   b. quartz
   c. gypsum
   d. feldspar

3. What is a crystal, and what determines a crystal's shape?

4. Describe the two major groups of minerals.

Math Skills

5. If there are approximately 3,600 known minerals and about 20 of the minerals are native elements, what percentage of all minerals are native elements?

Critical Thinking

6. **Applying Concepts** Explain why each of the following is not considered a mineral: water, oxygen, honey, and teeth.

7. **Applying Concepts** Explain why scientists consider ice to be a mineral.

8. **Making Comparisons** In what ways are sulfate and sulfide minerals the same. In what ways are they different?

SCiLINKS®

NSTA
Developed and maintained by the National Science Teachers Association

For a variety of links related to this chapter, go to www.scilinks.org

Topic: Gems
SciLinks code: HSM0640

Identifying Minerals

If you closed your eyes and tasted different foods, you could probably determine what the foods are by noting properties such as saltiness or sweetness. You can also determine the identity of a mineral by noting different properties.

In this section, you will learn about the properties that will help you identify minerals.

Color

The same mineral can come in a variety of colors. For example, in its purest state quartz is clear. Samples of quartz that contain various types of and various amounts of impurities, however, can be a variety of colors.

Besides impurities, other factors can change the appearance of minerals. The mineral pyrite, often called fool's gold, normally has a golden color. But if pyrite is exposed to air and water for a long period, it can turn brown or black. Because of factors such as impurities, color usually is not the best way to identify a mineral.

Luster

The way a surface reflects light is called **luster.** When you say an object is shiny or dull, you are describing its luster. Minerals have metallic, submetallic, or nonmetallic luster. If a mineral is shiny, it has a metallic luster. If the mineral is dull, its luster is either submetallic or nonmetallic. The different types of lusters are shown in **Figure 1.**

READING WARM-UP

Objectives

- Identify seven ways to determine the identity of minerals.
- Explain special properties of minerals.

Terms to Learn

luster   fracture
streak   hardness
cleavage   density

READING STRATEGY

Reading Organizer As you read this section, create an outline of the section. Use the headings from the section in your outline.

luster the way in which a mineral reflects light

Figure 1   Types of Mineral Luster

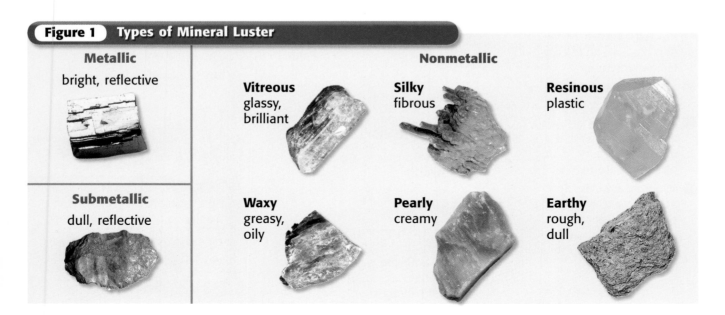

Metallic
bright, reflective

Submetallic
dull, reflective

Nonmetallic

Vitreous
glassy,
brilliant

Waxy
greasy,
oily

Silky
fibrous

Pearly
creamy

Resinous
plastic

Earthy
rough,
dull

Streak

The color of a mineral in powdered form is called the mineral's **streak.** A mineral's streak can be found by rubbing the mineral against a piece of unglazed porcelain called a *streak plate.* The mark left on the streak plate is the streak. The streak is a thin layer of powdered mineral. The color of a mineral's streak is not always the same as the color of the mineral sample. The difference between color and streak is shown in **Figure 2.** Unlike the surface of a mineral sample, the streak is not affected by air or water. For this reason, using streak is more reliable than using color in identifying a mineral.

✔ **Reading Check** Why is using streak more reliable in identifying a mineral than using color is? (*See the Appendix for answers to Reading Checks.*)

Figure 2 *The color of the mineral hematite may vary, but hematite's streak is always red-brown.*

Cleavage and Fracture

Different types of minerals break in different ways. The way a mineral breaks is determined by the arrangement of its atoms. **Cleavage** is the tendency of some minerals to break along smooth, flat surfaces. **Figure 3** shows the cleavage patterns of the minerals mica and halite.

Fracture is the tendency of some minerals to break unevenly along curved or irregular surfaces. One type of fracture is shown in **Figure 4.**

streak the color of the powder of a mineral

cleavage the splitting of a mineral along smooth, flat surfaces

fracture the manner in which a mineral breaks along either curved or irregular surfaces

Figure 3 *Cleavage varies with mineral type.*

Mica breaks easily ▶ into distinct sheets.

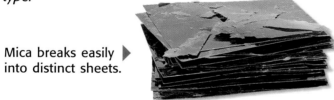

Halite breaks at 90° angles in three directions. ▼

Figure 4 *This sample of quartz shows a curved fracture pattern called* conchoidal fracture *(kahn KOYD uhl FRAK chuhr).*

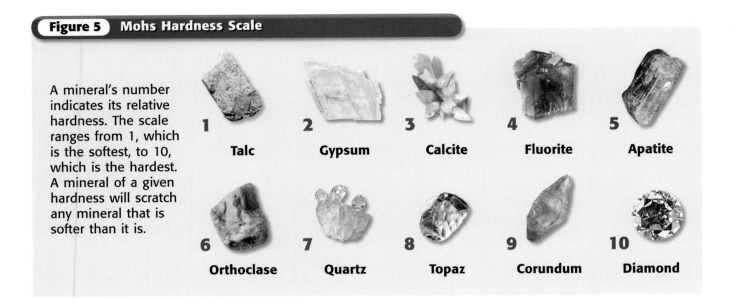

Figure 5 Mohs Hardness Scale

A mineral's number indicates its relative hardness. The scale ranges from 1, which is the softest, to 10, which is the hardest. A mineral of a given hardness will scratch any mineral that is softer than it is.

1 Talc
2 Gypsum
3 Calcite
4 Fluorite
5 Apatite
6 Orthoclase
7 Quartz
8 Topaz
9 Corundum
10 Diamond

hardness a measure of the ability of a mineral to resist scratching

density the ratio of the mass of a substance to the volume of the substance

Hardness

A mineral's resistance to being scratched is called **hardness**. To determine the hardness of minerals, scientists use *Mohs hardness scale,* shown in **Figure 5.** Notice that talc has a rating of 1 and diamond has a rating of 10. The greater a mineral's resistance to being scratched is, the higher the mineral's rating is. To identify a mineral by using Mohs scale, try to scratch the surface of a mineral with the edge of one of the 10 reference minerals. If the reference mineral scratches your mineral, the reference mineral is harder than your mineral.

✓ Reading Check How would you determine the hardness of an unidentified mineral sample?

Density

If you pick up a golf ball and a table-tennis ball, which will feel heavier? Although the balls are of similar size, the golf ball will feel heavier because it is denser. **Density** is the measure of how much matter is in a given amount of space. In other words, density is a ratio of an object's mass to its volume. Density is usually measured in grams per cubic centimeter. Because water has a density of 1 g/cm^3, it is used as a reference point for other substances. The ratio of an object's density to the density of water is called the object's *specific gravity.* The specific gravity of gold, for example, is 19. So, gold has a density of 19 g/cm^3. In other words, there is 19 times more matter in 1 cm^3 of gold than in 1 cm^3 of water.

Scratch Test

1. You will need a **penny,** a **pencil,** and your **fingernail.** Which one of these three materials is the hardest?

2. Use your fingernail to try to scratch the graphite at the tip of a pencil.

3. Now try to scratch the penny with your fingernail.

4. Rank the three materials in order from softest to hardest.

Special Properties

Some properties are particular to only a few types of minerals. The properties shown in **Figure 6** can help you quickly identify the minerals shown. To identify some properties, however, you will need specialized equipment.

Figure 6 **Special Properties of Some Minerals**

Fluorescence
Calcite and fluorite glow under ultraviolet light. The same fluorite sample is shown in ultraviolet light (top) and in white light (bottom).

Chemical Reaction
Calcite will become bubbly, or "fizz," when a drop of weak acid is placed on it.

Optical Properties
A thin, clear piece of calcite placed over an image will cause a double image.

Magnetism
Both magnetite and pyrrhotite are natural magnets that attract iron.

Taste
Halite has a salty taste.

Radioactivity
Minerals that contain radium or uranium can be detected by a Geiger counter.

SECTION Review

Summary

- Properties that can be used to identify minerals are color, luster, streak, cleavage, fracture, hardness, and density.
- Some minerals can be identified by special properties they have, such as taste, magnetism, fluorescence, radioactivity, chemical reaction, and optical properties.

Using Key Terms

1. Use each of the following terms in a separate sentence: *luster, streak,* and *cleavage.*

Understanding Key Ideas

2. Which of the following properties of minerals is expressed in numbers?
   a. fracture
   b. cleavage
   c. hardness
   d. streak

3. How do you determine a mineral's streak?

4. Briefly describe the special properties of minerals.

Math Skills

5. If a mineral has a specific gravity of 5.5, how much more matter is there in 1 cm^3 of this mineral than in 1 cm^3 of water?

Critical Thinking

6. **Applying Concepts** What properties would you use to determine whether two mineral samples are different minerals?

7. **Applying Concepts** If a mineral scratches calcite but is scratched by apatite, what is the mineral's hardness?

8. **Analyzing Methods** What would be the easiest way to identify calcite?

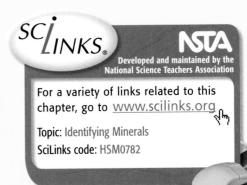

Developed and maintained by the National Science Teachers Association

For a variety of links related to this chapter, go to www.scilinks.org

Topic: Identifying Minerals
SciLinks code: HSM0782

The Formation, Mining, and Use of Minerals

If you wanted to find a mineral, where do you think you would look?

Minerals form in a variety of environments in the Earth's crust. Each of these environments has a different set of physical and chemical conditions. Therefore, the environment in which a mineral forms determines the mineral's properties. Environments in which minerals form may be on or near the Earth's surface or deep beneath the Earth's surface.

READING WARM-UP

Objectives

● Describe the environments in which minerals form.

● Compare the two types of mining.

● Describe two ways to reduce the effects of mining.

● Describe different uses for metallic and nonmetallic minerals.

Terms to Learn

ore
reclamation

READING STRATEGY

Discussion Read this section silently. Write down questions that you have about this section. Discuss your questions in a small group.

Limestones Surface water and groundwater carry dissolved materials into lakes and seas, where they crystallize on the bottom. Minerals that form in this environment include calcite and dolomite.

Evaporating Salt Water When a body of salt water dries up, minerals such as gypsum and halite are left behind. As the salt water evaporates, these minerals crystallize.

Metamorphic Rocks When changes in pressure, temperature, or chemical makeup alter a rock, *metamorphism* takes place. Minerals that form in metamorphic rock include calcite, garnet, graphite, hematite, magnetite, mica, and talc.

INTERNET ACTIVITY

For another activity related to this chapter, go to go.hrw.com and type in the keyword **HZ5MINW**.

Hot-Water Solutions

Groundwater works its way downward and is heated by magma. It then reacts with minerals to form a hot liquid solution. Dissolved metals and other elements crystallize out of the hot fluid to form new minerals. Gold, copper, sulfur, pyrite, and galena form in such hot-water environments.

Pegmatites As magma moves upward, it can form teardrop-shaped bodies called *pegmatites*. The mineral crystals in pegmatites become extremely large, sometimes growing to several meters across! Many gemstones, such as topaz and tourmaline, form in pegmatites.

Plutons As magma rises upward through the crust, it sometimes stops moving before it reaches the surface and cools slowly, forming millions of mineral crystals. Eventually, the entire magma body solidifies to form a *pluton*. Mica, feldspar, magnetite, and quartz are some of the minerals that form from magma.

Surface Coal Mining

Producing 1 metric ton of coal requires that up to 30 metric tons of earth be removed first. Some surface coal mines produce up to 50,000 metric tons of coal per day. How many metric tons of earth might have to be removed in order to mine 50,000 metric tons of coal?

ore a natural material whose concentration of economically valuable minerals is high enough for the material to be mined profitably

Mining

Many kinds of rocks and minerals must be mined to extract the valuable elements they contain. Geologists use the term **ore** to describe a mineral deposit large enough and pure enough to be mined for profit. Rocks and minerals are removed from the ground by one of two methods—surface mining or subsurface mining. The method miners choose depends on how close to the surface or how far down in the Earth the mineral is located.

Surface Mining

When mineral deposits are located at or near the surface of the Earth, surface-mining methods are used to remove the minerals. Types of surface mines include open pits, surface coal mines, and quarries.

Open-pit mining is used to remove large, near-surface deposits of economically important minerals such as gold and copper. As shown in **Figure 1,** ore is mined downward, layer by layer, in an open-pit mine. Explosives are often used to break up the ore. The ore is then loaded into haul trucks and transported from the mine for processing. Quarries are open pits that are used to mine building stone, crushed rock, sand, and gravel. Coal that is near the surface is removed by surface coal mining. Surface coal mining is sometimes known as strip mining because the coal is removed in strips that may be as wide as 50 m and as long as 1 km.

Figure 1 *In open-pit mines, the ore is mined downward in layers. The stair-step excavation of the walls keeps the sides of the mine from collapsing. Giant haul trucks (inset) are used to transport ore from the mine.*

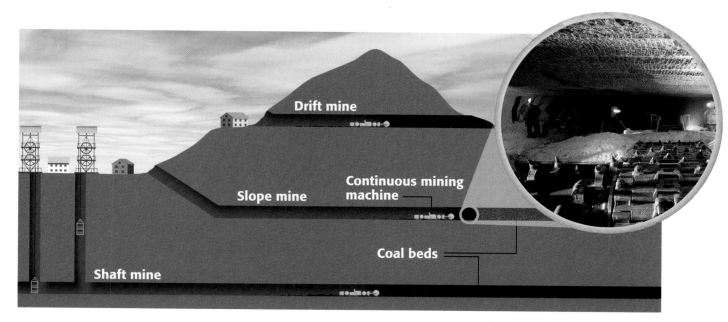

Drift mine

Continuous mining machine

Slope mine

Coal beds

Shaft mine

Subsurface Mining

Subsurface mining methods are used when mineral deposits are located too deep within the Earth to be surface mined. Subsurface mining often requires that passageways be dug into the Earth to reach the ore. As shown in **Figure 2,** these passageways may be dug horizontally or at an angle. If a mineral deposit extends deep within the Earth, however, a vertical shaft is sunk. This shaft may connect a number of passageways that intersect the ore at different levels.

✓ Reading Check Compare surface and subsurface mining.
(*See the Appendix for answers to Reading Checks.*)

Responsible Mining

Mining gives us the minerals we need, but it may also create problems. Mining can destroy or disturb the habitats of plants and animals. Also, the waste products from a mine may get into water sources, which pollutes surface water and groundwater.

Mine Reclamation

One way to reduce the potential harmful effects of mining is to return the land to its original state after the mining is completed. The process by which land used for mining is returned to its original state or better is called **reclamation.** Reclamation of mined public and private land has been required by law since the mid-1970s. Another way to reduce the effects of mining is to reduce our need for minerals. We reduce our need for minerals by recycling many of the mineral products that we currently use, such as aluminum.

Figure 2 *Subsurface mining is the removal of minerals or other materials from deep within the Earth. Passageways must be dug underground to reach the ore. Machines such as continuous mining machines (inset) are used to mine ore in subsurface mines.*

reclamation the process of returning land to its original condition after mining is completed

Recycling Minerals at Home

With your parent, locate products in your home that are made of minerals. Decide which of these products could be recycled. In your **science journal,** make a list of the products that could be recycled to save minerals.

The Use of Minerals

As shown in **Table 1,** some minerals are of major economic and industrial importance. Some minerals can be used just as they are. Other minerals must be processed to get the element or elements that the minerals contain. **Figure 3** shows some processed minerals used to make the parts of a bicycle.

Table 1	Common Uses of Minerals
Mineral	**Uses**
Copper	electrical wire, plumbing, coins
Diamond	jewelry, cutting tools, drill bits
Galena	batteries, ammunition
Gibbsite	cans, foil, appliances, utensils
Gold	jewelry, computers, spacecraft, dentistry
Gypsum	wallboards, plaster, cement
Halite	nutrition, highway de-icer, water softener
Quartz	glass, computer chips
Silver	photography, electronics products, jewelry
Sphalerite	jet aircraft, spacecraft, paints

Metallic Minerals

Some minerals are metallic. Metallic minerals have shiny surfaces, do not let light pass through them, and are good conductors of heat and electricity. Metallic minerals can be processed into metals that are strong and do not rust. Other metals can be pounded or pressed into various shapes or stretched thinly without breaking. These properties make metals desirable for use in aircraft, automobiles, computers, communications and electronic equipment, and spacecraft. Examples of metallic minerals that have many industrial uses are gold, silver, and copper.

Nonmetallic Minerals

Other minerals are nonmetals. Nonmetallic minerals have shiny or dull surfaces, may let light pass through them, and are good insulators of electricity. Nonmetallic minerals are some of the most widely used minerals in industry. For example, calcite is a major component of concrete, which is used in building roads, buildings, bridges, and other structures. Industrial sand and gravel, or silica, have uses that range from glassmaking to producing computer chips.

Figure 3 Some Materials Used in the Parts of a Bicycle

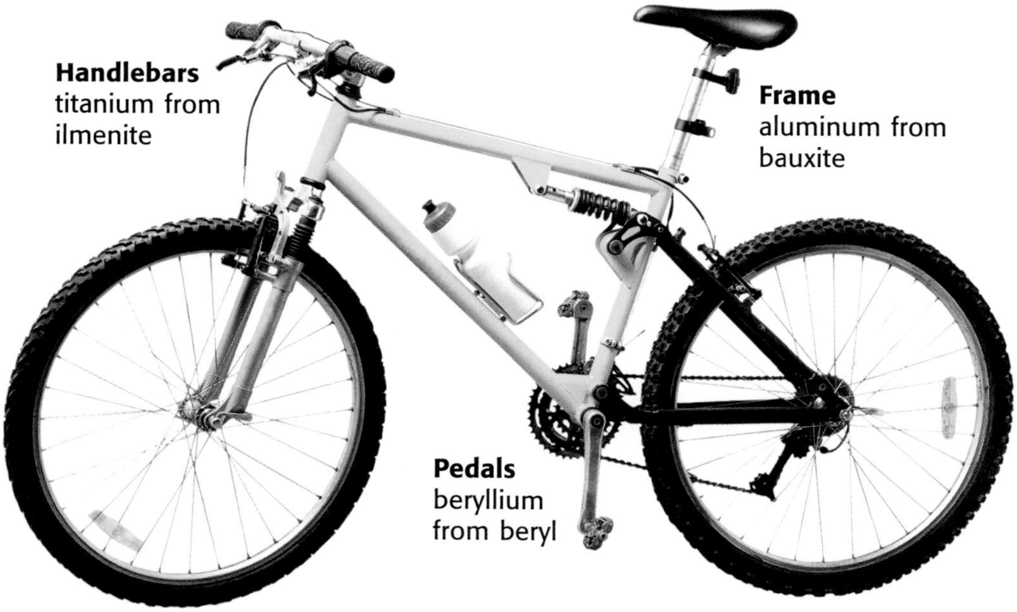

Handlebars
titanium from ilmenite

Frame
aluminum from bauxite

Spokes
iron from magnetite

Pedals
beryllium from beryl

Gemstones

Some nonmetallic minerals, called *gemstones*, are highly valued for their beauty and rarity rather than for their usefulness. Important gemstones include diamond, ruby, sapphire, emerald, aquamarine, topaz, and tourmaline. An example of a diamond is shown in **Figure 4.** Color is the most important characteristic of a gemstone. The more attractive the color is, the more valuable the gem is. Gemstones must also be durable. That is, they must be hard enough to be cut and polished. The mass of a gemstone is expressed in a unit known as a *carat*. One carat is equal to 200 mg.

Reading Check In your own words, define the term *gemstone*.

Figure 4 *The Cullinan diamond, at the center of this scepter, is part of the largest diamond ever found.*

SECTION Review

Summary

- Environments in which minerals form may be located at or near the Earth's surface or deep below the surface.
- The two types of mining are surface mining and subsurface mining.
- Two ways to reduce the effects of mining are the reclamation of mined land and the recycling of mineral products.
- Some metallic and nonmetallic minerals have many important economic and industrial uses.

Using Key Terms

Complete each of the following sentences by choosing the correct term from the word bank.

    ore   reclamation

1. _____ is the process of returning land to its original condition after mining is completed.

2. _____ is the term used to describe a mineral deposit that is large enough and pure enough to be mined for profit.

Understanding Key Ideas

3. Which of the following conditions is NOT important in the formation of minerals?
   a. presence of groundwater
   b. evaporation
   c. volcanic activity
   d. wind

4. What are the two main types of mining, and how do they differ?

5. List some uses of metallic minerals.

6. List some uses of nonmetallic minerals.

Math Skills

7. A diamond cutter has a raw diamond that weighs 19.5 carats and from which two 5-carat diamonds will be cut. How much did the raw diamond weigh in milligrams? How much will each of the two cut diamonds weigh in milligrams?

Critical Thinking

8. **Analyzing Ideas** How does reclamation protect the environment around a mine?

9. **Applying Concepts** Suppose you find a mineral crystal that is as tall as you are. What kinds of environmental factors would cause such a crystal to form?

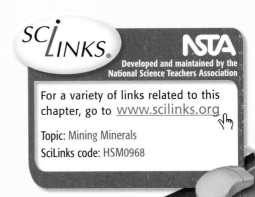

SCILINKS®

NSTA
Developed and maintained by the
National Science Teachers Association

For a variety of links related to this chapter, go to www.scilinks.org

Topic: Mining Minerals
SciLinks code: HSM0968

Skills Practice Lab

Is It Fool's Gold? A Dense Situation

Have you heard of fool's gold? Maybe you've seen a piece of it. This mineral is actually pyrite, and it was often passed off as real gold. However, there are simple tests that you can do to keep from being tricked. Minerals can be identified by their properties. Some properties, such as color, vary from sample to sample. Other properties, such as density and specific gravity, remain consistent across samples. In this activity, you will try to verify the identity of some mineral samples.

OBJECTIVES

Calculate the density and specific gravity of a mineral.

Explain how density and specific gravity can be used to identify a mineral specimen.

MATERIALS

- balance
- beaker, 400 mL
- galena sample
- pyrite sample
- ring stand
- spring scale
- string
- water, 400 mL

SAFETY

Ask a Question

1 How can I determine if an unknown mineral is not gold or silver?

Form a Hypothesis

2 Write a hypothesis that is a possible answer to the question above. Explain your reasoning.

Test the Hypothesis

3 Copy the data table. Use it to record your observations.

Observation Chart		
Measurement	**Galena**	**Pyrite**
Mass in air (g)		
Weight in air (N)		
Volume of mineral (mL)	DO NOT WRITE IN BOOK	
Weight in water (N)		

Galena

Pyrite

4 Find the mass of each sample by laying the mineral on the balance. Record the mass of each sample in your data table.

5 Attach the spring scale to the ring stand.

6 Tie a string around the sample of galena, and leave a loop at the loose end. Suspend the galena from the spring scale, and find its mass and weight in air. Do not remove the sample from the spring scale yet. Enter these data in your data table.

7 Fill a beaker halfway with water. Record the beginning volume of water in your data table.

8 Carefully lift the beaker around the galena until the mineral is completely submerged. Be careful not to splash any water out of the beaker! Do not allow the mineral to touch the beaker.

9 Record the new volume and weight in your data table.

10 Subtract the original volume of water from the new volume to find the amount of water displaced by the mineral. This is the volume of the mineral sample itself. Record this value in your data table.

11 Repeat steps 6—10 for the sample of pyrite.

Analyze the Results

1 **Constructing Tables** Copy the data table below. (Note: 1 mL = 1 cm^3)

Density Data Table		
Mineral	Density (g/cm^3)	Specific gravity
Silver	10.5	10.5
Galena	DO NOT WRITE IN BOOK	
Pyrite		
Gold	19.0	19.0

2 **Organizing Data** Use the following equations to calculate the density and specific gravity of each mineral, and record your answers in your data table.

$$density = \frac{mass\ in\ air}{volume}$$

$$specific\ gravity = \frac{weight\ in\ air}{weight\ in\ air - weight\ in\ water}$$

Draw Conclusions

3 **Drawing Conclusions** The density of pure gold is 19 g/cm^3. How can you use this information to prove that your sample of pyrite is not gold?

4 **Drawing Conclusions** The density of pure silver is 10.5 g/cm^3. How can you use this information to prove that your sample of galena is not silver?

5 **Applying Conclusions** If you found a gold-colored nugget, how could you find out if the nugget was real gold or fool's gold?

Chapter Review

USING KEY TERMS

1 Use each of the following terms in a separate sentence: *element, compound,* and *mineral.*

For each pair of terms, explain how the meanings of the terms differ.

2 *color* and *streak*

3 *mineral* and *ore*

4 *silicate mineral* and *nonsilicate mineral*

UNDERSTANDING KEY IDEAS

Multiple Choice

5 Which of the following properties of minerals does Mohs scale measure?

a. luster
b. hardness
c. density
d. streak

6 Pure substances that cannot be broken down into simpler substances by ordinary chemical means are called

a. molecules.
b. elements.
c. compounds.
d. crystals.

7 Which of the following properties is considered a special property that applies to only a few minerals?

a. luster
b. hardness
c. taste
d. density

8 Silicate minerals contain a combination of the elements

a. sulfur and oxygen.
b. carbon and oxygen.
c. iron and oxygen.
d. silicon and oxygen.

9 The process by which land used for mining is returned to its original state is called

a. recycling.
b. regeneration.
c. reclamation.
d. renovation.

10 Which of the following minerals is an example of a gemstone?

a. mica
b. diamond
c. gypsum
d. copper

Short Answer

11 Compare surface and subsurface mining.

12 Explain the four characteristics of a mineral.

13 Describe two environments in which minerals form.

14 List two uses for metallic minerals and two uses for nonmetallic minerals.

15 Describe two ways to reduce the effects of mining.

16 Describe three special properties of minerals.

17 Concept Mapping Use the following terms to create a concept map: *minerals, calcite, silicate minerals, gypsum, carbonates, nonsilicate minerals, quartz,* and *sulfates*.

18 Making Inferences Imagine that you are trying to determine the identity of a mineral. You decide to do a streak test. You rub the mineral across the streak plate, but the mineral does not leave a streak. Has your test failed? Explain your answer.

19 Applying Concepts Why would cleavage be important to gem cutters, who cut and shape gemstones?

20 Applying Concepts Imagine that you work at a jeweler's shop and someone brings in some gold nuggets for sale. You are not sure if the nuggets are real gold. Which identification tests would help you decide whether the nuggets are gold?

21 Identifying Relationships Suppose you are in a desert. You are walking across the floor of a dry lake, and you see crusts of cubic halite crystals. How do you suppose the halite crystals formed? Explain your answer.

The table below shows the temperatures at which various minerals melt. Use the table below to answer the questions that follow.

Melting Points of Various Minerals	
Mineral	Melting Point (°C)
Mercury	−39
Sulfur	+113
Halite	801
Silver	961
Gold	1,062
Copper	1,083
Pyrite	1,171
Fluorite	1,360
Quartz	1,710
Zircon	2,500

22 According to the table, what is the approximate difference in temperature between the melting points of the mineral that has the lowest melting point and the mineral that has the highest melting point?

23 Which of the minerals listed in the table do you think is a liquid at room temperature?

24 Pyrite is often called *fool's gold*. Using the information in the table, how could you determine if a mineral sample is pyrite or gold?

25 Convert the melting points of the minerals shown in the table from degrees Celsius to degrees Fahrenheit. Use the formula °F = (9/5 × °C) + 32.

Standardized Test Preparation

Read each of the passages below. Then, answer the questions that follow each passage.

Passage 1 In North America, copper was mined at least 6,700 years ago by the ancestors of the Native Americans who live on Michigan's upper peninsula. Much of this mining took place on Isle Royale, an island in Lake Superior. These <u>ancient</u> people removed copper from the rock by using stone hammers and wedges. The rock was sometimes heated first to make breaking it up easier. Copper that was mined was used to make jewelry, tools, weapons, fish hooks, and other objects. These objects were often marked with designs. The Lake Superior copper was traded over long distances along ancient trade routes. Copper objects have been found in Ohio, Florida, the Southwest, and the Northwest.

1. In the passage, what does *ancient* mean?
   A young
   B future
   C modern
   D early

2. According to the passage, what did the ancient copper miners do?
   F They mined copper in Ohio, Florida, the Southwest, and the Northwest.
   G They mined copper by cooling the rock in which the copper was found.
   H They mined copper by using stone tools.
   I They mined copper for their use only.

3. Which of the following statements is a fact according to the passage?
   A Copper could be shaped into different objects.
   B Copper was unknown outside of Michigan's upper peninsula.
   C Copper could be mined easily from the rock in which it was found.
   D Copper could not be marked with designs.

Passage 2 Most mineral names end in *-ite*. The <u>practice</u> of so naming minerals dates back to the ancient Romans and Greeks, who added *-ites* and *-itis* to common words to indicate a color, a use, or the chemistry of a mineral. More recently, mineral names have been used to honor people, such as scientists, mineral collectors, and even rulers of countries. Other minerals have been named after the place where they were discovered. These place names include mines, quarries, hills, mountains, towns, regions, and even countries. Finally, some minerals have been named after gods in Greek, Roman, and Scandinavian mythology.

1. In the passage, what does *practice* mean?
   A skill
   B custom
   C profession
   D use

2. According to the passage, the ancient Greeks and Romans did not name minerals after what?
   F colors
   G chemical properties
   H people
   I uses

3. Which of the following statements is a fact according to the passage?
   A Minerals are sometimes named for the country in which they are discovered.
   B Minerals are never named after their collectors.
   C All mineral names end in *-ite*.
   D All of the known minerals were named by the Greeks and Romans.

A sample of feldspar was analyzed to find out what it was made of. The graph below shows the results of the analysis. Use the graph below to answer the questions that follow.

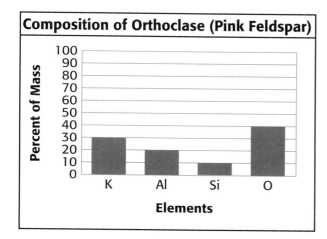

1. The sample consists of four elements: potassium, K, aluminum, Al, silicon, Si, and oxygen, O. Which element makes up the largest percentage of your sample?

   A potassium
   B aluminum
   C silicon
   D oxygen

2. Silicate minerals, such as feldspar, contain a combination of silicon and oxygen. What percentage of your sample is composed of silicon and oxygen combined?

   F 30%
   G 40%
   H 50%
   I 70%

3. If your sample has a mass of 10 g, how many grams of oxygen does it contain?

   A 1 g
   B 2 g
   C 4 g
   D 8 g

4. Your sample of orthoclase has a hardness of 6. Which of the following minerals will scratch your sample?

   F gypsum
   G corundum
   H calcite
   I apatite

MATH

Read each question below, and choose the best answer.

1. Gold classified as 24-karat is 100% gold. Gold classified as 18-karat is 18 parts gold and 6 parts another, similar metal. The gold is therefore 18/24, or 3/4, pure. What is the percentage of pure gold in 18-karat gold?

   A 10%
   B 25%
   C 50%
   D 75%

2. Gold's specific gravity is 19. Pyrite's specific gravity is 5. What is the difference in the specific gravities of gold and pyrite?

   F 8 g/cm^3
   G 10 g/cm^3
   H 12 g/cm^3
   I 14 g/cm^3

3. In a quartz crystal, there is one silicon atom for every two oxygen atoms. So, the ratio of silicon atoms to oxygen atoms is 1:2. If there were 8 million oxygen atoms in a sample of quartz, how many silicon atoms would there be in the sample?

   A 2 million
   B 4 million
   C 8 million
   D 16 million

Science in Action

Science Fiction

"The Metal Man" by Jack Williamson

In a dark, dusty corner of Tyburn College Museum stands a life-sized statue of a man. Except for its strange greenish color, the statue looks quite ordinary. But if you look closely, you will see the perfect detail of the hair and skin. On the statue's chest, you will also see a strange mark—a dark crimson shape with six sides. No one knows how the statue ended up in the dark corner. But most people in Tyburn believe that the metal man is, or once was, Professor Thomas Kelvin of Tyburn College's geology department. Read for yourself the strange story of Professor Kelvin and the Metal Man, which is in the *Holt Anthology of Science Fiction*.

Language Arts ACTiViTY

WRITING SKILL Read "The Metal Man" by Jack Williamson. Write a short essay explaining how the ideas in the story are related to what you are learning.

HOLT ANTHOLOGY OF
Science Fiction

HOLT, RINEHART AND WINSTON

Weird Science

Wieliczka Salt Mine

Imagine an underground city that is made entirely of salt. Within the city are churches, chapels, rooms of many kinds, and salt lakes. Sculptures of biblical scenes, saints, and famous historical figures carved from salt are found throughout the city. Even chandeliers of salt hang from the ceilings. Such a city is located 16 km southeast of Krakow, Poland, inside the Wieliczka (VEE uh LEETS kuh) Salt Mine. As the mine grew over the past 700 years, it turned into an elaborate underground city. Miners constructed chapels to patron saints so they could pray for a safe day in the mine. Miners also developed superstitions about the mine. So, images that were meant to bring good luck were carved in salt. In 1978, the mine was added to UNESCO's list of endangered world heritage sites. Many of the sculptures in the mine have begun to dissolve because of the humidity in the air. Efforts to save the treasures in the mine from further damage were begun in 1996.

Social Studies ACTiViTY

WRITING SKILL Research some aspect of the role of salt in human history. For example, subjects might include the Saharan and Tibetan salt trade or the use of salt as a form of money in ancient Poland. Report your findings in a one-page essay.

Jamie Hill

The Emerald Man Jamie Hill was raised in the Brushy Mountains of North Carolina. While growing up, Hill gained firsthand knowledge of the fabulous green crystals that could be found in the mountains. These green crystals were emeralds. Emerald is the green variety of the silicate mineral beryl and is a valuable gemstone. Emerald crystals form in pockets, or openings, in rock known as *pegmatite*.

Since 1985, Hill has been searching for pockets containing emeralds in rock near the small town of Hiddenite, North Carolina. He has been amazingly successful. Hill has discovered some spectacular emerald crystals. The largest of these crystals weighs 858 carats and is on display at the North Carolina Museum of Natural Science. Estimates of the total value of the emeralds that Hill has discovered so far are well in the millions of dollars. Hill's discoveries have made him a celebrity, and he has appeared both on national TV and in magazines.

Math ACTIVITY

An emerald discovered by Jamie Hill in 1999 was cut into a 7.85-carat stone that sold for $64,000 per carat. What was the total value of the cut stone?

To learn more about these Science in Action topics, visit go.hrw.com and type in the keyword **HZ5MINF.**

Current Science

Check out Current Science® articles related to this chapter by visiting go.hrw.com. **Just type in the keyword HZ5CS03.**

2

Rocks: Mineral Mixtures

About the PHOTO

Irish legend claims that the mythical hero Finn MacCool built the Giant's Causeway, shown here. But this rock formation is the result of the cooling of huge amounts of molten rock. As the molten rock cooled, it formed tall pillars separated by cracks called *columnar joints*.

PRE-READING ACTIVITY

Graphic Organizer

Spider Map Before you read the chapter, create the graphic organizer entitled "Spider Map" described in the **Study Skills** section of the Appendix. Label the circle "Rock." Create a leg for each of the sections in this chapter. As you read the chapter, fill in the map with details about the material presented in each section of the chapter.

START-UP ACTIVITY

Classifying Objects

Scientists use the physical and chemical properties of rocks to classify rocks. Classifying objects such as rocks requires looking at many properties. Do this exercise for some classification practice.

Procedure

1. Your teacher will give you a **bag** containing **several objects.** Examine the objects, and note features such as size, color, shape, texture, smell, and any unique properties.

2. Develop three different ways to sort these objects.

3. Create a chart that organizes objects by properties.

Analysis

1. What properties did you use to sort the items?

2. Were there any objects that could fit into more than one group? How did you solve this problem?

3. Which properties might you use to classify rocks? Explain your answer.

The Rock Cycle

You know that paper, plastic, and aluminum can be recycled. But did you know that the Earth also recycles? And one of the things that Earth recycles is rock.

Scientists define **rock** as a naturally occurring solid mixture of one or more minerals and organic matter. It may be hard to believe, but rocks are always changing. The continual process by which new rock forms from old rock material is called the **rock cycle.**

The Value of Rock

Rock has been an important natural resource as long as humans have existed. Early humans used rocks as hammers to make other tools. They discovered that they could make arrowheads, spear points, knives, and scrapers by carefully shaping rocks such as chert and obsidian.

Rock has also been used for centuries to make buildings, monuments, and roads. **Figure 1** shows how rock has been used as a construction material by both ancient and modern civilizations. Buildings have been made out of granite, limestone, marble, sandstone, slate, and other rocks. Modern buildings also contain concrete and plaster, in which rock is an important ingredient.

☑️ *Reading Check* Name some types of rock that have been used to construct buildings. (*See the Appendix for answers to Reading Checks.*)

READING WARM-UP

Objectives

● Describe two ways rocks have been used by humans.

● Describe four processes that shape Earth's features.

● Describe how each type of rock changes into another type as it moves through the rock cycle.

● List two characteristics of rock that are used to help classify it.

Terms to Learn

rock cycle   deposition
rock   composition
erosion   texture

READING STRATEGY

Reading Organizer As you read this section, make a flowchart of the steps of the rock cycle.

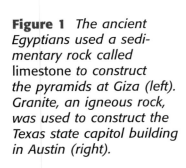
Figure 1 *The ancient Egyptians used a sedimentary rock called* limestone *to construct the pyramids at Giza (left). Granite, an igneous rock, was used to construct the Texas state capitol building in Austin (right).*

Processes That Shape the Earth

Certain geological processes make and destroy rock. These processes shape the features of our planet. These processes also influence the type of rock that is found in a certain area of Earth's surface.

Weathering, Erosion, and Deposition

The process in which water, wind, ice, and heat break down rock is called *weathering*. Weathering is important because it breaks down rock into fragments. These rock and mineral fragments are the sediment of which much sedimentary rock is made.

The process by which sediment is removed from its source is called **erosion.** Water, wind, ice, and gravity can erode and move sediments and cause them to collect. **Figure 2** shows an example of the way land looks after weathering and erosion.

The process in which sediment moved by erosion is dropped and comes to rest is called **deposition.** Sediment is deposited in bodies of water and other low-lying areas. In those places, sediment may be pressed and cemented together by minerals dissolved in water to form sedimentary rock.

Heat and Pressure

Sedimentary rock made of sediment can also form when buried sediment is squeezed by the weight of overlying layers of sediment. If the temperature and pressure are high enough at the bottom of the sediment, the rock can change into metamorphic rock. In some cases, the rock gets hot enough to melt. This melting creates the magma that eventually cools to form igneous rock.

How the Cycle Continues

Buried rock is exposed at the Earth's surface by a combination of uplift and erosion. *Uplift* is movement within the Earth that causes rocks inside the Earth to be moved to the Earth's surface. When uplifted rock reaches the Earth's surface, weathering, erosion, and deposition begin.

rock a naturally occurring solid mixture of one or more minerals or organic matter

rock cycle the series of processes in which a rock forms, changes from one type to another, is destroyed, and forms again by geological processes

erosion the process by which wind, water, ice, or gravity transports soil and sediment from one location to another

deposition the process in which material is laid down

Figure 2 *Bryce Canyon, in Utah, is an excellent example of how the processes of weathering and erosion shape the face of our planet.*

Illustrating the Rock Cycle

You have learned about various geological processes, such as weathering, erosion, heat, and pressure, that create and destroy rock. The diagram on these two pages illustrates one way that sand grains can change as different geological processes act on them. In the following steps, you will see how these processes change the original sand grains into sedimentary rock, metamorphic rock, and igneous rock.

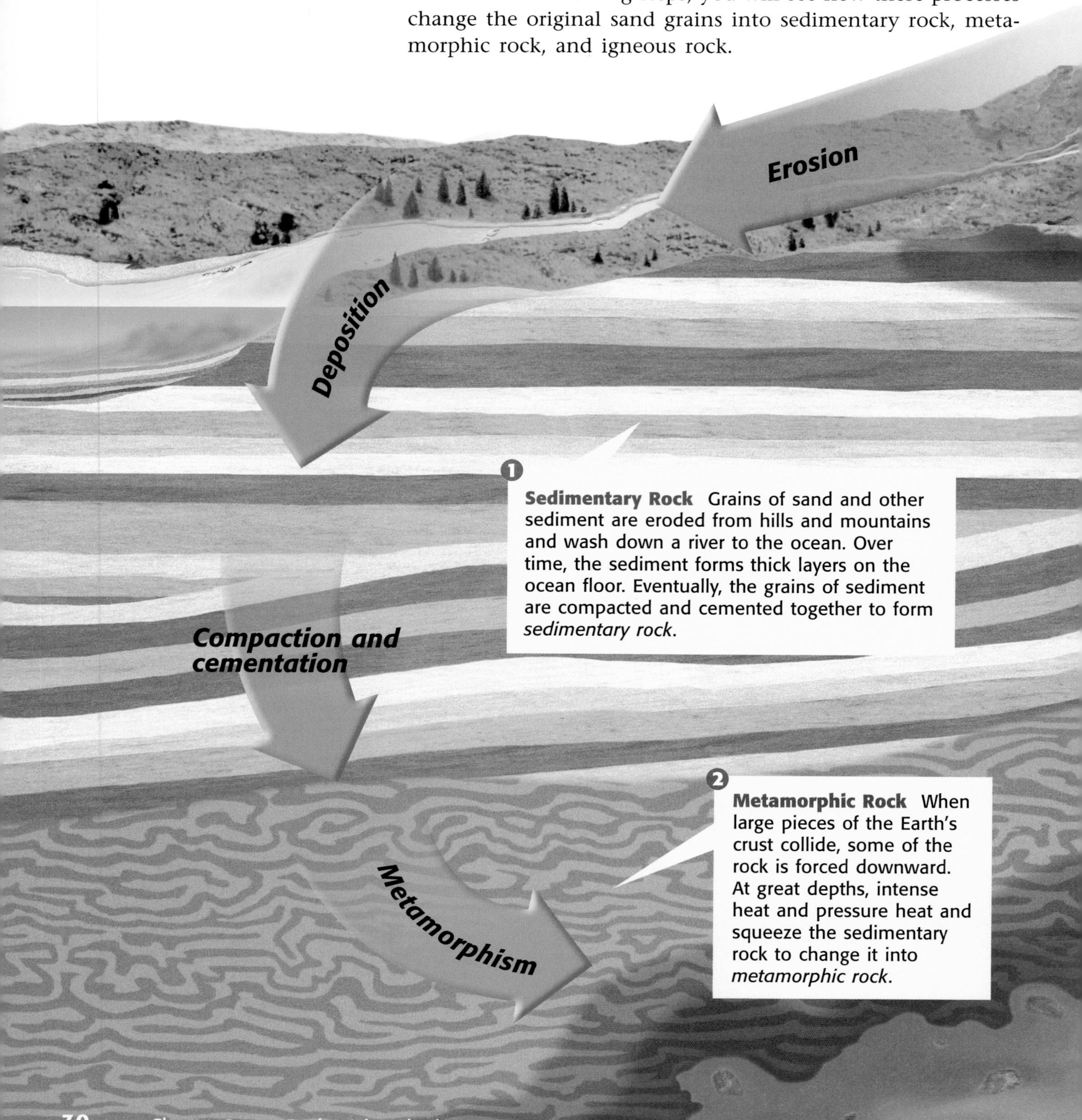

Erosion

Deposition

Compaction and cementation

Metamorphism

❶ Sedimentary Rock Grains of sand and other sediment are eroded from hills and mountains and wash down a river to the ocean. Over time, the sediment forms thick layers on the ocean floor. Eventually, the grains of sediment are compacted and cemented together to form *sedimentary rock*.

❷ Metamorphic Rock When large pieces of the Earth's crust collide, some of the rock is forced downward. At great depths, intense heat and pressure heat and squeeze the sedimentary rock to change it into *metamorphic rock*.

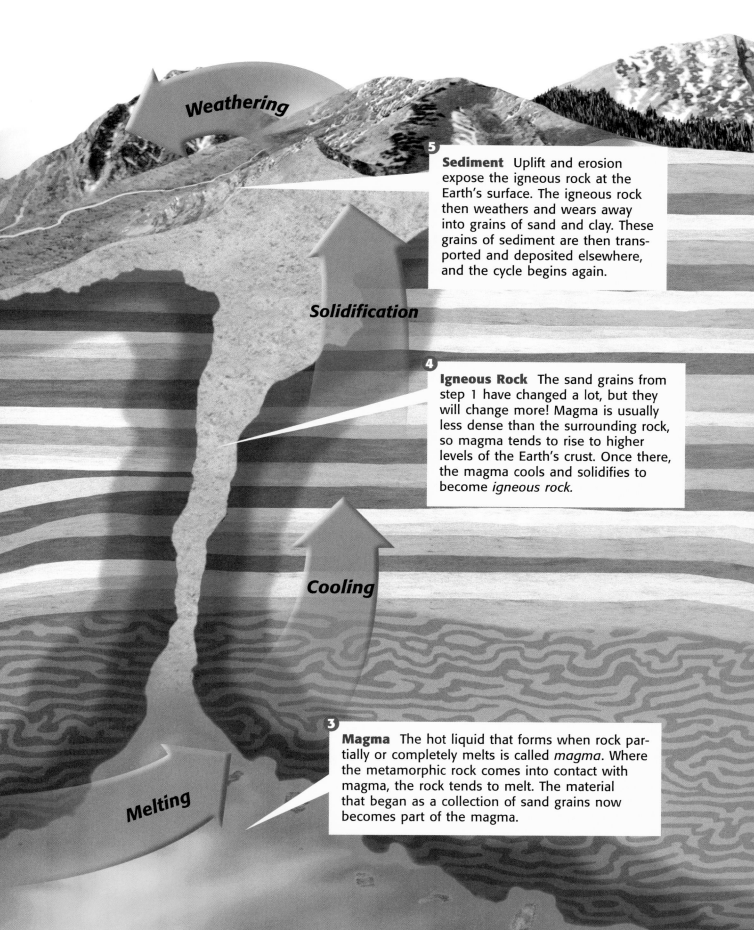

Weathering

5

Sediment Uplift and erosion expose the igneous rock at the Earth's surface. The igneous rock then weathers and wears away into grains of sand and clay. These grains of sediment are then transported and deposited elsewhere, and the cycle begins again.

Solidification

4

Igneous Rock The sand grains from step 1 have changed a lot, but they will change more! Magma is usually less dense than the surrounding rock, so magma tends to rise to higher levels of the Earth's crust. Once there, the magma cools and solidifies to become *igneous rock.*

Cooling

3

Magma The hot liquid that forms when rock partially or completely melts is called *magma.* Where the metamorphic rock comes into contact with magma, the rock tends to melt. The material that began as a collection of sand grains now becomes part of the magma.

Melting

Figure 3 The Rock Cycle

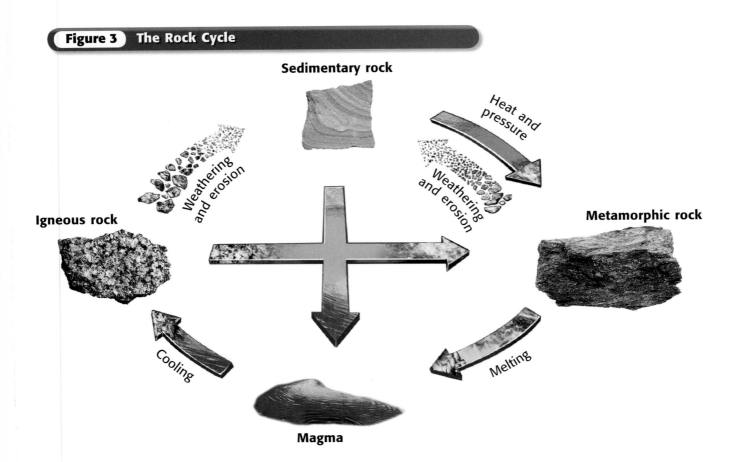

Sedimentary rock

Heat and pressure

Weathering and erosion

Weathering and erosion

Igneous rock

Metamorphic rock

Cooling

Melting

Magma

Round and Round It Goes

You have seen how different geological processes can change rock. Each rock type can change into one of the three types of rock. For example, igneous rock can change into sedimentary rock, metamorphic rock, or even back into igneous rock. This cycle, in which rock is changed by geological processes into different types of rock, is known as the rock cycle.

Rocks may follow various pathways in the rock cycle. As one rock type is changed to another type, several variables, including time, heat, pressure, weathering, and erosion may alter a rock's identity. The location of a rock determines which natural forces will have the biggest impact on the process of change. For example, rock at the Earth's surface is primarily affected by forces of weathering and erosion, whereas deep inside the Earth, rocks change because of extreme heat and pressure. **Figure 3** shows the different ways rock may change when it goes through the rock cycle and the different forces that affect rock during the cycle.

✓ Reading Check What processes change rock deep within the Earth?

Rock Classification

You have already learned that scientists divide all rock into three main classes based on how the rock formed: igneous, sedimentary, and metamorphic. But did you know that each class of rock can be divided further? These divisions are also based on differences in the way rocks form. For example, all igneous rock forms when magma cools and solidifies. But some igneous rocks form when magma cools *on* the Earth's surface, and others form when magma cools deep *beneath* the surface. Therefore, igneous rock can be divided again based on how and where it forms. Sedimentary and metamorphic rocks are also divided into groups. How do scientists know how to classify rocks? They study rocks in detail using two important criteria—composition and texture.

Composition

The minerals a rock contains determine the **composition** of that rock, as shown in **Figure 4.** For example, a rock made of mostly the mineral quartz will have a composition very similar to that of quartz. But a rock made of 50% quartz and 50% feldspar will have a very different composition than quartz does.

✓ **Reading Check** What determines a rock's composition?

What's in It?

Assume that a granite sample you are studying is made of 30% quartz and 55% feldspar by volume. The rest is made of biotite mica. What percentage of the sample is biotite mica?

composition the chemical makeup of a rock; describes either the minerals or other materials in the rock

---

Figure 4 Two Examples of Rock Composition

The composition of a rock depends on the minerals the rock contains.

Limestone

95% Calcite · 5% Aragonite

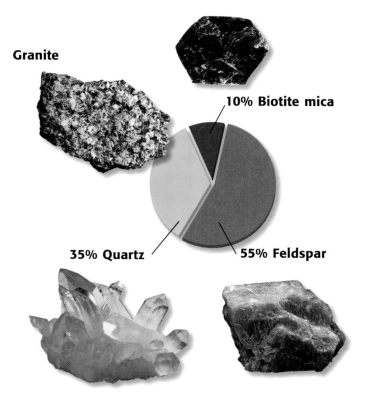

Granite

10% Biotite mica

35% Quartz · 55% Feldspar

Figure 5 Three Examples of Sedimentary Rock Texture

Fine-grained

Siltstone

Medium-grained

Sandstone

Coarse-grained

Conglomerate

Texture

texture the quality of a rock that is based on the sizes, shapes, and positions of the rock's grains

The size, shape, and positions of the grains that make up a rock determine a rock's **texture.** Sedimentary rock can have a fine-grained, medium-grained, or coarse-grained texture, depending on the size of the grains that make up the rock. Three samples of textures are shown in **Figure 5.** The texture of igneous rock can be fine-grained or coarse-grained, depending on how much time magma has to cool. Based on the degree of temperature and pressure a rock is exposed to, metamorphic rock can also have a fine-grained or coarse-grained texture.

The texture of a rock can provide clues as to how and where the rock formed. Look at the rocks shown in **Figure 6.** The rocks look different because they formed in very different ways. The texture of a rock can reveal the process that formed it.

✓ Reading Check Give three examples of sedimentary rock textures.

Figure 6 Texture and Rock Formation

Basalt, a fine-grained igneous rock, forms when lava that erupts onto Earth's surface cools rapidly.

Sandstone, a medium-grained sedimentary rock, forms when sand grains deposited in dunes, on beaches, or on the ocean floor are buried and cemented.

Summary

- Rock has been an important natural resource for as long as humans have existed. Early humans used rock to make tools. Ancient and modern civilizations have used rock as a construction material.

- Weathering, erosion, deposition, and uplift are all processes that shape the surface features of the Earth.

- The rock cycle is the continual process by which new rock forms from old rock material.

- The sequence of events in the rock cycle depends on processes, such as weathering, erosion, deposition, pressure, and heat, that change the rock material.

- Composition and texture are two characteristics that scientists use to classify rocks.

- The composition of a rock is determined by the minerals that make up the rock.

- The texture of a rock is determined by the size, shape, and positions of the grains that make up the rock.

Using Key Terms

Complete each of the following sentences by choosing the correct term from the word bank.

rock	composition
rock cycle	texture

1. The minerals that a rock is made of determine the ___ of that rock.

2. ___ is a naturally occurring, solid mixture of crystals of one or more minerals.

Understanding Key Ideas

3. Sediments are transported or moved from their original source by a process called
   a. deposition.
   b. erosion.
   c. uplift.
   d. weathering.

4. Describe two ways that rocks have been used by humans.

5. Name four processes that change rock inside the Earth.

6. Describe four processes that shape Earth's surface.

7. Give an example of how texture can provide clues as to how and where a rock formed.

Critical Thinking

8. **Making Comparisons** Explain the difference between texture and composition.

9. **Analyzing Processes** Explain how rock is continually recycled in the rock cycle.

Interpreting Graphics

10. Look at the table below. Sandstone is a type of sedimentary rock. If you had a sample of sandstone that had an average particle size of 2 mm, what texture would your sandstone have?

Classification of Clastic Sedimentary Rocks	
Texture	**Particle size**
coarse grained	> 2 mm
medium grained	0.06 to 2 mm
fine grained	< 0.06 mm

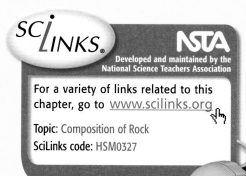

SCILINKS.

NSTA

Developed and maintained by the National Science Teachers Association

For a variety of links related to this chapter, go to www.scilinks.org

Topic: Composition of Rock
SciLinks code: HSM0327

Igneous Rock

Where do igneous rocks come from? Here's a hint: The word igneous *comes from a Latin word that means "fire."*

Igneous rock forms when hot, liquid rock, or *magma,* cools and solidifies. The type of igneous rock that forms depends on the composition of the magma and the amount of time it takes the magma to cool.

Origins of Igneous Rock

Igneous rock begins as magma. As shown in **Figure 1,** there are three ways magma can form: when rock is heated, when pressure is released, or when rock changes composition.

When magma cools enough, it solidifies to form igneous rock. Magma solidifies in much the same way that water freezes. But there are also differences between the way magma freezes and the way water freezes. One main difference is that water freezes at 0°C. Magma freezes between 700°C and 1,250°C. Also, liquid magma is a complex mixture containing many melted minerals. Because these minerals have different melting points, some minerals in the magma will freeze or become solid before other minerals do.

READING WARM-UP

Objectives

- Describe three ways that igneous rock forms.
- Explain how the cooling rate of magma affects the texture of igneous rock.
- Distinguish between igneous rock that cools within Earth's crust and igneous rock that cools at Earth's surface.

Terms to Learn

intrusive igneous rock
extrusive igneous rock

READING STRATEGY

Reading Organizer As you read this section, make a table comparing intrusive rock and extrusive rock.

Figure 1 The Formation of Magma

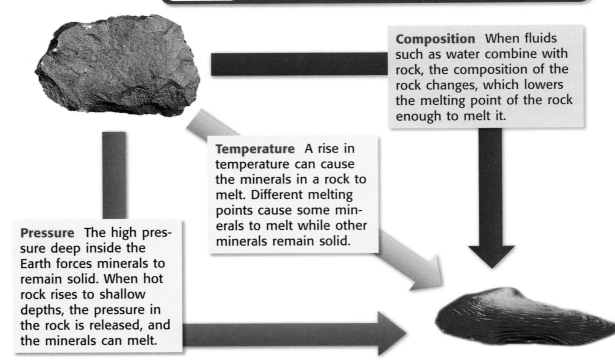

Composition When fluids such as water combine with rock, the composition of the rock changes, which lowers the melting point of the rock enough to melt it.

Temperature A rise in temperature can cause the minerals in a rock to melt. Different melting points cause some minerals to melt while other minerals remain solid.

Pressure The high pressure deep inside the Earth forces minerals to remain solid. When hot rock rises to shallow depths, the pressure in the rock is released, and the minerals can melt.

Figure 2 Igneous Rock Texture

	Coarse-grained	**Fine-grained**
Felsic	Granite	Rhyolite
Mafic	Gabbro	Basalt

Composition and Texture of Igneous Rock

Look at the rocks in **Figure 2.** All of the rocks are igneous rocks even though they look different from one another. These rocks differ from one another in what they are made of and how fast they cooled.

The light-colored rocks are less dense than the dark-colored rocks are. The light-colored rocks are rich in elements such as aluminum, potassium, silicon, and sodium. These rocks are called *felsic rocks.* The dark-colored rocks, called *mafic rocks,* are rich in calcium, iron, and magnesium, and poor in silicon.

Figure 3 shows what happens to magma when it cools at different rates. The longer it takes for the magma or lava to cool, the more time mineral crystals have to grow. The more time the crystals have to grow, the larger the crystals are and the coarser the texture of the resulting igneous rock is.

In contrast, the less time magma takes to cool, the less time crystals have to grow. Therefore, the rock that is formed will be fine grained. Fine-grained igneous rock contains very small crystals, or if the cooling is very rapid, it contains no crystals.

✓ Reading Check Explain the difference between felsic rock and mafic rock. (*See the Appendix for answers to Reading Checks.*)

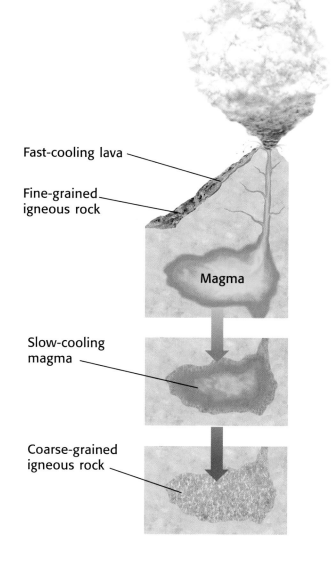

Figure 3 *The amount of time it takes for magma or lava to cool determines the texture of igneous rock.*

Fast-cooling lava

Fine-grained igneous rock

Magma

Slow-cooling magma

Coarse-grained igneous rock

For another activity related to this chapter, go to **go.hrw.com** and type in the keyword **HZ5RCKW**.

Igneous Rock Formations

Igneous rock formations are located above and below the surface of the Earth. You may be familiar with igneous rock formations that were caused by lava cooling on the Earth's surface, such as volcanoes. But not all magma reaches the surface. Some magma cools and solidifies deep within the Earth's crust.

Intrusive Igneous Rock

intrusive igneous rock rock formed from the cooling and solidification of magma beneath the Earth's surface

When magma *intrudes,* or pushes, into surrounding rock below the Earth's surface and cools, the rock that forms is called **intrusive igneous rock.** Intrusive igneous rock usually has a coarse-grained texture because it is well insulated by surrounding rock and cools very slowly. The minerals that form are large, visible crystals.

Masses of intrusive igneous rock are named for their size and shape. Common intrusive shapes are shown in **Figure 4.** *Plutons* are large, irregular-shaped intrusive bodies. The largest of all igneous intrusions are *batholiths.* *Stocks* are intrusive bodies that are exposed over smaller areas than batholiths. Sheetlike intrusions that cut across previous rock units are called *dikes,* whereas *sills* are sheetlike intrusions that are oriented parallel to previous rock units.

Figure 4 *Igneous intrusive bodies have different shapes and sizes.*

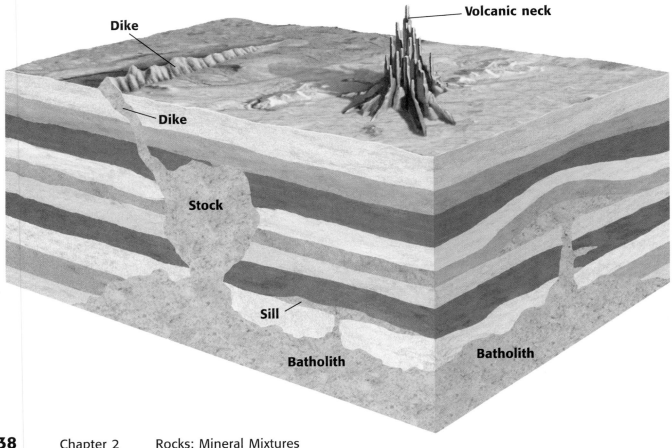

Extrusive Igneous Rock

Igneous rock that forms from magma that erupts, or extrudes, onto the Earth's surface is called **extrusive igneous rock.** Extrusive rock is common around volcanoes. It cools quickly on the surface and contains very small crystals or no crystals.

When lava erupts from a volcano, a *lava flow* forms. **Figure 5** shows an active lava flow. Lava does not always flow from volcanoes. Sometimes lava erupts and flows from long cracks in the Earth's crust called *fissures.* Lava flows from fissures on the ocean floor at places where tension is causing the ocean floor to be pulled apart. This lava cools to form new ocean floor. When a large amount of lava flows out of fissures onto land, the lava can cover a large area and form a plain called a *lava plateau.* Pre-existing landforms are often buried by these lava flows.

✓ Reading Check How does new ocean floor form?

Figure 5 *An active lava flow is shown in this photo. When exposed to Earth's surface conditions, lava quickly cools and solidifies to form a fine-grained igneous rock.*

extrusive igneous rock rock that forms as a result of volcanic activity at or near the Earth's surface

SECTION Review

Summary

- Igneous rock forms when magma cools and hardens.
- The texture of igneous rock is determined by the rate at which the rock cools.
- Igneous rock that solidifies at Earth's surface is extrusive. Igneous rock that solidifies within Earth's surface is intrusive.
- Shapes of common igneous intrusive bodies include batholiths, stocks, sills, and dikes.

Using Key Terms

1. In your own words, write a definition for each of the following terms: *intrusive igneous rock* and *extrusive igneous rock.*

Understanding Key Ideas

2. ___ is an example of a coarse-grained, felsic, igneous rock.
   a. Basalt
   b. Gabbro
   c. Granite
   d. Rhyolite

3. Explain three ways in which magma can form.

4. What determines the texture of igneous rocks?

Math Skills

5. The summit of a granite batholith has an elevation of 1,825 ft. What is the height of the batholith in meters?

Critical Thinking

6. **Making Comparisons** Dikes and sills are both types of igneous intrusive bodies. What is the difference between a dike and a sill?

7. **Predicting Consequences** An igneous rock forms from slow-cooling magma deep beneath the surface of the Earth. What type of texture is this rock most likely to have? Explain.

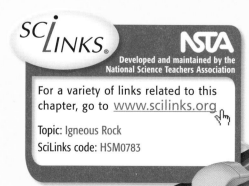

SCILINKS®

NSTA
Developed and maintained by the
National Science Teachers Association

For a variety of links related to this chapter, go to www.scilinks.org

Topic: Igneous Rock
SciLinks code: HSM0783

Sedimentary Rock

Have you ever tried to build a sand castle at the beach? Did you ever wonder where the sand came from?

Sand is a product of weathering, which breaks rock into pieces. Over time, sand grains may be compacted, or compressed, and then cemented together to form a rock called *sandstone*. Sandstone is just one of many types of sedimentary rock.

Origins of Sedimentary Rock

Wind, water, ice, sunlight, and gravity all cause rock to physically weather into fragments. Through the process of erosion, these rock and mineral fragments, called *sediment*, are moved from one place to another. Eventually, the sediment is deposited in layers. As new layers of sediment are deposited, they cover older layers. Older layers become compacted. Dissolved minerals, such as calcite and quartz, separate from water that passes through the sediment to form a natural cement that binds the rock and mineral fragments together into sedimentary rock.

Sedimentary rock forms at or near the Earth's surface. It forms without the heat and pressure that are involved in the formation of igneous and metamorphic rocks.

The most noticeable feature of sedimentary rock is its layers, or **strata.** A single, horizontal layer of rock is sometimes visible for many miles. Road cuts are good places to observe strata. **Figure 1** shows the spectacular views that sedimentary rock formations carved by erosion can provide.

READING WARM-UP

Objectives

- Describe the origin of sedimentary rock.
- Describe the three main categories of sedimentary rock.
- Describe three types of sedimentary structures.

Terms to Learn

strata
stratification

READING STRATEGY

Reading Organizer As you read this section, create an outline of this section. Use the headings from the section in your outline.

Figure 1 *The red sandstone "monuments" for which Monument Valley in Arizona has been named are the products of millions of years of erosion.*

Figure 2 Classification of Clastic Sedimentary Rock

Conglomerate   Sandstone   Siltstone   Shale

Coarse grained ← ————————————————————→ Fine grained

Composition of Sedimentary Rock

Sedimentary rock is classified by the way it forms. *Clastic sedimentary rock* forms when rock or mineral fragments, called *clasts,* are cemented together. *Chemical sedimentary rock* forms when minerals crystallize out of a solution, such as sea water, to become rock. *Organic sedimentary rock* forms from the remains of once-living plants and animals.

Clastic Sedimentary Rock

Clastic sedimentary rock is made of fragments of rocks cemented together by a mineral such as calcite or quartz. **Figure 2** shows how clastic sedimentary rock is classified according to the size of the fragments from which the rock is made. Clastic sedimentary rocks can have coarse-grained, medium-grained, or fine-grained textures.

Chemical Sedimentary Rock

Chemical sedimentary rock forms from solutions of dissolved minerals and water. As rainwater slowly makes its way to the ocean, it dissolves some of the rock material it passes through. Some of this dissolved material eventually crystallizes and forms the minerals that make up chemical sedimentary rock. Halite, one type of chemical sedimentary rock, is made of sodium chloride, NaCl, or table salt. Halite forms when sodium ions and chlorine ions in shallow bodies of water become so concentrated that halite crystallizes from solution.

Reading Check How does a chemical sedimentary rock such as halite form? (*See the Appendix for answers to Reading Checks.*)

strata layers of rock (singular, *stratum*)

CONNECTION TO Language Arts

WRITING SKILL **Salty Expressions** The word salt is used in many expressions in the English language. Some common examples include "the salt of the earth," "taken with a grain of salt," not worth his salt," "the salt of truth," "rubbing salt into a wound," and "old salt." Use the Internet or another source to research one these expressions. In your research, attempt to find the origin of the expression. Write a short paragraph that summarizes what you found.

Organic Sedimentary Rock

Most limestone forms from the remains, or *fossils*, of animals that once lived in the ocean. For example, some limestone is made of the skeletons of tiny organisms called *coral*. Coral are very small, but they live in huge colonies called *reefs*, shown in **Figure 3.** Over time, the skeletons of these sea animals, which are made of calcium carbonate, collect on the ocean floor. These animal remains eventually become cemented together to form *fossiliferous limestone* (FAH suhl IF uhr uhs LIEM STOHN).

Corals are not the only animals whose remains are found in fossiliferous limestone. The shells of mollusks, such as clams and oysters, commonly form fossiliferous limestone. An example of fossiliferous limestone that contains mollusks is shown in **Figure 4.**

Another type of organic sedimentary rock is *coal*. Coal forms underground when partially decomposed plant material is buried beneath sediment and is changed into coal by increasing heat and pressure. This process occurs over millions of years.

Figure 3 *Ocean animals called coral create huge deposits of limestone. As they die, their skeletons collect on the ocean floor.*

Figure 4 **The Formation of Organic Sedimentary Rock**

Marine organisms, such as brachiopods, get the calcium carbonate for their shells from ocean water. When these organisms die, their shells collect on the ocean floor and eventually form fossiliferous limestone (inset). Over time, huge rock formations that contain the remains of large numbers of organisms, such as brachiopods, form.

Sedimentary Rock Structures

Many features can tell you about the way sedimentary rock formed. The most important feature of sedimentary rock is stratification. **Stratification** is the process in which sedimentary rocks are arranged in layers. Strata differ from one another depending on the kind, size, and color of their sediment.

Sedimentary rocks sometimes record the motion of wind and water waves on lakes, oceans, rivers, and sand dunes in features called *ripple marks*, as shown in **Figure 5.** Structures called *mud cracks* form when fine-grained sediments at the bottom of a shallow body of water are exposed to the air and dry out. Mud cracks indicate the location of an ancient lake, stream, or ocean shoreline. Even raindrop impressions can be preserved in fine-grained sediments, as small pits with raised rims.

Reading Check What are ripple marks?

Figure 5 *These ripple marks were made by flowing water and were preserved when the sediments became sedimentary rock. Ripple marks can also form from the action of wind.*

stratification the process in which sedimentary rocks are arranged in layers

---

SECTION Review

Summary

- Sedimentary rock forms at or near the Earth's surface.

- Clastic sedimentary rock forms when rock or mineral fragments are cemented together.

- Chemical sedimentary rock forms from solutions of dissolved minerals and water.

- Organic limestone forms from the remains of plants and animals.

- Sedimentary structures include ripple marks, mud cracks, and raindrop impressions.

Using Key Terms

1. In your own words, write a definition for each of the following terms: *strata* and *stratification*.

Understanding Key Ideas

2. Which of the following is an organic sedimentary rock?
   - **a.** chemical limestone
   - **b.** shale
   - **c.** fossiliferous limestone
   - **d.** conglomerate

3. Explain the process by which clastic sedimentary rock forms.

4. Describe the three main categories of sedimentary rock.

Math Skills

5. A layer of a sedimentary rock is 2 m thick. How many years did it take for this layer to form if an average of 4 mm of sediment accumulated per year?

Critical Thinking

6. **Identifying Relationships** Rocks are classified based on texture and composition. Which of these two properties would be more important for classifying clastic sedimentary rock?

7. **Analyzing Processes** Why do you think raindrop impressions are more likely to be preserved in fine-grained sedimentary rock rather than in coarse-grained sedimentary rock?

SCiLINKS. **NSTA** Developed and maintained by the National Science Teachers Association

For a variety of links related to this chapter, go to www.scilinks.org

Topic: Sedimentary Rock
SciLinks code: HSM1365

Metamorphic Rock

Have you ever watched a caterpillar change into a butterfly? Some caterpillars go through a biological process called metamorphosis in which they completely change their shape.

Rocks can also go through a process called *metamorphism*. The word *metamorphism* comes from the Greek words *meta*, which means "changed," and *morphos*, which means "shape." Metamorphic rocks are rocks in which the structure, texture, or composition of the rock have changed. All three types of rock can be changed by heat, pressure, or a combination of both.

Origins of Metamorphic Rock

The texture or mineral composition of a rock can change when its surroundings change. If the temperature or pressure of the new environment is different from the one in which the rock formed, the rock will undergo metamorphism.

The temperature at which most metamorphism occurs ranges from 50°C to 1,000°C. However, the metamorphism of some rocks takes place at temperatures above 1,000°C. It seems that at these temperatures the rock would melt, but this is not true of metamorphic rock. It is the depth and pressure at which metamorphic rocks form that allows the rock to heat to this temperature and maintain its solid nature. Most metamorphic change takes place at depths greater than 2 km. But at depths greater than 16 km, the pressure can be 4,000 times greater than the pressure of the atmosphere at Earth's surface.

Large movements within the crust of the Earth cause additional pressure to be exerted on a rock during metamorphism. This pressure can cause the mineral grains in rock to align themselves in certain directions. The alignment of mineral grains into parallel bands is shown in the metamorphic rock in **Figure 1**.

READING WARM-UP

Objectives

- Describe two ways a rock can undergo metamorphism.
- Explain how the mineral composition of rocks changes as the rocks undergo metamorphism.
- Describe the difference between foliated and nonfoliated metamorphic rock.
- Explain how metamorphic rock structures are related to deformation.

Terms to Learn

foliated
nonfoliated

READING STRATEGY

Discussion Read this section silently. Write down questions that you have about this section. Discuss your questions in a small group.

Figure 1 *This metamorphic rock is an example of how mineral grains were aligned into distinct bands when the rock underwent metamorphism.*

Figure 2 *Metamorphism occurs over small areas, such as next to bodies of magma, and over large areas, such as mountain ranges.*

Contact metamorphism

Sedimentary rock

Magma

Regional metamorphism

Contact Metamorphism

One way rock can undergo metamorphism is by being heated by nearby magma. When magma moves through the crust, the magma heats the surrounding rock and changes it. Some minerals in the surrounding rock are changed into other minerals by this increase in temperature. The greatest change takes place where magma comes into direct contact with the surrounding rock. The effect of heat on rock gradually decreases as the rock's distance from the magma increases and as temperature decreases. *Contact metamorphism* occurs near igneous intrusions, as shown in **Figure 2.**

Regional Metamorphism

When pressure builds up in rock that is buried deep below other rock formations or when large pieces of the Earth's crust collide with each other, *regional metamorphism* occurs. The increased pressure and temperature causes rock to become deformed and chemically changed. Unlike contact metamorphism, which happens near bodies of magma, regional metamorphism occurs over thousands of cubic kilometers deep within Earth's crust. Rocks that have undergone regional metamorphism are found beneath most continental rock formations.

Reading Check Explain how and where regional metamorphism takes place. (*See the Appendix for answers to Reading Checks.*)

Stretching Out

1. Sketch the crystals in granite rock on a **piece of paper** with a **black-ink pen.** Be sure to include the outline of the rock, and fill it in with different crystal shapes.

2. Flatten some **plastic play putty** over your drawing, and slowly peel it off.

3. After making sure that the outline of your granite has been transferred to the putty, squeeze and stretch the putty. What happened to the crystals in the granite? What happened to the granite?

Figure 3 *The minerals calcite, quartz, and hematite combine and recrystallize to form the metamorphic mineral garnet.*

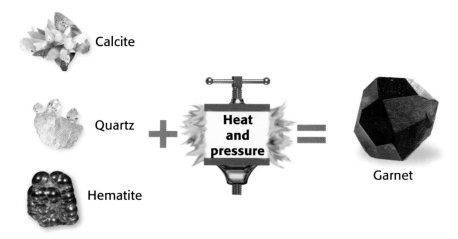

Calcite

Quartz

Hematite

+ Heat and pressure **=** Garnet

Making a Rock Collection

With a parent, try to collect a sample of each class of rock described in this chapter. You may wish to collect rocks from road cuts or simply collect pebbles from your garden or driveway. Try to collect samples that show the composition and texture of each rock. Classify the rocks in your collection, and bring it to class. With other members of the class, discuss your rock samples and see if they are accurately identified.

ACTIVITY

Composition of Metamorphic Rock

Metamorphism occurs when temperature and pressure inside the Earth's crust change. Minerals that were present in the rock when it formed may not be stable in the new temperature and pressure conditions. The original minerals change into minerals that are more stable in these new conditions. Look at **Figure 3** to see an example of how this change happens.

Many of these new minerals form only in metamorphic rock. As shown in **Figure 4,** some metamorphic minerals form only at certain temperatures and pressures. These minerals, known as *index minerals,* are used to estimate the temperature, depth, and pressure at which a rock undergoes metamorphism. Index minerals include biotite mica, chlorite, garnet, kyanite, muscovite mica, sillimanite, and staurolite.

 **Reading Check** What is an index mineral?

Figure 4 *Scientists can understand a metamorphic rock's history by observing the minerals the rock contains. For example, a metamorphic rock that contains garnet formed at a greater depth and under greater heat and pressure than a rock that contains only chlorite.*

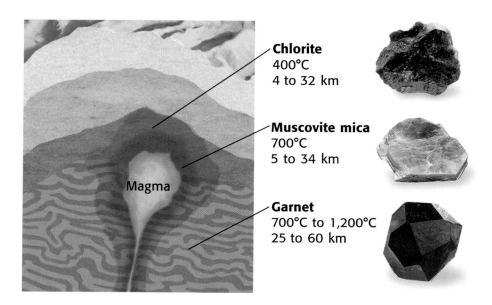

Magma

Chlorite
400°C
4 to 32 km

Muscovite mica
700°C
5 to 34 km

Garnet
700°C to 1,200°C
25 to 60 km

Textures of Metamorphic Rock

You have learned that texture helps scientists classify igneous and sedimentary rock. The same is true of metamorphic rock. All metamorphic rock has one of two textures—foliated or nonfoliated. Take a closer look at each of these types of metamorphic rock to find out how each type forms.

Foliated Metamorphic Rock

The texture of metamorphic rock in which the mineral grains are arranged in planes or bands is called **foliated.** Foliated metamorphic rock usually contains aligned grains of flat minerals, such as biotite mica or chlorite. Look at **Figure 5.** Shale is a sedimentary rock made of layers of clay minerals. When shale is exposed to slight heat and pressure, the clay minerals change into mica minerals. The shale becomes a foliated metamorphic rock called *slate*.

Metamorphic rocks can become other metamorphic rocks if the environment changes again. If slate is exposed to more heat and pressure, the slate can change into rock called *phyllite*. When phyllite is exposed to heat and pressure, it can change into *schist*.

If metamorphism continues, the arrangement of minerals in the rock changes. More heat and pressure cause minerals to separate into distinct bands in a metamorphic rock called *gneiss* (NIES).

foliated the texture of metamorphic rock in which the mineral grains are arranged in planes or bands

Sedimentary shale

Slate

Phyllite

Figure 5 *The effects of metamorphism depend on the heat and pressure applied to the rock. Here you can see what happens to shale, a sedimentary rock, when it is exposed to more and more heat and pressure.*

Schist

Gneiss

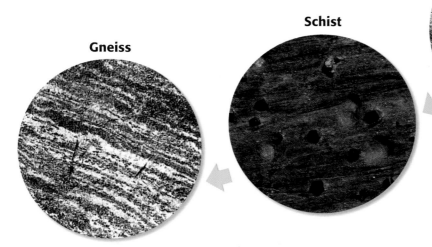

CONNECTION TO Biology

WRITING SKILL

Metamorphosis The term *meta-morphosis* means "change in form." When some animals undergo a dramatic change in the shape of their body, they are said to have undergone a metamorphosis. As part of their natural life cycle, moths and butterflies go through four stages. After they hatch from an egg, they are in the larval stage in the form of a cater-pillar. In the next stage, they build a cocoon or become a chrysalis. This stage is called the *pupal stage*. They finally emerge into the adult stage of their life, in which they have wings, antennae, and legs! Research other animals that undergo a metamorphosis, and summarize your findings in a short essay.

nonfoliated the texture of meta-morphic rock in which the mineral grains are not arranged in planes or bands

Nonfoliated Metamorphic Rock

The texture of metamorphic rock in which the mineral grains are not arranged in planes or bands is called **nonfoliated.** Notice that the rocks shown in **Figure 6** do not have mineral grains that are aligned. This lack of aligned mineral grains is the reason these rocks are called *nonfoliated rocks.*

Nonfoliated rocks are commonly made of one or only a few minerals. During metamorphism, the crystals of these minerals may change in size or the mineral may change in composition in a process called *recrystallization*. The quartzite and marble shown in **Figure 6** are examples of sedimentary rocks that have recrystallized during metamorphism.

Quartz sandstone is a sedimentary rock made of quartz sand grains that have been cemented together. When quartz sand-stone is exposed to the heat and pressure, the spaces between the sand grains disappear as the grains recrystallize to form quartzite. Quartzite has a shiny, glittery appearance. Like quartz sandstone, it is made of quartz. But during recrystallization, the mineral grains have grown larger than the original grains in the sandstone.

When limestone undergoes metamorphism, the same process that happened to the quartz happens to the calcite, and the limestone becomes marble. The calcite crystals in the marble are larger than the calcite grains in the original limestone.

Figure 6 **Two Examples of Nonfoliated Metamorphic Rock**

Marble and quartzite are nonfoliated metamorphic rocks. As you can see in the views through a microscope, the mineral crystals are not well aligned.

Marble

Quartzite

Metamorphic Rock Structures

Like igneous and sedimentary rock, metamorphic rock also has features that tell you about its history. In metamorphic rocks, these features are caused by deformation. *Deformation* is a change in the shape of a rock caused by a force placed on it. These forces may cause a rock to be squeezed or stretched.

Folds, or bends, in metamorphic rock are structures that indicate that a rock has been deformed. Some folds are not visible to the naked eye. But, as shown in **Figure 7,** some folds may be kilometers or even hundreds of kilometers in size.

✓ **Reading Check** How are metamorphic rock structures related to deformation?

Figure 7 *These large folds occur in metamorphosed sedimentary rock along Saglet Fiord in Labrador, Canada.*

SECTION Review

Summary

- Metamorphic rocks are rocks in which the structure, texture, or composition has changed.

- Two ways rocks can undergo metamorphism are by contact metamorphism and regional metamorphism.

- As rocks undergo metamorphism, the original minerals in a rock change into new minerals that are more stable in new pressure and temperature conditions.

- Foliated metamorphic rock has mineral crystals aligned in planes or bands, whereas nonfoliated rocks have unaligned mineral crystals.

- Metamorphic rock structures are caused by deformation.

Using Key Terms

1. In your own words, define the following terms: *foliated* and *nonfoliated.*

Understanding Key Ideas

2. Which of the following is not a type of foliated metamorphic rock?
   - **a.** gneiss
   - **b.** slate
   - **c.** marble
   - **d.** schist

3. Explain the difference between contact metamorphism and regional metamorphism.

4. Explain how index minerals allow a scientist to understand the history of a metamorphic rock.

Math Skills

5. For every 3.3 km a rock is buried, the pressure placed upon it increases 0.1 gigapascal (100 million pascals). If rock undergoing metamorphosis is buried at 16 km, what is the pressure placed on that rock? (Hint: The pressure at Earth's surface is .101 gigapascal.)

Critical Thinking

6. **Making Inferences** If you had two metamorphic rocks, one that has garnet crystals and the other that has chlorite crystals, which one could have formed at a deeper level in the Earth's crust? Explain your answer.

7. **Applying Concepts** Which do you think would be easier to break, a foliated rock, such as slate, or a nonfoliated rock, such as quartzite? Explain.

8. **Analyzing Processes** A mountain range is located at a boundary where two tectonic plates are colliding. Would most of the metamorphic rock in the mountain range be a product of contact metamorphism or regional metamorphism? Explain.

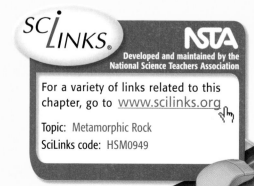

SCiLINKS®

NSTA
Developed and maintained by the
National Science Teachers Association

For a variety of links related to this chapter, go to www.scilinks.org

Topic: Metamorphic Rock
SciLinks code: HSM0949

Skills Practice Lab

Let's Get Sedimental

OBJECTIVES

Model the process of sedimentation.

Determine whether sedimentary rock layers are undisturbed.

MATERIALS

- clay
- dropper pipet
- gravel
- magnifying lens
- mixing bowl, 2 qt
- sand
- scissors
- soda bottle with a cap, plastic, 2 L
- soil, clay rich, if available
- water

SAFETY

How do we determine if sedimentary rock layers are undisturbed? The best way to do this is to be sure that fine-grained sediments near the top of a layer lie above coarse-grained sediments near the bottom of the layer. This lab activity will show you how to read rock features that will help you distinguish individual sedimentary rock layers. Then, you can look for the features in real rock layers.

Procedure

1. In a mixing bowl, thoroughly mix the sand, gravel, and soil. Fill the soda bottle about one-third full of the mixture.

2. Add water to the soda bottle until the bottle is two-thirds full. Twist the cap back onto the bottle, and shake the bottle vigorously until all of the sediment is mixed in the rapidly moving water.

3. Place the bottle on a tabletop. Using the scissors, carefully cut the top off the bottle a few centimeters above the water, as shown. The open bottle will allow water to evaporate.

4. Immediately after you set the bottle on the tabletop, describe what you see from above and through the sides of the bottle.

5. Do not disturb the container. Allow the water to evaporate. (You may speed up the process by carefully using the dropper pipet to siphon off some of the clear water after you allow the container to sit for at least 24 hours.) You may also set the bottle in the sun or under a desk lamp to speed up evaporation.

6. After the sediment has dried and hardened, describe its surface.

7. Carefully lay the container on its side, and cut a wide, vertical strip of plastic down the length of the bottle to expose the sediments in the container. You may find it easier if you place pieces of clay on either side of the container to stabilize it. (If the bottle is clear along its length, this step may not be required.)

8. Brush away the loose material from the sediment, and gently blow on the surface until it is clean. Examine the surface, and record your observations.

Analyze the Results

1 **Identifying Patterns** Do you see anything through the side of the bottle that could help you determine if a sedimentary rock is undisturbed? Explain your answer.

2 **Identifying Patterns** Can you observe a pattern of deposition? If so, describe the pattern of deposition of sediment that you observe from top to bottom.

3 **Explaining Events** Explain how these features might be used to identify the top of a sedimentary layer in real rock and to decide if the layer has been disturbed.

4 **Identifying Patterns** Do you see any structures through the side of the bottle that might indicate which direction is up, such as a change in particle density or size?

5 **Identifying Patterns** Use the magnifying lens to examine the boundaries between the gravel, sand, and silt. Do the size of the particles and the type of sediment change dramatically in each layer?

Draw Conclusions

6 **Making Predictions** Imagine that a layer was deposited directly above the sediment in your bottle. Describe the composition of this new layer. Will it have the same composition as the mixture in steps 1–5 in the Procedure?

Applying Your Data

With your class or with a parent, visit an outcrop of sedimentary rock. Apply the information that you have learned in this lab to see if you can determine whether the sedimentary rock layers are disturbed or undisturbed.

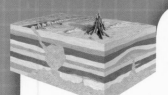

Chapter Review

USING KEY TERMS

1 In your own words, write a definition for the term *rock cycle*.

Complete each of the following sentences by choosing the correct term from the word bank.

stratification	foliated
extrusive igneous rock	texture

2 The ___ of a rock is determined by the sizes, shapes, and positions of the minerals the rock contains.

3 ___ metamorphic rock contains minerals that are arranged in plates or bands.

4 The most characteristic property of sedimentary rock is ___.

5 ___ forms plains called *lava plateaus*.

UNDERSTANDING KEY IDEAS

Multiple Choice

6 Sedimentary rock is classified into all of the following main categories except

a. clastic sedimentary rock.

b. chemical sedimentary rock.

c. nonfoliated sedimentary rock.

d. organic sedimentary rock.

7 An igneous rock that cools very slowly has a ___ texture.

a. foliated

b. fine-grained

c. nonfoliated

d. coarse-grained

8 Igneous rock forms when

a. minerals crystallize from a solution.

b. sand grains are cemented together.

c. magma cools and solidifies.

d. mineral grains in a rock recrystallize.

9 A ___ is a common structure found in metamorphic rock.

a. ripple mark   **c.** sill

b. fold   **d.** layer

10 The process in which sediment is removed from its source and transported is called

a. deposition.   **c.** weathering.

b. erosion.   **d.** uplift.

11 Mafic rocks are

a. light-colored rocks rich in calcium, iron, and magnesium.

b. dark-colored rocks rich in aluminum, potassium, silica, and sodium.

c. light-colored rocks rich in aluminum, potassium, silica, and sodium.

d. dark-colored rocks rich in calcium, iron, and magnesium.

Short Answer

12 Explain how composition and texture are used by scientists to classify rocks.

13 Describe two ways a rock can undergo metamorphism.

14 Explain why some minerals only occur in metamorphic rocks.

15 Describe how each type of rock changes as it moves through the rock cycle.

16 Describe two ways rocks were used by early humans and ancient civilizations.

17 **Concept Mapping** Use the following terms to construct a concept map: *rocks, metamorphic, sedimentary, igneous, foliated, nonfoliated, organic, clastic, chemical, intrusive,* and *extrusive.*

18 **Making Inferences** If you were looking for fossils in the rocks around your home and the rock type that was closest to your home was metamorphic, do you think that you would find many fossils? Explain your answer.

19 **Applying Concepts** Imagine that you want to quarry, or mine, granite. You have all of the equipment, but you have two pieces of land to choose from. One area has a granite batholith underneath it. The other has a granite sill. If both intrusive bodies are at the same depth, which one would be the better choice for you to quarry? Explain your answer.

20 **Applying Concepts** The sedimentary rock coquina is made up of pieces of seashells. Which of the three kinds of sedimentary rock could coquina be? Explain your answer.

21 **Analyzing Processes** If a rock is buried deep inside the Earth, which geological processes cannot change the rock? Explain your answer.

INTERPRETING GRAPHICS

The bar graph below shows the percentage of minerals by mass that compose a sample of granite. Use the graph below to answer the questions that follow.

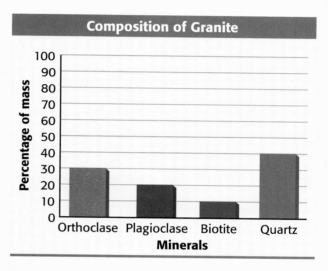

Composition of Granite

22 Your rock sample is made of four minerals. What percentage of each mineral makes up your sample?

23 Both plagioclase and orthoclase are feldspar minerals. What percentage of the minerals in your sample of granite are not feldspar minerals?

24 If your rock sample has a mass of 10 g, how many grams of quartz does it contain?

25 Use paper, a compass, and a protractor or a computer to make a pie chart. Show the percentage of each of the four minerals your sample of granite contains. (Look in the Appendix of this book for help on making a pie chart.)

Standardized Test Preparation

Read each of the passages below. Then, answer the questions that follow each passage.

Passage 1 The texture and composition of a rock can provide good clues about how and where the rock formed. Scientists use both texture and composition to understand the <u>origin</u> and history of rocks. For example, marble is a rock that is made when limestone is metamorphosed. Only limestone contains the mineral—calcite—that can change into marble. Therefore, wherever scientists find marble, they know the sediment that created the original limestone was deposited in a warm ocean or lake environment.

1. In the passage, what does the word *origin* mean?
  A size or appearance
  B age
  C location or surroundings
  D source or formation

2. Based on the passage, what can the reader conclude?
  F Marble is a sedimentary rock.
  G Limestone is created by sediments deposited in warm ocean or lake environments.
  H Marble is a rock that is made when sandstone has undergone metamorphism.
  I In identifying a rock, the texture of a rock is more important than the composition of the rock.

3. What is the main idea of the passage?
  A Scientists believe marble is the most important rock type to study.
  B Scientists study the composition and texture of a rock to determine how the rock formed and what happened after it formed.
  C Some sediments are deposited in warm oceans and lakes.
  D When limestone undergoes metamorphism, it creates marble.

Passage 2 Fulgurites are a rare type of natural glass found in areas that have quartz-rich sediments, such as beaches and deserts. A <u>tubular</u> fulgurite forms when a lightning bolt strikes material such as sand and melts the quartz into a liquid. The liquid quartz cools and solidifies quickly, and a thin, glassy tube is left behind. Fulgurites usually have a rough outer surface and a smooth inner surface. Underground, a fulgurite may be shaped like the roots of a tree. The fulgurite branches out with many arms that trace the zigzag path of the lightning bolt. Some fulgurites are as short as your little finger, but others stretch 20 m into the ground.

1. In the passage, what does the word *tubular* mean?
  A flat and sharp
  B round and long
  C funnel shaped
  D pyramid shaped

2. From the information in the passage, what can the reader conclude?
  F Fulgurites are formed above ground.
  G Sand contains a large amount of quartz.
  H Fulgurites are most often very small.
  I Fulgurites are easy to find in sandy places.

3. Which of the following statements best describes a fulgurite?
  A Fulgurites are frozen lightning bolts.
  B Fulgurites are rootlike rocks.
  C Fulgurites are glassy tubes found in deserts.
  D Fulgurites are natural glass tubes formed by lightning bolts.

Use the diagram below to answer the questions that follow.

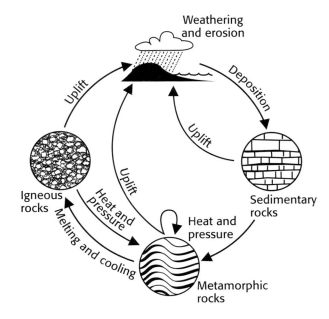

1. According to the rock cycle diagram, which of the following statements is true?
   A Only sedimentary rock gets weathered and eroded.
   B Sedimentary rocks are made from metamorphic, igneous, and sedimentary rock fragments and minerals.
   C Heat and pressure create igneous rocks.
   D Metamorphic rocks are created by melting and cooling.

2. A rock exists at the surface of the Earth. What would be the next step in the rock cycle?
   F cooling
   G weathering
   H melting
   I metamorphism

3. Which of the following processes brings rocks to Earth's surface, where they can be eroded?
   A burial
   B deposition
   C uplift
   D weathering

4. Which of the following is the best summary of the rock cycle?
   F Each type of rock gets melted. Then the magma turns into igneous, sedimentary, and metamorphic rock.
   G Magma cools to form igneous rock. Then, the igneous rock becomes sedimentary rock. Sedimentary rock is heated and forms metamorphic rock. Metamorphic rock melts to form magma.
   H All three rock types weather to create sedimentary rock. All three rock types melt to form magma. Magma forms igneous rock. All three types of rock form metamorphic rock because of heat and pressure.
   I Igneous rock is weathered to create sedimentary rock. Sedimentary rock is melted to form igneous rock. Metamorphic rock is weathered to form igneous rock.

MATH

Read each question below, and choose the best answer.

1. Eric has 25 rocks he has collected as a science project for class. Nine rocks are sedimentary, 10 are igneous, and 6 are metamorphic. If Eric chooses a rock at random, what is the probability that he will choose an igneous rock?
   A 1/2
   B 2/5
   C 3/8
   D 1/15

2. At a mineral and fossil show, Elizabeth bought two quartz crystals that cost $2.00 each and four trilobite fossils that cost $3.50 each. Which equation can be used to describe c, the total cost of her purchase?
   F $c = (2 \times 4) + (2.00 \times 3.50)$
   G $c = (2 \times 2.00) + (4 \times 3.50)$
   H $c = (4 \times 2.00) + (2 \times 3.50)$
   I $c = (2 + 2.00) + (4 + 3.50)$

Science in Action

Science, Technology, and Society

The Moai of Easter Island

Easter island is located in the Pacific Ocean more than 3,200 km from the coast of Chile. The island is home to mysterious statues that were carved from volcanic ash. The statues, called *moai,* have human heads and large torsos. The average moai weighs 14 tons and is more than 4.5 m tall, though some are as tall as 10 m! Altogether, 887 moai have been discovered. How old are the moai? Scientists believe that the moai were built between 500 and 1,000 years ago. What purpose did moai serve for their creators? The moai may have been religious symbols or gods.

Social Studies ACTiViTY

WRITING SKILL Research another ancient society or civilization, such as the ancient Egyptians, who are believed to have used stone to construct monuments to their gods or to important people. Report your findings in a short essay.

Scientific Discoveries

Shock Metamorphism

When a large asteroid, meteoroid, or comet collides with the Earth, extremely high temperatures and pressures are created in Earth's surface rock. These high pressures and temperatures cause minerals in the surface rock to shatter and recrystallize. The new minerals that result from this recrystallization cannot be created under any other conditions. This process is called *shock metamorphism.*

When large objects from space collide with the Earth, craters are formed by the impact. However, impact craters are not always easy to find on Earth. Scientists use shock metamorphism as a clue to locate ancient impact craters.

Language Arts ACTiViTY

WRITING SKILL The impact site caused by the asteroid strike in the Yucatán 65 million years ago has been named the Chicxulub (cheeks OO loob) structure. Research the origin of the name Chicxulub, and report your findings in a short paper.

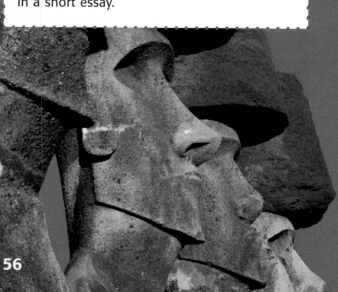

Robert L. Folk

Petrologist For Dr. Robert Folk, the study of rock takes place on the microscopic level. Dr. Folk is searching for tiny life-forms he has named nannobacteria, or dwarf bacteria, in rock. *Nannobacteria* may also be spelled *nanobacteria*. Because nannobacteria are so incredibly small, only 0.05 to 0.2 µm in diameter, Folk must use an extremely powerful 100,000× microscope, called a *scanning electron microscope,* to see the shape of the bacteria in rock. Folk's research had already led him to discover that a certain type of Italian limestone is produced by bacteria. The bacteria were consuming the minerals, and the waste of the bacteria was forming the limestone. Further research led Folk to the discovery of the tiny nannobacteria. The spherical or oval-shaped nannobacteria appeared as chains and grapelike clusters. From his research, Folk hypothesized that nannobacteria are responsible for many inorganic reactions that occur in rock. Many scientists are skeptical of Folk's nannobacteria. Some skeptics believe that the tiny size of nannobacteria makes the bacteria simply too small to contain the chemistry of life. Others believe that nannobacteria actually represent structures that do not come from living things.

Math ACTIVITY

If a nannobacterium is 1/10 the length, 1/10 the width, and 1/10 the height of an ordinary bacterium, how many nannobacteria can fit within an ordinary bacterium? (Hint: Draw block diagrams of both a nannobacterium and an ordinary bacterium.)

go.hrw.com

To learn more about these Science in Action topics, visit go.hrw.com and type in the keyword **HZ5RCKF.**

Current Science

Check out Current Science® articles related to this chapter by visiting go.hrw.com. Just type in the keyword HZ5CS04.

3

The Rock and Fossil Record

About the PHOTO

This extremely well preserved crocodile fossil
has been out of water for 49 million years. Its
skeleton was collected in an abandoned mine
pit in Messel, Germany.

PRE-READING ACTIVITY

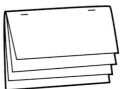

FOLDNOTES **Layered Book** Before
you read the chapter,
create the FoldNote entitled
"Layered Book" described in the **Study
Skills** section of the Appendix. Label the
tabs of the layered book with "Earth's
history," "Relative dating," "Absolute
dating," "Fossils," and "Geologic time."
As you read the chap-
ter, write information
you learn about each
category under the
appropriate tab.

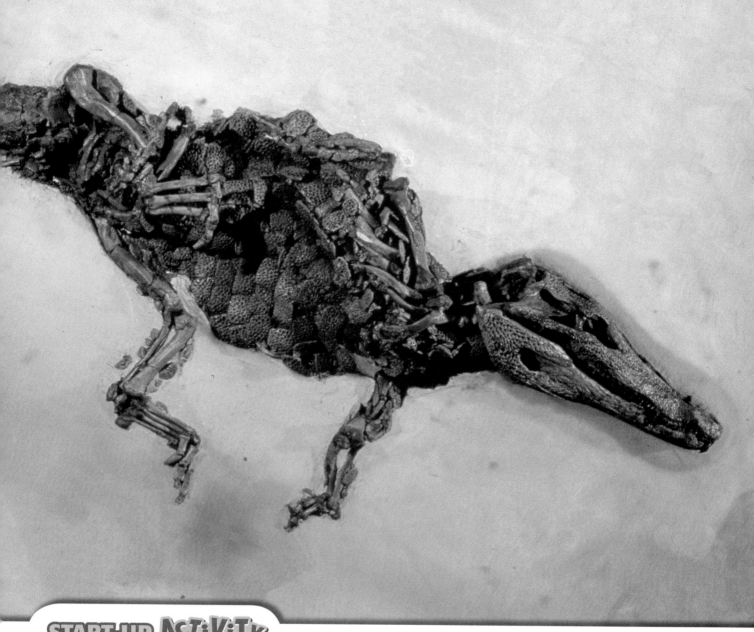

Making Fossils

How do scientists learn from fossils? In this activity, you will study "fossils" and identify the object that made each.

Procedure

1. You and three or four of your classmates will be given **several pieces** of **modeling clay** and a **paper sack** containing a few **small objects.**

2. Press each object firmly into a piece of clay. Try to leave a "fossil" imprint showing as much detail as possible.

3. After you have made an imprint of each object, exchange your model fossils with another group.

4. On a **sheet of paper,** describe the fossils you have received. List as many details as possible. What patterns and textures do you observe?

5. Work as a group to identify each fossil, and check your results. Were you right?

Analysis

1. What kinds of details were important in identifying your fossils? What kinds of details were not preserved in the imprints? For example, can you tell the materials from which the objects are made or their color?

2. Explain how scientists follow similar methods when studying fossils.

Earth's Story and Those Who First Listened

How do mountains form? How is new rock created? How old is the Earth? Have you ever asked these questions? Nearly 250 years ago, a Scottish farmer and scientist named James Hutton did.

Searching for answers to his questions, Hutton spent more than 30 years studying rock formations in Scotland and England. His observations led to the foundation of modern geology.

The Principle of Uniformitarianism

In 1788, James Hutton collected his notes and wrote *Theory of the Earth.* In *Theory of the Earth,* he stated that the key to understanding Earth's history was all around us. In other words, processes that we observe today—such as erosion and deposition—remain uniform, or do not change, over time. This assumption is now called uniformitarianism. **Uniformitarianism** is the idea that the same geologic processes shaping the Earth today have been at work throughout Earth's history. **Figure 1** shows how Hutton developed the idea of uniformitarianism.

READING WARM-UP

Objectives
- Compare uniformitarianism and catastrophism.
- Describe how the science of geology has changed over the past 200 years.
- Explain the role of paleontology in the study of Earth's history.

Terms to Learn
uniformitarianism
catastrophism
paleontology

READING STRATEGY

Reading Organizer As you read this section, make a table comparing uniformitarianism and catastrophism.

Figure 1 *Hutton observed gradual, uniform geologic change.*

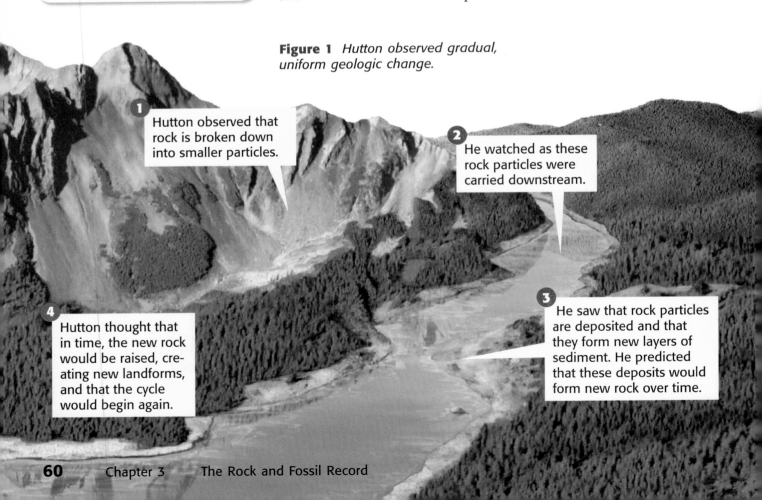

1 Hutton observed that rock is broken down into smaller particles.

2 He watched as these rock particles were carried downstream.

3 He saw that rock particles are deposited and that they form new layers of sediment. He predicted that these deposits would form new rock over time.

4 Hutton thought that in time, the new rock would be raised, creating new landforms, and that the cycle would begin again.

Figure 2 *This photograph shows Siccar Point on the coast of Scotland. Siccar Point is one of the places where Hutton observed results of geologic processes that would lead him to form his principle of uniformitarianism.*

Uniformitarianism Versus Catastrophism

Hutton's theories sparked a scientific debate by suggesting that Earth was much older than previously thought. In Hutton's time, most people thought that Earth was only a few thousand years old. A few thousand years was not nearly enough time for the gradual geologic processes that Hutton described to have shaped our planet. The rocks that he observed at Siccar Point, shown in **Figure 2,** were deposited and folded, indicating a long geological history. To explain Earth's history, most scientists supported catastrophism. **Catastrophism** is the principle that states that all geologic change occurs suddenly. Supporters of catastrophism thought that Earth's features, such as its mountains, canyons, and seas, formed during rare, sudden events called *catastrophes.* These unpredictable events caused rapid geologic change over large areas—sometimes even globally.

✓ Reading Check According to catastrophists, what was the rate of geologic change? (*See the Appendix for answers to Reading Checks.*)

A Victory for Uniformitarianism

Despite Hutton's work, catastrophism remained geology's guiding principle for decades. Only after the work of British geologist Charles Lyell did people seriously consider uniformitarianism as geology's guiding principle.

From 1830 to 1833, Lyell published three volumes, collectively titled *Principles of Geology,* in which he reintroduced uniformitarianism. Armed with Hutton's notes and new evidence of his own, Lyell successfully challenged the principle of catastrophism. Lyell saw no reason to doubt that major geologic change happened at the same rate in the past as it happens in the present—gradually.

uniformitarianism a principle that states that geologic processes that occurred in the past can be explained by current geologic processes

catastrophism a principle that states that geologic change occurs suddenly

CONNECTION TO Biology

WRITING SKILL **Darwin and Lyell** The theory of evolution was developed soon after Lyell introduced his ideas, which was no coincidence. Lyell and Charles Darwin were good friends, and their talks greatly influenced Darwin's theories. Similar to uniformitarianism, Darwin's theory of evolution proposes that changes in species occur gradually over long periods of time. Write a short essay comparing uniformitarianism and evolution.

Modern Geology—A Happy Medium

During the late 20th century, scientists such as Stephen J. Gould challenged Lyell's uniformitarianism. They believed that catastrophes do, at times, play an important role in shaping Earth's history.

Today, scientists realize that neither uniformitarianism nor catastrophism accounts for all geologic change throughout Earth's history. Although most geologic change is gradual and uniform, catastrophes that cause geologic change have occurred during Earth's long history. For example, huge craters have been found where asteroids and comets are thought to have struck Earth in the past. Some scientists think one such asteroid strike, approximately 65 million years ago, may have caused the dinosaurs to become extinct. **Figure 3** is an imaginary re-creation of the asteroid strike that is thought to have caused the extinction of the dinosaurs. The impact of this asteroid is thought to have thrown debris into the atmosphere. The debris spread around the entire planet and rained down on Earth for decades. This global debris cloud may have blocked the sun's rays, causing major changes in the global climate that doomed the dinosaurs.

Reading Check How can a catastrophe affect life on Earth?

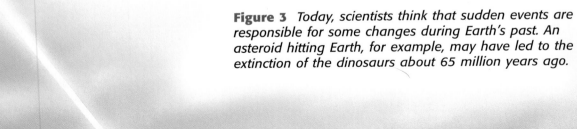

Figure 3 *Today, scientists think that sudden events are responsible for some changes during Earth's past. An asteroid hitting Earth, for example, may have led to the extinction of the dinosaurs about 65 million years ago.*

Paleontology—The Study of Past Life

The history of the Earth would be incomplete without a knowledge of the organisms that have inhabited our planet and the conditions under which they lived. The science involved with the study of past life is called **paleontology.** Scientists who study this life are called *paleontologists.* The data paleontologists use are fossils. Fossils are the remains of organisms preserved by geologic processes. Some paleontologists specialize in the study of particular organisms. Invertebrate paleontologists study animals without backbones, whereas vertebrate paleontologists, such as the scientist in **Figure 4,** study animals with backbones. Paleobotanists study fossils of plants. Other paleontologists reconstruct past ecosystems, study the traces left behind by animals, and piece together the conditions under which fossils were formed. As you see, the study of past life is as varied and complex as Earth's history itself.

Figure 4 *Edwin Colbert was a 20th-century vertebrate paleontologist who made important contributions to the study of dinosaurs.*

paleontology the scientific study of fossils

SECTION Review

Summary

- Uniformitarianism assumes that geologic change is gradual. Catastrophism is based on the idea that geologic change is sudden.
- Modern geology is based on the idea that gradual geologic change is interrupted by catastrophes.
- Using fossils to study past life is called *paleontology.*

Using Key Terms

1. Use each of the following terms in a separate sentence: *uniformitarianism, catastrophism,* and *paleontology.*

Understanding Key Ideas

2. Which of the following words describes change according to the principle of uniformitarianism?
   - **a.** sudden
   - **b.** rare
   - **c.** global
   - **d.** gradual

3. What is the difference between uniformitarianism and catastrophism?

4. Describe how the science of geology has changed.

5. Give one example of catastrophic global change.

6. Describe the work of three types of paleontologists.

Math Skills

7. An impact crater left by an asteroid strike has a radius of 85 km. What is the area of the crater? (Hint: The area of a circle is πr^2.)

Critical Thinking

8. **Analyzing Ideas** Why is uniformitarianism considered to be the foundation of modern geology?

9. **Applying Concepts** Give an example of a type of recent catastrophe.

SCiLINKS

NSTA
Developed and maintained by the National Science Teachers Association

For a variety of links related to this chapter, go to www.scilinks.org

Topic: Earth's Story
SciLinks code: HSM0450

Relative Dating: Which Came First?

Imagine that you are a detective investigating a crime scene. What is the first thing you would do?

You might begin by dusting the scene for fingerprints or by searching for witnesses. As a detective, you must figure out the sequence of events that took place before you reached the crime scene.

Geologists have a similar goal when investigating the Earth. They try to determine the order in which events have happened during Earth's history. But instead of relying on fingerprints and witnesses, geologists rely on rocks and fossils to help them in their investigation. Determining whether an object or event is older or younger than other objects or events is called **relative dating.**

The Principle of Superposition

Suppose that you have an older brother who takes a lot of photographs of your family and piles them in a box. Over the years, he keeps adding new photographs to the top of the stack. Think about the family history recorded in those photos. Where are the oldest photographs—the ones taken when you were a baby? Where are the most recent photographs—those taken last week?

Layers of sedimentary rock, such as the ones shown in **Figure 1,** are like stacked photographs. As you move from top to bottom, the layers are older. The principle that states that younger rocks lie above older rocks in undisturbed sequences is called **superposition.**

READING WARM-UP

Objectives

- Explain how relative dating is used in geology.
- Explain the principle of superposition.
- Describe how the geologic column is used in relative dating.
- Identify two events and two features that disrupt rock layers.
- Explain how physical features are used to determine relative ages.

Terms to Learn

relative dating
superposition
geologic column
unconformity

READING STRATEGY

Reading Organizer As you read this section, create an outline of the section. Use the headings from the section in your outline.

Figure 1 *Rock layers are like photos stacked over time—the younger ones lie above the older ones.*

Disturbing Forces

Not all rock sequences are arranged with the oldest layers on the bottom and the youngest layers on top. Some rock sequences are disturbed by forces within the Earth. These forces can push other rocks into a sequence, tilt or fold rock layers, and break sequences into movable parts. Sometimes, geologists even find rock sequences that are upside down! The disruptions of rock sequences pose a challenge to geologists trying to determine the relative ages of rocks. Fortunately, geologists can get help from a very valuable tool—the geologic column.

The Geologic Column

To make their job easier, geologists combine data from all the known undisturbed rock sequences around the world. From this information, geologists create the geologic column, as illustrated in **Figure 2.** The **geologic column** is an ideal sequence of rock layers that contains all the known fossils and rock formations on Earth, arranged from oldest to youngest.

Geologists rely on the geologic column to interpret rock sequences. Geologists also use the geologic column to identify the layers in puzzling rock sequences.

✓ **Reading Check** List two ways in which geologists use the geologic column. (*See the Appendix for answers to Reading Checks.*)

relative dating any method of determining whether an event or object is older or younger than other events or objects

superposition a principle that states that younger rocks lie above older rocks if the layers have not been disturbed

geologic column an arrangement of rock layers in which the oldest rocks are at the bottom

---

Figure 2 **Constructing the Geologic Column**

Here, you can see three rock sequences (A, B, and C) from three different locations. Some rock layers appear in more than one sequence. Geologists construct the geologic column by piecing together different rock sequences from all over the world.

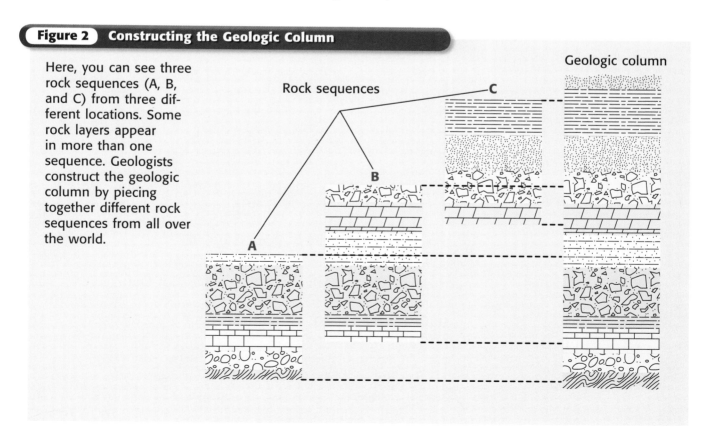

Figure 3 **How Rock Layers Become Disturbed**

Fault A *fault* is a break in the Earth's crust along which blocks of the crust slide relative to one another.

Intrusion An *intrusion* is molten rock from the Earth's interior that squeezes into existing rock and cools.

Folding *Folding* occurs when rock layers bend and buckle from Earth's internal forces.

Tilting *Tilting* occurs when internal forces in the Earth slant rock layers.

Disturbed Rock Layers

Geologists often find features that cut across existing layers of rock. Geologists use the relationships between rock layers and the features that cut across them to assign relative ages to the features and the layers. They know that the features are younger than the rock layers because the rock layers had to be present before the features could cut across them. Faults and intrusions are examples of features that cut across rock layers. A fault and an intrusion are illustrated in **Figure 3.**

Events That Disturb Rock Layers

Geologists assume that the way sediment is deposited to form rock layers—in horizontal layers—has not changed over time. According to this principle, if rock layers are not horizontal, something must have disturbed them after they formed. This principle allows geologists to determine the relative ages of rock layers and the events that disturbed them.

Folding and tilting are two types of events that disturb rock layers. These events are always younger than the rock layers they affect. The results of folding and tilting are shown in **Figure 3.**

Gaps in the Record—Unconformities

Faults, intrusions, and the effects of folding and tilting can make dating rock layers a challenge. Sometimes, layers of rock are missing altogether, creating a gap in the geologic record. To think of this another way, let's say that you stack your newspapers every day after reading them. Now, let's suppose you want to look at a paper you read 10 days ago. You know that the paper should be 10 papers deep in the stack. But when you look, the paper is not there. What happened? Perhaps you forgot to put the paper in the stack. Now, imagine a missing rock layer instead of a missing newspaper.

Missing Evidence

Missing rock layers create breaks in rock-layer sequences called unconformities. An **unconformity** is a surface that represents a missing part of the geologic column. Unconformities also represent missing time—time that was not recorded in layers of rock. When geologists find an unconformity, they must question whether the "missing layer" was never present or whether it was somehow removed. **Figure 4** shows how *nondeposition,* or the stoppage of deposition when a supply of sediment is cut off, and *erosion* create unconformities.

unconformity a break in the geologic record created when rock layers are eroded or when sediment is not deposited for a long period of time

✓ **Reading Check** Define the term unconformity.

Figure 4 How Unconformities Are Created

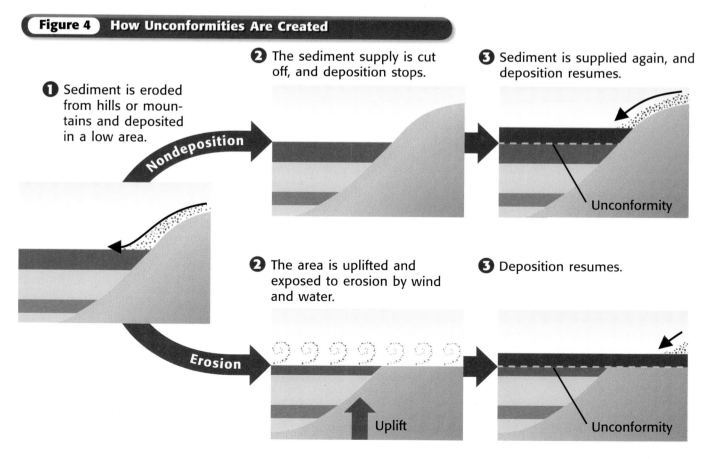

❶ Sediment is eroded from hills or mountains and deposited in a low area.

Nondeposition

❷ The sediment supply is cut off, and deposition stops.

❸ Sediment is supplied again, and deposition resumes.

Unconformity

Erosion

❷ The area is uplifted and exposed to erosion by wind and water.

Uplift

❸ Deposition resumes.

Unconformity

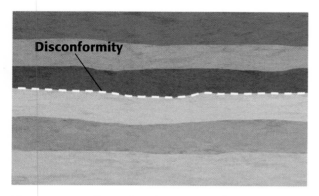

Figure 5 *A disconformity exists where part of a sequence of parallel rock layers is missing.*

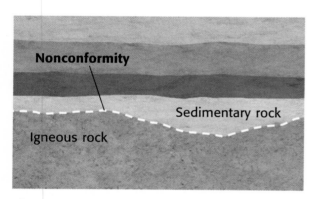

Figure 6 *A nonconformity exists where sedimentary rock layers lie on top of an eroded surface of nonlayered igneous or metamorphic rock.*

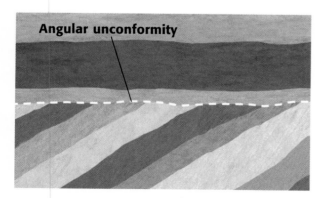

Figure 7 *An angular unconformity exists between horizontal rock layers and rock layers that are tilted or folded.*

Types of Unconformities

Most unconformities form by both erosion and nondeposition. But other factors can complicate matters. To simplify the study of unconformities, geologists place them into three major categories: disconformities, nonconformities, and angular unconformities. The three diagrams at left illustrate these three categories.

Disconformities

The most common type of unconformity is a disconformity, which is illustrated in **Figure 5.** *Disconformities* are found where part of a sequence of parallel rock layers is missing. A disconformity can form in the following way. A sequence of rock layers is uplifted. Younger layers at the top of the sequence are removed by erosion, and the eroded material is deposited elsewhere. At some future time, deposition resumes, and sediment buries the old erosion surface. The disconformity that results shows where erosion has taken place and rock layers are missing. A disconformity represents thousands to many millions of years of missing time.

Nonconformities

A nonconformity is illustrated in **Figure 6.** *Nonconformities* are found where horizontal sedimentary rock layers lie on top of an eroded surface of older intrusive igneous or metamorphic rock. Intrusive igneous and metamorphic rocks form deep within the Earth. When these rocks are raised to Earth's surface, they are eroded. Deposition causes the erosion surface to be buried. Nonconformities represent millions of years of missing time.

Angular Unconformities

An angular unconformity is shown in **Figure 7.** *Angular unconformities* are found between horizontal layers of sedimentary rock and layers of rock that have been tilted or folded. The tilted or folded layers were eroded before horizontal layers formed above them. Angular unconformities represent millions of years of missing time.

Reading Check Describe each of the three major categories of unconformities.

Rock-Layer Puzzles

Geologists often find rock-layer sequences that have been affected by more than one of the events and features mentioned in this section. For example, as shown in **Figure 8,** intrusions may squeeze into rock layers that contain an unconformity. Determining the order of events that led to such a sequence is like piecing together a jigsaw puzzle. Geologists must use their knowledge of the events that disturb or remove rock-layer sequences to help piece together the history of Earth as told by the rock record.

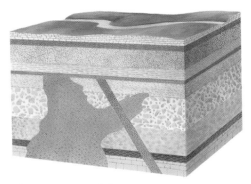

Figure 8 *Rock-layer sequences are often disturbed by more than one rock-disturbing feature.*

SECTION Review

Summary

- Geologists use relative dating to determine the order in which events happen.

- The principle of superposition states that in undisturbed rock sequences, younger layers lie above older layers.

- Folding and tilting are two events that disturb rock layers. Faults and intrusions are two features that disturb rock layers.

- The known rock and fossil record is indicated by the geologic column.

- Geologists examine the relationships between rock layers and the structures that cut across them in order to determine relative ages.

Using Key Terms

1. In your own words, write a definition for each of the following terms: *relative dating, superposition,* and *geologic column.*

Understanding Key Ideas

2. Molten rock that squeezes into existing rock and cools is called a(n)
   a. fold.
   b. fault.
   c. intrusion.
   d. unconformity.

3. List two events and two features that can disturb rock-layer sequences.

4. Explain how physical features are used to determine relative ages.

Critical Thinking

5. **Analyzing Concepts** Is there a place on Earth that has all the layers of the geologic column? Explain.

6. **Analyzing Ideas** Disconformities are hard to recognize because all of the layers are horizontal. How does a geologist know when he or she is looking at a disconformity?

Interpreting Graphics

Use the illustration below to answer the question that follows.

7. If the top rock layer were eroded and deposition later resumed, what type of unconformity would mark the boundary between older rock layers and the newly deposited rock layers?

For a variety of links related to this chapter, go to www.scilinks.org

Topic: Relative Dating
SciLinks code: HSM1288

Absolute Dating: A Measure of Time

Have you ever heard the expression "turning back the clock"? With the discovery of the natural decay of uranium in 1896, French physicist Henri Becquerel provided a means of doing just that. Scientists could use radioactive elements as clocks to measure geologic time.

The process of establishing the age of an object by determining the number of years it has existed is called **absolute dating.** In this section, you will learn about radiometric dating, which is the most common method of absolute dating.

Radioactive Decay

To determine the absolute ages of fossils and rocks, scientists analyze isotopes of radioactive elements. Atoms of the same element that have the same number of protons but have different numbers of neutrons are called **isotopes.** Most isotopes are stable, meaning that they stay in their original form. But some isotopes are unstable. Scientists call unstable isotopes *radioactive.* Radioactive isotopes tend to break down into stable isotopes of the same or other elements in a process called **radioactive decay. Figure 1** shows an example of how radioactive decay occurs. Because radioactive decay occurs at a steady rate, scientists can use the relative amounts of stable and unstable isotopes present in an object to determine the object's age.

READING WARM-UP

Objectives

- Describe how radioactive decay occurs.
- Explain how radioactive decay relates to radiometric dating.
- Identify four types of radiometric dating.
- Determine the best type of radiometric dating to use to date an object.

Terms to Learn

absolute dating
isotope
radioactive decay
radiometric dating
half-life

READING STRATEGY

Reading Organizer As you read this section, make a concept map by using the terms above.

Figure 1 Radioactive Decay

Unstable Isotope
6 protons, 8 neutrons

Radioactive Decay When some unstable isotopes decay, a neutron is converted into a proton. In the process, an electron is released.

Stable Isotope
7 protons, 7 neutrons

Dating Rocks—How Does It Work?

In the process of radioactive decay, an unstable radioactive isotope of one element breaks down into a stable isotope. The stable isotope may be of the same element or, more commonly, a different element. The unstable radioactive isotope is called the *parent isotope*. The stable isotope produced by the radioactive decay of the parent isotope is called the *daughter isotope*. The radioactive decay of a parent isotope into a stable daughter isotope can occur in a single step or a series of steps. In either case, the rate of decay is constant. Therefore, to date rock, scientists compare the amount of parent material with the amount of daughter material. The more daughter material there is, the older the rock is.

Radiometric Dating

If you know the rate of decay for a radioactive element in a rock, you can figure out the absolute age of the rock. Determining the absolute age of a sample, based on the ratio of parent material to daughter material, is called **radiometric dating.** For example, let's say that a rock sample contains an isotope with a half-life of 10,000 years. A **half-life** is the time that it takes one-half of a radioactive sample to decay. So, for this rock sample, in 10,000 years, half the parent material will have decayed and become daughter material. You analyze the sample and find equal amounts of parent material and daughter material. This means that half the original radioactive isotope has decayed and that the sample must be about 10,000 years old.

What if one-fourth of your sample is parent material and three-fourths is daughter material? You would know that it took 10,000 years for half the original sample to decay and another 10,000 years for half of what remained to decay. The age of your sample would be 2 × 10,000, or 20,000, years. **Figure 2** shows how this steady decay happens.

Reading Check What is a half-life? (*See the Appendix for answers to Reading Checks.*)

absolute dating any method of measuring the age of an event or object in years

isotope an atom that has the same number of protons (or the same atomic number) as other atoms of the same element do but that has a different number of neutrons (and thus a different atomic mass)

radioactive decay the process in which a radioactive isotope tends to break down into a stable isotope of the same element or another element

radiometric dating a method of determining the age of an object by estimating the relative percentages of a radioactive (parent) isotope and a stable (daughter) isotope

half-life the time needed for half of a sample of a radioactive substance to undergo radioactive decay

Figure 2 *After every half-life, the amount of parent material decreases by one-half.*

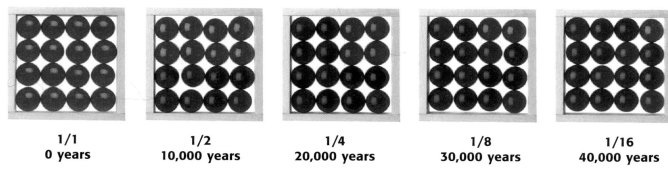

1/1	1/2	1/4	1/8	1/16
0 years	**10,000 years**	**20,000 years**	**30,000 years**	**40,000 years**

Types of Radiometric Dating

Imagine traveling back through the centuries to a time before Columbus arrived in America. You are standing along the bluffs of what will one day be called the Mississippi River. You see dozens of people building large mounds. Who are these people, and what are they building?

The people you saw in your time travel were Native Americans, and the structures they were building were burial mounds. The area you imagined is now an archaeological site called Effigy Mounds National Monument. **Figure 3** shows one of these mounds.

According to archaeologists, people lived at Effigy Mounds from 2,500 years ago to 600 years ago. How do archaeologists know these dates? They have dated bones and other objects in the mounds by using radiometric dating. Scientists use different radiometric-dating techniques based on the estimated age of an object. As you read on, think about how the half-life of an isotope relates to the age of the object being dated. Which technique would you use to date the burial mounds?

Figure 3 *This burial mound at Effigy Mounds resembles a snake.*

Potassium-Argon Method

One isotope that is used for radiometric dating is potassium-40. Potassium-40 has a half-life of 1.3 billion years, and it decays to argon and calcium. Geologists measure argon as the daughter material. This method is used mainly to date rocks older than 100,000 years.

Uranium-Lead Method

Uranium-238 is a radioactive isotope that decays in a series of steps to lead-206. The half-life of uranium-238 is 4.5 billion years. The older the rock is, the more daughter material (lead-206) there will be in the rock. Uranium-lead dating can be used for rocks more than 10 million years old. Younger rocks do not contain enough daughter material to be accurately measured by this method.

Rubidium-Strontium Method

Through radioactive decay, the unstable parent isotope rubidium-87 forms the stable daughter isotope strontium-87. The half-life of rubidium-87 is 49 billion years. This method is used to date rocks older than 10 million years.

Reading Check What is the daughter isotope of rubidium-87?

Carbon-14 Method

The element carbon is normally found in three forms, the stable isotopes carbon-12 and carbon-13 and the radioactive isotope carbon-14. These carbon isotopes combine with oxygen to form the gas carbon dioxide, which is taken in by plants during photosynthesis. As long as a plant is alive, new carbon dioxide with a constant carbon-14 to carbon-12 ratio is continually taken in. Animals that eat plants contain the same ratio of carbon isotopes.

Once a plant or an animal dies, however, no new carbon is taken in. The amount of carbon-14 begins to decrease as the plant or animal decays, and the ratio of carbon-14 to carbon-12 decreases. This decrease can be measured in a laboratory, such as the one shown in **Figure 4.** Because the half-life of carbon-14 is only 5,730 years, this dating method is used mainly for dating things that lived within the last 50,000 years.

Figure 4 *Some samples containing carbon must be cleaned and burned before their age can be determined.*

SECTION Review

Summary

- During radioactive decay, an unstable isotope decays at a constant rate and becomes a stable isotope of the same or a different element.

- Radiometric dating, based on the ratio of parent to daughter material, is used to determine the absolute age of a sample.

- Methods of radio-metric dating include potassium-argon, uranium-lead, rubidium-strontium, and carbon-14 dating.

Using Key Terms

1. Use each of the following terms in a separate sentence: *absolute dating, isotope,* and *half-life.*

Understanding Key Ideas

2. Rubidium-87 has a half-life of
   a. 5,730 years.
   b. 4.5 billion years.
   c. 49 billion years.
   d. 1.3 billion years.

3. Explain how radioactive decay occurs.

4. How does radioactive decay relate to radiometric dating?

5. List four types of radiometric dating.

Math Skills

6. A radioactive isotope has a half-life of 1.3 billion years. After 3.9 billion years, how much of the parent material will be left?

Critical Thinking

7. **Analyzing Methods** Explain why radioactive decay must be constant in order for radiometric dating to be accurate.

8. **Applying Concepts** Which radiometric-dating method would be most appropriate for dating artifacts found at Effigy Mounds? Explain.

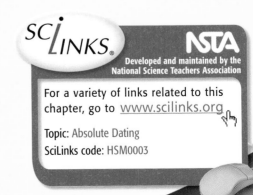

SC*i*LINKS.

NSTA
Developed and maintained by the National Science Teachers Association

For a variety of links related to this chapter, go to www.scilinks.org

Topic: Absolute Dating
SciLinks code: HSM0003

Looking at Fossils

Descending from the top of a ridge in the badlands of Argentina, your expedition team suddenly stops. You look down and realize that you are walking on eggshells— dinosaur eggshells!

A paleontologist named Luis Chiappe had this experience. He had found an enormous dinosaur nesting ground.

Fossilized Organisms

The remains or physical evidence of an organism preserved by geologic processes is called a **fossil.** Fossils are most often preserved in sedimentary rock. But as you will see, other materials can also preserve evidence of past life.

Fossils in Rocks

When an organism dies, it either immediately begins to decay or is consumed by other organisms. Sometimes, however, organisms are quickly buried by sediment when they die. The sediment slows down decay. Hard parts of organisms, such as shells and bones, are more resistant to decay than soft tissues are. So, when sediments become rock, the hard parts of animals are much more commonly preserved than are soft tissues.

Fossils in Amber

Imagine that an insect is caught in soft, sticky tree sap. Suppose that the insect gets covered by more sap, which quickly hardens and preserves the insect inside. Hardened tree sap is called *amber*. Some of our best insect fossils are found in amber, as shown in **Figure 1.** Frogs and lizards have also been found in amber.

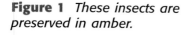 **Reading Check** Describe how organisms are preserved in amber. (*See the Appendix for answers to Reading Checks.*)

READING WARM-UP

Objectives

● Describe five ways that different types of fossils form.

● List three types of fossils that are not part of organisms.

● Explain how fossils can be used to determine the history of changes in environments and organisms.

● Explain how index fossils can be used to date rock layers.

Terms to Learn

fossil
trace fossil
mold
cast
index fossil

READING STRATEGY

Reading Organizer As you read this section, create an outline of the section. Use the headings from this section in your outline.

Figure 1 *These insects are preserved in amber.*

Figure 2 *Scientist Vladimir Eisner studies the upper molars of a 20,000-year-old woolly mammoth found in Siberia, Russia. The almost perfectly preserved male mammoth was excavated from a block of ice in October 1999.*

Petrifaction

Another way that organisms are preserved is by petrifaction. *Petrifaction* is a process in which minerals replace an organism's tissues. One form of petrifaction is called permineralization. *Permineralization* is a process in which the pore space in an organism's hard tissue—for example, bone or wood—is filled up with mineral. Another form of petrifaction is called *replacement,* a process in which the organism's tissues are completely replaced by minerals. For example, in some specimens of petrified wood, all of the wood has been replaced by minerals.

fossil the remains or physical evidence of an organism preserved by geological processes

Fossils in Asphalt

There are places where asphalt wells up at the Earth's surface in thick, sticky pools. The La Brea asphalt deposits in Los Angeles, California, for example, are at least 38,000 years old. These pools of thick, sticky asphalt have trapped and preserved many kinds of organisms for the past 38,000 years. From these fossils, scientists have learned about the past environment in southern California.

Frozen Fossils

In October 1999, scientists removed a 20,000-year-old woolly mammoth frozen in the Siberian tundra. The remains of this mammoth are shown in **Figure 2.** Woolly mammoths, relatives of modern elephants, became extinct approximately 10,000 years ago. Because cold temperatures slow down decay, many types of frozen fossils are preserved from the last ice age. Scientists hope to find out more about the mammoth and the environment in which it lived.

CONNECTION TO
Environmental Science

WRITING SKILL **Preservation in Ice** Subfreezing climates contain almost no decomposing bacteria. The well-preserved body of John Torrington, a member of an expedition that explored the Northwest Passage in Canada in the 1840s, was uncovered in 1984. His body appeared much as it did at the time he died, more than 160 years earlier. Research another well-preserved discovery, and write a report for your class.

Figure 3 *These dinosaur tracks are located in Arizona. They leave a trace of a dinosaur that had longer legs than humans do.*

trace fossil a fossilized mark that is formed in soft sediment by the movement of an animal

mold a mark or cavity made in a sedimentary surface by a shell or other body

cast a type of fossil that forms when sediments fill in the cavity left by a decomposed organism

Other Types of Fossils

Besides their hard parts—and in rare cases their soft parts—do organisms leave behind any other clues about their existence? What other evidence of past life do paleontologists look for?

Trace Fossils

Any naturally preserved evidence of animal activity is called a **trace fossil.** Tracks like the ones shown in **Figure 3** are a fascinating example of a trace fossil. These fossils form when animal footprints fill with sediment and are preserved in rock. Tracks reveal a lot about the animal that made them, including how big it was and how fast it was moving. Parallel trackways showing dinosaurs moving in the same direction have led paleontologists to hypothesize that dinosaurs moved in herds.

Burrows are another trace fossil. Burrows are shelters made by animals, such as clams, that bury in sediment. Like tracks, burrows are preserved when they are filled in with sediment and buried quickly. A *coprolite* (KAHP roh LIET), a third type of trace fossil, is preserved animal dung.

Molds and Casts

Molds and casts are two more examples of fossils. A cavity in rock where a plant or animal was buried is called a **mold.** A **cast** is an object created when sediment fills a mold and becomes rock. A cast shows what the outside of the organism looked like. **Figure 4** shows two types of molds from the same organism—and internal mold and an external mold.

✓ Reading Check How are a cast and a mold different?

Figure 4 *This photograph shows two molds from an ammonite. The image on the left is the internal mold of the ammonite, which formed when sediment filled the ammonite's shell, which later dissolved away. The image on the right is the external mold of the ammonite, which preserves the external features of the shell.*

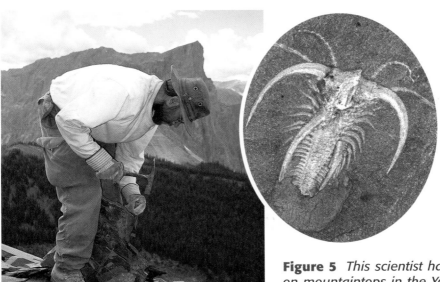

Figure 5 *This scientist has found marine fossils on mountaintops in the Yoho National Park in Canada. The fossil of* Marrella, *shown above, tells the scientist that these rocks were pushed up from below sea level millions of years ago.*

Using Fossils to Interpret the Past

Think about your favorite outdoor place. Now, imagine that you are a paleontologist at the same site 65 million years from now. What types of fossils would you dig up? Based on the fossils you found, how would you reconstruct this place?

The Information in the Fossil Record

The fossil record offers only a rough sketch of the history of life on Earth. Some parts of this history are more complete than others. For example, scientists know more about organisms that had hard body parts than about organisms that had soft body parts. Scientists also know more about organisms that lived in environments that favored fossilization. The fossil record is incomplete because most organisms never became fossils. And of course, many fossils have yet to be discovered.

History of Environmental Changes

Would you expect to find marine fossils on the mountaintop shown in **Figure 5**? The presence of marine fossils means that the rocks of these mountaintops in Canada formed in a totally different environment—at the bottom of an ocean.

The fossil record reveals a history of environmental change. For example, marine fossils help scientists reconstruct ancient coastlines and the deepening and shallowing of ancient seas. Using the fossils of plants and land animals, scientists can reconstruct past climates. They can tell whether the climate in an area was cooler or wetter than it is at present.

Make a Fossil

1. Find a **common object,** such as a shell, a button, or a pencil, to use to make a mold. Keep the object hidden from your classmates.

2. To create a mold, press the items down into **modeling clay** in a **shallow pan or tray.**

3. Trade your tray with a classmate's tray, and try to identify the item that made the mold.

4. Describe how a cast could be formed from your mold.

School to Home

Fossil Hunt

Go on a fossil hunt with your family. Find out what kinds of rocks in your local area might contain fossils. Take pictures or draw sketches of your trip and any fossils that you find.

ACTIVITY

index fossil a fossil that is found in the rock layers of only one geologic age and that is used to establish the age of the rock layers

History of Changing Organisms

By studying the relationships between fossils, scientists can interpret how life has changed over time. For example, older rock layers contain organisms that often differ from the organisms found in younger rock layers.

Only a small fraction of the organisms that have existed in Earth's history have been fossilized. Because the fossil record is incomplete, it does not provide paleontologists with a continuous record of change. Instead, they look for similarities between fossils, or between fossilized organisms and their closest living relatives, and try to fill in the blanks in the fossil record.

Reading Check How do paleontologists fill in missing information about changes in organisms in the fossil record?

Using Fossils to Date Rocks

Scientists have found that particular types of fossils appear only in certain layers of rock. By dating the rock layers above and below these fossils, scientists can determine the time span in which the organisms that formed the fossils lived. If a type of organism existed for only a short period of time, its fossils would show up in a limited range of rock layers. These types of fossils are called index fossils. **Index fossils** are fossils of organisms that lived during a relatively short, well-defined geologic time span.

Ammonites

To be considered an index fossil, a fossil must be found in rock layers throughout the world. One example of an index fossil is the fossil of a genus of ammonites (AM uh NIETS) called *Tropites*, shown in **Figure 6.** *Tropites* was a marine mollusk similar to a modern squid. It lived in a coiled shell. *Tropites* lived between 230 million and 208 million years ago and is an index fossil for that period of time.

Figure 6 Tropites *is a genus of coiled ammonites.* Tropites *existed for only about 20 million years, which makes this genus a good index fossil.*

Trilobites

Fossils of a genus of trilobites (TRIE loh BIETS) called *Phacops* are another example of an index fossil. Trilobites are extinct. Their closest living relative is the horseshoe crab. Through the dating of rock, paleontologists have determined that *Phacops* lived approximately 400 million years ago. So, when scientists find *Phacops* in rock layers anywhere on Earth, they assume that these rock layers are also approximately 400 million years old. An example of a *Phacops* fossil is shown in **Figure 7.**

✓ Reading Check Explain how fossils of *Phacops* can be used to establish the age of rock layers.

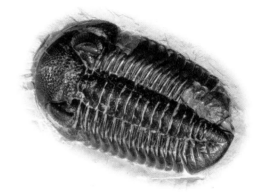

Figure 7 *Paleontologists assume that any rock layer containing a fossil of the trilobite* Phacops *is about 400 million years old.*

SECTION Review

Summary

- Fossils are the remains or physical evidence of an organism preserved by geologic processes.
- Fossils can be preserved in rock, amber, asphalt, and ice and by petrifaction.
- Trace fossils are any naturally preserved evidence of animal activity. Tracks, burrows, and coprolites are examples of trace fossils.
- Scientists study fossils to determine how environments and organisms have changed over time.
- An index fossil is a fossil of an organism that lived during a relatively short, well-defined time span. Index fossils can be used to establish the age of rock layers.

Using Key Terms

Complete each of the following sentences by choosing the correct term from the word bank.

| cast | index fossils |
| mold | trace fossils |

1. A ___ is a cavity in rock where a plant or animal was buried.

2. ___ can be used to establish the age of rock layers.

Understanding Key Ideas

3. Fossils are most often preserved in
   a. ice.
   b. amber.
   c. asphalt.
   d. rock.

4. Describe three types of trace fossils.

5. Explain how an index fossil can be used to date rock.

6. Explain why the fossil record contains an incomplete record of the history of life on Earth.

7. Explain how fossils can be used to determine the history of changes in environments and organisms.

Math Skills

8. If a scientist finds the remains of a plant between a rock layer that contains 400 million–year-old *Phacops* fossils and a rock layer that contains 230 million–year-old *Tropites* fossils, how old could the plant fossil be?

Critical Thinking

9. **Making Inferences** If you find rock layers containing fish fossils in a desert, what can you infer about the history of the desert?

10. **Identifying Bias** Because information in the fossil record is incomplete, scientists are left with certain biases concerning fossil preservation. Explain two of these biases.

SCI LINKS

NSTA
Developed and maintained by the
National Science Teachers Association

For a variety of links related to this chapter, go to www.scilinks.org

Topic: Looking at Fossils
SciLinks code: HSM0886

Time Marches On

How old is the Earth? Well, if the Earth celebrated its birthday every million years, there would be 4,600 candles on its birthday cake! Humans have been around only long enough to light the last candle on the cake.

Try to think of the Earth's history in "fast-forward." If you could watch the Earth change from this perspective, you would see mountains rise up like wrinkles in fabric and quickly wear away. You would see life-forms appear and then go extinct. In this section, you will learn that geologists must "fast-forward" the Earth's history when they write or talk about it. You will also learn about some incredible events in the history of life on Earth.

Geologic Time

Shown in **Figure 1** is the rock wall at the Dinosaur Quarry Visitor Center in Dinosaur National Monument, Utah. Contained within this wall are approximately 1,500 fossil bones that have been excavated by paleontologists. These are the remains of dinosaurs that inhabited the area about 150 million years ago. Granted, 150 million years seems to be an incredibly long period of time. However, in terms of the Earth's history, 150 million years is little more than 3% of the time our planet has existed. It is a little less than 4% of the time represented by the Earth's oldest known rocks.

READING WARM-UP

Objectives

● Explain how geologic time is recorded in rock layers.

● Identify important dates on the geologic time scale.

● Explain how environmental changes resulted in the extinction of some species.

Terms to Learn

geologic time scale   period
eon   epoch
era   extinction

READING STRATEGY

Brainstorming The key idea of this section is the geologic time scale. Brainstorm words and phrases related to the geologic time scale.

Figure 1 *Bones of dinosaurs that lived about 150 million years ago are exposed in the quarry wall at Dinosaur National Monument in Utah.*

Figure 2 *Well-preserved plant and animal fossils are common in the Green River formation. Clockwise from the upper right are a fossil leaf, a dragonfly, a fish, and a turtle.*

The Rock Record and Geologic Time

One of the best places in North America to see the Earth's history recorded in rock layers is in Grand Canyon National Park. The Colorado River has cut the canyon nearly 2 km deep in some places. Over the course of 6 million years, the river has eroded countless layers of rock. These layers represent almost half, or nearly 2 billion years, of Earth's history.

✓ Reading Check How much geologic time is represented by the rock layers in the Grand Canyon? (*See the Appendix for answers to Reading Checks.*)

The Fossil Record and Geologic Time

Figure 2 shows sedimentary rocks that belong to the Green River formation. These rocks, which are found in parts of Wyoming, Utah, and Colorado, are thousands of meters thick. These rocks were once part of a system of ancient lakes that existed for a period of millions of years. Fossils of plants and animals are common in these rocks and are very well preserved. Burial in the fine-grained lake-bed sediments preserved even the most delicate structures.

For another activity related to this chapter, go to **go.hrw.com** and type in the keyword **HZ5FOSW**.

Phanerozoic Eon

(543 million years ago to the present)
The rock and fossil record mainly represents the Phanerozoic eon, which is the eon in which we live.

Proterozoic Eon

(2.5 billion years ago to 543 million years ago)
The first organisms with well-developed cells appeared during this eon.

Archean Eon

(3.8 billion years ago to 2.5 billion years ago)
The earliest known rocks on Earth formed during this eon.

Hadean Eon

(4.6 billion years ago to 3.8 billion years ago)
The only rocks that scientists have found from this eon are meteorites and rocks from the moon.

Geologic Time Scale

Era	Period	Epoch	Millions of years ago
Cenozoic	Quaternary	Holocene	0.01
		Pleistocene	1.8
	Tertiary	Pliocene	5.3
		Miocene	23.8
		Oligocene	33.7
		Eocene	54.8
		Paleocene	65
Mesozoic	Cretaceous		144
	Jurassic		206
	Triassic		248
Paleozoic	Permian		290
	Pennsylvanian		323
	Mississippian		354
	Devonian		417
	Silurian		443
	Ordovician		490
	Cambrian		543

(PHANEROZOIC EON)

PROTEROZOIC EON — 2,500

ARCHEAN EON — 3,800

HADEAN EON — 4,600

Figure 3 *The geologic time scale accounts for Earth's entire history. It is divided into four major parts called eons. Dates given for intervals on the geologic time scale are estimates.*

The Geologic Time Scale

The geologic column represents the billions of years that have passed since the first rocks formed on Earth. Altogether, geologists study 4.6 billion years of Earth's history! To make their job easier, geologists have created the geologic time scale. The **geologic time scale,** which is shown in **Figure 3,** is a scale that divides Earth's 4.6 billion–year history into distinct intervals of time.

✓ Reading Check Define the term *geologic time scale.*

Divisions of Time

Geologists have divided Earth's history into sections of time, as shown on the geologic time scale in **Figure 3.** The largest divisions of geologic time are **eons** (EE AHNZ). There are four eons—the Hadean eon, the Archean eon, the Proterozoic eon, and the Phanerozoic eon. The Phanerozoic eon is divided into three **eras,** which are the second-largest divisions of geologic time. The three eras are further divided into **periods,** which are the third-largest divisions of geologic time. Periods are divided into **epochs** (EP uhks), which are the fourth-largest divisions of geologic time.

The boundaries between geologic time intervals represent shorter intervals in which visible changes took place on Earth. Some changes are marked by the disappearance of index fossil species, while others are recognized only by detailed paleontological studies.

geologic time scale the standard method used to divide the Earth's long natural history into manageable parts

eon the largest division of geologic time

era a unit of geologic time that includes two or more periods

period a unit of geologic time into which eras are divided

epoch a subdivision of a geologic period

extinction the death of every member of a species

The Appearance and Disappearance of Species

At certain times during Earth's history, the number of species has increased or decreased dramatically. An increase in the number of species often comes as a result of either a relatively sudden increase or decrease in competition among species. *Hallucigenia,* shown in **Figure 4,** appeared during the Cambrian period, when the number of marine species greatly increased. On the other hand, the number of species decreases dramatically over a relatively short period of time during a mass extinction event. **Extinction** is the death of every member of a species. Gradual events, such as global climate change and changes in ocean currents, can cause mass extinctions. A combination of these events can also cause mass extinctions.

Figure 4 Hallucigenia, *named for its "bizarre and dreamlike quality," was one of numerous marine organisms to make its appearance during the early Cambrian period.*

Figure 5 *Jungles were present during the Paleozoic era, but there were no birds singing in the trees and no monkeys swinging from the branches. Birds and mammals didn't evolve until much later.*

The Paleozoic Era—Old Life

The Paleozoic era lasted from about 543 million to 248 million years ago. It is the first era well represented by fossils.

Marine life flourished at the beginning of the Paleozoic era. The oceans became home to a diversity of life. However, there were few land organisms. By the middle of the Paleozoic, all modern groups of land plants had appeared. By the end of the era, amphibians and reptiles lived on the land, and insects were abundant. **Figure 5** shows what the Earth might have looked like late in the Paleozoic era. The Paleozoic era came to an end with the largest mass extinction in Earth's history. Some scientists believe that ocean changes were a likely cause of this extinction, which killed nearly 90% of all species.

The Mesozoic Era—The Age of Reptiles

The Mesozoic era began about 248 million years ago. The Mesozoic is known as the *Age of Reptiles* because reptiles, such as the dinosaurs shown in **Figure 6,** inhabited the land.

During this time, reptiles dominated. Small mammals appeared about the same time as dinosaurs, and birds appeared late in the Mesozoic era. Many scientists think that birds evolved directly from a type of dinosaur. At the end of the Mesozoic era, about 15% to 20% of all species on Earth, including the dinosaurs, became extinct. Global climate change may have been the cause.

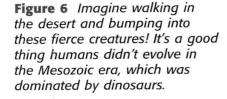

Figure 6 *Imagine walking in the desert and bumping into these fierce creatures! It's a good thing humans didn't evolve in the Mesozoic era, which was dominated by dinosaurs.*

✓ **Reading Check** Why is the Mesozoic known as the *Age of Reptiles*?

The Cenozoic Era—The Age of Mammals

The Cenozoic era, as shown in **Figure 7,** began about 65 million years ago and continues to the present. This era is known as the *Age of Mammals*. During the Mesozoic era, mammals had to compete with dinosaurs and other animals for food and habitat. After the mass extinction at the end of the Mesozoic era, mammals flourished. Unique traits, such as regulating body temperature internally and bearing young that develop inside the mother, may have helped mammals survive the environmental changes that probably caused the extinction of the dinosaurs.

Figure 7 *Thousands of species of mammals evolved during the Cenozoic era. This scene shows species from the early Cenozoic era that are now extinct.*

SECTION
Review

Summary

- The geologic time scale divides Earth's 4.6 billion–year history into distinct intervals of time. Divisions of geologic time include eons, eras, periods, and epochs.

- The boundaries between geologic time intervals represent visible changes that have taken place on Earth.

- The rock and fossil record represents mainly the Phanerozoic eon, which is the eon in which we live.

- At certain times in Earth's history, the number of life-forms has increased or decreased dramatically.

Using Key Terms

1. Use each of the following terms in the same sentence: *era, period,* and *epoch.*

Understanding Key Ideas

2. The unit of geologic time that began 65 million years ago and continues to the present is the
   a. Holocene epoch.
   b. Cenozoic era.
   c. Phanerozoic eon.
   d. Quaternary period.

3. What are the major time intervals represented by the geologic time scale?

4. Explain how geologic time is recorded in rock layers.

5. What kinds of environmental changes cause mass extinctions?

Critical Thinking

6. **Making Inferences** What future event might mark the end of the Cenozoic era?

7. **Identifying Relationships** How might a decrease in competition between species lead to the sudden appearance of many new species?

Interpreting Graphics

8. Look at the illustration below. On the Earth-history clock shown, 1 h equals 383 million years, and 1 min equals 6.4 million years. In millions of years, how much more time is represented by the Proterozoic eon than by the Phanerozoic eon?

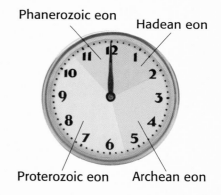

Phanerozoic eon

Hadean eon

Proterozoic eon

Archean eon

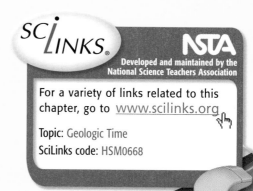

SCILINKS.

NSTA
Developed and maintained by the
National Science Teachers Association

For a variety of links related to this chapter, go to www.scilinks.org

Topic: Geologic Time
SciLinks code: HSM0668

Model-Making Lab

OBJECTIVES

Make a model of a geologic column.

Interpret the geologic history represented by the geologic column you have made.

MATERIALS

- paper, white
- pencil
- pencils or crayons, assorted colors
- ruler, metric
- scissors
- tape, transparent

SAFETY

How Do You Stack Up?

According to the principle of superposition, in undisturbed sequences of sedimentary rock, the oldest layers are on the bottom. Geologists use this principle to determine the relative age of the rocks in a small area. In this activity, you will model what geologists do by drawing sections of different rock outcrops. Then, you will create a part of the geologic column, showing the geologic history of the area that contains all of the outcrops.

Procedure

1. Use a metric ruler and a pencil to draw four boxes on a blank piece of paper. Each box should be 3 cm wide and at least 6 cm tall. (You can trace the boxes shown on the next page.)

2. With colored pencils, copy the illustrations of the four outcrops on the next page. Copy one illustration in each of the four boxes. Use colors and patterns similar to those shown.

3. Pay close attention to the contact between layers—straight or wavy. Straight lines represent bedding planes, where deposition was continuous. Wavy lines represent unconformities, where rock layers may be missing. The top of each outcrop is incomplete, so it should be a jagged line. (Assume that the bottom of the lowest layer is a bedding plane.)

4. Use a black crayon or pencil to add the symbols representing fossils to the layers in your drawings. Pay attention to the shapes of the fossils and the layers that they are in.

5. Write the outcrop number on the back of each section.

6. Carefully cut the outcrops out of the paper, and lay the individual outcrops next to each other on your desk or table.

7. Find layers that have the same rocks and contain the same fossils. Move each outcrop up or down to line up similar layers next to each other.

8. If unconformities appear in any of the outcrops, there may be rock layers missing. You may need to examine other sections to find out what fits between the layers above and below the unconformities. Leave room for these layers by cutting the outcrops along the unconformities (wavy lines).

86   Chapter 3   The Rock and Fossil Record

9 Eventually, you should be able to make a geologic column that represents all four of the outcrops. It will show rock types and fossils for all the known layers in the area.

10 Tape the pieces of paper together in a pattern that represents the complete geologic column.

Analyze the Results

1 **Examining Data** How many layers are in the part of the geologic column that you modeled?

2 **Examining Data** Which is the oldest layer in your column? Which rock layer is the youngest? How do you know? Describe these layers in terms of rock type or the fossils they contain.

3 **Classifying** List the fossils in your column from oldest to youngest. Label the youngest and oldest fossils.

4 **Analyzing Data** Look at the unconformity in outcrop 2. Which rock layers are partially or completely missing? How do you know?

Draw Conclusions

5 **Drawing Conclusions** Which (if any) fossils can be used as index fossils for a single layer? Why are these fossils considered index fossils? What method(s) would be required to determine the absolute age of these fossils?

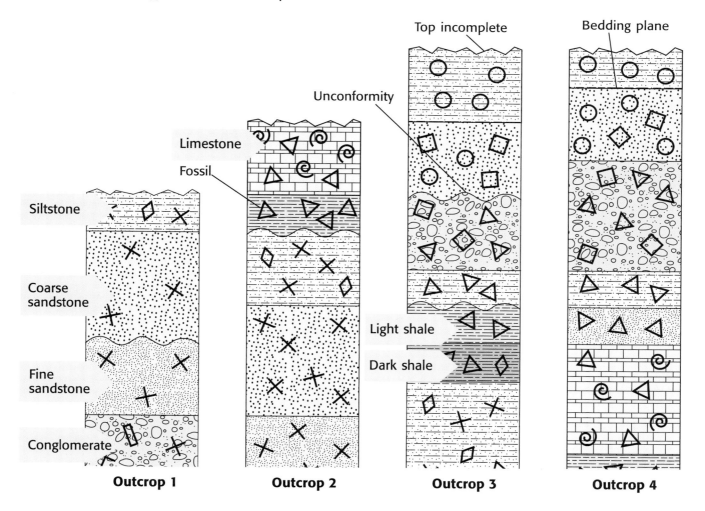

Outcrop 1   Outcrop 2   Outcrop 3   Outcrop 4

Chapter Review

USING KEY TERMS

1 In your own words, write a definition for each of the following terms: *superposition, geologic column,* and *geologic time scale.*

For each pair of terms, explain how the meanings of the terms differ.

2 *uniformitarianism* and *catastrophism*

3 *relative dating* and *absolute dating*

4 *trace fossil* and *index fossil*

UNDERSTANDING KEY IDEAS

Multiple Choice

5 Which of the following does not describe catastrophic change?

a. widespread

b. sudden

c. rare

d. gradual

6 Scientists assign relative ages by using

a. absolute dating.

b. the principle of superposition.

c. radioactive half-lives.

d. carbon-14 dating.

7 Which of the following is a trace fossil?

a. an insect preserved in amber

b. a mammoth frozen in ice

c. wood replaced by minerals

d. a dinosaur trackway

8 The largest divisions of geologic time are called

a. periods.

b. eras.

c. eons.

d. epochs.

9 Rock layers cut by a fault formed

a. after the fault.

b. before the fault.

c. at the same time as the fault.

d. There is not enough information to determine the answer.

10 Of the following isotopes, which is stable?

a. uranium-238

b. potassium-40

c. carbon-12

d. carbon-14

11 A surface that represents a missing part of the geologic column is called a(n)

a. intrusion.

b. fault.

c. unconformity.

d. fold.

12 Which method of radiometric dating is used mainly to date the remains of organisms that lived within the last 50,000 years?

a. carbon-14 dating

b. potassium-argon dating

c. uranium-lead dating

d. rubidium-strontium dating

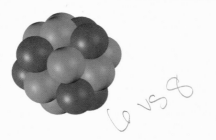  

6 vs 8

7 vs 7

Short Answer

13 Describe three processes by which fossils form.

14 Identify the role of uniformitarianism in Earth science.

15 Explain how radioactive decay occurs.

16 Describe two ways in which scientists use fossils to determine environmental change.

17 Explain the role of paleontology in the study of Earth's history.

CRITICAL THINKING

18 **Concept Mapping** Use the following terms to create a concept map: *age, half-life, absolute dating, radioactive decay, radiometric dating, relative dating, superposition, geologic column,* and *isotopes.*

19 **Applying Concepts** Identify how changes in environmental conditions can affect the survival of a species. Give two examples.

20 **Identifying Relationships** Why do paleontologists know more about hard-bodied organisms than about soft-bodied organisms?

21 **Analyzing Processes** Why isn't a 100 million–year-old fossilized tree made of wood?

INTERPRETING GRAPHICS

Use the diagram below to answer the questions that follow.

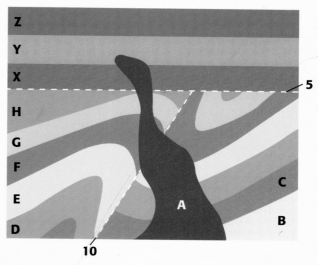

22 Is intrusion A younger or older than layer X? Explain. old

23 What feature is marked by 5? fault

24 Is intrusion A younger or older than fault 10? Explain. older

25 Other than the intrusion and faulting, what event happened in layers B, C, D, E, F, G, and H? Number this event, the intrusion, and the faulting in the order that they happened.

READING

Read each of the passages below. Then, answer the questions that follow each passage.

Passage 1 Three hundred million years ago, the region that is now Illinois had a different climate than it does today. Swamps and shallow bays covered much of the area. No fewer than 500 species of plants and animals lived in this environment. Today, the remains of these organisms are found beautifully preserved within nodules. Nodules are round or oblong structures usually composed of cemented sediments that sometimes contain the fossilized hard parts of plants and animals. The Illinois nodules are <u>exceptional</u> because the soft parts of organisms are found together with hard parts. For this reason, these nodules are found in fossil collections around the world.

1. In the passage, what is the meaning of the word *exceptional*?

  A beautiful

  B extraordinary

  C average

  D large

2. According to the passage, which of the following statements about nodules is correct?

  F Nodules are rarely round or oblong.

  G Nodules are usually composed of cemented sediment.

  H Nodules are not found in present-day Illinois.

  I Nodules always contain fossils.

3. Which of the following is a fact in the passage?

  A The Illinois nodules are not well known outside of Illinois.

  B Illinois has had the same climate throughout Earth's history.

  C Both the hard and soft parts of organisms are preserved in the Illinois nodules.

  D Fewer than 500 species of plants and animals have been found in Illinois nodules.

Passage 2 In 1995, paleontologist Paul Sereno and his team were working in an unexplored region of Morocco when they made an <u>astounding</u> find—an enormous dinosaur skull! The skull measured approximately 1.6 m in length, which is about the height of a refrigerator. Given the size of the skull, Sereno concluded that the skeleton of the animal it came from must have been about 14 m long—about as big as a school bus. The dinosaur was even larger than *Tyrannosaurus rex*! The newly discovered 90 million–year-old predator most likely chased other dinosaurs by running on large, powerful hind legs, and its bladelike teeth meant certain death for its prey.

1. In the passage, what does the word *astounding* mean?

  A important

  B new

  C incredible

  D one of a kind

2. Which of the following is evidence that the dinosaur described in the passage was a predator?

  F It had bladelike teeth.

  G It had a large skeleton.

  H It was found with the bones of a smaller animal nearby.

  I It is 90 million years old.

3. What types of information do you think that fossil teeth provide about an organism?

  A the color of its skin

  B the types of food it ate

  C the speed that it ran

  D the mating habits it had

Use the graph below to answer the questions that follow.

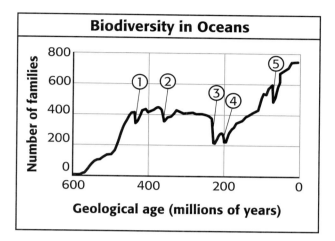

Biodiversity in Oceans

1. At which point in Earth's history did the greatest mass-extinction event take place?

   A at point 1, the Ordovician-Silurian boundary

   B at point 3, the Permian-Triassic boundary

   C at point 4, the Triassic-Jurassic boundary

   D at point 5, the Cretaceous-Tertiary boundary

2. Immediately following the Cretaceous-Tertiary extinction, represented by point 5, approximately how many families of marine organisms remained in the Earth's oceans?

   F 200 marine families

   G 300 marine families

   H 500 marine families

   I 700 marine families

3. Approximately how many million years ago did the Ordovician-Silurian mass-extinction event, represented by point 1, take place?

   A 200 million years ago

   B 250 million years ago

   C 350 million years ago

   D 420 million years ago

Read each question below, and choose the best answer.

1. Carbon-14 is a radioactive isotope with a half-life of 5,730 years. How much carbon-14 would remain in a sample that is 11,460 years old?

   A 12.5%

   B 25%

   C 50%

   D 100%

2. If a sample contains an isotope with a half-life of 10,000 years, how old would the sample be if 1/8 of the original isotope remained in the sample?

   F 20,000 years

   G 30,000 years

   H 40,000 years

   I 50,000 years

3. If a sample contains an isotope with a half-life of 5,000 years, how old would the sample be if 1/4 of the original isotope remained in the sample?

   A 10,000 years

   B 20,000 years

   C 30,000 years

   D 40,000 years

4. If Earth history spans 4.6 billion years and the Phanerozoic eon was 543 million years, what percentage of Earth history does the Phanerozoic eon represent?

   F about 6%

   G about 12%

   H about 18%

   I about 24%

5. Humans live in the Holocene epoch. If the Holocene epoch has lasted approximately 10,000 years, what percentage of the Quaternary period, which began 1.8 million years ago, is represented by the Holocene?

   A about 0.0055%

   B about 0.055%

   C about 0.55%

   D about 5.5%

Standardized Test Preparation

Science in Action

Scientific Debate

Feathered Dinosaurs

One day in 1996, a Chinese farmer broke open a rock he found in the bed of an ancient dry lake. What he found inside the rock became one of the most exciting paleontological discoveries of the 20th century. Preserved inside were the remains of a dinosaur. The dinosaur had a large head; powerful jaws; sharp, jagged teeth; and, most important of all, a row of featherlike structures along the backbone. Scientists named the dinosaur *Sinosauropteryx,* or "Chinese dragon wing." *Sinosauropteryx* and the remains of other "feathered" dinosaurs recently discovered in China have led some scientists to hypothesize that feathers evolved through theropod (three-toed) dinosaurs. Other paleontologists disagree. They believe the structures along the backbone of these dinosaurs are not feathers but the remains of elongated spines, like those that run down the head and back of an iguana.

Science, Technology, and Society

DNA and a Mammoth Discovery

In recent years, scientists have unearthed several mammoths that had been frozen in ice in Siberia and other remote northern locations. Bones, fur, food in the stomach, and even dung have all been found in good condition. Some scientists hoped that DNA extracted from the mammoths might lead to the cloning of this animal, which became extinct about 10,000 years ago. But the DNA might not be able to be duplicated by scientists. However, DNA samples may nevertheless help scientists understand why mammoths became extinct. One theory about why mammoths became extinct is that they were killed off by disease. Using DNA taken from fossilized mammoth bone, hair, or dung, scientists can check to see if it contains the DNA of a disease-causing pathogen that led to the extinction of the mammoths.

Language Arts ACTiViTY

Paleontologists often give dinosaurs names that describe something unusual about the animal's head, body, feet, or size. These names have Greek or Latin roots. Research the names of some dinosaurs, and find out what the names mean. Create a list of dinosaur names and their meanings.

Math ACTiViTY

The male Siberian mammoth reached a height of about 3 m at the shoulder. Females reached a height of about 2.5 m at the shoulder. What is the ratio of the maximum height of a female Siberian mammoth to the height of a male Siberian mammoth?

Lizzie May

Amateur Paleontologist For Lizzie May, summer vacations have meant trips into the Alaskan wilderness with her stepfather, geologist/paleontologist Kevin May. The purpose of these trips has not been for fun. Instead, Kevin and Lizzie have been exploring the Alaskan wilderness for the remains of ancient life—dinosaurs, in particular.

At age 18, Lizzie May has gained the reputation of being Alaska's most famous teenage paleontologist. It is a reputation that is well deserved. To date, Lizzie has collected hundreds of dinosaur bones and located important sites of dinosaur, bird, and mammal tracks. In her honor and as a result of her hard work in the field, scientists named the skeleton of a dinosaur discovered by the Mays "Lizzie." "Lizzie" is a duck-bill dinosaur, or hadrosaur, that lived approximately 90 million years ago. "Lizzie" is the oldest dinosaur ever found in Alaska and one of the earliest known duckbill dinosaurs in North America.

The Mays have made other, equally exciting discoveries. On one summer trip, Kevin and Lizzie located six dinosaur and bird track sites that dated back 97 million to 144 million years. On another trip, the Mays found a fossil marine reptile more than 200 million years old—an ichthyosaur—that had to be removed with the help of a military helicopter. You have to wonder what other exciting adventures are in store for Lizzie and Kevin!

Social Studies ACTiViTy

WRITING SKILL Lizzie May is not the only young person to have made a mark in dinosaur paleontology. Using the Internet or another source, research people such as Bucky Derflinger, Johnny Maurice, Brad Riney, and Wendy Sloboda, who as young people made contributions to the field of dinosaur study. Write a short essay summarizing your findings.

To learn more about these Science in Action topics, visit **go.hrw.com** and type in the keyword **HZ5FOSF**.

Current Science

Check out Current Science® articles related to this chapter by visiting **go.hrw.com**. Just type in the keyword **HZ5CS06**.

Plate Tectonics

About the PHOTO

The San Andreas fault stretches across the California landscape like a giant wound. The fault, which is 1,000 km long, breaks the Earth's crust from Northern California to Mexico. Because the North American plate and Pacific plate are slipping past one another along the fault, many earthquakes happen.

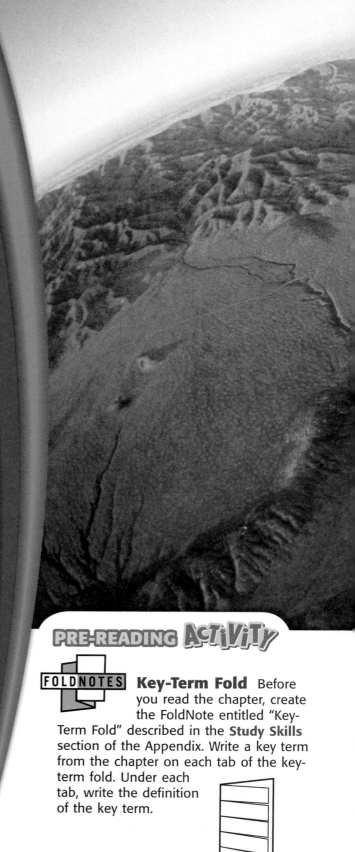

PRE-READING ACTIVITY

FOLDNOTES **Key-Term Fold** Before you read the chapter, create the FoldNote entitled "Key-Term Fold" described in the **Study Skills** section of the Appendix. Write a key term from the chapter on each tab of the key-term fold. Under each tab, write the definition of the key term.

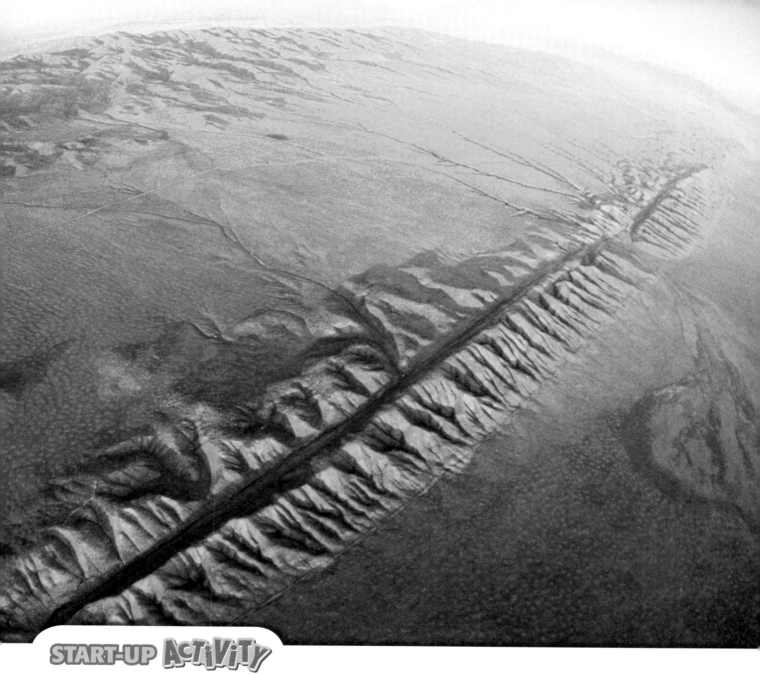

START-UP ACTIVITY

Continental Collisions

As you can see, continents not only move but can also crash into each other. In this activity, you will model the collision of two continents.

Procedure

1. Obtain **two stacks of paper** that are each about 1 cm thick.
2. Place the two stacks of paper on a **flat surface,** such as a desk.
3. Very slowly, push the stacks of paper together so that they collide. Continue to push the stacks until the paper in one of the stacks folds over.

Analysis

1. What happens to the stacks of paper when they collide with each other?
2. Are all of the pieces of paper pushed upward? If not, what happens to the pieces that are not pushed upward?
3. What type of landform will most likely result from this continental collision?

Inside the Earth

If you tried to dig to the center of the Earth, what do you think you would find? Would the Earth be solid or hollow? Would it be made of the same material throughout?

Actually, the Earth is made of several layers. Each layer is made of different materials that have different properties. Scientists think about physical layers in two ways—by their composition and by their physical properties.

READING WARM-UP

Objectives

● Identify the layers of the Earth by their composition.

● Identify the layers of the Earth by their physical properties.

● Describe a tectonic plate.

● Explain how scientists know about the structure of Earth's interior.

Terms to Learn

crust   asthenosphere
mantle   mesosphere
core   tectonic plate
lithosphere

READING STRATEGY

Reading Organizer As you read this section, create an outline of the section. Use the headings from the section in your outline.

The Composition of the Earth

The Earth is divided into three layers—the crust, the mantle, and the core—based on the compounds that make up each layer. A *compound* is a substance composed of two or more elements. The less dense compounds make up the crust and mantle, and the densest compounds make up the core. The layers form because heavier elements are pulled toward the center of the Earth by gravity, and elements of lesser mass are found farther from the center.

The Crust

The outermost layer of the Earth is the **crust.** The crust is 5 to 100 km thick. It is the thinnest layer of the Earth.

As **Figure 1** shows, there are two types of crust—continental and oceanic. Both continental crust and oceanic crust are made mainly of the elements oxygen, silicon, and aluminum. However, the denser oceanic crust has almost twice as much iron, calcium, and magnesium, which form minerals that are denser than those in the continental crust.

Figure 1 *Oceanic crust is thinner and denser than continental crust.*

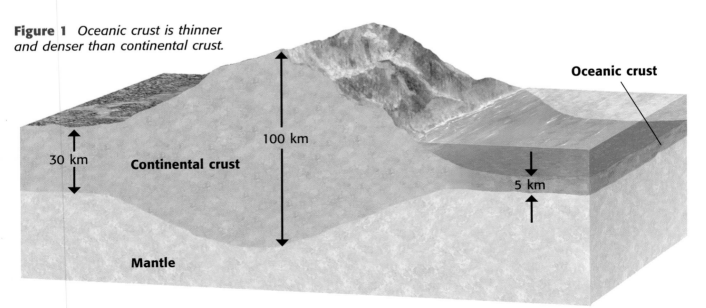

Oceanic crust

100 km

30 km

Continental crust

5 km

Mantle

The Mantle

The layer of the Earth between the crust and the core is the **mantle.** The mantle is much thicker than the crust and contains most of the Earth's mass.

No one has ever visited the mantle. The crust is too thick to drill through to reach the mantle. Scientists must draw conclusions about the composition and other physical properties of the mantle from observations made on the Earth's surface. In some places, mantle rock pushes to the surface, which allows scientists to study the rock directly.

As you can see in **Figure 2,** another place scientists look for clues about the mantle is the ocean floor. Magma from the mantle flows out of active volcanoes on the ocean floor. These underwater volcanoes have given scientists many clues about the composition of the mantle. Because the mantle has more magnesium and less aluminum and silicon than the crust does, the mantle is denser than the crust.

The Core

The layer of the Earth that extends from below the mantle to the center of the Earth is the **core.** Scientists think that the Earth's core is made mostly of iron and contains smaller amounts of nickel but almost no oxygen, silicon, aluminum, or magnesium. As shown in **Figure 3,** the core makes up roughly one-third of the Earth's mass.

Reading Check Briefly describe the layers that make up the Earth. (*See the Appendix for answers to Reading Checks.*)

Figure 2 *Volcanic vents on the ocean floor, such as this vent off the coast of Hawaii, allow magma to rise up through the crust from the mantle.*

crust the thin and solid outermost layer of the Earth above the mantle

mantle the layer of rock between the Earth's crust and core

core the central part of the Earth below the mantle

The **mantle** is 67% of Earth's mass and is 2,900 km thick.

The **crust** is less than 1% of Earth's mass and is 5 to 100 km thick.

The **core** is 33% of Earth's mass and has a radius of 3,430 km.

Figure 3 *The Earth is made up of three layers based on the composition of each layer.*

Using Models

Imagine that you are building a model of the Earth that will have a radius of 1 m. You find out that the average radius of the Earth is 6,380 km and that the thickness of the lithosphere is about 150 km. What percentage of the Earth's radius is the lithosphere? How thick (in centimeters) would you make the lithosphere in your model?

The Physical Structure of the Earth

Another way to look at the Earth is to examine the physical properties of its layers. The Earth is divided into five physical layers—the lithosphere, asthenosphere, mesosphere, outer core, and inner core. As shown in the figure below, each layer has its own set of physical properties.

✓ Reading Check What are the five physical layers of the Earth?

Lithosphere The outermost, rigid layer of the Earth is the **lithosphere.** The lithosphere is made of two parts—the crust and the rigid upper part of the mantle. The lithosphere is divided into pieces called *tectonic plates*.

Asthenosphere The **asthenosphere** is a plastic layer of the mantle on which pieces of the lithosphere move. The asthenosphere is made of solid rock that flows very slowly.

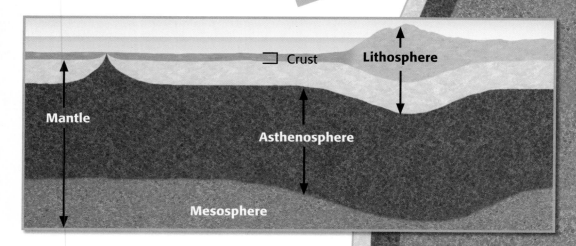

lithosphere the solid, outer layer of the Earth that consists of the crust and the rigid upper part of the mantle

asthenosphere the soft layer of the mantle on which the tectonic plates move

mesosphere the strong, lower part of the mantle between the asthenosphere and the outer core

Mesosphere Beneath the asthenosphere is the strong, lower part of the mantle called the **mesosphere**. The mesosphere extends from the bottom of the asthenosphere to the Earth's core.

Lithosphere
15–300 km

Asthenosphere
250 km

Mesosphere
2,550 km

Outer Core The Earth's core is divided into two parts—the outer core and the inner core. The outer core is the liquid layer of the Earth's core that lies beneath the mantle and surrounds the inner core.

Outer core
2,200 km

Inner Core The inner core is the solid, dense center of our planet that extends from the bottom of the outer core to the center of the Earth, which is about 6,380 km beneath the surface.

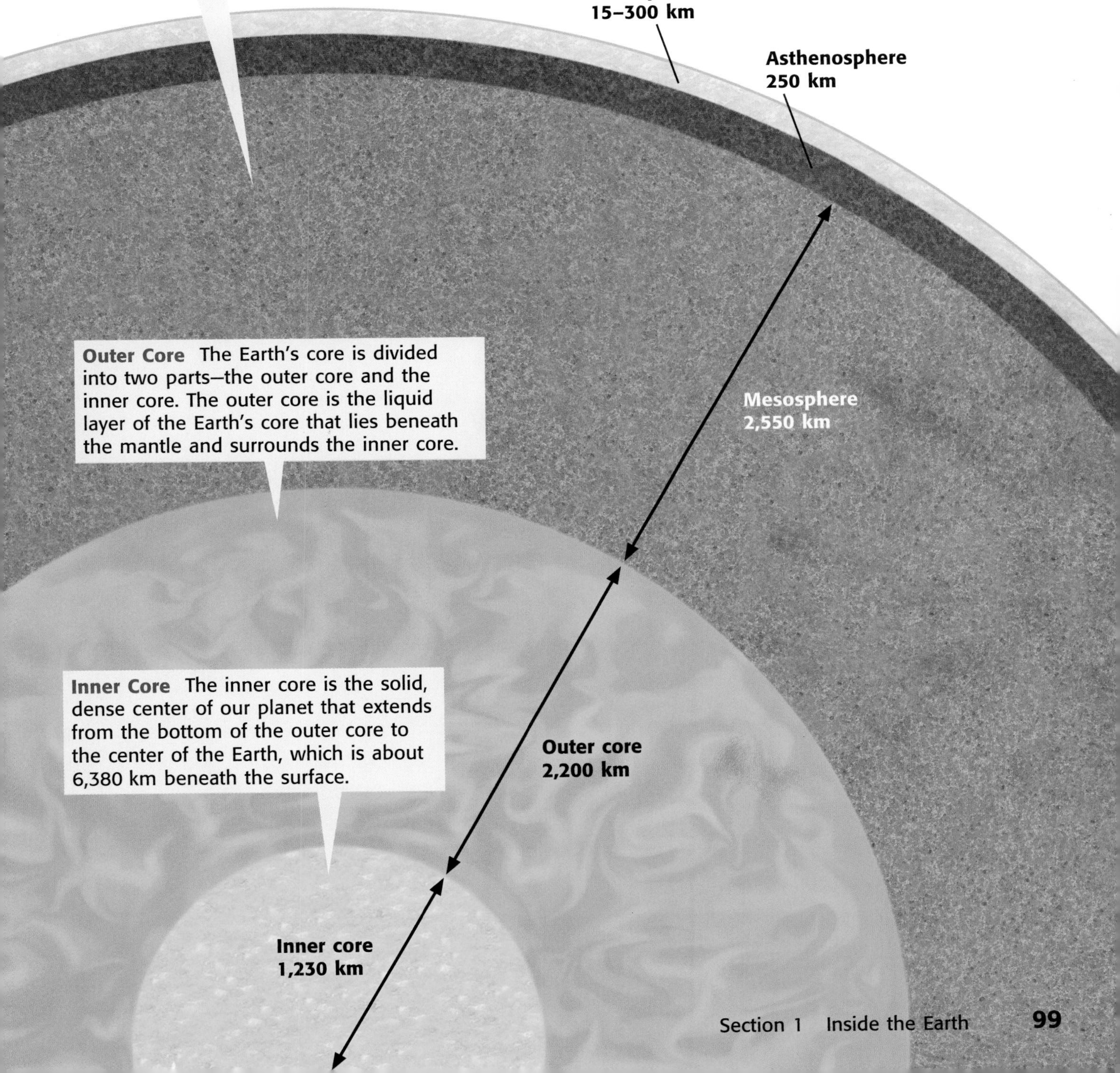

Inner core
1,230 km

Tectonic Plates

Pieces of the lithosphere that move around on top of the asthenosphere are called **tectonic plates**. But what exactly does a tectonic plate look like? How big are tectonic plates? How and why do they move around? To answer these questions, begin by thinking of the lithosphere as a giant jigsaw puzzle.

A Giant Jigsaw Puzzle

All of the tectonic plates have names, some of which you may already know. Some of the major tectonic plates are named on the map in **Figure 4.** Notice that each tectonic plate fits together with the tectonic plates that surround it. The lithosphere is like a jigsaw puzzle, and the tectonic plates are like the pieces of a jigsaw puzzle.

Notice that not all tectonic plates are the same. For example, compare the size of the South American plate with that of the Cocos plate. Tectonic plates differ in other ways, too. For example, the South American plate has an entire continent on it and has oceanic crust, but the Cocos plate has only oceanic crust. Some tectonic plates, such as the South American plate, include both continental and oceanic crust.

tectonic plate a block of lithosphere that consists of the crust and the rigid, outermost part of the mantle

Major Tectonic Plates

1. Pacific plate
2. North American plate
3. Cocos plate
4. Nazca plate
5. South American plate
6. African plate
7. Eurasian plate
8. Indian plate
9. Australian plate
10. Antarctic plate

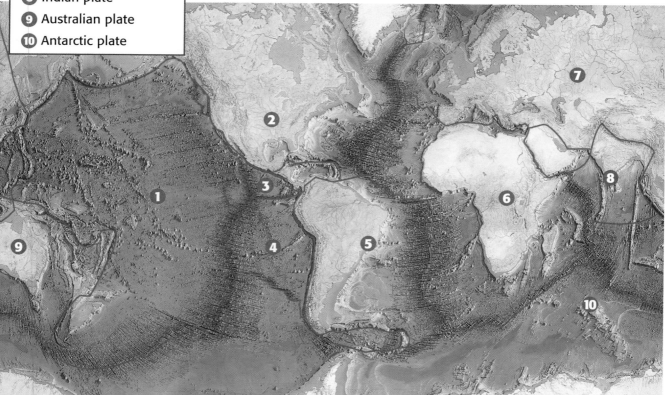

Figure 4 Tectonic plates fit together like the pieces of a giant jigsaw puzzle.

Figure 5 The South American Plate

This image shows what you might see if you could lift the South American plate out of its position between other tectonic plates.

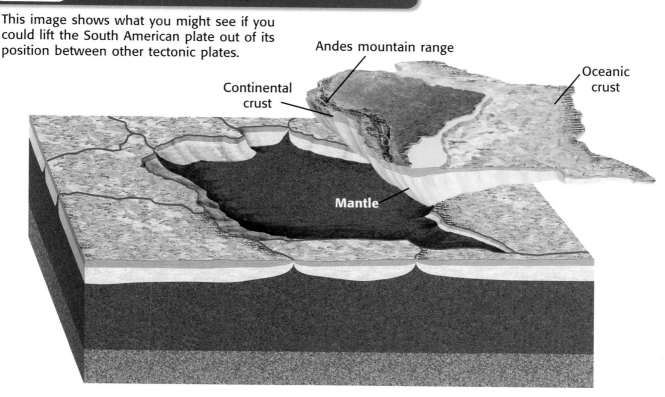

Andes mountain range

Continental crust

Oceanic crust

Mantle

A Tectonic Plate Close-Up

What would a tectonic plate look like if you could lift it out of its place? **Figure 5** shows what the South American plate might look like if you could. Notice that this tectonic plate not only consists of the upper part of the mantle but also consists of both oceanic crust and continental crust. The thickest part of the South American plate is the continental crust. The thinnest part of this plate is in the mid-Atlantic Ocean.

Like Ice Cubes in a Bowl of Punch

Think about ice cubes floating in a bowl of punch. If there are enough cubes, they will cover the surface of the punch and bump into one another. Parts of the ice cubes are below the surface of the punch and displace the punch. Large pieces of ice displace more punch than small pieces of ice. Tectonic plates "float" on the asthenosphere in a similar way. The plates cover the surface of the asthenosphere, and they touch one another and move around. The lithosphere displaces the asthenosphere. Thick tectonic plates, such as those made of continental crust, displace more asthenosphere than do thin plates, such as those made of oceanic lithosphere.

Reading Check Why do tectonic plates made of continental lithosphere displace more asthenosphere than tectonic plates made of oceanic lithosphere do?

Tectonic Ice Cubes

1. Take the bottom half of a clear, **2 L soda bottle** that has been cut in half. Make sure that the label has been removed.

2. Fill the bottle with **water** to about 1 cm below the top edge of the bottle.

3. Get **three pieces of irregularly shaped ice** that are small, medium, and large.

4. Float the ice in the water, and note how much of each piece is below the surface of the water.

5. Do all pieces of ice float mostly below the surface? Which piece is mostly below the surface? Why?

Build a Seismograph

Seismographs are instruments that seismologists, scientists who study earthquakes, use to detect seismic waves. Research seismograph designs with your parent. For example, a simple seismograph can be built by using a weight suspended by a spring next to a ruler. With your parent, attempt to construct a home seismograph based on a design you have selected. Outline each of the steps used to build your seismograph, and present the written outline to your teacher.

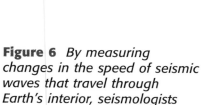

Mapping the Earth's Interior

How do scientists know things about the deepest parts of the Earth, where no one has ever been? Scientists have never even drilled through the crust, which is only a thin skin on the surface of the Earth. So, how do we know so much about the mantle and the core?

Would you be surprised to know that some of the answers come from earthquakes? When an earthquake happens, vibrations called *seismic waves* are produced. Seismic waves travel at different speeds through the Earth. Their speed depends on the density and composition of material that they pass through. For example, a seismic wave traveling through a solid will go faster than a seismic wave traveling through a liquid.

When an earthquake happens, machines called *seismographs* measure the times at which seismic waves arrive at different distances from an earthquake. Seismologists can then use these distances and travel times to calculate the density and thickness of each physical layer of the Earth. **Figure 6** shows how seismic waves travel through the Earth.

Reading Check What are some properties of seismic waves?

Figure 6 *By measuring changes in the speed of seismic waves that travel through Earth's interior, seismologists have learned that the Earth is made of different layers.*

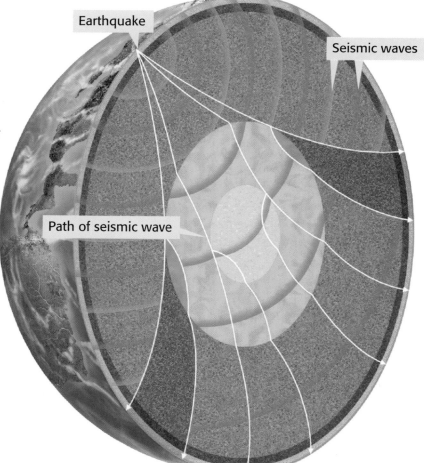

Earthquake

Seismic waves

Path of seismic wave

SECTION Review

Summary

- The Earth is made up of three layers—the crust, the mantle, and the core—based on chemical composition. Less dense compounds make up the crust and mantle. Denser compounds make up the core.

- The Earth is made up of five main physical layers: the lithosphere, the asthenosphere, the mesosphere, the outer core, and the inner core.

- Tectonic plates are large pieces of the lithosphere that move around on the Earth's surface.

- The crust in some tectonic plates is mainly continental. Other plates have only oceanic crust. Still other plates include both continental and oceanic crust.

- Thick tectonic plates, such as those in which the crust is mainly continental, displace more asthenosphere than do thin plates, such as those in which the crust is mainly oceanic.

- Knowledge about the layers of the Earth comes from the study of seismic waves caused by earthquakes.

Using Key Terms

For each pair of terms, explain how the meanings of the terms differ.

1. *crust* and *mantle*

2. *lithosphere* and *asthenosphere*

Understanding Key Ideas

3. The part of the Earth that is molten is the
   a. crust.
   b. mantle.
   c. outer core.
   d. inner core.

4. The part of the Earth on which the tectonic plates move is the
   a. lithosphere.
   b. asthenosphere.
   c. mesosphere.
   d. crust.

5. Identify the layers of the Earth by their chemical composition.

6. Identify the layers of the Earth by their physical properties.

7. Describe a tectonic plate.

8. Explain how scientists know about the structure of the Earth's interior.

Interpreting Graphics

9. According to the wave speeds shown in the table below, which two physical layers of the Earth are densest?

Speed of Seismic Waves in Earth's Interior	
Physical layer	**Wave speed**
Lithosphere	7 to 8 km/s
Asthenosphere	7 to 11 km/s
Mesosphere	11 to 13 km/s
Outer core	8 to 10 km/s
Inner core	11 to 12 km/s

Critical Thinking

10. **Making Comparisons** Explain the difference between the crust and the lithosphere.

11. **Analyzing Ideas** Why does a seismic wave travel faster through solid rock than through water?

SCI**LINKS**.

NSTA
Developed and maintained by the
National Science Teachers Association

For a variety of links related to this chapter, go to www.scilinks.org
Topic: Composition of the Earth;
    Structure of the Earth
SciLinks code: HSM0329; HSM1468

Restless Continents

Have you ever looked at a map of the world and noticed how the coastlines of continents on opposite sides of the oceans appear to fit together like the pieces of a puzzle? Is it just coincidence that the coastlines fit together well? Is it possible that the continents were actually together sometime in the past?

READING WARM-UP

Objectives

● Describe Wegener's hypothesis of continental drift.

● Explain how sea-floor spreading provides a way for continents to move.

● Describe how new oceanic lithosphere forms at mid-ocean ridges.

● Explain how magnetic reversals provide evidence for sea-floor spreading.

Terms to Learn

continental drift
sea-floor spreading

READING STRATEGY

Paired Summarizing Read this section silently. In pairs, take turns summarizing the material. Stop to discuss ideas that seem confusing.

Wegener's Continental Drift Hypothesis

One scientist who looked at the pieces of this puzzle was Alfred Wegener (VAY guh nuhr). In the early 1900s, he wrote about his hypothesis of *continental drift*. **Continental drift** is the hypothesis that states that the continents once formed a single landmass, broke up, and drifted to their present locations. This hypothesis seemed to explain a lot of puzzling observations, including the observation of how well continents fit together.

Continental drift also explained why fossils of the same plant and animal species are found on continents that are on different sides of the Atlantic Ocean. Many of these ancient species could not have crossed the Atlantic Ocean. As you can see in **Figure 1,** without continental drift, this pattern of fossils would be hard to explain. In addition to fossils, similar types of rock and evidence of the same ancient climatic conditions were found on several continents.

✓ **Reading Check** How did fossils provide evidence for Wegener's hypothesis of continental drift? (*See the Appendix for answers to Reading Checks.*)

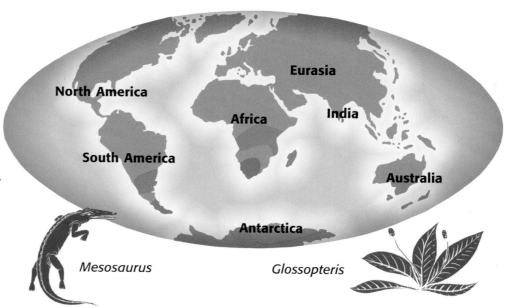

Figure 1 *Fossils of* Mesosaurus, *a small, aquatic reptile, and* Glossopteris, *an ancient plant species, have been found on several continents.*

Figure 2 **The Drifting Continents**

245 Million Years Ago
Pangaea existed when some of the earliest dinosaurs were roaming the Earth. The continent was surrounded by a sea called *Panthalassa*, which means "all sea."

180 Million Years Ago
Gradually, Pangaea broke into two big pieces. The northern piece is called *Laurasia*. The southern piece is called *Gondwana*.

65 Million Years Ago
By the time the dinosaurs became extinct, Laurasia and Gondwana had split into smaller pieces.

The Breakup of Pangaea

Wegener made many observations before proposing his hypothesis of continental drift. He thought that all of the present continents were once joined in a single, huge continent. Wegener called this continent *Pangaea* (pan JEE uh), which is Greek for "all earth." We now know from the hypothesis of plate tectonics that Pangaea existed about 245 million years ago. We also know that Pangaea further split into two huge continents—Laurasia and Gondwana—about 180 million years ago. As shown in **Figure 2,** these two continents split again and formed the continents we know today.

continental drift the hypothesis that states that the continents once formed a single landmass, broke up, and drifted to their present locations

Sea-Floor Spreading

When Wegener put forth his hypothesis of continental drift, many scientists would not accept his hypothesis. From the calculated strength of the rocks, it did not seem possible for the crust to move in this way. During Wegener's life, no one knew the answer. It wasn't until many years later that evidence provided some clues to the forces that moved the continents.

Figure 3 Sea-Floor Spreading

Sea-floor spreading creates new oceanic lithosphere at mid-ocean ridges.

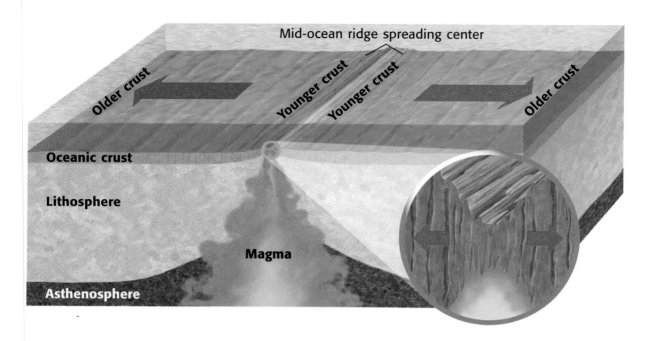

Mid-ocean ridge spreading center

Older crust

Younger crust

Younger crust

Older crust

Oceanic crust

Lithosphere

Magma

Asthenosphere

sea-floor spreading the process by which new oceanic lithosphere forms as magma rises toward the surface and solidifies

Mid-Ocean Ridges and Sea-Floor Spreading

A chain of submerged mountains runs through the center of the Atlantic Ocean. The chain is part of a worldwide system of mid-ocean ridges. Mid-ocean ridges are underwater mountain chains that run through Earth's ocean basins.

Mid-ocean ridges are places where sea-floor spreading takes place. **Sea-floor spreading** is the process by which new oceanic lithosphere forms as magma rises toward the surface and solidifies. As the tectonic plates move away from each other, the sea floor spreads apart and magma fills in the gap. As this new crust forms, the older crust gets pushed away from the mid-ocean ridge. As **Figure 3** shows, the older crust is farther away from the mid-ocean ridge than the younger crust is.

Evidence for Sea-Floor Spreading: Magnetic Reversals

Some of the most important evidence of sea-floor spreading comes from magnetic reversals recorded in the ocean floor. Throughout Earth's history, the north and south magnetic poles have changed places many times. When the poles change places, the polarity of Earth's magnetic poles changes, as shown in **Figure 4.** When Earth's magnetic poles change places, this change is called a *magnetic reversal.*

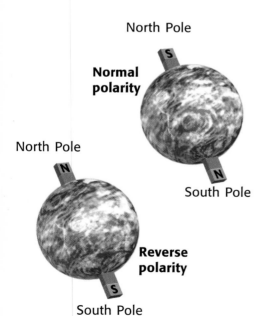

North Pole

Normal polarity

S

North Pole

N

South Pole

N

Reverse polarity

S

South Pole

Figure 4 *The polarity of Earth's magnetic field changes over time.*

Magnetic Reversals and Sea-Floor Spreading

The molten rock at the mid-ocean ridges contains tiny grains of magnetic minerals. These mineral grains contain iron and are like compasses. They align with the magnetic field of the Earth. When the molten rock cools, the record of these tiny compasses remains in the rock. This record is then carried slowly away from the spreading center of the ridge as sea-floor spreading occurs.

As you can see in **Figure 5,** when the Earth's magnetic field reverses, the magnetic mineral grains align in the opposite direction. The new rock records the direction of the Earth's magnetic field. As the sea floor spreads away from a mid-ocean ridge, it carries with it a record of magnetic reversals. This record of magnetic reversals was the final proof that sea-floor spreading does occur.

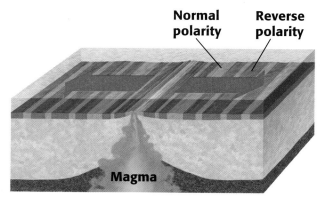

Normal polarity   Reverse polarity

Magma

Figure 5 *Magnetic reversals in oceanic crust are shown as bands of light blue and dark blue oceanic crust. Light blue bands indicate normal polarity, and dark blue bands indicate reverse polarity.*

Reading Check How is a record of magnetic reversals recorded in molten rock at mid-ocean ridges?

SECTION Review

Summary

- Wegener hypothesized that continents drift apart from one another and have done so in the past.
- The process by which new oceanic lithosphere forms at mid-ocean ridges is called sea-floor spreading.
- As tectonic plates separate, the sea floor spreads apart and magma fills in the gap.
- Magnetic reversals are recorded over time in oceanic crust.

Using Key Terms

1. In your own words, write a definition for each of the following terms: *continental drift* and *sea-floor spreading*.

Understanding Key Ideas

2. At mid-ocean ridges,
   a. the crust is older.
   b. sea-floor spreading occurs.
   c. oceanic lithosphere is destroyed.
   d. tectonic plates are colliding.

3. Explain how oceanic lithosphere forms at mid-ocean ridges.

4. What is magnetic reversal?

Math Skills

5. If a piece of sea floor has moved 50 km in 5 million years, what is the yearly rate of sea-floor motion?

Critical Thinking

6. **Identifying Relationships** Explain how magnetic reversals provide evidence for sea-floor spreading.

7. **Applying Concepts** Why do bands indicating magnetic reversals appear to be of similar width on both sides of a mid-ocean ridge?

8. **Applying Concepts** Why do you think that old rocks are rare on the ocean floor?

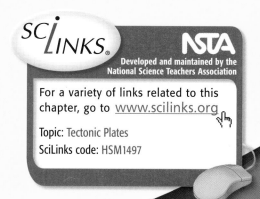

SCI*LINKS*.

NSTA

Developed and maintained by the National Science Teachers Association

For a variety of links related to this chapter, go to www.scilinks.org

Topic: Tectonic Plates
SciLinks code: HSM1497

The Theory of Plate Tectonics

It takes an incredible amount of force to move a tectonic plate! But where does this force come from?

As scientists' understanding of mid-ocean ridges and magnetic reversals grew, scientists formed a theory to explain how tectonic plates move. **Plate tectonics** is the theory that the Earth's lithosphere is divided into tectonic plates that move around on top of the asthenosphere. In this section, you will learn what causes tectonic plates to move. But first you will learn about the different types of tectonic plate boundaries.

Tectonic Plate Boundaries

A boundary is a place where tectonic plates touch. All tectonic plates share boundaries with other tectonic plates. These boundaries are divided into three types: convergent, divergent, and transform. The type of boundary depends on how the tectonic plates move relative to one another. Tectonic plates can collide, separate, or slide past each other. Earthquakes can occur at all three types of plate boundaries. The figure below shows examples of tectonic plate boundaries.

READING WARM-UP

Objectives

- Describe the three types of tectonic plate boundaries.
- Describe the three forces thought to move tectonic plates.
- Explain how scientists measure the rate at which tectonic plates move.

Terms to Learn

plate tectonics
convergent boundary
divergent boundary
transform boundary

READING STRATEGY

Brainstorming The key idea of this section is plate tectonics. Brainstorm words and phrases related to plate tectonics.

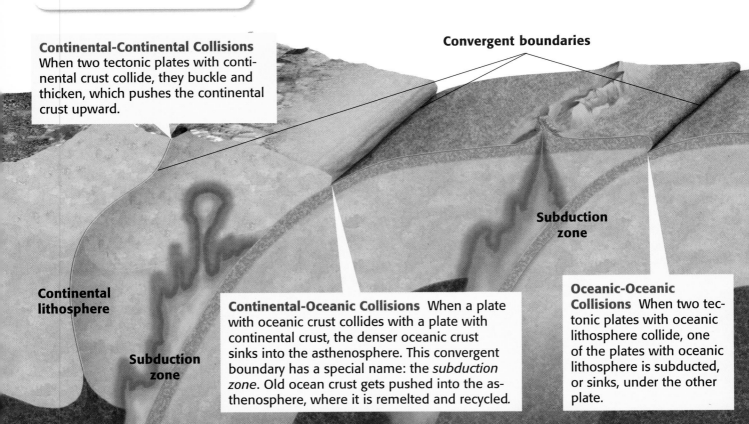

Continental-Continental Collisions When two tectonic plates with continental crust collide, they buckle and thicken, which pushes the continental crust upward.

Convergent boundaries

Continental lithosphere

Subduction zone

Continental-Oceanic Collisions When a plate with oceanic crust collides with a plate with continental crust, the denser oceanic crust sinks into the asthenosphere. This convergent boundary has a special name: the *subduction zone*. Old ocean crust gets pushed into the asthenosphere, where it is remelted and recycled.

Subduction zone

Oceanic-Oceanic Collisions When two tectonic plates with oceanic lithosphere collide, one of the plates with oceanic lithosphere is subducted, or sinks, under the other plate.

Convergent Boundaries

When two tectonic plates collide, the boundary between them is a **convergent boundary.** What happens at a convergent boundary depends on the kind of crust at the leading edge of each tectonic plate. The three types of convergent boundaries are continental-continental boundaries, continental-oceanic boundaries, and oceanic-oceanic boundaries.

Divergent Boundaries

When two tectonic plates separate, the boundary between them is called a **divergent boundary.** New sea floor forms at divergent boundaries. Mid-ocean ridges are the most common type of divergent boundary.

Transform Boundaries

When two tectonic plates slide past each other horizontally, the boundary between them is a **transform boundary.** The San Andreas Fault in California is a good example of a transform boundary. This fault marks the place where the Pacific and North American plates are sliding past each other.

✓ Reading Check Define the term *transform boundary*. (*See the Appendix for answers to Reading Checks.*)

plate tectonics the theory that explains how large pieces of the Earth's outermost layer, called *tectonic plates,* move and change shape

convergent boundary the boundary formed by the collision of two lithospheric plates

divergent boundary the boundary between two tectonic plates that are moving away from each other

transform boundary the boundary between tectonic plates that are sliding past each other horizontally

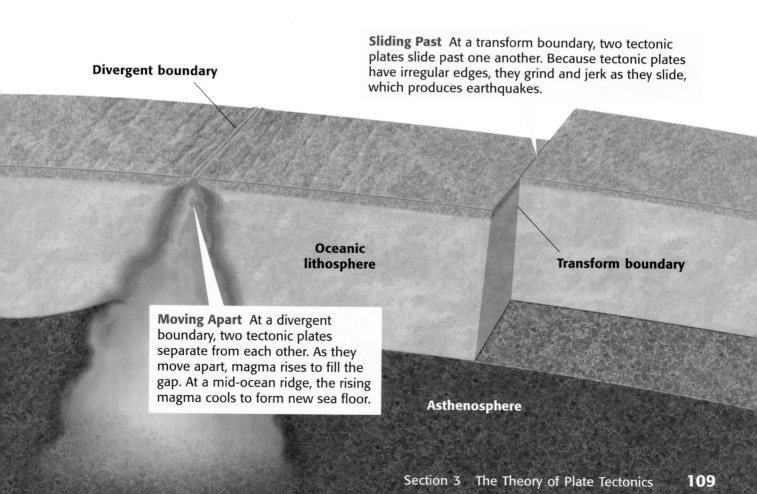

Divergent boundary

Sliding Past At a transform boundary, two tectonic plates slide past one another. Because tectonic plates have irregular edges, they grind and jerk as they slide, which produces earthquakes.

Oceanic lithosphere

Transform boundary

Moving Apart At a divergent boundary, two tectonic plates separate from each other. As they move apart, magma rises to fill the gap. At a mid-ocean ridge, the rising magma cools to form new sea floor.

Asthenosphere

Possible Causes of Tectonic Plate Motion

You have learned that plate tectonics is the theory that the lithosphere is divided into tectonic plates that move around on top of the asthenosphere. What causes the motion of tectonic plates? Remember that the solid rock of the asthenosphere flows very slowly. This movement occurs because of changes in density within the asthenosphere. These density changes are caused by the outward flow of thermal energy from deep within the Earth. When rock is heated, it expands, becomes less dense, and tends to rise to the surface of the Earth. As the rock gets near the surface, the rock cools, becomes more dense, and tends to sink. **Figure 1** shows three possible causes of tectonic plate motion.

Reading Check What causes changes in density in the asthenosphere?

Figure 1 Three Possible Driving Forces of Plate Tectonics

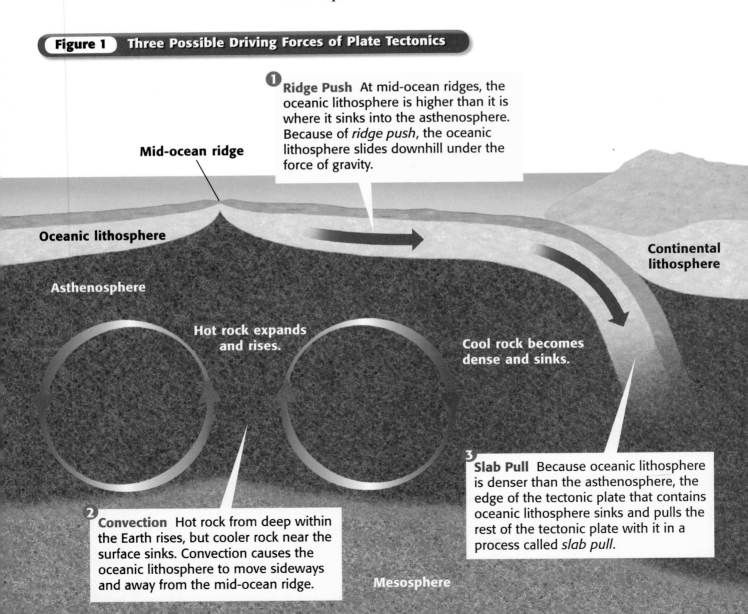

Mid-ocean ridge

1 Ridge Push At mid-ocean ridges, the oceanic lithosphere is higher than it is where it sinks into the asthenosphere. Because of *ridge push*, the oceanic lithosphere slides downhill under the force of gravity.

Oceanic lithosphere

Continental lithosphere

Asthenosphere

Hot rock expands and rises.

Cool rock becomes dense and sinks.

2 Convection Hot rock from deep within the Earth rises, but cooler rock near the surface sinks. Convection causes the oceanic lithosphere to move sideways and away from the mid-ocean ridge.

3 Slab Pull Because oceanic lithosphere is denser than the asthenosphere, the edge of the tectonic plate that contains oceanic lithosphere sinks and pulls the rest of the tectonic plate with it in a process called *slab pull*.

Mesosphere

Tracking Tectonic Plate Motion

How fast do tectonic plates move? The answer to this question depends on many factors, such as the type and shape of the tectonic plate and the way that the tectonic plate interacts with the tectonic plates that surround it. Tectonic plate movements are so slow and gradual that you can't see or feel them—the movement is measured in centimeters per year.

The Global Positioning System

Scientists use a system of satellites called the *global positioning system* (GPS), shown in **Figure 2,** to measure the rate of tectonic plate movement. Radio signals are continuously beamed from satellites to GPS ground stations, which record the exact distance between the satellites and the ground station. Over time, these distances change slightly. By recording the time it takes for the GPS ground stations to move a given distance, scientists can measure the speed at which each tectonic plate moves.

GPS satellite

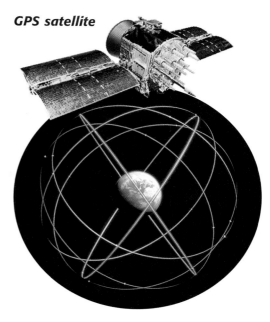

Figure 2 *The image above shows the orbits of the GPS satellites.*

SECTION Review

Summary

- Boundaries between tectonic plates are classified as convergent, divergent, or transform.
- Ridge push, convection, and slab pull are three possible driving forces of plate tectonics.
- Scientists use data from a system of satellites called the global positioning system to measure the rate of motion of tectonic plates.

Using Key Terms

1. In your own words, write a definition for the term *plate tectonics*.

Understanding Key Ideas

2. The speed a tectonic plate moves per year is best measured in
   a. kilometers per year.
   b. centimeters per year.
   c. meters per year.
   d. millimeters per year.

3. Briefly describe three possible driving forces of tectonic plate movement.

4. Explain how scientists use GPS to measure the rate of tectonic plate movement.

Math Skills

5. If an orbiting satellite has a diameter of 60 cm, what is the total surface area of the satellite? (Hint: *surface area* $= 4\pi r^2$)

Critical Thinking

6. **Identifying Relationships** When convection takes place in the mantle, why does cool rock material sink and warm rock material rise?

7. **Analyzing Processes** Why does oceanic crust sink beneath continental crust at convergent boundaries?

SCiLINKS.

NSTA

Developed and maintained by the
National Science Teachers Association

For a variety of links related to this chapter, go to www.scilinks.org

Topic: Plate Tectonics
SciLinks code: HSM1171

Deforming the Earth's Crust

Have you ever tried to bend something, only to have it break? Take long, uncooked pieces of spaghetti, and bend them very slowly but only a little. Now, bend them again, but this time, bend them much farther and faster. What happened?

How can a material bend at one time and break at another time? The answer is that the stress you put on the material was different each time. *Stress* is the amount of force per unit area on a given material. The same principle applies to the rocks in the Earth's crust. Different things happen to rock when different types of stress are applied.

Deformation

The process by which the shape of a rock changes because of stress is called *deformation*. In the example above, the spaghetti deformed in two different ways—by bending and by breaking. **Figure 1** illustrates this concept. The same thing happens in rock layers. Rock layers bend when stress is placed on them. But when enough stress is placed on rocks, they can reach their elastic limit and break.

Compression and Tension

The type of stress that occurs when an object is squeezed, such as when two tectonic plates collide, is called **compression.** When compression occurs at a convergent boundary, large mountain ranges can form.

Another form of stress is *tension*. **Tension** is stress that occurs when forces act to stretch an object. As you might guess, tension occurs at divergent plate boundaries, such as mid-ocean ridges, when two tectonic plates pull away from each other.

✓ **Reading Check** How do the forces of plate tectonics cause rock to deform? (*See the Appendix for answers to Reading Checks.*)

READING WARM-UP

Objectives

● Describe two types of stress that deform rocks.

● Describe three major types of folds.

● Explain the differences between the three major types of faults.

● Identify the most common types of mountains.

● Explain the difference between uplift and subsidence.

Terms to Learn

compression   fault
tension   uplift
folding   subsidence

READING STRATEGY

Discussion Read this section silently. Write down questions that you have about this section. Discuss your questions in a small group.

Figure 1 *When a small amount of stress is placed on uncooked spaghetti, the spaghetti bends. Additional stress causes the spaghetti to break.*

Figure 2 Folding: When Rock Layers Bend Because of Stress

Unstressed

Undeformed Rock Layers

Horizontal stress

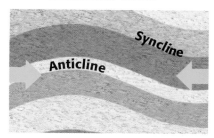

Anticline Syncline

Vertical stress

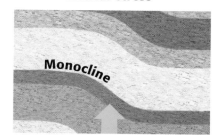

Monocline

Folding

The bending of rock layers because of stress in the Earth's crust is called **folding.** Scientists assume that all rock layers started as horizontal layers. So, when scientists see a fold, they know that deformation has taken place.

Types of Folds

Depending on how the rock layers deform, different types of folds are made. **Figure 2** shows the two most common types of folds—*anticlines*, or upward-arching folds, and *synclines*, downward, troughlike folds. Another type of fold is a *monocline*. In a monocline, rock layers are folded so that both ends of the fold are horizontal. Imagine taking a stack of paper and laying it on a table. Think of the sheets of paper as different rock layers. Now put a book under one end of the stack. You can see that both ends of the sheets are horizontal, but all of the sheets are bent in the middle.

Folds can be large or small. The largest folds are measured in kilometers. Other folds are also obvious but are much smaller. These small folds can be measured in centimeters. **Figure 3** shows examples of large and small folds.

compression stress that occurs when forces act to squeeze an object

tension stress that occurs when forces act to stretch an object

folding the bending of rock layers due to stress

Figure 3 *The large photo shows mountain-sized folds in the Rocky Mountains. The small photo shows a rock that has folds smaller than a penknife.*

Fault

Footwall

Hanging wall

Figure 4 *The position of a fault block determines whether it is a hanging wall or a footwall.*

fault a break in a body of rock along which one block slides relative to another

Faulting

Some rock layers break when stress is applied to them. The surface along which rocks break and slide past each other is called a **fault.** The blocks of crust on each side of the fault are called *fault blocks.*

When a fault is not vertical, understanding the difference between its two sides—the *hanging wall* and the *footwall*—is useful. **Figure 4** shows the difference between a hanging wall and a footwall. Two main types of faults can form. The type of fault that forms depends on how the hanging wall and footwall move in relationship to each other.

Normal Faults

A *normal fault* is shown in **Figure 5.** When a normal fault moves, it causes the hanging wall to move down relative to the footwall. Normal faults usually occur when tectonic forces cause tension that pulls rocks apart.

Reverse Faults

A *reverse fault* is shown in **Figure 5.** When a reverse fault moves, it causes the hanging wall to move up relative to the footwall. This movement is the reverse of a normal fault. Reverse faults usually happen when tectonic forces cause compression that pushes rocks together.

✓ Reading Check How does the hanging wall in a normal fault move in relation to a reverse fault?

Figure 5 **Normal and Reverse Faults**

Normal Fault When rocks are pulled apart because of tension, normal faults often form.

Reverse Fault When rocks are pushed together by compression, reverse faults often form.

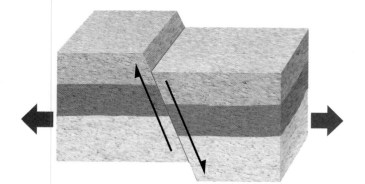

114   Chapter 4   Plate Tectonics

Figure 6 *The photo at left is a normal fault. The photo at right is a reverse fault.*

Telling the Difference Between Faults

It's easy to tell the difference between a normal fault and a reverse fault in drawings with arrows. But what types of faults are shown in **Figure 6**? You can certainly see the faults, but which one is a normal fault, and which one is a reverse fault? In the top left photo in **Figure 6,** one side has obviously moved relative to the other side. You can tell this fault is a normal fault by looking at the order of sedimentary rock layers. If you compare the two dark layers near the surface, you can see that the hanging wall has moved down relative to the footwall.

Strike-Slip Faults

A third major type of fault is called a *strike-slip fault*. An illustration of a strike-slip fault is shown in **Figure 7.** *Strike-slip faults* form when opposing forces cause rock to break and move horizontally. If you were standing on one side of a strike-slip fault looking across the fault when it moved, the ground on the other side would appear to move to your left or right. The San Andreas Fault in California is a spectacular example of a strike-slip fault.

Quick Lab

Modeling Strike-Slip Faults

1. Use **modeling clay** to construct a box that is 6 in. × 6 in. × 4 in. Use different colors of clay to represent different horizontal layers.

2. Using **scissors,** cut the box down the middle. Place **two 4 in. × 6 in. index cards** inside the cut so that the two sides of the box slide freely.

3. Using gentle pressure, slide the two sides horizontally past one another.

4. How does this model illustrate the motion that occurs along a strike-slip fault?

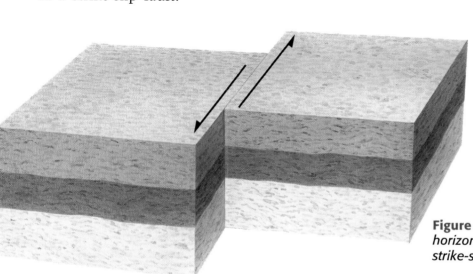

Figure 7 *When rocks are moved horizontally by opposing forces, strike-slip faults often form.*

Figure 8 *The Andes Mountains formed on the edge of the South American plate where it converges with the Nazca plate.*

Plate Tectonics and Mountain Building

You have just learned about several ways the Earth's crust changes because of the forces of plate tectonics. When tectonic plates collide, land features that start as folds and faults can eventually become large mountain ranges. Mountains exist because tectonic plates are continually moving around and colliding with one another. As shown in **Figure 8,** the Andes Mountains formed above the subduction zone where two tectonic plates converge.

When tectonic plates undergo compression or tension, they can form mountains in several ways. Take a look at three of the most common types of mountains—folded mountains, fault-block mountains, and volcanic mountains.

Folded Mountains

The highest mountain ranges in the world are made up of folded mountains. These ranges form at convergent boundaries where continents have collided. *Folded mountains* form when rock layers are squeezed together and pushed upward. If you place a pile of paper on a table and push on opposite edges of the pile, you will see how folded mountains form.

An example of a folded mountain range that formed at a convergent boundary is shown in **Figure 9.** About 390 million years ago, the Appalachian Mountains formed when the landmasses that are now North America and Africa collided. Other examples of mountain ranges that consist of very large and complex folds are the Alps in central Europe, the Ural Mountains in Russia, and the Himalayas in Asia.

Reading Check Explain how folded mountains form.

Figure 9 *The Appalachian Mountains were once as tall as the Himalaya Mountains but have been worn down by hundreds of millions of years of weathering and erosion.*

Figure 10 *When the crust is subjected to tension, the rock can break along a series of normal faults, which creates fault-block mountains.*

Fault-Block Mountains

When tectonic forces put enough tension on the Earth's crust, a large number of normal faults can result. *Fault-block mountains* form when this tension causes large blocks of the Earth's crust to drop down relative to other blocks. **Figure 10** shows one way that fault-block mountains form.

When sedimentary rock layers are tilted up by faulting, they can produce mountains that have sharp, jagged peaks. As shown in **Figure 11,** the Tetons in western Wyoming are a spectacular example of fault-block mountains.

Volcanic Mountains

Most of the world's major volcanic mountains are located at convergent boundaries where oceanic crust sinks into the asthenosphere at subduction zones. The rock that is melted in subduction zones forms magma, which rises to the Earth's surface and erupts to form *volcanic mountains*. Volcanic mountains can also form under the sea. Sometimes these mountains can rise above the ocean surface to become islands. The majority of tectonically active volcanic mountains on the Earth have formed around the tectonically active rim of the Pacific Ocean. The rim has become known as the *Ring of Fire.*

CONNECTION TO Social Studies

WRITING SKILL **The Naming of the Appalachian Mountains** How did the Appalachian Mountains get their name? It is believed that the Appalachian Mountains were named by Spanish explorers in North America during the 16th century. It is thought that the name was taken from a Native American tribe called *Appalachee,* who lived in northern Florida. Research other geological features in the United States, including mountains and rivers, whose names are of Native American origin. Write the results of your research in a short essay.

Figure 11 *The Tetons formed as a result of tectonic forces that stretched the Earth's crust and caused it to break in a series of normal faults.*

INTERNET ACTIVITY

For another activity related to this chapter, go to **go.hrw.com** and type in the keyword **HZ5TECW.**

uplift the rising of regions of the Earth's crust to higher elevations

subsidence the sinking of regions of the Earth's crust to lower elevations

Uplift and Subsidence

Vertical movements in the crust are divided into two types—uplift and subsidence. The rising of regions of Earth's crust to higher elevations is called **uplift.** Rocks that are uplifted may or may not be highly deformed. The sinking of regions of Earth's crust to lower elevations is known as **subsidence** (suhb SIED'ns). Unlike some uplifted rocks, rocks that subside do not undergo much deformation.

Uplifting of Depressed Rocks

The formation of mountains is one type of uplift. Uplift can also occur when large areas of land rise without deforming. One way areas rise without deforming is a process known as *rebound*. When the crust rebounds, it slowly springs back to its previous elevation. Uplift often happens when a weight is removed from the crust.

Subsidence of Cooler Rocks

Rocks that are hot take up more space than cooler rocks. For example, the lithosphere is relatively hot at mid-ocean ridges. The farther the lithosphere is from the ridge, the cooler and denser the lithosphere becomes. Because the oceanic lithosphere now takes up less volume, the ocean floor subsides.

Tectonic Letdown

Subsidence can also occur when the lithosphere becomes stretched in rift zones. A *rift zone* is a set of deep cracks that forms between two tectonic plates that are pulling away from each other. As tectonic plates pull apart, stress between the plates causes a series of faults to form along the rift zone. As shown in **Figure 12,** the blocks of crust in the center of the rift zone subside.

Figure 12 *The East African Rift, from Ethiopia to Kenya, is part of a divergent boundary, but you can see how the crust has subsided relative to the blocks at the edge of the rift zone.*

Summary

- Compression and tension are two forces of plate tectonics that can cause rock to deform.

- Folding occurs when rock layers bend because of stress.

- Faulting occurs when rock layers break because of stress and then move on either side of the break.

- Mountains are classified as either folded, fault-block, or volcanic depending on how they form.

- Mountain building is caused by the movement of tectonic plates. Folded mountains and volcanic mountains form at convergent boundaries. Fault-block mountains form at divergent boundaries.

- Uplift and subsidence are the two types of vertical movement in the Earth's crust. Uplift occurs when regions of the crust rise to higher elevations. Subsidence occurs when regions of the crust sink to lower elevations.

Using Key Terms

For each pair of key terms, explain how the meanings of the terms differ.

1. *compression* and *tension*

2. *uplift* and *subsidence*

Understanding Key Ideas

3. The type of fault in which the hanging wall moves up relative to the footwall is called a

   a. strike-slip fault.

   b. fault-block fault.

   c. normal fault.

   d. reverse fault.

4. Describe three types of folds.

5. Describe three types of faults.

6. Identify the most common types of mountains.

7. What is rebound?

8. What are rift zones, and how do they form?

Critical Thinking

9. **Predicting Consequences** If a fault occurs in an area where rock layers have been folded, which type of fault is it likely to be? Why?

10. **Identifying Relationships** Would you expect to see a folded mountain range at a mid-ocean ridge? Explain your answer.

Interpreting Graphics

Use the diagram below to answer the questions that follow.

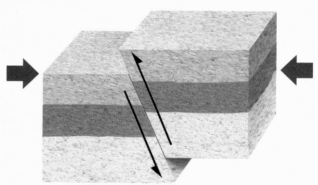

11. What type of fault is shown in the diagram?

12. At what kind of tectonic boundary would you most likely find this fault?

SCILINKS®

NSTA

Developed and maintained by the
National Science Teachers Association

For a variety of links related to this chapter, go to www.scilinks.org

Topic: Faults; Mountain Building
SciLinks code: HSM0566; HSM0999

Model-Making Lab

Convection Connection

Some scientists think that convection currents within the Earth's mantle cause tectonic plates to move. Because these convection currents cannot be observed directly, scientists use models to simulate the process. In this activity, you will make your own model to simulate tectonic plate movement.

Ask a Question

1 How can I make a model of convection currents in the Earth's mantle?

Form a Hypothesis

2 Turn the question above into a statement in which you give your best guess about what factors will have the greatest effect on your convection model.

Test the Hypothesis

3 Place two hot plates side by side in the center of your lab table. Be sure that they are away from the edge of the table.

4 Place the pan on top of the hot plates. Slide the wooden blocks under the pan to support the ends. Make sure that the pan is level and secure.

5 Fill the pan with cold water. The water should be at least 4 cm deep. Turn on the hot plates, and put on your gloves.

6 After a minute or two, tiny bubbles will begin to rise in the water above the hot plates. Gently place two craft sticks on the water's surface.

7 Use the pencil to align the sticks parallel to the short ends of the pan. The sticks should be about 3 cm apart and near the center of the pan.

8 As soon as the sticks begin to move, place a drop of food coloring in the center of the pan. Observe what happens to the food coloring.

OBJECTIVES

Model convection currents to simulate plate tectonic movement.

Draw conclusions about the role of convection in plate tectonics.

MATERIALS

- craft sticks (2)
- food coloring
- gloves, heat-resistant
- hot plates, small (2)
- pan, aluminum, rectangular
- pencil
- ruler, metric
- thermometers (3)
- water, cold
- wooden blocks

SAFETY

9. With the help of a partner, hold one thermometer bulb just under the water at the center of the pan. Hold the other two thermometers just under the water near the ends of the pan. Record the temperatures.

10. When you are finished, turn off the hot plates. After the water has cooled, carefully empty the water into a sink.

Analyze the Results

1. **Explaining Events** Based on your observations of the motion of the food coloring, how does the temperature of the water affect the direction in which the craft sticks move?

Draw Conclusions

2. **Drawing Conclusions** How does the motion of the craft sticks relate to the motion of the water?

3. **Applying Conclusions** How does this model relate to plate tectonics and the movement of the continents?

4. **Applying Conclusions** Based on your observations, what can you conclude about the role of convection in plate tectonics?

Applying Your Data

Suggest a substance other than water that might be used to model convection in the mantle. Consider using a substance that flows more slowly than water.

Chapter Review

USING KEY TERMS

1 Use the following terms in the same sentence: *crust*, *mantle*, and *core*.

Complete each of the following sentences by choosing the correct term from the word bank.

asthenosphere   uplift
tension   continental drift

2 The hypothesis that continents can drift apart and have done so in the past is known as ___.

3 The ___ is the soft layer of the mantle on which the tectonic plates move.

4 ___ is stress that occurs when forces act to stretch an object.

5 The rising of regions of the Earth's crust to higher elevations is called ___.

UNDERSTANDING KEY IDEAS

Multiple Choice

6 The strong, lower part of the mantle is a physical layer called the
- **a.** lithosphere.
- **b.** mesosphere.
- **c.** asthenosphere.
- **d.** outer core.

7 The type of tectonic plate boundary that forms from a collision between two tectonic plates is a
- **a.** divergent plate boundary.
- **b.** transform plate boundary.
- **c.** convergent plate boundary.
- **d.** normal plate boundary.

8 The bending of rock layers due to stress in the Earth's crust is known as
- **a.** uplift.
- **b.** folding.
- **c.** faulting.
- **d.** subsidence.

9 The type of fault in which the hanging wall moves up relative to the footwall is called a
- **a.** strike-slip fault.
- **b.** fault-block fault.
- **c.** normal fault.
- **d.** reverse fault.

10 The type of mountain that forms when rock layers are squeezed together and pushed upward is the
- **a.** folded mountain.
- **b.** fault-block mountain.
- **c.** volcanic mountain.
- **d.** strike-slip mountain.

11 Scientists' knowledge of the Earth's interior has come primarily from
- **a.** studying magnetic reversals in oceanic crust.
- **b.** using a system of satellites called the *global positioning system*.
- **c.** studying seismic waves generated by earthquakes.
- **d.** studying the pattern of fossils on different continents.

Short Answer

12 Explain how scientists use seismic waves to map the Earth's interior.

13 How do magnetic reversals provide evidence of sea-floor spreading?

14 Explain how sea-floor spreading provides a way for continents to move.

15 Describe two types of stress that deform rock.

16 What is the global positioning system (GPS), and how does GPS allow scientists to measure the rate of motion of tectonic plates?

CRITICAL THINKING

17 **Concept Mapping** Use the following terms to create a concept map: *sea-floor spreading, convergent boundary, divergent boundary, subduction zone, transform boundary,* and *tectonic plates.*

18 **Applying Concepts** Why does oceanic lithosphere sink at subduction zones but not at mid-ocean ridges?

19 **Identifying Relationships** New tectonic material continually forms at divergent boundaries. Tectonic plate material is also continually destroyed in subduction zones at convergent boundaries. Do you think that the total amount of lithosphere formed on the Earth is about equal to the amount destroyed? Why?

20 **Applying Concepts** Folded mountains usually form at the edge of a tectonic plate. How can you explain folded mountain ranges located in the middle of a tectonic plate?

INTERPRETING GRAPHICS

Imagine that you could travel to the center of the Earth. Use the diagram below to answer the questions that follow.

Composition	Structure
Crust (50 km)	Lithosphere (150 km)
Mantle (2,900 km)	
	Asthenosphere (250 km)
	Mesosphere (2,550 km)
Core (3,430 km)	Outer core (2,200 km)
	Inner core (1,228 km)

21 How far beneath the Earth's surface would you have to go before you were no longer passing through rock that had the composition of granite?

22 How far beneath the Earth's surface would you have to go to find liquid material in the Earth's core?

23 At what depth would you find mantle material but still be within the lithosphere?

24 How far beneath the Earth's surface would you have to go to find solid iron and nickel in the Earth's core?

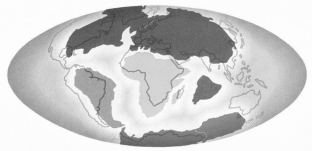

Standardized Test Preparation

Read each of the passages below. Then, answer the questions that follow each passage.

Passage 1 The Deep Sea Drilling Project was a program to retrieve and research rocks below the ocean to test the hypothesis of sea-floor spreading. For 15 years, scientists studying sea-floor spreading <u>conducted</u> research aboard the ship *Glomar Challenger*. Holes were drilled in the sea floor from the ship. Long, cylindrical lengths of rock, called *cores*, were obtained from the drill holes. By examining fossils in the cores, scientists discovered that rock closest to mid-ocean ridges was the youngest. The farther from the ridge the holes were drilled, the older the rock in the cores was. This evidence supported the idea that sea-floor spreading creates new lithosphere at mid-ocean ridges.

1. In the passage, what does *conducted* mean?
   A directed
   B led
   C carried on
   D guided

2. Why were cores drilled in the sea floor from the *Glomar Challenger*?
   F to determine the depth of the crust
   G to find minerals in the sea-floor rock
   H to examine fossils in the sea-floor rock
   I to find oil and gas in the sea-floor rock

3. Which of the following statements is a fact according to the passage?
   A Rock closest to mid-ocean ridges is older than rock at a distance from mid-ocean ridges.
   B One purpose of scientific research on the *Glomar Challenger* was to gather evidence for sea-floor spreading.
   C Fossils examined by scientists came directly from the sea floor.
   D Evidence gathered by scientists did not support sea-floor spreading.

Passage 2 The Himalayas are a range of mountains that is 2,400 km long and that <u>arcs</u> across Pakistan, India, Tibet, Nepal, Sikkim, and Bhutan. The Himalayas are the highest mountains on Earth. Nine mountains, including Mount Everest, the highest mountain on Earth, are more than 8,000 m tall. The formation of the Himalaya Mountains began about 80 million years ago. A tectonic plate carrying the Indian subcontinent collided with the Eurasian plate. The Indian plate was driven beneath the Eurasian plate. This collision caused the uplift of the Eurasian plate and the formation of the Himalayas. This process is continuing today.

1. In the passage, what does the word *arcs* mean?
   A forms a circle
   B forms a plane
   C forms a curve
   D forms a straight line

2. According to the passage, which geologic process formed the Himalaya Mountains?
   F divergence
   G subsidence
   H strike-slip faulting
   I convergence

3. Which of the following statements is a fact according to the passage?
   A The nine tallest mountains on Earth are located in the Himalaya Mountains.
   B The Himalaya Mountains are located within six countries.
   C The Himalaya Mountains are the longest mountain range on Earth.
   D The Himalaya Mountains formed more than 80 million years ago.

The illustration below shows the relative velocities (in centimeters per year) and directions in which tectonic plates are separating and colliding. Arrows that point away from one another indicate plate separation. Arrows that point toward one another indicate plate collision. Use the illustration below to answer the questions that follow.

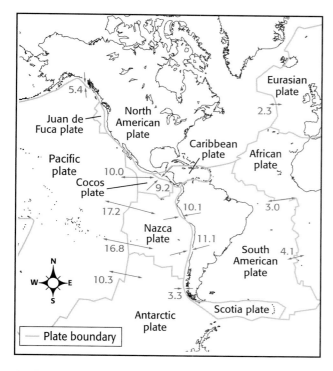

1. Between which two tectonic plates does spreading appear to be the fastest?

   A the Australian plate and the Pacific plate

   B the Antarctic plate and the Pacific plate

   C the Nazca plate and the Pacific plate

   D the Cocos plate and the Pacific plate

2. Where do you think mountain building is taking place?

   F between the African plate and the South American plate

   G between the Nazca plate and the South American plate

   H between the North American plate and the Eurasian plate

   I between the African plate and the North American plate

Read each question below, and choose the best answer.

1. The mesosphere is 2,550 km thick, and the asthenosphere is 250 km thick. If you assume that the lithosphere is 150 km thick and that the crust is 50 km thick, how thick is the mantle?

   A 2,950 km

   B 2,900 km

   C 2,800 km

   D 2,550 km

2. If a seismic wave travels through the mantle at an average velocity of 8 km/s, how many seconds will the wave take to travel through the mantle?

   F 318.75 s

   G 350.0 s

   H 362.5 s

   I 368.75 s

3. If the crust in a certain area is subsiding at the rate of 2 cm per year and has an elevation of 1,000 m, what elevation will the crust have in 10,000 years?

   A 500 m

   B 800 m

   C 1,200 m

   D 2,000 m

4. Assume that a very small oceanic plate is located between a mid-ocean ridge and a subduction zone. At the ridge, the plate is growing at a rate of 5 km every 1 million years. At the subduction zone, the plate is being destroyed at a rate of 10 km every 1 million years. If the oceanic plate is 100 km across, how long will it take the plate to disappear?

   F 100 million years

   G 50 million years

   H 20 million years

   I 5 million years

Science in Action

Science, Technology, and Society

Using Satellites to Track Plate Motion

When you think of laser beams firing, you may think of science fiction movies. However, scientists use laser beams to determine the rate and direction of motion of tectonic plates. From ground stations on Earth, laser beams are fired at several small satellites orbiting 5,900 km above Earth. From the satellites, the laser beams are reflected back to ground stations. Differences in the time it takes signals to be reflected from targets are measured over a period of time. From these differences, scientists can determine the rate and direction of plate motion.

Social Studies ACTIVITY

WRITING SKILL Research a society that lives at an active plate boundary. Find out how the people live with dangers such as volcanoes and earthquakes. Include your findings in a short report.

This scientist is using a laser to test one of the satellites that will be used to track plate motion.

Scientific Discoveries

Megaplumes

Eruptions of boiling water from the sea floor form giant, spiral disks that twist through the oceans. Do you think it's impossible? Oceanographers have discovered these disks at eight locations at mid-ocean ridges over the past 20 years. These disks, which may be tens of kilometers across, are called *megaplumes*. Megaplumes are like blenders. They mix hot water with cold water in the oceans. Megaplumes can rise hundreds of meters from the ocean floor to the upper layers of the ocean. They carry gases and minerals and provide extra energy and food to animals in the upper layers of the ocean.

Language Arts ACTIVITY

WRITING SKILL Did you ever wonder about the origin of the name *Himalaya*? Research the origin of the name *Himalaya*, and write a short report about what you find.

Alfred Wegener

Continental Drift Alfred Wegener's greatest contribution to science was the hypothesis of continental drift. This hypothesis states that continents drift apart from one another and have done so in the past. To support his hypothesis, Wegener used geologic, fossil, and glacial evidence gathered on both sides of the Atlantic Ocean. For example, Wegener recognized similarities between rock layers in North America and Europe and between rock layers in South America and Africa. He believed that these similarities could be explained only if these geologic features were once part of the same continent.

Although continental drift explained many of his observations, Wegener could not find scientific evidence to develop a complete explanation of how continents move. Most scientists were skeptical of Wegener's hypothesis and dismissed it as foolishness. It was not until the 1950s and 1960s that the discoveries of magnetic reversals and sea-floor spreading provided evidence of continental drift.

Math ACTIVITY

The distance between South America and Africa is 7,200 km. As new crust is created at the mid-ocean ridge, South America and Africa are moving away from each other at a rate of about 3.5 cm per year. How many millions of years ago were South America and Africa joined?

To learn more about these Science in Action topics, visit go.hrw.com and type in the keyword **HZ5TECF.**

Current Science

Check out Current Science® articles related to this chapter by visiting go.hrw.com. Just type in the keyword **HZ5CS07.**

Earthquakes

About the PHOTO

On January 17, 1995, an earthquake of magnitude 7.0 shook the area in and around Kobe, Japan. Though the earthquake lasted for less than a minute, more than 5,000 people lost their lives and another 300,000 people were left homeless. More than 200,000 buildings were damaged or destroyed. Large sections of the elevated Hanshin Expressway, shown in the photo, toppled when the columns supporting the expressway failed. The expressway passed over ground that was soft and wet, where the shaking was stronger and longer lasting.

PRE-READING ACTIVITY

Graphic Organizer

Spider Map Before you read the chapter, create the graphic organizer entitled "Spider Map" described in the **Study Skills** section of the Appendix. Label the circle "Earthquakes." Create a leg for each of the sections in this chapter. As you read the chapter, fill in the map with details about the material presented in each section of the chapter.

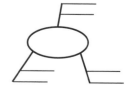

START-UP ACTIVITY

Bend, Break, or Shake

In this activity, you will test different materials in a model earthquake setting.

Procedure

1. Gather a **small wooden stick**, a **wire clothes hanger**, and a **plastic clothes hanger.**

2. Draw a straight line on a **sheet of paper.** Use a **protractor** to measure and draw the following angles from the line: 20°, 45°, and 90°.

3. Put on your **safety goggles.** Using the angles that you drew as a guide, try bending each item 20° and then releasing it. What happens? Does it break? If it bends, does it return to its original shape?

4. Repeat step 3, but bend each item 45°. Repeat the test again, but bend each item 90°.

Analysis

1. How do the different materials' responses to bending compare?

2. Where earthquakes happen, engineers use building materials that are flexible but that do not break or stay bent. Which materials from this experiment would you want building materials to behave like? Explain your answer.

What Are Earthquakes?

Have you ever felt the earth move under your feet? Many people have. Every day, somewhere within this planet, an earthquake is happening.

The word *earthquake* defines itself fairly well. But there is more to earthquakes than just the shaking of the ground. An entire branch of Earth science, called **seismology** (siez MAHL uh jee), is devoted to studying earthquakes. Earthquakes are complex, and they present many questions for *seismologists,* the scientists who study earthquakes.

Where Do Earthquakes Occur?

Most earthquakes take place near the edges of tectonic plates. *Tectonic plates* are giant pieces of Earth's thin, outermost layer. Tectonic plates move around on top of a layer of plastic rock. **Figure 1** shows the Earth's tectonic plates and the locations of recent major earthquakes.

Tectonic plates move in different directions and at different speeds. Two plates can push toward or pull away from each other. They can also slip slowly past each other. As a result of these movements, numerous features called faults exist in the Earth's crust. A *fault* is a break in the Earth's crust along which blocks of the crust slide relative to one another. Earthquakes occur along faults because of this sliding.

READING WARM-UP

Objectives

● Explain where earthquakes take place.

● Explain what causes earthquakes.

● Identify three different types of faults that occur at plate boundaries.

● Describe how energy from earthquakes travels through the Earth.

Terms to Learn

seismology   P waves
deformation   S waves
elastic rebound
seismic waves

READING STRATEGY

Paired Summarizing Read this section silently. In pairs, take turns summarizing the material. Stop to discuss ideas that seem confusing.

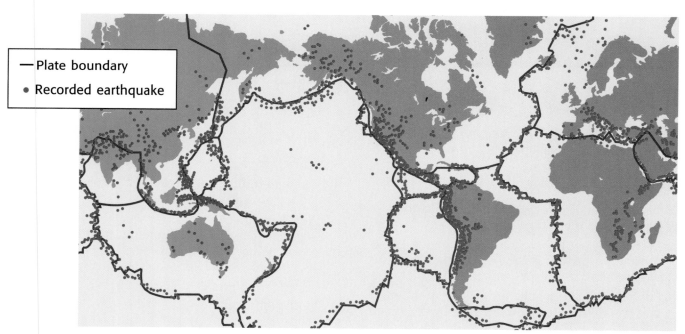

Figure 1 *The largest and most active earthquake zone lies along the plate boundaries surrounding the Pacific Ocean.*

- Plate boundary
- Recorded earthquake

What Causes Earthquakes?

As tectonic plates push, pull, or slip past each other, stress increases along faults near the plates' edges. In response to this stress, rock in the plates deforms. **Deformation** is the change in the shape of rock in response to stress. Rock along a fault deforms in mainly two ways. It deforms in a plastic manner, like a piece of molded clay, or in an elastic manner, like a rubber band. *Plastic deformation,* which is shown in **Figure 2,** does not lead to earthquakes.

Elastic deformation, however, does lead to earthquakes. Rock can stretch farther without breaking than steel can, but rock will break at some point. Think of elastically deformed rock as a stretched rubber band. You can stretch a rubber band only so far before it breaks. When the rubber band breaks, it releases energy. Then, the broken pieces return to their unstretched shape.

Figure 2 *This road cut is adjacent to the San Andreas Fault in southern California. The rocks in the cut have undergone deformation because of the continuous motion of the fault.*

Elastic Rebound

The sudden return of elastically deformed rock to its original shape is called **elastic rebound.** Elastic rebound is like the return of the broken rubber-band pieces to their unstretched shape. Elastic rebound occurs when more stress is applied to rock than the rock can withstand. During elastic rebound, energy is released. Some of this energy travels as seismic waves. These seismic waves cause an earthquake, as shown in **Figure 3.**

✓ Reading Check How does elastic rebound relate to earthquakes? (*See the Appendix for answers to Reading Checks.*)

seismology the study of earthquakes

deformation the bending, tilting, and breaking of the Earth's crust; the change in the shape of rock in response to stress

elastic rebound the sudden return of elastically deformed rock to its undeformed shape

---

Figure 3 **Elastic Rebound and Earthquakes**

Before earthquake

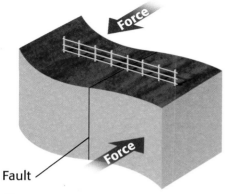

Fault

❶ Tectonic forces push rock on either side of the fault in opposite directions, but the rock is locked together and does not move. The rock deforms in an elastic manner.

After earthquake

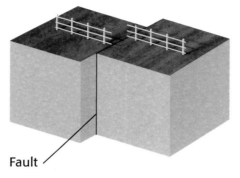

Fault

❷ When enough stress is applied, the rock slips along the fault and releases energy.

Faults at Tectonic Plate Boundaries

A specific type of plate motion takes place at different tectonic plate boundaries. Each type of motion creates a particular kind of fault that can produce earthquakes. Examine **Table 1** and the diagram below to learn more about plate motion.

Table 1 Plate Motion and Fault Types	
Plate motion	**Major fault type**
Transform	strike-slip fault
Convergent	reverse fault
Divergent	normal fault

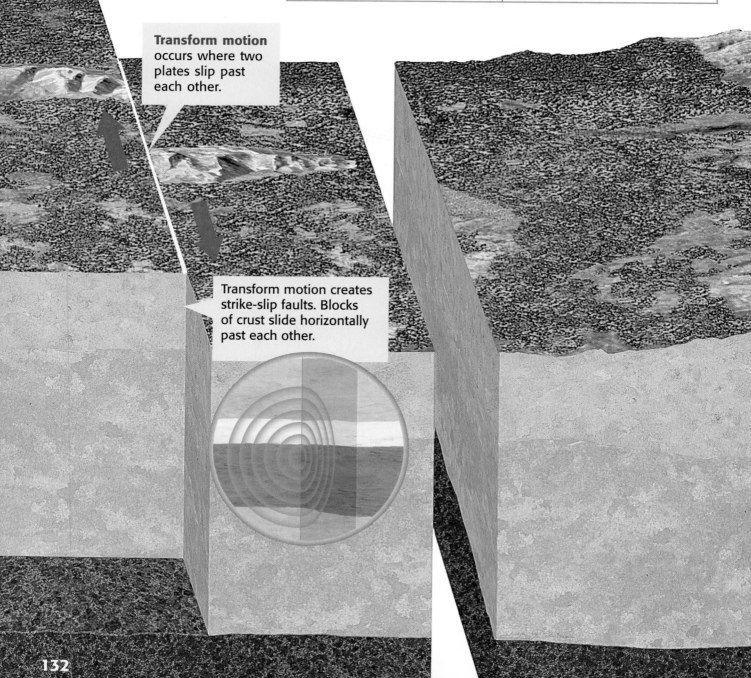

Transform motion occurs where two plates slip past each other.

Transform motion creates strike-slip faults. Blocks of crust slide horizontally past each other.

Earthquake Zones

Earthquakes can happen both near Earth's surface or far below it. Most earthquakes happen in the earthquake zones along tectonic plate boundaries. Earthquake zones are places where a large number of faults are located. The San Andreas Fault Zone in California is an example of an earthquake zone. But not all faults are located at tectonic plate boundaries. Sometimes, earthquakes happen along faults in the middle of tectonic plates.

✓ **Reading Check** Where are earthquake zones located?

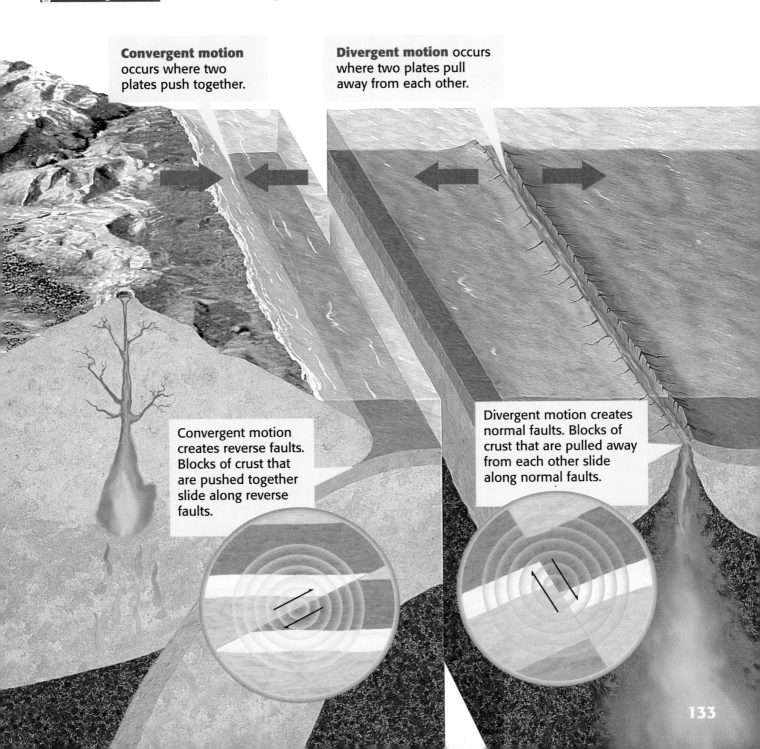

Convergent motion occurs where two plates push together.

Divergent motion occurs where two plates pull away from each other.

Convergent motion creates reverse faults. Blocks of crust that are pushed together slide along reverse faults.

Divergent motion creates normal faults. Blocks of crust that are pulled away from each other slide along normal faults.

Quick Lab

Modeling Seismic Waves

1. Stretch a **spring toy** lengthwise on a **table.**

2. Hold one end of the spring while a partner holds the other end. Push your end toward your partner's end, and observe what happens.

3. Repeat step 2, but this time shake the spring from side to side.

4. Which type of seismic wave is represented in step 2? in step 3?

---

seismic wave a wave of energy that travels through the Earth, away from an earthquake in all directions

P wave a seismic wave that causes particles of rock to move in a back-and-forth direction

S wave a seismic wave that causes particles of rock to move in a side-to-side direction

How Do Earthquake Waves Travel?

Waves of energy that travel through the Earth are called **seismic waves.** Seismic waves that travel through the Earth's interior are called *body waves.* There are two types of body waves: P waves and S waves. Seismic waves that travel along the Earth's surface are called *surface waves.* Each type of seismic wave travels through Earth's layers in a different way and at a different speed. Also, the speed of a seismic wave depends on the kind of material the wave travels through.

P Waves

Waves that travel through solids, liquids, and gases are called **P waves** (pressure waves). They are the fastest seismic waves, so P waves always travel ahead of other seismic waves. P waves are also called *primary waves,* because they are always the first waves of an earthquake to be detected. To understand how P waves affect rock, imagine a cube of gelatin sitting on a plate. Like most solids, gelatin is an elastic material. It wiggles if you tap it. Tapping the cube of gelatin changes the pressure inside the cube, which momentarily deforms the cube. The gelatin then reacts by springing back to its original shape. This process is how P waves affect rock, as shown in **Figure 4.**

S Waves

Rock can also be deformed from side to side. After being deformed from side to side, the rock springs back to its original position and S waves are created. **S waves,** or shear waves, are the second-fastest seismic waves. S waves shear rock side to side, as shown in **Figure 4,** which means they stretch the rock sideways. Unlike P waves, S waves cannot travel through parts of the Earth that are completely liquid. Also, S waves are slower than P waves and always arrive later. Thus, another name for S waves is *secondary waves.*

Figure 4   Body Waves

P waves move rock back and forth, which squeezes and stretches the rock, as they travel through the rock.

Direction of wave travel

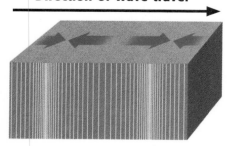

S waves shear rock side to side as they travel through the rock.

Direction of wave travel

Surface Waves

Surface waves move along the Earth's surface and produce motion mostly in the upper few kilometers of Earth's crust. There are two types of surface waves. One type of surface wave produces motion up, down, and around, as shown in **Figure 5.** The other type produces back-and-forth motion like the motion produced by S waves. Surface waves are different from body waves in that surface waves travel more slowly and are more destructive.

✓ Reading Check Explain the differences between surface waves and body waves.

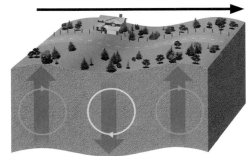

Figure 5 Surface Waves

Surface waves move the ground much like ocean waves move water particles.

Direction of wave travel

SECTION Review

Summary

- Earthquakes occur mainly near the edges of tectonic plates.

- Elastic rebound is the direct cause of earthquakes.

- Three major types of faults occur at tectonic plate boundaries: normal faults, reverse faults, and strike-slip faults.

- Earthquake energy travels as body waves through the Earth's interior or as surface waves along the surface of the Earth.

Using Key Terms

Complete each of the following sentences by choosing the correct term from the word bank.

| Deformation | P waves |
| Elastic rebound | S waves |

1. _____ is the change in shape of rock due to stress.

2. _____ always travel ahead of other waves.

Understanding Key Ideas

3. Seismic waves that shear rock side to side are called
   a. surface waves.
   b. S waves.
   c. P waves.
   d. Both (b) and (c)

4. Where do earthquakes occur?

5. What is the direct cause of earthquakes?

6. Describe the three types of plate motion and the faults that are characteristic of each type of motion.

7. What is an earthquake zone?

Math Skills

8. A seismic wave is traveling through the Earth at an average rate of speed of 8 km/s. How long will it take the wave to travel 480 km?

Critical Thinking

9. **Applying Concepts** Given what you know about elastic rebound, why do you think some earthquakes are stronger than others?

10. **Identifying Relationships** Why are surface waves more destructive to buildings than P waves or S waves are?

11. **Identifying Relationships** Why do you think the majority of earthquake zones are located at tectonic plate boundaries?

SCI**LINKS**®

NSTA
Developed and maintained by the
National Science Teachers Association

For a variety of links related to this chapter, go to www.scilinks.org

Topic: What Is an Earthquake?
SciLinks code: HSM1658

Earthquake Measurement

Imagine walls shaking, windows rattling, and glassware and dishes clinking and clanking. After only seconds, the vibrating stops and the sounds die away.

Within minutes, news reports give information about the strength, the time, and the location of the earthquake. You are amazed at how scientists could have learned this information so quickly.

Locating Earthquakes

How do seismologists know when and where earthquakes begin? They depend on earthquake-sensing instruments called seismographs. **Seismographs** are instruments located at or near the surface of the Earth that record seismic waves. When the waves reach a seismograph, the seismograph creates a seismogram. A **seismogram** is a tracing of earthquake motion and is created by a seismograph.

Determining Time and Location of Earthquakes

Seismologists use seismograms to calculate when an earthquake began. Seismologists find an earthquake's start time by comparing seismograms and noting the differences in arrival times of P waves and S waves. Seismologists also use seismograms to find an earthquake's epicenter. An **epicenter** is the point on the Earth's surface directly above an earthquake's starting point. A **focus** is the point inside the Earth where an earthquake begins. **Figure 1** shows the location of an earthquake's epicenter and its focus.

✔️ **Reading Check** How do seismologists determine an earthquake's start time? (*See the Appendix for answers to Reading Checks.*)

READING WARM-UP

Objectives

● Explain how earthquakes are detected.

● Describe how to locate an earthquake's epicenter.

● Explain how the strength of an earthquake is measured.

● Explain how the intensity of an earthquake is measured.

Terms to Learn

seismograph   epicenter
seismogram   focus

READING STRATEGY

Reading Organizer As you read this section, create an outline of the section. Use the headings from the section in your outline.

seismograph an instrument that records vibrations in the ground and determines the location and strength of an earthquake

seismogram a tracing of earthquake motion that is created by a seismograph

epicenter the point on Earth's surface directly above an earthquake's starting point, or focus

focus the point along a fault at which the first motion of an earthquake occurs

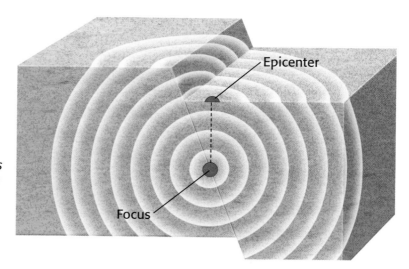

Figure 1 *An earthquake's epicenter is on the Earth's surface directly above the earthquake's focus.*

Epicenter

Focus

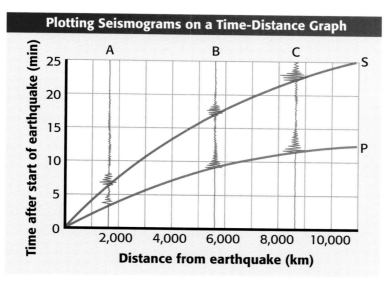

Plotting Seismograms on a Time-Distance Graph

Figure 2 *After identifying P and S waves, seismologists can use the time difference to determine an earthquake's start time and the distance from the epicenter to each station. The vertical axis tells how much time passed between the start of the earthquake and the arrival of seismic waves at a station. The horizontal axis tells the distance between a station and the earthquake's epicenter.*

The S-P Time Method

Perhaps the simplest method by which seismologists find an earthquake's epicenter is the *S-P time method*. The first step in this method is to collect several seismograms of the same earthquake from different locations. Then, the seismograms are placed on a time-distance graph. The seismogram tracing of the first P wave is lined up with the P-wave time-distance curve, and the tracing of the first S wave is lined up with the S-wave curve, as shown in **Figure 2.** The distance of each station from the earthquake can be found by reading the horizontal axis. After finding out the distances, a seismologist can locate an earthquake's epicenter, as shown in **Figure 3.**

Figure 3 **Finding an Earthquake's Epicenter**

1 A circle is drawn around a seismograph station. The radius of the circle equals the distance from the seismograph to the epicenter. (This distance is taken from the time-distance graph.)

2 When a second circle is drawn around another seismograph station, the circle overlaps the first circle in two spots. One of these spots is the earthquake's epicenter.

3 When a circle is drawn around a third seismograph station, all three circles intersect in one spot—the earthquake's epicenter. In this case, the epicenter was in San Francisco.

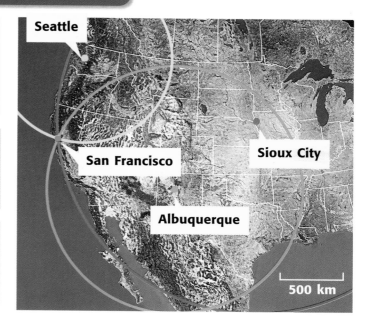

CONNECTION TO
Social Studies

WRITING SKILL **New Madrid Earthquakes**

During the winter of 1811–1812, three of the most powerful earthquakes in U.S. history were centered near New Madrid, Missouri, thousands of miles from the nearest tectonic plate boundary. Research the New Madrid earthquakes, and summarize your findings in a one-page essay.

Measuring Earthquake Strength and Intensity

"How strong was the earthquake?" is a common question asked of seismologists. This question is not easy to answer. But it is an important question for anyone living near an earthquake zone. Fortunately, seismograms can be used not only to determine an earthquake's epicenter and its start time but also to find out an earthquake's strength.

The Richter Magnitude Scale

Throughout much of the 20th century, seismologists used the *Richter magnitude scale*, commonly called the Richter scale, to measure the strength of earthquakes. Seismologist Charles Richter created the scale in the 1930s. Richter wanted to compare earthquakes by measuring ground motion recorded by seismograms at seismograph stations.

Earthquake Ground Motion

A measure of the strength of an earthquake is called *magnitude*. The Richter scale measures the ground motion from an earthquake and adjusts for distance to find its strength. Each time the magnitude increases by one unit, the measured ground motion becomes 10 times larger. For example, an earthquake with a magnitude of 5.0 on the Richter scale will produce 10 times as much ground motion as an earthquake with a magnitude of 4.0. Furthermore, an earthquake with a magnitude of 6.0 will produce 100 times as much ground motion (10 × 10) as an earthquake with a magnitude of 4.0. **Table 1** shows the differences in the estimated effects of earthquakes with each increase of one unit of magnitude.

Reading Check How are magnitude and ground motion related in the Richter scale?

Table 1 Effects of Different-Sized Earthquakes	
Magnitude	**Estimated effects**
2.0	can be detected only by seismograph
3.0	can be felt at epicenter
4.0	can be felt by most people in the area
5.0	causes damage at epicenter
6.0	can cause widespread damage
7.0	can cause great, widespread damage

Modified Mercalli Intensity Scale

A measure of the degree to which an earthquake is felt by people and the amount of damage caused by the earthquake, if any, is called *intensity*. Currently, seismologists in the United States use the Modified Mercalli Intensity Scale to measure earthquake intensity. This scale is a numerical scale that uses Roman numerals from I to XII to describe increasing earthquake intensity levels. An intensity level of I describes an earthquake that is not felt by most people. An intensity level of XII indicates total damage of an area. **Figure 4** shows the type of damage caused by an earthquake that has a Modified Mercalli intensity level of XI.

Because the effects of an earthquake vary from place to place, any earthquake will have more than one intensity value. Intensity values are usually higher near an earthquake's epicenter.

Figure 4 *Intensity values for the 1906 San Francisco earthquake varied from place to place. The maximum intensity level was XI.*

SECTION Review

Summary

- Seismologists detect seismic waves and record them as seismograms.
- The S-P time method is the simplest method to use to find an earthquake's epicenter.
- Seismologists use the Richter scale to measure an earthquake's strength.
- Seismologists use the Modified Mercalli Intensity Scale to measure an earthquake's intensity.

Using Key Terms

1. In your own words, write a definition for each of the following terms: *epicenter* and *focus*.

Understanding Key Ideas

2. What is the difference between a seismograph and a seismogram?

3. Explain how earthquakes are detected.

4. Briefly explain the steps of the S-P time method for locating an earthquake's epicenter.

5. Why might an earthquake have more than one intensity value?

Math Skills

6. How much more ground motion is produced by an earthquake of magnitude 7.0 than by an earthquake of magnitude 4.0?

Critical Thinking

7. **Making Inferences** Why is a 6.0 magnitude earthquake so much more destructive than a 5.0 magnitude earthquake?

8. **Identifying Bias** Which do you think is the more important measure of earthquakes, strength or intensity? Explain.

9. **Making Inferences** Do you think an earthquake of moderate magnitude can produce high Modified Mercalli intensity values?

SCILINKS

Developed and maintained by the National Science Teachers Association

For a variety of links related to this chapter, go to www.scilinks.org

Topic: Earthquake Measurement
SciLinks code: HSM0452

Earthquakes and Society

Imagine that you are in class and the ground begins to shake beneath your feet. What do you do?

READING WARM-UP

Objectives

● Explain how earthquake-hazard level is determined.

● Compare methods of earthquake forecasting.

● Describe five ways to safeguard buildings against earthquakes.

● Outline earthquake safety procedures.

Terms to Learn

gap hypothesis
seismic gap

READING STRATEGY

Discussion Read this section silently. Write down questions that you have about this section. Discuss your questions in a small group.

Seismologists are not able to predict the exact time when and place where an earthquake will occur. They can, at best, make forecasts based on the frequency with which earthquakes take place. Therefore, seismologists are always looking for better ways to forecast when and where earthquakes will happen. In the meantime, it is important for people in earthquake zones to be prepared before an earthquake strikes.

Earthquake Hazard

Earthquake hazard is a measurement of how likely an area is to have damaging earthquakes in the future. An area's earthquake-hazard level is determined by past and present seismic activity. The map in **Figure 1** shows that some areas of the United States have a higher earthquake-hazard level than others do. This variation is caused by differences in seismic activity. The greater the seismic activity, the higher the earthquake-hazard level. The West Coast, for example, has a very high earthquake-hazard level because it has a lot of seismic activity.

Look at the map. What earthquake-hazard level or levels are shown in the area in which you live? How do the hazard levels of nearby areas compare with your area's hazard level?

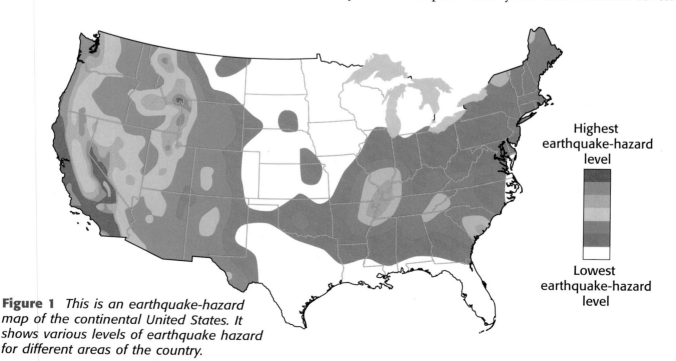

Highest
earthquake-hazard
level

Lowest
earthquake-hazard
level

Figure 1 *This is an earthquake-hazard map of the continental United States. It shows various levels of earthquake hazard for different areas of the country.*

Table 1 Worldwide Earthquake Frequency (Based on Observations Since 1900)		
Descriptor	**Magnitude**	**Average number annually**
Great	8.0 and higher	1
Major	7.0–7.9	18
Strong	6.0–6.9	120
Moderate	5.0–5.9	800
Light	4.0–4.9	about 6,200
Minor	3.0–3.9	about 49,000
Very minor	2.0–2.9	about 365,000

Earthquake Forecasting

Forecasting when and where earthquakes will occur and their strength is difficult. By looking carefully at areas of seismic activity, seismologists have discovered some patterns in earthquakes that allow them to make some general predictions.

Strength and Frequency

Earthquakes vary in strength. And you can probably guess that earthquakes don't occur on a set schedule. But what you may not know is that the strength of earthquakes is related to how often they occur. **Table 1** provides more detail about this relationship worldwide.

The relationship between earthquake strength and frequency is also at work on a local scale. For example, each year approximately 1.6 earthquakes with a magnitude of 4.0 on the Richter scale occur in the Puget Sound area of Washington State. Over this same time period, approximately 10 times as many earthquakes with a magnitude of 3.0 occur in this area. Scientists use these statistics to make forecasts about the strength, location, and frequency of future earthquakes.

Reading Check What is the relationship between the strength of earthquakes and earthquake frequency? (*See the Appendix for answers to Reading Checks.*)

The Gap Hypothesis

Another method of forecasting an earthquake's strength, location, and frequency is based on the gap hypothesis. The **gap hypothesis** is a hypothesis that states that sections of active faults that have had relatively few earthquakes are likely to be the sites of strong earthquakes in the future. The areas along a fault where relatively few earthquakes have occurred are called **seismic gaps.**

INTERNET ACTIVITY

For another activity related to this chapter, go to **go.hrw.com** and type in the keyword **HZ5EQKW.**

gap hypothesis a hypothesis that is based on the idea that a major earthquake is more likely to occur along the part of an active fault where no earthquakes have occurred for a certain period of time

seismic gap an area along a fault where relatively few earthquakes have occurred recently but where strong earthquakes have occurred in the past

Figure 2 A Seismic Gap on the San Andreas Fault

This diagram shows a cross section of the San Andreas Fault. Note how the seismic gap was filled by the 1989 Loma Prieta earthquake and its aftershocks. *Aftershocks* are weaker earthquakes that follow a stronger earthquake.

- Earthquakes prior to 1989 earthquake

- 1989 earthquake and aftershocks

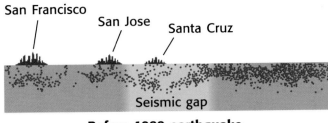

Before 1989 earthquake

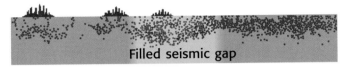

After 1989 earthquake

Using the Gap Hypothesis

Not all seismologists believe the gap hypothesis is an accurate method of forecasting earthquakes. But some seismologists think the gap hypothesis helped forecast the approximate location and strength of the 1989 Loma Prieta earthquake in the San Francisco Bay area. The seismic gap that they identified is illustrated in **Figure 2.** In 1988, these seismologists predicted that over the next 30 years there was a 30% chance that an earthquake with a magnitude of at least 6.5 would fill this seismic gap. Were they correct? The Loma Prieta earthquake, which filled in the seismic gap in 1989, measured 6.9 on the Richter scale. Their prediction was very close, considering how complicated the forecasting of earthquakes is.

Figure 3 *During the January 17, 1995, earthquake, the fronts of entire buildings collapsed into the streets of Kobe, Japan.*

Earthquakes and Buildings

Figure 3 shows what can happen to buildings during an earthquake. These buildings were not designed or constructed to withstand the forces of an earthquake.

Today, older structures in seismically active places, such as California, are being made more earthquake resistant. The process of making older structures more earthquake resistant is called *retrofitting*. A common way to retrofit an older home is to securely fasten it to its foundation. Steel can be used to strengthen structures made of brick.

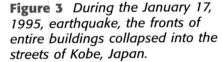 **Reading Check** Explain the meaning of the term *retrofitting*.

Earthquake-Resistant Buildings

A lot has been learned from building failure during earthquakes. Armed with this knowledge, architects and engineers use the newest technology to design and construct buildings and bridges to better withstand earthquakes. Carefully study **Figure 4** to learn more about this modern technology.

Figure 4 Earthquake-Resistant Building Technology

The **mass damper** is a weight placed in the roof of a building. Motion sensors detect building movement during an earthquake and send messages to a computer. The computer then signals controls in the roof to shift the mass damper to counteract the building's movement.

The **active tendon system** works much like the mass damper system in the roof. Sensors notify a computer that the building is moving. Then, the computer activates devices to shift a large weight to counteract the movement.

Base isolators act as shock absorbers during an earthquake. They are made of layers of rubber and steel wrapped around a lead core. Base isolators absorb seismic waves, preventing them from traveling through the building.

Steel **cross braces** are placed between floors. These braces counteract pressure that pushes and pulls at the side of a building during an earthquake.

Flexible pipes help prevent waterlines and gas lines from breaking. Engineers design the pipes with flexible joints so that the pipes are able to twist and bend without breaking during an earthquake.

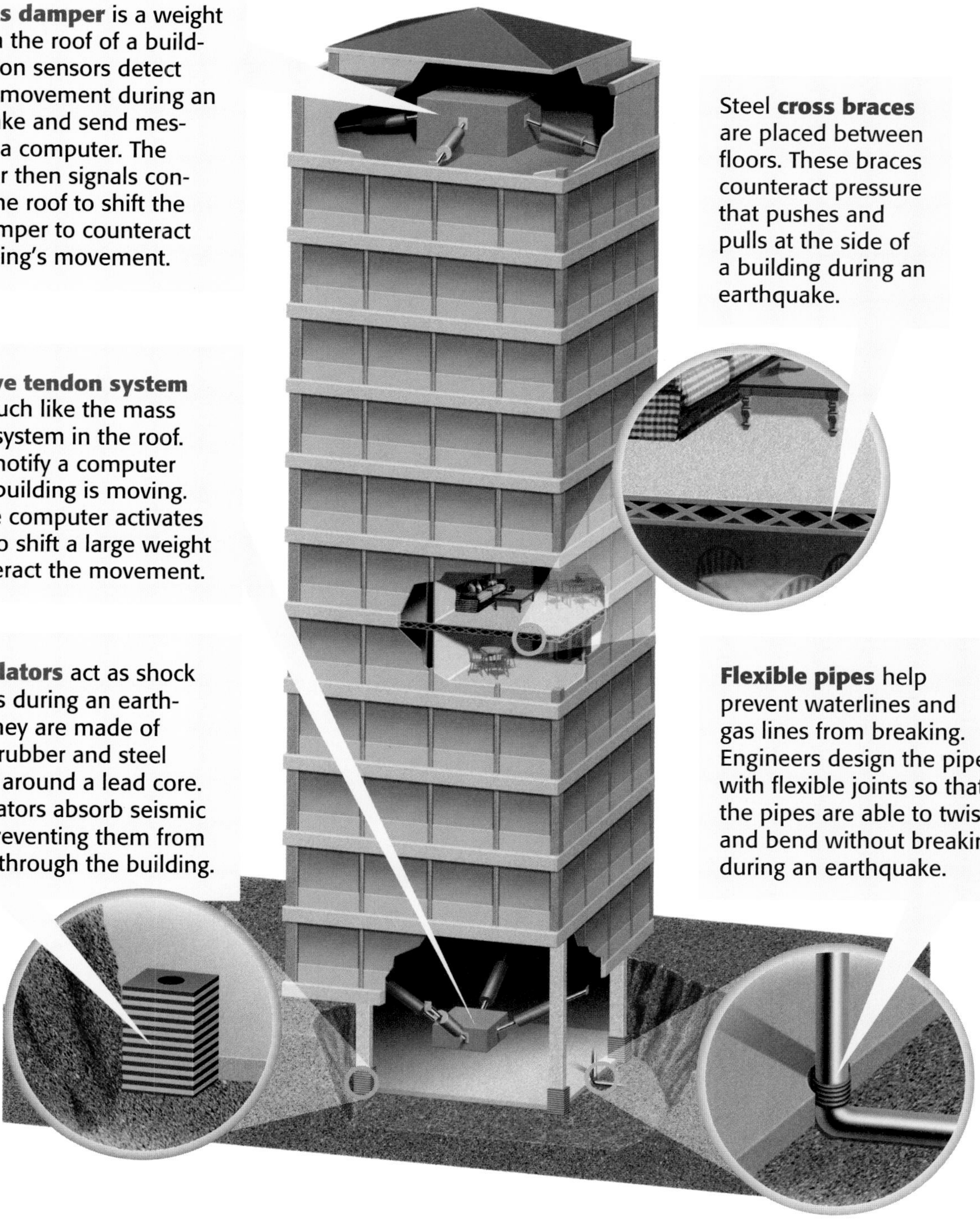

CONNECTION TO
Physics

WRITING SKILL **Earthquake Proof Buildings** During earthquakes, buildings often sway from side to side when the ground beneath them moves. This swaying can cause structural damage to buildings. Scientists and engineers are developing computer-controlled systems that counteract the swaying of buildings during earthquakes. Research a computer-controlled system that uses mass dampers or active tendons to reduce damage to buildings. Summarize your research in a short essay.

Are You Prepared for an Earthquake?

If you live in an area where earthquakes are common, there are many things you can do to protect yourself and your property from earthquakes. Plan ahead so that you will know what to do before, during, and after an earthquake. Stick to your plan as closely as possible.

Before the Shaking Starts

The first thing you should do is safeguard your home against earthquakes. You can do so by putting heavier objects on lower shelves so that they do not fall during the earthquake. You can also talk to a parent about having your home strengthened. Next, you should find safe places within each room of your home and outside of your home. Then, make a plan with others (your family, neighbors, or friends) to meet in a safe place after the earthquake is over. This plan ensures that you will all know who is safe. During the earthquake, waterlines, power lines, and roadways may be damaged. So, you should store water, nonperishable food, a fire extinguisher, a flashlight with batteries, a portable radio, medicines, and a first-aid kit in a place you can access after the earthquake.

When the Shaking Starts

The best thing to do if you are indoors when an earthquake begins is to crouch or lie face down under a table or desk in the center of a room, as shown in **Figure 5.** If you are outside, lie face down away from buildings, power lines, and trees and cover your head with your hands. If you are in a car on an open road, you should stop the car and remain inside.

✓ Reading Check Explain what you would do if you were in class and an earthquake began to shake the ground.

Figure 5 *These students are participating in an earthquake drill.*

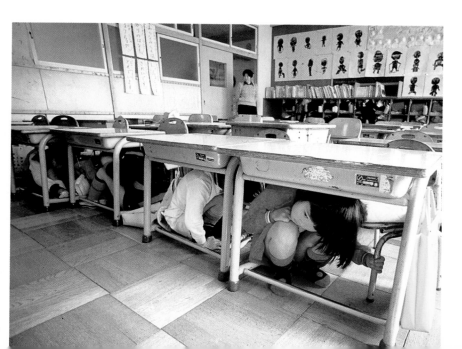

144

After the Shaking Stops

Being in an earthquake is a startling and often frightening experience for most people. After being in an earthquake, you should not be surprised to find yourself and others puzzled about what took place. You should try to calm down and get your bearings as quickly as possible. Then, remove yourself from immediate danger, such as downed power lines, broken glass, and fire hazards. Always stay out of damaged buildings, and return home only when you are told that it is safe to do so by someone in authority. Be aware that there may be aftershocks, which may cause more damage to structures. Recall your earthquake plan, and follow it.

SCHOOL to HOME

Disaster Planning

With your parent, create a plan that will protect your family in the event of a natural disaster, such as an earthquake. The plan should include steps to take before, during, and after a disaster. Present your disaster plan in the form of an oral report to your class.

ACTIVITY

SECTION Review

Summary

- Earthquake hazard is a measure of how likely an area is to have earthquakes in the future.
- Seismologists use their knowledge of the relationship between earthquake strength and frequency and of the gap hypothesis to forecast earthquakes.
- Homes and buildings and bridges can be strengthened to decrease earthquake damage.
- People who live in earthquake zones should safeguard their home against earthquakes.

Using Key Terms

1. In your own words, write a definition for each of the following terms: *gap hypothesis* and *seismic gap*.

Understanding Key Ideas

2. A weight that is placed on a building to make the building earthquake resistant is called a(n)
   a. active tendon system.
   b. cross brace.
   c. mass damper.
   d. base isolator.

3. How is an area's earthquake-hazard level determined?

4. Compare the strength and frequency method with the gap hypothesis method for predicting earthquakes.

5. What is a common way of making homes more earthquake resistant?

6. Describe four pieces of technology that are designed to make buildings earthquake resistant.

7. Name five items that you should store in case of an earthquake.

Math Skills

8. Of the approximately 420,000 earthquakes recorded each year, about 140 have a magnitude greater than 6.0. What percentage of total earthquakes have a magnitude greater than 6.0?

Critical Thinking

9. **Evaluating Hypotheses** Seismologists predict that there is a 20% chance that an earthquake of magnitude 7.0 or greater will fill a seismic gap during the next 50 years. Is the hypothesis incorrect if the earthquake does not happen? Explain your answer.

10. **Applying Concepts** Why is a large earthquake often followed by numerous aftershocks?

SCILINKS.

NSTA
Developed and maintained by the National Science Teachers Association

For a variety of links related to this chapter, go to www.scilinks.org

Topic: Earthquakes and Society
SciLinks code: HSM0455

Inquiry Lab

OBJECTIVES

Build a model of a structure that can withstand a simulated earthquake.

Evaluate ways in which you can strengthen your model.

MATERIALS

- gelatin, square, approximately 8 × 8 cm
- marshmallows (10)
- paper plate
- toothpicks (10)

SAFETY

Quake Challenge

In many parts of the world, people must have earthquakes in mind when they construct buildings. Each building must be designed so that the structure is protected during an earthquake. Architects have greatly improved the design of buildings since 1906, when an earthquake and the fires it caused destroyed much of San Francisco. In this activity, you will use marshmallows and toothpicks to build a structure that can withstand a simulated earthquake. In the process, you will discover some of the ways a building can be built to withstand an earthquake.

Ask a Question

1. What features help a building withstand an earthquake? How can I use this information to build my structure?

Form a Hypothesis

2. Brainstorm with a classmate to design a structure that will resist the simulated earthquake. Write two or three sentences to describe your design. Explain why you think your design will be able to withstand a simulated earthquake.

Test the Hypothesis

3. Follow your design to build a structure using the toothpicks and marshmallows.

4. Set your structure on a square of gelatin, and place the gelatin on a paper plate.

5. Shake the square of gelatin to test whether your building will remain standing during a quake. Do not pick up the gelatin.

6. If your first design does not work well, change it until you find a design that does. Try to determine why your building is falling so that you can improve your design each time.

7. Sketch your final design.

8 After you have tested your final design, place your structure on the gelatin square on your teacher's desk.

9 When every group has added a structure to the teacher's gelatin, your teacher will simulate an earthquake by shaking the gelatin. Watch to see which buildings withstand the most severe quake.

Analyze the Results

1 **Explaining Events** Which buildings were still standing after the final earthquake? What features made them more stable?

2 **Analyzing Results** How would you change your design in order to make your structure more stable?

Draw Conclusions

3 **Evaluating Models** This was a simple model of a real-life problem for architects. Based on this activity, what advice would you give to architects who design buildings in earthquake zones?

4 **Evaluating Models** What are some limitations of your earthquake model?

5 **Making Predictions** How could your research have an impact on society?

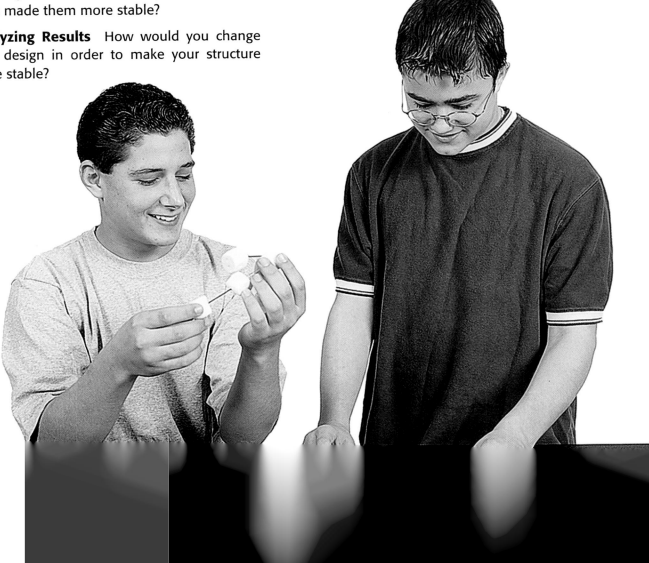

Chapter Review

USING KEY TERMS

1 Use each of the following terms in a separate sentence: *seismic wave*, *P wave*, and *S wave*.

For each pair of terms, explain how the meanings of the terms differ.

2 *seismograph* and *seismogram*

3 *epicenter* and *focus*

4 *gap hypothesis* and *seismic gap*

UNDERSTANDING KEY IDEAS

Multiple Choice

5 When rock is ___, energy builds up in it. Seismic waves occur as this energy is ___.
- **a.** plastically deformed, increased
- **b.** elastically deformed, released
- **c.** plastically deformed, released
- **d.** elastically deformed, increased

6 Reverse faults are created
- **a.** by divergent plate motion.
- **b.** by convergent plate motion.
- **c.** by transform plate motion.
- **d.** All of the above

7 The last seismic waves to arrive are
- **a.** P waves.
- **b.** body waves.
- **c.** S waves.
- **d.** surface waves.

8 If an earthquake begins while you are in a building, the safest thing for you to do is
- **a.** to run out into an open space.
- **b.** to get under the strongest table, chair, or other piece of furniture.
- **c.** to call home.
- **d.** to crouch near a wall.

9 How many major earthquakes (magnitude 7.0 to 7.9) happen on average in the world each year?
- **a.** 1
- **b.** 18
- **c.** 120
- **d.** 800

10 ___ counteract pressure that pushes and pulls at the side of a building during an earthquake.
- **a.** Base isolators
- **b.** Mass dampers
- **c.** Active tendon systems
- **d.** Cross braces

Short Answer

11 Can the S-P time method be used with one seismograph station to locate the epicenter of an earthquake? Explain your answer.

12 Explain how the Richter scale and the Modified Mercalli Intensity Scale are different.

13 What is the relationship between the strength of earthquakes and earthquake frequency?

14 Explain the way that different seismic waves affect rock as they travel through it.

15 Describe some steps you can take to protect yourself and your property from earthquakes.

CRITICAL THINKING

16 Concept Mapping Use the following terms to create a concept map: *focus, epicenter, earthquake start time, seismic waves, P waves,* and *S waves.*

17 Identifying Relationships Would a strong or light earthquake be more likely to happen along a major fault where there have not been many recent earthquakes? Explain. (Hint: Think about the average number of earthquakes of different magnitudes that occur annually.)

18 Applying Concepts Japan is located near a point where three tectonic plates converge. What would you imagine the earthquake-hazard level in Japan to be? Explain why.

19 Applying Concepts You learned that if you are in a car during an earthquake and are out in the open, it is best to stay in the car. Can you think of any situation in which you might want to leave a car during an earthquake?

20 Identifying Relationships You use gelatin to simulate rock in an experiment in which you are investigating the way different seismic waves affect rock. In what ways is your gelatin model limited?

INTERPRETING GRAPHICS

The graph below illustrates the relationship between earthquake magnitude and the height of tracings on a seismogram. Charles Richter initially formed his magnitude scale by comparing the heights of seismogram readings for different earthquakes. Use the graph below to answer the questions that follow.

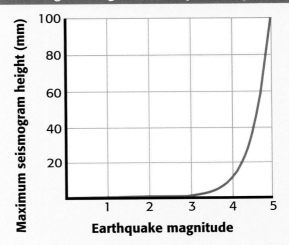

Seismogram Height Vs. Earthquake Magnitude

Maximum seismogram height (mm)

Earthquake magnitude

21 According to the graph, what would the magnitude of an earthquake be if its maximum seismograph height is 10 mm?

22 According to the graph, what is the difference in maximum seismogram height (in mm) between an earthquake of magnitude 4.0 and an earthquake of magnitude 5.0?

23 Look at the shape of the curve on the graph. What does this tell you about the relationship between seismogram heights and earthquake magnitudes? Explain.

READING

Read each of the passages below. Then, answer the questions that follow each passage.

Passage 1 At 5:04 P.M. on October 14, 1989, life in California's San Francisco Bay area seemed normal. While 62,000 fans filled Candlestick Park to watch the third game of the World Series, other people were rushing home from a day's work. By 5:05 P.M., the area had changed <u>drastically</u>. The area was rocked by the 6.9 magnitude Loma Prieta earthquake, which lasted 20 s and caused 68 deaths, 3,757 injuries, and the destruction of more than 1,000 homes. Considering that the earthquake was of such a high magnitude and that the earthquake happened during rush hour, it is amazing that more people did not die.

1. In the passage, what does the word *drastically* mean?
  A continuously
  B severely
  C gradually
  D not at all

2. Which of the following statements about the Loma Prieta earthquake is false?
  F The earthquake happened during rush hour.
  G The earthquake destroyed more than 1,000 homes.
  H The earthquake lasted for 1 min.
  I The earthquake had a magnitude of 6.9.

3. Which of the following statements is a fact in the passage?
  A Thousands of people were killed in the Loma Prieta earthquake.
  B The Loma Prieta earthquake happened during the morning rush hour.
  C The Loma Prieta earthquake was a light to moderate earthquake.
  D The Loma Prieta earthquake occurred during the 1989 World Series.

Passage 2 In the United States, seismologists use the Modified Mercalli Intensity Scale to measure the intensity of earthquakes. Japanese seismologists, however, use the Shindo scale to measure earthquake intensity. Earthquakes are <u>assigned</u> a number between 1 and 7 on the scale. Shindo 1 indicates a slight earthquake. Such an earthquake is felt by few people, usually people who are sitting. Shindo 7 indicates a severe earthquake. An earthquake that causes great destruction, such as the earthquake that struck Kobe, Japan, in January 1995, would be classified as Shindo 7.

1. In the passage, what does the word *assigned* mean?
  A named
  B voted
  C given
  D chosen

2. Which of the following statements about the Shindo scale is true?
  F The Shindo scale is used to measure earthquake strength.
  G The Shindo scale, which ranges from 1 to 7, is used to rank earthquake intensity.
  H The Shindo scale is the same as the Modified Mercalli Intensity Scale.
  I Seismologists all over the world use the Shindo scale.

3. Which of the following is a fact in the passage?
  A American seismologists use the Richter scale instead of the Shindo scale.
  B Japanese seismologists measure the intensity of large earthquakes only.
  C The Kobe earthquake was too destructive to be given a Shindo number.
  D Shindo 1 indicates a slight earthquake.

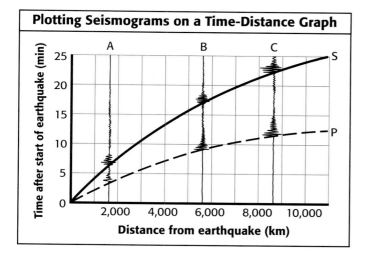

Plotting Seismograms on a Time-Distance Graph

1. According to the seismogram, which waves travel the **fastest**?

   A P waves travel the fastest.

   B S waves travel the fastest.

   C P waves and S waves travel at the same speed.

   D The graph does not show how fast P waves and S waves travel.

2. What is the approximate difference in minutes between the time the first P waves arrived at station B and the time the first S waves arrived at station B?

   F 22 1/2 min

   G 10 1/2 min

   H 8 min

   I 3 min

3. Station A is approximately how much closer to the epicenter than station B is?

   A 1,800 km

   B 4,000 km

   C 5,800 km

   D 8,600 km

MATH

Read each question below, and choose the best answer.

1. If a seismic wave travels at a rate of 12 km/s, how far will it travel away from the earthquake in 1 min?

   A 7,200 km

   B 720 km

   C 72 km

   D 7.2 km

2. If a P wave travels a distance of 70 km in 10 s, what is its speed?

   F 700 km/s

   G 70 km/s

   H 7 km/s

   I 0.7 km/s

3. Each time the magnitude of an earthquake increases by 1 unit, the amount of energy released is 31.7 times greater. How much greater is the energy for a magnitude 7.0 earthquake than a magnitude 5.0 earthquake?

   A 31,855 times as strong

   B 63.4 times as strong

   C 634 times as strong

   D 1,005 times as strong

4. An approximate relationship between earthquake magnitude and frequency is that when magnitude increases by 1.0, 10 times fewer earthquakes occur. Thus, if 150 earthquakes of magnitude 2.0 happen in your area this year, about how many 4.0 magnitude earthquakes will happen in your area this year?

   F 50

   G 10

   H 2

   I 0

5. If an average of 421,140 earthquakes occur annually, what percentage of these earthquakes are minor earthquakes if 49,000 minor earthquakes occur annually?

   A approximately .01%

   B approximately .12%

   C approximately 12%

   D approximately 86%

Standardized Test Preparation

Science in Action

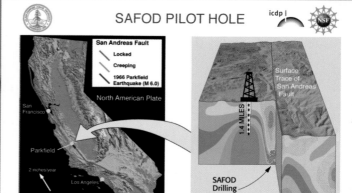

SAFOD PILOT HOLE

San Andreas Fault
Locked
Creeping
1966 Parkfield Earthquake (M 6.0)

North American Plate

San Francisco

Parkfield

2 inches/year

Los Angeles

Pacific Plate

1.4 MILES

Surface Trace of San Andreas Fault

SAFOD Drilling Target

Source: Martyn Unsworth

Weird Science

Can Animals Predict Earthquakes?

Is it possible that animals close to the epicenter of an earthquake are able to sense changes in their environment? And should we be paying attention to such animal behavior? As long ago as the 1700s, unusual animal activity prior to earthquakes has been recorded. Examples include domestic cattle seeking higher ground and zoo animals refusing to enter their shelters at night. Other animals, such as lizards, snakes, and small mammals, evacuate their underground burrows, and wild birds leave their usual habitats. These events occur days, hours, or even minutes before an earthquake.

Language Arts ACTIVITY

WRITING SKILL Create an illustrated field guide of animal activity to show how animal activity can predict earthquakes. Each illustration must have a paragraph that describes the activity of a specific animal.

Science, Technology, and Society

San Andreas Fault Observatory at Depth (SAFOD)

Seismologists are creating an underground observatory in Parkfield, California, to study earthquakes along the San Andreas Fault. The observatory will be named the San Andreas Fault Observatory at Depth (SAFOD). A deep hole will be drilled directly into the fault zone near a point where earthquakes of magnitude 6.0 have been recorded. Instruments will be placed at the bottom of the hole, 3 to 4 km beneath Earth's surface. These instruments will make seismological measurements of earthquakes and measure the deformation of rock.

Social Studies ACTIVITY

Research the great San Francisco earthquake of 1906. Find images of the earthquake on the Internet and download them, or cut them out of old magazines. Create a photo collage of the earthquake that shows San Francisco before and after the earthquake.

Hiroo Kanamori

Seismologist Hiroo Kanamori is a seismologist at the California Institute of Technology in Pasadena, California. Dr. Kanamori studies how earthquakes occur and tries to reduce their impact on our society. He also analyzes what the effects of earthquakes on oceans are and how earthquakes create giant ocean waves called *tsunamis* (tsoo NAH meez). Tsunamis are very destructive to life and property when they reach land. Kanamori has discovered that even some weak earthquakes can cause powerful tsunamis. He calls these events *tsunami earthquakes,* and he has learned to predict when tsunamis will form. In short, when tectonic plates grind together slowly, special waves called *long-period seismic waves* are created. When Kanamori sees a long-period wave recorded on a seismogram, he knows a tsunami will form. Because long-period waves travel faster than tsunamis, they arrive at recording stations earlier. When an earthquake station records an earthquake, information about that earthquake is provided to a tsunami warning center. The center determines if the earthquake may cause a tsunami and, if so, issues a tsunami warning to areas that may be affected.

Math ACTIVITY

An undersea earthquake causes a tsunami to form. The tsunami travels across the open ocean at 800 km/h. How long will the tsunami take to travel from the point where it formed to a coastline 3,600 km away?

To learn more about these Science in Action topics, visit go.hrw.com and type in the keyword HZ5EQKF.

Current Science

Check out Current Science® articles related to this chapter by visiting go.hrw.com. Just type in the keyword HZ5CS08.

6

Volcanoes

About the PHOTO

When you think of a volcanic eruption, you probably think of a cone-shaped mountain exploding and sending huge clouds of ash into the air. Some volcanic eruptions do just that! Most volcanic eruptions, such as the one shown here, which is flowing over a road in Hawaii, are slow and quiet. Volcanic eruptions happen throughout the world, and they play a major role in shaping the Earth's surface.

PRE-READING ACTIVITY

FOLDNOTES **Layered Book** Before you read the chapter, create the FoldNote entitled "Layered Book" described in the **Study Skills** section of the Appendix. Label the tabs of the layered book with "Volcanic eruptions," "Effects of eruptions," and "Causes of eruptions." As you read the chapter, write information you learn about each category under the appropriate tab.

START-UP ACTIVITY

Anticipation

In this activity, you will build a simple model of a volcano and you will try to predict an eruption.

Procedure

1. Place **10 mL of baking soda** on a **sheet of tissue.** Fold the corners of the tissue over the baking soda, and place the tissue packet in a **large pan.**

2. Put **modeling clay** around the top edge of a **funnel.** Press that end of the funnel over the tissue packet to make a tight seal.

3. After you put on **safety goggles,** add **50 mL of vinegar** and **several drops of liquid dish soap** to a **200 mL beaker** and stir.

4. Predict how long it will take the volcano to erupt after the liquid is poured into the funnel. Then, carefully pour the liquid into the funnel, and use a **stopwatch** to measure how long the volcano takes to begin erupting.

Analysis

1. Based on your observations, explain what happened to cause the eruption.

2. How accurate was your prediction? By how many seconds did the class predictions vary?

3. How do the size of the funnel opening and the amount of baking soda and vinegar affect the amount of time that the volcano takes to erupt?

Volcanic Eruptions

Think about the force released when the first atomic bomb exploded during World War II. Now imagine an explosion 10,000 times stronger, and you will get an idea of how powerful a volcanic eruption can be.

The explosive pressure of a volcanic eruption can turn an entire mountain into a billowing cloud of ash and rock in a matter of seconds. But eruptions are also creative forces—they help form fertile farmland. They also create some of the largest mountains on Earth. During an eruption, molten rock, or *magma,* is forced to the Earth's surface. Magma that flows onto the Earth's surface is called *lava.* **Volcanoes** are areas of Earth's surface through which magma and volcanic gases pass.

Nonexplosive Eruptions

At this moment, volcanic eruptions are occurring around the world—on the ocean floor and on land. Nonexplosive eruptions are the most common type of eruption. These eruptions produce relatively calm flows of lava, such as those shown in **Figure 1.** Nonexplosive eruptions can release huge amounts of lava. Vast areas of the Earth's surface, including much of the sea floor and the Northwest region of the United States, are covered with lava from nonexplosive eruptions.

READING WARM-UP

Objectives

- Distinguish between nonexplosive and explosive volcanic eruptions.
- Identify the features of a volcano.
- Explain how the composition of magma affects the type of volcanic eruption that will occur.
- Describe four types of lava and four types of pyroclastic material.

Terms to Learn

volcano   vent
magma chamber

READING STRATEGY

Reading Organizer As you read this section, make a table comparing types of lava and pyroclastic material.

volcano a vent or fissure in the Earth's surface through which magma and gases are expelled

Figure 1   Examples of Nonexplosive Eruptions

Sometimes, nonexplosive eruptions can spray lava into the air. Lava fountains, such as this one, pulse with the pressure of escaping gases.

▲ The speed of a lava flow can range from a slow creep to as fast as 60 km/h.

Explosive Eruptions

Explosive eruptions, such as the one shown in **Figure 2,** are much rarer than nonexplosive eruptions. However, the effects of explosive eruptions can be incredibly destructive. During an explosive eruption, clouds of hot debris, ash, and gas rapidly shoot out from a volcano. Instead of producing lava flows, explosive eruptions cause molten rock to be blown into tiny particles that harden in the air. The dust-sized particles, called *ash,* can reach the upper atmosphere and can circle the Earth for years. Larger pieces of debris fall closer to the volcano. An explosive eruption can also blast millions of tons of lava and rock from a volcano. In a matter of seconds, an explosive eruption can demolish an entire mountainside, as shown in **Figure 3.**

Reading Check List two differences between explosive and nonexplosive eruptions. (*See the Appendix for answers to Reading Checks.*)

Figure 2 *In what resembles a nuclear explosion, volcanic ash rockets skyward during the 1990 eruption of Mount Redoubt in Alaska.*

Figure 3 *Within seconds, the 1980 eruption of Mount St. Helens in Washington State caused the side of the mountain to collapse. The blast scorched and flattened 600 km² of forest.*

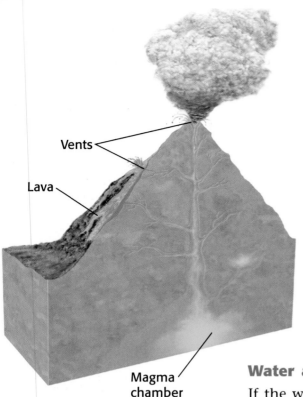

Vents

Lava

Magma chamber

Figure 4 *Volcanoes form when lava is released from vents.*

magma chamber the body of molten rock that feeds a volcano

vent an opening at the surface of the Earth through which volcanic material passes

What Is Inside a Volcano?

If you could look inside an erupting volcano, you would see the features shown in **Figure 4.** A **magma chamber** is a body of molten rock deep underground that feeds a volcano. Magma rises from the magma chamber through cracks in the Earth's crust to openings called **vents.** Magma is released from the vents during an eruption.

What Makes Up Magma?

By comparing the composition of magma from different eruptions, scientists have made an important discovery. The composition of the magma affects how explosive a volcanic eruption is. The key to whether an eruption will be explosive lies in the silica, water, and gas content of the magma.

Water and Magma Are an Explosive Combination

If the water content of magma is high, an explosive eruption is more likely. Because magma is underground, it is under intense pressure and water stays dissolved in the magma. If the magma quickly moves to the surface, the pressure suddenly decreases and the water and other compounds, such as carbon dioxide, become gases. As the gases expand rapidly, an explosion can result. This process is similar to what happens when you shake a can of soda and open it. When a can of soda is shaken, the CO_2 dissolved in the soda is released and pressure builds up. When the can is opened, the soda shoots out, just as lava shoots out of a volcano during an explosive eruption. In fact, some lava is so frothy with gas when it reaches the surface that its solid form, called *pumice,* can float in water!

Silica-Rich Magma Traps Explosive Gases

Magma that has a high silica content also tends to cause explosive eruptions. Silica-rich magma has a stiff consistency. It flows slowly and tends to harden in a volcano's vents. As a result, it plugs the vent. As more magma pushes up from below, pressure increases. If enough pressure builds up, an explosive eruption takes place. Stiff magma also prevents water vapor and other gases from easily escaping. Gas bubbles trapped in magma can expand until they explode. When they explode, the magma shatters and ash and pumice are blasted from the vent. Magma that contains less silica has a more fluid, runnier consistency. Because gases escape this type of magma more easily, explosive eruptions are less likely to occur.

✓ Reading Check How do silica levels affect an eruption?

What Erupts from a Volcano?

Magma erupts as either lava or pyroclastic (PIE roh KLAS tik) material. *Lava* is liquid magma that flows from a volcanic vent. *Pyroclastic material* forms when magma is blasted into the air and hardens. Nonexplosive eruptions produce mostly lava. Explosive eruptions produce mostly pyroclastic material. Over many years—or even during the same eruption—a volcano's eruptions may alternate between lava and pyroclastic eruptions.

Types of Lava

The viscosity of lava, or how lava flows, varies greatly. To understand viscosity, remember that a milkshake has high viscosity and a glass of milk has low viscosity. Lava that has high viscosity is stiff. Lava that has low viscosity is more fluid. The viscosity of lava affects the surface of a lava flow in different ways, as shown in **Figure 5.** *Blocky lava* and *pahoehoe* (puh HOY HOY) have a high viscosity and flow slowly. Other types of lava flows, such as *aa* (AH AH) and *pillow lava*, have lower viscosities and flow more quickly.

CONNECTION TO Social Studies

Fertile Farmlands Volcanic ash helps create some of the most fertile farmland in the world. Use a world map and reference materials to find the location of volcanoes that have helped create farmland in Italy, Africa, South America, and the United States. Make an illustrated map on a piece of poster board to share your findings.

ACTIVITY

Figure 5 Four Types of Lava

Aa is so named because of the painful experience of walking barefoot across its jagged surface. This lava pours out quickly and forms a brittle crust. The crust is torn into jagged pieces as molten lava continues to flow underneath.

Pahoehoe lava flows slowly, ▶ like wax dripping from a candle. Its glassy surface has rounded wrinkles.

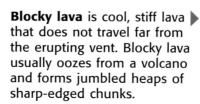

◀ **Pillow lava** forms when lava erupts underwater. As you can see here, this lava forms rounded lumps that are the shape of pillows.

Blocky lava is cool, stiff lava ▶ that does not travel far from the erupting vent. Blocky lava usually oozes from a volcano and forms jumbled heaps of sharp-edged chunks.

Figure 6 Four Types of Pyroclastic Material

◀ **Volcanic bombs** are large blobs of magma that harden in the air. The shape of this bomb was caused by the magma spinning through the air as it cooled.

◀ **Lapilli,** which means "little stones" in Italian, are pebblelike bits of magma that hardened before they hit the ground.

◀ **Volcanic ash** forms when the gases in stiff magma expand rapidly and the walls of the gas bubbles explode into tiny, glasslike slivers. Ash makes up most of the pyroclastic material in an eruption.

▼ **Volcanic blocks,** the largest pieces of pyroclastic material, are pieces of solid rock erupted from a volcano.

Types of Pyroclastic Material

Pyroclastic material forms when magma explodes from a volcano and solidifies in the air. This material also forms when powerful eruptions shatter existing rock. The size of pyroclastic material ranges from boulders that are the size of houses to tiny particles that can remain suspended in the atmosphere for years. **Figure 6** shows four types of pyroclastic material: volcanic bombs, volcanic blocks, lapilli (lah PIL IE), and volcanic ash.

✓ *Reading Check* Describe four types of pyroclastic material.

Modeling an Explosive Eruption

1. Inflate a **large balloon,** and place it in a **cardboard box.**

2. Spread a **sheet** on the floor. Place the box in the middle of the sheet. Mound a thin layer of **sand** over the balloon to make a volcano that is taller than the edges of the box.

3. Lightly mist the volcano with **water.** Sprinkle **tempera paint** on the volcano until the volcano is completely covered.

4. Place **small objects** such as **raisins** randomly on the volcano. Draw a sketch of the volcano.

5. Put on your **safety goggles.** Pop the balloon with a **pin.**

6. Use a **metric ruler** to calculate the average distance that 10 grains of sand and 10 raisins traveled.

7. How did the relative weight of each type of material affect the average distance that the material traveled?

8. Draw a sketch of the exploded volcano.

Pyroclastic Flows

One particularly dangerous type of volcanic flow is called a *pyroclastic flow*. Pyroclastic flows are produced when enormous amounts of hot ash, dust, and gases are ejected from a volcano. This glowing cloud of pyroclastic material can race downhill at speeds of more than 200 km/h—faster than most hurricane-force winds! The temperature at the center of a pyroclastic flow can exceed 700°C. A pyroclastic flow from the eruption of Mount Pinatubo is shown in **Figure 7**. Fortunately, scientists were able to predict the eruption and a quarter of a million people were evacuated before the eruption.

Figure 7 *The 1991 eruption of Mount Pinatubo in the Philippines released terrifying pyroclastic flows.*

SECTION Review

Summary

- Volcanoes erupt both explosively and nonexplosively.

- Magma that has a high level of water, CO_2, or silica tends to erupt explosively.

- Lava can be classified by its viscosity and by the surface texture of lava flows.

- Pyroclastic material, such as ash and volcanic bombs, forms when magma solidifies as it travels through the air.

Using Key Terms

1. In your own words, write a definition for each of the following terms: *volcano, magma chamber,* and *vent.*

Understanding Key Ideas

2. Which of the following factors influences whether a volcano erupts explosively?
   a. the concentration of volcanic bombs in the magma
   b. the concentration of phosphorus in the magma
   c. the concentration of aa in the magma
   d. the concentration of water in the magma

3. How are lava and pyroclastic material classified? Describe four types of lava.

4. Which produces more pyroclastic material: an explosive eruption or a nonexplosive eruption?

5. Explain how the presence of silica and water in magma increases the chances of an explosive eruption.

6. What is a pyroclastic flow?

Math Skills

7. A sample of magma is 64% silica. Express this percentage as a simplified fraction.

Critical Thinking

8. **Analyzing Ideas** How is an explosive eruption similar to opening a can of soda that has been shaken? Be sure to describe the role of carbon dioxide.

9. **Making Inferences** Predict the silica content of aa, pillow lava, and blocky lava.

10. **Making Inferences** Explain why the names of many types of lava are Hawaiian but the names of many types of pyroclastic material are Italian and Indonesian.

SCiLINKS®

NSTA
Developed and maintained by the
National Science Teachers Association

For a variety of links related to this chapter, go to www.scilinks.org

Topic: Volcanic Eruptions
SciLinks code: HSM1616

Effects of Volcanic Eruptions

In 1816, Chauncey Jerome, a resident of Connecticut, wrote that the clothes his wife had laid out to dry the day before had frozen during the night. This event would not have been unusual except that the date was June 10!

READING WARM-UP

Objectives

● Explain how volcanic eruptions can affect climate.

● Compare the three types of volcanoes.

● Compare craters, calderas, and lava plateaus.

Terms to Learn

crater
caldera
lava plateau

READING STRATEGY

Paired Summarizing Read this section silently. In pairs, take turns summarizing the material. Stop to discuss ideas that seem confusing.

At that time, residents of New England did not know that the explosion of a volcanic island on the other side of the world had severely changed the global climate and was causing "The Year Without a Summer."

Volcanic Eruptions and Climate Change

The explosion of Mount Tambora in 1815 blanketed most of Indonesia in darkness for three days. It is estimated that 12,000 people died directly from the explosion and 80,000 people died from the resulting hunger and disease. The global effects of the eruption were not felt until the next year, however. During large-scale eruptions, enormous amounts of volcanic ash and gases are ejected into the upper atmosphere.

As volcanic ash and gases spread throughout the atmosphere, they can block enough sunlight to cause global temperatures to drop. The Tambora eruption affected the global climate enough to cause food shortages in North America and Europe. More recently, the eruption of Mount Pinatubo, shown in **Figure 1,** caused average global temperatures to drop by as much as 0.5°C. Although this may seem insignificant, such a shift can disrupt climates all over the world.

✓ **Reading Check** How does a volcanic eruption affect climate? (*See the Appendix for answers to Reading Checks.*)

Figure 1 *Ash from the eruption of Mount Pinatubo blocked out the sun in the Philippines for several days. The eruption also affected global climate.*

Different Types of Volcanoes

Volcanic eruptions can cause profound changes in climate. But the changes to Earth's surface caused by eruptions are probably more familiar. Perhaps the best known of all volcanic landforms are the volcanoes themselves. The three basic types of volcanoes are illustrated in **Figure 2.**

Shield Volcanoes

Shield volcanoes are built of layers of lava released from repeated nonexplosive eruptions. Because the lava is very runny, it spreads out over a wide area. Over time, the layers of lava create a volcano that has gently sloping sides. Although their sides are not very steep, shield volcanoes can be enormous. Hawaii's Mauna Kea, the shield volcano shown here, is the tallest mountain on Earth. Measured from its base on the sea floor, Mauna Kea is taller than Mount Everest.

Cinder Cone Volcanoes

Cinder cone volcanoes are made of pyroclastic material usually produced from moderately explosive eruptions. The pyroclastic material forms steep slopes, as shown in this photo of the Mexican volcano Paricutín. Cinder cones are small and usually erupt for only a short time. Paricutín appeared in a cornfield in 1943 and erupted for only nine years before stopping at a height of 400 m. Cinder cones often occur in clusters, commonly on the sides of other volcanoes. They usually erode quickly because the pyroclastic material is not cemented together.

Composite Volcanoes

Composite volcanoes, sometimes called *stratovolcanoes,* are one of the most common types of volcanoes. They form from explosive eruptions of pyroclastic material followed by quieter flows of lava. The combination of both types of eruptions forms alternating layers of pyroclastic material and lava. Composite volcanoes, such as Japan's Mount Fuji (shown here), have broad bases and sides that get steeper toward the top. Composite volcanoes in the western region of the United States include Mount Hood, Mount Rainier, Mount Shasta, and Mount St. Helens.

Figure 2 Three Types of Volcanoes

Shield volcano

Cinder cone volcano

Composite volcano

Figure 3 *A crater, such as this one in Kamchatka, Russia, forms around the central vent of a volcano.*

crater a funnel-shaped pit near the top of the central vent of a volcano

caldera a large, semicircular depression that forms when the magma chamber below a volcano partially empties and causes the ground above to sink

Other Types of Volcanic Landforms

In addition to volcanoes, other landforms are produced by volcanic activity. These landforms include craters, calderas, and lava plateaus. Read on to learn more about these landforms.

Craters

Around the central vent at the top of many volcanoes is a funnel-shaped pit called a **crater.** An example of a crater is shown in **Figure 3.** During less explosive eruptions, lava flows and pyroclastic material can pile up around the vent creating a cone with a central crater. As the eruption stops, the lava that is left in the crater often drains back underground. The vent may then collapse to form a larger crater. If the lava hardens in the crater, the next eruption may blast it away. In this way, a crater becomes larger and deeper.

Calderas

Calderas can appear similar to craters, but they are many times larger. A **caldera** is a large, semicircular depression that forms when the chamber that supplies magma to a volcano partially empties and the chamber's roof collapses. As a result, the ground above the magma chamber sinks, as shown in **Figure 4.** Much of Yellowstone Park is made up of three large calderas that formed when volcanoes collapsed between 1.9 million and 0.6 million years ago. Today, hot springs, such as Old Faithful, are heated by the thermal energy left over from those events.

✓ Reading Check How do calderas form?

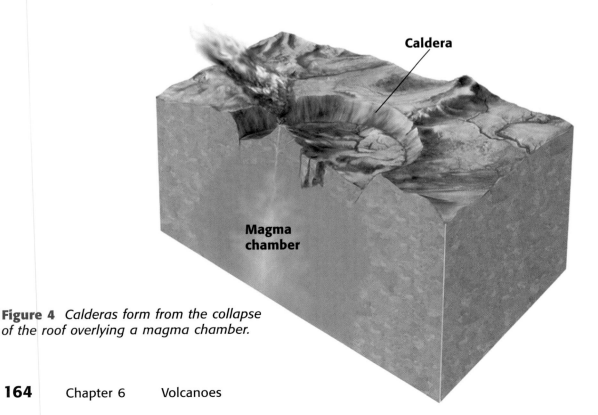

Caldera

Magma chamber

Figure 4 *Calderas form from the collapse of the roof overlying a magma chamber.*

Lava Plateaus

The most massive outpourings of lava do not come from individual volcanoes. Most of the lava on Earth's surface erupted from long cracks, or *rifts,* in the crust. In this type of eruption, runny lava can pour out for millions of years and spread over huge areas. A landform that results from repeated eruptions of lava spread over a large area is called a **lava plateau.** The Columbia River Plateau, part of which is shown in **Figure 5,** is a lava plateau that formed between 17 million and 14 million years ago in the northwestern region of the United States. In some places, the Columbia River Plateau is 3 km thick.

Figure 5 *The Columbia River Plateau formed from a massive outpouring of lava that began 17 million years ago.*

lava plateau a wide, flat landform that results from repeated nonexplosive eruptions of lava that spread over a large area

SECTION Review

Summary

- The large volumes of gas and ash released from volcanic eruptions can affect climate.
- Shield volcanoes result from many eruptions of relatively runny lava.
- Cinder cone volcanoes result from mildly explosive eruptions of pyroclastic material.
- Composite volcanoes result from alternating explosive and nonexplosive eruptions.
- Craters, calderas, and lava plateaus are volcanic landforms.

Using Key Terms

Complete each of the following sentences by choosing the correct term from the word bank.

caldera   crater

1. A ___ is a funnel-shaped hole around the central vent.

2. A ___ results when a magma chamber partially empties.

Understanding Key Ideas

3. Which type of volcano results from alternating explosive and nonexplosive eruptions?
   a. composite volcano
   b. cinder cone volcano
   c. rift-zone volcano
   d. shield volcano

4. Why do cinder cone volcanoes have narrower bases and steeper sides than shield volcanoes do?

5. Why does a volcano's crater tend to get larger over time?

Math Skills

6. The fastest lava flow recorded was 60 km/h. A horse can gallop as fast as 48 mi/h. Could a galloping horse outrun the fastest lava flow?
   (Hint: 1 km = 0.621 mi)

Critical Thinking

7. **Making Inferences** Why did it take a year for the effects of the Tambora eruption to be experienced in New England?

SCILINKS

NSTA
Developed and maintained by the
National Science Teachers Association

For a variety of links related to this chapter, go to www.scilinks.org

Topic: Volcanic Effects
SciLinks code: HSM1615

Causes of Volcanic Eruptions

More than 2,000 years ago, Pompeii was a busy Roman city near the sleeping volcano Mount Vesuvius. People did not see Vesuvius as much of a threat. Everything changed when Vesuvius suddenly erupted and buried the city in a deadly blanket of ash that was almost 20 ft thick!

Today, even more people are living on and near active volcanoes. Scientists closely monitor volcanoes to avoid this type of disaster. They study the gases coming from active volcanoes and look for slight changes in the volcano's shape that could indicate that an eruption is near. Scientists know much more about the causes of eruptions than the ancient Pompeiians did, but there is much more to be discovered.

The Formation of Magma

Understanding how magma forms helps explain why volcanoes erupt. Magma forms in the deeper regions of the Earth's crust and in the uppermost layers of the mantle where the temperature and pressure are very high. Changes in pressure and temperature cause magma to form.

Pressure and Temperature

Part of the upper mantle is made of very hot, puttylike rock that flows slowly. The rock of the mantle is hot enough to melt at Earth's surface, but it remains a puttylike solid because of pressure. This pressure is caused by the weight of the rock above the mantle. In other words, the rock above the mantle presses the atoms of the mantle so close together that the rock cannot melt. As **Figure 1** shows, rock melts when its temperature increases or when the pressure on the rock decreases.

READING WARM-UP

Objectives

● Describe the formation and movement of magma.

● Explain the relationship between volcanoes and plate tectonics.

● Summarize the methods scientists use to predict volcanic eruptions.

Terms to Learn

rift zone
hot spot

READING STRATEGY

Reading Organizer As you read this section, make a flowchart of the steps of magma formation in different tectonic environments.

Figure 1 *The curved line indicates the melting point of a rock. As pressure decreases and temperature increases, the rock begins to melt.*

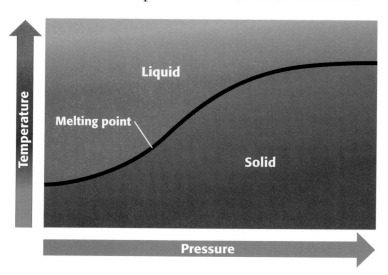

Magma Formation in the Mantle

Because the temperature of the mantle is fairly constant, a decrease in pressure is the most common cause of magma formation. Magma often forms at the boundary between separating tectonic plates, where pressure is decreased. Once formed, the magma is less dense than the surrounding rock, so the magma slowly rises toward the surface like an air bubble in a jar of honey.

Where Volcanoes Form

The locations of volcanoes give clues about how volcanoes form. The map in **Figure 2** shows the location of some of the world's major active volcanoes. The map also shows the boundaries between tectonic plates. A large number of volcanoes lie directly on tectonic plate boundaries. In fact, the plate boundaries surrounding the Pacific Ocean have so many volcanoes that the area is called the *Ring of Fire*.

Tectonic plate boundaries are areas where tectonic plates either collide, separate, or slide past one another. At these boundaries, it is possible for magma to form and travel to the surface. About 80% of active volcanoes on land form where plates collide, and about 15% form where plates separate. The remaining few occur far from tectonic plate boundaries.

Reading Check **Why are most volcanoes on plate boundaries?** (*See the Appendix for answers to Reading Checks.*)

Reaction to Stress

1. Make a pliable "rock" by pouring **60 mL of water** into a **plastic cup** and adding **150 mL of cornstarch,** 15 mL at a time. Stir well each time.

2. Pour half of the cornstarch mixture into a **clear bowl.** Carefully observe how the "rock" flows. Be patient—this process is slow!

3. Scrape the rest of the "rock" out of the cup with a **spoon.** Observe the behavior of the "rock" as you scrape.

4. What happened to the "rock" when you let it flow by itself? What happened when you put stress on the "rock"?

5. How is this pliable "rock" similar to the rock of the upper part of the mantle?

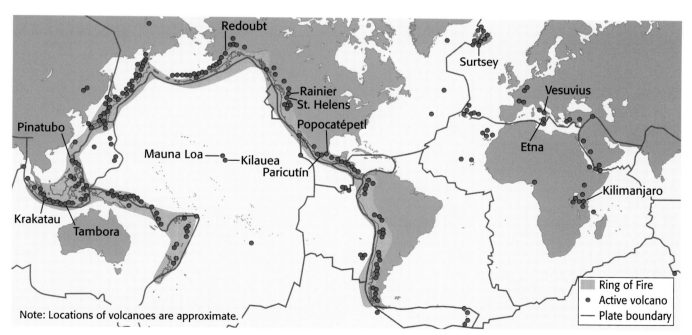

Figure 2 *Tectonic plate boundaries are likely places for volcanoes to form. The Ring of Fire contains nearly 75% of the world's active volcanoes on land.*

How Hot Is Hot?

Inside the Earth, magma can reach a burning-hot 1,400°C! You may be more familiar with Fahrenheit temperatures, so convert 1,400°C to degrees Fahrenheit by using the formula below.

°F = (°C ÷ 5 × 9) + 32

What is the temperature in degrees Fahrenheit?

rift zone an area of deep cracks that forms between two tectonic plates that are pulling away from each other

When Tectonic Plates Separate

At a *divergent boundary,* tectonic plates move away from each other. As tectonic plates separate, a set of deep cracks called a **rift zone** forms between the plates. Mantle rock then rises to fill in the gap. When mantle rock gets closer to the surface, the pressure decreases. The pressure decrease causes the mantle rock to melt and form magma. Because magma is less dense than the surrounding rock, it rises through the rifts. When the magma reaches the surface, it spills out and hardens, creating new crust, as shown in **Figure 3.**

Mid-Ocean Ridges Form at Divergent Boundaries

Lava that flows from undersea rift zones produces volcanoes and mountain chains called *mid-ocean ridges.* Just as a baseball has stitches, the Earth is circled with mid-ocean ridges. At these ridges, lava flows out and creates new crust. Most volcanic activity on Earth occurs at mid-ocean ridges. While most mid-ocean ridges are underwater, Iceland, with its volcanoes and hot springs, was created by lava from the Mid-Atlantic Ridge. In 1963, enough lava poured out of the Mid-Atlantic Ridge near Iceland to form a new island called *Surtsey.* Scientists watched this new island being born!

Figure 3 **How Magma Forms at a Divergent Boundary**

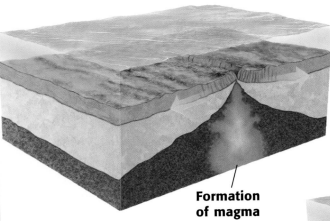

◀ Mantle material rises to fill the space opened by separating tectonic plates. As the pressure decreases, the mantle begins to melt.

New oceanic crust

Formation of magma

Because magma is less dense than the ▶ surrounding rock, it rises toward the surface, where it forms new crust on the ocean floor.

Figure 4 How Magma Forms at a Convergent Boundary

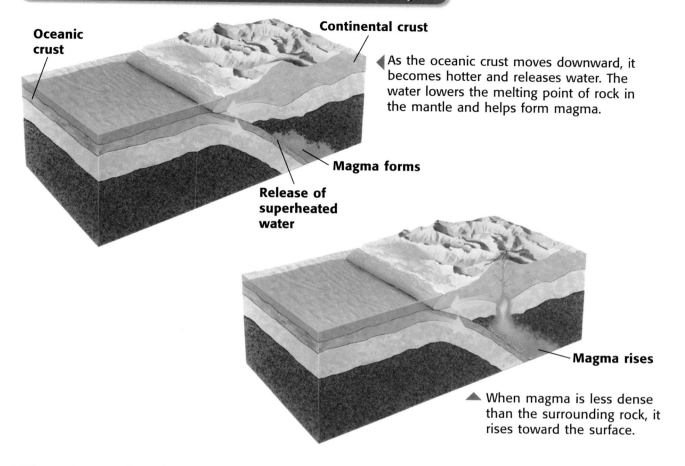

Oceanic crust

Continental crust

As the oceanic crust moves downward, it becomes hotter and releases water. The water lowers the melting point of rock in the mantle and helps form magma.

Magma forms

Release of superheated water

Magma rises

When magma is less dense than the surrounding rock, it rises toward the surface.

When Tectonic Plates Collide

If you slide two pieces of notebook paper into one another on a flat desktop, the papers will either buckle upward or one piece of paper will move under the other. This is similar to what happens at a convergent boundary. A *convergent boundary* is a place where tectonic plates collide. When an oceanic plate collides with a continental plate, the oceanic plate usually slides underneath the continental plate. The process of *subduction,* the movement of one tectonic plate underneath another, is shown in **Figure 4.** Oceanic crust is subducted because it is denser and thinner than continental crust.

Subduction Produces Magma

As the descending oceanic crust scrapes past the continental crust, the temperature and pressure increase. The combination of increased heat and pressure causes the water contained in the oceanic crust to be released. The water then mixes with the mantle rock, which lowers the rock's melting point, causing it to melt. This body of magma can rise to form a volcano.

Reading Check How does subduction produce magma?

Tectonic Models

Create models of convergent and divergent boundaries by using materials of your choice. Have your teacher approve your list before you start building your model at home with a parent. In class, use your model to explain how each type of boundary leads to the formation of magma.

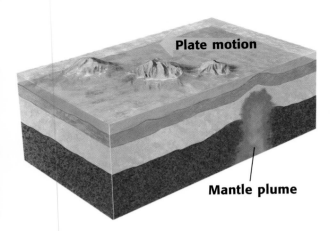

Plate motion

Mantle plume

Figure 5 *According to one theory, a string of volcanic islands forms as a tectonic plate passes over a mantle plume.*

hot spot a volcanically active area of Earth's surface far from a tectonic plate boundary

Figure 6 *As if being this close to an active volcano is not dangerous enough, the gases being collected are extremely poisonous.*

Hot Spots

Not all magma develops along tectonic plate boundaries. For example, the Hawaiian Islands, some of the most well-known volcanoes on Earth, are nowhere near a plate boundary. The volcanoes of Hawaii and several other places on Earth are known as *hot spots*. **Hot spots** are volcanically active places on the Earth's surface that are far from plate boundaries. Some scientists think that hot spots are directly above columns of rising magma, called *mantle plumes*. Other scientists think that hot spots are the result of cracks in the Earth's crust.

A hot spot often produces a long chain of volcanoes. One theory is that the mantle plume stays in the same spot while the tectonic plate moves over it, as shown in **Figure 5.** Another theory argues that hot-spot volcanoes occur in long chains because they form along the cracks in the Earth's crust. Both theories may be correct.

Reading Check Describe two theories that explain the existence of hot spots.

Predicting Volcanic Eruptions

You now understand some of the processes that produce volcanoes, but how do scientists predict when a volcano is going to erupt? Volcanoes are classified in three categories. *Extinct volcanoes* have not erupted in recorded history and probably never will erupt again. *Dormant volcanoes* are currently not erupting, but the record of past eruptions suggests that they may erupt again. *Active volcanoes* are currently erupting or show signs of erupting in the near future. Scientists study active and dormant volcanoes for signs of a future eruption.

Measuring Small Quakes and Volcanic Gases

Most active volcanoes produce small earthquakes as the magma within them moves upward and causes the surrounding rock to shift. Just before an eruption, the number and intensity of the earthquakes increase and the occurrence of quakes may be continuous. Monitoring these quakes is one of the best ways to predict an eruption.

As **Figure 6** shows, scientists also study the volume and composition of volcanic gases. The ratio of certain gases, especially that of sulfur dioxide, SO_2, to carbon dioxide, CO_2, may be important in predicting eruptions. Changes in this ratio may indicate changes in the magma chamber below.

Measuring Slope and Temperature

As magma moves upward prior to an eruption, it can cause the Earth's surface to swell. The side of a volcano may even bulge as the magma moves upward. An instrument called a *tiltmeter* helps scientists detect small changes in the angle of a volcano's slope. Scientists also use satellite technology such as the Global Positioning System (GPS) to detect the changes in a volcano's slope that may signal an eruption.

One of the newest methods for predicting volcanic eruptions includes using satellite images. Infrared satellite images record changes in the surface temperature and gas emissions of a volcano over time. If the site is getting hotter, the magma below is probably rising!

INTERNET ACTIVITY

For another activity related to this chapter, go to **go.hrw.com** and type in the keyword **HZ5VOLW.**

SECTION Review

Summary

- Temperature and pressure influence magma formation.

- Most volcanoes form at tectonic boundaries.

- As tectonic plates separate, magma rises to fill the cracks, or rifts, that develop.

- As oceanic and continental plates collide, the oceanic plate tends to subduct and cause the formation of magma.

- To predict eruptions, scientists study the frequency and type of earthquakes associated with the volcano as well as changes in slope, changes in the gases released, and changes in the volcano's surface temperature.

Using Key Terms

1. Use each of the following terms in a separate sentence: *hot spot* and *rift zone*.

Understanding Key Ideas

2. If the temperature of a rock remains constant but the pressure on the rock decreases, what tends to happen?

    a. The temperature increases.

    b. The rock becomes liquid.

    c. The rock becomes solid.

    d. The rock subducts.

3. Which of the following words is a synonym for *dormant*?

    a. predictable

    b. active

    c. dead

    d. sleeping

4. What is the Ring of Fire?

5. Explain how convergent and divergent plate boundaries cause magma formation.

6. Describe four methods that scientists use to predict volcanic eruptions.

7. Why does a oceanic plate tend to subduct when it collides with a continental plate?

Math Skills

8. If a tectonic plate moves at a rate of 2 km every 1 million years, how long would it take a hot spot to form a chain of volcanoes 100 km long?

Critical Thinking

9. **Making Inferences** New crust is constantly being created at mid-ocean ridges. So, why is the oldest oceanic crust only about 150 million years old?

10. **Identifying Relationships** If you are studying a volcanic deposit, would the youngest layers be more likely to be found on the top or on the bottom? Explain your answer.

SCiLINKS

Developed and maintained by the National Science Teachers Association

For a variety of links related to this chapter, go to www.scilinks.org

Topic: What Causes Volcanoes?
SciLinks code: HSM1654

Skills Practice Lab

Volcano Verdict

You will need to pair up with a partner for this exploration. You and your partner will act as geologists who work in a city located near a volcano. City officials are counting on you to predict when the volcano will erupt next. You and your partner have decided to use limewater as a gas-emissions tester. You will use this tester to measure the levels of carbon dioxide emitted from a simulated volcano. The more active the volcano is, the more carbon dioxide it releases.

OBJECTIVES

Build a working apparatus to test carbon dioxide levels.

Test the levels of carbon dioxide emitted from a model volcano.

MATERIALS

- baking soda, 15 mL
- bottle, drinking, 16 oz
- box or stand for plastic cup
- clay, modeling
- coin
- cup, clear plastic, 9 oz
- graduated cylinder
- limewater, 1 L
- straw, drinking, flexible
- tissue, bathroom (2 sheets)
- vinegar, white, 140 mL
- water, 100 mL

SAFETY

Procedure

1. Put on your safety goggles, and carefully pour limewater into the plastic cup until the cup is three-fourths full. You have just made your gas-emissions tester.

2. Now, build a model volcano. Begin by pouring 50 mL of water and 70 mL of vinegar into the drink bottle.

3. Form a plug of clay around the short end of the straw, as shown at left. The clay plug must be large enough to cover the opening of the bottle. Be careful not to get the clay wet.

4. Sprinkle 5 mL of baking soda along the center of a single section of bathroom tissue. Then, roll the tissue, and twist the ends so that the baking soda can't fall out.

5. Drop the tissue into the drink bottle, and immediately put the short end of the straw inside the bottle to make a seal with the clay.

6. Put the other end of the straw into the lime-water, as shown at right.

7. You have just taken your first measurement of gas levels from the volcano. Record your observations.

8. Imagine that it is several days later and you need to test the volcano again to collect more data. Before you continue, toss a coin. If it lands heads up, go to step 9. If it lands tails up, go to step 10. Write down the step that you follow.

9. Repeat steps 1–7. This time, add 2 mL of baking soda to the vinegar and water. (Note: You must use fresh water, vinegar, and limewater.) Write down your observations. Go to step 11.

10. Repeat steps 1–7. This time, add 8 mL of baking soda to the vinegar and water. (Note: You must use fresh water, vinegar, and limewater.) Write down your observations. Go to step 11.

11. Return to step 8 once. Then, answer the questions below.

Analyze the Results

1. **Explaining Events** How do you explain the difference in the appearance of the limewater from one trial to the next?

2. **Recognizing Patterns** What does the data that you collected indicate about the activity in the volcano?

Draw Conclusions

3. **Evaluating Results** Based on your results, do you think it would be necessary to evacuate the city?

4. **Applying Conclusions** How would a geologist use a gas-emissions tester to predict volcanic eruptions?

Chapter Review

USING KEY TERMS

For each pair of terms, explain how the meanings of the terms differ.

1 *caldera* and *crater*

2 *lava* and *magma*

3 *lava* and *pyroclastic material*

4 *vent* and *rift*

5 *cinder cone volcano* and *shield volcano*

UNDERSTANDING KEY IDEAS

Multiple Choice

6 The type of magma that tends to cause explosive eruptions has a

a. high silica content and high viscosity.

b. high silica content and low viscosity.

c. low silica content and low viscosity.

d. low silica content and high viscosity.

7 Lava that flows slowly to form a glassy surface with rounded wrinkles is called

a. aa lava.

b. pahoehoe lava.

c. pillow lava.

d. blocky lava.

8 Magma forms within the mantle most often as a result of

a. high temperature and high pressure.

b. high temperature and low pressure.

c. low temperature and high pressure.

d. low temperature and low pressure.

9 What causes an increase in the number and intensity of small earthquakes before an eruption?

a. the movement of magma

b. the formation of pyroclastic material

c. the hardening of magma

d. the movement of tectonic plates

10 If volcanic dust and ash remain in the atmosphere for months or years, what do you predict will happen?

a. Solar reflection will decrease, and temperatures will increase.

b. Solar reflection will increase, and temperatures will increase.

c. Solar reflection will decrease, and temperatures will decrease.

d. Solar reflection will increase, and temperatures will decrease.

11 At divergent plate boundaries,

a. heat from Earth's core causes mantle plumes.

b. oceanic plates sink, which causes magma to form.

c. tectonic plates move apart.

d. hot spots cause volcanoes.

12 A theory that helps explain the causes of both earthquakes and volcanoes is the theory of

a. pyroclastics.

b. plate tectonics.

c. climatic fluctuation.

d. mantle plumes.

Short Answer

13 How does the presence of water in magma affect a volcanic eruption?

14 Describe four clues that scientists use to predict eruptions.

15 Identify the characteristics of the three types of volcanoes.

16 Describe the positive effects of volcanic eruptions.

CRITICAL THINKING

17 **Concept Mapping** Use the following terms to create a concept map: *volcanic bombs, aa, pyroclastic material, pahoehoe, lapilli, lava,* and *volcano.*

18 **Identifying Relationships** You are exploring a volcano that has been dormant for some time. You begin to keep notes on the types of volcanic debris that you see as you walk. Your first notes describe volcanic ash. Later, your notes describe lapilli. In what direction are you most likely traveling—toward the crater or away from the crater? Explain your answer.

19 **Making Inferences** Loihi is a submarine Hawaiian volcano that might grow to form a new island. The Hawaiian Islands are located on the Pacific plate, which is moving northwest. Considering how this island chain may have formed, where do you think the new volcanic island will be located? Explain your answer.

20 **Evaluating Hypotheses** What evidence could confirm the existence of mantle plumes?

INTERPRETING GRAPHICS

The graph below illustrates the average change in temperature above or below normal for a community over several years. Use the graph below to answer the questions that follow.

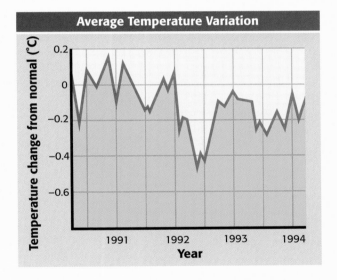

21 If the variation in temperature over the years was influenced by a major volcanic eruption, when did the eruption most likely take place? Explain.

22 If the temperature were measured only once each year (at the beginning of the year), how would your interpretation be different?

Standardized Test Preparation

Read each of the passages below. Then, answer the questions that follow each passage.

Passage 1 When the volcanic island of Krakatau in Indonesia exploded in 1883, a shock wave sped around the world seven times. The explosion was probably the loudest sound in recorded human history. What caused this enormous explosion? Most likely, the walls of the volcano ruptured, and ocean water flowed into the magma chamber of the volcano. The water instantly turned into steam, and the volcano exploded with the force of 100 million tons of TNT. The volcano ejected about 18 km³ of volcanic material into the air. The ash clouds blocked out the sun, and everything within 80 km of the volcano was plunged into darkness for more than two days. The explosion caused a <u>tsunami</u> that was nearly 40 m high. Detected as far away as the English Channel, the tsunami destroyed almost 300 coastal towns. In 1928, another volcano rose from the caldera left by the explosion. This volcano is called <u>Anak</u> Krakatau.

1. In the passage, what does *tsunami* mean?
   A a large earthquake
   B a shock wave
   C a giant ocean wave
   D a cloud of gas and dust

2. According to the passage, what was the size of the Krakatau explosion probably the result of?
   F pyroclastic material rapidly mixing with air
   G 100 million tons of TNT
   H an ancient caldera
   I the flow of water into the magma chamber

3. What does the Indonesian word *anak* probably mean?
   A father
   B child
   C mother
   D grandmother

Passage 2 Yellowstone National Park in Montana and Wyoming contains three overlapping calderas and evidence of the <u>cataclysmic</u> ash flows that erupted from them. The oldest eruption occurred 1.9 million years ago, the second eruption happened 1.3 million years ago, and the most recent eruption occurred 0.6 million years ago. Seismographs regularly detect the movement of magma beneath the caldera, and the hot springs and geysers of the park indicate that a large body of magma lies beneath the park. The geology of the area shows that major eruptions occurred about once every 0.6 or 0.7 million years. Thus, a devastating eruption is long overdue. People living near the park should be evacuated immediately.

1. In the passage, what does *cataclysmic* mean?
   A nonexplosive
   B ancient
   C destructive
   D characterized by ash flows

2. Which of the following clues are evidence of an active magma body beneath the park?
   F cataclysmic ash flows
   G the discovery of seismoclasts
   H minor eruptions
   I seismograph readings

3. Which of the following contradicts the author's conclusion that an eruption is "long overdue"?
   A Magma has been detected beneath the park.
   B With a variation of 0.1 million years, an eruption may occur in the next 100,000 years.
   C The composition of gases emitted indicates that an eruption is near.
   D Seismographs have detected the movement of magma.

The map below shows some of the Earth's major volcanoes and the tectonic plate boundaries. Use the map below to answer the questions that follow.

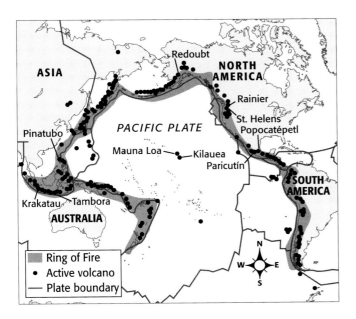

- Ring of Fire
- • Active volcano
- — Plate boundary

1. If ash from Popocatépetl landed on the west coast of the United States, what direction did the ash travel?
   - **A** northeast
   - **B** northwest
   - **C** southeast
   - **D** southwest

2. Why aren't there any active volcanoes in Australia?
   - **F** Australia is not located on a plate boundary.
   - **G** Australia is close to Krakatau and Tambora.
   - **H** Australia is near a plate boundary.
   - **I** Australia is near a rift zone.

3. If a scientist traveled along the Ring of Fire from Mt. Redoubt to Krakatau, which of the following most accurately describes the directions in which she traveled?
   - **A** west, southeast, east
   - **B** west, southeast, west
   - **C** west, southwest, east
   - **D** west, southwest, west

Read each question below, and choose the best answer.

1. Midway Island is 1,935 km northwest of Hawaii. If the Pacific plate is moving to the northwest at a rate of 9 cm per year, how long ago was Midway Island over the hot spot that formed the island?
   - **A** 215,000 years
   - **B** 2,150,000 years
   - **C** 21,500,000 years
   - **D** 215,000,000 years

2. In the first year that the Mexican volcano Paricutín appeared in a cornfield, it grew 360 m. The volcano stopped growing at about 400 m. What percentage of the volcano's total growth occurred in the first year?
   - **F** 67%
   - **G** 82%
   - **H** 90%
   - **I** 92%

3. A pyroclastic flow is moving down a hill at 120 km/h. If you lived in a town 5 km away, how much time would you have before the flow reached your town?
   - **A** 2 min and 30 s
   - **B** 1 min and 21 s
   - **C** 3 min and 12 s
   - **D** 8 min and 3 s

4. The Columbia River plateau is a lava plateau that contains 350,000 km^3 of solidified lava. The plateau took 3 million years to form. What was the average rate of lava deposition each century?
   - **F** 0.116 km^3
   - **G** 11.6 km^3
   - **H** 116 km^3
   - **I** 11,600 km^3

Science in Action

Weird Science

Pele's Hair

It is hard to believe that the fragile specimen shown below is a volcanic rock. This strange type of lava, called *Pele's hair,* forms when volcanic gases spray molten rock high into the air. When conditions are right, the lava can harden into strands of volcanic glass as thin as a human hair. This type of lava is named after Pele, the Hawaiian goddess of volcanoes. Several other types of lava are named in Pele's honor. Pele's tears are tear-shaped globs of volcanic glass often found at the end of strands of Pele's hair. Pele's diamonds are green, gemlike stones found in hardened lava flows.

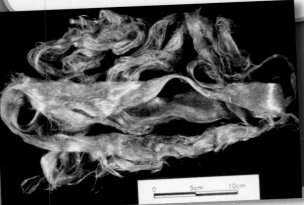

Science, Technology, and Society

Fighting Lava with Fire Hoses

What would you do if a 60 ft wall of lava was advancing toward your home? Most people would head for safety. But when an eruption threatened to engulf the Icelandic fishing village of Heimaey in 1973, some villagers held their ground and fought back. Working 14-hour days in conditions so hot that their boots would catch on fire, villagers used fire-hoses to spray sea water on the lava flow. For several weeks, the lava advanced toward the town, and it seemed as if there was no hope. But the water eventually cooled the lava fast enough to divert the flow and save the village. It took 5 months and about 1.5 billion gallons of water to fight the lava flow. When the eruption stopped, villagers found that the island had grown by 20%!

Language Arts ACTiViTY

Volcanic terms come from many languages. Research some volcanic terms on the Internet, and create an illustrated volcanic glossary to share with your class.

Social Studies ACTiViTY

WRITING SKILL To try to protect the city of Hilo, Hawaii, from an eruption in 1935, planes dropped bombs on the lava. Find out if this mission was successful, and write a report about other attempts to stop lava flows.

Tina Neal

Volcanologist Would you like to study volcanoes for a living? Tina Neal is a volcanologist at the Alaska Volcano Observatory in Anchorage, Alaska. Her job is to monitor and study some of Alaska's 41 active volcanoes. Much of her work focuses on studying volcanoes in order to protect the public. According to Neal, being near a volcano when it is erupting is a wonderful adventure for the senses. "Sometimes you can get so close to an erupting volcano that you can feel the heat, hear the activity, and smell the lava. It's amazing! In Alaska, erupting volcanoes are too dangerous to get very close to, but they create a stunning visual display even from a distance."

Neal also enjoys the science of volcanoes. "It's fascinating to be near an active volcano and become aware of all the chemical and physical processes taking place. When I'm watching a volcano, I think about everything we understand and don't understand about what is happening. It's mind-boggling!" Neal says that if you are interested in becoming a volcanologist, it is important to be well rounded as a scientist. So, you would have to study math, geology, chemistry, and physics. Having a good understanding of computer tools is also important because volcanologists use computers to manage a lot of data and to create models. Neal also suggests learning a second language, such as Spanish. In her spare time, Neal is learning Russian so that she can better communicate with research partners in Kamchatka, Siberia.

Math ACTIVITY

The 1912 eruption of Mt. Katmai in Alaska could be heard 5,620 km away in Atlanta, Georgia. If the average speed of sound in the atmosphere is 342 m/s, how many hours after the eruption did the citizens of Atlanta hear the explosion?

To learn more about these Science in Action topics, visit go.hrw.com and type in the keyword **HZ5VOLF**.

Current Science

Check out Current Science® articles related to this chapter by visiting go.hrw.com. **Just type in the keyword HZ5CS09.**

Skills Practice Lab

Mysterious Minerals

Imagine sitting on a rocky hilltop, gazing at the ground below you. You can see dozens of different types of rocks. How can scientists possibly identify the countless variations? It's a mystery!

In this activity, you'll use your powers of observation and a few simple tests to determine the identities of rocks and minerals. Take a look at the Mineral Identification Key on the next page. That key will help you use clues to discover the identity of several minerals.

MATERIALS

- gloves, protective
- iron filings
- minerals, samples
- slides, microscope, glass
- streak plate

SAFETY

Procedure

1 On a separate sheet of paper, create a data chart like the one below.

2 Choose one mineral sample, and locate its column in your data chart.

3 Follow the Mineral Identification Key to find the identity of your sample. When you are finished, record the mineral's name and primary characteristics in the appropriate column in your data chart. **Caution:** Put on your safety goggles and gloves when scratching the glass slide.

4 Select another mineral sample, and repeat steps 2 and 3 until your data table is complete.

Analyze the Results

1 Were some minerals easier to identify than others? Explain.

2 A streak test is a better indicator of a mineral's true color than visual observation is. Why isn't a streak test used to help identify every mineral?

3 On a separate sheet of paper, summarize what you learned about the various characteristics of each mineral sample you identified.

Mineral Summary Chart						
Characteristics	**1**	**2**	**3**	**4**	**5**	**6**
Mineral name						
Luster						
Color						
Streak			DO NOT WRITE IN BOOK			
Hardness						
Cleavage						
Special properties						

Mineral Identification Key

1. a. If your mineral has a metallic luster, **GO TO STEP 2.**
   b. If your mineral has a nonmetallic luster, **GO TO STEP 3.**

2. a. If your mineral is black, **GO TO STEP 4.**
   b. If your mineral is yellow, it is **PYRITE.**
   c. If your mineral is silver, it is **GALENA.**

3. a. If your mineral is light in color, **GO TO STEP 5.**
   b. If your mineral is dark in color, **GO TO STEP 6.**

4. a. If your mineral leaves a red-brown line on the streak plate, it is **HEMATITE.**
   b. If your mineral leaves a black line on the streak plate, it is **MAGNETITE.** Test your sample for its magnetic properties by holding it near some iron filings.

5. a. If your mineral scratches the glass microscope slide, **GO TO STEP 7.**
   b. If your mineral does not scratch the glass microscope slide, **GO TO STEP 8.**

6. a. If your mineral scratches the glass slide, **GO TO STEP 9.**
   b. If your mineral does not scratch the glass slide, **GO TO STEP 10.**

7. a. If your mineral shows signs of cleavage, it is **ORTHOCLASE FELDSPAR.**
   b. If your mineral does not show signs of cleavage, it is **QUARTZ.**

8. a. If your mineral shows signs of cleavage, it is **MUSCOVITE.** Examine this sample for twin sheets.
   b. If your mineral does not show signs of cleavage, it is **GYPSUM.**

9. a. If your mineral shows signs of cleavage, it is **HORNBLENDE.**
   b. If your mineral does not show signs of cleavage, it is **GARNET.**

10. a. If your mineral shows signs of cleavage, it is **BIOTITE.** Examine your sample for twin sheets.
   b. If your mineral does not show signs of cleavage, it is **GRAPHITE.**

Applying Your Data

Using your textbook and other reference books, research other methods of identifying different types of minerals. Based on your findings, create a new identification key. Give the key and a few sample minerals to a friend, and see if your friend can unravel the mystery!

Skills Practice Lab

Crystal Growth

Magma forms deep below the Earth's surface at depths of 25 km to 160 km and at extremely high temperatures. Some magma reaches the surface and cools quickly. Other magma gets trapped in cracks or magma chambers beneath the surface and cools very slowly. When magma cools slowly, large, well-developed crystals form. But when magma erupts onto the surface, it cools more quickly. There is not enough time for large crystals to grow. The size of the crystals found in igneous rocks gives geologists clues about where and how the rocks formed.

In this experiment, you will demonstrate how the rate of cooling affects the size of crystals in igneous rocks by cooling crystals of magnesium sulfate at two different rates.

Ask a Question

1 How does temperature affect the formation of crystals?

Form a Hypothesis

2 Suppose you have two solutions that are identical in every way except for temperature. How will the temperature of a solution affect the size of the crystals and the rate at which they form?

Test the Hypothesis

3 Put on your gloves, apron, and goggles.

4 Fill the beaker halfway with tap water. Place the beaker on the hot plate, and let it begin to warm. The temperature of the water should be between 40°C and 50°C. **Caution:** Make sure the hot plate is away from the edge of the lab table.

5 Examine two or three crystals of the magnesium sulfate with your magnifying lens. On a separate sheet of paper, describe the color, shape, luster, and other interesting features of the crystals.

6 On a separate sheet of paper, draw a sketch of the magnesium sulfate crystals.

- aluminum foil
- basalt
- beaker, 400 mL
- gloves, heat-resistant
- granite
- hot plate
- laboratory scoop, pointed
- magnesium sulfate ($MgSO_4$) (Epsom salts)
- magnifying lens
- marker, dark
- pumice
- tape, masking
- test tube, medium-sized
- thermometer, Celsius
- tongs, test-tube
- watch (or clock)
- water, distilled
- water, tap, 200 mL

SAFETY

7 Use the pointed laboratory scoop to fill the test tube about halfway with the magnesium sulfate. Add an equal amount of distilled water.

8 Hold the test tube in one hand, and use one finger from your other hand to tap the test tube gently. Observe the solution mixing as you continue to tap the test tube.

9 Place the test tube in the beaker of hot water, and heat it for approximately 3 min. **Caution:** Be sure to direct the opening of the test tube away from you and other students.

10 While the test tube is heating, shape your aluminum foil into two small boatlike containers by doubling the foil and turning up each edge.

11 If all the magnesium sulfate is not dissolved after 3 min, tap the test tube again, and heat it for 3 min longer. **Caution:** Use the test-tube tongs to handle the hot test tube.

12 With a marker and a piece of masking tape, label one of your aluminum boats "Sample 1," and place it on the hot plate. Turn the hot plate off.

13 Label the other aluminum boat "Sample 2," and place it on the lab table.

14 Using the test-tube tongs, remove the test tube from the beaker of water, and evenly distribute the contents to each of your foil boats. Carefully pour the hot water in the beaker down the drain. Do not move or disturb either of your foil boats.

15 Copy the table below onto a separate sheet of paper. Using the magnifying lens, carefully observe the foil boats. Record the time it takes for the first crystals to appear.

Crystal-Formation Table			
Crystal formation	**Time**	**Size and appearance of crystals**	**Sketch of crystals**
Sample 1			
Sample 2		DO NOT WRITE IN BOOK	

16 If crystals have not formed in the boats before class is over, carefully place the boats in a safe place. You may then record the time in days instead of in minutes.

17 When crystals have formed in both boats, use your magnifying lens to examine the crystals carefully.

Analyze the Results

1 Was your prediction correct? Explain.

2 Compare the size and shape of the crystals in Samples 1 and 2 with the size and shape of the crystals you examined in step 5. How long do you think the formation of the original crystals must have taken?

Draw Conclusions

3 Granite, basalt, and pumice are all igneous rocks. The most distinctive feature of each is the size of its crystals. Different igneous rocks form when magma cools at different rates. Examine a sample of each with your magnifying lens.

4 Copy the table below onto a separate sheet of paper, and sketch each rock sample.

5 Use what you have learned in this activity to explain how each rock sample formed and how long it took for the crystals to form. Record your answers in your table.

Igneous Rock Observations			
	Granite	**Basalt**	**Pumice**
Sketch			
How did the rock sample form?		DO NOT WRITE IN BOOK	
Rate of cooling			

Communicating Your Data

Describe the size and shape of the crystals you would expect to find when a volcano erupts and sends material into the air and when magma oozes down the volcano's slope.

184 Chapter 2 LabBook

Model-Making Lab

Metamorphic Mash

Metamorphism is a complex process that takes place deep within the Earth, where the temperature and pressure would turn a human into a crispy pancake. The effects of this extreme temperature and pressure are obvious in some metamorphic rocks. One of these effects is the reorganization of mineral grains within the rock. In this activity, you will investigate the process of metamorphism without being charred, flattened, or buried.

MATERIALS

- cardboard (or plywood), very stiff, small pieces
- clay, modeling
- knife, plastic
- sequins (or other small flat objects)

SAFETY

Procedure

1. Flatten the clay into a layer about 1 cm thick. Sprinkle the surface with sequins.

2. Roll the corners of the clay toward the middle to form a neat ball.

3. Carefully use the plastic knife to cut the ball in half. On a separate sheet of paper, describe the position and location of the sequins inside the ball.

4. Put the ball back together, and use the sheets of cardboard or plywood to flatten the ball until it is about 2 cm thick.

5. Using the plastic knife, slice open the slab of clay in several places. Describe the position and location of the sequins in the slab.

Analyze the Results

1. What physical process does flattening the ball represent?

2. Describe any changes in the position and location of the sequins that occurred as the clay ball was flattened into a slab.

Draw Conclusions

3. How are the sequins oriented in relation to the force you put on the ball to flatten it?

4. Do you think the orientation of the mineral grains in a foliated metamorphic rock tells you anything about the rock? Defend your answer.

Applying Your Data

Suppose you find a foliated metamorphic rock that has grains running in two distinct directions. Use what you have learned in this activity to offer a possible explanation for this observation.

Model-Making Lab

Oh, the Pressure!

When scientists want to understand natural processes, such as mountain formation, they often make models to help them. Models are useful in studying how rocks react to the forces of plate tectonics. A model can demonstrate in a short amount of time geological processes that take millions of years. Do the following activity to find out how folding and faulting occur in the Earth's crust.

MATERIALS

- can, soup (or rolling pin)
- clay, modeling, 4 colors
- knife, plastic
- newspaper
- pencils, colored
- poster board, 5 cm × 5 cm squares (2)
- poster board, 5 cm × 15 cm strip

SAFETY

Ask a Question

1. How do synclines, anticlines, and faults form?

Form a Hypothesis

2. On a separate piece of paper, write a hypothesis that is a possible answer to the question above. Explain your reasoning.

Test the Hypothesis

3. Use modeling clay of one color to form a long cylinder, and place the cylinder in the center of the glossy side of the poster-board strip.

4. Mold the clay to the strip. Try to make the clay layer the same thickness all along the strip; you can use the soup can or rolling pin to even it out. Pinch the sides of the clay so that the clay is the same width and length as the strip. Your strip should be at least 15 cm long and 5 cm wide.

5 Flip the strip over on the newspaper your teacher has placed across your desk. Carefully peel the strip from the modeling clay.

6 Repeat steps 3–5 with the other colors of modeling clay. Each person should have a turn molding the clay. Each time you flip the strip over, stack the new clay layer on top of the previous one. When you are finished, you should have a block of clay made of four layers.

7 Lift the block of clay, and hold it parallel to and just above the tabletop. Push gently on the block from opposite sides, as shown below.

8 Use the colored pencils to draw the results of step 6. Use the terms *syncline* and *anticline* to label your diagram. Draw arrows to show the direction that each edge of the clay was pushed.

9 Repeat steps 3–6 to form a second block of clay.

10 Cut the second block of clay in two at a 45° angle as seen from the side of the block.

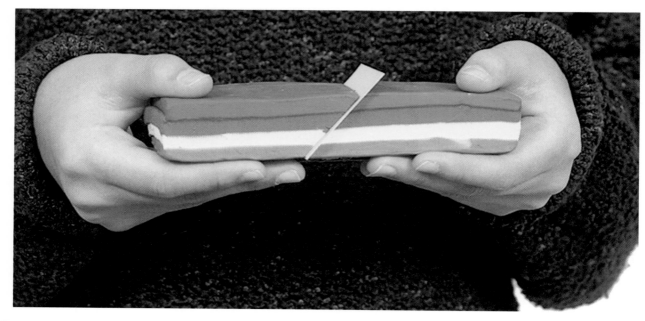

11 Press one poster-board square on the angled end of each of the block's two pieces. The poster board represents a fault. The two angled ends represent a hanging wall and a footwall. The model should resemble the one in the photograph above.

12 Keeping the angled edges together, lift the blocks, and hold them parallel to and just above the tabletop. Push gently on the two blocks until they move. Record your observations.

13 Now, hold the two pieces of the clay block in their original position, and slowly pull them apart, allowing the hanging wall to move downward. Record your observations.

Analyze the Results

1 What happened to the first block of clay in step 7? What kind of force did you apply to the block of clay?

2 What happened to the pieces of the second block of clay in step 12? What kind of force did you apply to them?

3 What happened to the pieces of the second block of clay in step 13? Describe the forces that acted on the block and the way the pieces of the block reacted.

Draw Conclusions

4 Summarize how the forces you applied to the blocks of clay relate to the way tectonic forces affect rock layers. Be sure to use the terms *fold, fault, anticline, syncline, hanging wall, footwall, tension,* and *compression* in your summary.

Skills Practice Lab

Earthquake Waves

The energy from an earthquake travels as seismic waves in all directions through the Earth. Seismologists can use the properties of certain types of seismic waves to find the epicenter of an earthquake.

P waves travel more quickly than S waves and are always detected first. The average speed of P waves in the Earth's crust is 6.1 km/s. The average speed of S waves in the Earth's crust is 4.1 km/s. The difference in arrival time between P waves and S waves is called *lag time.*

In this activity, you will use the S-P-time method to determine the location of an earthquake's epicenter.

MATERIALS

- calculator (optional)
- compass
- ruler, metric

SAFETY

Procedure

1 The illustration below shows seismographic records made in three cities following an earthquake. These traces begin at the left and show the arrival of P waves at time zero. The second set of waves on each record represents the arrival of S waves.

Seismographic Records

Austin

Bismarck

Portland

| 0 | 50 | 100 | 150 | 200 |

Time scale (seconds)

2 Copy the data table on the next page.

3 Use the time scale provided with the seismographic records to find the lag time between the P waves and the S waves for each city. Remember that the lag time is the time between the moment when the first P wave arrives and the moment when the first S wave arrives. Record this data in your table.

4 Use the following equation to calculate how long it takes each wave type to travel 100 km:

$$100 \text{ km} \div average\ speed\ of\ the\ wave = time$$

5 To find lag time for earthquake waves at 100 km, subtract the time it takes P waves to travel 100 km from the time it takes S waves to travel 100 km. Record the lag time.

6 Use the following formula to find the distance from each city to the epicenter:

$$distance = \frac{measured\ lag\ time\ (s) \times 100\ km}{lag\ time\ for\ 100\ km\ (s)}$$

In your data table, record the distance from each city to the epicenter.

7 Trace the map below onto a separate sheet of paper.

8 Use the scale to adjust your compass so that the radius of a circle with Austin at the center is equal to the distance between Austin and the epicenter of the earthquake.

Epicenter Data Table

City	Lag time (seconds)	Distance to the epicenter (km)
Austin, TX		
Bismarck, ND	*DO NOT WRITE IN BOOK*	
Portland, OR		

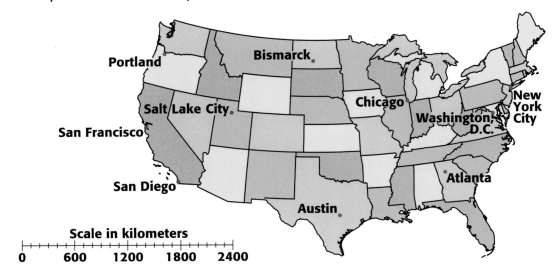

Scale in kilometers
0   600   1200   1800   2400

9 Put the point of your compass at Austin on your copy of the map, and draw a circle.

10 Repeat steps 8 and 9 for Bismarck and Portland. The epicenter of the earthquake is located near the point where the three circles meet.

Anayze the Results

1 Which city is closest to the epicenter?

Draw Conclusions

2 Why do seismologists need measurements from three different locations to find the epicenter of an earthquake?

Skills Practice Lab

Some Go "Pop," Some Do Not

Volcanic eruptions range from mild to violent. When volcanoes erupt, the materials left behind provide information to scientists studying the Earth's crust. Mild, or nonexplosive, eruptions produce thin, runny lava that is low in silica. During nonexplosive eruptions, lava simply flows down the side of the volcano. Explosive eruptions, on the other hand, do not produce much lava. Instead, the explosions hurl ash and debris into the air. The materials left behind are light in color and high in silica. These materials help geologists determine the composition of the crust underneath the volcanoes.

MATERIALS

- paper, graph (1 sheet)
- pencils (or markers), red, yellow, and orange
- ruler, metric

Procedure

1 Copy the map below onto graph paper. Take care to line the grid up properly.

2 Locate each volcano from the list on the next page by drawing a circle with a diameter of about 2 mm in the proper location on your copy of the map. Use the latitude and longitude grids to help you.

3 Review all the eruptions for each volcano. For each explosive eruption, color the circle red. For each quiet volcano, color the circle yellow. For volcanoes that have erupted in both ways, color the circle orange.

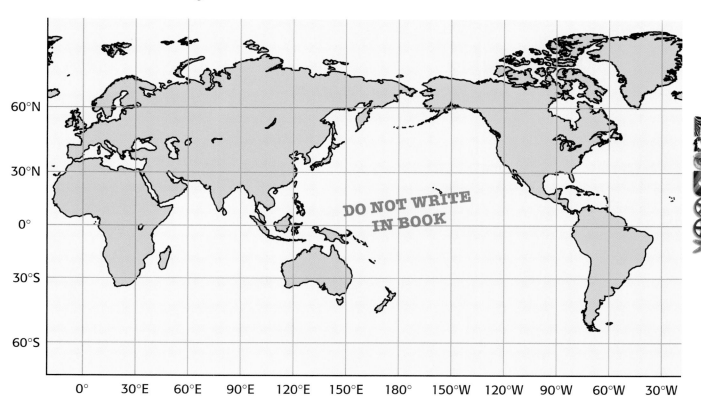

DO NOT WRITE IN BOOK

Volcanic Activity Chart		
Volcano name	**Location**	**Description**
Mount St. Helens	46°N 122°W	An explosive eruption blew the top off the mountain. Light-colored ash covered thousands of square kilometers. Another eruption sent a lava flow down the southeast side of the mountain.
Kilauea	19°N 155°W	One small eruption sent a lava flow along 12 km of highway.
Rabaul caldera	4°S 152°E	Explosive eruptions have caused tsunamis and have left 1–2 m of ash on nearby buildings.
Popocatépetl	19°N 98°W	During one explosion, Mexico City closed the airport for 14 hours because huge columns of ash made it too difficult for pilots to see. Eruptions from this volcano have also caused damaging avalanches.
Soufriere Hills	16°N 62°W	Small eruptions have sent lava flows down the hills. Other explosive eruptions have sent large columns of ash into the air.
Long Valley caldera	37°N 119°W	Explosive eruptions have sent ash into the air.
Okmok	53°N 168°W	Recently, there have been slow lava flows from this volcano. Twenty-five hundred years ago, ash and debris exploded from the top of this volcano.
Pavlof	55°N 161°W	Eruption clouds have been sent 200 m above the summit. Eruptions have sent ash columns 10 km into the air. Occasionally, small eruptions have caused lava flows.
Fernandina	42°N 12°E	Eruptions have ejected large blocks of rock from this volcano.
Mount Pinatubo	15°N 120°E	Ash and debris from an explosive eruption destroyed homes, crops, and roads within 52,000 km^2 around the volcano.

Analyze the Results

1. According to your map, where are volcanoes that always have nonexplosive eruptions located?

2. Where are volcanoes that always erupt explosively located?

3. Where are volcanoes that erupt in both ways located?

4. If volcanoes get their magma from the crust below them, what can you say about the silica content of Earth's crust under the oceans?

5. What is the composition of the crust under the continents? How do we know?

Draw Conclusions

6. What is the source of materials for volcanoes that erupt in both ways? How do you know?

7. Do the locations of volcanoes that erupt in both ways make sense, based on your answers to questions 4 and 5? Explain.

Applying Your Data

Volcanoes are present on other planets. If a planet had only nonexplosive volcanoes on its surface, what would we be able to infer about the planet? If a planet had volcanoes that ranged from nonexplosive to explosive, what might that tell us about the planet?

Contents

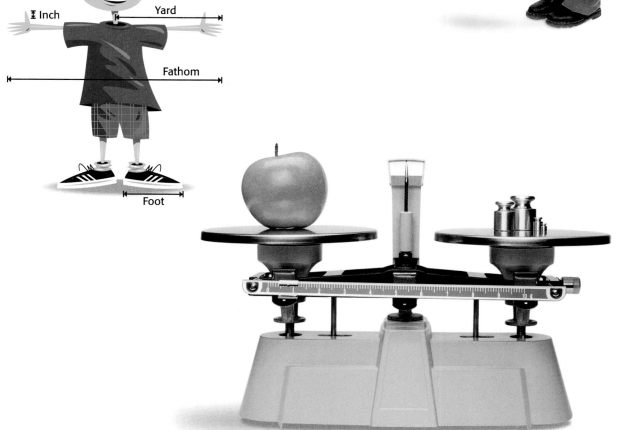

✓ *Reading Check* Answers

Chapter 1   Minerals of the Earth's Crust
Section 1
Page 5: An element is a pure substance that cannot be broken down into simpler substances by ordinary chemical means. A compound is a substance made of two or more elements that have been chemically bonded.

Page 6: Answers may vary. Silicate minerals contain a combination of silicon and oxygen; nonsilicate minerals do not contain a combination of silicon and oxygen.

Section 2
Page 9: A mineral's streak is not affected by air or water, but a mineral's color may be affected by air or water.

Page 10: Scratch the mineral with a series of 10 reference minerals. If the reference mineral scratches the unidentified mineral, the reference mineral is harder than the unidentified mineral.

Section 3
Page 15: Surface mining is used to remove mineral deposits that are at or near the Earth's surface. Subsurface mining is used to remove mineral deposits that are too deep to be removed by surface mining.

Page 17: Sample answer: Gemstones are nonmetallic minerals that are valued for their beauty and rarity rather than for their usefulness.

Chapter 2   Rocks: Mineral Mixtures
Section 1
Page 28: Types of rocks that have been used by humans to construct buildings include granite, limestone, marble, sandstone, and slate.

Page 32: Rock within the Earth is affected by temperature and pressure.

Page 33: The minerals that a rock contains determine a rock's composition.

Page 34: Fine-grained rocks are made of small grains, such as silt or clay particles. Medium-grained rocks are made of medium-sized grains, such as sand. Coarse-grained rocks are made of large grains, such as pebbles.

Section 2
Page 37: Felsic rocks are light-colored igneous rocks rich in aluminum, potassium, silicon, and sodium. Mafic rocks are dark-colored igneous rocks rich in calcium, iron, and magnesium.

Page 39: New sea floor forms when lava that flows from fissures on the ocean floor cools and hardens.

Section 3
Page 41: Halite forms when sodium and chlorine ions become so concentrated in sea water that halite crystallizes from the sea-water solution.

Page 43: Ripple marks are the marks left by wind and water waves on lakes, seas, rivers, and sand dunes.

Page 45: Regional metamorphism occurs when pressure builds up in rock that is buried deep below other rock formations or when large pieces of the Earth's crust collide. The increased pressure can cause thousands of square miles of rock to become deformed and chemically changed.

Page 46: An index mineral is a metamorphic mineral that forms only at certain temperatures and pressures and therefore can be used by scientists to estimate the temperature, pressure, and depth at which a rock undergoes metamorphosis.

Page 47: Increased heat and pressure cause metamorphic rocks to change from fine-grained rocks, such as slate and phyllite, to coarse-grained rocks, such as schist and gneiss.

Page 49: Deformation causes metamorphic structures, such as folds.

Chapter 3   The Rock and Fossil Record
Section 1
Page 61: Catastrophists believed that all geologic change occurs rapidly.

Page 62: A global catastrophe can cause the extinction of species.

Section 2
Page 65: Geologists use the geologic column to interpret rock sequences and to identify layers in puzzling rock sequences.

Page 67: An unconformity is a surface that represents a missing part of the geologic column.

Page 68: A disconformity is found where part of a sequence of parallel rock layers is missing. A nonconformity is found where horizontal sedimentary rock layers lie on top of an eroded surface of igneous or metamorphic rock. Angular unconformities are found between horizontal sedimentary rock layers and rock layers that have been tilted or folded.

Section 3
Page 71: A half-life is the time it takes one-half of a radioactive sample to decay.

Page 72: strontium-87

Section 4
Page 74: An organism is caught in soft, sticky tree sap, which hardens and preserves the organism.

Page 76: A mold is a cavity in rock where a plant or an animal was buried. A cast is an object created when sediment fills a mold and becomes rock.

Page 78: To fill in missing information about changes in organisms in the fossil record, paleontologists look for similarities between fossilized organisms or between fossilized organisms and their closest living relatives.

Page 79: *Phacops* can be used to establish the age of rock layers because *Phacops* lived during a relatively short, well-defined time span and is found in rock layers throughout the world.

Section 5

Page 81: approximately 2 billion years

Page 82: The geologic time scale is a scale that divides Earth's 4.6 billion–year history into distinct intervals of time.

Page 84: The Mesozoic era is known as the *Age of Reptiles* because reptiles, including the dinosaurs, were the dominant organisms on land.

Chapter 4 Plate Tectonics

Section 1

Page 97: The crust is the thin, outermost layer of the Earth. It is 5 km to 100 km thick and is mainly made up of the elements oxygen, silicon, and aluminum. The mantle is the layer between the crust and core. It is 2,900 km thick, is denser than the crust, and contains most of the Earth's mass. The core is the Earth's innermost layer. The core has a radius of 3,430 km and is made mostly of iron.

Page 98: The five physical layers of the Earth are the lithosphere, asthenosphere, mesosphere, outer core, and inner core.

Page 101: Although continental lithosphere is less dense than oceanic lithosphere is, continental lithosphere has a greater weight and will displace more asthenosphere than oceanic lithosphere.

Page 102: Answers may vary. A seismic wave traveling through a solid will go faster than a seismic wave traveling through a liquid.

Section 2

Page 104: Similar fossils were found on landmasses that are very far apart. The best explanation for this phenomenon is that the landmasses were once joined.

Page 107: The molten rock at mid-ocean ridges contains tiny grains of magnetic minerals. The minerals align with the Earth's magnetic field before the rock cools and hardens. When the Earth's magnetic field reverses, the orientation of the mineral grains in the rocks will also change.

Section 3

Page 109: A transform boundary forms when two tectonic plates slide past each other horizontally.

Page 110: The circulation of thermal energy causes changes in density in the asthenosphere. As rock is heated, it expands, becomes less dense, and rises. As rock cools, it contracts, becomes denser, and sinks.

Section 4

Page 112: Compression can cause rocks to be pushed into mountain ranges as tectonic plates collide at convergent boundaries. Tension can pull rocks apart as tectonic plates separate at divergent boundaries.

Page 114: In a normal fault, the hanging wall moves down. In a reverse fault, the hanging wall moves up.

Page 116: Folded mountains form when rock layers are squeezed together and pushed upward.

Chapter 5 Earthquakes

Section 1

Page 131: During elastic rebound, rock releases energy. Some of this energy travels as seismic waves that cause earthquakes.

Page 133: Earthquake zones are usually located along tectonic plate boundaries.

Page 135: Surface waves travel more slowly than body waves but are more destructive.

Section 2

Page 137: Seismologists determine an earthquake's start time by comparing seismograms and noting differences in arrival times of P and S waves.

Page 138: Each time the magnitude increases by 1 unit, the amount of ground motion increases by 10 times.

Section 3

Page 141: With a decrease of one unit in earthquake magnitude, the number of earthquakes occurring annually increases by about 10 times.

Page 142: Retrofitting is the process of making older structures more earthquake resistant.

Page 144: You should crouch or lie face down under a table or desk.

Chapter 6 Volcanoes

Section 1

Page 157: Nonexplosive eruptions are common, and they feature relatively calm flows of lava. Explosive eruptions are less common and produce large, explosive clouds of ash and gases.

Page 158: Because silica-rich magma has a high viscosity, it tends to trap gases and plug volcanic vents. This causes pressure to build up and can result in an explosive eruption.

Page 160: Volcanic bombs are large blobs of magma that harden in the air. Lapilli are small pieces of magma that harden in the air. Volcanic blocks are pieces of solid rock erupted from a volcano. Ash forms when gases in stiff magma expand rapidly and the walls of the gas bubbles shatter into tiny glasslike slivers.

Section 2

Page 162: Eruptions release large quantities of ash and gases, which can block sunlight and cause global temperatures to drop.

Page 164: Calderas form when a magma chamber partially empties and the roof overlying the chamber collapses.

Section 3

Page 167: Volcanic activity is common at tectonic plate boundaries because magma tends to form at plate boundaries.

Page 169: When a tectonic plate subducts, it becomes hotter and releases water vapor. The water lowers the melting point of the rock above the plate, causing magma to form.

Page 170: According to one theory, a rising body of magma, called a mantle plume, causes a chain of volcanoes to form on a moving tectonic plate. According to another theory, a chain of volcanoes forms along cracks in the Earth's crust.

Study Skills

Have you ever tried to study for a test or quiz but didn't know where to start? Or have you read a chapter and found that you can remember only a few ideas? Well, FoldNotes are a fun and exciting way to help you learn and remember the ideas you encounter as you learn science!

FoldNotes are tools that you can use to organize concepts. By focusing on a few main concepts, FoldNotes help you learn and remember how the concepts fit together. They can help you see the "big picture." Below you will find instructions for building 10 different FoldNotes.

Pyramid

1. Place a sheet of paper in front of you. Fold the lower left-hand corner of the paper diagonally to the opposite edge of the paper.

2. Cut off the tab of paper created by the fold (at the top).

3. Open the paper so that it is a square. Fold the lower right-hand corner of the paper diagonally to the opposite corner to form a triangle.

4. Open the paper. The creases of the two folds will have created an X.

5. Using scissors, cut along one of the creases. Start from any corner, and stop at the center point to create two flaps. Use tape or glue to attach one of the flaps on top of the other flap.

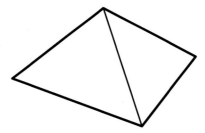

Double Door

1. Fold a sheet of paper in half from the top to the bottom. Then, unfold the paper.

2. Fold the top and bottom edges of the paper to the crease.

Copyright © by Holt, Rinehart and Winston. All rights reserved.

Booklet

1. Fold a sheet of paper in half from left to right. Then, unfold the paper.

2. Fold the sheet of paper in half again from the top to the bottom. Then, unfold the paper.

3. Refold the sheet of paper in half from left to right.

4. Fold the top and bottom edges to the center crease.

5. Completely unfold the paper.

6. Refold the paper from top to bottom.

7. Using scissors, cut a slit along the center crease of the sheet from the folded edge to the creases made in step 4. Do not cut the entire sheet in half.

8. Fold the sheet of paper in half from left to right. While holding the bottom and top edges of the paper, push the bottom and top edges together so that the center collapses at the center slit. Fold the four flaps to form a four-page book.

Layered Book

1. Lay one sheet of paper on top of another sheet. Slide the top sheet up so that 2 cm of the bottom sheet is showing.

2. Hold the two sheets together, fold down the top of the two sheets so that you see four 2 cm tabs along the bottom.

3. Using a stapler, staple the top of the FoldNote.

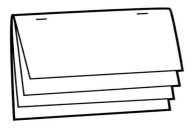

Key-Term Fold

1. Fold a sheet of lined notebook paper in half from left to right.

2. Using scissors, cut along every third line from the right edge of the paper to the center fold to make tabs.

Four-Corner Fold

1. Fold a sheet of paper in half from left to right. Then, unfold the paper.

2. Fold each side of the paper to the crease in the center of the paper.

3. Fold the paper in half from the top to the bottom. Then, unfold the paper.

4. Using scissors, cut the top flap creases made in step 3 to form four flaps.

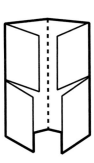

Three-Panel Flip Chart

1. Fold a piece of paper in half from the top to the bottom.

2. Fold the paper in thirds from side to side. Then, unfold the paper so that you can see the three sections.

3. From the top of the paper, cut along each of the vertical fold lines to the fold in the middle of the paper. You will now have three flaps.

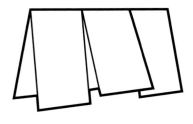

Appendix

Table Fold

1. Fold a piece of paper in half from the top to the bottom. Then, fold the paper in half again.

2. Fold the paper in thirds from side to side.

3. Unfold the paper completely. Carefully trace the fold lines by using a pen or pencil.

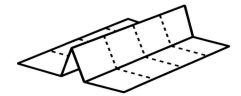

Two-Panel Flip Chart

1. Fold a piece of paper in half from the top to the bottom.

2. Fold the paper in half from side to side. Then, unfold the paper so that you can see the two sections.

3. From the top of the paper, cut along the vertical fold line to the fold in the middle of the paper. You will now have two flaps.

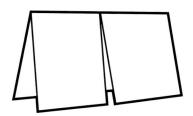

Tri-Fold

1. Fold a piece a paper in thirds from the top to the bottom.

2. Unfold the paper so that you can see the three sections. Then, turn the paper sideways so that the three sections form vertical columns.

3. Trace the fold lines by using a pen or pencil. Label the columns "Know," "Want," and "Learn."

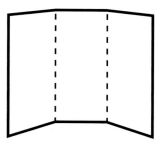

Copyright © by Holt, Rinehart and Winston. All rights reserved.

Appendix

Graphic Organizer Instructions

Have you ever wished that you could "draw out" the many concepts you learn in your science class? Sometimes, being able to *see* how concepts are related really helps you remember what you've learned. Graphic Organizers do just that! They give you a way to draw or map out concepts.

All you need to make a Graphic Organizer is a piece of paper and a pencil. Below you will find instructions for four different Graphic Organizers designed to help you organize the concepts you'll learn in this book.

Spider Map

1. Draw a diagram like the one shown. In the circle, write the main topic.

2. From the circle, draw legs to represent different categories of the main topic. You can have as many categories as you want.

3. From the category legs, draw horizontal lines. As you read the chapter, write details about each category on the horizontal lines.

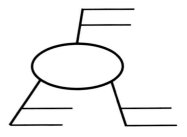

Comparison Table

1. Draw a chart like the one shown. Your chart can have as many columns and rows as you want.

2. In the top row, write the topics that you want to compare.

3. In the left column, write characteristics of the topics that you want to compare. As you read the chapter, fill in the characteristics for each topic in the appropriate boxes.

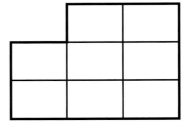

Appendix

Copyright © by Holt, Rinehart and Winston. All rights reserved.

Chain-of-Events-Chart

1. Draw a box. In the box, write the first step of a process or the first event of a timeline.

2. Under the box, draw another box, and use an arrow to connect the two boxes. In the second box, write the next step of the process or the next event in the timeline.

3. Continue adding boxes until the process or timeline is finished.

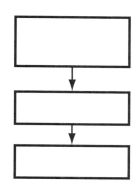

Concept Map

1. Draw a circle in the center of a piece of paper. Write the main idea of the chapter in the center of the circle.

2. From the circle, draw other circles. In those circles, write characteristics of the main idea. Draw arrows from the center circle to the circles that contain the characteristics.

3. From each circle that contains a characteristic, draw other circles. In those circles, write specific details about the characteristic. Draw arrows from each circle that contains a characteristic to the circles that contain specific details. You may draw as many circles as you want.

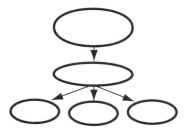

Copyright © by Holt, Rinehart and Winston. All rights reserved.

Appendix

SI Measurement

The International System of Units, or SI, is the standard system of measurement used by many scientists. Using the same standards of measurement makes it easier for scientists to communicate with one another.

SI works by combining prefixes and base units. Each base unit can be used with different prefixes to define smaller and larger quantities. The table below lists common SI prefixes.

SI Prefixes

Prefix	Symbol	Factor	Example
kilo-	k	1,000	kilogram, 1 kg = 1,000 g
hecto-	h	100	hectoliter, 1 hL = 100 L
deka-	da	10	dekameter, 1 dam = 10 m
		1	meter, liter, gram
deci-	d	0.1	decigram, 1 dg = 0.1 g
centi-	c	0.01	centimeter, 1 cm = 0.01 m
milli-	m	0.001	milliliter, 1 mL = 0.001 L
micro-	μ	0.000 001	micrometer, 1 μm = 0.000 001 m

SI Conversion Table

SI units	From SI to English	From English to SI
Length		
kilometer (km) = 1,000 m	1 km = 0.621 mi	1 mi = 1.609 km
meter (m) = 100 cm	1 m = 3.281 ft	1 ft = 0.305 m
centimeter (cm) = 0.01 m	1 cm = 0.394 in.	1 in. = 2.540 cm
millimeter (mm) = 0.001 m	1 mm = 0.039 in.	
micrometer (μm) = 0.000 001 m		
nanometer (nm) = 0.000 000 001 m		
Area		
square kilometer (km^2) = 100 hectares	1 km^2 = 0.386 mi^2	1 mi^2 = 2.590 km^2
hectare (ha) = 10,000 m^2	1 ha = 2.471 acres	1 acre = 0.405 ha
square meter (m^2) = 10,000 cm^2	1 m^2 = 10.764 ft^2	1 ft^2 = 0.093 m^2
square centimeter (cm^2) = 100 mm^2	1 cm^2 = 0.155 in.^{2}	1 in.^{2} = 6.452 cm^2
Volume		
liter (L) = 1,000 mL = 1 dm^3	1 L = 1.057 fl qt	1 fl qt = 0.946 L
milliliter (mL) = 0.001 L = 1 cm^3	1 mL = 0.034 fl oz	1 fl oz = 29.574 mL
microliter (μL) = 0.000 001 L		
Mass		
kilogram (kg) = 1,000 g	1 kg = 2.205 lb	1 lb = 0.454 kg
gram (g) = 1,000 mg	1 g = 0.035 oz	1 oz = 28.350 g
milligram (mg) = 0.001 g		
microgram (μg) = 0.000 001 g		

Measuring Skills

Using a Graduated Cylinder

When using a graduated cylinder to measure volume, keep the following procedures in mind:

1. Place the cylinder on a flat, level surface before measuring liquid.

2. Move your head so that your eye is level with the surface of the liquid.

3. Read the mark closest to the liquid level. On glass graduated cylinders, read the mark closest to the center of the curve in the liquid's surface.

Using a Meterstick or Metric Ruler

When using a meterstick or metric ruler to measure length, keep the following procedures in mind:

1. Place the ruler firmly against the object that you are measuring.

2. Align one edge of the object exactly with the 0 end of the ruler.

3. Look at the other edge of the object to see which of the marks on the ruler is closest to that edge. (Note: Each small slash between the centimeters represents a millimeter, which is one-tenth of a centimeter.)

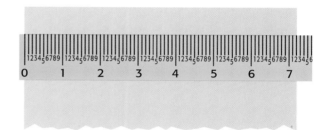

Using a Triple-Beam Balance

When using a triple-beam balance to measure mass, keep the following procedures in mind:

1. Make sure the balance is on a level surface.

2. Place all of the countermasses at 0. Adjust the balancing knob until the pointer rests at 0.

3. Place the object you wish to measure on the pan. **Caution:** Do not place hot objects or chemicals directly on the balance pan.

4. Move the largest countermass along the beam to the right until it is at the last notch that does not tip the balance. Follow the same procedure with the next-largest countermass. Then, move the smallest countermass until the pointer rests at 0.

5. Add the readings from the three beams together to determine the mass of the object.

6. When determining the mass of crystals or powders, first find the mass of a piece of filter paper. Then, add the crystals or powder to the paper, and remeasure. The actual mass of the crystals or powder is the total mass minus the mass of the paper. When finding the mass of liquids, first find the mass of the empty container. Then, find the combined mass of the liquid and container. The mass of the liquid is the total mass minus the mass of the container.

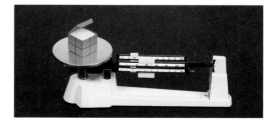

Scientific Methods

The ways in which scientists answer questions and solve problems are called **scientific methods.** The same steps are often used by scientists as they look for answers. However, there is more than one way to use these steps. Scientists may use all of the steps or just some of the steps during an investigation. They may even repeat some of the steps. The goal of using scientific methods is to come up with reliable answers and solutions.

Six Steps of Scientific Methods

1 Ask a Question

Good questions come from careful **observations.** You make observations by using your senses to gather information. Sometimes, you may use instruments, such as microscopes and telescopes, to extend the range of your senses. As you observe the natural world, you will discover that you have many more questions than answers. These questions drive investigations.

Questions beginning with *what, why, how,* and *when* are important in focusing an investigation. Here is an example of a question that could lead to an investigation.

Question: How does acid rain affect plant growth?

2 Form a Hypothesis

After you ask a question, you need to form a **hypothesis.** A hypothesis is a clear statement of what you expect the answer to your question to be. Your hypothesis will represent your best "educated guess" based on what you have observed and what you already know. A good hypothesis is testable. Otherwise, the investigation can go no further. Here is a hypothesis based on the question, "How does acid rain affect plant growth?"

Hypothesis: Acid rain slows plant growth.

The hypothesis can lead to predictions. A prediction is what you think the outcome of your experiment or data collection will be. Predictions are usually stated in an if-then format. Here is a sample prediction for the hypothesis that acid rain slows plant growth.

Prediction: If a plant is watered with only acid rain (which has a pH of 4), then the plant will grow at half its normal rate.

3 Test the Hypothesis

After you have formed a hypothesis and made a prediction, your hypothesis should be tested. One way to test a hypothesis is with a controlled experiment. A **controlled experiment** tests only one factor at a time. In an experiment to test the effect of acid rain on plant growth, the **control group** would be watered with normal rain water. The **experimental group** would be watered with acid rain. All of the plants should receive the same amount of sunlight and water each day. The air temperature should be the same for all groups. However, the acidity of the water will be a variable. In fact, any factor that is different from one group to another is a **variable.** If your hypothesis is correct, then the acidity of the water and plant growth are *dependant variables.* The amount a plant grows is dependent on the acidity of the water. However, the amount of water each plant receives and the amount of sunlight each plant receives are *independent variables.* Either of these factors could change without affecting the other factor.

Sometimes, the nature of an investigation makes a controlled experiment impossible. For example, the Earth's core is surrounded by thousands of meters of rock. Under such circumstances, a hypothesis may be tested by making detailed observations.

4 Analyze the Results

After you have completed your experiments, made your observations, and collected your data, you must analyze all the information you have gathered. Tables and graphs are often used in this step to organize the data.

5 Draw Conclusions

After analyzing your data, you can determine if your results support your hypothesis. If your hypothesis is supported, you (or others) might want to repeat the observations or experiments to verify your results. If your hypothesis is not supported by the data, you may have to check your procedure for errors. You may even have to reject your hypothesis and make a new one. If you cannot draw a conclusion from your results, you may have to try the investigation again or carry out further observations or experiments.

6 Communicate Results

After any scientific investigation, you should report your results. By preparing a written or oral report, you let others know what you have learned. They may repeat your investigation to see if they get the same results. Your report may even lead to another question and then to another investigation.

Scientific Methods in Action

Scientific methods contain loops in which several steps may be repeated over and over again. In some cases, certain steps are unnecessary. Thus, there is not a "straight line" of steps. For example, sometimes scientists find that testing one hypothesis raises new questions and new hypotheses to be tested. And sometimes, testing the hypothesis leads directly to a conclusion. Furthermore, the steps in scientific methods are not always used in the same order. Follow the steps in the diagram, and see how many different directions scientific methods can take you.

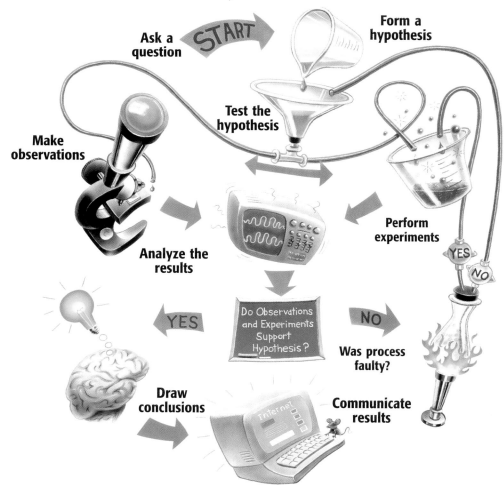

Math Refresher

Science requires an understanding of many math concepts. The following pages will help you review some important math skills.

Averages

An **average,** or **mean,** simplifies a set of numbers into a single number that *approximates* the value of the set.

> **Example:** Find the average of the following set of numbers: 5, 4, 7, and 8.

Step 1: Find the sum.
$$5 + 4 + 7 + 8 = 24$$

Step 2: Divide the sum by the number of numbers in your set. Because there are four numbers in this example, divide the sum by 4.

$$\frac{24}{4} = 6$$

The average, or mean, is **6.**

Ratios

A **ratio** is a comparison between numbers, and it is usually written as a fraction.

> **Example:** Find the ratio of thermometers to students if you have 36 thermometers and 48 students in your class.

Step 1: Make the ratio.
$$\frac{36 \text{ thermometers}}{48 \text{ students}}$$

Step 2: Reduce the fraction to its simplest form.

$$\frac{36}{48} = \frac{36 \div 12}{48 \div 12} = \frac{3}{4}$$

The ratio of thermometers to students is **3 to 4,** or $\frac{3}{4}$. The ratio may also be written in the form 3:4.

Proportions

A **proportion** is an equation that states that two ratios are equal.

$$\frac{3}{1} = \frac{12}{4}$$

To solve a proportion, first multiply across the equal sign. This is called *cross-multiplication.* If you know three of the quantities in a proportion, you can use cross-multiplication to find the fourth.

> **Example:** Imagine that you are making a scale model of the solar system for your science project. The diameter of Jupiter is 11.2 times the diameter of the Earth. If you are using a plastic-foam ball that has a diameter of 2 cm to represent the Earth, what must the diameter of the ball representing Jupiter be?
>
> $$\frac{11.2}{1} = \frac{x}{2 \text{ cm}}$$

Step 1: Cross-multiply.
$$\frac{11.2}{1} \diagdown \frac{x}{2}$$
$$11.2 \times 2 = x \times 1$$

Step 2: Multiply.
$$22.4 = x \times 1$$

Step 3: Isolate the variable by dividing both sides by 1.
$$x = \frac{22.4}{1}$$
$$x = 22.4 \text{ cm}$$

You will need to use a ball that has a diameter of **22.4** cm to represent Jupiter.

Percentages

A **percentage** is a ratio of a given number to 100.

> **Example:** What is 85% of 40?

Step 1: Rewrite the percentage by moving the decimal point two places to the left.

$$0.\underset{\smile}{85}$$

Step 2: Multiply the decimal by the number that you are calculating the percentage of.

$$0.85 \times 40 = 34$$

85% of 40 is **34.**

Decimals

To **add** or **subtract decimals,** line up the digits vertically so that the decimal points line up. Then, add or subtract the columns from right to left. Carry or borrow numbers as necessary.

> **Example:** Add the following numbers: 3.1415 and 2.96.

Step 1: Line up the digits vertically so that the decimal points line up.

$$\begin{array}{r} 3.1415 \\ + 2.96 \\ \hline \end{array}$$

Step 2: Add the columns from right to left, and carry when necessary.

$$\begin{array}{r} {\scriptstyle 1\ \ 1} \\ 3.1415 \\ + 2.96 \\ \hline 6.1015 \end{array}$$

The sum is **6.1015.**

Fractions

Numbers tell you how many; **fractions** tell you *how much of a whole*.

> **Example:** Your class has 24 plants. Your teacher instructs you to put 5 plants in a shady spot. What fraction of the plants in your class will you put in a shady spot?

Step 1: In the denominator, write the total number of parts in the whole.

$$\frac{?}{24}$$

Step 2: In the numerator, write the number of parts of the whole that are being considered.

$$\frac{5}{24}$$

So, $\frac{5}{24}$ of the plants will be in the shade.

Reducing Fractions

It is usually best to express a fraction in its simplest form. Expressing a fraction in its simplest form is called *reducing* a fraction.

> **Example:** Reduce the fraction $\frac{30}{45}$ to its simplest form.

Step 1: Find the largest whole number that will divide evenly into both the numerator and denominator. This number is called the *greatest common factor* (GCF).

Factors of the numerator 30:

    1, 2, 3, 5, 6, 10, **15,** 30

Factors of the denominator 45:

    1, 3, 5, 9, **15,** 45

Step 2: Divide both the numerator and the denominator by the GCF, which in this case is 15.

$$\frac{30}{45} = \frac{30 \div 15}{45 \div 15} = \frac{2}{3}$$

Thus, $\frac{30}{45}$ reduced to its simplest form is $\frac{2}{3}$.

Adding and Subtracting Fractions

To **add** or **subtract fractions** that have the **same denominator,** simply add or subtract the numerators.

Examples:

$$\frac{3}{5} + \frac{1}{5} = ? \quad \text{and} \quad \frac{3}{4} - \frac{1}{4} = ?$$

Step 1: Add or subtract the numerators.

$$\frac{3}{5} + \frac{1}{5} = \frac{4}{} \quad \text{and} \quad \frac{3}{4} - \frac{1}{4} = \frac{2}{}$$

Step 2: Write the sum or difference over the denominator.

$$\frac{3}{5} + \frac{1}{5} = \frac{4}{5} \quad \text{and} \quad \frac{3}{4} - \frac{1}{4} = \frac{2}{4}$$

Step 3: If necessary, reduce the fraction to its simplest form.

$$\frac{4}{5} \text{ cannot be reduced, and } \frac{2}{4} = \frac{1}{2}.$$

To **add** or **subtract fractions** that have **different denominators,** first find the least common denominator (LCD).

Examples:

$$\frac{1}{2} + \frac{1}{6} = ? \quad \text{and} \quad \frac{3}{4} - \frac{2}{3} = ?$$

Step 1: Write the equivalent fractions that have a common denominator.

$$\frac{3}{6} + \frac{1}{6} = ? \quad \text{and} \quad \frac{9}{12} - \frac{8}{12} = ?$$

Step 2: Add or subtract the fractions.

$$\frac{3}{6} + \frac{1}{6} = \frac{4}{6} \quad \text{and} \quad \frac{9}{12} - \frac{8}{12} = \frac{1}{12}$$

Step 3: If necessary, reduce the fraction to its simplest form.

The fraction $\frac{4}{6} = \frac{2}{3}$, and $\frac{1}{12}$ cannot be reduced.

Multiplying Fractions

To **multiply fractions,** multiply the numerators and the denominators together, and then reduce the fraction to its simplest form.

Example:

$$\frac{5}{9} \times \frac{7}{10} = ?$$

Step 1: Multiply the numerators and denominators.

$$\frac{5}{9} \times \frac{7}{10} = \frac{5 \times 7}{9 \times 10} = \frac{35}{90}$$

Step 2: Reduce the fraction.

$$\frac{35}{90} = \frac{35 \div 5}{90 \div 5} = \frac{7}{18}$$

Dividing Fractions

To **divide fractions,** first rewrite the divisor (the number you divide by) upside down. This number is called the *reciprocal* of the divisor. Then multiply and reduce if necessary.

Example:

$$\frac{5}{8} \div \frac{3}{2} = ?$$

Step 1: Rewrite the divisor as its reciprocal.

$$\frac{3}{2} \rightarrow \frac{2}{3}$$

Step 2: Multiply the fractions.

$$\frac{5}{8} \times \frac{2}{3} = \frac{5 \times 2}{8 \times 3} = \frac{10}{24}$$

Step 3: Reduce the fraction.

$$\frac{10}{24} = \frac{10 \div 2}{24 \div 2} = \frac{5}{12}$$

Scientific Notation

Scientific notation is a short way of representing very large and very small numbers without writing all of the place-holding zeros.

Example: Write 653,000,000 in scientific notation.

Step 1: Write the number without the place-holding zeros.

653

Step 2: Place the decimal point after the first digit.

6.53

Step 3: Find the exponent by counting the number of places that you moved the decimal point.

6.53000000

The decimal point was moved eight places to the left. Therefore, the exponent of 10 is positive 8. If you had moved the decimal point to the right, the exponent would be negative.

Step 4: Write the number in scientific notation.

$$\mathbf{6.53 \times 10^8}$$

Area

Area is the number of square units needed to cover the surface of an object.

Formulas:

area of a square = side × side
area of a rectangle = length × width
area of a triangle = $\frac{1}{2}$ × base × height

Examples: Find the areas.

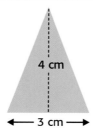

Triangle
area = $\frac{1}{2}$ × base × height
area = $\frac{1}{2}$ × 3 cm × 4 cm
area = **6 cm²**

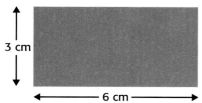

Rectangle
area = length × width
area = 6 cm × 3 cm
area = **18 cm²**

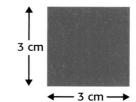

Square
area = side × side
area = 3 cm × 3 cm
area = **9 cm²**

Volume

Volume is the amount of space that something occupies.

Formulas:

volume of a cube =
side × side × side

volume of a prism =
area of base × height

Examples:

Find the volume
of the solids.

Cube
volume = side × side × side
volume = 4 cm × 4 cm × 4 cm
volume = **64 cm³**

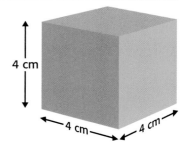

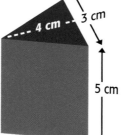

Prism
volume = area of base × height
volume = (area of triangle) × height
volume = ($\frac{1}{2}$ × 3 cm × 4 cm) × 5 cm
volume = 6 cm² × 5 cm
volume = **30 cm³**

Properties of Common Minerals

	Mineral	Color	Luster	Streak	Hardness
Silicate Minerals	Beryl	deep green, pink, white, bluish green, or yellow	vitreous	white	7.5–8
	Chlorite	green	vitreous to pearly	pale green	2–2.5
	Garnet	green, red, brown, black	vitreous	white	6.5–7.5
	Hornblende	dark green, brown, or black	vitreous	none	5–6
	Muscovite	colorless, silvery white, or brown	vitreous or pearly	white	2–2.5
	Olivine	olive green, yellow	vitreous	white or none	6.5–7
	Orthoclase	colorless, white, pink, or other colors	vitreous	white or none	6
	Plagioclase	colorless, white, yellow, pink, green	vitreous	white	6
	Quartz	colorless or white; any color when not pure	vitreous or waxy	white or none	7

	Mineral	Color	Luster	Streak	Hardness
Nonsilicate Minerals	**Native Elements**				
	Copper	copper-red	metallic	copper-red	2.5–3
	Diamond	pale yellow or colorless	adamantine	none	10
	Graphite	black to gray	submetallic	black	1–2
	Carbonates				
	Aragonite	colorless, white, or pale yellow	vitreous	white	3.5–4
	Calcite	colorless or white to tan	vitreous	white	3
	Halides				
	Fluorite	light green, yellow, purple, bluish green, or other colors	vitreous	none	4
	Halite	white	vitreous	white	2.0–2.5
	Oxides				
	Hematite	reddish brown to black	metallic to earthy	dark red to red-brown	5.6–6.5
	Magnetite	iron-black	metallic	black	5.5–6.5
	Sulfates				
	Anhydrite	colorless, bluish, or violet	vitreous to pearly	white	3–3.5
	Gypsum	white, pink, gray, or colorless	vitreous, pearly, or silky	white	2.0
	Sulfides				
	Galena	lead-gray	metallic	lead-gray to black	2.5–2.8
	Pyrite	brassy yellow	metallic	greenish, brownish, or black	6–6.5

Density (g/cm³)	Cleavage, Fracture, Special Properties	Common Uses
2.6–2.8	1 cleavage direction; irregular fracture; some varieties fluoresce in ultraviolet light	gemstones, ore of the metal beryllium
2.6–3.3	1 cleavage direction; irregular fracture	
4.2	no cleavage; conchoidal to splintery fracture	gemstones, abrasives
3.0–3.4	2 cleavage directions; hackly to splintery fracture	
2.7–3	1 cleavage direction; irregular fracture	electrical insulation, wallpaper, fireproofing material, lubricant
3.2–3.3	no cleavage; conchoidal fracture	gemstones, casting
2.6	2 cleavage directions; irregular fracture	porcelain
2.6–2.7	2 cleavage directions; irregular fracture	ceramics
2.6	no cleavage; conchoidal fracture	gemstones, concrete, glass, porcelain, sandpaper, lenses
8.9	no cleavage; hackly fracture	wiring, brass, bronze, coins
3.5	4 cleavage directions; irregular to conchoidal fracture	gemstones, drilling
2.3	1 cleavage direction; irregular fracture	pencils, paints, lubricants, batteries
2.95	2 cleavage directions; irregular fracture; reacts with hydrochloric acid	no important industrial uses
2.7	3 cleavage directions; irregular fracture; reacts with weak acid; double refraction	cements, soil conditioner, whitewash, construction materials
3.0–3.3	4 cleavage directions; irregular fracture; some varieties fluoresce	hydrofluoric acid, steel, glass, fiberglass, pottery, enamel
2.1–2.2	3 cleavage directions; splintery to conchoidal fracture; salty taste	tanning hides, salting icy roads, food preservation
5.2–5.3	no cleavage; splintery fracture; magnetic when heated	iron ore for steel, pigments
5.2	no cleavage; splintery fracture; magnetic	iron ore
3.0	3 cleavage directions; conchoidal to splintery fracture	soil conditioner, sulfuric acid
2.3	3 cleavage directions; conchoidal to splintery fracture	plaster of Paris, wallboard, soil conditioner
7.4–7.6	3 cleavage directions; irregular fracture	batteries, paints
5	no cleavage; conchoidal to splintery fracture	sulfuric acid

Glossary

A

absolute dating any method of measuring the age of an event or object in years (70)

asthenosphere the soft layer of the mantle on which the tectonic plates move (98)

C

caldera a large, semicircular depression that forms when the magma chamber below a volcano partially empties and causes the ground above to sink (164)

cast a type of fossil that forms when sediments fill in the cavity left by a decomposed organism (76)

catastrophism a principle that states that geologic change occurs suddenly (61)

cleavage the splitting of a mineral along smooth, flat surfaces (9)

composition the chemical makeup of a rock; describes either the minerals or other materials in the rock (33)

compound a substance made up of atoms of two or more different elements joined by chemical bonds (5)

compression stress that occurs when forces act to squeeze an object (112)

continental drift the hypothesis that states that the continents once formed a single landmass, broke up, and drifted to their present locations (104)

convergent boundary the boundary formed by the collision of two lithospheric plates (109)

core the central part of the Earth below the mantle (97)

crater a funnel-shaped pit near the top of the central vent of a volcano (164)

crust the thin and solid outermost layer of the Earth above the mantle (96)

crystal a solid whose atoms, ions, or molecules are arranged in a definite pattern (5)

D

deformation the bending, tilting, and breaking of the Earth's crust; the change in the shape of rock in response to stress (131)

density the ratio of the mass of a substance to the volume of the substance (10)

deposition the process in which material is laid down (29)

divergent boundary the boundary between two tectonic plates that are moving away from each other (109)

E

elastic rebound the sudden return of elastically deformed rock to its undeformed shape (131)

element a substance that cannot be separated or broken down into simpler substances by chemical means (4)

eon (EE AHN) the largest division of geologic time (83)

epicenter the point on Earth's surface directly above an earthquake's starting point, or focus (136)

epoch (EP uhk) a subdivision of a geologic period (83)

era a unit of geologic time that includes two or more periods (83)

erosion the process by which wind, water, ice, or gravity transports soil and sediment from one location to another (29)

extinction the death of every member of a species (83)

extrusive igneous rock rock that forms as a result of volcanic activity at or near the Earth's surface (39)

F

fault a break in a body of rock along which one block slides relative to another (114)

focus the point along a fault at which the first motion of an earthquake occurs (136)

folding the bending of rock layers due to stress (113)

foliated describes the texture of metamorphic rock in which the mineral grains are arranged in planes or bands (47)

fossil the remains or physical evidence of an organism preserved by geological processes (74)

fracture the manner in which a mineral breaks along either curved or irregular surfaces (9)

G

gap hypothesis a hypothesis that is based on the idea that a major earthquake is more likely to occur along the part of an active fault where no earthquakes have occurred for a certain period of time (141)

geologic column an arrangement of rock layers in which the oldest rocks are at the bottom (65)

geologic time scale the standard method used to divide the Earth's long natural history into manageable parts (82)

H

half-life the time needed for half of a sample of a radioactive substance to undergo radioactive decay (71)

hardness a measure of the ability of a mineral to resist scratching (10)

hot spot a volcanically active area of Earth's surface far from a tectonic plate boundary (170)

I

index fossil a fossil that is found in the rock layers of only one geologic age and that is used to establish the age of the rock layers (78)

intrusive igneous rock rock formed from the cooling and solidification of magma beneath the Earth's surface (38)

isotope an atom that has the same number of protons (or the same atomic number) as other atoms of the same element do but that has a different number of neutrons (and thus a different atomic mass) (70)

L

lava plateau a wide, flat landform that results from repeated nonexplosive eruptions of lava that spread over a large area (165)

lithosphere the solid, outer layer of the Earth that consists of the crust and the rigid upper part of the mantle (98)

luster the way in which a mineral reflects light (8)

M

magma chamber the body of molten rock that feeds a volcano (158)

mantle the layer of rock between the Earth's crust and core (97)

mesosphere the strong, lower part of the mantle between the asthenosphere and the outer core (99)

mineral a naturally formed, inorganic solid that has a definite chemical structure (4)

mold a mark or cavity made in a sedimentary surface by a shell or other body (76)

N

nonfoliated describes the texture of metamorphic rock in which the mineral grains are not arranged in planes or bands (48)

nonsilicate mineral a mineral that does not contain compounds of silicon and oxygen (6)

O

ore a natural material whose concentration of economically valuable minerals is high enough for the material to be mined profitably (14)

P

paleontology the scientific study of fossils (63)

period a unit of geologic time into which eras are divided (83)

plate tectonics the theory that explains how large pieces of the Earth's outermost layer, called *tectonic plates,* move and change shape (108)

P wave a seismic wave that causes particles of rock to move in a back-and-forth direction (134)

R

radioactive decay the process in which a radioactive isotope tends to break down into a stable isotope of the same element or another element (70)

radiometric dating a method of determining the age of an object by estimating the relative percentages of a radioactive (parent) isotope and a stable (daughter) isotope (71)

reclamation the process of returning land to its original condition after mining is completed (15)

relative dating any method of determining whether an event or object is older or younger than other events or objects (64)

rift zone an area of deep cracks that forms between two tectonic plates that are pulling away from each other (168)

rock a naturally occurring solid mixture of one or more minerals or organic matter (28)

rock cycle the series of processes in which a rock forms, changes from one type to another, is destroyed, and forms again by geological processes (28)

S

sea-floor spreading the process by which new oceanic lithosphere forms as magma rises toward the surface and solidifies (106)

seismic gap an area along a fault where relatively few earthquakes have occurred recently but where strong earthquakes have occurred in the past (141)

seismic wave a wave of energy that travels through the Earth and away from an earthquake in all directions (134)

seismogram a tracing of earthquake motion that is created by a seismograph (136)

seismograph an instrument that records vibrations in the ground and determines the location and strength of an earthquake (136)

seismology (siez MAHL uh jee) the study of earthquakes (130)

silicate mineral a mineral that contains a combination of silicon, oxygen, and one or more metals (6)

strata layers of rock (singular, *stratum*) (40)

stratification the process in which sedimentary rocks are arranged in layers (43)

streak the color of the powder of a mineral (9)

subsidence (suhb SIED′ns) the sinking of regions of the Earth's crust to lower elevations (118)

superposition a principle that states that younger rocks lie above older rocks if the layers have not been disturbed (64)

S wave a seismic wave that causes particles of rock to move in a side-to-side direction (134)

T

tectonic plate a block of lithosphere that consists of the crust and the rigid, outermost part of the mantle (100)

tension stress that occurs when forces act to stretch an object (112)

texture the quality of a rock that is based on the sizes, shapes, and positions of the rock's grains (34)

trace fossil a fossilized mark that is formed in soft sediment by the movement of an animal (76)

transform boundary the boundary between tectonic plates that are sliding past each other horizontally (109)

U

unconformity a break in the geologic record created when rock layers are eroded or when sediment is not deposited for a long period of time (67)

uniformitarianism a principle that states that geologic processes that occurred in the past can be explained by current geologic processes (60)

uplift the rising of regions of the Earth's crust to higher elevations (118)

V

vent an opening at the surface of the Earth through which volcanic material passes (158)

volcano a vent or fissure in the Earth's surface through which magma and gases are expelled (156)

Glossary

Spanish Glossary

A

absolute dating/datación absoluta cualquier método que sirve para determinar la edad de un suceso u objeto en años (70)

asthenosphere/astenosfera la capa blanda del manto sobre la que se mueven las placas tectónicas (98)

C

caldera/caldera una depresión grande y semicircular que se forma cuando se vacía parcialmente la cámara de magma que hay debajo de un volcán, lo cual hace que el suelo se hunda (164)

cast/molde un tipo de fósil que se forma cuando un organismo descompuesto deja una cavidad que es llenada por sedimentos (76)

catastrophism/catastrofismo un principio que establece que los cambios geológicos ocurren súbitamente (61)

cleavage/exfoliación el agrietamiento de un mineral en sus superficies lisas y planas (9)

composition/composición la constitución química de una roca; describe los minerales u otros materiales presentes en ella (33)

compound/compuesto una substancia formada por átomos de dos o más elementos diferentes unidos por enlaces químicos (5)

compression/compresión estrés que se produce cuando distintas fuerzas actúan para estrechar un objeto (112)

continental drift/deriva continental la hipótesis que establece que alguna vez los continentes formaron una sola masa de tierra, se dividieron y se fueron a la deriva hasta terminar en sus ubicaciones actuales (104)

convergent boundary/límite convergente el límite que se forma debido al choque de dos placas de la litosfera (109)

core/núcleo la parte central de la Tierra, debajo del manto (97)

crater/cráter una depresión con forma de embudo que se encuentra cerca de la parte superior de la chimenea central de un volcán (164)

crust/corteza la capa externa, delgada y sólida de la Tierra, que se encuentra sobre el manto (96)

crystal/cristal un sólido cuyos átomos, iones o moléculas están ordenados en un patrón definido (5)

D

deformation/deformación el proceso de doblar, inclinar y romper la corteza de la Tierra; el cambio en la forma de una roca en respuesta a la tensión (131)

density/densidad la relación entre la masa de una substancia y su volumen (10)

deposition/deposición el proceso por medio del cual un material se deposita (29)

divergent boundary/límite divergente el límite entre dos placas tectónicas que se están separando una de la otra (109)

E

elastic rebound/rebote elástico ocurre cuando una roca deformada elásticamente vuelve súbitamente a su forma no deformada (131)

element/elemento una substancia que no se puede separar o descomponer en substancias más simples por medio de métodos químicos (4)

eon/eón la mayor división del tiempo geológico (83)

epicenter/epicentro el punto de la superficie de la Tierra que queda justo arriba del punto de inicio, o foco, de un terremoto (136)

epoch/época una subdivisión de un período geológico (83)

era/era una unidad de tiempo geológico que incluye dos o más períodos (83)

erosion/erosión el proceso por medio del cual el viento, el agua, el hielo o la gravedad transporta tierra y sedimentos de un lugar a otro (29)

extinction/extinción la muerte de todos los miembros de una especie (83)

extrusive igneous rock/roca ígnea extrusiva una roca que se forma como resultado de la actividad volcánica en la superficie de la Tierra o cerca de ella (39)

F

fault/falla una grieta en un cuerpo rocoso a lo largo de la cual un bloque se desliza respecto a otro (114)

focus/foco el punto a lo largo de una falla donde ocurre el primer movimiento de un terremoto (136)

folding/plegamiento fenómeno que ocurre cuando las capas de roca se doblan debido a la compresión (113)

foliated/foliada término que describe la textura de una roca metamórfica en la que los granos de mineral están ordenados en planos o bandas (47)

fossil/fósil los restos o las pruebas físicas de un organismo preservados por los procesos geológicos (74)

fracture/fractura la forma en la que se rompe un mineral a lo largo de superficies curvas o irregulares (9)

G

gap hypothesis/hipótesis del intervalo una hipótesis que se basa en la idea de que es más probable que ocurra un terremoto importante a lo largo de la parte de una falla activa donde no se han producido terremotos durante un determinado período de tiempo (141)

geologic column/columna geológica un arreglo de las capas de roca en el que las rocas más antiguas están al fondo (65)

geologic time scale/escala de tiempo geológico el método estándar que se usa para dividir la larga historia natural de la Tierra en partes razonables (82)

H

half-life/vida media el tiempo que tarda la mitad de la muestra de una substancia radiactiva en desintegrarse por desintegración radiactiva (71)

hardness/dureza una medida de la capacidad de un mineral de resistir ser rayado (10)

hot spot/mancha caliente un área volcánicamente activa de la superficie de la Tierra que se encuentra lejos de un límite entre placas tectónicas (170)

I

index fossil/fósil guía un fósil que se encuentra en las capas de roca de una sola era geológica y que se usa para establecer la edad de las capas de roca (78)

intrusive igneous rock/roca ígnea intrusiva una roca formada a partir del enfriamiento y solidificación del magma debajo de la superficie terrestre (38)

isotope/isótopo un átomo que tiene el mismo número de protones (o el mismo número atómico) que otros átomos del mismo elemento, pero que tiene un número diferente de neutrones (y, por lo tanto, otra masa atómica) (70)

L

lava plateau/meseta de lava un accidente geográfico amplio y plano que se forma debido a repetidas erupciones no explosivas de lava que se expanden por un área extensa (165)

lithosphere/litosfera la capa externa y sólida de la Tierra que está formada por la corteza y la parte superior y rígida del manto (98)

luster/brillo la forma en que un mineral refleja la luz (8)

M

magma chamber/cámara de magma la masa de roca fundida que alimenta un volcán (158)

mantle/manto la capa de roca que se encuentra entre la corteza terrestre y el núcleo (97)

mesosphere/mesosfera la parte fuerte e inferior del manto que se encuentra entre la astenosfera y el núcleo externo (99)

mineral/mineral un sólido natural e inorgánico que tiene una estructura química definida (4)

mold/molde una marca o cavidad hecha en una superficie sedimentaria por una concha u otro cuerpo (76)

N

nonfoliated/no foliada término que describe la textura de una roca metamórfica en la que los granos de mineral no están ordenados en planos ni bandas (48)

nonsilicate mineral/mineral no-silicato un mineral que no contiene compuestos de sílice y oxígeno (6)

O

ore/mena un material natural cuya concentración de minerales con valor económico es suficientemente alta como para que el material pueda ser explotado de manera rentable (14)

P

paleontology/paleontología el estudio científico de los fósiles (63)

period/período una unidad de tiempo geológico en la que se dividen las eras (83)

plate tectonics/tectónica de placas la teoría que explica cómo se mueven y cambian de forma las placas tectónicas, que son grandes porciones de la capa más externa de la Tierra (108)

P wave/onda P una onda sísmica que hace que las partículas de roca se muevan en una dirección de atrás hacia delante (134)

R

radioactive decay/desintegración radiactiva el proceso por medio del cual unlos isótopos radiactivos tienden a desintegrarse y formar un isótopos estables del mismo elemento o de otros elementos (70)

radiometric dating/datación radiométrica un método para determinar la edad de un objeto estimando los porcentajes relativos de un isótopo radiactivo (precursor) y un isótopo estable (hijo) (71)

reclamation/restauración el proceso de hacer que la tierra vuelva a su condición original después de que se terminan las actividades de explotación minera (15)

relative dating/datación relativa cualquier método que se utiliza para determinar si un acontecimiento u objeto es más viejo o más joven que otros acontecimientos u objetos (64)

rift zone/zona de rift un área de grietas profundas que se forma entre dos placas tectónicas que se están alejando una de la otra (168)

rock/roca una mezcla sólida de uno o más minerales o de materia orgánica que se produce de forma natural (28)

rock cycle/ciclo de las rocas la serie de procesos por medio de los cuales una roca se forma, cambia de un tipo a otro, se destruye y se forma nuevamente por procesos geológicos (28)

S

sea-floor spreading/expansión del suelo marino el proceso por medio del cual se forma nueva litosfera oceánica a medida que el magma se eleva hacia la superficie y se solidifica (106)

seismic gap/brecha sísmica un área a lo largo de una falla donde han ocurrido relativamente pocos terremotos recientemente, pero donde se han producido terremotos fuertes en el pasado (141)

seismic wave/onda sísmica una onda de energía que viaja a través de la Tierra y se aleja de un terremoto en todas direcciones (134)

seismogram/sismograma una gráfica del movimiento de un terremoto elaborada por un sismógrafo (136)

seismograph/sismógrafo un instrumento que registra las vibraciones en el suelo y determina la ubicación y la fuerza de un terremoto (136)

seismology/sismología el estudio de los terremotos (130)

silicate mineral/mineral silicato un mineral que contiene una combinación de sílice, oxígeno y uno o más metales (6)

strata/estratos capas de roca (40)

stratification/estratificación el proceso por medio del cual las rocas sedimentarias se acomodan en capas (43)

streak/veta el color del polvo de un mineral (9)

subsidence/hundimiento del terreno el hundimiento de regiones de la corteza terrestre a elevaciones más bajas (118)

superposition/superposición un principio que establece que las rocas más jóvenes se encontrarán sobre las rocas más viejas si las capas no han sido alteradas (64)

S wave/onda S una onda sísmica que hace que las partículas de roca se muevan en una dirección de lado a lado (134)

T

tectonic plate/placa tectónica un bloque de litosfera formado por la corteza y la parte rígida y más externa del manto (100)

tension/tensión estrés que se produce cuando distintas fuerzas actúan para estirar un objeto (112)

texture/textura la cualidad de una roca que se basa en el tamaño, la forma y la posición de los granos que la forman (34)

trace fossil/fósil traza una marca fosilizada que se forma en un sedimento blando debido al movimiento de un animal (76)

transform boundary/límite de transformación el límite entre placas tectónicas que se están deslizando horizontalmente una sobre otra (109)

Spanish Glossary

U

unconformity/disconformidad una ruptura en el registro geológico, creada cuando las capas de roca se erosionan o cuando el sedimento no se deposita durante un largo período de tiempo (67)

uniformitarianism/uniformitarianismo un principio que establece que es posible explicar los procesos geológicos que ocurrieron en el pasado en función de los procesos geológicos actuales (60)

uplift/levantamiento la elevación de regiones de la corteza terrestre a elevaciones más altas (118)

V

vent/chimenea una abertura en la superficie de la Tierra a través de la cual pasa material volcánico (158)

volcano/volcán una chimenea o fisura en la superficie de la Tierra a través de la cual se expulsan magma y gases (156)

Spanish Glossary

Index

Boldface page numbers refer to illustrative material, such as figures, tables, margin elements, photographs, and illustrations.

Index

Index   **221**

Index   **223**

Index

Index

W

water
  density of, 10
  in volcanic eruptions, 158, 169,
    169
waxy luster, **8**
weathering, in the rock cycle, 29,
  29, 31
Wegener, Alfred, 104–105, 127
Wieliczka salt mine, 24
Williamson, Jack, 24
woolly mammoths, 75, **75,** 92

Y

Yellowstone National Park, 164
Yoho National Park, **77**

Index

Credits

Abbreviations used: (t) top, (c) center, (b) bottom, (l) left, (r) right, (bkgd) background

PHOTOGRAPHY

Front Cover Doug Scott/Age Fotostock

Skills Practice Lab Teens Sam Dudgeon/HRW

Connection to Astrology Corbis Images; **Connection to Biology** David M. Phillips/Visuals Unlimited; **Connection to Chemistry** Digital Image copyright © 2005 PhotoDisc; **Connection to Environment** Digital Image copyright © 2005 PhotoDisc; **Connection to Geology** Letraset Phototone; **Connection to Language Arts** Digital Image copyright © 2005 PhotoDisc; **Connection to Meteorology** Digital Image copyright © 2005 PhotoDisc; **Connection to Oceanography** © ICONOTEC; **Connection to Physics** Digital Image copyright © 2005 PhotoDisc

Table of Contents iv (yellow), E. R. Degginger/Color–Pic, Inc.; iv (purple), Mark A. Schneider/Photo Researchers, Inc.; (green), Dr. E.R. Degginger/Bruce Coleman Inc.; iv (bl), The G.R. "Dick" Roberts Photo Library; v (b), ©National Geographic Image Collection/Robert W. Madden; x (bl), Sam Dudgeon/HRW; xi (tl), John Langford/HRW; xi (b), Sam Dudgeon/HRW; xii (tl), Victoria Smith/HRW; xii (bl), Stephanie Morris/HRW; xii (br), Sam Dudgeon/HRW; xiii (tl), Patti Murray/Animals, Animals; xiii (tr), Jana Birchum/HRW; xiii (b), Peter Van Steen/HRW

Chapter One 2–3, Terry Wilson; 4, Sam Dudgeon/HRW; 5, Dr. Rainer Bode/Bode–Verlag Gmb; 6 (tr), Victoria Smith/HRW; 6 (bc), Sam Dudgeon/HRW; 6 (tl), Sam Dudgeon/HRW; 7, (copper), E. R. Degginger/Color–Pic, Inc.; 7, (calcite), E. R. Degginger/Color–Pic, Inc.; 7, (fluorite), E. R. Degginger/Color–Pic, Inc.; 7, (corundum), E. R. Degginger/Color–Pic, Inc.; 7, (gypsum), SuperStock; 7, (galena), Visuals Unlimited/Ken Lucas; 8, (vitreous), Biophoto Associates/Photo Researchers, Inc.; 8, (waxy), Biophoto Associates/Photo Researchers, Inc.; 8, (silky), Dr. E.R. Degginger/Bruce Coleman Inc.; 8, (submetallic), John Cancalosi 1989/DRK Photo; 8 (bl), Kosmatsu Mining Systems; 8, (resinous), Charles D. Winters/Photo Researchers, Inc.; 8, (pearly), Victoria Smith/HRW; 8, (metallic), Victoria Smith/HRW; 8, (earthy), Sam Dudgeon/HRW; 9 (tr, c, bl), Sam Dudgeon/HRW; 9, Tom Pantages; 10, (1), Visuals Unlimited/Ken Lucas; 10, (3), Visuals Unlimited/Dane S. Johnson; 10, (7), Carlyn Iverson/Absolute Science Illustration and Photography; 10, (8), Mark A. Schneider/Visuals Unlimited; 10, (9), Charles D. Winters/Photo Researchers, Inc.; 10, (10), Bard Wrisley; 10, (5), Biophoto Associates/Photo Researchers, Inc.; 10, (6), Victoria Smith/HRW; 10, (4), Mark A. Schneider/Photo Researchers, Inc.; 10, (2), Sam Dudgeon/HRW; 11 (tc), Sam Dudgeon/HRW; 11 (tr), Sam Dudgeon/HRW, Courtesy Science Stuff, Austin, TX; 11 (br), Tom Pantages Photography; 11 (bc), Sam Dudgeon/HRW; 11 (tl), Mark A. Schneider/Photo Researchers, Inc.; 11 (tl), Mark A. Schneider/Photo Researchers, Inc.; 11 (bl), 12 (t), Sam Dudgeon/HRW; 12 (bl), Victoria Smith/HRW Photo, Courtesy Science Stuff, Austin, TX; 12 (c), Breck P. Kent; 13 (br), Sam Dudgeon/HRW; 13 (c), Breck P. Kent; 13 (t), Visuals Unlimited/Ken Lucas; 14 (br), Wernher Krutein; 15, Stewart Cohen/Index Stock Photography, Inc.; 16, Digital Image copyright © 2005 PhotoDisc; 17, Historic Royal Palaces; 18 (c), Russell Dian/HRW; 18 (b), 19 (tr), Sam Dudgeon/HRW; 20, Digital Image copyright © 2005 PhotoDisc; 21 (b), E. R. Degginger/Color–Pic, Inc.; 24 (t), Stephan Edelbroich; 25 (t), Will & Dennie McIntyre/McIntyre Photography; 25 (b), Mark Schneider/Visuals Unlimited

Chapter Two 26–27, Tom Till; 28 (bl), Michael Melford/Getty Images/The Image Bank; 28 (br), Joseph Sohm; Visions of America/CORBIS; 29, CORBIS Images/HRW; 32 (t), Joyce Photographics/Photo Researchers, Inc.; 32 (l), Pat Lanza/Bruce Coleman Inc.; 32 (r), Sam Dudgeon/HRW ; 32 (b), James Watt/Animals Animals/Earth Scenes; 32 (l), Pat Lanza/Bruce Coleman Inc.; 33, (granite), Pat Lanza/Bruce Coleman Inc.; 33, (mica), E. R. Degginger/Color–Pic, Inc.; 33, (aragonite), Breck P. Kent; 33, (limestone), Breck P. Kent; 33, (calcite), Mark Schneider/Visuals Unlimited; 33, (feldspar), Mark Schneider/Visuals Unlimited; 33, (quartz), Digital Image copyright © 2005 PhotoDisc; 34 (tl), Sam Dudgeon/HRW; 34 (tc), Dorling Kindersley; 34 (tr, br), Breck P. Kent; 34 (bl), E. R. Degginger/Color–Pic, Inc.; 35, Joseph Sohm; Visions of America/CORBIS; 36 (l), E. R. Degginger/Color–Pic, Inc.; 37 (tr, tl, bl), Breck P. Kent; 37 (br), Victoria Smith/HRW; 39, J.D. Griggs/USGS; 40, CORBIS Images/HRW; 41, (conglomerate), Breck P. Kent; 41, (siltstone), Sam Dudgeon/HRW; 41, (sandstone), Joyce Photographics/Photo Researchers, Inc.; 41, (shale), Sam Dudgeon/HRW; 42 (tl), Stephen Frink/Corbis; 42 (br), Breck P. Kent; 42 (bc), David Muench/CORBIS; 43, Franklin P. OSF/Animals Animals/Earth Scenes; 44, George Wuerthner; 46, (calcite), Dane S. Johnson/Visuals Unlimited; 46, (quartz), Carlyn Iverson/Absolute Science Illustration and Photography; 46, (hematite), Breck P. Kent; 46, (garnet), Breck P. Kent/Animals Animals/Earth Scenes; 46, (chlorite), Sam Dudgeon/HRW; 46, (mica), Tom Pantages; 47, (shale), Ken Karp/HRW; 47, (slate), Sam Dudgeon/HRW; 47, (phyllite), Sam Dudgeon/HRW; 47, (gneiss), Breck P. Kent; 47, (schist), Sam Dudgeon/HRW; 48 (tl), E. R. Degginger/Color–Pic, Inc.; 48 (bl), Ray Simmons/Photo Researchers, Inc; 48 (tr), The Natural History Museum, London; 48 (br), Breck P. Kent; 49, Jim Wark/Airphoto; 51 (t), Sam Dudgeon/HRW; 51 (b), James Tallon; 56 (l), Wolfgang Kaehler/CORBIS; 56 (tr), Dr. David Kring/Science Photo Library/Photo Researchers, Inc.; 57 (r), James Miller/Courtesy Robert Folk, Department of Geological Sciences, University of Texas at Austin; 57 (l), Dr. Philppa Uwins, Whistler Research PTY/SPL/Photo Researchers, Inc.

Chapter Three 58, National Geographic Image Collection/Jonathan Blair, Courtesy Hessian Regional Museum, Darmstadt, Germany; 61, GeoScience Features Picture Library; 63, Museum of Northern Arizona; 64 (l), Sam Dudgeon/HRW; 64 (r), Andy Christiansen/HRW; 66 (tl), Fletcher & Baylis/Photo Researchers, Inc.; 66 (tr), Ken M. Johns/Photo Researchers, Inc.; 66 (bl), Glenn M. Oliver/Visuals Unlimited; 66 (br), Francois Gohier/Photo Researchers, Inc.; 71, Sam Dudgeon/HRW; 72, Tom Till/DRK Photo; 73, Courtesy Charles S. Tucek/University of Arizona at Tucson; 74, Howard Grey/Getty Images/Stone; 75, Francis Latreille/Nova Productions/AP/Wide World Photos; 76 (b), The G.R. "Dick" Roberts Photo Library; 76 (t), © Louie Psihoyos/psihoyos.com; 77 (l), Brian Exton; 77 (r), Chip Clark/Smithsonian; 78 (l), ; 79, Thomas R. Taylor/Photo Researchers, Inc.; 80, James L. Amos/CORBIS; 81 (tl), Tom Till Photography; 81 (fish), Tom Bean/CORBIS; 81 (leaf), James L. Amos/CORBIS; 81 (turtle), Layne Kennedy/CORBIS; 81 (fly), Ken Lucas/Visuals Unlimited; 83, Chip Clark/Smithsonian; 84 (t), Neg. no. 5793 Courtesy Dept. of Library Services, American Museum of Natural History; 84 (b), Neg. no. 5799 Courtesy Department of Library Services., American Museum of Natural History; 85, Neg. no. 5801 Courtesy Department of Library Services, American Museum of Natural History; 86, Jonathan Blair/CORBIS; 88 (b), The G.R. "Dick" Roberts Photo Library; 89 (fly), Ken Lucas/Visuals Unlimited; 92 (tl), Beth A. Keiser/AP/Wide World Photos; 92 (tr), Jonathan Blair/CORBIS; 93, Courtesy Kevin C. May

Chapter Four 94–95, James Balog/Getty Images/Stone; 97 (t), James Wall/Animals Animals/Earth Scenes; 100, Bruce C. Heezen and Marie Tharp; 111 (tc), ESA/CE/Eurocontrol/Science Photo Library/Photo Researchers, Inc.; 111 (tr), NASA; 112 (bl, br), Peter Van Steen/HRW; 113 (bc), Visuals Unlimited/SylvesterAllred; 113 (br), G.R. Roberts Photo Library; 115 (tl), Tom Bean; 115 (tr), Landform Slides; 116, Jay Dickman/CORBIS; 117 (b), Michele & Tom Grimm Photography; 118, Y. Arthus–B./Peter Arnold, Inc.; 119, Peter Van Steen/HRW; 121, Sam Dudgeon/HRW; 126 (bl), NASA/Science Photo Library/Photo Researchers, Inc.; 126 (c), Ron Miller/Fran Heyl Associates; 126 (tr), Photo by S. Thorarinsson/Solar–Filma/Sun Film–15/3/courtesy of Edward T. Baker, Pacific Marine Environmental Laboratory, NOAA; 127 (r), Bettman/CORBIS

Chapter Five 128–129, Robert Patrick/Sygma/CORBIS; 131, Roger Ressmeyer/CORBIS; 137, Earth Images/Getty Images/Stone; 139, Bettmann/CORBIS; 142, Michael S. Yamashita/CORBIS; 144, Paul Chesley/Getty Images/Stone; 146, NOAA/NGDC; 147, Sam Dudgeon/HRW; 149, Bettmann/CORBIS; 152, Sam Dudgeon/HRW; 152 (t), Courtesy Stephen H. Hickman, USGS; 153 (t), Todd Bigelow/HRW; 153 (b), Corbis Images

Chapter Six 154–155, Carl Shaneff/Pacific Stock; 156 (bl), National Geographic Image Collection/Robert W. Madden; 156 (br), Ken Sakamoto/Black Star; 157 (b), Breck P. Kent/Animals Animals/Earth Scenes; 157, Joyce Warren/USGS Photo Library; 159 (tl), Tui De Roy/Minden Pictures; 159 (bl), B. Murton/Southampton Oceanography Centre/Science Photo Library/Photo Researchers, Inc.; 159 (tr), Visuals Unlimited/Martin Miller; 159 (br), Buddy Mays/CORBIS; 160 (tr), Tom Bean/DRK Photo; 160 (tl), Francois Gohier/Photo Researchers, Inc.; 160, (tlc), Visuals Unlimited Inc./Glenn Oliver; 160, (tlb), E. R. Degginger/Color–Pic, Inc.; 161 (tr), Alberto Garcia/SABA/CORBIS; 161, Robert W. Madden/National Geographic Society; 162, Images & Volcans/Photo Researchers, Inc.; 163 (br), SuperStock; 163 (cr), SuperStock; 163 (tr), Roger Ressmeyer/CORBIS; 164 (tl), Yann Arthus–Bertrand/CORBIS; 165, Joseph Sohm; ChromoSohm Inc./CORBIS; 170 (bl), Robert McGimsey/USGS Alaska Volcano Observatory; 174 (tr), Alberto Garcia/SABA/CORBIS; 178 (bl), CORBIS; 178 (tr), Photo courtesy of Alan V. Morgan, Department of Earth Sciences, University of Waterloo; 178 (tc), © Sigurgeir Jonasson; Frank Lane Picture Agency/CORBIS; 179 (bl), Courtesy Christina Neal; 179 (r), Courtesy Alaska Volcano Observatory

Lab Book/Appendix "LabBook Header", "L", Corbis Images; "a", Letraset Phototone; "b", and "B", HRW; "o", and "k", images ©2006 PhotoDisc/HRW; 181 (tr), Victoria Smith/HRW, Courtesy of Science Stuff, Austin, TX; 181, (galena), Ken Lucas/Visuals Unlimited Inc.; 181 (cr), Charlie Winters/HRW; 181, 182, 183 (hematite, br), Sam Dudgeon/HRW; 184 (all), Andy Christiansen/HRW; 185, Sam Dudgeon/HRW; 186, Tom Bean; 187, 188, Sam Dudgeon/HRW; 189, Andy Christiansen/HRW; 193 (tr) Sam Dudgeon/HRW

D1466449

GOURMET FOOD NATURALLY

Heather and Zune Bampfylde

LAROUSSE

Measurement conversions

Quantities throughout are given in metric, imperial and US cup measures. Although the exact conversion for 1oz is 28.5g, for the sake of convenience we have rounded it down to 25g, which is a more handy measure for conversion purposes. For successful results in your cookery, you should use *either* metric *or* imperial *or* US cup measurements, not a mixture of all three, as the measures are not interchangeable. For example, whereas the British and Australian pint = 20floz, the American pint is only 16floz/2 US cups.

All spoon measurements throughout are level, and although the British, American and Australian teaspoons differ slightly in volume, we have used the following conversion: 1 tablespoon = 15ml; 1 teaspoon = 5ml; ½ teaspoon = 2.5ml; and ¼ teaspoon = 1.25ml capacity. You can buy special handy measuring spoons in these volumes.

Art director: Al Rockall
Illustrations: Al Rockall
Photographer: Barry Bullough
Home economist: Elaine Bastable

Tableware by Josiah Wedgwood & Sons Ltd, Coalport and Mason's Ironstone on pages 33, 133, 149
Brassware and pans by Smiffs Antiques, East Finchley, London N2 on pages 28, 29, 45, 165
Photograph courtesy of British Chicken Federation on page 113

First published in the U.K. in 1983
by William Collins Sons & Co Ltd
London · Glasgow · Sydney
Auckland · Johannesburg

First published in the United States by Larousse & Co., Inc.,
572 Fifth Avenue, New York, NY 10036
ISBN 0 88332 331 1
Library of Congress No. 83-48932

© Sackville Design Group Ltd 1983

Designed and produced by Sackville Design Group Ltd
32-34 Great Titchfield Street, London W1P 7AD
Typeset in Plantin by Sackville Design Group Ltd

All rights reserved. No part of this publication may be reproduced, stored in a retrieval system, or transmitted, in any form or by any means, electronic, mechanical, photocopying, recording or otherwise, without the prior written permission of the publishers.

Printed in Italy by New Interlitho

Contents

Introduction

This book is dedicated to good food — delicious recipes made with natural, fresh ingredients which will help us to achieve a more balanced and healthy diet. To some extent, our health is only as good as the food we eat, and in spite of our sophisticated Western diet and the wide range of foods available, we are not as healthy as we should be. Medical opinion now accepts that many physical disorders and diseases are diet-related, especially heart disease, diabetes, strokes and some forms of cancer. These were less common in the past and have grown significantly in this century since the advent of modern farming methods and food processing techniques. Many of these lifestyle diseases are still rare in less developed countries where fewer animal fats and a higher proportion of unrefined carbohydrates are eaten. We have developed a sweet tooth and a taste for soft refined foods, and our over-consumption of sugar, fats and animal products and lack of dietary fibre may be detrimental to our health. Even the less serious disorders that most of us suffer from at some time or another, such as constipation, tooth and gum disease, varicose veins, haemorrhoids and peptic ulcers, may be directly related to the food we eat.

To improve our health we must change our diet and eat more natural, less refined foods which are both nutritious and high in fibre. A well-balanced diet need not be boring — far from it, as it should include a wide variety of healthy foods, each with its own natural goodness, flavour, colour and texture. Eating the natural way can be enjoyable and interesting as more people are finding out. The trend towards a healthier diet and the growing interest in wholefood ingredients is evident in the meteoric spread of health food stores in our towns and cities, and even supermarkets now sell such healthy foods as wholemeal flour, dried beans, wholewheat pasta and muesli breakfast cereals. So good ingredients are not hard to find.

The essential nutrients needed for the maintenance of good health are: protein, unrefined carbohydrate, vitamins, minerals and some fat. Most of us have a tendency to eat too much protein and fats and insufficient unrefined carbohydrates, vitamins and minerals.

Protein is essential for growth, the repair of body cells and tissues, healthy blood and firm muscle tone. Proteins are made up of chains of amino acids. High biological protein chains, found in meat, fish and animal produce (eggs, milk and cheese) and soya beans resemble the chains in our own bodies, whereas low biological protein chains, found in some vegetables, beans and pulses, grains, nuts and seeds, are incomplete. Their deficiencies can be overcome by eating these vegetable foods in combination with animal proteins or soya beans.

Carbohydrates provide us with most of our energy needs, in the form of starch, sugar and cellulose. Starches are the main source of carbohydrates in our diet, followed closely by sugar. Cellulose, the indigestible fibrous parts of plants, provides roughage and bulk to keep our bowels healthy and working more efficiently. Refined carbohydrates like sugar and white flour are full of empty calories which are stored as fat if they outnumber the body's energy requirements. Unrefined carbohydrates, such as whole grains beans and pulses, seeds and starchy vegetables, contain fibre and help prevent many diseases, especially piles, diverticular disease, constipation, appendicitis, hiatus hernia and bowel cancer, while helping us to maintain a steady weight or even to lose weight in the case of some people.

Fats play a protective role in the body, maintaining cell structure, organs, nerves and body temperature and transporting the fat-soluble vitamins A, D, E and K. Although some fats are essential for promoting good health, we tend to eat too much fat, and doctors have discovered that a high fat intake may be linked to diabetes, most liver diseases, coronary heart disease, atheriosclerosis and cancer. There are three types of fats — saturated, polyunsaturated and monounsaturated. Saturated fats are found in meat, butter, cheese, egg yolks, lard and hard margarine made from animal fats. They raise the cholesterol levels in our blood which may lead to a build-up of fatty cholesterol deposits in the arteries leading to the heart and eventually block them. Polyunsaturated fats, on the other hand, actually lower the blood's cholesterol level and cell structures. These fats are found in vegetable and maintaining cell These fats are found in vegetable oils, nuts, oily fish, soya beans, fish livers and soft margarines. Monounsaturated fats, which include olive oil, are neutral.

Vitamins are organic substances which help promote good health. They are only present in small amounts but deficiencies of any one can lead to ill-health. In a varied diet, you should obtain all the essential vitamins your body needs without resorting to pills and supplements (in fact, some vitamins, notably A and D, can even be harmful if taken in excess). Vitamin A, found in carrots, oily fish, fish liver oils, eggs, dairy food and green vegetables, promotes healthy skin and good vision. The seven B vitamins are necessary for growth, releasing energy from proteins, carbohydrates and fats, maintaining healthy skin, muscles and nerves, and making red blood cells. Thiamine (B1) is found in meat, whole grains, some vegetables and potatoes. Riboflavin (B2) can be obtained from meat, dairy foods, especially milk, whole grains, liver and kidney. Niacin is present in meat, whole grains, fish and milk. Pyridoxine (B6) is found in meat, nuts, fish, yeast, milk, whole grains and some vegetables. Pantothenic acid is obtained from meat, whole grains, eggs and yeast. Folic acid which maintains healthy blood is present in liver, green vegetables, pulses, oranges and yeast. Cyanocobalamin (B12) is found only in meat and animal products.

Vitamin C, often invested with magical powers by many people, helps to heal damaged tissue and cells, resist infection, absorb iron and keep gums and teeth healthy. It is found in citrus fruits, soft fruits and many green vegetables. Vitamin D, present in sunshine, fish liver oils, oily fish, eggs and margarine, assists in the building of healthy bones and teeth. Vitamin E, found in vegetable oils, whole grains, eggs and nuts, helps to maintain healthy muscles and probably fertility, whereas vitamin K, found in leafy green vegetables and oils, is needed for blood clotting.

Minerals, like vitamins, are found only in very small amounts in the food we eat but they too play an important part in maintaining good health. Calcium, iodine, iron, chlorine, magnesium, potassium, phosphorus and sulphur are all major elements in our diet, whereas some trace elements needed in smaller quantities include copper, chromium, cobalt, fluorine, manganese and zinc. They are found in a wide range of foods in varying quantities and a balanced diet should include them all.

By becoming more health-conscious and learning to balance the nutrients and different foods in your diet, you can develop a new style of healthy eating. Here are some basic guidelines for you to follow:

1 Eat less meat
Meat is high in saturated fat, especially red meats (lamb and beef), so cut down on these and eat fish and poultry instead. Fish is particularly good for you as it contains polyunsaturated fats, protein, vitamins and minerals. It is one of the most delicious protein foods and can add great variety to your diet as there are so many different fish and ways of cooking and serving them. Unrefined carbohydrates, whole grains, beans, pulses, vegetables, brown rice and wholewheat pasta, are other ways of introducing protein into your meals. These foods, which are high in fibre, vitamins and minerals, were advocated by the US Senate Committee on Nutrition and Human Needs which met in 1977 to discuss our dietary problems and ways in which we can improve our health. You need not eliminate meat from your diet and become a vegetarian — just eat it less often and gradually increase the meatless meals you eat.

2 Eat more fibre
Fibre has been seized upon recently as the magic formula for losing weight and preventing numerous diet-related diseases, notably constipation, diverticular disease, bowel disorders and heart disease. Fibre comprises a group of complex cellular substances found in plant food together with complex carbohydrates. Our digestive enzymes cannot break down these fibrous substances and so they absorb water and stay bulky as they pass through our bodies. Scientific research has shown that fibre not only helps dilute and quickly expel any poisonous substances in the body but it is also beneficial in its effect on harmful bacteria in the bowel. You can increase your consumption of fibre by eating wholewheat bread, sprinkling 15ml/1 tablespoon bran on your muesli or granola breakfast cereal each day and eating more whole grains, brown rice, beans, fresh fruit and vegetables. Foods which contain no fibre are meat, fat, eggs and sugar.

3 Cut down on sugar
Most of us have grown up with a sweet taste for sugar and favour sweet desserts, cakes, puddings and cookies. So when you next add a spoonful of sugar to your cup of coffee, reflect on the fact that 99 per cent of white sugar is empty calories, or sucrose, and its only function is to provide us with quick energy — great for marathon runners, perhaps, but not for the more sedentary among us. Too much sugar may lead to diabetes as well as tooth decay and weight problems. Instead of cutting out sugar completely, eat less and use unrefined light and dark raw sugars, such as Barbados and Muscovado, or molasses and malt extract in cooking. At least they contain B vitamins, calcium and potassium. Better still are honey and fresh fruits which contain fructose and less calories. Honey is rich in vitamins and minerals.

4 Eat less fat
As we said earlier, most of us eat too much fat and

thereby make ourselves vulnerable to a wide range of affluent diseases, particularly atheriosclerosis and heart disease. You can cut down your saturated fats intake in several ways:

● by cooking with polyunsaturated margarine and vegetable oils instead of lard and butter
● by reducing the amount of cream in your diet — use yoghurt for topping desserts, and cook meat and fish in simpler ways so that they do not need a rich cream sauce to mask their natural flavour
● by mixing yoghurt into salad dressings and sauces
● by making mayonnaise with olive oil and poly-unsaturated oils
● by spreading either soft margarine or special low-fat spreads on bread instead of butter
● by eating more low-fat cheeses and skimmed milk
● by eating less red meat and cutting off the surplus fat and eating only the lean flesh

The best oils for cooking and salads are sunflower, safflower, corn and ground nut oils. Avoid those labelled simply as 'vegetable oil' — these may contain solvent extracted oils. The most delicious oils of all for salads are olive, walnut and hazelnut oils.

5 Use less salt

Reducing the amount of cooking and table salt in your diet is also beneficial to health. A high intake of salt can predispose a person to hypertension, high blood pressure and even arthritis. Although salt is an essential mineral and is present in our body fluids, it is finely balanced with potassium in the body. Too much salt can damage this delicate equilibrium and actually displace the potassium, resulting sometimes in water retention, kidney disorders and even muscle damage. Obviously, if you live in a very hot climate you will lose a certain amount of salt through perspiration and will need more salt than people in temperate lands. Most of us eat 4 or 5 times as much salt as we need and we should try to ration our daily intake to about 4 grams (less than 1 teaspoonful per day). Use sea salt crystals in preference to table salt. They are rich in iodine and do not contain additives, such as phosphate of lime and starch which are sometimes mixed into finely ground table salt to make it free-flowing. Remember that if food is seasoned correctly, there is no need to salt it again on your plate, so leave the salt grinder off the table at mealtimes. Make more use of natural flavourings like aromatics, herbs and spices in your cooking. Each has its own distinctive aroma and flavour, many pungent and exotic. Fresh herbs are more flavoursome than dried, and spices should be purchased whole and freshly ground just before using.

6 Cut out processed foods

Refined processed foods are usually soft in texture and indifferently flavoured, lacking both fibre and natural goodness. The shelves and freezers of supermarkets are stacked with packets, tubs and cans of processed foods, which are likely to be high in sugar, salt, saturated fats and unnecessary additives. With their colourful, cheerful covers and packaging, they are labelled as 'convenience foods', the argument being that they were formulated specially to help busy people who haven't the time to spend in the kitchen preparing lengthy meals. However, many health-promoting dishes can be quickly prepared (in less than 30 minutes) as proven by many of the recipes in this book, especially with the aid of modern labour-saving gadgets. Study the ingredients listed on the side of most packets and you may be surprised to discover a whole array of additives — artificial flavourings and colourings, stabilisers, preserving agents, emulsifiers and other chemicals which have no nutritional value. Although there are safety limits and regulations set by most countries regarding the type and amounts of additives permissible in processed foods, many are toxic if eaten in large quantities and may cause allergies in some people. There are over 3000 additives currently permissible, so if you *have* to buy processed foods, check the packet first.

7 Use simpler, healthier cooking methods

The quality and nutritional value of food is affected by the cooking method you select. For example, frying, especially deep-fat frying at high heat, can destroy essential vitamins as well as adding unwanted calories. Shallow-frying in polyunsaturated fats and oils is preferable to saturated fats, such as butter and lard/shortening, whereas grilling/broiling with the minimum of oil is healthier still. Choose simple cooking methods such as grilling, poaching, steaming and casseroling to gain maximum nutritional benefit and minimum loss of true flavour. Instead of frying fish, try baking it in wine, tomatoes herbs and aromatics, poach it in a court-bouillon or marinate it and thread onto kebab skewers with peppers, onions, tomatoes and mushrooms. Cook meat and poultry in its own juices with fresh vegetables or fruit and stock or wine, and do not overcook vegetables. The best cooking method is the one that enhances the natural flavour of the fresh food without significantly reducing its food value.

Grains & Cereals

Grains and cereals have been Man's staple food since ancient times. The early civilisations of Egypt and Mesopotamia both sprang up around fertile river valleys (the Nile, Tigris and Euphrates rivers) where grain crops were grown. Various gods and goddesses of mythology have been worshipped as the providers of bountiful grain harvests, such as the Roman goddess Ceres, from whom the word 'cereal' evolved.

All the maincrop cereals belong to the botanical family *Graminaciae*. They are grown all over the world, and the type of grain cultivated is determined by the prevailing climate and location. Thus maize, millet and rice are products of the tropics and subtropics, whereas wheat, rye, oats and barley are the staples of temperate regions. Grains are eaten whole, crushed in groats, ground into flour, boiled into cereal, flaked or fermented in alcoholic drinks. They are among the best ingredients we can eat and feature significantly in most people's daily diet. However, they must be whole and of good quality if they are to be nutritious.

Cereals are extremely valuable foods, containing protein, dietary fibre, minerals, B vitamins, and vitamin E in the case of wheat. However, processing can reduce the vitamin and mineral content of the grain and completely eliminate the fibre (the bran contained in the grain's outer layer) which is so important for preventing constipation and diseases of the bowel. The best example of this disturbing trend is the preference for white bread which has been prevalent since the nineteenth centruy in Europe and North America, although the Romans too were culprits. Most of the white bread we eat today is made from wheat flour. In order to obtain the desired whiteness and soft texture, all the natural wheatgerm and bran are removed, together with most of the B vitamins which are contained in the surface endosperm. The vitamin E and fatty acids in the germ, which keep our tissues, skin and muscles healthy and prevent blood clotting, are also removed. The ground flour is then bleached with chlorine dioxide and some additives, usually calcium, iron, niacin and thiamine, are used to enrich it. This, then, is the flour we eat in white bread, cakes, biscuits, pastry and puddings. It is not only less nutritious than wholewheat flour but also less tasty and satisfying as many people are now beginning to discover.

Wheat

This grain, which is the staple food of half the world, evolved at the end of the Ice Age in its wild form. Its earliest cultivation was in the fertile Eastern Mediterranean coutries. The ancient Egyptians were the first to crush the grain and bake it into unleavened bread. Later they used wild yeasts to make the wheat bread rise, and their bread-making techniques were adopted by the Romans, whose legions brought the wheat seeds to Gaul and Britain. Throughout the Middle Ages, however, the staple European cereal was rye, much enjoyed by the Saxons and Scandinavians.

Wheat is the best flour for bread-making because of its high gluten content. This mixture of proteins (gliadin and glutenin) absorbs water and stretches out to form an elastic dough. Gluten also traps the carbon-dioxide produced when the dough is leavened with yeast and causes the dough to blow up and hold its shape. It is present in rye also but to a lesser extent and thus rye loaves are denser and not so light as wheat loaves. There is a wide range of wheat flours for sale:

Wholemeal flour which contains the whole wheat grain, including the bran and wheatgerm. The stone-ground wholemeal flours are best as the flour is ground between stone burrstones rather than steel rollers to ensure a better distribution of wheat germ oil. Buy 100 per cent stoneground wholemeal flour for preference. This is the pure ground grains with all their natural goodness. Many of the brown or wholemeal loaves you buy in the shops are coloured with caramel and may not contain all the brain and wheatgerm of the grain, so buy reputable loaves sold as being made with 100 per cent wholemeal flour. Many companies make these now and some supermarkets have their own brands.

White all-purpose flour is made up of the grain's starchy endosperm, which has been roller-milled, refined and bleached. Nearly all of the bran and wheatgerm are removed in the processing. Special strong white bread flours are made by most manufacturers with a high gluten content. To try and compensate for its loss of natural goodness, additives are mixed into the flour, notably calcium and thiamine.

Self-raising flour may be bleached or unbleached and has chemical raising agents added to it during its manufacture. Cream of tartar and bicarbonate of soda/baking soda are the usual leaveners. This flour is commonly used for baking cakes but ordinary wholemeal flour may be substituted if a raising agent is added to it.

Wheat can also be purchased as cracked wheat for adding to granary loaves and scattering over the top of bread, wholewheat berries for savoury dishes, kibbled wheat for cereals, durum wheat for pasta-making, and burghul, beloved of Middle Eastern cookery.

Buckwheat

Sometimes known as saracen corn, this is not a true wheat but is really a starchy plant in the sorrel, dock and rhubarb family. It can be cooked like rice, or roasted and eaten as kasha as in Eastern Europe and the Soviet Union, or may be ground into flour to make muffins, blinis and crêpes. It is rich in iron and also contains a glucoside called rutin which may be beneficial in treating high blood pressure. It is native to Asiatic Russia and was brought back to Europe by the Crusaders, hence its other name of saracen corn.

Barley

The world's oldest cultivated grain, barley was grown by the ancient Hebrews, Greeks and Romans. It was so highly valued that the Sumerians even used it as a currency. Unlike wheat flour, barley flour contains little gluten and is rarely used in bread-making nowadays as it produces a flat unleavened loaf. It is still widely grown in the Balkan states, the Middle East and some parts of the Third World. Pearl and pot barley are used to bulk out savoury stews and soups, or may be made into barley water — a soft drink. Barley is also grown, as in Scotland, for distilling into whisky. It contains protein, traces of B vitamins, phosphorus, calcium and iron.

Rye

This hardy grain seems to thrive in the coldest climates and poorest soils. It was the staple cereal of northern Europe throughout the Middle Ages when most loaves were made of rye or a mixture of rye and barley. It is still popular in Germany, the Soviet Union, the Baltic countries and Scandinavia where people enjoy its dark, heavy texture and its characteristically sour flavour. In North America, it is distilled into whisky, or bourbon. It probably originated in the Middle East in the cornfields around Mount Ararat and was later grown by the Romans. Although it has a better bread-making capacity than barley, it contains less protein and gluten than wheat. Unfortunately, rye can become infected and poisoned by ergot, a mould that induces hallucinations and madness. This phenomenon may account for many of the mediaeval plagues and the high incidence of so-called witches who may have self-induced a trance-like state from eating diseased rye.

Oats

This cereal has been cultivated since the Bronze Age and grows well in the coldest climates, including those of Scandinavia and Alaska. Although it is grown mainly for animal feed, it is still popular in Scotland where it was once the staple food. Oats are made into oatcakes, flapjacks, haggis, porridge and even *boudin blanc* sausages. They are not suitable for bread-making but are delicious in home-made muesli breakfast cereals, giving them a nutty, slightly sweet flavour.

Maize

The only cereal of American origin, maize, or Indian corn as it is sometimes called, is the staple food of Central and South America. The Spanish brought it back to Europe and later it was taken to the Middle East. It is now grown all over the world. Worshipped by the South and North American Indians as the 'daughter of life', it may be ground into cornmeal and made into tortillas as in Mexico and Central America, eaten as a vegetable(sweetcorn or corn on the cob), ground into flour for the Italian *polenta* or as a thickening agent for sauces and stews, flaked as a popular breakfast cereal, and made into corn oil and corn syrup. The grains may be heated until they pop and eaten as popcorn.

Muesli

Formulated by Dr Bircher-Benner at his Zurich Health Clinic at the turn of the century, muesli is now a popular breakfast cereal on sale in most supermarkets as well as health food shops. It is not only high in fibre but it is also rich in protein, vitamins and minerals and thus makes an ideal breakfast dish. However, Dr Bircher-Benner advocated muesli as a complete meal in itself at any time of the day and prescribed it for his patients. Most modern nutritionists agree that Dr Bircher-Benner was correct in thinking that a combination of fibre and milk or yoghurt helps maintain a healthy digestive tract. It is more economical to make your own muesli than to buy it, and it tastes fresher and better than many of the packaged varieties. More-over, you can mix in your favourite ingredients in larger quantities. Try our recipe below and do not be afraid to experiment with it to obtain the version you like best. Serve with milk, sliced fruit (apple, pear or banana) or soft fruits (strawberries, blackberries, raspberries or blueberries), topped with a swirl of yoghurt.

350g/12oz/4 cups jumbo oats
75g/3oz/¾ cup rye flakes
50g/2oz/⅔ cup bran
25g/1oz/⅓ cup wheatgerm
100g/4oz/⅔ cup raisins
100g/4oz/⅔ cup chopped dried dates
50g/2oz/½ cup chopped hazelnuts
50g/2oz/½ cup chopped walnuts
25g/1oz/¼ cup chopped cashew nuts
50g/2oz/½ cup chopped Brazil nuts
50g/2oz/⅜ cup chopped dried apricots

Mix all the ingredients together and store in a large airtight container. Serve as a breakfast cereal or as a dessert with milk, yoghurt and fruit.

Makes approximately 1kg/2lb muesli

Granola

This is a form of toasted muesli in which the grains and nuts are mixed with sesame seeds, coated with oil and honey and baked in the oven until crisp and golden. Like muesli, it is served with milk, fruit and yoghurt as a breakfast cereal. You can, if wished, mix granola and muesli together in equal quantities for a more interesting texture and flavour.

300g/11oz/3⅔ cups jumbo oats
50g/2oz/⅔ cup bran
25g/1oz/⅓ cup wheatgerm
50g/2oz/½ cup chopped hazelnuts
100g/4oz/1¼ cups desiccated coconut
2.5ml/½ teaspoon salt
50g/2oz sesame seeds
100ml/4floz/½ cup vegetable oil
100ml/4floz/½ cup honey
2-3 drops vanilla essence
150g/5oz/¾ cup raisins
50g/2oz/½ cup chopped Brazil nuts
30ml/2 tablespoons chopped cashew nuts

Mix the jumbo oats, bran, wheatgerm, hazelnuts, coconut, salt and sesame seeds in a large bowl. Heat the oil and honey together in a small pan over a low heat until thoroughly blended. Add the vanilla essence and pour over the granola mixture. Mix well so that all the nuts, grains and seeds are well-coated.

Spread this mixture over a shallow baking tin and bake in a preheated oven at 140°C, 275°F, gas 1 for 35 - 40 minutes, stirring occasionally. Cool the granola, stir in the raisins, Brazil and cashew nuts and store in an airtight container.

Makes approximately 1kg/2lb granola

Lebanese tabbouleh

A colourful pyramid of lemony tabbouleh, garnished with cucumber slices, red pepper and black olives on a bed of cabbage leaves makes a beautiful party dish or a good first course salad. It derives its characteristically earthy flavour and texture from the main ingredient — cracked wheat burghul, which is sold at most health food shops.

225g/8oz/1⅓ cups burghul
300ml/½ pint/1¼ cups water
60ml/4 tablespoons chopped fresh mint
5 spring onions/shallots, finely chopped
small bunch parsley, finely chopped
juice of 1 lemon
30ml/2 tablespoons olive oil
salt and pepper
Garnish:
4 or 5 cabbage leaves
½ red pepper, thinly sliced
6 black olives
¼ cucumber, thinly sliced

Soak the burghul in the water for 30-40 minutes until

it soaks up the liquid and expands. Mix with the chopped mint, onions, parsley, lemon juice, oil and seasoning to taste.

Arrange a bed of cabbage leaves on a large plate and pile the tabbouleh into a pyramid shape in the centre. Decorate the sides with the sliced red pepper, olives and cucumber, and serve.

Serves 6

Algerian couscous

Throughout the Maghreb countries of North Africa, Tunisia, Algeria and Morocco, couscous is a favourite dish, served with a lamb and vegetable stew and a fiery red-hot sauce, flavoured with *harissa* paste and tomato. Couscous, a sort of wheat grain semolina, and *harissa* can be bought in many delicatessens or shops that specialise in Eastern foods. The basic method, which is common to all the regional variations of this dish, is to steam the couscous above the cooking stew, either in the upper half of a double steamer or in a sieve which fits over the pan. You can make infinite additions and changes to this dish — try adding sliced pumpkin, aubergine, red peppers, peas, runner beans, apricots, quinces, fresh dates or sliced apple. Serve with a bowl of cool yoghurt, if wished, to counter the hot sauce.

Lamb stew:
75g/3oz/ cup chick peas
2 onions, chopped
1 carrot, sliced
1 leek, sliced
1 green pepper, deseeded and chopped
550g/1lb 4oz lamb, cubed
45ml/3 tablespoons oil
2.5ml/½ teaspoon each of ground ginger and cinnamon
1 small packet powdered saffron
550ml/1 pint/2½ cups water
15ml/1 tablespoon tomato paste
2 courgettes/zucchini, sliced
2 tomatoes, skinned and chopped
100g/4oz French beans
50g/2oz/⅓ cup raisins
2 pears, peeled, cored and sliced
few sprigs, of parsley, chopped
Couscous:
225g/8oz/ cup couscous
300ml/½ pint/1¼ cups cold water
salt and pepper
15g/½ oz/1 tablespoon butter (optional)

Hot sauce:
30ml/2 tablespoons tomato paste
2.5ml/½ teaspoon harissa paste
pinch of paprika

Soak the chick peas in water overnight. Drain well. Sauté the onion, carrot, leek, green pepper and lamb in the oil for 5-6 minutes (until the vegetables are tender and the lamb is browned). Add the spices, saffron and water and bring to the boil. Reduce the heat to a simmer and add the drained chick peas. Leave to simmer gently for 1 hour.

Soak the couscous in a bowl of cold water for 10 minutes. Gently separate the grains a little with your fingers. Put the couscous in a metal sieve or the upper half of a steamer and place over the pan of cooking stew. Do not cover but leave open to steam gently. After about 20 minutes add the tomato paste and the remaining ingredients to the stew. Cook gently for a further 30 minutes.

At the point when you add the vegetables, you can remove the couscous, season it with salt and pepper and add a little cold water. Gently break up any lumps with your fingers and replace in the sieve or steamer over the stew.

Just before serving, work the butter into the couscous. Take 100ml/4floz/½ cup of the cooking liquid from the stew and blend with the tomato paste and harissa. Season with paprika and place in a small bowl. Serve the stew within a border of couscous, with the hot sauce in a separate bowl.

Serves 4

Kasha

Roasted buckwheat is known as kasha in Eastern Europe, the Soviet Union and central Asia. Kasha is eaten as a savoury dish either as an accompaniment to a main course, or mixed with vegetables, herbs and seasonings. Here is a recipe for basic kasha but you can add sautéed chopped onion, sliced mushrooms, herbs and spices for a more substantial dish. Top with grated cheese if wished and finish it off under the grill/broiler until golden and bubbling.

225g/8oz buckwheat
100g/4oz/½ cup margarine
550ml/1 pint/2½ cups boiling water
sea salt and freshly ground black pepper
chopped fresh herbs to garnish (chives, parsley)

Place the buckwheat in a heavy pan and stir over

medium heat until the buckwheat is golden-brown, crisp and nutty in texture. Shake the pan occasionally to prevent the buckwheat burning. Pour into an oven-proof dish with the margarine, boiling water and seasoning. Cover and place in a preheated oven at 150°C, 300°F, gas 2 for 1½ hours, or until all the water is absorbed and the buckwheat is cooked. Serve sprinkled with chopped fresh herbs.

Serves 4

Tyro pitta

Wafer-thin filo paste is used throughout the Middle East and the Balkans for savoury dishes and desserts. You have probably eaten it many times in the Greek dessert *baklava* with nuts and honey, but have you ever tried it in a savoury form with feta cheese, yoghurt and nuts? Tyro pitta makes a great party dish — delicious and unusual. You can buy the filo pastry sheets in most Greek food stores and delicatessens. It freezes well so when you discover a supply, buy a couple of boxes and freeze until required.

2 large eggs, separated
100ml/4floz/½ cup plain or apricot yoghurt
100g/4oz fresh or dried apricots
100g/4oz/1 cup chopped walnuts
150g/5oz feta cheese, crumbled
good pinch of ground cinnamon
225g/8oz filo pastry
175g/6oz/¾ cup margarine, melted

Make the filling: whisk the egg yolks with the yoghurt and chop the apricots, removing the stones/pits. Soak them overnight if you are using dried ones. Add to the mixture with the chopped nuts. Mix in the cheese with a fork. Whisk the egg whites separately until they stand in stiff peaks and gently fold into the mixture with the ground cinnamon.

Carefully unfold the pastry and lay one sheet across the base of a well-greased rectangular baking tin. Brush with margarine and lay another sheet of filo on top, and brush with more melted margarine. Spread a third of the filling over the top and cover with 2-3 more sheets of filo pastry brushing each with melted margarine. Cover with another layer of filling, top with filo paste in the same way and then spread with the remaining filling and filo paste. Brush the top layer of filo with the remaining melted margarine and place in a preheated oven at 220°C, 425°F, gas 7 for 5 minutes and then reduce the heat to 190°C, 375°F,

gas 5 and bake for a further 45-50 minutes until crisp and golden-brown.

To ensure that the tyro pitta is cooked right through to the centre, you can raise it at a slight angle in the tin with a palette knife or fish slice and bake it for a further 5-10 minutes at 150°C, 300°F, gas 2. Remove from the tin and cut in slices or squares and serve warm.

Savoury buckwheat bake

Buckwheat was brought back to Europe from Asia by the Crusaders and for this reason it is sometimes known as saracen corn. Use ordinary buckwheat for this recipe but roast it first by heating it in a heavy frying pan (with 15ml/1 tablespoon oil if wished) until golden-brown, nutty and crisp.

30ml/2 tablespoons long-grain brown rice
1 onion, chopped
1 clove of garlic, crushed
30ml/2 tablespoons oil
4 tomatoes, skinned and chopped
50g/2oz mushrooms, chopped
75g/3oz/¾ cup roasted buckwheat
300ml/½ pint/1¼ cups chicken stock
pinch of powdered saffron
5ml/1 teaspoon thyme
2.5ml/½ teaspoon basil
2.5ml/½ teaspoon oregano
salt and pepper

Boil the rice in salted water for 10 minutes and drain. Sauté the onion and garlic in the oil until soft and transparent. Add the tomatoes and mushrooms and cook gently for 1 minute. Stir in the roasted buckwheat and drained rice. Add the stock, herbs and seasoning.

Transfer the buckwheat mixture to a greased oven-proof dish and bake in a preheated oven at 180°C, 350°F, gas 4 for 30 minutes until crisp and golden. For a more substantial dish, you can pour thick béchamel sauce flavoured with plenty of grated Parmesan cheese across the top of the buckwheat bake. Sprinkle with more grated cheese and breadcrumbs and bake until golden.

Serves 4

Opposite: muesli and granola (recipes on page 10) are both healthy breakfast cereals. Serve them with milk or yoghurt, sweetened with honey and chopped fresh fruit, including chopped banana and apple, orange segments, strawberries, blackberries and apricots

Pizzas

The Neapolitan pizza has been exported all over the world and the range of toppings is seemingly limitless. Of course, to make a really authentic pizza you need to use an old-fashioned bread oven with a brick floor. This lends the pizza its charcoaly flavour. This is obviously impractical in your own kitchen at home but you can still create some very tasty pizzas which are always appreciated for supper and parties. A good idea is to make an extra large batch and freeze some to heat up later. The quantity of dough makes two large pizzas (enough to feed 4 people), and we have suggested a different topping for each.

450g/1lb basic wholemeal bread dough (see recipe on page 25)
15ml/1 tablespoon olive oil
Basic tomato sauce:
½ small onion, finely chopped
1-2 cloves garlic, crushed
30ml/2 tablespoons oil
675g/1½lb tomatoes, skinned and chopped or canned tomatoes
salt and pepper
Four seasons topping:
50g/2oz button mushrooms, thinly sliced
50g/2oz spicy Italian peperoni sausage, sliced
½ small onion, thinly sliced
5ml/1 teaspoon capers
5ml/1 teaspoon pine nuts
5ml/1 teaspoon sultanas/seedless raisins
50g/2oz/⅜ cup peeled shrimps
1 spring onion/shallot, chopped
100g/4oz mozzarella cheese, thinly sliced
few anchovy fillets
black olives to garnish
1 egg (optional)
Marinara topping
100g/4oz/¾ cup peeled shrimps
5ml/1 teaspoon basil
3 spring onions/shallots, chopped
100g/4oz mozzarella cheese, sliced
5 unpeeled prawns/shrimps
5 black olives

First make the tomato sauce: sauté the onion and garlic in the oil until soft. Add the tomatoes and seasoning and cook over high heat for about 10-15 minutes until the sauce is thick. You can add a little tomato paste to improve the colour.

Divide the basic wholemeal dough into 2 portions and roll each out thinly, about 5mm/¼in thick. Brush both dough circles with a little olive oil and spread thickly with the tomato sauce.

Assemble the four seasons pizza: arrange the sliced mushrooms on one-quarter of the pizza; spread the sliced sausage across another quarter; then the onion slices, capers, pine nuts and sultanas on another quarter; and the shrimps and spring onion on the remaining section. Scatter the mozzarella across the top with the black olives and a few criss-crossing anchovy fillets.

Assemble the marinara pizza: scatter the shrimps across the top and then the basil and spring onions. Top with the sliced mozzarella, unpeeled prawns and black olives. Place both pizzas on well-greased baking trays and bake in a preheated oven at 200°C 400°F, gas 6 for 20-30 minutes until the bases are crisp and the tops are sizzling. If wished, you can break an egg on top of the four seasons pizza about 5 minutes before it is ready. Replace in the oven until the egg is set. Serve immediately.
Serves 4

Burghul wheat pilaff

This is an interesting variation on a rice pilaff, but with a crisp, chewy texture and earthy flavour. It is a good accompaniment for a North African tagine (a stew of meat and fruit) or it can make a tasty meatless meal served with a salad. The recipe comes from Armenia.

225g/8oz/1½ cups burghul wheat
550ml/1 pint/2½ cups boiling water
30ml/2 tablespoons oil
1 large onion, chopped
1 clove garlic, crushed
1 red pepper, chopped
50g/2oz button mushrooms, sliced
45ml/3 tablespoons pine nuts
50g/2oz/⅓ cup raisins
25g/1oz/¼ cup cashew nuts
salt and pepper
25g/1oz/¼ cup grated Swiss cheese
Topping:
50g/2oz/½ cup chopped cashew nuts
50g/2oz/½ cup grated Swiss cheese.

Soak the wheat in the boiling water for 20 minutes until it swells and absorbs the liquid. Meanwhile, heat the oil in a flameproof dish and sauté the onion, garlic and pepper until tender. Add the sliced mushroom, pine nuts, raisins, cashews and seasoning and cook for

2 minutes. Then stir in the drained and soaked wheat and cheese. Sprinkle with the topping of chopped nuts and grated cheese and bake in a preheated oven at 150°C, 300°F, gas 2 for 15 minutes, or until the topping is crunchy and golden.

Serves 4

Tacos

Mexican tacos make a wonderful party dish and look very colourful if offered with a choice of two fillings: chilli beef or guacamole. They consist of tortillas which are wrapped around a tasty filling and quickly crisped just before serving. They are best eaten in your hand without the aid of knives and forks as the tortilla casing will hold the sauce inside. For the guacamole filling, refer to the recipe on page 127 and garnish each taco with black olives and chopped parsley. If you are in a hurry, you can buy ready-made taco shells in many delicatessens. Just heat them through according to the instructions on the packet and fill with guacamole or chilli beef sauce.

8 cooked tortillas
Chilli beef filling:
15ml/1 tablespoon oil
1 onion, finely chopped
1 clove garlic, crushed
225g/8oz/1 cup minced/ground beef
3 tomatoes, skinned and chopped
½ red pepper, chopped
45ml/3 tablespoons tomato paste
2 dried chillis, seeds removed and chopped
pinch of sugar
30ml/2 tablespoons raisins
salt and pepper
8 pimento stuffed green olives, thinly sliced

To make the chilli sauce: heat the oil and sauté the onion and garlic until tender. Add the beef and brown lightly. Stir in the chopped tomato, red pepper, tomato paste, chilli, sugar, raisins and seasoning. Cover the pan and simmer gently for about 40 minutes until the beef is cooked and the sauce is thick. If it gets too thick, thin it down with a little water, but the finished sauce should not be too wet or it will make the taco shells soggy. Mix the olives into the sauce.

Take 4 of the tortillas. If they were made in advance, replace them in a hot, ungreased pan for a few seconds to heat them up. Place a good dollop of sauce along the middle of each tortilla and fold the two sides around it up into the centre. Arrange the tacos in an ovenproof dish and place in a preheated oven at 200°C, 400°F, gas 6 for about 5 minutes to crisp them, or fry them quickly in a little oil. Fill the remaining warm tortillas with guacamole and roll up and cook in the same way. Serve the tacos together on a dish. They look most attractive with their contrasting red and green fillings.

Makes 4 beef and 4 guacamole tacos

Mexican tortillas

Tortillas are the staple Mexican food, served at nearly every meal as a sort of bread, or rolled around meat and vegetable fillings and baked or fried. Made from finely ground maize or corn flour, tortillas have been adopted enthusiastically as a 'fast food' on the West Coast of the United States. However, tortillas are one of the few fast foods that does you good, and they make an excellent party dish rolled into tacos and filled with guacamole or a chilli beef sauce, or simply topped with a fried egg and sliced avocado. To ensure success, you must use a very finely ground flour — masa harina is the best and can be bought in many delicatessens and health food shops.

225g/8oz/2 cups masa harina
225ml/8floz/1 cup water
good pinch of salt

Mix the masa harina and water to a smooth, pliable dough. You can do this by hand or in a food mixer or processor. Divide the dough into about 12 small balls and keep covered to prevent them drying out.

Place a ball of dough between 2 sheets of polythene or inside a polythene bag and roll out to a circle, about 15cm/6in wide. Slide the tortilla into an *ungreased* heavy frying pan or griddle and cook over medium heat for about 2 minutes until the underside is beginning to brown and the edges lift away from the pan. Flip the tortilla over and cook the other side for 2 minutes. Remove from the pan, wrap in foil and keep warm while you cook the remaining tortillas in the same way. Serve warm in a linen napkin, either buttered, or topped with fried eggs, guacamole or rolled into tacos.

> **Tip:** Make Mexican enchiladas by rolling cooked tortillas around picadillo mixture (see page 118). Cover with tomato sauce (cook fresh tomatoes slowly with onions and garlic until thick) and sprinkle with cheese. Bake in a medium oven for 20 minutes.

Basic strudel paste

This strudel paste can be used in most savoury and sweet strudel recipes. It is essential to knead the dough well so that it is really soft and elastic. You can mix it by hand or in a food mixer or processor for a really thorough mix. You will need warm hands to keep the dough really supple. Although we tend to associate strudel paste with Austria and its sumptuous apple strudels, this method of making wafer thin pastry layers probably evolved from the filo paste of Arab and Middle Eastern cookery.

450g/1lb/4½ cups plain flour
pinch of salt
150ml/¼ pint/⅝ cup warm water
25g/1oz/2 tablespoons softened lard/shortening

Mix the flour and salt together on a clean work surface and make a well in the centre. Whisk 15ml/1 tablespoon of the flour into the warm water. Place the softened lard with a little of the water in the well and gradually blend in the flour from around the sides with a palette knife, adding more water as you go along and drawing in the flour until you have a smooth, elastic dough.

Shape into a ball and bang it hard 5 or 6 times to bring any excess water to the surface. Knead the dough for about 10 minutes until it is very smooth, cover with a cloth or a bowl to keep it warm and leave to relax for about 30 minutes while you prepare the filling.

Makes 450g/1lb basic strudel paste

Savoury vegetable strudel

Savoury cheese, meat or vegetable strudels are sometimes eaten in Eastern Europe and served with soured cream sprinkled with caraway seeds. This vegetable strudel makes an interesting family meal.

175g/6oz bacon or gammon, diced
60ml/4 tablespoons olive oil
1 large onion, chopped
1 courgette/zucchini, sliced
100g/4oz button mushrooms, sliced
2.5ml/½ teaspoon paprika
1.25ml/¼ teaspoon mixed herbs
225g/8oz shredded white cabbage
salt and pepper
150ml/¼ pint/⅝ cup soured cream
100g/4oz/1 cup grated Gruyère/Swiss cheese
½ red pepper, seeded and diced
450g/1lb prepared basic strudel paste

Fry the bacon in its own fat until browned. Add 15ml/1 tablespoon of the oil and sauté the onion until tender. Add the courgette/zucchini and mushrooms and cook for 2-3 minutes. Stir in the paprika and herbs and cook for 1 minute. Add the shredded cabbage and cook gently over low heat for a few minutes until tender. Season to taste and fold in the soured cream with half the quantity of grated cheese and the diced red pepper.

Roll out the strudel paste on a tea-towel, as in the apple strudel recipe above, and brush with olive oil. Spread the filling across the paste to within 2.5cm/1in of the border and roll up in the same manner, brushing wth oil at every turn. Lift the strudel onto a well-greased baking sheet, brush with oil and sprinkle with grated cheese. Bake in a preheated oven at 190°C, 375°F, gas 5 until crisp and golden. Serve hot with soured cream and salad.

Serves 6

Spicy beef strudel

The minced beef filling in this tasty strudel is flavoured with spices and dried apricots in the Middle Eastern manner. Serve it with a green salad or spicy red cabbage.

450g/1lb/2 cups lean minced/ground beef
60ml/4 tablespoons olive or sunflower oil
2 onions, finely chopped
1 clove garlic, crushed
10ml/2 teaspoons tomato paste
2.5ml/½ teaspoon dark molasses sugar
1.25ml/¼ teaspoon each of ground cinnamon, cumin and paprika
60ml/4 tablespoons beef stock or red wine
100g/4oz/¾ cup dried apricots, soaked overnight
3 tomatoes, skinned and chopped
salt and pepper
450g/1lb prepared basic strudel paste

Fry the meat in 15ml/1 tablespoon of the oil until lightly browned. Add the onions and garlic and sauté until soft and translucent. Stir in the tomato paste, sugar and spices and cook for 1 minute. Moisten with the stock or red wine and simmer gently for 4-5 minutes. Drain and chop the apricots and add to the meat mixture with the tomatoes and seasoning.

Roll out the strudel paste on a clean floured tea-towel as described in the apple strudel recipe and spread the meat filling across it to within 2.5cm/1in of the border. Roll up in the same way, brushing with oil at each turn. Place on a greased baking sheet and brush with the remaining oil. Bake in a preheated oven at 190°C, 375°F, gas 5 for 30-35 minutes until crisp and golden. Serve immediately.

Serves 6

West country teabread

In the south-western counties of Devon and Somerset teabreads are sometimes flavoured with cider for these are the principal English cider-producing regions. A bowl of thick, clotted cream is traditionally served with the teabread along with jam and butter.

150g/5oz/1 cup currants
150g/5oz/1 cup sultanas
300ml/½ pint/1¼ medium-sweet cider
150g/5oz/⅝ cup soft brown sugar
20ml/4 teaspoons oil
1 egg, beaten
2.5ml/½ teaspoon each of ground ginger and nutmeg
250g/9oz/2⅜ cups wholemeal flour
5ml/1 teaspoon baking powder

Place the dried fruit and cider in a bowl and let it stand for at least one hour. Beat in the sugar, oil, egg and spices, and the fold in the flour and baking powder.

Pour the mixture into a greased 20cm/8in square or round baking tin and bake in a preheated oven at 170°C, 325°F, gas 3 for 1-1¼ hours. Turn out of the tin and cool. Serve sliced and buttered with jam or honey.

Apple strudel

If you have ever visited Austria, you have almost certainly eaten warm apple strudel with lashings of whipped cream. Well, it is less difficult to make than it looks and tastes best eaten straight from the oven. You can have fun experimenting with other fruits such as cherries, apricots and gooseberries.

675g/1½lb cooking/green apples
juice and grated rind of 1 lemon
2.5ml/½ teaspoon cinnamon
75g/3oz/⅓ cup soft brown sugar
75g/3oz/½ cup sultanas/seedless raisins
75g/3oz/1½ cups fresh breadcrumbs
100g/4oz/½ cup margarine
450g/1lb prepared basic strudel paste

25g/1oz/¼ cup chopped hazelnuts
100g/4oz/¾ cup ground almonds
icing/confectioner's sugar for dusting

Peel and core the apples and slice them thinly. Mix with the lemon juice and grated rind, cinnamon, sugar and sultanas. Cook the breadcrumbs in half the margarine until golden and remove from the heat. Melt the remaining margarine in a clean pan.

Cover the work surface with a clean tea-towel and dredge with flour. Roll out the prepared strudel paste as thinly as possible, working from the centre outwards and gently pulling the dough out until the cloth is covered. It should be so thin that you can read a newspaper through it, although this ideal state of affairs takes practice! Take care that you do not make any holes in the paste. Brush it all over with plenty of melted margarine.

Mix the breadcrumbs, hazelnuts and ground almonds into the apple mixture and spread this filling across the paste to within 2.5cm/1in of the edge. Fold one end of the paste over the filling and the side borders inwards to seal it. Then start rolling up the strudel as you would a Swiss roll by lifting the tea-towel, and brushing wth melted margarine at regular intervals. Place the strudel on a well-greased baking sheet with the folded edge underneath. Brush with more melted margarine and bake in a preheated oven at 190°C, 375°F, gas 5 for about 30 minutes until golden-brown and crisp. Dust with icing/confectioner's sugar and serve warm.

Serves 6

Wholemeal sponge cake

Most of us are easily deceived into thinking that cooking with wholemeal flour produces a heavier, more stodgy result than does white flour. However, this cake, made with wholemeal flour, is as light and airy as any standard fatless sponge cake and the flavour is even better. Fill it with home-made jam or fresh fruit and just a *little* whipped cream, or better still with lemon curd.

75g/3oz/⅜ cup soft brown sugar
3 large eggs
75g/3oz/¾ cup wholemeal flour
jam or cream for filling
caster/superfine sugar for dusting

Whisk the sugar and eggs until they leave a trail from the beaters of the whisk. Fold in the flour lightly, a little at a time, with a metal spoon. Do not over-mix.

Butter two 17.5cm/7in sandwich cake tins and line

the bases with greaseproof paper. Pour in the sponge mixture, smooth the top and bake in a preheated oven at 190°C, 375°F, gas 5 on the middle shelf for about 25 minutes until well-risen and cooked. Allow to cool on a wire cake rack. Sandwich the sponges together with your favourite filling and dust the top of the cake with sugar or decorate with fruit.

Date and rum slices

The addition of rum gives these date slices an unusual flavour. Take care not to overcook them as the texture should be soft, not crisp.

100g/*4oz/1¼ cups wholemeal flour*
pinch salt
5ml/1 teaspoon bicarbonate of soda
150g/5oz/⅝ cup margarine
25g/1oz/⅓ cup wheatgerm
25g/1oz/⅓ cup desiccated coconut
25g/1oz/¼ cup chopped nuts
75g/3oz/⅜ cup molasses sugar
100g/4oz/1⅓ cups oats
150g/5oz/1 cup chopped dried dates
15ml/1 tablespoon dark rum
30ml/2 tablespoons honey

Mix the flour, salt and bicarbonate of soda in a large mixing bowl and rub in the margarine. Stir in the wheatgerm, coconut, nuts, molasses sugar and oats. Press half of the mixture into a 19cm/7½in square shallow, greased baking tin. Press down firmly.

Simmer the dates gently in a small pan with the rum and honey for a few minutes. Spread the date mixture over the crumble mixture and cover with the rest of the crumble, pressing down firmly.

Bake in a preheated oven at 180°C, 350°F, gas 4 for 30 minutes. Cut into slices and allow to cool in the tin before serving.

Makes 10-12 slices

Fruit cake

Probably the most popular cake of all, fruit cake has been eaten in Britain ever since the English discovered the tea plant and invented the custom of taking afternoon tea. Whether tea was an elegant affair served at four o'clock or a family evening meal (high tea), fruit cake was, and still is, a favourite cake. This recipe departs from the norm and uses wholemeal flour, brown sugar, spices and orange juice for a delicious flavour and moist texture.

200g/7oz/⅞ cup margarine
200g/7oz/1 cup soft brown sugar
3 eggs
75g/3oz/¾ cup chopped walnuts
50g/2oz/½ cup chopped hazelnuts
100g/4oz/1¼ cups desiccated coconut
50g/2oz/⅜ cup ground almonds
2.5ml/½ teaspoon ground ginger
1.25ml/¼ teaspoon ground cinnamon
100g/4oz/⅓ cup glacé cherries, halved
200g/7oz/1⅛ cups mixed fruit (currants, sultanas, raisins)
250g/9oz/2⅜ cups wholemeal flour
10ml/2 teaspoons baking powder
150ml/¼ pint/⅝ cup orange juice
30ml/2 tablespoons water
caster sugar for dusting

Cream the margarine and sugar and gradually beat in the eggs. Add the nuts, spices, cherries and dried fruit. Stir in the flour and baking powder and fold in the orange juice and water. The mixture should be of a soft, dropping consistency.

Line a greased 20cm/8in cake tin with baking paper. Bake in a preheated oven at 170°C, 325°F, gas 3 for about 1½ hours until the cake is well-risen and thoroughly cooked. Place on a low shelf of the oven throughout cooking — the top of the tin should not be higher than half-way up the oven if the cake is to rise and not collapse. Cool in the tin and turn out onto a serving plate. Dust the top with caster sugar. This cake improves if it is kept in an airtight tin for 2 or 3 days before cutting.

Special dark chocolate cake

This rich, dark cake is flavoured with ginger, apricots and nuts. The result is a sensational cake — deliciously moist and spicy. You need only eat thin slices because it is so rich. It will keep for 2-3 weeks if stored in an airtight tin or container.

50g/2oz/⅜ cup dried apricots
225g/8oz/1 cup margarine
225g/8oz/1 cup soft brown sugar
3 eggs, beaten
225g/8oz/2¼ cups wholemeal flour
pinch of salt

10ml/2 teaspoons baking powder
30ml/2 tablespoons cocoa powder
30ml/2 tablespoons water
50g/2oz/½ cup chopped walnuts
25g/1oz stem ginger in syrup, chopped
25g/1oz crystallised ginger, chopped
Coating:
75g/3oz plain chocolate
15g/½oz/1 tablespoon margarine
walnut halves and chopped crystallised ginger

Soak the dried apricots overnight. Cream the margarine and sugar until soft and light. Gradually beat in the eggs and then gently fold in the flour with a metal spoon. Add the salt and baking powder. Mix the cocoa with the water to form a soft paste and add to the mixture with the drained apricots, walnuts and ginger. Mix to a soft, dropping consistency with a little water. Pour the mixture into a greased and lined 20cm/8in round cake tin and bake in a preheated oven at 170°C, 325°F, gas 3 for about 1½ hours, or until cooked through. The top of the tin should not come above the centre of the oven.

Leave the cake to cool in the tin for 30 minutes and then turn out onto a wire cooling tray. Prepare the chocolate coating: place the chocolate and margarine in a double boiler or in a basin over a pan of cold water. Bring the water slowly to the boil and then remove from the heat. When the coating mixture has melted and blended, spread it over the top and around the sides of the cake. Decorate with walnuts and crystallised ginger and leave to harden.

Old-fashioned shortbread

We tend to associate shortbread with Scotland although several versions of it exist in other parts of the British Isles. In Scotland it is sometimes referred to as bride's cake after the old custom of showering the bride with crumbled shortbread as she crossed the threshold of the marital home for the first time. You can vary this recipe by adding chopped nuts, a little vanilla essence or even chopped candied peel.

150g/5oz/1½ cups wholemeal flour
25g/1oz/3 tablespoons rice flour or semolina
50g/2oz/¼ cup soft brown sugar
100g/4oz/½ cup margarine or butter

Place the flours and brown sugar in a mixing bowl and rub in the margarine. Mix to a firm dough and turn out onto a lightly floured board and knead. Roll the short-

bread out on a baking sheet and cut into a round, fluted cake about 5mm/¼in thick, using a fluted metal flan ring as a cutter. Prick all over with a fork.

Bake in a preheated oven at 180°C, 350°F, gas 4 for 20-25 minutes until the shortbread is pale on top and golden-brown underneath. Divide into triangle-shaped wedges while warm and leave to cool. Do not worry if the shortbread seems a little soft when you take it out of the oven. It will crisp up and harden as it cools. Dredge the shortbread with caster sugar.

Kourabiedes

These small Greek shortbreads, each topped with a tiny clove and dusted with icing/confectioner's sugar, are traditionally made at Christmas to honour the spices brought by the Three Kings to Bethleham. They are usually eaten late in the afternoon after the siesta but, of course, you can enjoy them any time.

225g/8oz/1 cup butter
45ml/3 tablespoons caster sugar
1 egg yolk
15ml/1 tablespoon ouzo or brandy
50g/2oz/½ cup chopped toasted almonds
65g/2½oz/½ cup ground almonds
225g/8oz/2¼ cups plain flour
5ml/1 teaspoon baking powder
cloves for decoration
350g/12oz/2 cups icing/confectioner's sugar

Cream the butter and sugar until creamy and light. Beat in the egg yolk and then add the ouzo or brandy and chopped and ground almonds. Gently fold in the sieved flour and baking powder. Chill the mixture in the refrigerator for 15 minutes.

Roll into balls the size of a walnut and place on an *ungreased* baking sheet. Pinch the top of each ball twice to make two small indentations. This gives them their characteristic shape when cooked. Place a small clove in the centre of each. Bake in a preheated oven at 170°C, 325°F, gas 3 for 20 minutes, taking care that they do not brown.

Allow them to cool for 10 minutes on the baking sheet before transferring to foil or vegetable parchment which has been well dusted with icing/confectioner's sugar. Dredge the kourabiedes with the remaining sugar and leave until completely cool. Pack into an airtight tin with a little more sugar and resist the temptation to eat them for 48 hours. This allows the spicy flavour to develop.

Ginger and orange shortbread

The addition of grated citrus fruit rind and spice to a basic shortbread mixture produces delicious crisp biscuits. An interesting variation is to substitute the grated rind of a lemon and 2.5ml/½ teaspoon cinnamon for the orange rind and ginger in this recipe, and follow the method below.

100g/4oz/½ cup margarine
50g/2oz/¼ cup soft brown sugar
grated rind of 1 orange
5ml/1 teaspoon ground ginger
25g/1oz/3 tablespoons rice flour/semolina
150g/5oz/1¼ cups plain flour

Cream the butter and sugar until smooth and creamy. Add the orange rind, ginger and the two flours. Knead well and roll out to fill a 20cm/8in square greased baking tin. Prick the shortbread all over with a fork and bake in a preheated oven at 180°C, 350°F, gas 4 for about 20 minutes or until lightly browned. Placed on the centre shelf of the oven.

Cut into squares or fingers and leave the shortbread to cool in the tin. Store in an airtight container.

Apricot honey squares

These delicious squares make nutritious snacks between meals or can be served at afternoon tea. They are simple to make and well worth the effort as they are heathier than most cakes and biscuits.

100g/4oz/¾ cup dried apricots
100g/4oz/1⅛ cups wholemeal flour + pinch salt
100g/4oz/1⅓ cups rolled oats
25g/1oz/⅓ cup wheatgerm
150g/5oz/⅝ cup margarine
75g/3oz/⅜ cup dark Barbados sugar
50g/2oz/¼ cup Demerara or soft brown sugar
50g/2oz/⅔ cup dessicated coconut
5ml/1 teaspoon bicarbonate of soda
10ml/2 teaspoons boiling water

Soak the apricots in sufficient water to cover them for about two hours. Then gently simmer over a low heat until softened but still firm. Drain off the liquid.

Place the flour, oats and wheatgerm in a bowl and rub in the margarine. Add the sugars and coconut. Dissolve the bicarbonate of soda in the boiling water and stir into the mixture.

Grease a 19cm/7½in square shallow baking tin and press half of the crumble mixture over the base. Press down hard and cover with a layer of the cooked, drained apricots. Top with the remaining crumble mixture and press down firmly so that the surface is smooth and even.

Bake in a preheated oven at 180°C, 350°F, gas 4 for 30-35 minutes, taking care that the top does not overcook and brown. Cool and cut into squares.

Makes 18 squares

Florentines

We always make florentines at Christmas-time. Eaten in large quantities they are obviously not among the healthiest foods as they are very rich, but we find them irresistible with coffee at the end of a meal.

100g/4oz/½ cup margarine
100g/4oz/½ cup caster sugar
15ml/1 tablespoon plain flour
100g/4oz/¾ cup flaked almonds, chopped
75g/3oz/⅓ cup glacé cherries, chopped
50g/2oz/⅓ cup sultanas/seedless raisins
50g/2oz/½ cup, candied peel (citron, lemon or orange), chopped
25g/1oz/¼ cup nibbed almonds
15ml/1 tablespoon cream
50g/2oz plain chocolate

Melt the fat over low heat and add the sugar. Stir gently until completely dissolved. Bring to the boil and boil hard for 1 minute, stirring all the time. Mix in the flour and remove from the heat. Add the remaining ingredients (except the chocolate).

Line a baking tray/cookie sheet with silicone or non-stick baking paper and drop the mixture in little heaps onto the tray. Keep the mounds well apart as they will spread out while they cook. Bake in a preheated oven at 180°C, 350°F, gas 4 for 10 minutes. Remove from the oven and using a well-oiled palette knife or plain round cutter, shape the florentines into neat circles. Return to the oven for another 2-3 minutes and then allow to cool.

When the florentines are set and cold, remove them from the paper. Heat the chocolate until it melts in a bain-marie or in a basin suspended over hot water. Coat the base of each florentine with melted chocolate and run a fork or a confectionery comb across it before the chocolate hardens. Leave to cool.

Opposite: Wholemeal sponge (see page 17), savoury cheese scones (see page 22), nut and raisin muffins (see page 32)

Carrot cake

Although we tend to eat carrots only in savoury dishes nowadays, they used to be made into cakes and puddings in the eighteenth century. The growing interest in healthy eating and wholefoods has led to a revival in some of the old recipes, and carrot cake, which has been popular for a long time in the United States, is now being eaten again in Britain and Australia. This particular version is very moist and keeps well.

175g/6oz/¾ cup margarine
175g/6oz/¾ cup soft brown sugar
3 eggs
100g/4oz finely grated carrot
50g/2oz/⅓ cup raisins
50g/2oz/⅓ cup chopped dates
2.5ml/½ teaspoon ground cinnamon
1.25ml/¼ teaspoon ground nutmeg
25g/1oz/⅛ cup desiccated coconut
25g/1oz/¼ cup chopped walnuts
175g/6oz/1½ cups wholemeal flour
pinch of salt
5ml/1 teaspoon baking powder
Topping:
25g/1oz/¼ cup chopped nuts (walnuts, hazelnuts or
    almonds)

Cream the margarine and sugar until soft and fluffy and gradually beat in the eggs. Fold in the grated carrot, fruit, spices and nuts. Sift the flour with the salt and baking powder and fold into the cake mixture, which should be of a soft, dropping consistency. Add a little orange or lemon juice to moisten it if necessary.

Pour the mixture into a well-greased 20cm/8in square cake tin and sprinkle the chopped nuts over the top. Bake in a preheated oven at 180°C, 350°F, gas 4 for 40-45 minutes. Cool and serve.

Honey squares

These delicious little cakes are flavoured with honey and spices and are always popular. Perhaps because of its unique antiseptic nature, various mystic and almost magical properties have been attributed to honey since ancient times. But in addition to being a great healer, honey is deliciously moist in cakes and a natural sweetener.

225g/8oz/2¼ cups wholemeal flour
pinch of salt
grated rind of 1 lemon
2.5ml/½ teaspoon ground cinnamon

1.25ml/¼ teaspoon ground nutmeg
pinch of mixed spice
75g/3oz/6 tablespoons margarine
225ml/8floz/1 cup honey
1 large egg, beaten
juice of ½ lemon
60ml/4 tablespoons milk
5ml/1 teaspoon bicarbonate of soda/baking soda
45ml/3 tablespoons flaked almonds

Mix the flour and salt with the grated lemon rind and spices. Gently heat the margarine in a pan and add the honey. Warm the mixture gently without overheating it. Pour onto the flour mixture and mix thoroughly with the beaten egg and lemon juice. Do not beat.

Heat the milk and bicarbonate of soda/baking soda until frothy and stir into the flour and honey mixture. Pour into a greased square or rectangular cake tin and scatter with flaked almonds. Bake in a preheated oven at 180°C, 350°F, gas 4 for 25 minutes, or until golden and firm to the touch. Cool in the tin for 10 minutes and then cut into squares and cool thoroughly on a wire rack.

Savoury cheese scones

These unusual scones have a crisp, golden cheese topping and are particularly moist due to the addition of a small carton of plain yoghurt. Eat them at tea-time, or split them and fill with salad, prawns and curd cheese, or egg and cress for a lunch or supper snack.

225g/8oz/2½ cups wholewheat flour
2.5ml/½ teaspoon salt
5ml/1 teaspoon baking powder
2.5ml/½ teaspoon dry mustard
pinch cayenne pepper
40g/1½ oz/¼ cup margarine
15ml/1 tablespoon grated Parmesan cheese
100g/4oz/1 cup grated Swiss (or Cheddar) cheese
45ml/3 tablespoons milk
150ml/¼ pint/⅝ cup plain yoghurt

Place the flour, salt, baking powder, mustard and cayenne in a bowl and rub in the margarine until the mixture resembles fine breadcrumbs. Add the grated Parmesan and 75g/3oz/¾ cup of the grated Gruyère cheese. Mix in the milk and yoghurt to form a soft, pliable dough.

Turn the dough onto a lightly floured board and knead lightly. Roll the mixture out to a thickness of 1.25cm/½in and cut out the scones with a 5cm/2in plain cutter. Place the scones on a well-greased baking sheet, brush with a little milk and sprinkle the tops with the remaining grated cheese.

Bake in a preheated oven at 200°C, 400°F, gas 6 for 15-20 minutes until well-risen and golden-brown. Serve hot with butter or fill when cold with the filling of your choice. If stored in an airtight tin, the scones will keep for two to three days, but they are at their best when eaten really fresh.

Makes 10-12 scones

Greek semolina cakes

These diamond-shaped cakes have a tangy sweet flavour as they are steeped in a lime-flavoured syrup before serving. Semolina and almonds are common ingredients in Greek cakes and pastries.

100g/4oz/½ cup margarine
175g/6oz/¾ cup soft brown sugar
2 drops vanilla essence
2 eggs
350g/12oz/2 cups semolina
5ml/1 teaspoon cream of tartar
2.5ml/½ teaspoon bicarbonate of soda/baking soda
200ml/6floz/¾ cup plain yoghurt
30ml/2 tablespoons split almonds
Syrup:
150g/5oz/⅔ cup sugar
100ml/4floz/½ cup water
juice of 1 lime

Cream the butter and sugar and then beat in the vanilla and the eggs, one at a time. Sieve the semolina, cream of tartar and bicarbonate of soda and fold gently into the mixture. Stir in the yoghurt and pour into a greased 25cm/10in square baking tin. Arrange the split almonds in diagonal lines across the top of the cake mixture. Bake in a preheated oven at 180°C, 350°F, gas 4 for 30 minutes and allow to cool in the tin.

Meanwhile, make the syrup: place the sugar, water and lime juice in a pan and stir over low heat until the sugar has completely dissolved. Bring to the boil and boil rapidly until thick and syrupy. Remove from the heat and cool. Spoon the syrup over the warm cake and leave in the tin until it is quite cold before cutting the cake into diamond shapes and serving.

Date and walnut loaf

This old favourite always goes down well with everybody. It has a pleasantly moist texture and is usually served sliced and buttered.

225ml/8 floz/1 cup water
175g/6oz/¾ cup soft brown sugar
25g/1oz/2 tablespoons margarine
5ml/1 teaspoon bicarbonate of soda/baking soda
100g/4oz/¾ cup chopped dates
2 eggs, beaten
225g/8oz/2¼ cups plain or wholemeal flour
100g/4oz/¾ cup chopped walnuts

Bring the water to the boil in a pan and add the brown sugar, margarine, baking soda and dates. Reduce the heat and stir over low heat until the sugar dissolves. Mix in the beaten egg and then the flour and walnuts. Pour the mixture into a greased and lined baking tin and bake in a preheated oven at 190°C, 375°F, gas 5 for about 25 minutes.

Dundee cake

This rich traditional fruit cake will stay fresh and moist for several months if wrapped in foil and stored in an airtight tin. Leave it a few days before cutting.

225g/8oz/1 cup margarine
225g/8oz/1 cup soft brown sugar
5 eggs
grated rind of 1 lemon and 1 orange
100g/4oz/1 cup ground almonds
275g/10oz/2¾ cups plain flour
100g/4oz/1 cup chopped mixed candied peel
175g/6oz/1 cup sultanas/seedless raisins
175g/6oz/1 cup currants
175g/6oz/1 cup raisins
100g/4oz/½ cup glacé cherries
50g/2oz/½ cup chopped walnuts
pinch each of ground ginger and nutmeg
juice of 1 lemon or 1 orange
2-3 drops almond essence
50ml/2 floz/¼ cup sherry
25g/1oz/¼ cup split blanched almonds

Cream the margarine and sugar until soft and fluffy. Beat in the eggs, one at a time. Beat in the grated lemon and orange rind and fold in the ground almonds. Fold in the flour and the fruit and nuts alternately, until both are mixed into the cake mixture. Add the spices and the fruit juice together with the almond essence and sherry. The mixture should be of a soft dropping consistency. Add more lemon or orange juice if the mixture is too stiff. Pour into a prepared (greased and lined) 20cm/8in cake tin. Arrange the split almonds in concentric circles on top (see picture on page 33) and bake in a preheated oven at 170°C, 325°F, gas 3 for 30 minutes, and then reduce the heat to 150°C, 300°F, gas 2 for a further 1½ hours. Be sure to place the cake on the lowest shelf in the oven.

Bread-making

Bread is still the 'staff of life' to many people and is eaten at most, if not all, of our meals — toasted for breakfast, sliced and buttered for lunch, and in crusty pieces or rolls with dinner. It is so easy to bake your own fragrant, crusty loaves that it seems a shame to buy bread, especially the mass-produced, ready-sliced polystyrene textured sort. There is nothing to compare with the delicious aroma of hot, freshly baked crisp loaves. More people are now baking their own bread and discovering that it is really very simple and satisfying and not the complicated process they imagined it to be. All you need are four basic ingredients — flour, yeast, salt and liquid.

Flour
Your choice of flour is all-important and will affect the flavour and quality of the bread you wish to bake. The important thing is to use a strong bread flour with a high gluten content. Gluten is a rubber-like substance which stretches when it is heated. It traps the carbon-dioxide released by the yeast and gives the dough its volume and texture. Hard wheat flours like strong plain white flour, wholemeal, granary and stone-ground wholewheat flours are all high in gluten and suitable for bread-making. For your health's sake, choose a wholemeal or granary flour containing bran and wheatgerm to which nothing has been added or taken away. For more information refer to page 8.

Yeast
This is the living organism that causes bread to rise. In warm, moist conditions, it grows and produces carbon-dioxide which is trapped by gluten in the flour. Yeast comes in various guises. Fresh putty-like yeast can be purchased at most bakeries and health food stores. It should be moist, not dry and crumbly. Store what you don't use straight away in a polythene bag in the refrigerator. It will stay fresh for 2-3 weeks.

Dried yeast is available in most supermarkets and has a shelf life of 6 months. Sugar is needed to activate it. Always sprinkle dried yeast onto tepid water in which the sugar has been dissolved. Leave for about 10-15 minutes to go frothy before adding the flour. It is more concentrated than fresh yeast so, as a general rule, 15ml/1 tablespoon dried yeast is equivalent to 25g/1oz fresh yeast.

A new dried yeast which does not need reconstituting before use is now available. It may be mixed directly into the flour with the liquid to make a dough and gives excellent results.

Salt
This is very important in bread-making and all too often forgotten when you are in a hurry. Not only does salt improve the flavour of the loaves but using too little can cause the dough to rise too fast and produce a crumbly texture. Too much salt, on the other hand, can retard the action of the yeast and causes an uneven textured, heavy loaf with holes.

Liquid
Water or milk are the usual liquids used in bread-making, and it is vitally important that the liquid should be at the right temperature. Heat, not cold, kills yeast, and the liquid should never be warmer than blood heat (37°C). So always use tepid liquids and test with your finger before adding the yeast. The amount used will vary according to the type of flour. Wholemeal and strong white flours that have a high gluten content absorb more liquid than softer flours. Milk gives the bread a softer crust than water and helps it to stay fresher longer.

Enriching the dough
You can enrich bread dough with fat, eggs, malt, molassses, honey or oil. These will all improve the colour and flavour and give a moister texture.

Mixing
Place the flour and salt in a large mixing bowl and make a well in the centre. Add the yeast mixture and any enriching agents and stir well with your hands or a wooden spoon to form a soft dough that leaves the sides of the bowl clean. You can use the dough hook on an electric food mixer or the plastic dough blades of a food processor.

Kneading
The way in which you knead the dough and the length of time taken affects the finished texture of the bread. Kneading strengthens the dough, develops the elasticity

of the gluten in the flour and gives a better rise. Knead the dough on a clean, lightly floured surface, folding the dough inwards towards you with one hand while pushing it away from you with the other. Give the dough a quarter-turn and repeat. After 10 minutes or so, the dough should be really smooth and elastic. You can be rough with dough and slap it around.

Rising

Yeast dough should always be allowed to rise at least once before it is baked. During this time it should be covered to keep it moist and warm and to prevent a skin forming on top. The temperature should be constant, whether it is at room temperature or in a warm place to speed up the process. Place the dough in a bowl and cover with a clean cloth or put inside a large oiled poythene bag. Stand it on a sunny window sill, on top of the central heating boiler, on the back of a warm stove or even in the airing cupboard. We usually stand the bowl containing the dough in a larger bowl of warm water. It takes about one hour for the dough to rise in a warm place or 2-3 hours at room temperature. It is ready when it has doubled in bulk and springs back into shape when pressed lightly.

Knocking back and shaping

After the dough has risen you must knock it back to its original size. Knead well for 3-4 minutes to knock out the air bubbles or your finished loaf will have an uneven texture full of holes. Shape the dough into loaves or rolls and place in well-greased loaf tins or on greased baking sheets. The dough can be shaped in any way you like — plaited, slashed, indented, with a cottage top-knot, in crescents or whirls.

Proving

The dough should be allowed to rise a second time before baking. Cover the tins or baking sheets with a clean cloth or place in a greased polythene bag and leave in a warm place until the dough doubles in size or rises to the top of the tins. If the oven is heated ready for baking, place the tins on top of the cooker. Do not over-prove the dough or the finished bread will have an uneven texture. Glaze the loaves with salt water for a crisp crust; beaten egg or milk for a softer, shinier crust. For an attractive finish, you can sprinkle the dough with sesame, poppy, caraway, celery or fennel seeds, cracked wheat or crushed sea salt.

Baking and storing

Always bake bread in a very hot preheated oven (usually 230°C, 450°F, gas 8). The bread is ready when you tap the base of the loaf with your knuckles and it sounds hollow. Remove from the tins and cool on a wire rack. Store in an airtight tin or container, or wrap in foil and freeze until required.

Avoiding failure

Bread-making needs practice and you may not get it right the first time. Here are some of the things that can go wrong and some hints on how to avoid them.

A cracked crust may be caused by using too soft a flour, insufficient fermentation or cramming too much dough into a small tin. So use a strong flour and give the yeast time to work.

If your bread has a heavy texture, you may have used too much salt, left it in too warm a place to rise or kneaded it insufficiently. Kneading is important as too little can cause an uneven texture with large holes, as can over-proving and excessive salt.

If your bread does not keep well and goes stale quickly, you may be using too much yeast or too soft a flour. So do not rush your bread-making and follow the instructions given in the recipes carefully. In this way, you can avoid the pitfalls and produce perfect loaves every time.

Basic wholemeal bread

This recipe for wholemeal bread can be used to make one large loaf or 16 rolls. It also makes a good base for pizzas if rolled out very thinly.

450g/1lb/4½ cups wholemeal flour
2.5ml/½ teaspoon salt
25g/1oz/2 tablespoons margarine or lard/shortening
15g/½oz fresh yeast or 10ml/2 teaspoons dried yeast
2.5ml/½ teaspoon sugar
300ml/½ pint/1¼ cups tepid water
milk or beaten egg to glaze

Tip the flour and salt into a mixing bowl and rub in the fat. Blend the fresh yeast with the sugar and tepid water, or sprinkle the dried yeast onto the water in which the sugar has been dissolved and leave until frothy. Mix the yeast mixture into the flour to form a ball of dough and knead until smooth and elastic. Replace the dough in the bowl, cover and leave in a warm place to rise (about 1 hour).

Turn the risen dough out onto a lightly floured surface and knock back to its original size, kneading lightly for 2-3 minutes. Shape into a large loaf or small rolls and place in a greased loaf tin or on greased baking sheets. Leave in a warm place to prove, covered with a cloth or some greased polythene. When the dough rises to the top of the tin, glaze it with milk or beaten egg and bake near the top of a preheated oven at 230°C, 450°F, gas 8. After 15 minutes, reduce the temperature to 200°C, 400°F, gas 6 for a further 30 minutes until the bread is cooked and turns out of the tin easily and the base sounds hollow when tapped with your knuckles. Turn the loaf out onto a wire tray and cool. Bread rolls will require less cooking time — test them after 20 minutes.

Makes one 450g/1lb loaf

Basic white bread

Although wholemeal or granary bread made with stoneground 100 per cent wholemeal flour is better for you than white bread, we have included a basic recipe should you want to make one of the speciality breads pictured on page 28. Both the harvest wheat sheave loaf and the plate of loaves and fishes look complicated but they are simple to make and assemble if you have the patience and the application. This basic milk bread recipe can be used for either, as well as for white loaves and rolls.

675g/1½lb/6¾ cups strong white bread flour
5ml/1 teaspoon salt
40g/1½oz/3 tablespoons margarine
25g/1oz fresh yeast or 15ml/1 tablespoon dried yeast
2.5ml/½ teaspoon sugar
400ml/14floz/1¾ cups warm milk
beaten egg to glaze

Sift the flour into a large mixing bowl and rub in the margarine. Blend the fresh yeast with the sugar to a cream and mix with the warm (at blood heat) milk. Or sprinkle the dried yeast onto the warm milk to which the sugar has been added and leave until frothy. Add the yeast liquid to the flour and mix to form an elastic dough.

Knead the dough on a lightly floured work-top for about 10 minutes until smooth and pliable, adding more flour if necessary. Place the dough in a large oiled polythene bag or in a clean bowl, cover with a cloth and leave in a warm place to rise. When it has doubled in bulk, knock it back and then shape into loaves or rolls. Place in greased baking tins or on a well-greased baking sheet, cover with a cloth and leave in a warm place to prove.

When the loaves rise to the top of the tins, brush them with beaten egg and bake in a very hot preheated oven at 230°C, 450°F, gas 8 for 10-15 minutes, and then lower the temperature to 200°C, 400°F, gas 6 for a further 25-30 minutes. When they are crisp and golden, remove from the tins and tap the bases with your knuckles. If they sound hollow, they are cooked. Remove and cool on a wire rack. Rolls will need less cooking time (about 25-30 minutes in total).

Makes 675g/1½lb dough or 2 loaves

Granary bread

This moist, nutty flavoured loaf is made from wholewheat flour mixed with cracked wheat, bran and wheatgerm for added goodness and a crunchy texture. It keeps well (up to a week in a bread bin) and freezes successfully so that you can bake a large batch and freeze any loaves you do not mean to eat immediately. All the ingredients are readily available from good health food stores.

1.5kg/3lb/13½ cups wholewheat flour
15ml/1 tablespoon salt
50g/2oz/¼ cup vegetable margarine
350g/12oz/2 cups cracked wheat
25g/1oz/⅓ cup wheatgerm
50g/2oz/⅔ cup bran
45ml/3 tablespoons dark brown sugar
30ml/2 tablespoons molasses
900ml/1½ pints/3¾ cups warm water
40g/1½oz fresh yeast (or 20g/¾oz dried yeast)
beaten egg, milk or salt water to glaze
cracked wheat for decoration

Place the flour and salt in a large mixing bowl and rub in the margarine. Stir in the cracked wheat, wheatgerm, bran and brown sugar.

Blend the molasses and warm water and add 30ml/2 tablespoons of this mixture to the fresh yeast and stir until mixed. If you are using dried yeast, sprinkle it onto the molasses and water mixture and leave in a warm place until it bubbles up the sides of the dish and goes frothy.

Make a well in the centre of the flour and dried ingredients and pour in the yeast and the remaining liquid. Mix to form a smooth dough which leaves the sides of the bowl clean. Add more water if necessary as the dough must not be dry. Turn out onto a lightly floured board and knead well. Return the kneaded dough to the bowl, cover with a cloth and leave at room temperature for 2 hours. Alternatively, for a quick rise, place the bowl in a warm place and leave for about 45 minutes until well-risen.

Knock the dough back and knead again. Cut into 3 pieces and shape into loaves. Put each in a well-greased 450g/1lb loaf tin and leave to prove until the dough rises to the top of the tins. Glaze the tops with beaten egg, milk or salt water. Sprinkle over a little cracked wheat if wished for an attractive finish. Place in a preheated oven at 230°C, 450°F, gas 8 for 30-45 minutes. The loaves are cooked when they are brown and crusty on the outside and the base sounds hollow when tapped with your knuckles. Cool on a wire tray.

Makes three 450g/1lb loaves

Malt bread

This sticky, sweet bread, flavoured with malt extract, fruit and nuts, is delicious at tea-time served with butter and jam. It stays moist for up to a week if stored in an airtight tin. Malt is made from fermented barley and brings a characteristically strong flavour to bread.

150g/5oz malt extract
100g/4oz molasses
25g/1oz/2 tablespoons margarine
350ml/12floz/1½ cups water
25g/1oz fresh yeast
400g/14oz/4 cups wholemeal flour
5ml/1 teaspoon salt
225g/8oz/1⅓ cups sultanas/seedless raisins
50g/2oz/½ cup chopped walnuts
Glaze:
15ml/1 tablespoon milk
15ml/1 tablespoon water
15ml/1 tablespoon sugar

Weigh a small saucepan and then measure in the malt extract and molasses. Add the water and margarine and warm gently over low heat until the margarine melts. Cool to blood heat, and then pour a little onto the yeast. Mix well.

Place the flour, salt, nuts and sultanas in a mixing bowl. Make a well in the centre and pour in the yeast mixture and the remaining liquid. Beat well for about 8-10 minutes.

Pour the mixture into 2 greased 450g/1lb loaf tins and leave in a warm place to prove. When the dough rises to the top of the tins, bake the loaves in a preheated oven at 200°C, 400°F, gas 6 for 45 minutes.

Stir the ingredients for the glaze in a small pan over low heat until the sugar dissolves. Brush over the top of the cooked loaves and leave to cool.

Makes two 450g/1lb loaves

Herb and garlic bread

A fragrant, warm herb loaf is the perfect complement to cheese, olives and pâté. Spread it with unsalted butter or margarine and just enjoy it.

350g/12oz/3½ cups wholemeal flour
1.25ml/¼ teaspoon salt
2.5ml/½ teaspoon each of chopped dill, basil, oregano and thyme
1 small onion, finely chopped
1 clove garlic, crushed
15g/½oz fresh yeast or 10ml/2 teaspoons dried yeast
200ml/6floz/¾ cup milk and water
30ml/2 tablespoons vegetable oil
1 egg, beaten
milk or beaten egg to glaze

Place the flour, salt and herbs in a large mixing bowl and mix in the onion and garlic. Blend the fresh yeast with the tepid water and milk *or* sprinkle the dried yeast onto the tepid liquid and leave until it becomes frothy. Make a well in the centre of the flour and gradually mix in the yeast mixture, vegetable oil and beaten egg to form a ball of dough, which leaves the sides of the bowl clean. Knead well until the dough is really elastic and leave to rise in a warm place until doubled in size.

Knock the dough back and knead well. Shape into a loaf and place in a well-greased loaf tin. Leave to prove in a warm place covered with a cloth or some oiled polythene. When the dough rises to the top of the tin, glaze with milk or beaten egg and bake in a preheated oven at 230°C, 450°F, gas 8 for about 30-40 minutes.

Overleaf: a selection of unusual breads and rolls:

1 Wholemeal bread	5 Granary bread	9 Malt bread
2 Cheese and walnut loaf	6 Rye bread	10 Plate of loaves and fishes
3 Limpa bread	7 Smoked mackerel loaf	11 White bread
4 Harvest sheave	8 Wholemeal rolls	

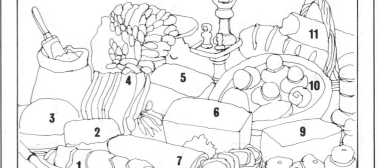

Rye bread

This is a closely-textured square loaf which tends to be fairly dense and heavy as there is little gluten in rye flour to allow the bread to rise. We have used equal quantities of dark rye and wholewheat flours for a really dark, characteristically rye-flavoured loaf. Rye bread is eaten widely in the Soviet Union, Eastern Europe, Scandinavia and Germany. It is often served with smoked or marinated fish, caviare, gherkins and soured cream, or as a bread base for smorrebrod (the Danish open sandwich). It is sometimes flavoured with anise caraway or fennel seeds and darkened with black treacle or molasses. To produce a traditional 'sour' rye bread, you can keep a little dough from the first baking and place it in a covered container. Put in a warm place for 2-3 days to 'sour' the dough and add to the next fresh lot of dough with the new yeast. This sourdough starter will produce a characteristic 'sour' flavour as in the American sourdough breads. We have chosen a German version of rye bread in which the loaf is weighted in the baking tin during cooking to prevent it rising further. This produces a densely textured loaf which is deliciously moist.

400g/14oz/4 cups dark rye flour
400g/14oz/4 cups wholewheat flour
2.5ml/½ teaspoon salt
5ml/1 teaspoon anise seed
5ml/1 teaspoon caraway seed
50g/2oz/¼ cup margarine
15g/¼oz fresh yeast
5ml/1 teaspoon honey
15ml/1 tablespoon molasses
550ml/1 pint/2½ cups warm water

Mix the flours and salt in a large mixing bowl. Add the anise and caraway seeds and rub in the fat. Blend the fresh yeast and honey until creamy. Mix the molasses into the warm water. Add the yeast and molasses mixtures to the flour and mix to form a soft dough. Knead lightly for about 5 minutes, replace in a bowl, cover with a cloth and leave in a warm place to rise for about 1 hour.

Knock back the dough and knead well. Divide into 2 pieces and shape into loaves. Grease two 450g/1lb baking tins and half-fill each with the dough. Leave in a warm place to prove for about 30 minutes or so until the loaves rise about three-quarters of the way up the tins. Place the tins upside-down on a greased baking sheet with weights on top of each tin.

Bake in a preheated oven at 230°C, 450°F, gas 8 and after 15 minutes reduce the oven temperature to 200°C, 400°F, gas 6. Bake for a further 30 minutes until the loaves are golden-brown and sound hollow when you tap the base. Cool on a wire tray and serve with smoked fish, or slice thinly for smorrebrod.

Makes two 450g/1lb loaves

Smoked mackerel loaf

Long, thin bread loaves flavoured with smoked fish and herbs are extremely popular in Germany. Fragrant and savoury, they always go down well at informal buffets, picnics and barbecues.

225g/8oz wholemeal bread dough (see recipe on page 25)
350g/12oz smoked mackerel fillets
15ml/1 tablespoon chopped fennel herb
freshly ground black pepper
beaten egg to glaze

Roll out the dough on a lightly floured board to a 30cm/12in square. Remove any skin and tiny bones from the mackerel and flake the flesh with a fork. Scatter the flaked fish and chopped feathery fennel over the dough square and sprinkle with freshly ground black pepper. Roll up tightly as you would a Swiss roll. Brush with beaten egg to glaze and place on a greased baking sheet. Leave in a warm place to prove for about 15-20 minutes.

Bake in a preheated oven at 220°C, 425°F, gas 7 for 30-40 minutes until cooked and golden-brown. Serve warm or cold cut into slices and buttered.

Plate of loaves and fishes

This traditional bread derives from the feeding of the five thousand by Christ when he turned the five loaves and two fishes into enough food to feed the assembled crowds. It is fun to make and serve at Easter. Make it with the basic white bread dough (see recipe on page 26).

675g/1½lb basic white bread dough
beaten egg to glaze, mixed with 2.5ml/½ teaspoon salt
2 currants

Divide the dough into 2 pieces. Set one aside and roll out the other into a large circle to make the base (or 'plate'). This should be as large as your baking sheet will allow. Grease the baking sheet and gently place the circle of dough on top.

Divide the remaining dough into 9 pieces. Shape 5 into cottage loaves with little topknots. To do this, cut off one-third of each piece of dough and shape the remaining dough into a perfectly round roll. Shape the smaller piece of dough into a smaller roll. Moisten the larger roll with beaten egg or water and place the smaller one on top, pressing down through the centre with your forefinger. Make the remaining 4 cottage rolls in the same way.

Use another 2 pieces of dough to make the 2 fish. Roll each out to an oval shape and then flatten them slightly, and use a sharp knife or scissors to cut out the tail. Cut out the scales on top with a sharp knife or scissors and use currants for the eyes.

Brush the circular dough base with the beaten egg and arrange the cottage rolls and fishes on top (see photograph on page 29). Take one of the remaining 2 pieces of dough and divide into 3. Roll each piece out into a long sausage shape and plait together. Do the same with the remaining piece of dough. Join the plaits together with beaten egg and use to encircle the dough 'plate' on the baking sheet. Brush the whole thing with the beaten egg and salt mixture, cover loosely with a cloth and leave in a warm place to prove.

When it is well-risen, brush with more beaten egg and bake in a preheated oven at 230°C, 450°F, gas 8 for 10-15 minutes, and then lower the temperature to 200°C, 400°F, gas 6 for a further 30 minutes until crisp and golden-brown. Cool and serve with butter.

Bagels

These traditional Jewish circular bread rolls were first made in Eastern Europe and Russia and eaten at fairs and festivals. Now they are made by Jewish communities all over the world, especially in the United States where they are split and filled with 'lox' — a mixture of cream cheese and chopped smoked salmon. Their distinctive shape (round with a central hole) is symbolic of the life cycle which has no beginning and no end. They are eaten warm sprinkled with poppy, caraway or sesame seeds. Sometimes they are flavoured with chocolate or dried fruits for a sweeter mixture.

225g/8oz/2¼ cups strong plain bread flour
2.5ml/½ teaspoon salt
25g/1oz/2 tablespoons margarine
15g/½oz fresh yeast
5ml/1 teaspoon honey
150ml/¼ pint/⅝ cup warm milk
1 egg, beaten
poppy, caraway or sesame seeds

Sieve the flour and salt and rub in the fat. Blend the yeast and honey together and add to the flour mixture with the warm milk and half the quantity of beaten egg (keep the rest for glazing the bagels). Mix to a smooth dough and knead well. Cover the dough and place in a warm place for 45 minutes to rise.

Knock back the dough, then knead until it is really elastic and then divide into 8 pieces. Flatten each piece and roll out into a cigar shape. Pull the ends round and press together to form a dough ring. Place the bagels on a lightly floured baking tray, cover with a cloth and leave to prove for about 15 minutes.

Half-fill a large pan with water and bring to the boil. Drop the bagels, one by one, into the boiling water and remove with a slotted spoon when they rise to the surface. Place them on a greased baking tray, brush with beaten egg and sprinkle with poppy, caraway or sesame seeds. Prove for a few more minutes and then bake in a preheated oven at 200°C, 400°F, gas 6 for about 15 minutes until golden. Serve warm with butter, cream cheese or lox.

Makes 8 bagels

Limpa bread

This unusual dark bread, flavoured with orange rind and anise, originated in Norway. It is excellent served at tea-time, especially when made into banana sandwiches. Rye flour can be obtained from most health food stores and good delicatessens.

400ml/14floz/1¾ cups water
50g/2oz/¼ cup molasses
50g/2oz/¼ cup Demerara or soft brown sugar
50g/2oz/¼ cup margarine
25g/1oz fresh yeast or 15ml/1 tablespoon dried yeast
350g/12oz/3 cups rye flour
grated rind of 1 large orange
5ml/1 teaspoon anise seed
50g/2oz/½ cup chopped walnuts
350g/12oz/3 cups wholemeal flour
1 egg, beaten

Place the water, molasses, sugar and margarine in a pan and heat very gently until the sugar dissolves and the margarine melts. Do *not* allow to boil. Stand the pan in cold water and cool to blood head. Mix a little of the cooled liquid with the yeast and blend well (if you are using dried yeast, sprinkle it over the liquid and leave until it starts to froth).

Pour all the liquid and the yeast mixture into a large

mixing bowl and gradually add the rye flour, orange rind, anise and nuts. Beat well and then gradually add the wholemeal flour. Turn the dough out onto a lightly floured board and knead well until the dough is smooth and elastic.

Cover the dough and leave in a warm place to prove — until it has risen and doubled in bulk. This takes about 1 hour. Knock the dough back and divide into 2 pieces. Shape into round loaves and place on a greased baking sheet. Cover with a clean cloth and leave to prove until doubled in size. Glaze the loaves with beaten egg and sprinkle with some chopped nuts if wished. Bake in a preheated oven at 200°C, 400°F, gas 6 for 35-40 minutes. Cool on wire trays.

Nut and raisin muffins

Muffins are essentially English although they are now more widely eaten as a breakfast dish in North America than they are at tea-time in Britain. The very idea of muffins conjures up homely pictures of a blazing fire in an old fireplace over which is suspended a griddle with the cooking muffins before they are brought hot to the tea-table and split and buttered. Never cut muffins — just pull them apart and eat them warm and oozing with melted butter. You can buy many commercial brands but none taste as good as these home-made ones fresh from the griddle. Toast any left-over muffins for breakfast the following day.

450g/1lb/4½ cups wholemeal flour
2.5ml/½ teaspoon salt
25g/1oz fresh yeast
5ml/1 teaspoon honey
1 egg, beaten
30ml/2 tablespoons oil
300ml/½ pint/1¼ cups water
50g/2oz/⅓ cup raisins
25g/1oz/¼ cup chopped walnuts

Put the flour and salt in a mixing bowl. Blend the yeast and honey together (if you are using dried yeast follow the instructions on the packet and when frothy, mix with the honey). Mix this into the flour with the beaten egg, oil and the water (do not add all the water at once as you may not need quite this much — the amount will vary according to the flour used). Mix in the raisins and nuts and knead to form a soft, pliable dough. Replace the dough in the bowl, cover with a lid or a cloth and leave in a warm place for about 1 hour until well-risen and doubled in size.

Knock the dough back and roll out on a board sprinkled with ground rice or flour to 1.25cm/½in thickness. Cut out the muffins with a 7.5cm/3in plain cutter and place on a lightly greased tray or griddle to prove for 30 minutes. Cook the muffins over a gentle heat on a greased griddle or in a heavy-bottomed frying pan for about 6 minutes each side until risen, golden-brown and puffed up. Serve hot with butter and jam.

Makes approximately 8 muffins

Cheese and walnut loaf

Savoury walnut loaves and bread are a feature of traditional European country cooking. In France they are sometimes eaten with fresh walnuts and a glass of dry white wine. You can make this loaf more savoury by adding a little grated onion and some chopped fresh herbs — chives and parsley are very good.

225g/8oz/2¼ cups wholemeal flour
2.5ml/½ teaspoon salt
5ml/1 teaspoon baking powder
5ml/1 teaspoon dry mustard
pinch of cayenne pepper
75g/3oz/⅜ cup margarine
100g/4oz/1 cup grated Gruyère cheese
50g/2oz/½ cup chopped walnuts
2 eggs, beaten
150ml/¼ pint/⅝ cup milk

Place the flour, salt, baking powder, mustard and cayenne in a bowl and rub in the margarine until the mixture resembles fine breadcrumbs. Add the grated cheese and walnuts.

Mix the beaten eggs and milk and beat into the loaf mixture. Pour into a greased loaf tin and bake in a preheated oven at 180°C, 350°F, gas 4 for about 50 minutes until the loaf is cooked and golden-brown. You can, if wished, sprinkle a little grated cheese over the top about 10 minutes before the end of the cooking time. Cool on a wire tray and serve cold, sliced and buttered.

Opposite: a plate of colourful Danish pastries in the foreground (see page 35), including chocolate nut pinwheels, apple triangles and fruit windmills, all decorated with flaked almonds and glacé icing and glazed with apricot jam. A rich, moist Dundee cake (see page 23) with its traditional almond topping is pictured behind the pastries

Hot cross buns

These spicy fruit buns are an English speciality and have been served traditionally on Good Friday since the eighteenth century. They are usually marked with a pastry dough or marzipan cross in honour of the festival. They are delicious eaten hot straight from the oven, sticky with sugar syrup and fragrant with spices. You can make the bun mixture at any time of year, of course, and just omit the crosses on top. If using dried yeast, follow the instructions on the packet and mix into the flour mixture in the same way.

15g/½oz fresh yeast
2.5ml/½ teaspoon caster sugar
225g/8oz/2¼ cups wholemeal flour
2.5ml/½ teaspoon salt
10ml/2 teaspoons mixed spice
2.5ml/½ teaspoon each of ground cinnamon and nutmeg
50g/2oz/¼ cup margarine
75g/3oz/½ cup mixed sultanas, currants and candied peel
50g/2oz/¼ cup soft brown sugar
150ml/¼ pint/⅝ cup mixed water and milk
1 egg, beaten
Sugar syrup:
150ml/¼ pint/⅝ cup water
65g/2½oz/⅓ cup sugar

Cream the yeast and sugar. Place the flour, salt and spices in a mixing bowl and rub in the fat. Add the mixed fruit and peel and sugar.

Heat the water and milk until just tepid and add to the bowl with the beaten egg and yeast. Beat to form a smooth, soft dough. Knead well until the dough is slack and elastic, adding more water if necessary. Cover and leave in a warm place for about 1 hour or until the dough has doubled in size.

Knock back the dough and knead lightly. Divide it into 10 pieces and roll each into a ball. Place the dough buns on a greased baking sheet and flatten slightly with your hand. Now, either cut a cross in the top of each with the point of a knife or make some dough or marzipan crosses to decorate the tops. Place in a warm place to prove and when puffed up, bake in a preheated oven at 200°C, 400°F, gas 6 for about 20 minutes until cooked and golden-brown underneath.

Make the sugar syrup: dissolve the sugar in the water over a low heat, stirring constantly. Bring to the boil and boil hard for 4-5 minutes until thick and syrupy. Use to coat the warm buns. Eat fresh, or store in an airtight tin and serve toasted and buttered.

Makes 10 buns

Blinis

These Russian yeast pancakes are eaten with soured cream, salt herring, smoked salmon and, traditionally, fine Beluga caviare. Not many of us nowadays can afford good caviare, but you can substitute salmon roe ('red caviare') or even the cheaper red or black lumpfish roe. Melted butter is another traditional accompaniment but this is too high in cholesterol for our liking. Blinis are smaller and thicker than the thin, lacy pancakes to which we are accustomed. They are made from a yeast batter of buckwheat flour which is left to rise for several hours before the blinis are cooked and served. Buckwheat flour produces a very dark, heavy sort of pancake, so we have mixed it with a strong plain white bread flour to get a lighter, more digestible result. They look very attractive as a first course, served with a large bowl of soured cream flavoured with chopped chives or anchovies, and thin slices of pink smoked salmon, black lumpfish roe, grated hard-boiled egg yolks and whites, chopped onion and salted herring, and, of course, a glass of vodka.

100/4oz/1⅛ cups buckwheat flour
100g/4oz/1⅛ cups strong plain white bread flour
5ml/1 teaspoon salt
350ml/12floz/1½ cups warm milk
15g/½oz fresh yeast
5ml/1 teaspoon sugar
2 egg yolks
30ml/2 tablespoons soured cream
2 egg whites
5ml/1 teaspoon oil

Sift the flours and salt into a mixing bowl. When the warm milk is about blood heat, mix in the yeast, sugar and egg yolks. Make a well in the centre of the flour and pour in the yeast mixture and the soured cream. Mix well until you have a thick, smooth batter. Cover the bowl with a clean cloth and leave in a warm place for about 1½ hours until the batter seems to be thicker and bubbles appear on the surface.

Whisk the egg whites until they are really stiff and gently fold into the batter. Cover the bowl and leave in a warm place for 2-3 hours. Heat a lightly oiled omelette pan over medium heat and when hot, drop in about 30-45ml/2-3 tablespoons of batter. It will spread out a little and small holes and bubbles will appear on the surface as it cooks. When the underside is set and golden-brown, flip the blini over and cook the other side. Place in a buttered dish and keep warm, Cook the remaining blinis in the same way.

Serve hot with soured cream and any of the following:

caviare, smoked salmon, lumpfish roe, salted herring, crisply fried bacon, grated hard-boiled egg, chopped onion and anchovies.
Serves 4

Pitta bread

Soft oval-shaped pitta bread is eaten throughout the Middle East. It can be split open and the pocket filled with fresh salad or hot meat in a spicy sauce. Or use it as a pizza base for a quick meal. Just top the cooked pitta bread with tomatoes, cheese, olives, anchovies and chopped onion and place under a hot grill/broiler until the cheese melts and bubbles.

450g/1lb/4½ cups wholemeal flour
2.5ml/½ teaspoon salt
15g/½oz fresh yeast or 10g dried yeast
2.5ml/½ teaspoon sugar
300ml/½ pint/1¼ cups tepid water
15ml/1 tablespoon oil

Mix the flour and salt together in a bowl. Cream the fresh yeast and sugar and add a little of the tepid water. Mix into the flour with the remaining liquid to form a soft dough. If using dried yeast, sprinkle it onto the tepid water to which the sugar has been added and leave until frothy. Mix into the flour in the same way.

Turn the dough out onto a lightly floured board and knead for 10-15 minutes until the dough has an elastic, silky texture. Place in an oiled bowl, rolling the dough around it so that it is well-oiled. Cover and leave in a warm place to rise until it doubles in bulk.

Knock back the dough on a lightly floured board and divide into 8 pieces. Roll each piece of dough into a ball and then flatten it with a rolling pin into an oval shape, approximately 5mm/¼in thick. Dust with flour and place on an upside down baking tray covered with aluminium foil. The reasons for this will become obvious when you transfer the proved pitta bread to hot sheets for baking. Cover with a cloth and leave in a warm place to rise.

Preheat the oven to 240°C, 475°F, gas 9 for 20 minutes and heat 2 more baking sheets to which the pitta bread will be transferred. When well-risen, slide the pitta bread carefully onto the hot baking sheets and spray them with water to prevent them browning. Bake in the preheated oven for 7-10 minutes, being careful not to open the door for at least 7 minutes. The pitta breads are ready when it is well-risen and cooked with a pouch inside. Remove immediately to a cooling

tray and cover with a clean cloth to keep them soft.
Makes 8 pitta breads

Danish pastries

These are always popular at teatime and there is a wide range of fillings, toppings and shapes to choose from. We have made our Danish pastries with wholemeal flour and filled them with chocolate, nuts and cherries; peaches and almonds; and apple purée. The shapes we have chosen are windmills, pin wheels and triangles. They are all quite easy to make with a little practice.

Basic dough:
450g/1lb/4½ cups wholemeal flour
good pinch of salt
25g/1oz/2 tablespoons lard/shortening
25g/1oz fresh yeast or 15ml/1 tablespoon dried yeast
25g/1oz/2 tablespoons soft brown sugar
300ml/½ pint/1¼ cups tepid water
1 egg, beaten
225g/8oz/1 cup mixed margarine and butter

Place the flour and salt in a large mixing bowl and rub in the lard/shortening. Blend the fresh yeast with a little sugar and some of the water. Add to the flour with the remaining sugar and water and beaten egg and mix to form an elastic dough. If you are using dried yeast, sprinkle it onto the tepid water in which a little of the sugar has been dissolved and leave to go frothy. Add to the flour in the same way.

Turn the dough out onto a lightly floured surface and knead until the dough is really smooth and elastic. Return the dough to the bowl, cover and place in the refrigerator for 10-15 minutes to rest. While the dough is resting, slice the butter and margarine and scatter over half of a sheet of dampened greaseproof/baking paper. Fold the other half of the paper over the top and press down with a rolling pin. Roll out so that the fat forms an oblong shape, 30cm/12in long x 20cm/8in wide. Neaten the edges.

Roll out the rested dough, 30cm/12in square. Cover two-thirds of it with the sheet of fat and fold the bottom uncovered third of the dough up over half of the fat and then the top third down over the top, so that you end up with a neat layered parcel of dough, fat, dough, fat, dough. Seal the edges with the rolling pin and roll out to its original size. Fold into three again in the same way, give the dough a half-turn and roll out once more. Fold again, give it another half-turn and roll out again. Fold, seal the edges and chill in the refrigerator for 20-30 minutes.

Roll out the dough and fold in three again. Replace in the refrigerator for 10 minutes. Roll out the dough for the last time and fill and shape the Danish pastries as described below. Place the prepared Danish pastries on a greased baking sheet, cover and leave in a warm place to prove for 15-20 minutes. Bake in a preheated oven at 200°C, 400°F, gas 6 for 15-20 minutes, or until the pastries are cooked and golden-brown underneath. Cool and then decorate with glacé icing or glaze with apricot jam as described below.

Makes 16 pastries

Chocolate nut pinwheels

75g/3oz chocolate
75g/3oz/¾ cup chopped walnuts
45ml/3 tablespoons oil
100g/4oz/½ cup soft brown sugar
100g/4oz/⅔ cup sultanas/seedless raisins
50g/2oz/¼ cup chopped glacé cherries
glacé icing and flaked almonds to decorate

Melt the chocolate in a double-boiler or in a basin suspended over a pan of hot water. Do not boil or overheat as this will cause the chocolate to separate. Stir in 25g/1oz/¼ cup of the chopped walnuts. Take a narrow piece of aluminium foil, 30cm/12in long, and pour the chocolate mixture along its length. Fold the foil over the top and roll it so that you end up with a long chocolate nut sausage shape wrapped in foil. Chill in the freezer or the freezing compartment of the refrigerator for at least 30 minutes. Brush the rolled out sheet of dough with oil. Remove the foil from the chocolate sausage shape and lay it along one short end of the dough. Sprinkle the remaining dough with the rest of the chopped nuts, sugar, sultanas and cherries and roll up, starting from the chocolate end, as you would roll a Swiss roll. Cut into slices and place them flat on greased baking sheets. Prove and cook as

described above in the basic Danish pastries recipe. Decorate the cooked pastries when cool with glacé icing and flaked almonds.

Apple triangles

2 cooking apples/green apples, peeled, cored and sliced
15ml/1 tablespoon water
15ml/1 tablespoon soft brown sugar
1.25ml/¼ teaspoon ground cinnamon
squeeze of lemon juice
apricot jam to glaze
glacé icing and flaked almonds to decorate

Place the sliced apple in a pan with the water. Cover and cook over gentle heat until the apple is soft and pulpy. Beat in the sugar, cinnamon and a squeeze of lemon juice, beating until the purée is smooth. Cut the prepared dough into squares and place a good spoonful of the apple filling in the centre of each. Fold in half diagonally and press the edges together lightly to seal in the filling. Place the triangles on greased baking sheets, 4 or 5 to a sheet, and prove and cook as described in the basic Danish pastries recipe above. Cool and brush with hot apricot jam to glaze, and decorate with glacé icing and flaked almonds.

Fruit windmills

50g/2oz marzipan or almond paste (optional)
beaten egg
16 canned or fresh apricot or peach halves
apricot jam to glaze
glacé icing and flaked almonds to decorate

Cut the prepared dough into 10cm/4in squares. Place a little marzipan or almond paste in the centre of each square. Make a diagonal cut from each corner of the square to within 1cm/½in of the centre. Fold one corner of each cut section into the centre, pressing each down firmly into the almond paste. Brush with a little beaten egg and place on greased baking sheets, 4 to a sheet, and prove and cook as described above in the basic Danish pastries recipe. Place a peach or apricot half in the centre of each windmill. Glaze with apricot jam and decorate the windmill with glacé icing and flaked almonds.

Wholemeal croissants

Although we normally associate croissants with French cookery, they weremade first by the Hungarians to commemorate their victory over the Turks in 1686. Bakers working in the early morning in Budapest heard the Turks tunnelling through the city walls and raised the alarm. They created a yeast bread in the crescent shape of the emblem on the Turkish flag, which we still eat today. Croissants should have a flaky, melt-in-the-mouth texture and may be filled with chocolate, grated cheese or puréed apple if wished.

25g/1 oz fresh yeast or 15ml/1 tablespoon dried yeast
5ml/1 teaspoon sugar
300ml/½ pint/1¼ cups tepid water
450g/1lb/4½ cups wholemeal flour
2.5ml/½ teaspoon salt
350g/12oz/1½ cups margarine
1 egg, beaten
beaten egg to glaze
Fillings:
150g/5oz plain chocolate
100g/4oz/1 cup grated Cheddar or Gruyère/Swiss cheeses

Blend the fresh yeast with the sugar and add a little of the tepid water. Or dissolve the sugar in about 50ml/2floz/¼ cup of tepid water and sprinkle over the dried yeast. Leave for about 15 minutes until the mixture is frothy and cool.

Place the flour and salt in a mixing bowl and rub in 25g/1oz/2 tablespoons of the fat. Add the cold yeast mixture, the remaining water and the egg and mix to form an elastic dough. Knead well and then chill in the refrigerator.

Moisten a sheet of greaseproof paper/baking paper with a little water. Slice the remaining fat into thin pieces and lay across half of the damp paper. Fold the other half of the paper over the top and flatten with a rolling pin. Roll out evenly so that the softened fat becomes one thin piece. Neaten the edges.

Roll out the chilled croissant dough into an oblong three times longer than its width. Place the sheet of fat over two-thirds of the oblong, leaving 5mm/¼ in border on three sides (see diagram). Fold the uncovered bottom third of the dough up over half of the fat, and the top third (covered with fat) down over the dough. You should end up with 5 neat layers of dough/fat/dough/

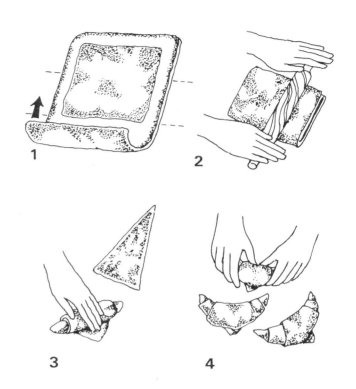

fat/dough. Seal the open edges with a rolling pin, pressing down firmly to seal in the air. Roll out thinly and then fold into three again in the same way. Give the dough a half turn, roll out to the original size and fold in three again. Repeat the process once more and then return to the refrigerator for 30 minutes to relax.

Roll out the dough again to its original size and fold in three and return to the refrigerator for 10 minutes only. Roll out the dough for the last time and cut into triangular shapes as shown. The sides must be longer than the base (15cm/6in long x 10cm/4in wide at the base). Roll the triangles up loosely, starting from the base and tucking the tip underneath. Curve the rolled-up dough into a crescent shape, glaze with beaten egg and place on a well-greased baking sheet. Cover lightly with a clean cloth and leave in a warm place to prove for 15-20 minutes. Bake in a preheated oven at 220°C, 425°F, gas 7 for about 20 minutes until puffy, crisp and golden-brown. Cool slightly and serve warm.

If you wish to fill the croissants, place a small heap of grated chocolate or grated cheese on each rolled-out triangle near the base and roll up loosely, shape into crescents and prove and bake in exactly the same way as described above.

Makes approximately 10-12 croissants

Rice and pasta have an important role to play in natural, healthy eating. These cereals can be made into a wide range of savoury and sweet dishes, from cold salads and hot pilaffs to creamy puddings. They are both ancient foods with a long history which stretches back at least 5000 years.

Rice

The birthplace of rice was probably India but it was first cultivated in China about 5000 years ago. Since then, it has become a symbol of happiness and fertility in the Far East and the staple diet of much of Asia, China, South America and even Spain and northern Italy. Although we usually associate rice with the monsoon belt of the tropics and vast paddy fields and terraces, it is grown also in temperate lands such as northern Italy. The Arab traders and conquerors brought the grain back from Asia and introduced it into Spain and from there it travelled to Italy in the fifteenth century. It was much later, in 1700, that rice reached North America, and South Carolina soon became another important rice-growing area.

Rice is now eaten throughout the world and most countries have their own special, national rice dish — the Spanish seafood *paella*, the spicy, sticky *pilaffs* of the Middle East, the golden *pilaus* of India, the colourful rice and bean dishes of the Caribbean, the creamy Italian *risotto*, the fried rice dishes of China and the baked rice pudding of Great Britain.

Rice usually takes its name from the district in which it is grown, and there are several thousand varieties of rice of which we eat only a few: long-, short- or medium-grain white and brown rice. Thus we have Carolina, Basmati, Arborio, Patna and Valencia rice. The grain, which is enclosed by a tough outer husk, has a similar structure to that of wheat, although it contains less protein. The outer layers of the grain are lost during the milling process together with their valuable nutrients, including vitamin B1 (thiamine). Brown rice, which has only the husk removed, is more nutritious than white rice. Rice is a good source of energy, being three-quarters starch, and it also contains essential minerals, fats and protein. It can be bought in different forms.

Brown rice has a pleasantly chewy, nutty texture and flavour and is used in many savoury dishes. Mixed with chopped apricots, nuts and herbs, it makes an excellent stuffing for poultry. It is the whole grain with only the indigestible husk removed and can be obtained in long- and short-grain varieties.

White rice loses its husk, germ and outer layers together with much of its protein, minerals and B vitamins in the milling process. To make it really shiny white, it is sometimes polished with talc or glucose. It may be purchased as long-, short- or medium-grains. The moister, stickier short-grain varieties, such as Carolina pudding rice, are used in desserts and rice moulds, whereas the long-grain varieties, which vary from the plump Italian risotto rice (arborio) to the slender separate fluffy Basmati and Patna grains, are used in savoury dishes. Although white rice is essential for some risottos, pilaffs and puddings, brown can usually be substituted with good results and this applies to most of the recipes in this section.

Wild rice is not really a cereal but the green seeds of a wild grass grown in the northern United States. Nutritionally, it is better for you than brown rice, but its scarcity and hand-harvesting by the Indians makes its price prohibitively high. It is served with game, as a stuffing or as a savoury pilaff.

How to cook rice

Rice may be boiled, steamed or parboiled and fried. Always bear in mind when cooking rice that brown grains need more time than white. To boil rice, allow 550ml/1pint/2½cups water for every 50g/2oz/¼ cup rice. Add 5ml/1 teaspoon salt to the water, bring to the boil and tip in the rice. Boil rapidly until the rice is tender but not over-cooked and mushy. Drain and rinse under hot water to separate the grains and wash out any excess starch.

Another way of cooking rice, which uses less water, is the absorption method. Allow 2 cups of liquid (water or stock) to every cup of rice. Add 5ml/1 teaspoon salt to the water, bring to the boil and tip in the rice. Reduce the heat to a bare simmer and cover the pan. Cook gently until the rice is tender and all the water has been absorbed (about 15 minutes for white rice, 40 minutes for brown).

Rice can be cooked in chicken stock, beef stock or water. You can add a little white wine or Marsala to the liquid if using the absorption method, as in a *risotto*. Boiled rice can be coloured with saffron or turmeric.

Pasta

Pasta is even older than rice and was probably invented in China about 6000 years ago. However, it was also eaten by the Romans in the Eastern Byzantine Empire and this seems to discount the theory that Marco Polo introduced it to Italy when he returned from his fabulous journey to the court of Kublai Khan in 1295. It is difficult to envisage Italian food without pasta, indeed it is almost a way of life in southern Italy, but it was not a widely eaten national food there until the beginning of this century. Now, Italy without pasta is inconceivable and you can sit down in any family-run *trattoria* in any Italian town and enjoy some home-made pasta.

Pasta is the generic name for the many foods that are made from a durum wheat flour and water dough. The traditional pasta flour is hard to obtain outside Italy, but strong white or wholemeal bread flour to which semolina is sometimes added, will give good results. Eggs are often used to enrich the dough. The hundreds of varieties of pasta, which come in all shapes and sizes, are all made from this basic dough, sometimes coloured green with puréed spinach or pink with tomato paste.

You do not need a special machine to make pasta, although there are several economically priced hand-cranked and electric-powered models on the market which knead, roll and cut the noodles. Pasta can be made by hand or in a food mixer or processor, and if you have never tasted fresh pasta, then you are in for a pleasant surprise. Its flavour and texture are far superior to dried pasta. Fresh spaghetti, ravioli and noodles are sold in many Italian delicatessens.

Types of pasta

Spaghetti —these long thin strings of pasta may be served simply dressed with olive oil, garlic and grated Parmesan, or in a creamy or tomato sauce.

Tagliatelle — these long thick noodles are sometimes coloured green and served with a creamy cheese sauce.

Fettuccine — these ribbon noodles are thinner than tagliatelle but are also served with cheese or creamy sauces, the best known being *fettuccine Alfredo*.

Trenette — these matchstick thin noodles are made in Genoa and are served traditionally with the Genovese pesto sauce.

Lasagne — these sheets of pasta, often coloured green and known as *lasagne verdi*, are boiled and then layered with rich *ragú* and béchamel sauces in a baked dish.

Ravioli — these are little squares of pasta filled with a savoury meat or spinach and ricotta filling and then cooked in a cheese or tomato sauce.

Of course, there are many other varieties of pasta, all with beautiful evocative names: conchiglie (little shells), amorini (little cupids) and farfalletti (little bows), to name but a few.

Cooking pasta

Timing is the secret of good pasta. It is ready when it is *al dente* (to the tooth), or when you can bite into it and it is still firm but tender. It should *never* be soft or mushy. Cook it in plenty of water. Allow 550ml/1pint/ 2½cups water to every 50g/2oz pasta. Salt the water and add 15ml/1 tablespoon oil to prevent the pasta pieces or strands from sticking together. When the water comes to a rolling boil, throw, or coil, in the pasta. Fresh pasta will need only a fraction of the cooking time of dried pasta. As soon as the pasta is cooked, drain it and toss it in garlic-flavoured olive oil, or coat with a sauce and serve immediately. Pasta should never be kept waiting or it will lose its fine flavour and texture. Neither should it be served swimming in sauce — the sauce is only a flavouring and each pasta strand or piece should be just coated. It is usually served with a bowl of grated Parmesan. Guests can help themselves and use a spoon and fork to manoeuvre any long strands into their mouths!

Storing pasta

Dried pasta of all varieties will keep for several months if stored in a cool, dry place. It is an invaluable item for your store cupboard, for quick meals and unexpected guests. Fresh pasta can be dried out and stored in a larder or refrigerator for 2-3 weeks or it can be frozen until required. When freezing ravioli, always separate the sheets into individual squares before putting them in a freezer bag or container. To cook, just plunge the frozen pasta into boiling water and cook uncovered until tender.

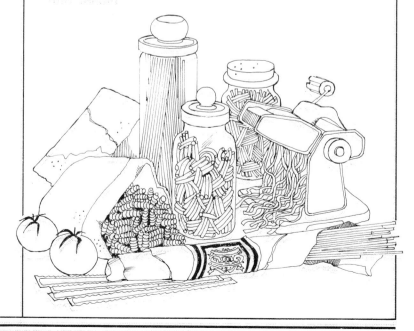

Rice

Dolmades

Lemony flavoured, tender vine leaves rolled around a spicy stuffing of rice, herbs, currants and pine nuts are a delicious way to start a summer meal. Alternatively, you can serve them as a snack with pre-dinner cocktails, or with *ouzo* as an aperitif. Dolmades, stuffed with a variety of fillings, are popular throughout Greece, Turkey and the Middle East. They are easily made in advance and frozen until required. If you cannot obtain fresh vine leaves, then use canned or pickled leaves, which are available in most good delicatessens and Greek specialist shops.

175g/6oz fresh or pickled vine leaves
100g/4oz/½ cup long-grain rice
1 small onion, chopped
1 tomato, skinned, deseeded and chopped
few sprigs of parsley, chopped
15ml/1 tablespoon each of chopped mint and chives
1.25ml/¼ teaspoon each of ground cinnamon, allspice and cumin
25g/1oz/⅓ cup pine nuts
75g/3oz/½ cup currants
salt and pepper
2 cloves of garlic, sliced
50ml/2floz/¼ cup olive oil
150ml/¼ pint/⅝ cup water
10ml/2 teaspoons sugar
juice of 1 lemon

If you are using fresh vine leaves, boil them for 3-4 minutes in water and drain. Pickled vine leaves should be soaked for 20-30 minutes in hot water.

Pat the leaves dry, remove the stalks and spread them out with the veined underside facing upwards. Soak the rice in boiling water for a few minutes, drain and mix with the onion, tomato, herbs, spices, pine nuts, currants and seasoning. Place a little of the filling in the centre of each leaf, fold the sides into the middle and roll up quickly. Line the base of a heavy saucepan with any broken or left-over leaves and pack in the dolmades tightly in layers. Pack the sliced garlic between the stuffed leaves. Pour in the olive oil, water, sugar and lemon juice, press a plate down over the dolmades to anchor them, and cover the pan with a close-fitting lid.

Simmer gently for about 1½ hours, adding more boiling water as it is absorbed by the filling. Leave the dolmades in the pan to cool, and when cold arrange them on a serving dish. Dress them with a little olive oil and lemon juice if wished. You can serve the dolmades secured with a cocktail stick/toothpick.

Makes approximately 18 dolmades

Rice and almond salad

This cold rice salad is flavoured with cucumber and nuts and tossed in a cool yoghurt dressing. It makes a refreshing first course or a good accompaniment to cold fish and poultry.

225g/8oz/1 cup long-grain brown rice
1 cucumber
6 spring onions/shallots, thinly sliced
150ml/¼ pint/⅝ cup natural yoghurt
salt and pepper
juice of ½ lemon
75g/3oz/½ cup flaked almonds (or chopped cashews)
15ml/1 tablespoon chopped parsley

Boil the rice in plenty of salted water until tender but not mushy. Drain and rinse in hot water. Leave to cool, and mix with the chopped onions/shallots.

Make the dressing: peel and dice the cucumber and sprinkle lightly with salt to drain off excess moisture. Pat lightly dry with absorbent kitchen paper. Mix the yoghurt with the seasoning and lemon juice and pour over the cold rice. Gently toss the rice in the dressing, stir in the cucumber and sprinkle with the almonds and parsley.

Serves 4

Caribbean rice and beans

Rice and bean dishes are popular throughout the Caribbean islands. You can use cooked or canned kidney beans in this recipe. Serve it with Tropical chicken (see recipe on page 107) and fried bananas. Add a hot chilli pepper if you enjoy hot spicy food.

15g/½oz/1 tablespoon lard
2 rashers streaky bacon, chopped
1 onion + 1 clove garlic, finely chopped
½ green pepper, chopped
1 tomato, skinned, seeded and chopped
225g/8oz cooked or canned kidney beans
175g/6oz/¾ cup long-grain rice
400ml/14floz/1¾ cups chicken stock
salt and pepper
juice of 1 lemon

strip of lemon peel
small packet powdered saffron
15ml/1 tablespoon chopped parsley

Heat the lard in a heavy pan and sauté the bacon, onion, garlic and green pepper until cooked but not browned. Add the tomato and beans and heat through gently for 2-3 minutes. Stir in the rice and mix well so that all the grains are glistening. Now add the stock, seasoning, lemon juice and peel and saffron. Cover the pan and cook gently until the rice is cooked and fluffy and all the liquid has been absorbed. Remove the lemon peel, sprinkle with parsley and serve.

Serves 4

Chinese egg fried rice

It is best to cook the rice the day before you make this dish in order that it may dry out thoroughly before frying. Although rice is the staple food of China, it is never eaten on its own. It is served at every meal — breakfast, lunch and dinner — with a wide range of meat, fish and vegetable dishes. Fried rice should be flavoursome, aromatic and with contrasting colours and textures. The scrambled eggs add a degree of creaminess to the tender, firm rice, whereas vegetables, shrimps and meat add colour and crunchiness. You can mix almost anything with fried rice — left-over chicken, pork, bacon, beef, shrimps, spring onions or leeks are just a few examples.

225g/8oz/1 cup long-grain rice
550ml/1 pint/2½ cups water
salt
1 onion, chopped
1 clove garlic, chopped
4 rashers streaky bacon, chopped
100g/4oz cooked ham, diced
45ml/3 tablespoons oil
2 eggs, beaten
100g/4oz peeled, cooked shrimps
45ml/3 tablespoons peas, fresh or frozen and thawed
salt and pepper
30ml/2 tablespoons soya sauce
2 spring onions/shallots, chopped

Cook the rice in boiling salted water until tender. Drain and rinse well under cold running water to remove any starch grains. Drain and spread the rice out to dry thoroughly.

Sauté the onion, garlic, bacon and ham in the oil and stir-fry over high heat for 2-3 minutes until tender.

Pour in the beaten egg and stir lightly until the eggs set and start to scramble. Add the shrimps and peas and stir in the cooked rice. Season with salt and pepper and stir-fry for 3 minutes over high heat. Season and flavour with soya sauce. Stir the rice mixture well and turn out onto a hot serving dish. Garnish with the chopped spring onions/shallots.

Serves 4

Persian chicken and rice

This is based on a recipe given to us by a Persian friend. Not only is it an exquisitely flavoured dish but also every grain of rice stays separate if it is cooked correctly. Many traditional Persian and Middle Eastern dishes which trace their origins back to the Middle Ages feature a combination of meat and fruit, and this theme is now coming back into vogue in modern cookery. Here, the chicken is cooked in water only with dried fruit and spices for a unique result. This makes an ideal buffet party dish. The rice can be prepared in advance, and the whole dish can be frozen successfully until required.

225g/8oz/1 cup Basmati or good-quality long-grain rice
25ml/5 teaspoons salt
1 onion, finely chopped
30ml/2 tablespoons oil
4 chicken portions, skinned and boned
25g/1oz/2 tablespoons raisins
50g/2oz/⅜ cup dried apricots
30ml/2 tablespoons pine nuts
2.5ml/½ teaspoon each ground coriander and cinnamon
salt and pepper
25g/1oz/2 tablespoons margarine
30ml/2 tablespoons chopped fresh parsley

First prepare the rice. Wash the rice in boiling water and then place it in a bowl with 15ml/3 teaspoons salt and cover with cold water. Set aside for a minimum of 2 hours. Drain and rinse the rice and then cook in a pan of boiling water to which the remaining salt has been added for about 10 minutes, or until the rice is just tender but still firm. Drain.

Sauté the onion in the oil until it starts to brown. Add the chicken portions and brown on both sides. Next stir in the dried fruit, nuts, spices and seasoning. Pour in enough water to barely cover the chicken, cover the pan and simmer for 1 hour.

Heat the margarine and add half of the cooked rice. Place the chicken and the sauce on top and cover with

the remaining rice. Cover with a clean cloth and then a lid and steam over very low heat for 25 minutes. Serve immediately sprinkled with chopped parsley.
Serves 4

Risotto alla Milanese

Many versions of this classic rice dish exist, but whether you use white wine, Marsala or just chicken stock to cook the rice, the basic risotto technique remains the same. The aim is to produce a creamy-textured risotto, which is neither too sticky nor soggy, by adding the cooking liquid a little at a time as it is gradually absorbed by the rice. The rice is cooked when it is judged *al dente* (meaning literally 'to the bite'). We have used Marsala in our version but you can substitute an equal quantity of white wine for a different flavour — this is particularly good in a seafood risotto if you add prawns, mussels, squid and lobster meat. Risotto is such a versatile dish that you can use practically any meat, fish or vegetables, especially left-over cooked, cold chicken, ham, duck or game. For a more substantial dish, add sliced red pepper, artichoke hearts, sliced courgettes/zucchini, spicy Italian sausage and aubergine/eggplant. But on *no* account forget the saffron, which is always used as a flavouring.

25g/1oz/2 tablespoons butter
30ml/2 tablespoons olive oil
2 onions, chopped
1 clove garlic, crushed
350g/12oz/1½ cups Italian Arborio rice
150ml/¼ pint/⅝ cup sweet Marsala
750ml/1¼ pints/3 cups chicken stock
1 small packet powdered saffron
salt and pepper
5-6 dried Boletus mushrooms
225g/8oz chopped cooked chicken or ham
50g/2oz sliced button mushrooms
15g/½ oz/1 tablespoon butter
50g/2oz/⅓ cup freshly grated Parmesan cheese

Heat the butter and oil in a large, heavy-bottomed frying pan and sauté the onion and garlic until soft and translucent. Add the rice and stir until it is glistening with oil and butter. Cook gently for two to three minutes and then add the Marsala. Cook over a moderate heat until it has all evaporated, and then add a little of the stock. As it is absorbed by the rice, gradually add some more, about 150ml/¼ pint/⅝ cup at a time, stirring occasionally to prevent the rice sticking to the pan.

Season with saffron, salt and pepper and the dried Boletus mushrooms. When the rice is nearly cooked, stir in the chicken or ham and the mushrooms, and heat through gently.

Just before serving, check the seasoning, then pile the risotto into a serving dish and stir in the butter. Sprinkle generously with Parmesan and serve immediately. A dressed green salad makes a good accompaniment if the risotto is to be served as a main course.
Serves 4

Spicy kedgeree

Kedgeree, eaten widely as a breakfast dish in Victorian times, was derived by the English in India from the Hindi dish of *Khichri*, a simple meal of spiced rice and lentils. There are many versions of kedgeree, each claiming its own authenticity and many resembling the flavourless, institutionalised food of our school-days. However, a good kedgeree is quickly and easily prepared and makes a lovely lunch or supper dish. Most cooks add generous helpings of cream and butter but these are optional in our recipe for health reasons. For a more crunchy, interesting texture, you can try substituting brown rice for white. Indian Basmati or Italian Arborio rices are the best ones to use.

3 shallots (or 1 small onion), chopped
45ml/3 tablespoons olive oil
225g/8oz/1 cup long-grain rice
2.5ml/½ teaspoon nutmeg
5ml/1 teaspoon good quality curry powder
pinch ground ginger
salt and pepper
50g/2oz/⅓ cup sultanas
900ml/1½ pints/3 cups water
450g/1lb smoked haddock
25g/1oz/¼ cup chopped walnuts
30ml/2 tablespoons double cream (optional)
2 hard-boiled eggs, finely chopped
30ml/2 tablespoons chopped parsley
lemon wedges

Sauté the shallots in oil in a large frying pan until soft and translucent. Add the rice and cook gently for 2 or 3 minutes until it begins to look transparent and all the grains are coated with oil. Add the spices, seasoning, sultanas and water. Bring to the boil, reduce the heat and cook gently until all the water has been absorbed and the rice is cooked but not soggy. The grains should be separate and fluffy.

Boil the haddock for 3 minutes, drain, remove the bones and flake it. Add it to the rice, when it has been cooking for 15 minutes, with the chopped nuts. Stir the rice occasionally to prevent it sticking to the pan and add more water if necessary.

Lastly, stir in the cream (if used) and transfer the kedgeree to a serving dish. Sprinkle over the chopped hard-boiled egg and parsley. Garnish with lemon wedges and serve with mango chutney.
Serves 4

Wild rice pilaff

Wild rice is harvested exclusively by the American Indians of the Minnesota lakes area. They use long poles to knock the rice into their flat-bottomed boats as they sail along the shores of the lakes and creeks. Wild rice is not really a rice at all but a separate botanical species with twice the protein of refined white rice and six times more iron and vitamins B1 and B3. As well as being nutritionally superior to ordinary rice, it is less fattening and more tasty with an interesting nutty flavour and texture. Unfortunately, because of its rarity and fine flavour it has achieved the status of a gourmet food and is very expensive to buy. If you see a small packet in a delicatessen or health food store, it is well worth buying for a special occasion. Use it as a stuffing for game birds or serve it as a delicious pilaff.

100g/4oz/⅔ cup wild rice
350ml/12floz/1½ cups water
1 onion, chopped
100g/4oz mushrooms, chopped
30ml/2 tablespoons oil
50g/2oz/½ cup chopped walnuts
salt and pepper
pinch of ground allspice
chopped chives and parsley to garnish

Wash the wild rice thoroughly in a sieve under running cold water. Bring the water to the boil in a pan and tip in the wild rice. Reduce the heat to a bare simmer, cover with a tightly fitting lid and simmer gently for about 30-40 minutes until all the water is absorbed.

Meanwhile, sauté the onion and mushroom in the oil until soft. Stir into the cooked rice with the walnuts, seasoning and chopped herbs. Serve with roast chicken or game birds. Vary the flavour of the pilaff by adding

chopped green pepper, currants or sliced celery.
Serves 4

Nasi goreng

This colourful dish of fried rice served with omelette strips, baked bananas, peanuts, sliced tomato and fried eggs, comes from Indonesia. Cook the rice ahead, either a few hours before preparing the dish or even the previous day. The flavour will be more authentic if you can get hold of some *trasi* (a spicy shrimp flavouring) or even a nasi goreng sambal mix — these are available in many good food stores and delicatessens and Chinese and Indian shops.

225g/8oz/1 cup long-grain basmati rice
550ml/1 pint/2½ cups salted water
1 small onion, chopped
2 cloves garlic, crushed
4 anchovy fillets
1 dried chilli, seeded (or 1 fresh)
45ml/3 tablespoons peanut oil
2.5ml/½ teaspoon trasi or nasi goreng sambal (optional)
225g/8oz cooked ham or pork, diced
100g/4oz shelled prawns/shrimps
15ml/1 tablespoon soya sauce
2 spring onions/shallots, chopped
Baked bananas:
4 bananas
juice of ½ lemon
15g/½oz/1 tablespoon margarine
Omelette:
2 eggs
salt and pepper
Garnish:
4 fried eggs
2 tomatoes, sliced
½ cucumber, cut in chunks
100g/4oz/1 cup salted peanuts

Cook the rice in the salted water in a covered pan until tender and all the water has been absorbed. Refresh under running water to get rid of any excess starch, and leave to cool.

Cut the bananas in half lengthwise and arrange them in a greased ovenproof dish, sprinkled with lemon juice and dotted with margarine. Bake in a preheated oven at 200°C, 400°F, gas 6 for 12-15 minutes until soft and golden-brown.

Liquidise the onion, garlic, anchovies, chilli and peanut oil to a smooth paste. Heat the paste in a wok or frying pan until it starts to soften and brown. Add the trasi (optional) and the diced meat. Cook for 4-5 minutes and then stir in the prawns/shrimps. Add the cooked rice and the soya sauce and mix thoroughly, adding more peanut oil if necessary to keep the mixture moist. Heat through over a gentle heat while you prepare the omelette strips.

Beat the eggs with the seasoning and make a moist omelette in another pan. Roll the cooked omelette up and cut into thin strips. Transfer the rice to a serving dish and arrange the omelette strips across the top in a criss-cross pattern and sprinkle with the chopped onions.

Serve garnished with the fried eggs, bananas, sliced tomato, cucumber chunks and peanuts.

Serves 4

Paella

Paella is the traditional Sunday dish in the southern Spanish regions of Alicante and Valencia. Its name is derived from the large, shallow iron or aluminium pan in which it is cooked and served — the *paellera*. There is no set recipe for a paella — countless variations exist which make use of local meat and shellfish and seasonal vegetables. The only two ingredients common to all versions of this colourful dish are saffron and rice. The Italian Arborio rice is superior to the Spanish Valencia type and should be used in preference as it is plumper and moister. You can vary the paella ingredients to produce a sumptuous, expensive party dish with crab and lobster as well as prawns, pork and chicken, or a more modest family meal with spicy Spanish chorizo sausage, prawns and chicken. We have added some giant Mediterranean prawns for a colourful flourish. You can serve the paella with a crisp green salad.

50ml/2floz/¼ cup olive oil
4 chicken pieces
225g/8oz lean salt pork, cubed
100g/4oz chorizo sausage, thinly sliced
2 onions, chopped
2 cloves garlic, crushed
1 red pepper, sliced in rings
1 green pepper, sliced in rings
450g/1lb tomatoes, skinned and roughly chopped
550ml/1 pint/2½ cups chicken stock
2.5ml/½ teaspoon powdered saffron
salt and pepper
pinch hot paprika
100g/4oz peeled prawns/shrimps

4 large Mediterranean/Pacific prawns/shrimps
50g/2oz French green beans, halved
275g/10oz/1¼ cups long-grain Arborio rice
50ml/2floz/¼ cup white wine
150ml/¼ pint mussels
30ml/2 tablespoons chopped parsley

Heat the olive oil and fry the chicken, pork and chorizo until golden-brown (about 15 minutes). Remove and keep warm while you sauté the onion, garlic and peppers until tender. Add the tomato and fry for 3-4 minutes and then replace the chicken, pork and chorizo in the pan and add the stock. For a traditional, authentic paella you should leave the chicken on the bone, but if your pan is quite small, add the boned meat.

Add the chicken stock and saffron and seasoning and bring to the boil. Reduce the heat a little and stir in the prawns/shrimps, green beans and rice. Cook gently over a medium heat until all the liquid is absorbed. Add a little white wine and continue cooking until the grains of rice are separate, moist and fluffy. Stir the paella occasionally to prevent the rice sticking to the base of the pan.

Meanwhile, scrub the mussels, discarding any that are open. Place the mussels in a large pan with a little water or wine over high heat. Cover the pan and shake occasionally until the mussels open in the steam. Use the mussels in their shells to garnish the paella and sprinkle with plenty of chopped parsley before serving the paella straight out of the pan.

Serves 4

Tip: Rice can also be served cold in salads:

1 Mix 225g/8oz cooked brown rice with segments of 2 large oranges, 1 chopped spring onion/shallot, chopped walnuts, chives and parsley and toss in a French dressing flavoured with orange juice.

2 Mix 225g/8oz cooked saffron rice with 225g/8oz flaked smoked haddock, 2 chopped tomatoes, 2 chopped spring onions/shallots and toss in a garlicy French dressing. Garnish with olives and parsley.

3 Mix 225g/8oz cooked rice with 2.5ml/½ teaspoon turmeric, 5ml/1 teaspoon curry powder, 100g/4oz chopped pineapple, 30ml/2 tablespoons sultanas/ seedless raisins, 30ml/2 tablespoons peanuts and toss in a French dressing and pineapple juice.

Saffron rice, shellfish, pork, chicken and vegetables make a vividly coloured paella (see this page) for a family meal or buffet party dish. Serve it straight from the pan

Baked stuffed peppers

Red, green and yellow bell peppers filled with a piquant rice stuffing make a colourful party dish. Choose peppers that will stand up easily and not fall over in the baking dish while cooking. If you prefer a meatless filling, then omit the pork or lamb and reduce the amount of stock very slightly.

2 large bell peppers (red, green or yellow)
100g/4oz/½ cup long-grain brown rice
1 onion, finely chopped
1 clove garlic, crushed
30ml/2 tablespoons oil
100g/4oz/½ cup minced/ground lamb or pork
150ml/¼ pint/⅝ cup chicken stock
salt and pepper
50g/2oz button mushrooms, thinly sliced
2.5ml/½ teaspoon paprika
450g/1lb canned tomatoes or fresh tomatoes, skinned and chopped
2.5ml/½ teaspoon brown sugar
2.5ml/½ teaspoon basil
1 bay leaf
150ml/¼ pint/⅝ cup natural yoghurt or soured cream

Wash and dry the peppers and slice off the tops with the stalk attached. These will be used as lids. Carefully scoop out and discard all the seeds inside and set aside.

Boil the rice in salted water for 15-20 minutes and drain. Sauté the onion and garlic in the oil until tender. Stir in the meat and brown lightly. Add the stock, and seasoning and simmer gently for 10 minutes. Stir in the drained rice, mushrooms and paprika. Fill the peppers with this mixture and cover with the 'lids'. Place in a deep ovenproof dish, standing upright. Place the tomatoes, sugar, herbs and seasoning in the base of the dish around the peppers, spooning a little of the tomato mixture over the top and bake in a preheated oven at 170°C, 325°F, gas 3 for 40-45 minutes, or until the peppers are tender and cooked.

Transfer the cooked peppers to a serving dish and boil the tomato sauce up on top of the cooker until it reduces slightly. Season to taste and stir in the soured cream or yoghurt. Pour the sauce around the peppers and serve hot.
Serves 2

Alternative filling

An equally good alternative filling can be made with feta cheese, pine nuts and ham.

2 large bell peppers (red, green or yellow)
100g/4oz/½ cup long-grain brown rice
4 shallots or 1 onion, finely chopped
15ml/1 tablespoon oil
150ml/¼ pint/⅝ cup chicken stock or red wine
100g/4oz ham, diced
5ml/1 teaspoon oregano
25g/1oz/¼ cup pine nuts
100g/4oz feta cheese, crumbled
25g/1oz/3 tablespoons grated Parmesan cheese
salt and pepper
pinch of paprika

Prepare the peppers in the same way and cook the rice in boiling, salted water for 15-20 minutes and drain. Sauté the shallots in the oil until soft and translucent. Add the stock or red wine, the diced ham, oregano and pine nuts. Gently stir in the feta and Parmesan cheeses. Mix in the drained rice and season to taste. Fill the peppers with this mixture and cook in tomato sauce as outlined in the previous recipe.
Serves 2

Stuffed aubergines

Vegetables stuffed with spicy rice fillings are popular throughout southern Europe, the Balkans and the Middle East. Here are two alternative stuffings for aubergines/eggplants, one spicy, the other fruity with dates and feta cheese. If you cannot get any feta, then try using another firm goat's cheese or even ricotta. Aubergines/eggplants should always be sprinkled with salt and put aside for at least 30 minutes before using to drain off any excess moisture and to prevent the final dish from being too wet.

2 aubergines/eggplants
salt
100g/4oz/½ cup long-grain brown rice
5ml/1 teaspoon turmeric
60ml/4 tablespoons olive oil
2 onions, finely chopped
1 clove garlic, crushed
1 small green pepper, diced
50g/2oz button mushrooms, chopped
1.25ml/¼ teaspoon each of ground cinnamon and allspice
1.25ml/¼ teaspoon dill
2 tomatoes, skinned, seeded and chopped
50g/2oz/½ cup pine nuts
50g/2oz/½ cup grated Swiss cheese
15ml/1 tablespoon grated Parmesan cheese

Wash the aubergines/eggplants, remove the stalks and split in half lengthwise. Carefully hollow out the central flesh to leave a thin outer casing to be filled. Sprinkle the hollowed-out shell and the chopped inner flesh with salt and leave to drain for about 30 minutes. Rinse well and dry on absorbent kitchen paper.

Meanwhile, cook the rice in boiling, salted water for 15-20 minutes until just tender. Drain, colour with turmeric and set aside. Sauté the chopped aubergine/eggplant in 30ml/2 tablespoons of the oil until golden. Remove and keep warm. Add the onion and garlic and sauté until soft and translucent. Stir in the chopped pepper and cook for 2 minutes, and then add the mushrooms. After another 2 minutes, remove the pan from the heat and mix in the cooked rice, sautéed aubergine/eggplant, spices, dill, chopped tomato and pine nuts. Stir well and season to taste.

Fill the prepared aubergines/eggplants with the rice mixture. Place in a shallow baking tin and sprinkle with grated cheese and about 5ml/1 teaspoon oil. Pour a little water into the pan with the remaining oil to reach halfway up the sides of the aubergines/eggplants. Bake in a preheated oven at 180°C, 350°F, gas 4 for 1 hour, or until the aubergines are tender and the topping is crisp and golden.

Serves 2

Alternative filling

An alternative filling with a Middle Eastern flavour is given here. Take care when seasoning the dish as the feta cheese is already salty.

2 aubergines/eggplants
100g/4oz/½ cup long-grain brown rice
salt
5ml/1 teaspoon turmeric
15ml/1 tablespoon olive oil
4 shallots or 1 onion, chopped
5ml/1 teaspoon oregano
2.5ml/½ teaspoon basil
15ml/1 tablespoon parsley
100g/4oz feta cheese, crumbled
50g/2oz/⅓ cup chopped dates
2 tomatoes, skinned and sliced
60ml/4 tablespoons grated Parmesan cheese
5ml/1 teaspoon oil

Prepare the aubergine/eggplants and rice in the same way as described above in the previous recipe. Sauté the chopped aubergine until golden and remove from the pan. Add the shallot and sauté until soft. Remove

from the heat and stir in the herbs, feta cheese, sautéed aubergine and dates. Mix in the cooked rice and fill the aubergine/eggplant shells with this mixture. Lay the sliced tomato on top and sprinkle with grated cheese and oil. Bake in the same way as outlined above.

Serves 2

Traditional rice pudding

No section on rice would be complete without a recipe for a really creamy, delicately spiced rice pudding covered by a thick, golden-brown skin. Aim for a thick and creamy texture with pale caramel coloured rice. We can guarantee that this will bear no resemblance to the school puddings of your childhood and that you will soon be converted. The secret lies in the addition of a cinnamon stick and nutmeg, and in the slow cooking in a low oven. You can serve the pudding with fresh or stewed fruit or a spoonful of your favourite jam.

50g/2oz/¼ cup round-grain Carolina pudding rice
50g/2oz/¼ cup caster/superfine or soft brown sugar
900ml/1½ pints/3½ cups milk
1 cinnamon stick, 2.5cm/1in long
15g/½oz/1 tablespoon butter
1.25ml/¼ teaspoon ground nutmeg

Put the rice and sugar in a well-buttered deep ovenproof dish. Pour in the milk with the cinnamon stick. Dot the top with tiny pieces of butter and sprinkle with ground nutmeg. Place in a preheated oven at 140°C, 275°F, gas 1 for about 3 hours. After 1 hour, give the pudding a gentle stir to distribute the rice throughout the pudding. Keep an eye on the pudding to ensure that the skin does not burn — it should be a rich golden-brown. Remember to remove the cinnamon stick before serving.

Serves 4

Pasta

Home-made pasta

If you cannot buy freshly made pasta in your local shops, it is a good idea to make your own. It is a simple process and all you need are eggs and strong plain bread flour. You can colour the pasta green with spinach, or pink with tomato paste. We make our pasta in a food processor and roll and cut it by hand. Of course, an electric pasta-maker takes all the effort out of this and kneads, thins out the pasta and cuts it to the desired width. However, it is an expensive item and not worthwhile unless you are a great pasta lover and eat it several times a week. Our method is very easy and as long as you knead the dough until it is really elastic and silky in texture and roll it correctly, you will not experience any problems. If you want to keep the pasta, dry the noodles thoroughly and and store in a dry, cool larder where they will keep for 2-3 weeks before cooking.

Standard pasta:
3 eggs
225g/8oz/2¼ cups strong plain bread flour
Pasta verdi:
150g/5oz leaf spinach, frozen and thawed
2 eggs
225g/8oz/2¼ cups strong plain bread flour

If making pasta verdi, cook the spinach with a pinch of salt over medium heat for about 5 minutes. Drain and squeeze all the water out. Allow to cool.

Beat the eggs in the food mixer or processor bowl, with the spinach if you are making pasta verdi. With the machine in motion, gradually add the flour, a little at a time, until the mixture forms a soft dough which comes away from the sides of the bowl.

Turn the dough out onto a lightly floured surface and knead well until the dough is really smooth and silky (about 10 minutes). Roll the dough out on a large floured surface, giving it a quarter-turn every so often. Curl one end of the dough around the rolling pin occasionally and, holding the other end down, roll it towards you to stretch it out. The dough should be very thin like a sheet of cloth, about 3mm/⅛in thick at most, paper-thin and almost transparent.

Lay the pasta out on the board with about one-third overhanging the edge of the table or work-top. Leave for 10-12 minutes to dry out. Turn the pasta and repeat with another third for 10-12 minutes, and then finally with the remaining third. It should not get too dry or it will crack. Roll the pasta up loosely like a Swiss roll and cut through it horizontally at regular intervals, about 3mm/⅛in for thin noodles (fettuccine) or 5mm/¼in for wider noodles (tagliatelle). Unroll the noodles carefully and spread them over a clean cloth to dry out a little more. After 10 minutes, they are ready for cooking. To cook, slide them into boiling salted water to which you have added a spoonful of oil. They will cook incredibly quickly — about 10 seconds after the boiling liquid in which they are dropped returns to

the boil. Stir with a wooden spoon to prevent them sticking together and drain as soon as they are cooked.
4 servings

Curried tuna and pasta salad

This faintly curry flavoured salad served in a tangy mayonnaise dressing makes a tasty snack or side-salad. Use large pasta shells for their interesting shape and texture. Although a home-made mayonnaise tastes best, you can achieve good results with some of the commercial low-calorie versions.

175g/6oz pasta shells
200g/7oz tuna canned in brine
100ml/4floz/½ cup mayonnaise
salt and pepper
5ml/1 teaspoon curry powder
juice of ½ lemon
2 spring onions, chopped
few sprigs of parsley, chopped

Cook the pasta shells in boiling salted water until tender. Drain and cool. Cut the tuna into small chunks. Blend the mayonnaise with the seasonings and lemon juice and mix with the tuna chunks, pasta shells and chopped spring onions.

Pile the salad onto a serving dish and scatter over some chopped parsley.
Serves 3-4

Conchiglie with ricotta and walnut sauce

You have probably eaten ricotta as a filling for pasta but not as a sauce. However, it is an excellent way of serving pasta shells with a garnish of chopped walnuts and fresh parsley. The dish is quite rich and should be served as a small first course. Ricotta is a very soft cheese made from ewe's milk and is widely eaten in Italy on its own or served in sweet and savoury dishes. It is available from most Italian food suppliers and good delicatessens.

225g/8oz conchiglie/pasta shells
175g/6oz/1 cup ricotta cheese
45ml/3 tablespoons grated Parmesan cheese
salt and pepper
good pinch of ground nutmeg
15g/½oz/1 tablespoon margarine or butter
25g/1oz/¼ cup chopped walnuts
15ml/1 tablespoon chopped parsley

Cook the pasta shells in boiling salted water until tender. Drain. While they are cooking, mix the ricotta, 30ml/2 tablespoons grated Parmesan and seasonings to a smooth paste. Melt the margarine or butter in a small pan and stir in the ricotta mixture. Heat through very gently over low heat. Toss the cooked, drained pasta in this mixture with the walnuts and pile into a serving dish. Sprinkle with the remaining Parmesan and pop under a hot grill/broiler for 3-4 minutes until really hot. Sprinkle with chopped parsley and serve immediately with a big bowl of Parmesan.

Serves 4

Fettuccine with walnut and parsley sauce

This sauce is really a variation on the more familiar pesto made with basil and pine nuts. When fresh basil is hard to find in the winter, a parsley and walnut sauce makes a good substitute although the flavour is not so delicate as that of pesto. Serve as a first course with grated Parmesan.

350g/12oz fettuccine or home-made noodles
75g/3oz/¾ cup shelled walnuts
1 large bunch or 2 cups of parsley
salt and pepper
15g/½oz/1 tablespoon melted butter
1 thick slice white bread, crusts removed
50ml/2floz/¼ cup olive oil
juice of ½ lemon
15ml/1 tablespoon cream
grated Parmesan to serve

Place the walnuts, parsley and seasoning in a food processor or blender and process to a smooth paste. Add the melted butter with the bread through the feed tube while the machine is operating. Then add the olive oil in a steady, thin trickle as for mayonnaise. Stir in the lemon juice. The sauce should be smooth and thick with a lovely fresh green colour.

Cook the fettuccine in boiling salted water in the usual way until tender. Drain and toss well in the walnut sauce with the cream. Season with plenty of freshly ground black pepper and serve with grated Parmesan.

Serves 4

Hungarian pasta au gratin

This typically Hungarian way of serving pasta with curd cheese and soured cream flavoured with paprika and caraway seeds makes a filling supper dish. To cut down on calories we have added yoghurt and reduced the quantity of soured cream. To make the dish more substantial you can add chopped spicy sausage and hard-boiled eggs. Serve with a crisp, green salad.

225g/8oz lasagne or lasagnette, broken up roughly
15g/½oz/1 tablespoon margarine
175g/6oz smoked bacon or gammon, diced
10ml/2 teaspoons oil
225g/8oz/1⅓ cups curd cheese
100ml/4floz/½ cup natural yoghurt
50ml/2floz/¼ cup soured cream
freshly ground black pepper
30ml/2 tablespoons caraway seeds
25g/1oz/½ cup fresh breadcrumbs
5ml/1 teaspoon paprika

Cook the lasagne in boiling salted water until tender. Drain and mix with the margarine. Meanwhile, sauté the bacon or gammon in the oil or its own fat until browned. Place the cooked lasagne and bacon in a buttered ovenproof gratin dish.

Blend the curd cheese, yoghurt and soured cream and season with black pepper and caraway seeds. Spread this mixture over the lasagne. Scatter with breadcrumbs and dribble a little olive oil over the top or dot with tiny knobs of margarine. Sprinkle with paprika and bake in a preheated oven at 200°C, 400°F, gas 6 for 15-20 minutes until the top is crisp, golden and bubbling. Serve immediately.

Serves 3-4

Spaghetti in blue cheese sauce

Use a creamy, mellow dolcelatte or gorgonzola cheese to make this sauce. You can substitute other blue cheeses such as a soft blue brie or a creamy torta san gaudenzio. Your choice of pasta is optional too — fettuccine, tagliatelle or trenette can all be used, as can macaroni.

450g/1lb wholemeal or fresh spaghetti
100g/4oz/1 cup creamy dolcelatte or gorgonzola cheese
15g/½oz/1 tablespoon margarine
75ml/3floz/⅜ cup milk
15ml/1 tablespoon double/heavy cream
salt and pepper
pinch of ground nutmeg
30ml/2 tablespoons chopped parsley
45ml/3 tablespoons grated Parmesan cheese

Cook the spaghetti in boiling salted water until it is *al dente*, and drain. The time taken will depend on whether you use fresh or dry pasta. Mash the blue cheese with the margarine and milk in a heavy pan and heat gently until it melts to a thick, creamy sauce. Stir in the cream and seasoning and toss the cooked spaghetti in this cheesy sauce until all the strands are well-coated. Sprinkle with plenty of chopped parsley and grated Parmesan and serve hot with a bowl of grated Parmesan for guests to help themselves.

Serves 4

Spaghetti alla carbonara

This dish is popular in the friendly little *trattorias* of Rome and it is easy to make in your own kitchen using simple, economical ingredients — basically, spaghetti, ham or bacon, and eggs. It is less rich than many pasta dishes which are tossed in cream or tomato sauces, and makes a delicious light lunch or supper dish.

450g/1lb spaghetti
8 rashers streaky bacon, chopped or 100g/4oz ham, diced
30ml/2 tablespoons olive oil
3 eggs, beaten
salt and pepper
50g/2oz/1 cup grated Parmesan cheese
45ml/3 tablespoons cream (optional)
15ml/1 tablespoon chopped parsley

Cook the spaghetti in boiling salted water in the usual way until tender. Drain and keep warm. Fry the chopped bacon or ham gently in the olive oil until golden-brown. Add the cooked spaghetti to the pan and stir in the beaten eggs and seasoning. Stir gently over low heat with a wooden spoon until the egg starts to set and thicken. It should be slightly thickened and not so set as scrambled eggs. Stir in a little of the Parmesan and the cream (optional). Pile the carbonara mixture onto a serving dish, sprinkle with parsley and serve with the remaining Parmesan in a separate dish for guests to help themselves.

Serves 4

Lasagne al forno

Many variations of this multi-layered pasta dish exist but the classic version comes from the province of Emilia-Romagna, the home of good Italian cooking. The Bolognese layer up *lasagne verdi* (pasta sheets made from eggs, flour and a purée of fresh spinach) with rich *ragù* and creamy béchamel sauces. It is best to prepare the pasta dough and ragù sauces in advance to make the assembly of ingredients easier. You can even made the ragù in large quantities and freeze some for further use. It can be served with spaghetti or tagliatelle as well as lasagne. Fresh home-made pasta will keep in the refrigerator for a week or more.

225g/8oz freshly made (or bought) lasagne verdi
50g/2oz/⅓ cup freshly grated Parmesan cheese
15g/½oz/1 tablespoon butter
Ragù sauce:
1 onion, chopped
1 clove garlic, crushed
4 slices streaky bacon, chopped
1 carrot, diced
1 stick of celery, diced
30ml/2 tablespoons oil
225g/8oz/1 cup minced/ground beef
100g/4oz/½ cup minced/ground gammon
150ml/¼ pint/⅝ cup red wine
few dried Boletus mushrooms, crumbled
salt and pepper
100ml/4floz/1 cup milk
2.5ml/½ teaspoon ground nutmeg
450g/1lb tomatoes, skimmed and chopped (or canned)
15ml/1 tablespoon sugar
good pinch of oregano
Béchamel sauce:
25g/1oz/2 tablespoons butter
25g/1oz/3 tablespoons flour
300ml/½ pint/1¼ cups milk
salt and pepper
pinch of ground nutmeg

Make the ragù sauce — this takes about 4 hours to cook so make it well in advance of preparing the lasagne, even the day before. Sauté the onion, garlic, bacon, carrot and celery in the oil until tender. Add the beef and gammon and cook quickly until they are faintly browned. Then add the wine, dried mushrooms and seasoning and cook over medium heat until the wine has evaporated.

Add the milk and nutmeg and continue cooking until absorbed by the meat mixture. Now add the tomatoes, sugar and oregano and turn up the heat until the tomatoes start bubbling and the sauce thickens a little. Reduce the heat to a bare simmer and cook gently for about 4 hours, stirring occasionally, until the sauce is reduced and richly coloured.

To make the béchamel sauce, melt the butter and

stir in the flour to make a roux. Cook over gentle heat for 3 minutes, taking care that it does not brown, and then gradually beat in the milk until you have a thick, smooth, glossy sauce. Bring to the boil and then reduce to a simmer. Add the seasoning and nutmeg and cook gently for a few minutes.

Cook the lasagne sheets in boiling salted water until tender (take care not to over-cook them or they will go mushy). Drain and pat dry.

Now assemble the lasagne in a buttered gratin dish. Put a little hot ragù in the bottom and cover with pasta, then another layer of ragù topped with some béchamel sauce. Continue layering in this way until all the pasta and sauces are used up, ending with a layer of béchamel sauce. Sprinkle with plenty of grated Parmesan and dot the top with butter.

Bake in a preheated oven at 230°C, 450°F, gas 8 for 20 minutes until the lasagne is bubbling and golden-brown. Serve hot with a green salad. This dish freezes successfully.

Serves 4

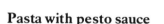

Pasta with pesto sauce

This is the classic Genoese pasta dish — the most magnificent of all Italian dishes in our opinion. It has been exported from Italy all over the world and is a great favourite in New York, for instance. Although you can buy ready-made pesto sauce in bottles in many Italian delicatessens it is only an apology for the real thing, and when basil is plentiful in summer it is a good idea to make up a large quantity of sauce and freeze some if you are a pesto lover. You can serve it with any pasta — tagliatelle, spaghetti, fettuccine, trenette or gnocchi.

50g/2oz/2 cups fresh basil leaves
50g/2oz/½ cup pine nuts
75g/3oz/½ cup grated Parmesan cheese
1 clove garlic, crushed
juice of ½ lemon
100ml/4floz/½ cup olive oil
salt and pepper
450g/1lb pasta of your choice

You can make the pesto sauce in a mortar but it is easier nowadays to use a blender or food processor. Wash and dry the basil and set aside. Spread the pine nuts out across a baking sheet and place in a preheated oven at 220°C, 425°F, gas 7 for 12-15 minutes until slightly golden-brown. This helps to bring out their

flavour. Chop them very finely or grind to a powder in a food processor. Mix with the Parmesan cheese.

Put the basil leaves, garlic and lemon juice in the blender or processor and process for 20 seconds. Pour the oil in a thin, steady stream as you would for a mayonnaise through the feed tube onto the basil mixture. Process until thick and smooth. Pour the basil sauce onto the ground nuts and cheese and blend well. Season with salt and pepper. You will probably have twice as much pesto as you need to dress the pasta, so store what you don't use in an airtight jar in the refrigerator, or freeze until needed.

Cook the pasta until tender in boiling, salted water and drain and refresh. Toss in the pesto sauce and serve sprinkled with grated Parmesan.

Serves 4

Tagliatelle in avocado sauce

You can use home-made or commercial pasta in this recipe, although the former tastes better, of course. It serves six people as a first course or three as a main course. Tagliatelle are the long egg noodles beloved of the Bolognese and usually served with a ragù sauce. However, this recipe departs from the traditional Italian pasta theme and the tagliatelle are served in an exquisite sauce of bacon, mushrooms and sliced avocado. It is especially attractive if you use a mixture of green and yellow noodles. It is important to choose an avocado which is not over-ripe but is still tender enough to slice easily and retain its firmness and distinctive pale green colouring.

450g/1lb mixed green and yellow tagliatelle
30ml/2 tablespoons olive oil
100g/4oz streaky bacon or unsmoked ham, diced
100g/4oz button mushrooms, thinly sliced
1 shallot, finely chopped
100ml/4floz/½ cup single/light cream
salt and freshly ground black pepper
pinch of ground nutmeg
1 avocado, peeled, stoned and thinly sliced
squeeze of lemon juice
50g/2oz/⅓ cup grated Parmesan cheese

Cook the tagliatelle in plenty of boiling salted water until it is *al dente*. Drain and keep warm. Heat the oil in the same large pan and sauté the bacon, mushroom and shallot quickly until tender. Replace the pasta in the pan and gently stir in the cream and seasonings. Heat through gently, tossing the tagliatelle in the sauce.

Pile in a warm serving dish and decorate with the avocado slices. Sprinkle with a little lemon juice and plenty of freshly grated Parmesan. Serve immediately with a bowl of Parmesan for guests to help themselves.

Serves 3-6

Spaghetti with salmon and mange-tout peas

This is a departure from the traditional ways of serving pasta in a rich tomato or creamy sauce. Served in small quantities, it is an appetising way to begin a meal. If you are a pasta-lover you will find it irresistible. Use spaghetti or long, thin home-made noodles. To reduce the cost of the dish, you can make it with smoked salmon trimmings, which are available from many fishmongers and delicatessens.

350g/12oz spaghetti
1 small onion, chopped
15ml/1 tablespoon oil
15g/½oz/1 tablespoon margarine
175g/6oz mange-tout/sugar peas
75g/3oz smoked salmon, chopped roughly
45ml/3 tablespoons single/light cream
pinch of ground nutmeg
salt and pepper
30ml/2 tablespoons chopped parsley
50g/2oz/⅓ cup grated Parmesan cheese

Cook the spaghetti in a large pan of boiling salted water until tender. Drain and rinse in boiling water. Meanwhile, sauté the onion in the oil and margarine until soft, and cook the mange-tout peas for 2 - 3 minutes in boiling, salted water until just tender but still crunchy.

Add the mange-tout peas and salmon to the onion in the pan and gently stir in the spaghetti until every strand is separate and glistening with oil. Toss it lightly in the cream and season with nutmeg, salt and freshly ground pepper. Stir in the chopped parsley and pile onto a serving dish. Sprinkle with plenty of Parmesan and serve immediately.

Serves 4

Sweet fruit and macaroni pudding

If you always associate macaroni with savoury dishes, you will be surprised at how well it adapts to this sweet treatment. You can vary the recipe by adding ground cinnamon and chopped candied peel for a more spicy, interesting flavour, or by cooking the macaroni slowly in milk (550ml/1 pint/2½ cups) for about 20 minutes, or until all the liquid is absorbed. Serve the pudding with yoghurt or custard.

225g/8oz/1½ cups dried fruit (apricots, peaches or pears)
50g/2oz/⅓ cup raisins
15ml/1 tablespoon dark rum
225g/8oz wholemeat macaroni
50g/2oz/¼ cup margarine
2 dessert apples, peeled, cored and diced
juice of 1 lemon
50g/2oz/¼ cup soft brown sugar
pinch of ground cloves
2 eggs, separated
25g/1oz/½ cup fresh breadcrumbs
25g/1oz/¼ cup chopped nuts (almonds, walnuts, hazelnuts)

Soak the dried fruit for several hours and drain. Place in a pan, cover with a little water and simmer until tender. Drain and set aside. Macerate the raisins in the rum for at least 30 minutes. Cook the macaroni in boiling water for 10 minutes, or simmer in milk (as described above) for 20 minutes. Drain and mix in the margarine, diced apple, lemon juice and raisins.

Whisk the sugar, ground cloves and egg yolk until light and frothy. Whisk the egg whites separately until glossy and standing in stiff peaks. Fold into the yolk mixture with a metal spoon and gently mix into the cooked macaroni.

Pour the macaroni mixture into a well-greased 900ml/1½ pint/3¼ cup capacity ovenproof dish and sprinkle with breadcrumbs and chopped nuts. Dot the top with a little margarine and bake in a preheated oven at 180°C 350°F, gas 4 for 30 minutes.

Serves 4

Opposite: tagliatelle in avocado sauce (see page 51) can be served as a first course for a dinner party, whereas lasagne al forno (see page 50) makes a tasty supper dish

Beans & Pulses

Beans are really the seeds of the Leguminae family, the second largest group of plants in the world with over 15,000 species. They are one of the most ancient foods known to Man with a colourful history. Not only were they placed in the Egyptian pharaohs' tombs to nourish them in the after-life, but they were also used as voting chips by the ancient Greeks and Romans — white broad beans were a positive 'for' vote whereas black beans were a vote 'against' a motion for the candidate. The only beans known in the Middle East and Europe until the sixteenth century and the opening of the new trade routes to the Americas were broad beans, peas, lentils and chick peas. With the discovery of America, Spanish and Portuguese explorers brought back new colourful beans and they became a delicacy in many European courts.

Soon, haricot, red and black kidney beans, creamy butter beans and colourful scarlet runner beans, so beloved of the English, were widely grown in European gardens. These New World beans were more versatile and varied in texture, flavour and colour than the old dried beans which were the staple winter diet of the poor in mediaeval Europe. Some beans actually travelled in the opposite direction across the Atlantic from east to west. African slaves took the seeds of black-eyed beans with them to Jamaica and from there to the Deep South states of the USA where they are still popular and an essential ingredient in such dishes as Hoppin' John.

There are two genera of beans: *vigna*, the smaller group which includes mung beans, aduki beans and black-eyed beans (or cow peas); and *phaseolus*, a larger group of which all the New World beans are members. The beauty of beans lies in their ability to thrive in almost any climate and their relatively high protein content, which varies from 17 to 38 per cent depending on the type of bean — higher than that of some fish and meat and double that of many cereals. Beans contain little fat and, being a good source of B vitamins, iron and calcium, they can play an important role in a healthy diet.

Do not fall intro the trap of thinking that beans are boring — on the contrary, they are probably the most versatile of all vegetables and can be served in so many ways. They can be puréed as a party dip, casseroled with meat and vegetables, served in filling, hearty soups, or dressed with olive oil and lemon in summer salads. They are among the most useful ingredients you can keep in your store-cupboard.

Types of beans and pulses

Aduki beans are natives of Japan where they are the second most important food crop. These small red beans are popular with many vegetarians who adhere to a strictly macrobiotic diet. Their nutty flavour lends itself well to savoury stews and casseroles. They require less soaking than most beans — only 2-3 hours.

Black beans, widely eaten in South America and Spain, belong to the haricot family. They require overnight soaking before cooking.

Black-eyed beans reached Jamaica in 1675 from their tropical home in Africa. Their soft texture and creamy flavour make them a good accompaniment to rice and vegetables. They are still an important staple food in many African countries as well as Central America. They require overnight soaking.

Borlotti beans, with their beautiful brown and pink speckled appearance, are used in many Italian bean dishes and soups. Soak overnight.

Broad beans are probably the most ancient vegetable in the Western world although they were held in low esteem by the Romans and Greeks and eaten only by the poor. In fact, Pythagoras, the ancient Greek philosopher, told his followers to abstain from these beans, and he later died at the hands of his pursuers beside a broad bean field through which he did not dare to venture. Broad beans sometimes caused favism in many Mediterranean peoples and it is possible that Pythagoras was afraid of this. The soft, floury texture of broad beans goes down well in salads, soups and stews. They can be used fresh or dried. Fresh young broad beans are one of the pleasures of early summer.

Butter beans, otherwise known as lima beans, originally came from Peru. The largest of all the beans and pulses, they are kidney-shaped and may be creamy-white, pale green, brown or red. They have a delicate flavour which goes well with fish and chicken in salads, or with creamy vegetable sauces. They require overnight soaking but are widely available precooked in cans.

Chick peas, also known as garbanzo beans in Spain and South America, are native to western Asia and were eaten in Egypt at the time of the pharaohs. Six million tonnes of chick peas are now grown in dry climates throughout the world, from the Middle East and India to southern Europe and South America. They may be cooked and puréed as in the Mediterranean *hummus*, toasted and salted and served with drinks, ground with flour to make couscous, or served in spicy stews and curries. In India they are split as *dahl* and then curried. They have a pleasant nutty flavour and crunchy texture and require overnight soaking.

Flageolets, subtly flavoured and pale green in colour, are grown in France and Italy and often served as an accompaniment to roast lamb. Soak them overnight.

Ful medames are eaten throughout Egypt and have become almost a national dish sold on every street corner. These small coffee coloured broad beans should be soaked overnight.

Haricot beans are a large family which includes dark red kidney and pink speckled pinto beans. All these beans are used in salads and casseroles, and the creamy white haricot beans are the main ingredient in such classic dishes as the American Boston baked beans and the French *cassoulet*. They are probably the most widely eaten beans in the world as they are also the famous canned beans in tomato sauce.

Lentils are one of the oldest pulses and are the small seeds of an Eastern Mediterranean plant. Now grown in Italy, India and the Middle East, they come in two varieties: the Continental brown or greyish seeds; and the orange-red Egyptian or Syrian seeds without a seed coat. Over one million tonnes are produced annually for use in salads, stews, curries and soups. Many people prefer red lentils to brown for purées and soups. They cook more quickly and break down in the cooking process to thicken the mixture. They do not require soaking.

Mung beans are a native of India and may be sprouted for use in salads. They are used as a dried bean in India and as a sprout by the Chinese. Dried mung beans require overnight soaking.

Peas, fresh or dried, are a good source of protein and have been cultivated since ancient times. Dried split green and yellow peas are usually made into hearty, warming winter soups. They do not require soaking.

Soya beans, weight for weight, have a much higher protein content than steak and are thus the most nutritious beans of all. Native to China, they have long been eaten in the Far East where they were sometimes known as 'the meat of the earth'. Now in the West, they are often eaten in the form of TVP (texturised vegetable protein) as a meat substitute. They need overnight soaking.

Buying and cooking beans
Beans come in all shapes, sizes and colours and can be purchased in most health food stores, continental and oriental delicatessens and many supermarkets. Go to a shop which has a quick turnover in stock to ensure that the beans have not been stored too long on the shelves before you buy them. Always check beans and lentils over before cooking to sort out any which are blemished or shrunken and remove small stones and grit.

All dried beans require soaking, usually overnight, although some varieties of beans, such as aduki beans, need less time. Don't soak for more than a maximum of 12 hours, however, or the beans may become sticky. Beans can also be soaked in boiling water and left for 3-4 hours to speed up the soaking process. All beans double in weight after soaking. Use double the amount of cold water to beans and pour away the soaking liquid afterwards and cook the beans in fresh water. The cooking time will be determined by the size and the age of the beans used. Kidney beans require special cooking (see page 63)

Beans may be flavoured with herbs, aromatics and vegetables while cooking but salt should *never* be added to the cooking liquid as this hardens the beans. Always season with salt *after* cooking. Beans also respond well to pressure-cooking.

Dried beans should be stored in airtight glass jars or containers in a cool, dry place well away from moisture and heat, and will keep well for 9-12 months. After this, they will get tougher, require longer soaking and lose their flavour.

Sprouting beans
The best sprouting beans are the tiny mung beans which have a really sweet flavour, but soya beans and alfalfa seeds are also suitable for sprouting. Just soak 60ml/4 tablespoons of the mung beans in water overnight. Discard any that float to the surface (these are infertile). Drain the remaining beans and place in a wide-necked jar covered with muslin or cheesecloth and secured with a rubber band. Leave it on its side, and then the following day pour in some tepid water through the muslin to rinse the beans. Pour out the excess through the muslin. Repeat this procedure every day for 4-5 days, or until the beans are 2.5cm/1in — 5cm/2in long. Remove the bean sprouts from the jar, rinse in fresh water and use in salads, in sandwiches or Chinese stir-fried dishes. Bean sprouts are high in vitamins and a good, healthy food to include in your diet. They contain B and C vitamins and some amino acids as well as 37 per cent protein. The beans do not gain nutritional value after the fourth day of sprouting.

Beans

Broad bean and rice salad

This Middle Eastern dish of broad beans is dressed with yoghurt to make a refreshing summer salad. Serve it as a first course on a bed of raw spinach leaves.

450g/1lb broad beans, fresh or frozen
50g/2oz/¼cup long-grain brown rice
150ml/¼ pint/⅝ cup yoghurt
1 clove garlic, crushed
pinch of paprika
25g/1oz/¼ cup pine nuts
salt and pepper
1 egg yolk
few well-washed spinach leaves
few chopped chives

Boil the beans until tender and drain. Do not add salt to the cooking water as this will harden the beans. Boil the rice in salted water until tender. Drain and mix with the cooked beans.

Mix the yoghurt, garlic, paprika, pine nuts and seasoning, and blend a little of this mixture with the egg yolk. Stir the cooked beans and rice into the remaining mixture and heat through very gently. Add the blended egg yolk and stir over low heat until the sauce thickens. Do not boil or the sauce will curdle. Cool and chill. Serve on a bed of spinach leaves sprinkled with chopped chives.

Serves 4

Tonno con fagiole

This earthy dish of tuna and beans from Tuscany in Italy is a tasty way to start a meal. Using canned tuna and dried butter beans it is a good way of utilising store cupboard ingredients. Serve it on a bed of crisp lettuce.

225g/8oz/1⅓ cups butter beans
1 onion, thinly sliced in rings
200g/7oz canned tuna in brine, drained
45ml/3 tablespoons chopped parsley
Dressing:
60ml/4 tablespoons olive oil
15ml/1 tablespoon wine vinegar
juice of ½ lemon
pinch of sugar
salt and pepper

Soak the butter beans overnight. Drain and cook in boiling water until tender but not mushy. Drain the beans and cool. Place in a salad dish with the sliced

onion and tuna, cut into chunks. Mix the dressing and pour over the beans. Toss well so that all the beans are coated and glistening. Scatter over the chopped parsley and serve.

Serves 4

Hummus bi tahina

This smooth, creamy chick pea purée is eaten throughout the Middle East with pitta bread (see recipe on page 35). It makes a delicious party or before-dinner dip served with bread, biscuits, crudités or slices of fried aubergine/eggplant. Tahina paste is available at most delicatessens, Greek shops and health food stores.

175g/6oz/1 cup chick peas
juice of 2 large lemons
2 small cloves of garlic, crushed
100ml/4floz/½ cup tahina paste
salt and pepper
Garnish:
5 or 6 cooked chick peas
15ml/1 tablespoon sesame or olive oil
15ml/1 tablespoon chopped parsley
good pinch of cayenne

Soak the chick peas in water overnight. Drain and cook in boiling water in a covered pan until tender (about 1 hour). Drain the cooked chick peas and set aside to cool, reserving 5 or 6 for the garnish.

Place the cooked chick peas, lemon juice, garlic, and half the tahina paste in a blender or food processor and purée them. Add the remaining tahina and process again until the purée is thick and smooth and creamy, adding more lemon juice or tahina if necessary. Season to taste. Pour the hummus into a serving dish. Level the top and swirl it attractively with a fork. Place the reserved chick peas in the centre, dribble over the oil and sprinkle with chopped parsley and cayenne.

Makes approximately 300ml/½pint/1¼ cups hummus

Egyptian ful medames

This earthy bean dish is reputed to have been served in Egypt since ancient times. Ful medames, or fava beans, are essential for an authentic flavour, and these are available from many delicatessens and Greek stores. Eaten throughout Egypt, this dish is always served with hard-boiled eggs, lemon juice and olive oil.

225g/8oz/1⅓ cups ful medame or fava beans
750ml/1¼ pints/3 cups water
1 onion, chopped
2 cloves garlic, crushed
7.5ml/½ tablespoon ground cumin
100g/4oz/⅔ cup red lentils
salt and pepper
30ml/2 tablespoons chopped parsley
Garnish:
olive oil
lemon juice
hard-boiled eggs

Soak the beans overnight. Strain and place in a pan of fresh water with the onion, garlic and cumin. Bring to the boil and then simmer for 1½ hours, or place in a low oven at 150°C, 300°F, gas 2.

Add the lentils and cook gently for 1 hour. Drain and garnish with chopped parsley, sprinkled with olive oil, lemon juice and chopped hard-boiled egg.

Serves 4

Salade niçoise

There are so many versions of this French salad that we hesitate to include a recipe for it. However, this is based on a salad enjoyed one hot day in a little restaurant in Pennsylvania. Small chunks of garlic sausage are mixed in with the tuna. You need the really thin stringless French beans for this dish and waxy, not floury, potatoes.

225g/8oz stringless French beans
2 medium-sized waxy potatoes
3 spring onions/shallots, chopped
225g/8oz tomatoes, quartered
100g/4oz garlic sausage, cut in chunks
175g/6oz canned tuna fish, drained and cut in chunks
3 hard-boiled eggs, shelled and halved
12 black olives
45ml/3 tablespoons chopped parsley
Dressing:
60ml/4 tablespoons olive oil
15ml/1 tablespoon wine vinegar
juice of ½ lemon
1.25ml/¼ teaspoon Dijon mustard
salt and pepper

Top and tail the French beans and cook in boiling, salted water until tender with the pan uncovered (this helps keep the fresh, green colour). Drain and cool.

Peel the potatoes and cook in boiling water until tender but *not* mushy. You can use tiny new potatoes, if you prefer. Leave to cool and cut the large potatoes into chunks.

Mix the beans and potatoes with the onions, tomato quarters, garlic sausage and tuna in a salad bowl. Mix the dressing and toss the salad in it. Garnish with the hard-boiled eggs, black olives and chopped parsley.

Serves 4

West Indian black bean soup

Beans are one of the staple foods of the West Indian and Caribbean islands. This tasty soup is economical to make and is full of natural fibre and goodness. You can make it hot and spicy if you wish in the real West Indian manner by adding some fiery chilli powder or chopped fresh chillis.

100g/4oz/⅔ cup black beans
1 bay leaf
22.5ml/1½ tablespoons oil
1 small onion, chopped
1 stick celery, chopped
550ml/1 pint/2½ cups water or vegetable stock
good pinch of thyme
2.5ml/½ teaspoon oregano
pinch each of cayenne pepper, dry mustard and ground nutmeg
salt and pepper
100g/4oz/½ cup long-grain brown rice
45ml/3 tablespoons tomato juice (or 2 puréed tomatoes)
5ml/1 teaspoon honey
225ml/8floz/1 cup milk

Soak the beans in water for several hours. Drain and place in a pan covered with fresh water. Bring to the boil and boil hard for about 3 minutes. Drain and replace the beans in the pan with more fresh water. Add the bay leaf, bring to the boil and simmer until tender (approximately 1¼ hours).

Meanwhile, heat the oil and sauté the onion and celery until soft. Add the water (or stock) and the herbs, spices and seasoning. Bring to the boil and add the rice. Simmer gently for about 30 minutes. Add the cooked beans, tomato juice and honey and simmer for a further 10 minutes or until the rice is tender and cooked. Just before serving, stir in the milk and check the seasoning. Serve with crusty granary bread.

Serves 4

Kidney bean and sausage salad

This dish of kidney beans and chunks of garlic sausage is flavoured with paprika and tossed in a soured cream and yoghurt dressing. Serve it with cold meats or sausages as a supper dish.

225g/8oz/1⅓ cups kidney beans
2 onions, chopped
1 large clove garlic, chopped
45ml/3 tablespoons oil
10ml/2 teaspoons sweet paprika
5ml/1 teaspoon hot paprika
225g/8oz garlic sausage, cut in chunks
50ml/2floz/¼ cup natural yoghurt
50ml/2floz/¼ cup soured cream
salt and pepper
15ml/1 tablespoon lemon juice
30ml/2 tablespoons chopped parsley

Soak the kidney beans overnight and drain. Place in a pan with fresh water, bring to the boil and boil for 10 minutes. Drain the beans and refresh under running water. Replace in the pan with more fresh water and bring to the boil, reduce the heat and simmer for 1 hour or until tender. Drain.

Sauté the chopped onion and garlic in the oil until soft and golden. Add the paprika and cook gently for 2 minutes. Mix the beans and onion mixture with the garlic sausage in a serving dish. Blend the yoghurt, soured cream, seasoning and lemon juice and toss the bean salad in this mixture. Season to taste and sprinkle with plenty of chopped parsley.

Serves 4

Bean and pepper salad

Glossy dark red kidney beans mixed with thin rings of bright green and red pepper make this a spectacular and beautiful salad. You can cheat if you really are in a hurry by using canned, precooked kidney beans but freshly cooked dried beans taste better.

175g/6oz/1 cup kidney beans
1 small red pepper
1 small green pepper
1 onion, thinly sliced in rings
1 spring onion/shallot chopped
chopped chives and parsley
Dressing:
45ml/3 tablespoons olive oil
juice of 1 lemon

15ml/1 tablespoon wine vinegar
salt and pepper

Soak the dried kidney beans overnight and then drain and rinse them. Place in a pan of cold water (do not add salt as this will harden the beans) and bring to the boil. Boil hard for 10 minutes. Drain and rinse the beans and transfer to a pan of fresh cold water. Bring to the boil and simmer for about one hour until tender. Drain and cool.

Cut out the core and seeds of the peppers and slice horizontally in thin rings. Place in a salad bowl with the beans and onion.

Mix the dressing and toss with the bean salad and sprinkle with chopped chives.

Serves 4

French country-style beans

This earthy dish of haricot beans cooked in wine with smoked pork is eaten in many French country districts. To obtain the best results, you should use a respectable, if not a good, red wine. This will elevate the dish considerably, especially if you choose a good claret or a burgundy. The France use smoked Bayonne ham but Italian Parma ham or even cubed smoked gammon will do as Bayonne ham is difficult to buy.

225g/8oz/1⅓ cups haricot beans
2.5ml/½ teaspoon basil
2 bay leaves
1 onion, chopped
¼ fennel bulb, cubed
30ml/2 tablespoons olive oil
300ml/½ pint/1¼ cups red wine
100g/4oz diced smoked ham
salt and pepper
chopped parsley to garnish

Soak the haricot beans overnight. Drain and cook in fresh water until tender with the basil and bay leaves. Be careful not to overcook the beans or they will become mushy. Strain and put aside.

Fry the onion and fennel in the oil until golden, and add the wine and beans. Bring to the boil and mix in the ham and seasoning. Cover the pan and remove from the heat. Place in a preheated oven at 170°C, 325°F, gas 3 for 30-40 minutes until the beans are really tender and the sauce has thickened. Sprinkle with chopped parsley and serve with crusty brown bread, a crisp, green salad and red wine.

Serves 4

German beans and red cabbage

This colourful dish of red cabbage and beans flavoured with apple and spices is usually eaten in Germany with sausages as a warming winter's supper. Follow the instructions for cooking the kidney beans carefully.

225g/8oz/1⅓ cups red kidney beans
350g/12oz/4½ cups shredded red cabbage
1 onion, finely chopped
1 clove garlic, crushed
2 sticks celery, chopped
50g/2oz fennel bulb, chopped
2 cooking/green apples, peeled, cored and diced
1.25ml/¼ teaspoon each of ground coriander, cinnamon, allspice and thyme
30ml/2 tablespoons soft brown sugar
salt and pepper
300ml/½ pint/1¼ cups red wine
15ml/1 tablespoon wine vinegar
50ml/2floz/¼ cup hot water

Soak the kidney beans overnight. Drain and boil in fresh water for 10 minutes. Drain and wash under running water. Cover with fresh water and bring to the boil again. Reduce the heat and cook gently for about 1 hour until tender. Strain.

Boil the shredded cabbage in a covered pan for 5 minutes and drain. Place a layer of cabbage across the base of an ovenproof casserole dish, cover with chopped onion, garlic, celery, fennel, apple and spices and then a layer of cooked beans on top. Continue layering up the ingredients in this way, finishing with a layer of cabbage. Sprinkle with brown sugar and season well. Pour in the wine, vinegar and hot water. Cover the casserole dish and bake in a preheated oven at 170°C 325°F, gas 3 for 1 hour. Serve hot with spicy sausages.
Serves 4

Greek bean casserole

This casserole of black-eyed beans, tomatoes and honey is lightly spiced with coriander and cloves. It should be served hot with a traditional Greek salad of lettuce, tomatoes, cucumber, black olives and feta cheese tossed in an oil and lemon dressing flavoured with oregano.

225g/8oz/1⅓ cups black-eyed beans
1 onion, chopped
1 clove garlic, crushed
45ml/3 tablespoons tomato paste
300ml/½ pint/1¼ cups water
2 tomatoes, skinned and sliced

pinch each of ground cloves and coriander
15ml/1 tablespoon wine vinegar
30ml/2 tablespoons honey
salt and pepper

Soak the beans overnight. Drain and cook in boiling water for about 1 hour or until just tender. Drain and set aside. Sauté the onion and garlic in the oil until soft and translucent. Stir in the tomato paste and then the water, sliced tomato and spices. Cook for 2 minutes, add the vinegar and honey and season to taste. Stir in the beans and transfer to an ovenproof casserole dish. Cover with a lid and cook in a preheated oven at 170°C 325°F, gas 3 for 30 minutes. Serve hot.
Serves 4

Chilli con carne

This South American dish of chilli, meat and beans has become popular in the West, especially with young people. It freezes well and makes a good party dish. It should be very fiery indeed but this will not suit everyone's tastes, so we have given a recipe for a medium-hot dish. Chilli powder varies in strength and some brands are red-hot so add only a little initially and keep tasting and adding until you get the right flavour and degree of heat and spiciness. Fresh hot chillis will give a better flavour than chilli powder.

225g/8oz/1⅓ cups red kidney beans
2 onions, finely chopped
1 clove garlic, crushed
2 carrots, diced
550g/1¼lb/2½ cups lean minced/ground beef
15ml/1 tablespoon paprika
5ml/1 teaspoon ground cumin
10ml/2 teaspoons chilli powder or 1 fresh red chilli pepper, seeded and diced
45ml/3 tablespoons tomato paste
450g/1lb canned tomatoes, chopped
5ml/1 teaspoon sugar
5ml/1 teaspoon oregano
salt and pepper

Soak the kidney beans overnight. Drain and cook in the usual way (see page 58). Sauté the onion and garlic until soft and golden with the diced carrot. Add the beef and cook for 5 minutes or so until browned. Add the spices and tomato paste and cook gently for 2 minutes. Stir in the tomatoes, sugar and oregano. Bring to the boil and then reduce the heat to a simmer and cook gently for 45 minutes with the pan covered.

Add the cooked, drained kidney beans about 10 minutes before serving and heat through gently in the meat sauce. Serve with plain boiled rice and salad.

Serves 4

Bean cassoulet

This is not the classical great cassoulet of south-western France, which is flavoured with *confit d'oie* (preserved goose) and smoked sausages, but a simpler more economical version without any meat. You don't have to be a vegetarian to enjoy it, although you can add a little salt pork or diced bacon if you *must*. Serve it with a fresh green salad as a tasty supper dish.

225g/8oz/1⅓ cups haricot beans
1 small onion studded with 3 cloves
1 bay leaf
30ml/2 tablespoons oil
1 large onion, chopped
1 clove garlic, crushed
22.5ml/1½ tablespoons tomato paste
2.5ml/½ teaspoon each of chopped basil, oregano and parsley
50ml/2floz/¼ cup red wine
225g/8oz tomatoes, skinned and chopped (or canned)
5ml/1 teaspoon brown sugar
salt and pepper
few drops Worcestershire sauce
15ml/1 tablespoon brandy
15ml/1 tablespoon lemon juice
Topping:
15ml/1 tablespoon wheatgerm
15ml/1 tablespoon chopped Brazil nuts
25g/1oz/3 tablespoons Parmesan cheese

Cover the beans with water and soak overnight. Drain and wash the beans in fresh water. Place them in a pan with the clove-studded onion and bay leaf, cover with water and bring to the boil. Do not add salt to the water as this will harden the beans. Simmer for 2 hours or until the beans are tender but not mushy. Drain, reserving 100ml/4floz/½ cup of the cooking liquid and discarding the onion and bay leaf.

Heat the oil in a flameproof casserole dish, and sauté the onion and garlic until tender. Stir in the tomato paste, herbs, red wine, tomatoes, sugar and seasoning. Bring to the boil, reduce the heat and add the reserved cooking liquid, Worcestershire sauce, brandy, lemon juice and the beans. Stir well. Cover the dish and place in a preheated oven at 180°C, 350°F, gas 4.

After an hour, remove the dish and add more wine or water if too much liquid is evaporating. Sprinkle the top with the wheatgerm, nuts and cheese and bake uncovered for a further 10-15 minutes until crisp and golden-brown.

Serves 4

Boston baked beans

This classic American dish was the forerunner of the canned beans in tomato sauce which are now sold all over the world. It became the daily meal of the brave pioneers who set out across the continent to discover new land in the West or to join the Californian gold rush. Every night a fire would be lit and a pot of beans and salt pork prepared. Boston baked beans is ideal for *al fresco* barbecues. Serve it with hamburgers, steaks or sausages and salad in the American manner.

450g/1lb/2⅔ cups haricot beans
1 large onion, studded with 3 cloves
1 large onion, chopped
15ml/1 tablespoon oil
60ml/4 tablespoons black treacle or molasses
100g/4oz/½ cup soft brown sugar
45ml/3 tablespoons tomato paste
15ml/1 tablespoon Dijon mustard
salt and pepper
225g/8oz salt belly pork or gammon

Soak the beans overnight. Drain and cover with fresh water (approximately 1 litre/1¾ pints/4¼ cups water). Add the clove-studded onion and bring to the boil. Simmer for about 50 minutes or until the beans are tender. Drain, reserving the onion and cooking liquor.

Sauté the chopped onion in the oil until soft and golden. Add the treacle, sugar, tomato paste, mustard, seasoning and 400ml/14floz/1¾ cups of the reserved cooking liquor. Finally, add the whole piece of belly pork or gammon and bring to the boil. Cover the pan and place in a very low preheated oven at 130°C, 250°F, gas ½ for 3½ hours. Remove the pork and cut into small pieces, discarding any excess fat. Replace in the bean pot and return to the oven, uncovered, for another 30 minutes.

Serves 4

Opposite: bean and pepper salad in an oil and lemon dressing (see page 58) and a tasty casserole of Boston baked beans (see this page) are interesting bean dishes

Butter beans in chilli sauce

This tasty dish is cheap to make and was inspired by the fiery bean dishes of central America. You can add more chilli powder or dried chillis if it is not hot enough for your taste. It freezes well and thus makes a quick, warming supper dish when you have no time to cook.

225g/8oz/1⅓ cups butter beans
100g/4oz streaky bacon, chopped
2 onions, chopped
30ml/2 tablespoons oil
450g/1lb fresh tomatoes, skinned and sliced (or canned)
200g/7oz canned sweetcorn kernels
5ml/1 teaspoon chilli powder
2.5ml/½ teaspoon dried oregano
salt and pepper
50ml/2floz/¼ cup black treacle
150ml/¼ pint/⅝ cup boiling water

Soak the beans in cold water overnight, drain and place in a saucepan. Cover with fresh water and bring to the boil. Reduce the heat and cook gently for about 1 hour until tender but firm. Drain and set aside.

Sauté the chopped onion and bacon in the oil until soft and place in a shallow ovenproof casserole dish. Cover with the beans and then a layer of tomato and finally the sweetcorn. Gently stir in the chilli, oregano and seasoning.

Mix the black treacle and boiling water and pour into the casserole dish. Bake in a preheated oven at 170°C, 325°F, gas 3 for about 45 minutes. Serve sprinkled with grated cheese if wished.

Serves 4

Butter beans in mushroom sauce

One of the best ways of serving butter beans is in a delicious mushroom sauce. This simple, tasty dish is quickly prepared and is very economical. Serve with a crisp green salad.

225g/8oz/1⅓ cups butter beans
550ml/1 pint/2½ cups coating béchamel sauce (see recipe
*   on page 171)*
150ml/¼ pint/⅝ cup chicken stock (optional)
350g/12oz mushrooms, finely chopped
5ml/1 teaspoon oregano
15ml/1 tablespoon chopped parsley
salt and pepper
pinch of ground nutmeg
10ml/2 teaspoons mushroom ketchup

Soak the butter beans overnight, drain and place in a pan. Cover with water and bring to the boil. Reduce the heat and simmer until tender. Take care not to overcook them. They should be firm and not mushy.

While the butter beans are cooking, prepare the mushroom sauce. Make the béchamel coating sauce and cook gently for 3 minutes. Add the strained beans and thin with a little stock, if necessary. Stir in the chopped mushrooms, herbs, seasoning and ketchup and cook gently for 5 minutes. Serve with green salad.

Serves 4

Chick pea curry

Chick peas make an interesting alternative to meat in a curry because of their unusual flavour and texture. They contain 20 per cent protein so you need not worry about missing out on valuable nutrients. Serve with sambals, rice and other curry dishes of contrasting flavours and textures.

225g/8oz/1⅓ cups chick peas, soaked overnight
45ml/3 tablespoons oil
1 large onion, chopped
2 cloves garlic, crushed
salt
15ml/1 tablespoon good-quality curry powder
5ml/1 teaspoon cumin seed
1.25ml/¼ teaspoon each ground cumin and coriander
22.5ml/1½ tablespoons flour
300ml/½ pint/1¼ cups boiling water
45ml/3 tablespoons desiccated coconut
7.5ml/½ tablespoon brown sugar
100g/4oz dates, pitted/stoned
juice of ½ lemon

Drain and wash the chick peas. Cover them with water and bring to the boil. Reduce the heat to a simmer, cover the pan and cook for 1½-2 hours, or until tender. Strain, reserving the cooking liquid.

Heat the oil, add the onion and garlic and sauté until soft and translucent. Stir in the curry powder and spices and aromatise for 1 minute. Now add the flour and cook for 1 minute. Add the coconut milk (made by infusing the coconut in boiling water and then straining, or making the same volume up with creamed tablet coconut). Stir until the mixture thickens, adding some of the strained chick pea liquid if necessary. Stir in the sugar and seasoning and then the chick peas.

Cover the pan and cook for 25 minutes over low

heat. Add the stoned/pitted dates and cook for a further 15 minutes. Add the lemon juice and serve.

Serves 4

Mexican garbanzo bean casserole

In Mexico, chick peas are known as garbanzo beans and they feature in many cold dressed salads and spicy chilli dishes. This recipe is less fiery than most and goes well with hot buttered tortillas and salad.

225g/8oz/1⅓ cups chick peas, soaked overnight
350g/12oz belly pork, diced
1 onion, chopped
1 bay leaf
pinch each of chervil, paprika, ground cinnamon and
*   cloves*
7.5ml/½ tablespoon dry mustard
15ml/1 tablespoon molasses
salt and pepper
1 small packet powdered saffron
15ml/1 tablespoon chopped parsley

Drain the chick peas and place in an ovenproof dish with the pork, onion, herbs and spices. Pour in enough water to cover the beans and meat. Cover the dish and cook in a prehated oven at 150°C, 300°F, gas 2 for 3 hours. Add the mustard, molasses, seasoning and saffron and turn up the oven to 180°C, 350°F, gas 4. Replace the casserole in the oven and bake uncovered for 30 minutes or until most of the liquid has been absorbed and the sauce has thickened. Sprinkle with chopped parsley and serve.

Serves 4

Black-eyed beans and nuts

This crunchy-textured casserole makes a tasty supper served with natural yoghurt and a crisp salad. You can buy black-eyed beans in most health food stores.

225g/8oz/1⅓ cups black-eyed beans
1 large onion, chopped
1 clove garlic, crushed
30ml/2 tablespoons oil
15ml/1 tablespoon tomato paste
4 tomatoes, skinned and chopped
100g/4oz/1 cup chopped mixed nuts (walnuts, hazelnuts,
*   almonds)*
salt and pepper
15ml/1 tablespoon chopped parsley

Soak the beans overnight, drain and cook in a covered pan of boiling water for about 1 hour, or until the beans are tender. Drain and set aside.

Sauté the onion and garlic in the oil until golden-brown. Stir in the tomato paste and tomatoes, and cook for 4-5 minutes. Add the chopped nuts, seasoning and parsley. Stir in the beans and simmer gently for 15 minutes until the sauce has reduced slightly. Serve with salad and yoghurt.

Serves 4

Chick peas Italienne

Here's a delicious bean dish in a Mediterranean-style spicy tomato sauce. You can serve it hot with plain boiled rice or cold as a salad accompaniment to fish, chicken or lamb. When eaten hot, it is better known in Italy as *risi e bisi*.

175g/6oz/1 cup chick peas
1 large onion, chopped
1 clove garlic, crushed
45ml/3 tablespoons olive oil
7.5ml/½ tablespoon tomato paste
450g/1lb canned or fresh tomatoes, skinned and chopped
5ml/1 teaspoon brown sugar
good pinch each of powdered saffron and cinnamon
2.5ml/½ teaspoon oregano or basil
salt and pepper
30ml/2 tablespoons chopped parsley

Soak the chick peas overnight. Drain and cook in plenty of water for about 2 hours, or until tender. Drain and set aside. Sauté the onion and garlic in the oil until soft and translucent. Stir in the tomato paste and chopped tomato, the sugar, spices and herbs. Bring to the boil and cook over high heat until the sauce reduces and thickens (about 10-15 minutes). Season to taste and mix with the cooked chick peas. Serve hot on a bed of rice or cold as a salad sprinkled with parsley.

Serves 4

Tip: Red kidney beans require careful cooking as they contain a toxic substance in their dried form. Soak them overnight and weed out any discoloured or shrivelled beans that float to the surface. Drain and place in a pan with fresh water. Bring to the boil and boil hard for not less than 10 minutes. Drain again and refresh under running water. Bring to the boil in fresh water and simmer gently for about 1 hour. Cooked in this way, they are perfectly safe to eat.

Pulses

Split pea and ham soup

Dried split pea soups flavoured with ham or bacon are a common feature of European cookery, especially in Scandinavia, France and Britain. Although a piece of smoked gammon probably constitutes the best flavouring of all, you can use salt pork or even good-quality sausages — the choice is up to you. This is definitely a winter soup from the cold, northern countries, with a thick, coarse texture which makes it extremely warming and satisfying on a really cold day. Served with crusty bread and with the addition of sausages, it makes a meal in itself and requires no main course to follow.

175g/6oz/1 cup yellow split peas
175g/6oz/1 cup green split peas
1 onion, chopped
1 carrot, chopped
1 leek, chopped
1 stick of celery, chopped
1 parsnip, chopped
15g/½oz/1 tablespoon margarine
1.6litres/2¾ pints/6½ cups chicken stock
450g/1lb smoked gammon or bacon
salt and pepper
2.5ml/½ teaspoon thyme
4 sausages or frankfurters (optional)

Soak the split peas for a minimum of 2 hours. Then sauté the vegetables in the fat until soft and tender. Add the stock, the drained split peas and the piece of gammon. Bring to the boil, skim the surface and reduce to a simmer. Season the soup.

Cover the pan and cook gently over very low heat for 2 hours, stirring occasionally. The peas will cook down to thicken the soup. Remove the gammon and trim off and discard any fat. Cut the meat into small pieces and return to the soup. Check the seasoning and serve. If you wish to make the soup more wholesome by adding sausages, then pop in some spicy or Toulouse sausages about 45 minutes before the end of cooking time, or add frankfurters 5 minutes before serving.

Serves 6

Spanish spicy lentil soup

This warming substantial soup is flavoured with spices, tomatoes and sliced Chorizo sausage. Serve it with crusty bread and cheese. You can add shredded cabbage if wished or poach an egg in the broth about 5 minutes before serving to make it more filling.

100g/4oz Chorizo sausage
45ml/3 tablespoons oil
100g/4oz smoked streaky bacon, diced
2 onions, chopped
1 clove garlic, crushed
1 carrot, diced
1 red pepper, seeded and chopped
175g/6oz/1 cup brown continental lentils
450g/1lb canned or fresh tomatoes
900ml/1½ pints/3¾ cups chicken stock
1 bay leaf
2.5ml/½ teaspoon each of ground cumin, thyme and basil
salt and pepper
5ml/1 teaspoon brown sugar

Remove the thin skin from the Chorizo and fry it in the oil until most of the fat has run out. Add the bacon and brown well. Stir in the onion, garlic, carrot and red pepper and cook over low heat until tender. Remove the Chorizo and put aside. Add the lentils and stir over low heat for 1 minute until coated and glistening with oil. Stir in the tomatoes (skin and chop them if you are using fresh ones), stock, bay leaf, cumin, thyme and basil, seasoning and sugar. Bring to the boil and then cook gently over low heat for about 1 hour.

Dice the Chorizo sausage and stir it into the soup. Check the seasoning and simmer for a further 30 minutes. Add some shredded cabbage or eggs, if wished, 5 minutes before serving.

Serves 4

Autumn lentil soup

This thick, earthy soup is flavoured with game stock and thickened with lentils and root vegetables. It is cheap and easy to make and very filling. The addition of pheasant stock creates its distinctive flavour (although you can cheat and use a chicken stock/bouillon cube). You can make the stock in advance with the carcase of a roasted pheasant and freeze it. Game and root vegetables have a natural affinity as is demonstrated well in this delicious soup.

Stock:
1 pheasant carcase
1 onion, halved
1 carrot, sliced
1 leek, halved
1 stick celery
salt and pepper

Soup:
15g/½oz/1 tablespoon dripping or margarine
15ml/1 tablespoon oil
3 streaky bacon rashers, chopped
1 onion, chopped
2 carrots, chopped
1 turnip, chopped
2 sticks of celery, chopped
1 parsnip, chopped
350g/12oz pumpkin, deseeded and chopped
175g/6oz/1 cup brown continental lentils
1 litre/1¾ pints/4¼ cups pheasant stock
salt and pepper
1 bay leaf
sprig of parsley
2 tomatoes, skinned and chopped
50ml/2floz/¼ cup red wine
5ml/1 teaspoon brown sugar

Make the stock: place the pheasant and vegetables in a pan and cover with water (about 1.5litres/2½ pints/6 cups). Bring to the boil, season and reduce the heat to a simmer. Cover the pan and cook gently for 2½ hours. Strain.

To make the soup: heat the dripping and oil in a large pan and sauté the bacon and vegetables until tender. Add the lentils and stir until they are coated with oil. Pour in the reserved pheasant stock and bring to the boil. Season and add the bay leaf, parsley and tomatoes. Stir in the red wine and sugar, cover the pan and simmer gently for about 50 minutes until thick and flavoursome. Remove the bay leaf and parsley before serving.

Serves 6

Lentil and tomato salad

Lentils make a lovely summer salad served with tomato and onion in an oil dressing — a nice change from lettuce salads. Serve with cold poultry or fish, or as a first course.

225g/8oz/1⅓ cups brown Continental lentils
1 small onion, chopped
2 spring onions/shallots, chopped
3 tomatoes, quartered
75ml/5 tablespoons olive oil
10ml/2 teaspoons white wine vinegar (optional)
salt and pepper
30ml/2 tablespoons chopped parsley and mint

Soak the lentils for about 1 hour and remove any gritty pieces. Drain and cook in fresh water for about 1¼ hours, or until tender. Strain and mix with the chopped onion and tomatoes. Mix the olive oil with the vinegar, if used, and season. Toss the lentil salad in this dressing and sprinkle with parsley and mint. Serve with crusty brown bread and hard-boiled eggs.

Serves 4

Lentil and nut roast

This dish is usually associated with cranky vegetarianism in the minds of the meat-eating general public, but it is, in fact, a delicious meal when served with a crisp salad and home-baked bread. Economical and filling, it makes a tasty supper dish.

100g/4oz/⅔ cup lentils
1 large onion, chopped
15ml/1 tablespoon oil
175g/6oz/1½ cups mixed ground nuts (walnuts, hazelnuts, almonds, pine nuts, cashews, peanuts etc)
10ml/2 teaspoons yeast extract
2.5ml/½ teaspoon each basil and oregano
5ml/1 teaspoon chopped parsley
2 tomatoes, skinned and sliced
75g/3oz/¾ cup grated hard cheese (Cheddar or Swiss)
15ml/1 tablespoon grated Parmesan cheese
25g/1oz/½ cup fresh breadcrumbs

Cook the lentils in simmering water for about 30 minutes until tender. Drain, keeping 150ml/¼ pint/⅝ cup of the cooking liquor. Sauté the onion in the oil until translucent and add the drained lentils and the ground nuts. Stir in the yeast extract and the reserved cooking liquor. Add the herbs and spoon the mixture into a well-greased shallow ovenproof dish. Cover with thinly sliced tomatoes and sprinkle with grated cheese and breadcrumbs. Dribble a little oil over the top. Bake in a preheated oven at 180°C, 350°F, gas 4 for about 30 minutes until crisp and golden.

Serves 4

Tip: You can make a delicious lentil purèe (dhal) for serving with curries and Indian dishes. Just cook 100g/4oz/⅔ cup red lentils in water until tender. Sauté an onion until soft in a little oil with spices of your choice. Mix with the cooked, softened lentils and stir to form a soft purée, or liquidise until smooth. Season to taste.

Milk, cheese and yoghurt are the dairy foods. They are all full of goodness and are very important natural ingredients in a well-balanced diet. We have included eggs in this section too, as they have a natural affinity with dairy foods. Both cheese and yoghurt have their base in milk, which is a good source of high biological protein, carbohydrate, calcium and vitamin A. Most of the milk we use has been pasteurised to destroy the bacteria within it and make it safe to drink. Fresh milk has a tendency to go sour quickly, separating into a thick curd and a liquid whey. These curds are the raw materials of cheese-making.

Cheese

Cheese is made all over the world from cow's, goat's, ewe's and even buffalo's milk. It is one of the oldest foods and was enjoyed by the ancient Greeks and Romans. There is a fanciful story that the first cheeses were probably made inadvertently by Asian nomads who lined their travelling pouches with the stomachs of goats. The rennin in the lining clotted the milk in the pouch, causing it to turn into curds and whey.

In ancient times, the curds were hung in a porous cloth above a basket to catch the whey. The European words for cheese are derived from the Greek and Latin names for this basket. The French *fromage* and Italian *formaggio* evolved from the Greek word *formos*, whereas the German *käse*, Dutch *kaas* and English 'cheese' all come from the Latin *caseus*. There are literally hundreds of varieties of cheeses. They may be hard, soft and creamy, blue-veined or flavoured with aromatic spices, herbs and garlic. However, all cheeses start with a curd, and their texture and flavour are determined by the milk used, the manufacturing process, the method of aging and even the environment in which they are matured. For example, whereas most blue-veined cheeses are injected with a mould, Roquefort, the greatest blue cheese of all, is left to ripen in the caves below the volcanic Massif Central in France and acquires its mould naturally without any assistance from Man.

The simplest way to make cheese is to tie the curd of some skimmed, soured milk in a piece of cheesecloth through which the whey can drip. However, in most manufacturing processes, a starter culture is used to sour the milk and convert the lactose into lactic acid. The enzyme rennet is then introduced to coagulate the milk, and the curds and whey separate when the milk reaches the right degree of acidity. The curd is cut at wide intervals for a soft cheese, or finely for a hard cheese, and then it is salted, moulded and matured. The maturing and aging process varies, and different cheeses may need weeks, months or even years before they are ready to eat.

Types of cheese

Cheeses are usually divided into fresh, hard, soft and blue-veined types:

Fresh cheeses, such as cottage cheese, fromage blanc, ricotta and mozzarella, do not travel well and may be stored for only 3-4 days in the refrigerator.

Hard cheeses are excellent for cooking and grating. The best known are Cheddar, Parmesan (the hardest cheese of all) and the Swiss Gruyère and Emmenthal with their large distinctive holes caused by fermentation during the ripening process.

Soft cheeses come in literally hundreds of varieties from crumbly goat's cheeses to ripe, creamy Camembert and Brie. The whey is drained only partially from the curds to create a moist, soft texture.

Blue-veined cheeses, the most famous of which are Roquefort and Stilton, may have a soft, creamy or crumbly texture. For example, Gorgonzola is soft whereas Stilton is firm.

Buying and storing cheese

Cheese should be bought freshly cut from the block rather than in prepackaged sections. Never buy browning or discoloured cheese with a slightly ammoniac smell. Always wrap cheese in foil or store in an airtight container to prevent it drying out. Store in a cool, dry place — a larder or refrigerator are ideal. Remove it from the refrigerator at least one hour before serving to allow the natural flavours to develop fully. Hard cheeses stay fresh longer than soft ones, but if they become very hard and dry, grate them and store in a screwtop jar in the refrigerator for cooking. They will stay fresh for several weeks stored in this way. Remember also that cheese has a natural affinity with wine, especially crisp, dry white wines and even some sweet dessert wines such as Monbazillac and Sauternes. Port goes well with stronger blue-veined cheeses such as Stilton and Roquefort.

Yoghurt

Yoghurt is another ancient food and it is said that it was first revealed by an angel to the prophet Abraham which accounts for his longevity(he lived to the ripe old age of 175). It has been used for many centuries in the countries of the Middle East, the Balkans, North Africa and India. Its popularity in the West is relatively short-lived, although the shelves of most supermarkets and health food stores now carry yoghurts of all flavours, textures and colours. However, yoghurt was enjoyed by the ancient Greeks, Egyptians, Arabs and Romans and was praised by the early Greek physician Galen for its healthy properties.

It is an important health food due to its ability to destroy harmful bacteria within the large intestine. The friendly lactobacillus in the yoghurt fights off diseased bacteria and indeed manufactures most of the B vitamins in the intestine, thus creating a really healthy environment there. To achieve this, you must eat yoghurt regularly and so it's a good idea to include some in your daily diet. Some Italian doctors even prescribe it in preference to antibiotics.

The best and cheapest yoghurt is home-made(see recipe on page 78). Most commercial brands contain white sugar and artificial colourings. Home-made natural yoghurt can be sweetened with honey or raw brown sugar and mixed with chopped nuts, fresh fruit, muesli or granola for a healthy breakfast dish.

Eggs

Eggs are so versatile that they make wonderful quick snacks, hors d'oeuvres, main courses, desserts and drinks. It is almost impossible to imagine many of our everyday meals and dishes made without eggs — for example, custards, cakes, soufflés, omelettes, mousses and many sauces. In addition, eggs are a meal in themselves, served boiled, poached, scrambled, fried or baked. They have been an important part of our diet since ancient times and were long regarded as a symbol of fertility and life itself.

Over 90 per cent of the eggs for sale are produced by factory farming methods, notably the battery system of keeping hens inside in cages and feeding them with processed foods. Their more fortunate free-range sisters are allowed to roam free in the open air and scratch for seeds and fodder in the traditional way. The battery system is obviously more economical and profitable on a large scale — egg production per bird has doubled since it was introduced and the eggs are easier to collect, although many animal lovers claim that the cost in suffering is too high to justify this.

Whatever your view, and we buy only free-range eggs, extensive scientific research has shown that the protein and fat values are exactly the same for both free-range and battery eggs. However, free-range eggs are 50 per cent higher in folic acid and contain more vitamin B12 than battery ones. On the other hand, battery eggs often contain more iron and sodium. But no matter which eggs you buy, there can be no doubt that battery eggs lack the flavour and colour of their free-range counterparts. Also, a local free-range source is likely to supply fresher eggs than supermarket battery ones. Beware of buying eggs that are labelled as being 'farm-fresh' — this is not a synonym for 'free-range' and may mean only that they are fresh from the battery farm.

Most people have a colour preference when it comes to eggs, discriminating between white and brown. Let us dispel this myth by stating that there is no difference whatsoever in flavour, the shell colour being determined by the breed of hen and not the quality of the egg itself.

There has been some controversy recently about the cholesterol content of eggs and whether over-consumption may be related to the incidence of high cholesterol levels in the bloodstream and atherio-sclerosis. Yes, egg yolks are rich in cholesterol (between 194 and 200mg) but egg whites are high in lecithin, a natural substance that disperses fat and helps the body to utilise cholesterol. Thus the cholesterol in the yolk is kept flowing by the lecithin in the white and does not build up in fatty deposits on the artery walls.

Storing eggs

Always store eggs in a cool place with a constant temperature — in a cool larder or the least coldest part of the refrigerator are best. They will stay fresh for about 3 weeks in the refrigerator but only 12 days at room temperature. A simple test for freshness is to put the egg in water: it will sink if fresh and float if old.

Eggs

Koko's Yorkshire breakfast

This filling, tasty breakfast was always prepared for us by an old, eccentric aunt. Although it is a delicious way to start the day, you can eat it at any time — as a supper snack or for high tea.

40g/1½oz/¾ cup fresh breadcrumbs
25g/1oz/3 tablespoons grated Parmesan cheese
100ml/4floz/½ cup milk
salt and pepper
2 eggs, separated
2 slices bacon (optional)

Mix the breadcrumbs, cheese, milk and seasoning together. Beat in the egg yolks. Whisk the egg whites until they form stiff peaks and fold into the mixture. Pour into a greased ovenproof dish and bake in a preheated oven at 190°C, 375°F, gas 5 for 30 minutes. Serve with bacon rashers if wished.

Serves 2

Haddock and mushroom roulade

A beautifully light supper dish, this fluffy roulade is filled with a tasty smoked haddock and mushroom sauce. Use the pale silvery smoked Finnan haddock for its delicate flavour. Working on the same basic roulade principle, you can vary the filling — try crabmeat and cheese, or chicken and mushroom. Serve the roulade with a fresh geen salad.

65g/2½oz/5 tablespoons margarine
65g/2½oz/½ cup plain flour
350ml/12floz/1½ cups milk
225g/8oz Finnan haddock, flaked
25g/1oz/¼ cup grated Gruyère/Swiss cheese
15g/½oz/2 tablespoons grated Parmesan cheese
salt and pepper
4 eggs, separated
Filling:
100g/4oz mushrooms, finely chopped
1 small onion, chopped
75ml/2½floz/⅓ cup white wine
25g/1oz/¼ cup grated Gruyère/Swiss cheese
45ml/3 tablespoons grated Parmesan cheese
salt and pepper
pinch of nutmeg
Garnish:
15ml/1 tablespoon grated Parmesan cheese
15ml/1 tablespoon chopped parsley

To make the roulade: melt the fat over low heat, stir in the flour and cook for 1 minute. Gradually beat in the milk until the sauce is thick and smooth. Put two-thirds of the sauce in a bowl and cover to prevent a skin forming. Ser this aside to make the filling.

Mix the flaked haddock, cheese and seasoning into the remaining sauce in the pan and beat in the egg yolks, one at a time. Whisk the egg whites stiffly and fold in gently with a metal spoon. Spread the mixture over a greased and lined Swiss roll tin (approx, 35cm/14in x 25cm/10in), and bake in a preheated oven at 200°C, 400°F, gas 6 for 15 minutes, or until the roulade is firm to the touch.

While the roulade is cooking, prepare the filling. Place the chopped mushrooms and onion in a pan and cover with the wine. Cook gently for 5 minutes until the wine reduces a little. Stir into the reserved sauce with the grated cheese and seasoning. Bring to the boil and cook gently for a few minutes until thick and smooth.

Turn the roulade out onto a sheet of greaseproof/baking paper and spread the filling across it, leaving a clear border of at least 2.5cm/1in all round. Roll the roulade up as you would a Swiss roll and transfer to a warm serving dish. Srpinkle with grated cheese and chopped parsley and serve.

Serves 4

Spinach quiche

Spinach tarts have been eaten for centuries in Europe, but usually a sweetened version as a dessert. However, savoury spinach tarts and quiches are now becoming popular as a first course, or as a light luncheon or supper dish. This quiche has a creamy texture and the dark green strands of spinach and diced pink gammon make it especially attractive.

675g/1½lb fresh spinach
1 large onion, chopped
100g/4oz gammon or streaky bacon rashers, diced
30ml/2 tablespoons oil
3 eggs, beaten
100ml/4floz/½ cup single/light cream
200ml/8floz/1 cup milk
salt and pepper
pinch of ground nutmeg
50g/2oz/½ cup grated Cheddar or Swiss cheese
one 25cm/10in uncooked shortcrust flan case
(for recipe see page 169)

Pick the spinach over and discard any tough stalks or discoloured leaves. Wash the leaves thoroughly in two or three changes of water. Shake dry and place in a saucepan over low heat. Cover and cook gently for about 5 minutes until the leaves turn bright green and soften. Drain and squeeze out any excess water.

Sauté the chopped onion and gammon in the oil until soft. Beat the eggs with the cream and milk and season well. Scatter the sautéed onion across the base of a lined 25cm/10in flan case. Arrange the cooked spinach, cheese and gammon dice on top and pour in the beaten egg mixture.

Cook in a preheated oven at 200°C, 400°F, gas 6 for 15 minutes and then reduce the temperature to 180°C, 350°F, gas 4 for a further 20-25 minutes until the filling is well-risen, firm and golden. Serve the quiche either hot or cold.

Serves 6

Curried crab soufflé

This makes an unusual first course and is a useful standby dish if you keep some canned crabmeat in your store cupboard. Serve it with a sharp tartare sauce (see tip in next column).

40g/1½oz/3 tablespoons margarine
40g/1½oz/4 tablespoons flour
5ml/1 teaspoon curry powder
225ml/8floz/1 cup milk
pinch of salt
3 eggs, separated
350g/12oz/1½ cups canned crabmeat
tartare sauce

Melt the fat and stir in the flour. Cook gently over low heat for 2 minutes and stir in the curry powder. Cook for 30 seconds and then gradually add the milk, beating well until you have a smooth sauce. Beat in the salt and the egg yolks, one at a time, and then fold in the crabmeat.

Whisk the egg whites until they form stiff peaks, and fold very gently in a figure-of-eight movement into the soufflé mixture. Pour the mixture into a lightly buttered 550ml/1 pint/2½ cup soufflé dish or four individual, small soufflé dishes. Bake in a preheated oven at 190°C, 375°F, gas 5 for 45 minutes until well-risen and golden-brown. Serve with tartare sauce.

Serves 4

Tip: To make a quick and easy tartare sauce, just mix 300ml/½pint/1¼cups mayonnaise with 50g/2oz/¼cup chopped gherkins, 25g/1oz/2 tablespoons chopped capers and 30ml/2 tablespoons chopped parsley. Flavour with lemon juice.

Orange crème renversée

This orange-flavoured cream in a slightly bitter caramel sauce is for special occasions. Serve it with fresh fruit: strawberries, sliced oranges or peaches. You can use skimmed milk to make a custard which is less rich. Baked custards have been a popular pudding since the Middle Ages, especially in France and Britain. They were sometimes flavoured with orange juice or brandy or topped with burnt sugar (the English 'burnt cream' or *crème brulée*).

700ml/1¼ pints/3 cups milk
150ml/¼ pint/⅝ cup cream
piece of vanilla pod
strip of orange peel
6 eggs
100g/4oz/½ cup caster/superfine sugar
2-3 drops vanilla essence
grated rind of 1 orange
15ml/1 tablespoon orange juice
Caramel:
75g/3oz/⅜ cup soft brown sugar
45ml/3 tablespoons hot water

Heat the milk, cream, vanilla pod and orange peel in a saucepan to boiling point. Meanwhile, whisk the eggs, sugar and vanilla essence in a large bowl. Whisk the boiling milk and cream into the egg mixture. Stir in the grated orange rind and juice. Leave to cool.

Make the caramel: put the sugar in a pan and just cover with cold water. Bring slowly to the boil over a moderate heat, stirring all the time until the sugar dissolves. Boil gently until the syrup thickens and starts to turn a rich golden-brown colour. Remove from the heat and, standing well back from the pan because it will spit, add the hot water. Return to the pan and stir over a gentle heat for 1-2 minutes to break down any caramel lumps.

Pour the syrup into an ovenproof dish or mould (1.1litre/2pint/5 cup capacity). Turn the dish slowly to swirl the syrup around the base and sides so that they are evenly covered. Strain the custard through a sieve into the dish and stand in a water bath. Bake in a preheated oven at 170°C, 325°F, gas 3 for about 50 minutes until set. Test whether the custard is set with a sharp knife. It is ready when it comes out clean.

Remove the custard from the water bath, and cool a little. Chill in the refrigerator before turning out onto a serving dish. Gently ease a sharp knife around the edge of the custard and invert the mould onto a dish. The caramel sauce will flow down the sides.

Serves 6

Black cherry soufflé omelette

A light and airy dessert from Hungary, this is one of the best sweet omelettes of all. Use fresh cherries in the summer or canned cherries when these are not available. A little kirsch liqueur (a white brandy made from cherries) or some cherry brandy gives the soufflé omelette a lift. Allow a little time for cooking as the omelettes have to be cooked individually.

225g/8oz black cherries, canned or fresh
15ml/1 tablespoon kirsch or cherry brandy
4 eggs, separated
15ml/1 tablespoon cold water
25g/1oz/2 tablespoons caster/superfine sugar
1.25ml/¼ teaspoon ground cinnamon
butter for cooking
icing/confectioner's sugar for dredging

Stone/pit the cherries (drain if canned) and marinate in the kirsch or cherry brandy. Beat the egg yolks until pale and frothy with the water, sugar and cinnamon. Whisk the egg whites until they stand in stiff peaks and beat 15ml/1 tablespoon of beaten egg white into the yolk mixture. Gently fold in the remaining egg white in a figure-of-eight movement. Warm the cherries gently in the liqueur.

Heat a small knob of butter in a proved omelette pan and add about one-quarter of the mixture, spreading it out to cover the base of the pan. Cook over moderate heat for 2 minutes, or until the underside is set and golden. Place the pan under a preheated grill/broiler and leave until fluffy and well-risen. Spoon a few of the warmed cherries onto one side of the omelette and fold the other half over the top. Slide onto a serving dish and dredge with icing/confectioner's sugar and serve immediately. Repeat with the remaining omelette mixture to make 4 omelettes in total. If preferred, you can finish the omelette in a preheated oven at 220°C, 425°F, gas 7 on the top shelf for 5-7 minutes instead of placing it under the grill.

Serves 4

Chilled orange soufflé

Unlike most soufflés, this one contains no fattening cream. It is made with simple, pure ingredients — orange juice, sugar and eggs. A dash of brandy or your favourite orange liqueur lifts it out of the ordinary into a special class of dessert. It makes the perfect finish to a filling meal.

400ml/14 floz/1¾ cups fresh orange juice
15g/½oz/3 heaped teaspoons powdered gelatine
50g/2oz/¼ cup caster/superfine sugar
3 eggs, separated
15-30ml/1-2 tablespoons brandy or orange liqueur

Place the orange juice in a saucepan and sprinkle with the gelatine. Leave on the side for 15-20 minutes. Stir gently and then place over the heat and bring the mixture *almost* to the boil. Remove from the heat immediately and stir in the sugar.

Beat the egg yolks and whisk in the orange gelatine mixture. Leave to cool. Meanwhile, whisk in the egg whites until glossy and standing in stiff peaks. When the gelatine mixture is almost setting, stir in the brandy and gently fold in the beaten egg white and pour into a soufflé dish. Chill well until set and decorate with caramelised orange slices (see Tart Citron recipe on page 150) or fresh fruit.

Serves 4

Chocolate and orange soufflé

This hot soufflé is a light and healthy way to end a meal. It should be served piping hot from the oven before it collapses. Serve it with hot orange sauce (see recipe on page 172).

25g/1oz/2 tablespoons margarine
25g/1oz/3 tablespoons flour
4 eggs, separated
225ml/8 floz/1 cup milk
60g/2½oz dark plain chocolate
30ml/2 tablespoons rum
grated rind of 1 orange

Melt the fat and stir in the flour over low heat. Gradually beat in the milk until the sauce is glossy and smooth. Leave to cool a little and then beat in the egg yolks, one at a time.

Melt the chocolate in the top of a bain-marie over hot water, and stir into the sauce with the rum and orange rind. Beat the egg whites until stiff and gently fold into the sauce. Pour the mixture into a buttered

550ml/1 pint/2½ cup soufflé dish and bake in a preheated oven at 180°C, 350°F, gas 4 for 45 minutes until cooked and well-risen. Serve immediately with orange sauce.
Serves 4

Banana and rum soufflé omelette

Soufflé omelettes make a light but filling dessert. This one is particularly good made with rum and bananas. The quantities given are enough for 2 people, so double up if you are cooking for 4 or more. Remember when timing the meal that each omelette has to be cooked individually. To ensure that the omelettes never stick to the pan, make sure that it is well proved. You can do this by covering the base with salt and placing it over low heat for about 1 hour. Tip out the salt and the pan is ready to use. If you keep this pan for omelettes, you need not wash it. Just wipe it round with a soft cloth or kitchen paper after use.

3 eggs, separated
50g/2oz/¼ cup soft brown sugar
25g/1oz/2 tablespoons butter
icing/confectioner's sugar for dusting
Filling:
40g/1½oz/3 tablespoons butter or margarine
2 bananas, cut in half lengthwise
25g/1oz/2 tablespoons soft brown sugar
30ml/2 tablespoons dark rum

Prepare the filling first and keep it warm while you make the omelettes. Melt the butter and fry the bananas gently until golden-brown with the sugar, stirring lightly until the sugar dissolves. Add the rum, bring to the boil and cook until reduced and slightly syrupy. Keep warm while you prepare the omelettes.

Whisk the egg yolks with the sugar until creamy. Whisk the egg whites separately until the mixture stands in stiff peaks and fold into the yolk mixture with a metal spoon. Melt half the butter in an omelette pan and pour in half of the omelette mixture. Spread it out across the base of the pan and cook until golden underneath. Cover the pan with a lid if you want the mixture to rise a great deal.

Place the pan under a hot grill/broiler or in a preheated oven at 200°C, 400°F, gas 6 for 1-2 minutes until fluffy and well-risen. Gently slide the omelette out of the pan onto a serving dish and spoon half the banana filling across one side of the omelette. Fold the other half over the top of the filling and dredge with sugar

and serve immediately. Repeat the process with the remaining mixture to make a second omelette and fill in the same way.
Serves 2

Orange custard

This light, refreshing custard is covered with a thin, crisp layer of caramel in the manner of a *crème brulée*. It is best to make the custard a day in advance of eating to chill it thoroughly. The caramel crust can be prepared a few hours before serving. If you are really health-conscious, you can substitute skimmed milk for whole milk in this dish.

2 whole eggs and 2 yolks
75g/3oz/⅜ cup caster sugar
grated rind of 2 oranges
350ml/12floz/1½ cups milk
2 drops of vanilla essence
4 oranges
15ml/1 tablespoon pistachio nuts
soft brown sugar for topping

Beat the eggs and yolks with the sugar and orange rind. Heat the milk almost to boiling point and pour over the beaten egg mixture. Whisk well and strain into a double-boiler or a basin suspended over a pan of hot water. Cook gently over the hot water, stirring well until the custard thickens and coats a spoon. Stand the basin in cold water to cool it quickly and then add the vanilla essence to the mixture.

Peel the oranges, removing all the white pith, and cut into segments. Place them in the base of a serving dish with the pistachio nuts and pour over the cooled custard. Chill overnight until set.

The following day, dredge the top of the custard with an even layer of sugar. Flash the dish under a *very* hot grill quickly, rotating the dish until all the sugar has melted evenly and turned golden-brown and caramelised. This operation should be performed at great speed so that the custard does not go soft. Cool the dish and chill for 2-3 hours before serving.
Serves 4

Pancakes/crêpes

Elegant, lacy-edged, paper-thin pancakes make a delicious dessert served with the traditional wedges of lemon and sugar, or with a fruit or nut filling. Pancakes have been a favourite European dish for several centuries and used to be flavoured at rich tables with wine, sherry or rose water. Many French chefs still add brandy to the batter when making *crêpes Suzette*.

Basic pancake batter:
100g/4oz/1⅛ cups plain flour
pinch salt
2 eggs
300ml/½ pint/1¼ cups milk
15g/½oz/1 tablespoon lard/shortening

Sift the flour and salt into a mixing bowl and make a well in the centre. Add the eggs and milk, a little at a time, beating well until the batter is smooth and creamy. Leave to stand for 30 minutes.

Heat a tiny knob of lard in a small omelette pan — just enough to coat the bottom. When it is sizzling, pour enough batter into the pan to cover the base thinly, tilting the pan to spread the batter evenly. When the underside of the pancake is cooked and golden, toss it over and cook the other side. Slide onto a warm plate and repeat the process until all the batter is used up. Although you can cook the pancakes in advance and keep them warm, they are at their best when eaten hot and fresh from the pan with lemon and sugar or honey, or rolled around one of the fillings below.

Makes approximately 12 pancakes

Fillings for pancakes/crêpes

There are many delicious fruit and nut fillings for pancakes, some of which are served with sauces. Our favourite way of eating pancakes is to fill them with a crushed walnut mixture and top with a chocolate sauce in the Hungarian manner.

Hungarian nut filling:

100g/4oz/1 cup finely chopped walnuts
grated rind of 1 orange
60ml/4 tablespoons Demerara or soft brown sugar
75ml/3 fl oz/⅜ cup double/thick cream
30ml/2 tablespoons brandy
Chocolate sauce:
100g/4oz chocolate polka dots or block chocolate
30ml/2 tablespoons dark golden syrup
15g/½oz/1 tablespoon brandy
2 drops vanilla essence

Mix together the filling ingredients and put aside while you make the chocolate sauce. Melt the chocolate in a basin suspended over a pan of hot water. Remove from the heat as soon as the water starts to boil. Mix in the syrup, butter, brandy and vanilla over the hot water until you have a thick, glossy sauce.

Place a little of the filling on each pancake. Roll up quickly and serve with the chocolate sauce. You can sprinkle the pancakes with more chopped nuts if liked.

Fills 12 pancakes

Apple and cinnamon filling:

2 large cooking/green apples, peeled, cored and sliced
45ml/3 tablespoons soft brown sugar
30ml/2 tablespoons rum
grated rind of 1 lemon
good pinch of cinnamon
sugar for dusting

Cook the apple slices and brown sugar in the rum over low heat until soft. Add the lemon rind and cinnamon, and fill the pancakes with this mixture. Roll up and dust with sugar. Serve with lemon wedges if wished, or pour over a little flaming rum for a real treat.

Fills 12 pancakes

Cream

Farmhouse clotted cream

Although you should try to cut down on the amount of cream and other fats that you include in your diet, it is nice to spoil yourself occasionally and to indulge in some real home-made clotted cream. It can be made easily with creamy milk (gold top Channel Islands milk in the United Kingdom) or with ordinary pasteurised milk to which single/light cream is added. All you need is the creamy top of 4 litres or 5 pints (12½ cups) of milk — only the top, not the ordinary thin milk underneath. If you are using plain pasteurised milk add 150ml/¼ pint/⅝ cup of single cream to this and place in a wide saucepan. Stand the milk for 2 days in the refrigerator and then heat gently *almost* to boiling point. Take care that you do not shake the pan. Leave the milk to cool and then chill in the refrigerator for about 18-24 hours.

A thick, creamy crust will form on top of the liquid underneath. Skim this off and use as clotted cream to serve with scones and jam or desserts. You can use the milk underneath for rice pudding (recipe see page 47).

Opposite: gougères: seafood filling in the foreground (see page 75) and crab and mushroom filling (see page 76)

Cheese

American mozzarella salad

Tomato and mozzarella salads have long been popular in Italy, but sliced avocado is sometimes added as an interesting variation in the United States. The pale green flesh of the avocado combined with the bright red tomato and creamy mozzarella make this a colourful dish. The best Italian mozzarella is made from buffalo milk, but the cheaper cow's milk varieties are also good provided that they are fresh and moist and preferably dripping with buttermilk.

450g/1lb tomatoes (or 2 large 225g/8oz Italian tomatoes)
15ml/1 tablespoon sugar
few leaves basil, chopped (or chopped parsley)
175g/6oz mozzarella
1 avocado
10ml/2 teaspoons dried oregano
salt and pepper
30ml/2 tablespoons olive oil
juice of ½ lemon

Skin and thinly slice the tomatoes. Place on a serving plate and sprinkle with sugar and chopped basil. Slice the mozzarella and peel and slice the avocado. Arrange on top of the tomato, scatter over the oregano and season well with salt and plenty of freshly ground black pepper. Mix the oil and lemon juice and dribble over the top. Serve immediately as an appetizer.
Serves 4

Cheese straws

These are always a favourite with adults and children. Serve with party dips or even with soups, or just munch then when you feel hungry — they are better for you and less fattening than sweet biscuits.

100g/4oz/1 cup plain or wholemeal flour
1.25ml/¼ teaspoon salt
pinch of cayenne
65g/2½oz/5 tablespoons margarine
50g/2oz/⅓ cup grated Parmesan cheese
a little egg yolk to blend

Sieve the flour, salt and cayenne into a bowl and rub in the fat until the mixture resembles fine breadcrumbs. Stir in the grated cheese and mix to a stiff paste with some egg yolk (about half of one yolk). Knead lightly and roll out 5mm/¼in thick. Cut the paste into long strips, 5mm/½in wide x 7.5cm/3in long.

Place the cheese straws on a well-greased baking sheet and cook in a preheated oven at 180°C, 350°F, gas 4 for 5-7 minutes only until crisp and golden-brown. Cool and serve.

Blue cheese and walnut quiche

You can use any blue-veined cheese in this savoury flan — Gorgonzola, Stilton, Roquefort or even Danish blue. Serve with a fresh green salad and brown rice or a mixture of chopped apple, nuts, celery and diced potato in a creamy mayonnaise sprinkled with chives.

Pastry:
100g/4oz/½cup soft margarine, cut in pieces
30ml/2 tablespoons water
225g/8oz/2¼ cups wholemeal flour
pinch of salt
Filling:
100g/4oz blue cheese
50g/2oz/½ cup chopped walnuts
8 spring onions, chopped
2 large eggs
150ml/¼ pint/⅝ cup milk
salt and pepper
pinch of ground coriander

Make the pastry: place the margarine, water and 15ml/1 tablespoon of the flour in a mixing bowl. Mix well with a fork and gradually blend in the remaining flour and salt, adding more water if necessary, to make a soft, pliable dough. Knead lightly on a floured surface and then leave the dough in the refrigerator for 10 minutes to relax it.

Roll it out and line a 20cm/8in flan ring or dish. Prick the base with a fork and bake 'blind' for 10 minutes in a preheated oven at 200°C, 400°F, gas 6.

Crumble or mash the cheese and place in the flan ring. Sprinkle with the walnuts and chopped onion. Beat the eggs and milk and stir in the seasoning. Pour into the flan and bake in a preheated oven on the middle shelf at 200°C, 400°F, gas 6 for 10 minutes. Reduce the heat to 180°C, 350°F, gas 4 and bake for 25-30 minutes until set, risen and golden-brown.
Serves 4

Stilton cheese soufflé

The beauty of this soufflé is that it is low in calories as it uses skimmed milk and no fat. However, this departure from the traditional method and ingredients does not result in any loss in flavour, and the golden, puffed-up soufflé which emerges triumphantly from the oven tastes as good as it looks.

10ml/2 teaspoons cornflour/cornstarch
150ml/¼ pint/⅝ cup skimmed milk
salt and pepper
good pinch of paprika
2.5ml/½ teaspoon dry mustard
2 eggs, separated
100g/4oz Stilton (or other blue cheese), grated
2.5ml/½ teaspoon grated Parmesan

Blend the cornflour and milk and stir in the seasoning, paprika and mustard. Stir over a gentle heat until the mixture thickens. Beat well until the sauce is smooth, then beat in the egg yolks and lastly the Stilton cheese.

Beat the egg whites until stiff, and beat about 15ml/ 1 tablespoon of the egg white into the cheese sauce. Fold in the rest with a metal spoon — very *gently*. Pour the soufflé mixture into a well-buttered 550ml/1pint/ 2½ cup soufflé dish or six individual ramekin dishes. Sprinkle the top with Parmesan and bake in the centre of a preheated oven at 190°C, 375°F, gas 5 for 30-35 minutes until well-risen and golden. Serve immediately. This soufflé serves two as a main course or six people as a first course.

Cheese fritters

When you cut into these golden fritters all the lovely melted cheese sauce inside oozes out. They make a delicious first course served with parsley and lemon wedges, and are a popular dish in France and Belgium. You can use any grated hard cheese but always include a little Parmesan for its strong, distinctive flavour.

300ml/½ pint/1¼ cups basic béchamel sauce (see recipe
*   on page 171)*
175g/6oz/1½ cups grated hard cheese (Swiss, Cheddar or
*   Parmesan)*
5ml/1 teaspoon made mustard
good pinch of ground nutmeg
2 egg yolks
salt and pepper
flour for dusting
1 egg, beaten
100g/4oz/1½ cups breadcrumbs
oil for deep-frying
parsley sprigs and lemon wedges to garnish

Make the basic béchamel sauce and cook for 2-3 minutes

over gentle heat. Gradually add the grated cheese and then the mustard and nutmeg. Beat well and remove from the heat. Beat in the egg yolks and season to taste. Line a 20cm/8in square shallow tin with foil and pour the cheese sauce into it. Chill thoroughly.

Cut the chilled cheese mixture into squares, dust with flour and dip in beaten egg. Coat with breadcrumbs and deep-fry at 190°C, 375°F until golden-brown. Drain and serve immediately, garnished with sprigs of parsley and lemon wedges.

Serves 4-6

Gougère

This is the great cheese dish of Burgundy — a delicious golden ring of cheesy choux pastry. The traditional gougère is served cut into slices but we have devised some colourful fillings to make it a more substantial supper dish. Do not be tempted, on any account, to open the oven door and have a peep at the cooking gougère until the cooking time has elapsed, however good and cooked it may smell. If you do succumb, it will probably collapse, so be patient and wait if you want good results.

Choux pastry:
225ml/8floz/1 cup water
75g/3oz/⅜ cup butter or margarine
100g/4oz/1⅛ cups wholemeal flour
2 egg yolks
1 whole egg
75g/3oz/¾ cup grated Gruyère/Swiss cheese
salt and pepper
pinch cayenne pepper

Seafood filling:
175g/6oz salmon
275g/10oz monkfish
300ml/½ pint/1¼ cups water
22.5ml/1½ tablespoons oil
4-5 shallots, chopped
22.5ml/1½ tablespoons flour
salt and pepper
pinch each oregano and ground nutmeg
75g/3oz peeled prawns/shrimps
2 tomatoes, skinned and sliced
5ml/1 teaspoon lemon juice
small packet powdered saffron
15ml/1 tablespoon grated Parmesan
¼ green pepper cut in julienne strips
4 whole prawns for garnish

First, make the choux pastry: put the water and fat in a small pan and bring to a rolling boil. Quickly add the flour, all at one go, and beat well until you have a smooth, glossy paste which leaves the sides of the pan clean. Cook for 30 seconds and remove from the heat.

When the mixture has cooled slightly, add the egg yolks, one at a time, beating well. The first yolk must be thoroughly mixed with the paste before the second is added. Then beat in the whole egg, and when the paste is smooth and shiny add the grated cheese, reserving about 15ml/1 tablespoonful for the top. Season with salt and pepper and cayenne, cover the pan with a lid and put aside while you make the filling.

Skin and bone the fish and poach gently in a pan of water for 15 - 20 minutes. Although we have suggested that you use salmon and monkfish you can use any firm-fleshed white fish of your choice, including cod, turbot, whiting, halibut, sole and John Dory. Mussels, lobster and squid could also be added. When the fish is cooked, strain off and keep the stock to make the sauce.

Heat the oil in a large frying pan and sauté the shallot until soft and translucent. Stir in the flour and cook for about 3 minutes. Add the reserved fish stock, seasoning and herbs, stirring well until the sauce thickens. Add the fish, cut into cubes, with the prawns, sliced tomato, lemon juice and saffron.

Place in the centre of a well-buttered, deep ovenproof plate or shallow pie dish. Sprinkle with grated Parmesan and decorate the top with julienne strips of green pepper and whole prawns. Pipe the choux pastry in large decorative swirls around the edge, using a vegetable star tube. Sprinkle the choux pastry with the remaining grated Gruyère cheese and bake in a preheated oven at 200°C, 400°F, gas 6 for 40 minutes until the gougère is puffed up and golden-brown. Serve immediately with a salad.

Serves 4

Crab and mushroom filling

A delicious alternative filling for gougère is made with crabmeat and mushrooms. Although you can use fresh crabmeat, for the sake of economy and convenience we have substituted canned crabmeat, which still produces tasty results. Make the choux pastry border in the same way and fill with the following:

1 shallot, chopped
30ml/2 tablespoons oil
150g/5oz sliced large field mushrooms
25g/1oz/3 tablespoons flour

150ml/¼ pint/⅝ cup fish or chicken stock
1.25ml/¼ teaspoon ground nutmeg
salt and pepper
5ml/1 teaspoon lemon juice
30ml/2 tablespoons white wine
3 tomatoes, skinned and sliced
200g/7oz/1 cup canned crabmeat
25g/1oz/¼ cup grated Gruyère/Swiss cheese
10ml/2 teaspoons grated Parmesan

Sauté the shallot in the oil for a few minutes and add the mushrooms. Cook for 2 minutes, stir in the flour and cook for another 2 minutes. Add the stock, a little at a time, stirring well until the sauce has thickened and is smooth. Add the nutmeg, seasoning, lemon juice and wine.

Arrange the sliced tomato in the centre of a buttered deep ovenproof plate or shallow pie dish. Cover with half of the sauce, then a layer of half the crabmeat, another layer of sauce and the remaining crabmeat. Sprinkle with grated Gruyère and Parmesan cheese, pipe the choux paste around the edge and bake in a preheated oven as described in the previous recipe.

Serves 4

Vegetable filling

A more economical filling can be made with fresh vegetables. You can follow our recipe or substitute your favourite seasonal vegetables. The filling below is especially good in the autumn when pumpkin is cheap and plentiful.

30ml/2 tablespoons oil
1 onion, chopped
½ leek, chopped
1 stick celery, chopped
225g/8oz tomatoes, skinned and sliced
100g/4oz pumpkin, diced
90g/3½oz/½ cup canned corn kernels
salt and pepper
25g/1oz/2 tablespoons flour
100ml/4floz/½ cup white wine
good pinch each of cinnamon, cayenne and allspice
30ml/2 tablespoons grated Parmesan cheese
½ red pepper, cut in julienne strips
8 canned asparagus tips

Heat the oil and sauté the onion, leek and celery until tender. Do not allow them to colour. Add the prepared tomato slices, pumpkin and drained corn kernels, season and cook gently for 5 minutes.

Stir in the flour and cook for 2 minutes over low

heat. Then add the wine and bring to the boil, stirring well. Remove from the heat and add the spices. Check the seasoning and spoon the prepared filling onto a shallow pie dish or deep ovenproof plate. Sprinkle with Parmesan and arrange the red pepper slices on top. Pipe the choux paste in large, decorative swirls around the edge of the dish. Bake in a preheated oven at 200°C, 400°F, gas 6 as in the previous recipes. After 30 minutes arrange the drained asparagus tips on top of the gougère in a star pattern and return to the oven for a further 10 minutes. Serve with a green salad.

Serves 4

Potted herb cheese

Potted cheese can be covered with clarified butter and stored for long periods. It is delicious spread on biscuits and served with crisp celery at the end of a meal. You can use hard cheese as in the recipe below or simply cream some blue cheese (Roquefort or Stilton) with a little butter and some port wine or Armagnac. Most herbs are suitable according to which are in season

100g/4oz/1 cup grated hard cheese (Cheddar, Cheshire etc)
2.5ml/½ teaspoon grated Parmesan cheese
30ml/2 tablespoons double/heavy cream
45ml/3 tablespoons port wine
30ml/2 tablespoons finely chopped fresh herbs (sage, thyme, parsley, basil, oregano, marjoram, lemon balm etc)
salt and black pepper

Place the cheese in a small pan with the cream, port wine and herbs. Heat gently until the cheese melts and the mixture turns a delicate pale green. Season with salt and pepper and pour into a small hot jar or pot. Seal with a lid and cool, then store in the refrigerator. Alternatively, seal with clarified butter and store in a cool place.

Pashka

This is a traditional Russian dessert which is served at Easter. A candle is usually lit and placed in the top of the pashka. We don't suggest that you do this but you may like to decorate the sides with toasted flaked almonds. This is one dish that is better made by hand than in a food mixer or processor, which grinds the glacé fruits and nuts to a powder. They should be evenly distributed throughout the pashka in colourful, recognisable pieces.

100ml/4floz/½ cup double/heavy cream
1 vanilla pod
3 eggs, separated
75g/3oz/⅓ cup sugar
450g/1lb/2⅔ cups curd cheese
50g/2oz/¼ cup unsalted butter, softened
50g/2oz/½ cup chopped blanched almonds
75g/3oz/¾ cup chopped glacé/candied fruits (cherries, pineapple, citron peel)
30ml/2 tablespoons dried apricots, chopped
toasted flaked almonds

Place the cream and vanilla pod in a pan and bring to the boil. Remove from the heat, take out the vanilla pod and set aside. Beat the egg yolks and sugar until pale and frothy and whisk in the hot cream. Pour into a double boiler and stir over gentle heat until the custard thickens. Do not allow the custard to boil. Remove from the heat and cool.

Beat the curd cheese and softened butter until well-blended and stir in the chopped nuts, glacé fruits and apricots. Fold in the cooled custard. Beat the egg whites stiffly and gently fold into the pashka mixture. Line a clean plastic flower pot with a damp muslin cloth and spoon the mixture into the pot. Stand in a bowl and leave to drain in the refrigerator overnight.

Turn the pashka out onto a serving dish and carefully remove the cloth without damaging it. Decorate the top and sides with toasted flaked almonds and serve.

Serves 6

Lemon cheesecake

This is the most economical and slimming cheesecake that we know. Don't be put off by the use of cottage instead of cream cheese — it gives the cheesecake an unusual texture and flavour. It is quick and easy to make and freezes well.

175g/6oz digestive biscuits/Graham crackers
25g/1oz/2 tablespoons soft brown sugar
75g/3oz/6 tablespoons margarine
Filling:
100g/4oz/⅔ cup cottage cheese
25g/1oz/2 tablespoons soft brown sugar
1 egg, beaten
150ml/¼ pint/⅝ cup soured or double/heavy cream
grated rind and juice of 1 large lemon

Crush the biscuits and mix the crumbs with the sugar.

Heat the fat until it melts and mix with the biscuit crumbs. Spread across the base of a 20cm/8in loose-bottomed flan ring and press down well. Bake in a preheated oven at 180°C, 350°F, gas 4 for 10 minutes and cool.

Mash the cottage cheese and sugar and beat in the egg, a little at a time. Mix with the cream and grated lemon rind and juice. Pour into the prepared flan ring and bake in a preheated oven at 180°C, 350°F, gas 4 for 30 minutes or until set. Cool and remove from the flan ring. Decorate with caramelised lemon slices (see tart citron recipe on page 150) or with fresh fruit.
Serves 6

Prune cheesecake

Do not be put off trying this dessert if you still have horrifying childhood memories of prunes and custard. Served in this way in a pale golden tart with nuts and lemon rind, prunes are really delicious. However, you can substitute dried apricots or fresh raspberries.

25g/1oz/¼ cup chopped walnuts
25g/8oz/1⅓ cups curd cheese
75g/3oz/⅓ cup soft brown sugar
grated rind of 1 lemon
2 eggs, beaten
15ml/1 tablespoon rum
150ml/¼ pint/⅝ cup soured cream or natural yoghurt
12 large prunes, soaked overnight
Rum sugar paste:
100g/4oz/½ cup soft margarine
50g/2oz/¼ cup soft brown sugar
1 egg, beaten
grated rind of ½ lemon
25g/1oz/¼ cup ground almonds
225g/8oz/2¼ cups wholemeal flour
pinch of salt
22.5ml/1½ tablespoons rum

Make the rum sugar paste: cream the margarine and sugar until soft and fluffy and add the beaten egg. Beat well and then mix in the lemon rind, ground almonds, sieved flour, salt and rum. Form into a ball and leave in the refrigerator for at least 30 minutes before rolling out.

Line a 20cm/8in flan case with the pastry and prick the base. Scatter the chopped nuts into the flan. Beat the curd cheese with a fork and add the sugar, lemon rind and then, gradually, the beaten egg. Stir in the rum and gently fold in the soured cream or yoghurt. Pour the cheese filling into the flan case.

Drain the prunes and remove the stones/pits if necessary. Cut each prune in half and arrange in the flan. Bake in a preheated oven at 190°C, 375°F, gas 5 for about 1 hour or until the curdcake is set. Serve warm.
Serves 6

Yoghurt

Home-made yoghurt

Although you can buy yoghurt in a wide range of flavours, home-made yoghurt tastes better and does not contain white sugar, preservatives and colourings unlike most commercial brands. You do not need a special yoghurt-maker — a wide-necked thermos flask is equally suitable and the best way to maintain a steady temperature during the incubation period. Yoghurt bacteria are destroyed at temperatures over 48°C, 120°F and inactive below 32°C, 90°F.

550ml/1 pint/2½ cups milk
30ml/2 tablespoons natural yoghurt
15ml/1 tablespoon skimmed milk powder

Heat the milk until it comes to the boil. Remove from the heat and cool to 43°C, 112°F. Use a sugar thermometer to measure the temperature. Blend the natural yoghurt with the milk powder until smooth, and stir into the warm milk. Pour into a *warmed* wide-necked thermos flask. Seal and leave for a minimum of 6 hours. When the yoghurt has thickened to a custard-like consistency, transfer it to a clean container and refrigerate for about 24 hours before serving. Do not incubate the yoghurt for too long or it will turn sour.

Makes approximately 550ml/1 pint/2½ cups yoghurt

Chilled yoghurt and cucumber soup

Yoghurt soups are popular throughout the Balkans and the Middle East. This version is served chilled with plenty of chopped fresh mint. You can use less yoghurt (say, 300ml/½ pint/1¼ cups mixed with the same ingredients) to make *cacik*, a cucumber and yoghurt dish which is served as a dip or with couscous and other hot dishes.

1 large cucumber
salt
3 spring onions/shallots, chopped
15ml/1 tablespoon chopped dill
30ml/2 tablespoons chopped fresh mint
550ml/1 pint/2½ cups natural yoghurt
freshly ground black pepper

juice of ½ lemon
25g/1oz/¼ cup chopped walnuts (optional)
25g/1oz/2 tablespoons raisins (optional)
fresh mint leaves to garnish

Peel and dice the cucumber and sprinkle with plenty of salt to draw out the excess moisture. Leave for 10-15 minutes and then rinse well in a colander under running water. Drain and pat dry.

Chop the spring onions, using a little of the green tops, and mix with the chopped herbs. Fold into the yoghurt and season to taste. Add the lemon juice and drained cucumber. Stir well and chill in the refrigerator. Serve garnished with chopped nuts and raisins, if wished, and few sprigs of fresh mint. You can use dried mint and dill in this recipe, but there will be a loss of flavour. Make it in the summer when mint and dill are plentiful.
Serves 4

Circassian chicken

There are many versions of this classic Turkish recipe, but chicken, walnuts and yoghurt are always included. Served cold with a crisp salad, this makes a light lunch on a warm summer's day.

4 chicken portions
1 carrot, sliced
2 sticks celery, quartered
3 parsley stalks
2.5ml/½ teaspoon each of chopped chervil, basil and dill
Walnut paste:
175g/6oz/1½ cups walnuts
175g/6oz/1½ cups chopped onion or shallots
175g/6oz/3 cups fresh breadcrumbs
15ml/1 tablespoon margarine or butter
5ml/1 teaspoon paprika
300ml/½ pint/1¼ cups apricot yoghurt
salt and pepper
chopped parsley and paprika to garnish

Wash and dry the chicken pieces and place in a large pan with the vegetables and herbs. Cover with water and bring to the boil. Lower the heat to a simmer, cover the pan and cook gently for about 1 hour. Let the chicken cool in the stock and then remove, reserving 300ml/½ pint/1¼ cups of strained stock to make the walnut paste. Cut the chicken meat off the bone and dice, discarding the skin. Set aside.

Make the walnut paste: grind the walnuts almost to a powder in a mortar, blender or, better still, a food processor. Sauté them gently with the chopped onion and breadcrumbs in the margarine until the onion is soft and the breadcrumbs are golden. Add the reserved stock and paprika and cook gently for 2-3 minutes. Mix in the yoghurt and season with salt and pepper. Then mix one-third of this paste with the chopped chicken and shape into 4 ovals. Arrange on a serving dish and spread each oval with the remaining paste. Smooth it over with a knife and sprinkle with a little chopped parsley and paprika. Serve cold with salad.
Serves 4

Lemon yoghurt cake

Yoghurt cakes are popular in Greece, Armenia and the Balkans, often flavoured with lemon, cinnamon and other spices. This is a light, moist cake which is seeped in lemon syrup before eating. Use good quality natural yoghurt for the best results.

225g/8oz/1 cup soft brown sugar
175g/6oz/¾cup soft margarine
grated rind of 1 lemon
4 eggs, separated
225g/8oz/2¼ cups plain flour
10ml/2 teaspoons baking powder
2.5ml/½ teaspoon bicarbonate of soda/baking soda
225ml/8floz/1 cup plain yoghurt
Syrup:
100g/4oz/½ cup sugar
juice of 2 lemons
long strip of lemon rind
2.5cm/1in piece cinnamon stick
15ml/1 tablespoon flaked almonds

Cream the sugar and margarine with the lemon rind until light and fluffy. Beat in the egg yolks, one at a time. Sieve the flour, baking powder and bicarbonate of soda, and fold into the cake mixture. Beat in the yoghurt. Whisk the egg whites until they stand in stiff peaks and gently fold into the mixture.

Pour into a well-buttered 20cm/8in cake tin and bake in a preheated oven at 180°C, 350°F, gas 4 for about 50 minutes. Let the cake cool in the tin for 5 minutes and then turn out onto a deep plate.

Make the syrup: put all the ingredients in a small pan and stir over low heat until the sugar dissolves. Bring to the boil and boil for 8-10 minutes until the syrup thickens. Remove the lemon rind and cinnamon stick and pour over the warm cake. Sprinkle over the flaked almonds and leave to cool.

Fish&Shellfish

Freshly caught fish is delicious, wholesome and nutritious and can be eaten in so many ways. Its protein content is as high as that of meat (between 15 and 20 per cent) and it is more easily digestible. The amount of fat varies according to the species. Thus cod, a white fish, has less than one per cent fat, whereas herring, an oily fish, contains between 5 and 22 per cent fat, depending on the season and the spawning cycle. Unlike meat, the fat is polyunsaturated and this helps to lower the body's cholesterol level. White fish, especially flat fish that live on the sea-bed, are low in calories, most of the oil being concentrated in the liver, which is also a rich source of vitamins A and D. Oily fish that feed on the surface are higher in fat. All fish and shellfish are rich in B vitamins and a good source of minerals, especially phosphorus, iodine and copper.

There is a wide range of fish to choose from, each with its own distinctive flavour and texture. The same fish do not flourish in all seas, of course, and this adds variety although it causes problems for cookery writers! Even if the same fish is not found in both the Atlantic and Pacific oceans, there is always another that can be substituted in a recipe with good results. For example, most firm-fleshed white fish are interchangeable as are flat fish and oily fish, and jumbo Pacific shrimps can be used instead of king prawns.

Fresh fish has been declining in popularity since the mass introduction of frozen fish fingers and cutlets, which require no preparation and are easy to cook even though they are relatively tasteless and high in calories when deep-fried. Over-fishing and pollution, especially in the North Atlantic and the Mediterranean, have diminished some fish stocks, and prices of over-fished species have risen accordingly. However, many fish are still economical and your choise will probably depend on the occasion for which it is to be cooked and how much money you are prepared to spend. Most fish can now be bought frozen but fresh fish always tastes better. For classification purposes, fish are usually divided into 3 categories: white fish, oily fish and shellfish.

White fish may be flat or round and are sold whole, filleted or cut into steaks and cutlets. They make the perfect low-calorie meal when grilled/broiled with fresh herbs or baked with aromatics and vegetables. Steaming and cooking *en papillote* (in a foil or paper parcel) are other healthy ways of preparing white fish.

Oily fish are usually eaten whole or smoked, although large oily fish such as salmon are sometimes cut into steaks and cutlets. They are higher in calories than white fish and may be cooked in similar ways. Some oily fish, such as trout and salmon, are now bred in fish farms for year-round availability.

Shellfish are divided into two groups: the bi-valves with hinged double shells, such as mussels, oysters, scallops, clams and cockles; and the crustaceans with jointed shells, such as crabs, lobsters, crayfish, scampi, prawns and shrimps. Shellfish is seasonal but it may also be bought frozen. It should be purchased live to ensure absolute freshness, but crabs, lobsters, prawns and shrimps are often sold precooked. It is an excellent source of protein and minerals but is relatively high in cholesterol, so it should not be eaten too often. Most shellfish, especially shrimps and prawns, are found all over the world, the largest shrimps coming from Africa and the Pacific.

Choosing fish and shellfish
The important thing when buying fish is that it should be really fresh because it putrefies rapidly. It should smell faintly and pleasantly fishy with a slight aroma of the sea. Avoid fish that smells unpleasantly strong, especially of ammonia. The scales should be firm, bright, shiny and should not cling tightly. The flesh should be elastic to the touch with tight, glowing skin. The eyes shold be clear, bright and sparkling — they should never be sunken, dull or cloudy. Look for bright red feathery gills free from slime and check that the flesh, when exposed, is clear without a bluish or greenish tinge.

Shellfish may be bought live, or precooked by the fishmonger, in which case it should have a bright, shiny shell with all the legs and claws attached. Shake a cooked crab gently to ensure that there is no water inside — it should always feel heavy for its size. Although crabs, lobsters, prawns, shrimps, crayfish and langoustines may be bought precooked, it is essential that mussels are bought live to ensure safety and freshness. The shells should be undamaged and closed tightly without any cracks.

Cleaning and preparing fish
You can ask most fishmongers to clean the fish for you if you are squeamish about doing so. They will also bone and fillet it if you ask. To clean fish yourself, just scrape off the scales with a wire brush or by pushing them the wrong way with a knife from the tail end towards the head. Rinse under running cold water and then slit the fish along its belly and remove the innards

(entrails) and blood, retaining the liver and roes as these are delicious and a good source of vitamins. Cut off any fins, spikes and gills with a pair of sharp kitchen scissors. Rinse again under cold running water.

The fish can now be lightly floured and fried or grilled/broiled, or the cavity filled with herbs and the fish baked in wine or stock with tomatoes and aromatics. To bone the fish, cut off its head and place it, cut-side down, on a clean surface. Press along the backbone with your fingers and then turn the fish over and gently remove the backbone.

To fillet a flatfish, cut off the fins and trim the edges with a sharp knife. Slice through the dark skin at the tail end of the fish and lift it up slightly to separate it from the flesh. Holding the skin in one hand and keeping the fish flat, gently pull off the skin from tail to head. Insert the blade of the knife between the white flesh and the slightly pink edge just below the head and cut along the length of the fish. Then cut down the centre along the backbone, working from head to tail, to separate the top two fillets. Make small cuts from the backbone towards the sides and lift the fillets up. Turn the fish over and fillet the other side

Cleaning and preparing shellfish

The methods of preparing shellfish for cooking vary according to the type of shellfish used. Live mussels should be washed several times in fresh water, and any with broken or gaping shells thrown away. Scrub the shells with a wire brush to remove any seaweed, mud and barnacles, and then remove the 'beard'. They are now ready for steaming.

Live lobsters and crabs can be plunged into boiling water or killed instantly by inserting the point of a sharp knife between the eyes. However, many people maintain that it is kinder to put them in tepid water

and bring them gently to the boil so that they are gradually overcome by the heat and pass out before the water boils. To remove crabmeat from a cooked crab, twist off the legs and claws and crack them open with the handle of a heavy knife or a hammer. Remove the white meat inside with a lobster pick or meat skewer. Turn the crab over onto its back and, holding the shell with the head away from you, push the body upwards and out of the shell with your thumbs. Remove and throw away the poisonous greyish-white stomach sac from behind the head and the feathery gills known as 'dead men's fingers'. Scrape out the soft creamy brown meat and put aside. Cut the body in half and remove the white meat from the sockets. Mix with the white meat from the claws and legs.

Cooking fish and shellfish

There are so many ways of cooking fish and shellfish, and there is literally no wastage as the bones, skin, trimmings and shell can be used to make delicious fish stock, or as flavourings for soups and sauces. Fish is economical to cook as it takes less time than meat and poultry and therefore fuel costs are lower. Never over-cook fish — the flesh should be firm and moist and slightly opaque; not mushy and falling off the bone.

Firm-fleshed fish can be cut into chunks, marinated in oil, wine, lemon juice and herbs and then threaded onto skewers with vegetables, bacon and prunes. Grill/broil and serve with rice and salad. Whole fish can be filled with herbs and seasoned, brushed with oil and grilled/broiled for about 5 minutes each side until the skin is crisp and the flesh cooked. Or it can be poached in stock, wine or court-bouillon, or wrapped up in buttered foil or baking paper with herbs, chopped onion, lemon juice and a little white wine and baked in the oven until tender.

Scottish smoked haddock soup

The picturesque Scottish name for this rich but delicately flavoured soup is 'cullen skink'. It is traditionally made with the pale silvery coloured Finnan haddock which, unlike the dyed yellow smoked haddock usually seen in the shops, is lightly cool-smoked for a more subtle flavour. Finnan haddock derives its name from the small fishing village of Findon south of Aberdeen on Scotland's eastern coast.

1 smoked Finnan haddock (about 450g/1lb)
15g/½oz/1 tablespoon butter
1 onion, finely chopped
30ml/2 tablespoons flour
550ml/1 pint/2½ cups milk
225g/8oz monkfish, cod or any other firm white fish, cubed
salt and pepper
dash of anchovy essence
juice of ½ lemon
15ml/1 tablespoon chopped parsley

Soak the haddock in boiling water for 15 minutes. Melt the butter in a large saucepan and sauté the onion until soft and translucent. Stir in the flour and cook gently for 2-3 minutes. Gradually add the milk, a little at a time, stirring all the while over a gentle heat. Add the monkfish.

Flake the haddock, carefully picking out all the bones. Add the flaked haddock to the soup and thin, if necessary, with a little of the haddock water. Season with salt and pepper and a dash of anchovy essence. Cook gently for 20 minutes.

Stir in the lemon juice and heat through over low heat. Serve sprinkled with chopped parsley.

Serves 4

Bouillabaisse

This classic French dish from Marseilles is served with garlic bread and *ailloli*, a garlic mayonnaise. Many versions of the recipe exist and as Mediterranean fish are sometimes hard to buy, you may have to use your favourites or whatever is plentiful at your local fishmonger. Fish and shellfish are included and the bouillabaisse is flavoured with saffron, fresh herbs and strips of orange peel. It is very filling and is better served as a main course than as a starter. Serve it with salad if you like. Although it is difficult to recreate a really authentic bouillabaisse away from the Mediterranean, you can still produce a delicious soup. Some people would argue that it is more of a stew than a soup, and fast boiling will reduce the liquid.

1.5kg/3lb fresh mixed fish (monkfish, John Dory, conger eel, gurnard, turbot, whiting, langoustines, mussels, mullet, scampi or squid)
50ml/2floz/¼ cup olive oil
2 onions, chopped
2 cloves garlic, crushed
2 leeks, thinly sliced
4 tomatoes, skinned and chopped
1 bay leaf
2-3 sprigs parsley
2 sprigs of fennel leaves
1 small packet powdered saffron
salt and pepper
2 large potatoes, thinly sliced
few strips of orange peel
1.1 litres/2 pints/5 cups water
8 slices French bread
olive oil and garlic

Clean and prepare the fish. Cut the white fish in good-sized chunks. Leave the mussels, langoustines and prawns in their shells although you may remove any legs and heads. Heat the oil in a large, heavy pan and add the vegetables and herbs. Add the saffron, seasoning and the soft fish. Cover with the thinly sliced potatoes, orange peel and the water and bring to the boil. Boil furiously for 15-20 minutes until the oil and water amalgamate and the liquid reduces and thickens slightly. Add the shellfish (mussels, scampi, prawns, langoustines) about 5 minutes before the end.

While the bouillabaisse is cooking, toast the slices of bread and fry in olive oil until crisp and golden. Rub lightly with a cut clove of garlic. Remove the fish from the bouillabaisse and arrange in a hot tureen or serving dish. Season the soup and boil hard for 3-4 minutes and then pour it over the fish (traditionally, it is strained through a sieve but we like to eat the vegetables). Pour it over the fried bread into large bowls and serve with ailloli (see recipe on page 173). Sprinkle with chopped parsley if wished.

Serves 6

Striped fish terrine

Delicately striped pink, golden and cream fish terrine, served with a pale green-flecked mayonnaise, is a sumptuous way to start a summer dinner party. Although it looks impressive and tastes exquisite, this dish is surprisingly easy to make if you have a good blender or food processor. It is served chilled in slices with a fresh herb mayonnaise and brown bread. You can use different combinations of fish and shellfish to create the creamy farce and the central pink and golden layers — monkfish, sole, whiting, cod, eel or scallops are all suitable for the creamy farce; and prawns/shrimps, salmon and scallop corals can all be used in the pink layer. We have even created an additional golden-yellow layer, with smoked yellow haddock. The most important thing to bear in mind when assembling the terrine is to keep all the farce ingredients well-chilled and even to chill the blender goblet or processor bowl before blending.

Creamy farce:
225g/8oz scallops
225g/8oz white fish, diced
2 egg whites
300ml/½ pint/1¼ cups double/thick or whipping cream
salt and pepper
30ml/2 tablespoons chopped tarragon, parsley and chives
Pink layer:
175g/6oz peeled prawns/shrimps
few scallop corals
50g/2oz chopped smoked salmon
Golden layer:
175g/6oz smoked haddock

Wash the scallops, separating the corals from the white parts. Chill the white scallops with the diced white fish and egg whites and cream. Also chill the processor bowl or blender goblet in the refrigerator or freezer.

While the farce ingredients are chilling, chop up the prawns/shrimps and mix with the corals and smoked salmon. Set aside. Pour boiling water over the smoked haddock and leave for 10 minutes before removing the skin and bones, flaking the meat and setting it aside.

When the bowl or blender and the farce ingredients are well-chilled, liquidise the scallops and white fish with the egg whites, and then add the cream. Blend until thick, smooth and creamy. Season and stir in the chopped herbs.

Spread a layer of farce across the base of a well-buttered terrine or baking tin. Cover with a layer of smoked haddock, then a very thin layer of farce, topped with the pink fish layer and finishing with the remaining farce. Cover with a sheet of buttered foil or baking paper and the lid of the terrine. Bake in a water bath in a preheated oven at 180°C, 350°F, gas 4 for about 35 minutes until the farce is set and firm to the touch.

Leave the terrine to cool and then chill overnight in the refrigerator. This will allow the farce to set further so that it will be firm when sliced the next day and not crumble on cutting. Decorate the top of the terrine with plenty of fresh chopped parsley and chopped chives. Serve with a herb-flavoured green mayonnaise (see recipe on page 173).

Seafood quiche

The classic quiche Lorraine is now familiar to all of us but how many people have experimented with different fillings for a standard fluted savoury flan case? In France there are many regional specialities and this seafood flan is based on a Normandy variation. Although monkfish is the best white fish to use in this recipe owing to its firmness, you can use any firm-fleshed white fish which does not flake easily.

75g/3oz monkfish (or any firm-fleshed white fish)
50ml/2floz/¼cup dry cider
50g/2oz peeled prawns/shrimps
50g/2oz button mushrooms, sliced
2 spring onions, chopped
2 eggs
150ml/¼ pint/⅝ cup milk
75ml/3floz/⅜ cup cream
salt and pepper
pinch ground nutmeg
50g/2oz/½ cup grated Gruyère/Swiss cheese
chopped chives
one 20cm/8inch wholemeal pastry flan case
  (see recipe on page 169)

Cube the monkfish and poach in the cider for a few minutes until tender. Drain off the cider and put aside. Place the fish, prawns, mushroom and spring onion in the flan case.

Beat together the eggs, milk and cream and season with salt and pepper and nutmeg. Stir in the reserved cider and pour into the flan case. Sprinkle with cheese and chopped chives, and bake in a preheated oven at 200°C, 400°F, gas 6. Reduce heat to 180°C, 350°F, gas 4 after 15 minutes and then continue baking for another 30 minutes until the filling is golden-brown and puffed up above the edge of the flan. Serve hot or cold with salad and a glass of cider.

Serves 4

Overleaf: a spread of delicious fish dishes: monkfish kebabs (see page 87) and bouillabaisse (see page 82) with stewed scallops in orange juice (see page 95) in the foreground

Fish escabeche

This pickled fish dish, known as *caveach* in eighteenth century England, is a recurring theme in Latin American and Caribbean cookery. Any fresh white fish can be used — sole, haddock, flounder, whiting, plaice, hake, cod or snapper. The principle of an escabeche is that the fish fillets or chunks are lightly fried and then marinated in citrus juice, oil, spices and herbs for at least 12 hours. It makes a refreshing and pretty first course served in real scallop shells and garnished with tiny pink shrimps and slices of creamy-green avocado.

4 fillets of sole, flounder or any white fish
salt and pepper
60ml/4 tablespoons olive oil
1 bay leaf
juice of 3 lemons or limes
juice of 2 oranges
1 orange, peeled and thinly sliced
½ green pepper, seeded and finely chopped
30ml/2 tablespoons chopped parsley
3 spring onions/shallots, chopped
pinch of ground nutmeg
Garnish:
50g/2oz peeled shrimps
1 avocado, peeled and thinly sliced

Season the skinned and boned fish fillets and cut into thin strips. Fry them in half the olive oil until just cooked and turning golden-brown. Drain and place in a shallow dish with the bay leaf. Pour the fruit juice and remaining olive oil over the top (just enough to cover them). Arrange the sliced orange and green pepper over the fish and sprinkle with chopped parsley, spring onion, seasoning and nutmeg. Cover the dish with a lid or clingfilm and chill in the refrigerator for at least 12 hours. Add a little more olive oil and remove the bay leaf just before serving.

Serve in scallop shells or small dishes garnished with shrimps and sliced avocado. You can vary the flavour of the dish by adding a little tarragon vinegar or finely chopped chilli peppers.

Serves 4

Sicilian-baked sardines

This Sicilian baked dish, known as *sarde a beccafico* throughout southern Italy, derives its name from the Italian word for warbler (*beccafico*), to which the sardines bear only a passing resemblance when laid out together in a baking dish. The sardines are rolled around the delicious sweet-sour stuffing, baked in oil, and then sprinkled with lemon and orange juice. The flavour is unusual and piquant and makes these little sardines an interesting first course for a dinner party.

450g/1lb fresh sardines
60ml/4 tablespoons fresh wholemeal breadcrumbs
60ml/4 tablespoons olive oil
3 anchovy fillets, chopped
30ml/2 tablespoons sultanas
25g/1oz/¼ cup pine nuts
few sprigs parsley, chopped
salt and pepper
5ml/1 teaspoon soft brown sugar
olive oil
juice of 1 orange
juice of 1 lemon

With a sharp knife, remove the scales from the sardines and then slit them open along the belly, removing the head and guts. Wash them under cold running water. Open each sardine out like a book, back up and flesh down, and press down firmly on the backbone. Turn the fish over and carefully remove the bone.

Sauté the breadcrumbs in the olive oil until crisp and lightly browned and mix with the chopped anchovy, sultanas, pine nuts, parsley, seasoning and sugar.

Place a little of the mixture on each sardine and roll up and secure with a cocktail stick/toothpick. Place the stuffed sardines in a well-oiled baking dish, sprinkle with any remaining stuffing and pour over just a trickle of olive oil. Bake in a preheated oven at 180°C, 350°F, gas 4 for 30 minutes. Arrange on a serving dish, pour over the citrus juice and serve.

Serves 4

Smoked salmon pâté

This is easily and quickly prepared and should be served in tiny white porcelain ramekin dishes. Serve it with wedges of lemon and thinly sliced wholemeal or granary bread.

15g/½oz/1 tablespoon butter or margarine
225g/8oz smoked salmon trimmings
30ml/2 tablespoons olive oil
juice of 1 lemon
salt and pepper
15ml/1 tablespoon natural yoghurt
50g/2oz/⅓ cup curd cheese
smoked salmon to garnish

Put the butter, smoked salmon trimmings, olive oil and lemon juice in a blender or food processor and process until smooth. Add the yoghurt and curd cheese and process for about 30 seconds. Season to taste and divide the mixture between little ramekin dishes. Swirl the top of the pâté decoratively with a fork and garnish each with a twist of smoked salmon.

Serves 4

Rollmop herring and soured cream

Spiced rollmop herrings are very popular in the Scandinavian countries and are sometimes made into unusual salads such as this one, which is mixed with apple and onion and tossed in soured cream and yoghurt. You can substitute diced salted herring fillets if you prefer them.

3 rollmop herrings, sliced thinly
4 spring onions/shallots, chopped
2 red-skinned dessert apples, diced
75ml/3floz/⅜ cup natural yoghurt
75ml/3floz/⅜ cup soured cream
salt and pepper
juice of ½ lemon
30ml/2 tablespoons chopped parsley

Mix the sliced herring, chopped onion and apple in a salad bowl and blend the dressing ingredients — the yoghurt, soured cream, seasoning and lemon juice. Toss the herring salad lightly in this dressing and sprinkle with plenty of chopped parsley. Chill in the refrigerator before serving.

Serves 4

Salmon trout parcels

Salmon trout, or brown trout as it is known in the United States, is a superb fish with sweet, moist pink flesh. Its flavour is so distinctive and delicate that it seems a shame to disguise it in a rich sauce and there is no better way to eat it than grilled with fresh herbs or, even better, baked *en papillote* with white wine, herbs and a little butter. This cooking method entails sealing the fish inside some foil or strong baking paper, thus allowing it to cook in its own juices without any loss of flavour, goodness or aroma. You can try it out with other fish, including white fish fillets, red mullet, salmon and sea-bass.

two 675g/1½lb or one 1.5kg/3lb salmon trout

30ml/2 tablespoons oil or melted butter
salt and pepper
*30-45ml/2-3 tablespoons chopped fresh herbs (rosemary,
    thyme, basil etc)*
2 bay leaves
1 shallot, chopped
60ml/4 tablespoons white wine
good squeeze lemon juice
15g/½oz/1 tablespoon butter

Wash, scale and gut the fish. Wash again under running water and pat dry. Cut out a large piece of foil (2 if you are cooking 2 small fish) and brush it lightly with oil or melted butter. Lay the fish on top and season the cavity with salt and pepper and a few of the herbs. Sprinkle the remaining herbs on top with the bay leaves and shallot and moisten with white wine and lemon juice. Dot the top with small knobs of butter and fold the foil up over the top to meet in the centre, twisting the edges to make a secure parcel which cannot leak while cooking.

Place the foil parcel in a baking dish and bake in a preheated oven at 180°C 350°F, gas 4 for about 45 minutes (take a peep at the fish after 30 minutes if you are cooking 2 smaller ones). Serve hot or cold with a cucumber salad, dressed with yoghurt or soured cream and dill, hard-boiled eggs and avocado sauce (see recipe on page 172).

Serves 4

Monkfish kebabs

Monkfish is ideal for threading onto kebabs as its flesh is so firm and does not fall apart or flake. Its sweet flavour and texture are reminiscent of scampi. If you cannot obtain monkfish, substitute cod or any other firm-fleshed white fish.

675g/1½lb monkfish, skinned and boned
4 rashers smoked, streaky bacon
8 prunes, soaked overnight
2 small onions, quartered
1 red pepper, cut in chunks
1 green pepper, cut in chunks
chopped fresh chives or parsley
Marinade:
50ml/2floz/¼ cup olive oil
juice of 1 lemon
50ml/2floz/¼ cup white wine
1 clove garlic, crushed

1 spring onion/shallot, chopped
salt and pepper

Cut the monkfish into cubes and place in a bowl with the marinade. Stir well and leave to marinate in a cool place for at least an hour.

Cut each bacon rasher in half and remove the rind. Stone/pit the prunes and then wrap some bacon around each prune. Thread onto 4 kebab skewers, alternating with cubes of monkfish, onion quarters and chunks of red and green pepper. Baste with the marinade and place under a hot grill for 10-15 minutes, turning occasionally and basting with more marinade if necessary.

Serve the kebabs lying diagonally across a serving dish with carrot purée (see recipe on page 138) on either side. Sprinkle with chives and decorate, if wished, with lettuce curls.

Serves 4

Kulebiaka

This is a very grand Russian fish pie wrapped up in a brioche crust. Impressive, rich and filling, it makes a spectacular party dish although it is relatively inexpensive to make. Boiling soured cream is poured into the pie immediately before serving as the finishing touch. Roast buckwheat, or *kasha*, is traditionally used but we have substituted brown rice as it is easier to buy and we feel that its crunchy texture is more suited to the dish. You can use other smoked or fresh white fish in this dish according to what is available.

Brioche dough:
350g/12oz/3½ cups wholemeal flour
2.5ml/½ teaspoon salt
15ml/1 tablespoon sugar
15g/½oz fresh yeast
30ml/2 tablespoons warm water
2 eggs, beaten
50g/2oz/¼ cup melted butter
Filling:
350g/12oz smoked haddock (or other smoked fish)
100g/4oz mushrooms, chopped
1 onion, chopped
30ml/2 tablespoons oil
juice of ½ lemon
salt and pepper
good pinch of ground nutmeg
100g/4oz/¾ cup long-grain brown rice

550ml/1 pint/2½ cups chicken stock
30ml/2 tablespoons dried dill
few sprigs of parsley, chopped
100g/4oz peeled prawns/shrimps
2 hard-boiled eggs, chopped
beaten egg to glaze
150ml/¼ pint/⅝ cup soured cream

Make the brioche dough: place the flour and salt in a mixing bowl. Cream the sugar and yeast and mix with the warm water. Add with the egg and melted butter to the flour and mix to form a soft dough. Knead lightly on an unfloured surface for a few minutes and then replace in the bowl, cover with a cloth and leave to rise in a warm place for about 1-1½ hours until risen and doubled in size.

Knock back the dough and knead well on a lightly floured board. Divide into two balls and roll out to two equal-sized oblong shapes.

While the dough is rising, make the filling. Poach the smoked haddock in a little water for about 10 minutes. Remove and cool and flake with a fork into chunks. Sauté the mushroom and onion in the oil until soft and stir in the lemon juice, seasoning and nutmeg. Cook the brown rice in the chicken stock until tender but still firm. All the stock should be absorbed by the cooking rice — add more liquid if necessary. Stir the chopped herbs into the rice and season.

Arrange the filling in layers in the centre of one of the oblong dough shapes. Start with half of the brown rice, leaving at least a 2.5cm/1in dough border around the filling. Cover with a layer of mushroom mixture, then the chopped egg, the flaked haddock and prawns, more egg and the remaining mushroom mixture and the cooked rice.

Brush the dough border with some beaten egg and cover with the other piece of dough. Seal the edges and plait neatly. Brush the pie with beaten egg and make a small central hole in the top.

Bake in a preheated oven at 200°C, 400°F, gas 6 for about 50-55 minutes until the brioche case is golden-brown. Just before serving, heat the soured cream to boiling point and pour through a funnel into the top of the pie. Serve very hot with more soured cream and a fresh green salad.

Serves 6

Opposite: for an impressive Russian meal, try serving blinis with soured cream, smoked salmon, hard-boiled eggs and caviare (see page 34) followed by kulebiaka (see this page) in a crisp, golden brioche crust

Baked salmon en croûte

You are probably familiar with the idea of meat baked en croûte but have you ever tried fish cooked in this way? A small tail-end of salmon can be made to feed several people if boned and skinned and cooked in a puff pastry case. Serve it with a fresh herb sauce and you have a lovely meal for when you are entertaining friends. This is an English West Country recipe and dates from mediaeval times when fish was often flavoured with spices and served in pastry.

1kg/2lb tail-end of fresh or frozen salmon
salt and pepper
juice of ½ lemon
50g/2oz/¼ cup softened maragarine or butter
45ml/ 3 tablespoons chopped parsley
15ml/ 1 tablespoon chopped chives
45ml/ 3 tablespoons chopped parsley
2.5ml/½ teaspoon chopped tarragon
1.25ml/¼ teaspoon each of ground cinnamon and allspice
small knob of stem ginger in syrup, chopped
225g/8oz fresh or frozen puff pastry
beaten egg to glaze
Fresh herb sauce:
2 shallots or 1 small onion, finely chopped
15g/½oz/1 tablespoon margarine
45ml/3 tablespoons chopped parsley
30ml/2 tablespoons chopped chives
15ml/1 tablespoon flour
300ml/½ pint/1¼ cups milk
1 egg yolk
30ml/2 tablespoons cream
salt and pepper
good pinch of ground nutmeg
15ml/1 tablespoon lemon juice

Skin and bone the salmon so that you have 2 thick fillets. Season with salt and freshly ground black pepper and sprinkle with lemon juice. Blend the softened butter with the chopped herbs, seasoning, spices and ginger, adding a little of the syrup if you are keen on ginger. Sandwich the 2 fillets together with this mixture.

Roll out the pastry thinly and place the salmon in the centre. Dot the top with a little butter and fold one side of the pastry over it. Brush the edge with beaten egg and fold the other side of the pastry over the top and seal. Turn the ends up, plait and seal securely to prevent the juices escaping while the salmon is cooking. Decorate the top with pastry leaves and brush the salmon parcel with beaten egg. Place on a well-greased baking sheet and bake in a preheated oven at 220°C,

425°F, gas 7 for 15 minutes and then reduce the temperature to 180°C, 350°F, gas 4 for a further 20 minutes until the pastry is well-risen and golden-brown.

While the salmon is cooking, make the sauce: sauté the shallots gently in the margarine until soft and translucent. Stir in the chopped herbs, cook for 1 minute and add the flour. Cook for 2 minutes and then add the milk, a little at a time, beating until the sauce is smooth. Simmer over a gentle heat for 10-15 minutes, stirring occasionally. Mix the egg yolk with the cream and stir into the sauce. Heat very gently until the sauce thickens. Season to taste and add the nutmeg and lemon juice. Serve hot with the cooked salmon en croûte.
Serves 6

Scandinavian fish mould with prawn sauce

This is a delicious variation on the French quenelles, using white fish and salmon for a delicate pink moulded dish. You bake it in a moderate oven in a water bath until set and turn out onto a plate and serve with prawn sauce. The result is sensational and it is a good way of stretching a small amount of fish around several people. If you have a processor or a good blender, nothing could be simpler.

175g/6oz salmon, skin and bone removed
175g/6oz white fish (sole, cod, scallops, whiting,
*   flounder, haddock or monkfish), skin and bone removed*
3 large eggs, separated
45ml/3 tablespoons flour
25g/1oz/2 tablespoons softened butter or margarine
5ml/1 teaspoon salt
1.25ml/¼ teaspoon ground nutmeg
few drops anchovy essence
5ml/1 teaspoon sugar
150ml/¼ pint/⅝ cup milk
150ml/¼ pint/⅝ cup double/heavy cream
45ml/3 tablespoons finely chopped parsley
45ml/3 tablespoons fresh white breadcrumbs
300ml/½ pint/1¼ cups prawn sauce (see recipe on
*   page 91)*

Process the fish with the egg yolks, flour, fat, salt, nutmeg, anchovy essence, sugar, milk and cream to a smooth purée. Whisk the egg whites until glossy and standing in stiff peaks and gently fold into the fish purée with a metal spoon. Stir in 30ml/2 tablespoons of the chopped parsley.

Butter a mould or basin lavishly (this will prevent the fish sticking to it) and tip in the remaining parsley and the breadcrumbs. Rotate the mould so that the sides are well-covered and shake out any excess crumbs. Pour in the fish mixture and stand in a water bath (the water should come halfway up the sides of the mould). Cover the mould with some buttered paper and bake in a preheated oven at 180°C, 350°F, gas 4 for 1¼ hours until well-set. You can insert a skewer to test whether it is cooked. It should be firm to the touch. Ease the point of a sharp knife around the sides of the mould and turn it out onto a serving dish. Serve hot with prawn sauce (see recipe below).

Serves 4

Quenelles in prawn sauce

Quenelles are light and creamy and easy to make in an electric blender or food processor. You can make them in advance as they freeze successfully. Served with a delicate prawn sauce, they make an impressive first course. Although they are traditionally made with pike, we prefer to use white fish fillets or salmon.

275g/10oz white fish fillets (cod, monkfish, whiting etc)
salt and pepper
good pinch of nutmeg
150ml/¼ pint/⅝ cup double/heavy cream
1 egg + 1 egg white
Sauce:
225g/8oz prawns/shrimps in their shells
400ml/14 fl oz/1¾ cups water
25g/1oz/2 tablespoons margarine
30ml/2 tablespoons flour
15ml/1 tablespoon tomato paste
2.5ml/½ teaspoon sugar
100ml/4 fl oz/½ cup single/light cream
100ml/4 fl oz/½ cup Madeira or Marsala
salt and pepper

Cut the fillets into small pieces, discarding any skin and bones. Process to a smooth purée in your liquidiser or processor. Add the seasoning, nutmeg, cream and egg, and process for about 30 seconds until thick and creamy. Chill in the refrigerator for at least an hour.

Meanwhile, make the prawn sauce: peel the prawns and place the shells in a pan with the water. Cover and simmer for about 25-30 minutes. Liquidise or process the shells and then rub through a fine sieve. Heat the margarine in a clean pan and stir in the flour. Cook gently for a couple of minutes. Add the sieved shell mixture and stir over a low heat until you have a smooth sauce. Simmer gently for 14 minutes and add the

tomato paste, sugar and cream. Simmer gently for 5 minutes and add the Madeira or Marsala and season to taste. Stir in the reserved prawns, which have been chopped into small pieces.

Bring a pan of salted water to the boil and then reduce the heat to a simmer. Slide 15ml/1 tablespoon of the chilled quenelle mixture into *simmering* water. Do not drop them into boiling water or they will break up. Add as many quenelles as the pan will take. They will sink at first and then float to the surface. Cook gently for about 8 minutes until the quenelles are set and cooked. Remove and keep warm and repeat until all the mixture is used up.

Serve the quenelles in the prawn sauce. If you wish to freeze the quenelles, pack them in polythene bags and freeze the sauce separately.

Serves 4

Fillets of sole Marsala

The Italians have an unusual and delicious way of cooking sole in Marsala wine with mushrooms. Not only is it easy to cook but it also makes a quick meal which is good enough to serve to special guests. To save time, ask the fishmonger to fillet the sole for you. Other fish can be cooked in this way, including flounder or even small pieces of monkfish and cod.

2 soles, filleted
30ml/2 tablespoons flour
salt and pepper
25g/1oz/2 tablespoons butter or margarine
30ml/2 tablespoons oil
100g/4oz button mushrooms, thinly sliced
100ml/4 fl oz/½ cup Marsala
15ml/1 tablespoon cream (optional)
15ml/1 tablespoon chopped parsley

Cut each of the sole fillets in half down the middle so that you end up with 8 pieces of fish. Turn the fillets in the flour and seasoning so that they are lightly coated. Heat the butter and oil in a large frying pan and gently fry the fish fillets until golden on both sides. Add the mushrooms and sauté gently until golden. Pour in the Marsala and cook over a medium heat until the sauce reduces and becomes slightly syrupy (about 10 minutes). Remove the fish fillets and arrange on a serving dish. Stir the cream into the sauce if wished and pour over the fish. Sprinkle with chopped parsley and serve with freshly cooked buttered noodles.

Serves 4

Mediterranean-style red mullet

Along the Mediterranean coastline of France and Italy, fish are often baked in wine with tomatoes and herbs and served in a piquant sauce. Red mullet has been a highly prized fish since Roman times and is always worth buying when it appears in your local fishmonger's or market. The liver, in particular, is a great delicacy and should never be discarded. Try our delicious recipe with its garnish of garlic croûtons. It is based on a dish that we enjoyed in a small restaurant near St Tropez.

2 large (450g/1lb) or 4 small (225g/8oz) red mullet
5ml/1 teaspoon olive oil
1 large onion, chopped
1 clove garlic, crushed
450g/1lb tomatoes, skinned and chopped
1 bay leaf
1 sprig parsley
5ml/1 teaspoon sugar
salt and pepper
300ml/½ pint/1¼ cups red wine
chopped parsley to garnish
Garlic croûtons:
4 slices of bread, crusts removed
2 cloves garlic
olive or sunflower oil for frying

Scale and clean the red mullet. Brush an ovenproof dish with olive oil and lay the cleaned mullet in the dish, sprinkled with the onion, garlic, tomatoes, herbs, sugar and seasoning. Pour in the red wine, cover with foil and bake in a preheated oven at 200°C, 400°F, gas 6 for 25-30 minutes until the mullet are cooked.

Remove the mullet and arrange in a serving dish and keep warm. Boil up the cooking liquid and vegetables to thicken the sauce (you can use a beurre manié, if wished) and then strain through a sieve to make a smooth, pink sauce. Pour over the mullet and sprinkle with chopped parsley.

Serve with garlic croûtons: cut each slice of bread into 4 triangles, rub both sides well with the garlic cloves and fry gently in the oil until crisp and golden.

Serves 4

Old-fashioned eel pie

Eel pies were once popular throughout the British Isles, and many regional variations existed. They were made at home or purchased at markets and traditional country fairs. Use conger eel if you cannot obtain freshwater eels. Ideally, eels should be bought alive and killed immediately before cooking, but if you are squeamish about this, then ask your fishmonger to kill and skin them for you. He will also cut the eel into good-sized portions. This version is rather more elaborate than the traditional dish, and we have added prunes in the French manner.

3 shallots, chopped
2 leeks, sliced
6 rashers streaky bacon, chopped
25g/1oz/2 tablespoons butter
1kg/2lb skinned eel, cut in 4 pieces
150ml/¼ pint/⅝ cup white wine
150ml/¼ pint/⅝ cup water or fish stock
25g/1oz/3 tablespoons flour
25g/1oz/2 tablespoons softened butter
pinch ground nutmeg
salt and pepper
few sprigs parsley, chopped
15ml/1 tablespoon lemon juice
30ml/2 tablespoons double cream
175g/6oz puff pastry (frozen or fresh)
beaten egg to glaze
8 large prunes, soaked overnight

Sauté the shallot, leek and bacon in the butter until soft. Add the eel and enough white wine and water to cover. Bring to the boil and remove the eel to a buttered pie dish. Keep warm.

Blend the flour and softened butter to make a *beurre manié*. Add tiny pieces of this to the cooking liquid, stirring well, until the sauce thickens. Flavour with the nutmeg, seasoning, parsley and lemon juice and stir in the cream.

Pour the sauce over the eel and add the prunes. Roll out the puff pastry and use to cover the pie dish. Brush with beaten egg and bake in a preheated oven at 225°C, 450°F, mark 7. After 20 minutes, reduce the heat to 190°C, 375°F, mark 5 and then continue cooking for a further 30 minutes until the pie is well-risen and golden-brown. If the pie starts to over-brown, then cover with foil or buttered paper. Serve with green vegetables.

Serves 4

Opposite: striped fish terrine (see page 82) and fish escabeche (see page 86) are both unusual and refreshing ways to start a meal. Serve the terrine with a green-flecked creamy herb mayonnaise (see page 173)

Sole in saffron sauce

This is a marvellous dinner party dish which always delights guests. Served in a pale golden sauce, garnished with pink prawns/shrimps and blue-black shells containing little orange mussels, it is one of the most attractive of fish dishes. You can vary the flavour by substituting a dry cider for white wine in the style of the great Normandy fish recipes. It is very filling and requires few vegetables to accompany it — just some French beans and puréed potatoes.

4 large fillets of sole (lemon sole, plaice or other white
   flat fish)
1 onion, chopped
100g/4oz button mushrooms, thinly sliced
100g/4oz peeled prawns1/shrimps
300ml/½ pint/1¼ cups white wine
150ml/¼ pint/⅝ cup fish stock or water
salt and pepper
1 bay leaf
15g/½oz/1 tablespoon butter
30ml/2 tablespoons flour
75ml/3floz/⅜ cup thin cream
juice of ½ lemon
small packet powdered saffron
550ml/1 pint mussels, washed and scrubbed
4 large whole prawns/shrimps for garnish
10ml/2 teaspoons chopped parsley

Lay the fillets of sole in a well-buttered large, shallow ovenproof dish. Scatter over the onion, mushrooms and peeled prawns and cover with the wine and stock (made from the bones and fish trimmings). Season with salt and pepper and the bay leaf. Cover the dish with some buttered aluminium foil and bake in a pre-heated oven at 180°C, 350°F, gas 4 for about 15-20 minutes until the fish is cooked and the onion tender.

Strain off the cooking liquor and keep for the sauce. Remove the bay leaf and keep the fish and vegetables warm. Melt the butter in a pan and add the flour to make a roux. Cook for 2-3 minutes without browning. Add the reserved fish liquor, a little at a time, beating over a low heat until you have a thick, smooth sauce. Bring to the boil, reduce to a simmer and stir in the cream and lemon juice. Season to taste and add the saffron. Cook gently for 3-4 minutes. Pour over the fish fillets and pop the dish under a hot grill for a few seconds to glaze it.

Meanwhile, place the washed and scrubbed mussels in a pan with a little water over medium heat. Cover tightly with the lid and shake the pan gently until the mussels start to open. Remove the mussels, discarding any that fail to open. Garnish the sole with the whole prawns and mussels and sprinkle with chopped parsley.

serves 4

Grecian-style baked fish

In Greece, whole fish or fish steaks are often baked in red wine with tomatoes and herbs. This method of cooking fish is known as *plaki*. You can use almost any sort of white fish for this recipe, including halibut, cod, sea-bass, bream and monkfish. It is best made with really fresh ingredients — fresh tomatoes, herbs and fennel — but you can use canned or dried equivalents.

4 white fish steaks or 1 whole (1.5kg/3lb) fish
30ml/2 tablespoons lemon juice
45ml/3 tablespoons oil
3 shallots, or 1 small onion, chopped
50g/2oz chopped fennel bulb
2 cloves garlic, crushed
10ml/2 teaspoons tomato paste
450g/1lb tomatoes, skinned and chopped (or canned)
pinch of sugar
15ml/1 tablespoon chopped parsley
5ml/1 teaspoon oregano
2.5ml/½ teaspoon fresh thyme
1 sprig rosemary
good pinch each of ground cinnamon and allspice
100ml/4floz/½ cup red wine (or port wine)
50g/2oz mushrooms, sliced
30ml/2 tablespoons fresh breadcrumbs
few black olives and chopped parsley to garnish

Wash the fish steaks or clean, scale and gut the whole fish. Sprinkle with lemon juice and set aside. Heat 30ml/2 tablespoons of the oil in a pan and sauté the shallots, fennel and garlic until tender and golden. Stir in the tomato paste and cook gently for 1 minute.

Add the chopped tomatoes and sugar and bring to the boil. Stir in the herbs and spices and the wine and cook gently for a few minutes.

Place the fish in an ovenproof dish. If using a whole fish, season the cavity and stuff it with fresh herbs. Season the sauce and pour it over the fish. Scatter with the mushrooms and then the breadcrumbs and dribble over the remaining oil. Bake in a moderate preheated oven at 180°C, 350°F, gas 4 for 20-25 minutes or until the fish is cooked and the topping is golden-brown and crisp. Garnish with olives and chopped parsley, and serve with a Greek salad of lettuce, tomatoes, onions, olives and feta cheese in a lemon-flavoured oil dressing.

Serves 4

Grilled sole with bananas

You can use sole, flounder or any flat fish in this recipe. It is also very good with lightly fried skate if you can find a source of really fresh fish. Simple to prepare and absolutely delicious, this dish should be served with a crisp, green salad.

4 small or *2 large sole or flounder*
15ml/1 tablespoon flour
15g/½oz/1 tablespoon butter
4 bananas
30ml/2 tablespoons oil
100ml/4floz/½ cup mango chutney

Wash and trim the sole or flounder, dry on absorbent kitchen paper and dust lightly with flour. Place on a grill pan and dot the top with butter. Grill/broil for about 5-6 minutes each side until golden-brown and cooked.

Meanwhile, peel the bananas and cut each in half lengthwise. Fry in the oil until slightly crisp and golden-brown outside and soft inside (you can lightly flour them to prevent them sticking to the pan). Heat the mango chutney gently over low heat until hot.

Serve the sole with the fried bananas arranged on either side, and the warmed chutney.

Serves 4

Shellfish

Grilled scallops

This is a tasty hot main course if you are in a hurry. Use the little bay scallops, or queens as they are sometimes called, for preference. It is best to use fresh scallops but it is often more economical to buy them in bulk in frozen packs and keep them in the freezer.

350g/12oz bay scallops or *8 large scallops*
juice of 1 lemon
15ml/1 tablespoon oil
50g/2oz/1 cup fresh white breadcrumbs
salt and pepper
1 clove garlic, crushed
15ml/1 tablespoon olive oil
15ml/1 tablespoon butter
chopped parsley to garnish
lemon wedges

Leave the bay scallops to marinate for about 1 hour in the lemon juice and oil. Gently mix in the breadcrumbs until they are well coated. Season with salt and plenty of freshly ground black pepper. If you are using large scallops, you will have to slice the whites and detach them from the corals.

Sauté the garlic in the oil and butter until it starts to brown. Pile the breadcrumbed scallops into 4 scallop shells and pour the hot garlic-flavoured oil over the top. Place under a very hot grill/broiler for about 5 minutes until golden-brown and crisp. Sprinkle with plenty of chopped parsley and serve immediately with lemon wedges.

Serves 4

Stewed scallops in orange juice

A delicious way of cooking scallops is to be found in Hannah Glasse's *The Art of Cookery*, which advocates stewing the scallops in 'a little white wine, a little vinegar, two or three blades of mace, two or three cloves, a piece of butter rolled in flour and the juice of a Seville orange'. Here is a modern version of the dish, served on a bed of crunchy brown rice in scallop shells as a subtly flavoured first course.

450g/1lb scallops
150ml/¼ pint/⅝ cup dry white wine
150ml/¼ pint/⅝ cup water
5ml/1 teaspoon wine vinegar
pinch of mace + 2 cloves
1 large orange
juice of ½ lemon
50ml/2floz/¼ cup single/light cream
1 egg yolk
salt and pepper
4 spring onions/scallions, chopped or *30ml/2 tablespoons chopped chives*

Detach the corals from the white parts of the scallops and cut each white piece in half. Heat the wine, water, vinegar and spices for about 10 minutes, and add the white parts of the scallops and cook gently for *no* more than 4 minutes, adding the corals for the last minute or so. It is very important not to overcook the scallops or they will become tough.

Remove the scallops and keep warm. Discard the cloves. Pare the peel off the orange with a potato peeler and cut into very thin julienne strips. Blanch them in boiling water for 5 minutes or so to soften them and drain. Squeeze the peeled orange and add the juice together with the lemon juice to the sauce. Boil it up to reduce it a little, and blend the cream and egg yolk to make a liaison. Reduce the heat to a simmer and stir in the liaison. Continue stirring over low heat until the sauce thickens a little. Add the scallops and serve on a bed of brown rice in 4 individual scallop shells. Sprinkle with the blanched strips of peel, chopped onion or chives and serve.

Serves 4

Crab and avocado crêpes

Savoury crêpes make an economical meal and a pleasant change from meat and fish dishes. You can buy canned crabmeat in supermarkets — it is almost as good as fresh crabmeat in this sort of recipe. The crêpe mixture can be prepared in seconds in a good processor, or in minutes by hand, and even the filling can be made in advance and frozen until needed.

75g/3oz/⅔ cup flour
2.5ml/½ teaspoon salt
3 eggs
400ml/14floz/¾ cup milk
30ml/2 tablespoons melted butter
15ml/1 tablespoon brandy
1 avocado, stoned/pitted and sliced
juice of ½ lemon
lemon wedges to garnish
Crabmeat filling:
300ml/½ pint/1¼ cups béchamel sauce (see recipe on
*   page 171)*
50g/2oz/½ cup grated Swiss or Cheddar cheese
1 egg yolk
juice of 1 small lemon
1.25ml/¼ teaspoon paprika
10ml/2 teaspoons anchovy sauce
225g/8oz canned or fresh crabmeat
salt and pepper

Make the crêpes by processing the flour, salt, eggs, milk, melted butter and brandy in a food processor. Or put the flour and salt in a bowl, make a well in the centre, and gradually beat in the eggs, milk, butter and brandy until the batter is smooth. Set aside while you make the filling.

Make the béchamel sauce in the usual way and stir in the grated cheese and egg yolk. Beat well and then add the lemon juice, paprika and anchovy sauce. Fold in the crabmeat and season to taste. Keep warm while you cook the crêpes.

Heat a little fat in a proved omelette pan and pour in enough crêpe mixture to cover the base and sides of the pan. Cook gently until golden underneath and flip it over and cook the other side. Keep warm. Cook all the crêpes in this way until the mixture is used up. Spread some of the warm crabmeat filling onto each crêpe and roll up. Garnish with the avocado slices dipped in lemon juice, and the lemon wedges. Alternatively, you can lay the avocado slices on top of the filling inside the crêpes, roll them up and place in an ovenproof dish. Sprinkle with a little grated cheese and flash under a hot grill/broiler until golden and bubbling.

Serves 4-6

Glazed king prawns with pineapple

Many people have never seen scampi in its shell — they only recognise it in its frozen state or crisp batter coating. However, Dublin bay prawns, or *langoustines* as scampi is also known, are sold fresh or frozen in their shells in many good fishmongers and quality food-stores and they are well worth the expense. In this recipe, we allow two prawns per person.

450g/1lb (or 8) cooked king prawns in their shells
1 small pineapple
15g/½oz/1 tablespoon clarified butter
2-3 leeks, thinly sliced horizontally
15ml/1 tablespoon dark rum
salt and pepper
chopped chives to garnish

Remove the heads from the king prawns and wash them under running water. Dry thoroughly. Tear off the feathery 'legs' underneath and cut down through the belly lengthwise, leaving the shell at the back intact. Open the prawn out like a book and remove the black vein running along the back. Slice the pineapple thinly and remove the outer skin. Heat the butter in a heavy pan and sauté the pineapple until golden-brown and tender. Add the king prawns and sauté gently.

Parboil the leeks in lightly salted water for 2 minutes and add to the pan. Stir-fry until golden and just tender. Add the rum and boil up the pan juices. Season to taste and arrange the prawns on a serving dish surrounded by the pineapple slices and leeks. Pour over the pan juices, sprinkle with chives and serve.

Serves 4

Opposite: Chinese crab with ginger (see page 99) is served
*   with egg fried rice (see page 41) and some China tea*

Shrimps in tomato sauce with feta cheese

Shrimps are sometimes served in a rich tomato sauce with feta cheese in Greece. Eaten with rice and a Greek salad, this makes a tasty summer meal. You can use tiny shrimps, large prawns/shrimps or even king prawns.

3 shallots or 1 small onion, chopped
1 clove garlic, crushed
15ml/1 tablespoon oil
450g/1lb tomatoes, skinned and chopped (or canned)
10ml/2 teaspoons tomato paste
5ml/1 teaspoon sugar
100ml/4floz/½ cup dry white wine
15ml/1 tablespoon chopped parsley
2.5ml/½ teaspoon each thyme and oregano
good pinch of cayenne pepper
freshly ground black pepper
450g/1lb peeled, cooked shrimps
225g/8oz feta cheese, crumbled
15ml/1 tablespoon chopped parsley to garnish

Sauté the shallots and garlic in the oil until tender and golden. Add the tomatoes and tomato paste — if using canned tomatoes, strain off the juice. Stir in the sugar and bring to the boil. Cook hard for 1 minute and then add the wine, herbs and cayenne pepper. Bring back to the boil and then reduce the heat to a simmer. Season with black pepper (not salt, as the later addition of feta cheese makes the dish quite salty), cover the pan and cook gently for 15 minutes until the sauce has reduced and thickened. Add the shrimps and cook for 5 minutes.

Crumble the feta cheese into an ovenproof dish and pour the shrimp sauce over the top. Bake in a preheated oven at 180°C, 350°F, gas 4 for 10 minutes. Sprinkle with chopped parsley and serve with boiled brown rice and Greek salad.

Serves 4

Shrimp rissoles

Crisp-fried little rissoles filled with shrimps in a piquant sauce are popular in Spain and Portugal. Eat them as a first course or as a hot snack with drinks.

225g/8oz/2¼ cups flour
pinch of salt
45ml/3 tablespoons grated Parmesan cheese
50g/2oz/¼ cup margarine
50g/2oz/¼ cup lard/shortening
60ml/4 tablespoons water

1 egg, beaten
100g/4oz breadcrumbs for coating
oil for deep-frying
Shrimp filling:
300ml/½ pint/1¼ cups béchamel sauce (see recipe on page 171)
15ml/1 tablespoon anchovy sauce
juice of ½ lemon
15ml/1 tablespoon chopped parsley
pinch each of fennel herb and paprika
salt and pepper
150g/5oz peeled, cooked shrimps

Make the pastry coatings for the rissoles: sieve the flour and salt, mix with the cheese and rub in the fat. Blend with water to a smooth paste. Put aside to relax in the refrigerator for 30 minutes while you prepare the filling.

Make the béchamel sauce in the usual way and stir in the anchovy sauce, lemon juice, herbs and seasoning. Fold in the shrimps and keep warm. The sauce should be thick and fairly stiff.

Roll out the pastry dough thinly and cut out 8 circles, using a 10cm/4in pastry cutter. Place a spoonful of the shrimp filling on each pastry circle and brush the edges with beaten egg. Fold the pastry over the filling and seal the edges with the back of a knife. Dip the rissoles in the beaten egg and then in the breadcrumbs so that they are well-coated. Shake off any excess crumbs.

Heat the oil to 190°C, 375°F, (you can measure the temperature with a sugar thermometer) and deep-fry the rissoles until crisp and golden-brown. Drain on absorbent paper and serve hot. The rissoles can be cooked in advance and heated up in the oven later without any loss of flavour.

Makes 8 rissoles

King prawn kebabs with curry sauce

Wrapped in bacon and threaded onto kebab skewers with onions, tomatoes and peppers, then served on a bed of saffron rice with curry sauce and fried bananas, a few king prawns go further and make a lovely meal. Use them fresh or frozen — it is sometimes cheaper to buy frozen ones in bulk.

12 king prawns/shrimps
6 rashers smoked streaky bacon
2 small onions, quartered

4 small tomatoes, halved
½ green pepper, cut in chunks
juice of ½ lemon
30ml/2 tablespoons olive oil
225g/8oz/1 cup long-grain rice
550ml/1 pint/2½ cups water
1 chicken stock/bouillon cube
1 small packet powdered saffron
4 bananas
45ml/3 tablespoons oil
15ml/1 tablespoon chopped parsley
Curry sauce:
25g/1oz/2 tablespoons margarine
1 small onion, chopped
10ml/2 teaspoons curry powder
25g/1oz/3 tablespoons flour
300ml/½ pint/1¼ cups milk
salt and pepper
squeeze of lemon juice

Peel the prawns/shrimps and remove the rind from the bacon rashers. Stretch out the rashers over the back of a knife, cut each in half and wrap around the prawns. Thread onto 4 kebab skewers with the onions, tomatoes and peppers and brush with lemon juice and olive oil. Put aside while you prepare the rice and sauce.

Cook the rice in a covered pan with the water, stock cube and saffron until tender and fluffy and all the water has been absorbed. Meanwhile, make the curry sauce: sauté the onion in the fat until it softens and starts to brown. Stir in the curry powder and cook for 2 minutes before adding the flour. Cook for 1 minute and gradually beat in the milk until the sauce is smooth and glossy. Season to taste and add a squeeze of lemon juice. Cook over a very low heat for about 5 minutes.

Place the kebabs under a hot grill/broiler and cook, turning frequently, for about 10 minutes until tender. Cut the bananas in half lengthwise and fry in the oil until golden-brown. Serve the kebabs on a bed of saffron rice with the fried bananas and the curry sauce. Sprinkle with a little chopped parsley.

Serves 4

Chinese crab with ginger

This makes an impressive centrepiece if you are serving a Chinese meal — glistening crab claws in a sharp, ginger sauce. Serve it with egg-fried rice (see recipe on page 41) and a pot of delicately scented China tea.

1 large cooked crab

45ml/3 tablespoons sesame oil
2.5cm/1in piece fresh ginger, chopped
1 large red pepper, seeded and sliced in rings
200ml/6floz/¾ cup chicken stock
10ml/2 teaspoons soy sauce
15ml/1 tablespoon sherry
5ml/1 teaspoon oyster sauce
10ml/2 teaspoons cornflour/cornstarch
salt and pepper
6 spring onions/shallots, chopped

Wash the crab and dry thoroughly. Cut off the claws and twist off the legs. Crack the claws or bash them with a hammer to break the hard shell and reveal the meat within. Cut each large claw into 2 or 3 pieces and the smaller legs in half. Now press on the sides of the shell with your thumbs to push the body up and out of the shell. Remove the poisonous stomach from behind the eyes and the 16 greyish gills, or 'dead men's fingers', and discard. Chop the body in half and then each half into 3 sections and put aside with the claws and legs. Scoop out any remaining meat in the shell.

Heat the sesame oil in a wok or frying pan and sauté the ginger and slices of pepper for 2 minutes. Add the crab and stir-fry for 1 minute until it is glistening with oil. Add the chicken stock, reserving 50ml/2floz/¼ cup for a later stage. Pour in the soy sauce, sherry and oyster sauce and cook over low heat for 5 minutes. Blend the cornflour with the remaining chicken stock and add to the wok. Raise the heat and stir for 2-3 minutes until the sauce thickens. Season to taste and sweeten with a little sugar if necessary. Sprinkle with the chopped spring onions and serve with fried rice.

Serves 4

Tip: To dress a crab, prepare it as described on page 81. Remove any white meat from the leg sockets and mix with the meat from the claws. Place the brown creamy meat in a separate bowl. Now, using the handle of a heavy knife, tap away the shell around the rim along the natural dark line. Wash, scrub and dry the shell and rub with oil. Mix 15ml/1 tablespoon chopped parsley and 30ml/2 tablespoons fresh white breadcrumbs into the brown meat and season well. Add some lemon juice and cayenne. Arrange the brown meat down the centre of the shell with the white on either side. Garnish with cayenne, chopped parsley and chopped hard-boiled egg yolk.

Meat, poultry and game are all excellent sources of high-biological protein and contain all the amino acids our bodies need. However, as vegetarians have discovered, they are not essential items in our diet and many people lead healthy lives without them, preferring to eat vegetable and cereal proteins or fish and animal products such as eggs and cheese. In the Western world we eat more meat than is necesary for our health — in fact, so much red meat containing saturated fats that over-consumption may even be detrimental to good health. It is hard to change the habits of a lifetime and we are not suggesting that you should eliminate meat from your diet altogether, but it is a good idea to eat meat less often and to gradually introduce some meatless days into your weekly eating programme. We enjoy meat ourselves but eat it only two or three times a week, preferring fish, vegetables, beans, eggs and cheese on meatless days. These foods provide us with all the protein and goodness of meat, although it may be necessary to include additional vitamin B12 in the form of eggs, milk or cheese.

Even the leanest meat contains 20 per cent fat, although chicken, turkey and game all have less concentrated fats than red meats. A correlation has been drawn between the high level of saturated fat in people's diets and the incidence of heart disease, so try and cut down on meat and use simpler cooking methods. The best poultry are free-range — not only have they a better flavour than factory-farmed birds, but they often contain less saturated fat. Some butchers specialise in free-range poultry and naturally reared meat from cattle grazed in healthy, organic pastures without hormones and antibiotics. Although it is more expensive, it has a good flavour and the percentage of fat is lower than that of intensively reared cattle.

Try eating meat in smaller quantities accompanied by delicious vegetables, whole grains, brown rice or wholemeal pasta. These unrefined carbohydrates are high in natural fibre and speed up the passage of food through our bodies. Meat protein in surplus of about 50g/2oz cannot be used by the body for the vital functions of building cell walls and repairing tissue, and is used up instead as energy or converted into fat and stored by the body.

As well as being a good source of protein, meat is rich in iron, phosphorus, potassium, sodium, magnesium and B vitamins, especially thiamine, niacin and B12. Because it is digested slowly, it can delay hunger pangs between meals and is favoured by many slimmers. The cholesterol-rich saturated fat is deposited between the muscle fibres to give the flesh of red meat a marbled effect.

Poultry

Poultry, which includes chicken, turkey, duck, goose and guinea-fowl, is rich in protein, vitamin B and iron. Duck and goose are more fatty than chicken and turkey and for this reason we have not included any recipes for them. Chicken and turkey are sold fresh or frozen, whole, quartered or in small joints (breasts, drumsticks etc) and may be cooked in so many ways — roasted, grilled/broiled, casseroled, barbecued, fried, boiled, pot-roasted, braised or served cold in salads. Our modern chickens, which are descended from small bantam-sized Asian jungle birds, may be bought free-range or factory-farmed, although these have less flavour than the former. The flavour of the bird is also affected by its age (old birds being tougher and less tasty) and the feedstuffs it was fed. For instance, maize-fed chickens have a more golden flesh and a better flavour than battery birds.

Baby chickens of four to six weeks old are known as poussins or broilers. They have little taste and are usually grilled/broiled or spit-roasted. Allow one per person. Poulets, or spring chickens, of three months old are larger and usually roasted, whereas roasting chickens are larger still (about 1.5kg/3lb - 3kg/6lb). Boiling fowls are the oldest, toughest birds, over 12 months old and suitable for boiling only.

When buying chicken, choose a bird with a plump white breast, smooth legs and a pliable breastbone. The legs get more scaly and the breastbone hardens with age. Chickens are usually sold oven-ready but can also be bought plucked but not drawn and trussed. Most butchers will do this for you. Like chicken, turkey is also available throughout the year and is sold whole or in joints. It is as nutritious as chicken and the best buys are hen birds of about seven to nine months with a plump pale breast.

Game

This term applies to all the game birds and furred animals that are hunted and then eaten. Game birds include pheasant, quail, ptarmigan, partridge, pigeon, wild goose, teal, mallard and snipe, whereas the most commonly hunted furred game animals are rabbits, hares and deer. Game tends to be expensive and is regarded by many people as a luxury, yet it is a traditional country food which has been eaten for centuries. The fashion in mediaeval times was for roast swan, peacock and wild boar and these were usually eaten at Christmas and on feast-days.

Some countries have special seasons when game can be hunted and closed seasons when this is forbidden. Thus the delicate natural balance of conservation in the countryside is maintained. In Britain, for example, it is only permissible to shoot game birds in the autumn and winter, each bird having its own season. Pheasants are the most commonly eaten birds, young ones being roasted and older, tougher birds made into soups, stocks, pâtés and pies. All game birds must be hung by the neck for about one week before plucking, drawing and cooking, but most butchers will do this for you. If you do it yourself, pepper the feathers to keep any flies away from the hanging bird.

Beef
This is the only meat to have the distinction of having been knighted — by the British king Henry VIII, and since then the hind-quarters have been known as the *baronne de boeuf*. Cuts of beef are not international and vary from country to country. The most tender cuts are invariably the most expensive. Quality beef may be bought fresh or frozen. Look for lean, moist red meat with a slightly brownish tinge and creamy fat. It may be kept in the refrigerator for two to three days wrapped loosely in plastic film, or it may be frozen for up to eight months. The cheaper cuts of beef are equally nutritious but require longer, slower cooking methods to tenderise them. Beef is often served under-done and slightly pink, or rare, or even *bleu*, very rare.

This is a matter of personal taste. It can be made more tender by marinating it in fruit juice or wine with herbs and aromatics prior to cooking.

Pork
This highly nutritious meat contains more B vitamins than beef or lamb. It is ideal for raised pies, pâtés and sausages as well as for baking, roasting and casseroling. Bacon and ham come from specially reared pigs and may be bought smoked or unsmoked. Pork is available throughout the year, either fresh or frozen. It may be stored in the refrigerator for two days or a maximum of four months in the freezer. The lean flesh should be firm and pale pink with milky-white fat. It should look smooth and slightly moist. Fruit, especially oranges, apples and gooseberries, go well with pork, as do most herbs, spices, garlic and ginger. Always eat it well-cooked and never underdone.

Lamb
Delicately flavoured fresh lamb is popular throughout Europe, the Middle East, Australia and New Zealand. Before the advent of modern refrigeration methods, it was referred to as 'spring lamb', being available only in the spring and early summer months. Now much of the lamb we eat is deep-frozen, often from Australia and New Zealand. Choose lamb with pale pink lean meat and firm, creamy-white fat. The redder the meat, the older the lamb. Lamb may be served well cooked or slightly underdone in the Continental manner. It may be seasoned with garlic and herbs, especially oregano, rosemary, marjoram and thyme. Uncooked meat can be wrapped loosely in plastic film and stored in the refrigerator for three days.

Pâtés

Chicken liver pâté

Served in individual gleaming white ramekin dishes, this makes an economical, tasty first course or a snack with biscuits and cheese. To make the pâté more attractive we suggest that you cover the top with a thin layer of parsley jelly.

100g/4oz/½ cup margarine
100g/4oz/½ cup chopped onion
225g/8oz chicken livers
1 clove garlic, crushed
pinch of ground nutmeg
15ml/1 tablespoon chopped parsley
1 bay leaf
salt and pepper
30ml/2 tablespoons brandy
Topping:
15g/½oz powdered aspic
15ml/1 tablespoon chopped parsley

Melt half the margarine in a frying pan/skillet, add the onion and sauté for a few minutes until soft. Wash and chop the chicken livers and add to the pan with the garlic, nutmeg, parsley and bay leaf. Season and cook gently for about 5 minutes, stirring well.

Remove from the heat and discard the bay leaf. Liquidise or process the chicken liver mixture until really smooth. Add the remaining margarine and the brandy and beat well. Check the seasoning and spoon into little ramekins and chill in the refrigerator.

When chilled, make the topping: bring 75ml/3floz/ ¾ cup water to the boil, remove from the heat and then sprinkle the aspic on top. Leave until dissolved and then stir and allow to cool a little. Just before it sets, stir in the chopped parsley and spread a little over the top of each ramekin. Leave to cool and serve.

Serves 6

Pork and ham pâté

This is not so rich and highly seasoned as the pheasant pâté opposite, and it is cheaper to make with belly pork and ham. Serve it as a light lunch, first course or party dish with crusty wholemeal or granary bread (much more substantial and tasty than thin pieces of dry toast!) and black olives. A food processor will take all the hard work out of mincing/grinding the meat and mixing the pâté. Make it the day before your party in order that it may be chilled and weighted overnight before decorating with orange slices.

1kg/2lb fat belly pork
350g/12oz ham or gammon
1 onion, chopped
2 cloves of garlic, crushed
2 eggs, beaten
100ml/4floz/½ cup Madeira wine or brandy
15ml/1 tablespoon chopped parsley
15ml/1 tablespoon thyme
salt and pepper
good pinch each of ground nutmeg and allspice
Garnish:
3 slices orange
3 bay leaves
9 juniper berries

Remove the skin and bones from the pork and ham. Mince the meat finely in a grinder or processor. Mix with the chopped onion, garlic, beaten eggs, wine, herbs, seasoning and spices. Place the mixture in a greased pâté dish and level the top. Cover with foil and stand in a water bath. The water level should come halfway up the sides of the dish. Bake in a preheated oven at 200°C, 400°F, gas 6 for 10 minutes and then reduce the heat to 180°C, 350°F, gas 4 for a further 1½ hours, or until the pâté shrinks away from the sides of the dish and appears to be swimming in fat. Pour off the excess fat and meat juices and and keep to make the topping the following day. Weight the pâté and leave to cool thoroughly and then chill overnight with the weights in place.

The following day, remove the weights and arrange the orange slices and bay leaves on top with 3 juniper berries on the centre of each slice of orange. Heat the meat juices and then cool until almost setting and pour over the top of the pâté. Cool and serve.

Serves 6-8

Pheasant pâté

You can make a delicious pâté with pheasant or other game birds. It sounds extravagant, but a little pheasant goes a long way in a pâté and the carcase can be used to make a warming soup, so there is no waste. Pâtés should be highly seasoned with spices, wines and spirits. You can have great fun experimenting with different ingredients: try adding chopped, parboiled chestnuts, grated orange or lemon rind, a variety of fresh herbs or even chopped mushrooms. Pâtés are best kept in the refrigerator for 2-3 days under a weight before eating. In fact, you can keep a pâté for up to two months by covering the top with a thick layer of melted lard or butter. It looks most attractive turned out on a serving plate in its jacket of striped bacon rashers, served with fresh granary bread or melba toast.

1 pheasant
675g/1½lb belly pork
175g/6oz flair fat or fat green bacon
45ml/3 tablespoons brandy
200ml/6floz/¾ cup red wine (mixed with port or madeira wine, if wished)
1 egg, beaten
2.5ml/½ teaspoon thyme
10ml/2 teaspoons chopped parsley
10ml/2 teaspoons salt
10 black peppercorns
10 juniper berries
1 clove garlic
good pinch of ground mace
225g/8oz streaky bacon rashers or thin strips back fat

Roast the pheasant for about 30 minutes in a preheated oven at 200°C, 400°F, gas 6. Cool before stripping off the meat (use the carcase for making soup or game stock). Cut the meat into thin strips and put aside.

Mince/grind the belly pork and the fat in a mincer or food processor until finely ground. Place in a large bowl with the chopped pheasant meat, brandy, wine, beaten egg, herbs and salt. Crush the peppercorns, juniper berries and garlic in a mortar and add to the pâté mixture with the mace. Stir well, cover and leave in a cool place overnight.

Next day, line 2 terrines or ovenproof dishes with the bacon or fat strips and fill with the pâté mixture. Top with criss-crossing strips of bacon and cover with aluminium foil. Stand the terrines in a water bath and cook in a preheated oven at 170°C, 325°F, gas 3 for about 1½ hours. The pâté is cooked when it appears to be swimming in its own fat and it has come away from the sides of the terrine. Another test is to insert a skewer or larding needle — the pâté is ready when it comes out clean.

Allow the pâté to cool a little and then place some heavy weights on top of the foil. Place in the refrigerator for at least 24 hours before eating.

Serves 8

Raised meat pies

Raised pork pie

Pork pies are easy to make, delicious hot or cold and are the ideal choice for picnics, buffets and summer meals. Once you have tasted the real thing, you will never want to buy another commercially produced pie again. For a home-made pork pie enclosed in a crisp, succulent crust is moist and full of tasty chunks of meat. The traditional way to make a pork pie is to use a wooden pie mould and to shape the pastry crust around the mould. However, it is much easier to use a hinged pie mould (available from most good kitchen suppliers), a large round cake tin or small individual pie tins. Take your pick, according to how many people you are going to feed and the nature of the occasion. Pork pies freeze successfully so it is well worth making double the quantity and having a few spare in the freezer.

1kg/2lb lean pie pork
2 large onions, finely chopped
2.5ml/½ teaspoon chopped sage
1.25ml/¼ teaspoon allspice
2.5ml/½ teaspoon salt
freshly ground black pepper
1 egg, beaten
150ml/¼ pint/⅝ cup water
15ml/1 tablespoon aspic powder
Hot-water crust paste:
450g/1lb/4½ cups wholemeal flour
5ml/1 teaspoon salt
225ml/8floz/1 cup water
100ml/4floz/½ cup milk
175g/6oz/¾ cup lard/shortening

Prepare the filling: remove most of the fat from the pork and cut the meat into small cubes. Mix in a large bowl with the onion, sage, allspice and seasoning.

To make the hot-water crust paste, sieve the flour and salt. Heat the water, milk and lard in a pan until it comes to a rolling boil and the lard has completely melted. Tip in the flour and beat well with a wooden spoon until you have a smooth ball of dough. Allow to cool a little and knead well while it is still warm. Replace the pastry in the pan or a warm bowl, cover with a lid or a cloth and keep warm.

Grease a large pie mould or a 15cm/6in cake tin, and roll out two-thirds of the pastry to line the tin. Make sure that there are no holes through which the filling and meat juices can escape. Fill the pie with the prepared pork filling right up to the rim, and then roll out the remaining pastry to make a lid. Damp the pastry edges with beaten egg and seal well. Decorate with pastry leaves made from the trimmings, and glaze with beaten egg. Make a small hole in the centre.

Bake in a preheated oven at 220°C, 425°F, gas 7, and after 10 minutes, reduce the temperature to 180°C, 350°F, gas 4 for 1½ hours. Then lower the oven temperature to 170°C, 325°F, gas 3 for a further 30 minutes. Cover with foil if the pie seems to be getting too brown. If you are making small individual pies bake at 220°C, 425°F, gas 7 for 15 minutes and then at 190°C, 375°F, gas 5 for a further 45 minutes.

Just before removing the pie from the oven, bring the water to the boil and sprinkle on the aspic powder. Leave until dissolved and then stir until smooth. Pour the warm aspic mixture through the central hole into the hot, cooked pie and leave until it cools and sets to a jelly. Serve cold in slices with chutney or pickle.
Serves 8

Cranberry and asparagus turkey pies

These individual turkey pies with their attractive green asparagus and rich red cranberry coverings are perfect picnic fare. Use the hot-water crust paste recipe on page 103 for pork pies but halve the quantities.

225g/8oz hot-water crust paste
350g/12oz/1½ cups minced/ground turkey
1 onion, finely chopped
2.5ml/½ teaspoon salt
freshly ground black pepper
1.25ml/¼ teaspoon each of ground nutmeg and cinnamon
100ml/4floz/½ cup port wine
300ml/½ pint/1¼ cups aspic jelly (see recipe on page 103)
Asparagus topping:
1 hard-boiled egg, sliced
175g/6oz canned asparagus tips
Cranberry topping:
100g/4oz fresh cranberries
15ml/1 tablespoon cranberry sauce
salt and pepper

Line 8 well-greased small pie tins with hot-water crust paste. Mix the turkey, onion, seasoning, spices and port wine together and divide this filling between the pie tins so that each is about two-thirds full. Cover the pies with foil and bake in a preheated oven at 200°C 400°F, gas 6 for 20 minutes, and then lower the oven to 180°C, 350°F, gas 4 for a further 45 minutes.

Remove the pies from their tins when completely cold. Place a slice of egg in the centre of 4 of the pies and arrange the asparagus tips around the egg in concentric circles. Heat the cranberries in a little water or orange juice and simmer gently until tender. Drain and mix in the cranberry sauce. Spread the cranberry topping across the remaining 4 pies. Pour a little of the aspic jelly across the top of each pie and chill until set.
Serves 8

Chicken, ham and egg pie

This pie always looks especially attractive when cut because of the hard-boiled eggs running through its centre. It is made in exactly the same way as the raised pork pie and is perfect for picnics and summer lunches.

450g/1lb hot-water crust paste (see recipe on page 103)
350g/12oz raw chicken, diced
275g/10oz/1¼ cups minced /ground ham
salt and freshly ground black pepper
3 hard-boiled eggs
1 egg, beaten

Prepare the hot-water crust paste in the usual way and keep warm while you make the filling. Mix the diced chicken, ham and seasoning together. Roll out the paste to line a large pie mould and spread a layer of filling across the base. Shell the hard-boiled eggs and line them up, end to end, along the centre of the pie. Pack the sides with more filling and cover with the rest of the meat filling. Roll out the remaining pastry to make a lid. Cover the pie and seal the edges. Decorate with pastry leaves made from the trimmings and brush with beaten egg. Make a small hole in the top.

Bake in a preheated oven at 220°C, 425°F, gas 7 for 10 minutes and then reduce the temperature to 180°C, 350°F, gas 4 for a further 1 hour 20 minutes or until the pastry is cooked and golden-brown. Cool and remove from the mould. If wished, you can make an aspic jelly as in the recipe for raised pork pie (see page 103) and pour the warm aspic liquid through the hole in the top into the pie. Leave to go cold and set and cut into slices to serve.

Serves 8

Opposite: pâtés can be eaten with granary bread as tasty snacks or as a first course. Here are some unusual pâtés for you to try, reading clockwise: pheasant pâté with its striped jacket of bacon rashers (see page 102), pork and ham pâté garnished with orange slices (see page 102), individual chicken liver pâtés (see page 102) and little ramekins filled with smoked salmon pâté (see page 86). Serve as a first course with toasted wholemeal bread

Poultry and game

Chicken and chicory salad

Crisp, slightly bitter chicory leaves mixed with strips of chicken, fruit, cheese and diced avocado and tossed in a lemony mayonnaise make a tasty winter salad — ideal for using up cold, cooked poultry and for serving over the Christmas holidays when you can try it with cold turkey instead. For additional colour, arrange on a bed of rich-red *radicchio* (red chicory) leaves. This is often available in good greengrocers and supermarkets in the winter months.

350g/12oz cooked chicken meat, cut in strips
2 heads of chicory, washed and sliced
2 red-skinned dessert apples, cored and diced
100g/4oz Roquefort or other blue cheese, cubed
1 avocado pear, cubed
50ml/2floz/¼ cup mayonnasie
juice of 1 lemon
75ml/3floz/⅓ cup yoghurt
freshly ground black pepper
30ml/2 tablespoons chopped parsley

Place the chicken, chicory, apple, cheese and avocado in a salad bowl. Mix the mayonnaise (see recipe on page 173) with lemon juice and yoghurt and season . Toss the salad in the dressing lightly and sprinkle with chopped parsley. Serve as a first course or snack. You can make a more slimming dressing by substituting natural yoghurt for mayonnaise.
Serves 4

Chicken Marsala

This is so delicious and simple and quick to prepare that it is perfect for evenings when you rush in and haven't the time or the inclination to cook a complicated or time-consuming meal. This takes literally 20 minutes from start to finish and you are sure to be complimented on the result. Always keep a bottle of Marsala handy in the cupboard for such occasions (it can also be used for flavouring sauces and gravies, fruit salads and trifles).

4 large chicken or turkey breasts, skinned and boned
15ml/1 tablespoon flour
15g/½oz/1 tablespoon margarine
30ml/2 tablespoons oil
175g/6oz button mushrooms, thinly sliced
salt and pepper
150ml/¼ pint/⅝ cup Marsala
15ml/1 tablespoon chopped parsley

Beat the chicken breasts out flat and dust with flour. Sauté them over medium heat in the margarine and oil until golden-brown (about 5 minutes each side). Add the sliced mushrooms and fry gently for 2 minutes. Season and pour in the Marsala. Bring the liquid to the boil and then reduce the heat slightly so that the sauce bubbles and thickens to a dark syrup. Add a little chicken stock if it thickens too much. Turn the chicken in the sauce so that it is well coated. Serve hot sprinkled with chopped parsley with green vegetables.
Serves 4

Stuffed chicken with chestnuts

You can use either chicken or turkey breasts for this dish. It is a good idea to make double the quantity given and freeze half until needed. The combination of chestnuts and apricots is very successful.

4 chicken or turkey breasts, skinned and boned
30ml/2 tablespoons oil
100g/4oz chestnuts
50g/2oz/⅔ cup dried apricots, soaked
15ml/1 tablespoon redcurrant jelly
Stuffing:
1 small onion, finely chopped
50g/2oz/1 cup fresh breadcrumbs
5ml/1 teaspoon each oregano and parsley
2.5ml/½ teaspoon each marjoram and thyme
salt and pepper
25g/1oz/⅓ cup dried apricots, soaked and chopped
1 egg, beaten
salt and pepper
Sauce:
50g/2oz mushrooms, finely chopped
2 shallots or 1 small onion, finely chopped
150ml/¼ pint/⅝ cup white wine
25g/1oz/2 tablespoons margarine
25g/1oz/3 tablespoons flour
400ml/14floz/1¾ cups chicken stock
100ml/4floz/½ cup port wine
salt and pepper

Mix all the stuffing ingredients together. Make a slit in each chicken breast and insert a finger to enlarge the cavity inside. Fill the chicken breasts with the stuffing and secure with wooden cocktail sticks/toothpicks. Heat the oil in a flameproof dish and brown the chicken breasts. Put aside and keep warm.

Make the sauce: heat the mushrooms and shallots in the white wine and bring to the boil. Simmer gently until the liquid is reduced by half. Make a roux with the fat and flour, cook 2-3 minutes and then gradually beat in the chicken stock until you have a smooth sauce. Strain the white wine into the sauce, discarding the shallots and mushrooms, and stir in the port. Season to taste. Pour the sauce over the chicken breasts, cover the dish and cook in a preheated oven at 170°C, 325°F, gas 3 for 1½ hours.

While the chicken is cooking, prepare the chestnuts. Make an incision in the pointed end of each nut, cover with water and bring to the boil. Boil for 2 minutes only and then remove from the heat and shell, removing the skin as well as the hard outer casing. Place the shelled chestnuts in a pan of fresh, salted water and simmer gently until cooked and tender. Drain and keep warm.

Gently stew the apricots until tender and keep warm also. Just before serving, remove the chicken from the sauce and throw away the cocktail stick/toothpicks. Add the redcurrant jelly to the sauce and boil hard on top of the cooker until it reduces and thickens. Correct the seasoning and pour over the chicken. Garnish with the chestnuts and apricots and serve with rice and a green vegetable.

Serves 4

Tropical chicken

Chicken cooked with pineapple, tomatoes, peppers and rum is served throughout the Caribbean, although most islands have their own special variation on this common theme. Fresh or canned pineapple are suitable and the addition of chilli powder is optional.

4 chicken breasts
juice and grated rind of 1 lemon or *lime*
salt and pepper
30ml/2 tablespoons oil
1 onion, chopped
1 clove garlic, crushed
1 red pepper, seeded and chopped
1 green pepper, seeded and chopped
3 tomatoes, skinned, seeded and chopped
60ml/4 tablespoons raisins
50g/2oz water chestnuts, sliced
450g/1lb fresh or canned pineapple, cubed
1 small hot chilli pepper, chopped (optional)
150ml/¼ pint/⅝ cup chicken stock
30ml/2 tablespoons dark rum
2-3 drops Angostura bitters (optional)
30ml/2 tablespoons chopped chives

Leave the chicken to marinate in the citrus juice, rind and seasoning for 1 hour. Heat the oil in a flameproof dish and sauté the chicken until well-browned. Remove and keep warm. Sauté the onion, garlic and pepper until tender and then add the tomato. Heat through for about 5 minutes. Add the remaining ingredients (except the chives) and replace the chicken in the dish. Cover and simmer gently or place in a preheated oven at 180°C, 350F, gas 4 for 1 hour until the chicken is tender and cooked.

Remove the chicken to a serving dish and boil the sauce up on top of the stove until it reduces. Pour over the chicken, scatter over some chopped chives and serve with fried bananas and beans and rice (see recipe on page 40).

Serves 4

Kentish chicken pudding

This boiled suet pudding is filled with a tasty mixture of chicken, pork, apple and fresh herbs. Although you can use a roasting chicken, a boiling fowl is less expensive and more flavoursome. It is an old English dish, dating back to the seventeenth century.

1.5kg/3lb boiling chicken
1 bay leaf
few fresh herbs: parsley, thyme, rosemary
1 onion, quartered
Suet pastry:
225g/8oz/2¼ cups wholemeal flour
2.5ml/½ teaspoon salt
20ml/4 teaspoons baking powder
100g/4oz/1 cup shredded suet
150ml/¼ pint/⅝ cup water
Chicken filling:
1 large onion, chopped
225g/8oz belly pork, cubed
2 large cooking apples, peeled and sliced
15ml/1 tablespoon chopped parsley
pinch of ground mace
salt and pepper
2.5ml/½ teaspoon brown sugar
45ml/3 tablespoons white wine

Place the boiling chicken, herbs, onion quarters and seasoning in a large pan and cover with water. Bring to the boil and skim the surface of the liquid. Cover the pan and simmer gently for 2 hours. This can be done the day before you prepare the pudding.

Cool the chicken in the stock. Remove the skin from

the chicken and cut the meat into chunks. Mix with the onion, pork, sliced apple, parsley, mace, seasoning and sugar in a large bowl. Use the stock for making soup or flavouring a casserole.

Make the suet pastry: mix all the ingredients together to form a soft dough. Knead lightly and line a greased 1.2 litre/2 pint/5 cup pudding basin, reserving a little pastry for the lid.

Pile the filling into the lined basin and add the wine. Dampen the pastry edges and cover with the lid, pressing the edges together well to seal them. Cover the basin with a piece of buttered, folded foil and a pudding cloth, tied securely with string around the edge of the basin.

Lower the basin into a large pan of boiling water. The level should be about three-quarters of the way up the sides of the basin. Boil for 3-4 hours, adding more water if necessary. Remove the cloth and foil to serve and wrap a clean napkin around the basin.

Serves 4

Chicken, leek and apricot pie

This may sound an unusual combination of ingredients but meat and fruit pies, often heavily spiced, were extremely popular in the Middle Ages and still are in North Africa and the Middle East. This pie makes an economical and tasty family meal with its delicate tangy flavour. Make the pastry in bulk in advance and freeze until needed if you like.

100g/4oz/¾ cup dried apricots
150ml/¼pint/⅝ cup water
3 boned and skinned chicken breasts
25g/1oz/3 tablespoons flour
salt and pepper
45ml/3 tablespoons oil
225g/8oz chopped leek
300ml/½pint/1¼cups hot chicken stock
2.5ml/½ teaspoon dried basil
few sprigs parsley, chopped
1 egg yolk
225g/8oz wholemeal shortcrust pastry dough (see recipe on page 169)
1 egg beaten

Soak the apricots for a few hours in water. Drain and reserve the juice.

Cut the chicken meat into strips and toss in the seasoned flour, reserving any flour left over. Sauté the chicken in the oil for about 5 minutes until golden.

Add the leek, sauté for 3 minutes and add any remaining flour. Cook gently for 1 minute and then add the hot stock and apricot juice, stirring until the sauce thickens and becomes smooth. Bring to the boil, then cover and simmer for 45 minutes.

Add the apricots and herbs and season to taste. Allow the sauce to cool a little and beat in the egg yolk. Pour into a pie dish right up to the rim to prevent the pastry collapsing when cooking.

Roll out the pastry on a floured board. Butter the edge of the pie dish, and top the pie with the pastry so that it covers the rim of the dish. Damp the pastry edge, seal and flute. Glaze with beaten egg and decorate with pastry leaves made from the dough trimmings. Bake in a preheated oven at 200°C, 400°F, gas 6 for 15 minutes and then reduce the heat to 180°C, 350°F gas 4 for a further 20 minutes or until crisp and golden-brown. Serve immediately with green vegetables or a green salad.

Serves 4

Chicken and fruit brochettes

Sweet and savoury fruit and meat brochettes may sound an unlikely combination but they complement each other extremely well and make a light, healthy and colourful meal. The chicken is marinated in fruit juice with herbs before cooking to make it moist and tender, and the brochettes are delicious served with either a cold avocado sauce or a hot Russian mushroom sauce (for recipes see page 172).

4 chicken breasts, skinned and boned
juice of 1 lemon
juice of 1 orange
45ml/3 tablespoons white wine
2.5ml/½teaspoon each of basil and thyme
freshly ground black pepper
pinch of ground mace
1 green pepper
2 small onions
8 prunes, soaked overnight
1 banana
6 rashers streaky bacon

Cut the chicken into good-sized cubes and place in a bowl with the fruit juice, white wine, herbs and

Opposite: reading clockwise: spinach quiche (see page 68), raised pork pie (see page 103), cranberry and asparagus turkey pies and chicken, ham and egg pie (see page 104)

seasoning. Cover and leave to marinate for an hour or so. Meanwhile, prepare the other brochette ingredients. Cut the pepper into chunks, quarter the onions and drain the prunes. Cut the banana in half and then slice each piece in half again horizontally. Stretch each bacon rasher over a knife and cut each in half. Wind a piece of bacon around each prune and banana.

Now assemble the brochettes: thread the chicken, pepper, onion, prunes and banana onto 4 long skewers. Line a grill pan with foil and place the brochettes above it. Brush with the marinade and place under a hot grill for 12-15 minutes, turning occasionally until they are evenly cooked. Keep an eye on them to make sure that they do not over-brown or burn. Serve hot with avocado or mushroom sauce.

Serves 4

Spanish chicken pie

Chicken pies cooked with spices and peppers in a yeast dough are popular in Spain. The dough can be made in advance and frozen until needed to cut down on preparation time. If you like earthy, country-style food, then this pie will make a delicious summer lunch served with a crisp salad and washed down with a fruity red Spanish wine.

350g/12oz basic wholemeal bread dough (see recipe on
page 25)
3 chicken breasts, skinned and boned (or 450g/1lb cooked
chicken meat)
150ml/¼ pint/⅝ cup chicken stock
1 onion, chopped
1 clove garlic, crushed
30ml/2 tablespoons oil
450g/1lb tomatoes, skinned and chopped
5ml/1 teaspoon tomato paste
2.5ml/½ teaspoon brown sugar
1 small red pepper, chopped
1 small green pepper, chopped
50g/2oz/½ cup stuffed olives, sliced
1 fresh or dried chilli pepper, chopped
50g/2oz smoked ham, chopped (optional)
7.5cm/3in chorizo sausage, skinned and cubed
good pinch of paprika
small packet powdered saffron
salt and pepper
5ml/1 teaspoon each of chopped oregano and parsley
1 egg, beaten

Skin the chicken breasts, cut each in two and place in a pan with the stock. Bring to the boil, then cover the

pan and simmer for 30 minutes. Remove the chicken and set aside. You can use left-over cooked chicken if you wish, which will not require further cooking.

Sauté the onion and garlic in the oil until soft and then add the tomatoes, tomato paste and sugar. Next add the peppers, olives and chilli and cook over a medium heat until the liquid evaporates and you are left with a thick sauce. Add the ham, sausage, chicken and seasonings and then put aside to cool while you roll out the dough.

Divide the dough into 2 pieces and roll each out on a lightly floured board to a circle 22.5cm/9in wide. Pile the filling into the centre and brush the border with beaten egg. Cover with the remaining dough and seal the edges. Decorate the top with any trimmings, cut out into leaf shapes, and brush with beaten egg. Carefully lift the dough onto a lightly greased baking tray and leave in a warm place to prove for 15 minutes. Bake in a preheated oven at 200°C, 400°F, gas 6 for 45-50 minutes until golden-brown. Reduce the oven temperature or cover the pie with some foil if it browns too quickly.

Serves 6

Italian stuffed chicken

Here is a truly delicious dish which is quick and simple to prepare and cook. If you have no Gorgonzola, you can cheat by substituting Stilton or any other blue-veined cheese. Make the velouté sauce in advance if wished. As you can see, it is much more healthy and slimming than using a traditional white sauce. For a real Italian flavour, serve the dish with noodles (tagliatelle or fettucine) and fried zucchini (courgettes).

4 chicken breasts, skinned and boned
75g/3oz Gorgonzola cheese, sliced into 4 pieces
15ml/1 tablespoon flour
15ml/1 tablespoon oil
15g/½oz/1 tablespoon margarine
100g/4oz button mushrooms, sliced
100ml/4floz/½ cup sweet Marsala
30ml/2 tablespoons chopped parsley
Veloute sauce:
15g/½oz/1 tablespoon margarine
15g/½oz/2 tablespoons flour
300ml/½ pint/1¼ cups chicken stock
salt and pepper
squeeze of lemon juice

Make a slit in each of the chicken breasts, insert a

finger and gently make a cavity large enough to stuff with a slice of cheese. Insert the cheese and secure with a cocktail stick/toothpick. Lightly flour the chicken.

Heat the oil and fat in a large frying pan and sauté the chicken until browned on both sides. Add the mushrooms and continue cooking over a low heat for several minutes.

Meanwhile, make the velouté sauce: make a roux with the fat and flour, cook for 2-3 minutes and then gradually beat in the chicken stock until you have a thick, smooth sauce. Season and add a squeeze of lemon juice.

Add the sauce and Marsala to the pan containing the chicken and mushrooms and bring to the boil. Reduce the heat, cover the pan and cook very gently for about 15 minutes, stirring often to prevent it burning or sticking to the base. Arrange the chicken on a serving dish, spoon over the sauce and sprinkle with chopped parsley. Serve with buttered noodles.

Serves 4

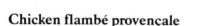

Chicken flambé provençale

Here is a delicious dish for a dinner party — stuffed chicken drumsticks flamed in brandy and served with colourful ratatouille and crunchy brown rice. Some alternative fillings for the chicken include creamy Gorgonzola cheese, and chopped ham, grated Swiss cheese and fresh sage. However, the filling below is more French, especially if you use fresh chopped herbs. We have used very little oil in the ratatouille so that the vegetables cook in their own juices.

8 chicken drumsticks
45ml/3 tablespoons clarified butter or olive oil
60ml/4 tablespoons brandy
15ml/1 tablespoon chopped parsley
Ratatouille:
1 aubergine/eggplant, sliced
salt
2 onions, chopped
1 clove garlic, crushed
1 red pepper, seeded and sliced
1 green pepper, seeded and sliced
30ml/2 tablespoons olive oil
3 courgettes/zucchini, sliced
450g/1lb tomatoes, skinned and chopped
2.5ml/½ teaspoon ground coriander seeds
1 bay leaf
10ml/2 teaspoons basil

freshly ground black pepper
5ml/1 teaspoon sugar
15ml/1 tablespoon chopped parsley
Herb cheese:
100g/4oz/⅔ cup fromage blanc or ricotta cheese
45ml/3 tablespoons chopped parsley, basil, tarragon
pinch of ground nutmeg
juice and grated rind of ½ lemon
salt and pepper

Make the ratatouille: sprinkle the aubergine/eggplant slices with salt and set aside for 30 minutes. Wash and dry them. Sauté the onion, garlic and sliced pepper in the oil until soft. Add the courgettes/zucchini and sliced aubergine/eggplant and sauté for 2-3 minutes. Stir in the remaining ingredients and cook over a low heat for 45 minutes until the vegetables are tender.

Meanwhile, bone the chicken drumsticks with a sharp knife. Blend the ingredients for the herb cheese to a smooth paste and fill the chicken cavities. Sew up the open ends with black thread or secure with cocktail sticks/toothpicks.

Fry the stuffed drumsticks in the clarified butter or oil over low heat for about 20 minutes until cooked and golden-brown, turning them occasionally. Remove the thread or cocktail sticks/toothpicks. Pour off any excess fat or oil and arrange the ratatouille in a border around the chicken. Heat the brandy, set it alight and pour it, flaming, over the chicken. When the flames die down sprinkle with chopped parsley and serve with plain brown rice.

Serves 4

Game pie

Many people tend to shy away from game because of the expense and its strong, distinctive flavour. However, served in a traditional pie in a tasty sauce, game adds a cheering, seasonal touch of luxury to everyday cookery. Most game is suitable for this dish and you can vary it by using different meat and birds, including rabbit, partridge, grouse and pigeon. If cooked in advance, the filling can be frozen successfully until assembling and cooking the pie. Cold, cooked game may also be used up in pies. Just bone and cut up the meat and make a sauce with 2 onions sautéed in oil, thickened with flour and moistened with 150ml/¼ pint/⅝ cup each of red wine and game stock and a touch of brandy. Add herbs and nutmeg to flavour, a little redcurrant or quince jelly and stir in the cold game. Cover with puff pastry and cook in a hot oven for 40 minutes until puffed-up and golden.

1 pheasant, jointed and boned
450g/1lb stewing venison, cut into 2.5cm/1in cubes
225g/8oz puff pastry
1 egg, beaten
Marinade:
150ml/¼ pint/⅝ cup red wine
30ml/2 tablespoons oil
12 juniper berries
1 bay leaf
Sauce:
30ml/2 tablespoons oil
2 onions, finely chopped
2 sticks of celery, diced
25g/1oz/3 tablespoons flour
300ml/½ pint/1¼ cups game or beef stock
1.25ml/¼ teaspoon each basil and thyme
pinch of ground nutmeg
few drops Worcestershire sauce
salt and pepper
100g/4oz mushrooms, sliced
15ml/1 tablespoon redcurrant jelly

Leave the pheasant and venison in the marinade for at least 24 hours. Drain the meat and reserve the marinade for the sauce.

Make the sauce: heat the oil and sauté the onion and celery until soft and lightly browned. Stir in the flour and cook for 1 minute over low heat. Gradually add the hot stock and the reserved marinade, stirring until the sauce thickens. Add the herbs, Worcestershire sauce and seasoning, the mushrooms and redcurrant jelly. Add the meat and simmer gently for 5 minutes. Pour into a large pie-dish and fill almost up to the rim to prevent the pastry crust sinking.

Roll out the puff pastry, about 1.25cm/½in thick. Cut a thin strip to place around the edge of the dish and dampen it with water. Cover the dish with the remaining pastry, press down the edges and seal firmly. Make a small hole in the centre and flute the edges with a fork. Decorate with pastry leaves made from the trimmings and brush with beaten egg. Bake in a preheated oven at 220°C, 425°F, gas 7 for 10 minutes and then reduce to 180°C, 350°F, gas 4 for 2-2½ hours. Cover the pastry with a piece of greaseproof paper or foil to prevent it burning. Alternatively, you can simmer the filling over a low heat for about 1½ hours and then cover with pastry and bake it for 40-45 minutes.

Serves 4-5

Chinese stir-fried chicken

The best cooking utensil to use for this dish is a real Chinese *wok*. You can buy the genuine article quite cheaply in Chinese shops and supermarkets, and most kitchen suppliers and department stores now sell electric woks. However, bear in mind that woks work better on gas stoves than on an electric hotplate. Food can be fried quickly in a wok in the minimum of time to just the right degree of crispness. The curved base of the wok distributes the heat evenly and ensures rapid evaporation, which is essential for most Chinese dishes.

3 chicken breasts, skinned and boned
30ml/2 tablespoons oil
1 onion, quartered and divided into layers
1 red pepper, seeded and cut in chunks
1 green pepper, seeded and cut in chunks
225g/8oz water chestnuts, sliced
225g/8oz bean sprouts
3 spring onions/shallots, chopped
small piece fresh root ginger, grated
15ml/1 tablespoon cornflour/cornstarch
150ml/¼ pint/⅝ cup water
15ml/1 tablespoon sherry
15ml/1 tablespoon soya sauce
5ml/1 teaspoon oyster sauce
½ chicken stock/bouillon cube
salt and pepper
chopped chives to garnish

Cut the chicken meat into chunks and stir-fry in the oil in a wok or heavy frying pan over high heat until tender. Add all the vegetables and the ginger and stir-fry for 3-4 minutes until tender but still crisp. Mix the cornflour/cornstarch with the remaining ingredients and stir into the pan, cooking until the sauce thickens. Season to taste and cook for 2 minutes. Remove from the pan and garnish with chopped chives. Serve with egg-fried rice (see recipe on page 41).

Serves 3-4

Opposite: a colourful Mediterranean dish of chicken flambé provençale (see page 111). The stuffed chicken drumsticks are flamed in brandy and served with a tasty vegetable ratatouille and boiled brown rice. Turkey drumsticks can be stuffed and served in the same way

Chicken saté

Many variations of this classic dish are served throughout Malaysia and Indonesia. The saté itself reflects the different cultures and traditions of Southeast Asia: the Muslim influenced skewered chicken, and the Indian influenced spicy nut sauce. Arrange the skewers of chicken in a fan shape around the edge of a large wicker/basketware tray or plate with chunks of fresh cucumber and cubes of rice cake or *lontong* in the centre and a dish of saté sauce for dipping.

450g/1lb chicken breasts, skinned, boned and cubed
1 small onion, chopped
1 clove garlic, crushed
30ml/2 tablespoons soya sauce
2.5ml/½ teaspoon each ground ginger and coriander
15ml/1 tablespoon lime or lemon juice
salt and pepper
5ml/1 teaspoon brown sugar
½ cucumber, cut in chunks
Saté sauce:
15ml/1 tablespoon arachide or vegetable oil
100g/4oz/1 cup peanuts
1 onion, chopped
1 clove garlic, chopped
300ml/½ pint/1¼ cups boiling water
100g/4oz creamed coconut, grated finely
juice of ½ lime or lemon
10ml/2 teaspoons soya sauce
salt and pepper
½ teaspoon each ground cumin and coriander
chilli powder to taste or 2 drops Tabasco sauce

Place the chicken cubes and marinade ingredients (onion, garlic, soya sauce, spices, lime juice, seasoning and sugar) in a bowl and leave for at least 1 hour. Make the sauce: heat the oil and sauté the peanuts for 3-4 minutes until golden-brown. Remove from the pan with a slotted spoon and cool. Sauté the onion and garlic in the oil until golden and liquidise or process in a processor with the peanuts to a smooth paste.

Pour the boiling water over the coconut and let it stand for 15 minutes. Strain the coconut milk into a saucepan and stir in the peanut and onion paste and the remaining ingredients. Bring the sauce to the boil, stirring until it becomes thick. Reduce the heat to a bare simmer and cook gently for 5-10 minutes. Check the seasoning and add more chilli, if wished.

Meanwhile, thread the chicken onto small wooden skewers and place under a hot grill/broiler for 6-8 minutes until golden-brown and cooked, turning occasionally. Serve with the saté sauce, cucumber chunks and boiled or *lontong* rice. To make the authentic *lontong* rice cubes, cook boil-in-the-bag rice for about 1 hour and then cool for several hours so that the rice becomes solid. Remove from the bag and cut in cubes.
Serves 4

Venison in cider

This is a really old-fashioned country recipe which probably dates from the eighteenth century when deer poaching was common. While the wealthy roasted their venison or cooked it in claret or port, the country folk would stew it with root vegetables in cider. To our way of thinking, this makes a tastier dish than when served with grand sauces.

675g/1½lb stewing venison, cubed
400ml/14floz/1¾ cups cider/applejack
30ml/2 tablespoons oil
450g/1lb parsnips, peeled and quartered
45ml/3 tablespoons flour
15ml/1 tablespoon black treacle
30ml/2 tablespoons soft brown sugar
15ml/1 tablespoon redcurrant jelly (or quince jelly)
salt and pepper

Marinate the venison in the cider for 2-3 hours (or overnight). Heat the oil and lightly brown the parsnips. Transfer them to an ovenproof dish. Drain the venison, reserving the marinade, and toss the meat in 15ml/1 tablespoon of the flour. Sauté in the oil until browned, and then remove and place on top of the parsnips in the ovenproof dish. Add the remaining flour to the pan and cook gently for 2-3 minutes. Gradually stir in the marinade with the black treacle, sugar and seasoning until you have a thick, smooth sauce. Add more cider if necessary. Pour the sauce over the venison and parsnips and cover the dish. Bake in a preheated slow oven at 150°C, 300°F, gas 2 for 2 hours. Stir in the redcurrant jelly, correct the seasoning and serve hot.
Serves 4

Beef and offal

Gulyas leves

A fiery red goulash soup from Hungary makes a warming winter meal. Remember that there are many varieties of paprika ranging from delicate to very hot indeed, so choose one that is right for you. Paprika is widely used in Hungarian cookery and was probably introduced by the Turks.

2 onions, chopped
45ml/3 tablespoons oil
1 large green pepper, chopped
1 carrot, diced
450g/1lb stewing beef (chuck steak or skirt), diced
2.5ml/½ teaspoon salt
15ml/1 tablespoon paprika
2.5ml/½ teaspoon caraway seeds
900ml/1½ pints/3½ cups beef stock
3 tomatoes, skinned and chopped
450g/1lb potatoes, peeled and diced
100ml/4floz/½ cup red wine
salt and pepper
60ml/4 tablespoons soured cream
chopped chives to garnish (optional)

Sauté the onion, pepper and carrot in the oil until soft. Add the diced beef, salt, paprika and caraway seeds and fry gently until browned. Pour in half of the stock and simmer gently for 30 minutes.

Add the remaining stock, cover the pan and simmer for 45 minutes. Now add the chopped potato, tomato, red wine and seasoning. Simmer for another 30 minutes until the potato is tender and cooked and the soup has thickened a little. Check the seasoning, pour into serving dishes and drop 15ml/1 tablespoon of soured cream into each. Garnish with chopped chives if wished.

Serves 4

Cornish pasties

Real Cornish pasties, as they are eaten in the Cornish countryside, bear little resemblance to their bland, stodgy namesakes which are sold in cafeterias, canteens and supermarkets throughout Britain. A real pasty should be large enough to overlap a dinner plate at both ends. It should be made with swede, not turnip; and the vegetable filling should be grated, not diced. Pasties were eaten as a 'packed lunch' by the men working in the fields and the tin mines — they could be eaten easily in the hands without wrappings and knives and forks. Sometimes a pastry divider would be placed across the centre of the pasty to separate a savoury from a sweet filling at opposite ends of the same pasty. The two great things about pasties are that there is virtually no washing-up afterwards, and that they emit a wonderful, fragrant aroma while they are cooking. This recipe was given to us by an old lady who grew up by Cape Cornwall. The quantities are for two pasties.

Pastry:
450g/1lb/4 cups self-raising wholemeal flour
100g/4oz/½ cup mixed lard and margarine
60ml/4 tablespoons water
pinch of salt
Filling:
2 large potatoes
1 medium swede
350g/12oz chuck steak or skirt
2 onions, chopped
15g/½oz/1 tablespoon lard
salt and freshly ground black pepper

Make the pastry in the usual way. Place the flour and salt in a mixing bowl and rub in the fat. Mix to a soft dough with the water. Knead lightly and put aside to rest.

Peel the potatoes and swede and grate coarsely with the cucumber grating side of the grater, or peel off into thin strips with a potato peeler. Dice the steak and chop up the onions.

Roll out the pastry and cut into 2 large ovals. Place the rolling pin half-way under one of the ovals and droop the pastry on either side. Using the rolling pin as a divider and back-rest, start piling up the filling on one side, starting with the potato, then the swede, steak and lastly the onion. Sprinkle with lots of freshly ground pepper and salt and place tiny knobs of lard along the top. This will keep the pasty moist during cooking.

Dampen the edges of the pasty and fold the top over to meet the bottom and seal the edges securely, pressing between finger and thumb. Then curl the edges back and 'plait' them so that they are really sealed and no filling or meat juices can leak out during cooking. Place on a well-greased baking sheet and brush with beaten egg. Repeat the process with the other pasty. Bake in a preheated oven at 180°C, 350°F, gas 4 for 1¾-2 hours until the pastry is golden and cooked. Serve hot or cold.

Serves 2

Wholemeal steak and kidney pudding

Savoury suet puddings came into vogue in Victorian times and it was Mrs Beeton who first published a recipe for a steak and kidney pudding in 1859. Now steak and kidney pudding is almost the British national dish and comes with a variety of fillings and crusts. In those far-off days when oysters were cheap and plentiful they were used as additional flavouring. We decided to make our pudding with a wholemeal flour suet crust for extra roughage and goodness; and to make the pudding a little special we added red wine and mushrooms. The result was a dish fit for a king — good enough to serve at the most elaborate, sophisticated dinner party or to enjoy at any time.

225g/8oz/2¼ cups wholemeal flour
2.5ml/½ teaspoon salt
20ml/ 4 teaspoons baking powder
100g/4oz/1 cup shredded suet
150ml/¼ pint/⅝ cup water
Filling:
275g/10oz lean chuck steak or skirt
225g/8oz ox or pig's kidney
25g/1oz/3 tablespoons flour
salt and pepper
1 onion, chopped
75g/3oz mushrooms, sliced
150ml/¼ pint/⅝ cup red wine
50ml/2floz/¼ cup beef stock

To make the suet crust, mix the flour, salt, baking powder and suet together in a large mixing bowl and gradually stir in the water to form a smooth dough (or process in a food processor). Knead the dough lightly and roll out on a floured surface, putting a little aside for the lid of the pudding.

Generously butter a 1.2litre/2pint/5 cup pudding basin and line with suet pastry, allowing about 1.25cm/½in to overhang the basin's rim. Cube the steak, wash the kidney in salted water, remove the core and cut in chunks. Toss in seasoned flour and mix with the onion and mushrooms. Put the filling inside the lined basin and pour in the red wine and stock. It is important that the level of the filling should be no more than 1.25cm/½in below the basin's rim or it may leak in cooking. Cut the remaining suet pastry into a circle and cover the basin, pressing the pastry edges firmly together.

Cut out a circle of aluminium foil with a diameter about 7.5cm/3in larger than the pudding basin. Make a fold in the centre of the foil, butter it and press down over the basin (this will allow the pudding to expand during steaming). Cover with a pudding cloth or tea-towel and tie a string securely around the rim. You can even make a handle with the string to make lifting the basin in and out of the saucepan easier.

Heat some water in a large saucepan and when it is boiling, lower the pudding into the pan. The water level should remain just below the level of the string throughout, so add more water when necessary as the level drops. Cook the pudding in this way for about 4 hours. To serve, remove the pudding cloth and foil

and wrap a checked tea-towel around the sides of the basin. Serve immediately with puréed potato or carrot and Brussels sprouts.

Serves 4

Calves liver with apricots and avocado

If you enjoy offal, then you will like this unusual recipe in which thin slices of calves liver are quickly sautéed with fresh apricots and sliced avocado, and then served in a thin Marsala sauce. Even if you are not a great liver fan, you might find that it is a very palatable way of including it in your weekly diet. This is a good idea as liver is high in iron.

8 thin slices calves liver
30ml/2 tablespoons oil
1 shallot or ½ small onion, finely chopped
8 fresh apricots, stoned/pitted and halved
1 avocado, peeled, stoned/pitted and sliced
15ml/1 tablespoon lemon juice
90ml/6 tablespoons Marsala
salt and pepper
15ml/1 tablespoon chopped parsley

Wash the liver and remove the fine membrane if there is any by lifting a corner and, with your thumb underneath, gently pulling it across the liver. Sauté the liver and shallot in the oil for about 2 minutes. Turn the liver over and cook the other side. Add the prepared apricots and avocado and cook gently. Be careful not to overcook the liver or it will become hard and tough.

Remove the liver and avocado and keep warm on a serving dish. Add the lemon juice and Marsala to the pan and bring to the boil. Cook over medium heat until the sauce starts to get thick and syrupy and season to taste. Pour over the liver and arrange the avocado slices around the sides of the dish or overlapping along the top of the liver. Sprinkle with chopped parsley and serve with a fresh green salad.

Serves 4

Opposite: a North African feast of couscous (see page 11) in the foreground with its tasty stew of lamb, chick peas and vegetables, served with fresh minty Lebanese tabbouleh (see page 10), a dish of fiery harissa sauce and some cooling cucumber and yoghurt cacik (see page 78)

Spiced braised steak with chick peas

This unusual way of braising steak comes from North Africa although we have added wine to the original recipe (wine is not used in Muslim cookery). Serve it with steamed couscous (see method on page 11) or rice.

1 onion, chopped
1 clove garlic, crushed
30ml/2 tablespoons oil
450g/1lb braising steak or skirt, diced
5ml/1 teaspoon ground cumin
2.5ml/½ teaspoon ground ginger
1.25ml/¼ teaspoon ground coriander seeds
1 cardamom, crushed
150ml/¼ pint/⅝ cup beef stock
100g/4oz/¾ cup chick peas, soaked overnight
100ml/4floz/½ cup red wine
salt and pepper
50g/2oz dates, stoned

Sauté the onion and garlic in the oil until soft. Add the steak and spices (using only the seeds of the crushed cardamom) and lightly brown. Transfer to an ovenproof casserole and add the beef stock, soaked, drained chick peas, wine and seasoning. Cook in a preheated oven at 170°C, 325°F, gas 3 for about 3 hours, adding the dates about 30 minutes before serving the dish. Serve hot with couscous.
Serves 4

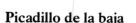

Picadillo de la baja

Picadillo is a term which embraces a variety of meat dishes served throughout Central and South America. This colourful version, which comes from Mexico, combines tender meat, vegetables, tropical fruit and spices. In Mexico, various ingredients are added according to what is seasonal or readily available. You can adjust the amount of chilli to your ideal level — we have used only a little for a medium-hot dish. If you cannot obtain fresh chillis, use a good chilli powder.

225g/8oz lean stewing beef, cubed
225g/8oz pork fillet or tenderloin, cubed
good pinch of salt
1 onion, chopped
1 clove garlic, crushed
½ red pepper, chopped
½ green pepper, chopped
1 fresh hot red chilli, deseeded and chopped
30ml/2 tablespoons oil
2 tomatoes, skinned and chopped

salt and pepper
pinch each of ground cloves and cinnamon
10ml/2 teaspoons white wine vinegar
30ml/2 tablespoons raisins
8 pimento stuffed green olives
175g/6oz cubed pineapple (fresh or canned in natural juice)
1 banana, sliced
30ml/2 tablespoons flaked almonds
15ml/1 tablespoon olive oil

Place the meat in a pan with the salt and cover with cold water. Bring to the boil, then lower the heat to a gentle simmer, cover the pan and cook for 1¼ hours. Remove the lid and cook for 10 minutes until the cooking liquid evaporates. Put the meat aside. You can cook the meat a day in advance if wished and refrigerate overnight.

Sauté the onion, garlic, peppers and chilli in the oil until tender. Add the tomato, seasonings and vinegar and cook for about 10 minutes over a medium heat until the tomato forms a thick sauce. Add the raisins, olives and fruit and cook for a further 10 minutes over low heat.

In another pan, fry the almonds in the oil until golden-brown. Serve the picadillo in a border of rice garnished with the sautéed almonds, with tortillas (see recipe on page 15) and a fresh green salad .
Serves 4

Pork

Stuffed pork in cider

This is a delicious way to serve pork, sandwiched together with dried fruits and cheese and baked in cider. Be sure to baste the meat frequently during cooking to keep it moist. It is delicious served with jacket-potatoes topped with soured cream, or rosti. Allow one pork fillet for two people.

8 dried apricots
8 large dried prumes
300ml/½ pint/1¼ cups medium-sweet cider
2 pork fillets or tenderloins
100g/4oz/1 cup grated Gruyère/Swiss cheese
salt and pepper
30ml/2 tablespoons chopped parsley and thyme
1 large onion, chopped
6 thin rashers smoked streaky bacon

Soak the dried fruits for a few hours or overnight in the cider. Pour into a small pan and cook gently for about 5 minutes over low heat to soften the fruit. Drain, reserving the cider for the sauce, and stone/pit the fruit.

Cut each pork fillet into three lengthwise. Sandwich two of the pork strips with the prunes and apricots, then a layer of grated cheese, reserving about 30ml/2 tablespoons for the topping, and herbs, and the remaining pork strip on top. Tie up with string at 5cm/2in intervals to secure the pork fillets firmly and keep the filling in place. Repeat with the other fillet.

Scatter the onion over the base of the baking tin and place the fillets on top. Cover with the bacon slices and pour in the cider. Bake in a preheated oven at 190°C, 375°F, gas 5 for about 1 hour until cooked, basting the meat from time to time.

Remove the fillets, top with the remaining cheese and place until a hot grill/broiler until melted, bubbling and golden. Remove the string and keep warm. Boil up the cidery meat juices on top of the stove until thickened and reduced. Serve with the pork.

Serves 4

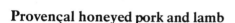

Provençal honeyed pork and lamb

This recipe combines sweet and savoury elements and· is well worth trying. Although the pork and lamb provide contrasting flavours, you can use just one meat in preference to the other. Use a respectable white wine in this dish as it will make all the difference to the flavour. You can enjoy drinking the rest of the bottle with the meal.

350g/12oz pork spare rib chops
350g/12oz boned lamb
45ml/3 tablespoons flour
salt and pepper
30ml/2 tablespoons olive or vegetable oil
2 cloves garlic, crushed
150ml/¼ pint/⅔ cup chicken stock
150ml/¼ pint/⅔ cup white wine
100g/4oz mushrooms, sliced
15ml/1 tablespoon honey
15ml/1 tablespoon redcurrant jelly

Trim off the fat and cut the meat into large cubes. Dust with seasoned flour. Fry the meat in the oil until golden-brown, remove and keep warm. Sauté the garlic for 2 minutes and then stir in the remaining flour. Cook for 1 minute and gradually add the stock and wine. Bring to the boil and then reduce the heat to a simmer. Cover the pan and cook for 1 hour. Add the mushrooms and honey and check the seasoning.

Sprinkle with basil and simmer for a further 40 minutes. Stir in the redcurrant jelly and serve with French beans and grilled/broiled tomatoes.

Serves 4

Herb and ham pie

This tasty pie is best made with fresh herbs, although you can use dried ones if you halve the quantities given below. Served hot as a supper dish or cold for a picnic, it is equally delicious. You can experiment with different fresh herbs, according to which ones are in season.

Pastry:
100g/4oz/½ cup vegetable margarine
225g/8oz/2¼ cups wholemeal flour
pinch of salt
water to mix
Herb and ham filling:
15ml/1 tablespoon oil
50g/2oz smoked streaky bacon rashers
1 onion, chopped
150g/5oz cooked ham, diced
15ml/1 tablespoon each of chopped parsley and chives
2.5ml/½ teaspoon each of chopped chervil, marjoram and oregano
5ml/1 teaspoon chopped basil
50g/2oz/½ cup grated Gruyère/Swiss cheese
2 large eggs
225g/8floz/1 cup skimmed or whole milk
15ml/1 tablespoon white wine
salt and pepper
beaten egg to glaze

Make the pastry: rub the margarine into the flour and salt. Mix to a soft dough with water. Knead lightly and roll out on a floured board. Use half the pastry to line a 20cm/8in flan ring or pie dish. Prick the base and bake 'blind' for 10 minutes in a preheated oven at 200°C 400°F, gas 6. Allow to cool.

Heat the oil and sauté the bacon and onion until soft — do not allow them to brown. Place them in the pie case with the ham, herbs and cheese. Whisk the eggs, milk and wine and season well. Pour into the pie case and cover the pie with the remaining pastry. Seal the edges and decorate the top with pastry leaves. Glaze with a little beaten egg.

Bake in a preheated oven at 200°C, 400°F, gas 6 for 15 minutes and then reduce the heat to 180°C, 350°F, gas 4 for a further 25 minutes. Serve hot or cold with a fresh green salad.

Serves 4-5

Pork steaks in orange sauce

Pork, wine and fruit casseroles are eaten in the western and south-western regions of France. The usual fruit are prunes or apples but in this recipe we have used oranges for a delicious result. Use cheap cooking wine and pork spare rib chops or steaks. You can substitute a dry cider for the white wine if you like.

30ml/2 tablespoons oil
2 onions, thinly sliced
15g/½oz/ 1 tablespoon butter
5ml/1 teaspoon Dijon mustard
15ml/1 tablespoon soft brown sugar
grated rind of 2 oranges
4 pork steaks
30ml/2 tablespoons flour
300ml/½ pint/1¼ cups chicken stock
150ml/¼ pint/⅝ cup white wine
juice of 2 oranges
salt and pepper
100g/4oz button mushrooms, sliced
1 large orange
chopped parsley

Heat the oil in a flameproof casserole dish and sauté the onion until soft and translucent. Remove from the pan and keep warm. Mix the butter, mustard, sugar and orange rind to a thick paste. Add to the pan with the pork steaks and sauté until browned on both sides. Remove from the pan and keep warm.

Stir the flour into the pan juices and cook for 3 minutes. Add the stock and wine, a little at a time, stirring over a medium heat until the sauce thickens. Bring to the boil, add the orange juice and seasoning and return the onions and meat to the pan. Cover with a lid and place in a preheated oven at 180°C, 350°F, gas 4 for about 1¼-1½ hours.

Add the sliced mushrooms to the casserole about 10 minutes before the end of the cooking time. Remove the pith and peel from the orange and separate into segments. Add these to the cooked casserole and sprinkle with chopped parsley just before serving.
Serves 4

Lamb

Nepalese lamb

This is a spicy dish of lamb served in a yoghurt sauce. Even if you do not usually like curries, you can enjoy this dish which is only mildly hot and aromatic. Serve it with a selection of small side-dishes in the Nepalese style: different chutneys, fried sliced bananas and apple rings, cashew nuts, fresh pineapple, poppadums and chapatis.

550g/1¼lb lean lamb
30ml/2 tablespoons ghee/clarified butter
1 onion, finely chopped
1 clove of garlic, chopped
15ml/1 tablespoon garam masala
2.5ml/½ teaspoon each of turmeric and cinnamon
1.25ml/¼ teaspoon each of ginger and cayenne
2 cloves
1 dried chilli
salt and pepper
30ml/2 tablespoons lemon juice
150ml/¼ pint/⅝ cup chicken stock
5ml/1 teaspoon mango chutney
75ml/3floz/⅓ cup natural yoghurt
30ml/2 tablespoons flaked almonds
15ml/1 tablespoon ghee/clarified butter

Remove any excess fat from the lamb and cut the meat into small chunks. Heat the ghee in a large pan and sauté the onion and garlic until soft and translucent. Add the lamb and fry gently for a few minutes until well-browned.

Add the spices to the pan and stir well. Remove the hot seeds from the chilli and chop it finely. Toss it into the pan and cook gently for 2-3 minutes, stirring often. Season and add the lemon juice, stock and chutney. Cover the pan and simmer gently for 20 minutes. Check the liquid level from time to time and add more stock if necessary.

Gently stir in the yoghurt and heat through very gently so that the sauce stays creamy and smooth and does not curdle. Do *not* allow it to boil. Meanwhile, brown the almonds in a little ghee. Serve the lamb on a bed of plain, boiled rice, sprinked with the fried almonds.
serves 4

Lamb and orange ragoût

The delicious, aromatic flavour of this recipe is the result of the lamb and vegetables being marinated in red wine with fresh herbs and orange peel for several hours before cooking. Ragoûts have been a popular feature of French and English cookery for at least three centuries. These richly seasoned, robust stews were often flavoured with orange or lemon, as in Hannah Glasse's recipe for a 'ragoo of lamb', published in her famous *The Art of Cookery Made Plain and Easy* in 1747. Mrs Glasse used lemon juice, anchovies and oysters as well as spices, herbs and red wine to flavour her stew. We have adapted her recipe to modern requirements (omitting the oysters which are now, alas, far too expensive to contemplate as a flavouring for a stew) but following some of her excellent suggestions.

1.5kg/3lb leg of lamb, boned and cubed
1 large onion, chopped
1 carrot, diced
1 leek, thinly sliced
1 clove of garlic, crushed
2 long strips thinly pared orange peel
fresh herbs: basil, thyme, rosemary, sage, parsley
30ml/2 tablespoons olive oil
2-3 whole cloves
good pinch of ground mace
450ml/16floz/2 cups red wine
salt and pepper
1 beef stock cube, crumbled
15ml/1 tablespoon tomato paste
2 tomatoes, skinned and chopped
2 anchovy fillets, chopped
100g/4oz button mushrooms, halved or quartered
50g/2oz black olives
30ml/2 tablespoons chopped parsley
Beurre manié:
15g/½oz/1 tablespoon butter
30ml/2 tablespoons flour

Place the lamb, vegetables, orange peel, herbs, olive oil, spices, red wine and seasoning in a large flameproof casserole dish. Cover and leave to marinate for 4 hours.

Crumble in the stock cube, add enough water to cover the meat and vegetables, and the tomato paste and tomatoes. Cover the casserole and place in a pre-heated oven at 180°C, 350°F, gas 4 and cook for 2 hours. Add the anchovy fillets, mushrooms and olives to the ragoût for the last 30 minutes of the cooking time.

Blend the butter and flour to a smooth paste. On top of the stove, over high heat, add the *beurre manié*, to the casserole, a little at a time, stirring until the sauce starts to thicken. Boil it up for 5-10 minutes until it is thick and smooth. Remove the herbs and orange peel, sprinkle over a little chopped parsley and serve with green vegetables and creamed potatoes.

Serves 4

Mediterranean lamb

This stuffed fillet of lamb is marinated in red wine and roasted on a bed of root vegetables. Serve it with flageolet beans to evoke the colour and flavours of the South of France.

1kg/2lb boned fillet end of leg of lamb
150ml/¼ pint/⅜ cup red wine
1 bay leaf
few parsley stalks
1 clove garlic, crushed
50g/2oz/¼ cup meat dripping
2 parsnips, quartered lengthwise
2 rashers bacon, diced
2 cloves garlic
2 sticks of celery, halved
450g/1lb potatoes, peeled and cubed
30ml/2 tablespoons flour
300ml/½ pint/1¼ cups beef stock or vegetable water
Stuffing:
1 onion, finely chopped
25g/1oz mushrooms, chopped
50g/2oz/1 cup fresh breadcrumbs
1 clove garlic, crushed
7.5ml/½ tablespoon chopped parsley
good pinch each of oregano and marjoram
75g/3oz/½ cup minced/ground pork
salt and pepper
15ml/1 tablespoon stock

Bone the lamb or get your butcher to do this for you. Place the joint in a large dish and pour over the marinade (red wine, bay leaf, parsley and garlic). Leave for 12 hours in a cool place, turning the lamb occasionally. Drain, reserving the marinade to make the gravy.

Make the stuffing: mix all the ingredients together and fill the cavity of the boned lamb with this mixture. Secure the open end with meat skewers. Melt the fat in a roasting pan and add the parsnips, bacon, garlic, celery and potatoes. Place the lamb on top of this bed of vegetables and roast in a preheated oven at 220°C, 425°F, gas 7 for 30 minutes and then reduce the heat to 190°C, 375°F, gas 5 for 1 hour. Remove the joint to a serving dish and allow to stand for 5 minutes. Take out the skewers. Remove the vegetables, discarding the garlic cloves, and keep warm.

Meanwhile, make the gravy: pour off most of the pan juices and stir the flour into the remaining fat (about 30ml/2 tablespoons) in the pan. Allow to brown and then gradually add the boiling stock or vegetable water and the reserved marinade. Bring to the boil and then cook over medium heat for a few minutes until thickened and smooth. Season to taste (you can add 5ml/1 teaspoon redcurrant jelly for a sweeter flavour).

Serve the lamb surrounded by the root vegetables with a dish of flageolet beans and the gravy separately.

Serves 4-6

Moroccan apricot and prune tagine

Many North African meat dishes closely resemble the mediaeval cookery of England and France when meats were spiced and flavoured with fruit and honey to suit the sweet tooth of the time. These meat and fruit stews, much favoured by the present-day Moroccans, were developed by ancient Arab and Persian civilisations and spread throughout the Islamic empire in the Middle Ages. Many dried and fresh fruits are used, including apples, quinces, pears, apricots, cherries, raisins, dates and prunes. Sometimes almonds or pistachio nuts, chick peas or honey are also added — there are countless variations. They are served traditionally with plain boiled rice. Although lamb is the usual meat, chicken can also be treated in this way.

50g/2oz/⅜ cup dried apricots
75g/3oz/½ cup prunes
675g/1½lb lean lamb, boned and diced (or 4 chicken joints)
1 onion, chopped
good pinch each of ground ginger and saffron
2.5ml/½ teaspoon ground cinnamon
1.25ml/¼ teaspoon ground coriander
salt and black pepper
few sprigs parsley, chopped
50g/2oz/⅓ cup dried dates
15ml/1 tablespoon honey

Soak the apricots and prunes overnight. Place the lamb (or chicken) in a flameproof casserole dish with the onion, spices and seasoning (and 15ml/1 tablespoon butter if you are using chicken). Cover with water, bring to the boil on top of the stove and then cover with a lid and place in a preheated oven at 170°C, 325°F, gas 3 and cook until tender (about 1½ hours for lamb; 1 hour for chicken). Add the parsley and dried fruit and bake for a further 30 minutes.

Stir in the honey and simmer gently on top of the stove for at least 10 minutes. Serve with rice (crunchy brown rice tastes good). Cider-baked onions go particularly well with this dish (see recipe on page 139).
Serves 4

Persian lamb kebabs

These are served with a spicy pilaff flavoured with dried fruit and nuts. Chicken can be used instead of lamb in this dish. You may serve it with hot chilli or barbecue sauce (see recipe on page 171).

450g/1lb lean lamb, cut in chunks
8 button onions or 2 small onions, quartered
12 button mushrooms
4 bay leaves
4 cherry tomatoes
30ml/2 tablespoons sesame or olive oil
juice of 1 lemon
salt and pepper
pinch each of ground cumin and cinnamon
5ml/1 teaspoon oregano
30ml/2 tablespoons chopped parsley
Rice pilaff:
175g/6oz/¾ cup long-grain brown rice
50g/2oz/⅜ cup dried apricots, soaked overnight
50g/2oz/½ cup chopped walnuts
50g/2oz/⅓ cup currants
salt and pepper
½ red pepper, seeded and diced
good pinch of ground cinnamon
30ml/2 tablespoons chopped parsley

Thread the lamb, onions, mushrooms, bay leaves and small cherry tomatoes onto 4 kebab skewers. Blend the oil, lemon juice, seasoning, spices and oregano and brush over the kebabs. Put aside while you prepare the rice pilaff.

Cook the rice in salted water with the chopped apricots until tender but still crunchy (about 20-25 minutes). Drain and mix with the remaining pilaff ingredients. Cover the dish and put in a low oven to keep warm and heat through.

Place the kebabs under a hot grill/broiler, turning occasionally until they are cooked. Brush with a little of the marinade while they are cooking to keep them moist. Sprinkle with chopped parsley and serve with the pilaff and a fresh green salad.
Serves 4

Turkish lamb in aubergine sauce

This is an unusual and attractive dish, the lamb being served in a spicy tomato and pepper mixture with a cheese and aubergine/eggplant sauce border. You can serve it with boiled rice and a lemony salad.

450g/1lb lean lamb, cubed
45ml/3 tablespoons oil
1 onion, chopped
½ red pepper, seeded and diced
½ green pepper, seeded and diced
1.25ml/¼ teaspoon each of ground cumin and allspice
15ml/1 tablespoon tomato paste
225g/8oz tomatoes, skinned and sliced or canned

300ml/½ pint/1¼ cups water
salt and pepper
2.5ml/½ teaspoon brown sugar
30ml/2 tablespoons chopped parsley
Sauce:
1 aubergine/eggplant
15ml/1 tablespoon lemon juice
50ml/2floz/¼ cup oil
50g/2oz/6 tablespoons flour
300ml/½ pint/1¼ cups milk infused with 1 clove-studded
  onion
50g/2oz/½ cup grated Gruyère/Swiss cheese
45ml/3 tablespoons grated Parmesan cheese
salt and pepper

Fry the lamb in the oil until browned. Remove and keep warm while you sauté the onion and chopped peppers until soft. Add the spices and fry for 2-3 minutes. Stir in the tomato paste and tomatoes and then gradually add the water, the lamb, sugar, seasoning and 15ml/1 tablespoon of the parsley. Bake in a covered ovenproof dish in a preheated oven at 170°C, 325°F, gas 3 for 1½ hours.

While the lamb is cooking, make the aubergine sauce. Place the aubergine/eggplant under a very hot grill/broiler, turning occasionally until the skin is soft and charred. Peel the skin off under running water and blend the aubergine flesh with the lemon juice in a liquidiser or food processor to a smooth, creamy purée. Heat the oil and stir in the flour to make a roux. Cook for 1 minute and then gradually beat in the infused milk until the sauce is thick and glossy. Add the aubergine purée and cook over gentle heat for 5 minutes. Beat in the grated cheeses and season to taste.

Arrange the lamb in the centre of a serving dish and pour the aubergine sauce around it in a border. Sprinkle with the remaining parsley and serve with buttered noodles or rice.

Serves 4

Moussaka with yoghurt

This is a slimming version of the traditional Greek moussaka with a yoghurt custard topping instead of a creamy béchamel sauce. Dried apricots, pine nuts and spices are added to the lamb and tomato sauce for an unusual flavour and texture. You can use left-over cooked minced/ground lamb in the sauce, or may even substitute beef. Do ensure that it is moist without being oily or watery — it should be thick and flavoursome.

50g/2oz/⅜ cup dried apricots
2 large aubergines/eggplants, thinly sliced
salt
olive oil for frying
2 onions, chopped
30ml/2 tablespoons oil
450g/1lb minced/ground lean lamb
450g/1lb canned tomatoes + juice
5ml/1 teaspoon brown sugar
15ml/1 tablespoon oregano
2.5ml/½ teaspoon each of ground cinnamon, allspice and
  cumin
30ml/2 tablespoons tomato paste
60ml/4 tablespoons pine nuts
50ml/2floz/¼ cup red wine
salt and pepper
100g/4oz feta cheese, crumbled
30ml/2 tablespoons grated Parmesan cheese
Yoghurt topping:
150ml/¼ pint/⅝ cup natural yoghurt
2 eggs, beaten
50ml/2 floz/¼ cup milk
salt and pepper

Soak the dried apricots overnight, drain and chop. Spread the sliced aubergine/eggplant out on a plate or colander and sprinkle generously with salt. Leave for at least 30 minutes to drain away their bitter excess moisture. Rinse thoroughly in cold water and pat dry. Fry gently in a little olive oil until golden-brown. Drain and set aside.

Make the meat sauce: sauté the onion in the oil until soft and translucent. Add the lamb and brown it. Add the tomatoes and their juice, sugar, herbs, spices, chopped apricots and tomato paste. Bring to the boil and cook rapidly for about 15 minutes until the sauce thickens. Stir in the pine nuts and red wine, continue boiling and then season to taste.

Grease a shallow ovenproof dish and arrange the fried aubergine/eggplant slices across the base in a layer, then a layer of meat sauce, another layer of aubergine and the remaining meat sauce. Crumble the feta cheese across the top. Beat the yoghurt, eggs and milk together and season. Pour over the moussaka and sprinkle with grated Parmesan cheese. Bake uncovered in a preheated oven at 180°C, 350°F, gas 4 for 45-50 minutes, until the topping is set, golden-brown and slightly risen. Serve with a crisp green salad and yoghurt dressing.

Serves 4-5

Vegetables have been cultivated as a food plant since ancient times when Man became a farmer as well as a gatherer. The great conquering empires of Rome and Islam introduced their favourite vegetables and food plants to their new colonies and settlements, and later the seafaring city states and nations of the Mediterranean brought back new exotic vegetables from their expanding trade markets.

However, it was not until 1492 and Columbus's momentous discovery of the Americas that the now-familiar New World food crops appeared in Europe. Many of the vegetables that we take for granted and indeed form the basis of the national cookery traditions of many Mediterranean and Balkan countries were unknown until the sixteenth century. It is difficult to conceive of Italian cookery without tomatoes, for example, or Hungarian cuisine without sweet peppers and paprika. The new vegetables were viewed with a mixture of delight and suspicion by the cooks, gardeners and consumers of the time, but tomatoes, potatoes, sweetcorn, beans, chillis, avocado pears, Jerusalem artichokes and peppers soon became essential ingredients in European cooking.

The great gardeners and horticulturists of the seventeenth century developed new and better strains of vegetables from the seeds brought back by explorers and traders and it was very fashionable to grow one's own exotic fruits and vegetables. However, many of these interesting vegetables practically disappeared from England and many other European countries in the nineteenth century as the Victorians extended their puritanical attitudes to food as well as good manners. Now, thanks to genetic science and new farming methods, and the growing interest in food and healthy eating, a wide range of vegetables is again available in the shops, and also in seed form to grow yourself.

Vegetables such as courgettes/zucchini, avocado pears, artichokes and colourful bell peppers are no longer an exotic and unfamiliar novelty. They are commonplace on supermarket shelves, even away from the big towns and cities. But despite the new enthusiasm for vegetables, their quality has declined as they are cultivated on a grand scale for their appearance — colour, plumpness, size and uniformity of shape — rather than their flavour. Tomatoes provide a good example of this disturbing trend. Short of growing your own it is becoming increasingly difficult to find really sweet and scented, flavoursome tomatoes. Most are grown for the wrong reasons as far as the cook is concerned, who is forced to buy tasteless, watery varieties because growers and supermarket chains have decreed that the general public distrusts misshapen vegetables and wants only uniformity. Thus most tomatoes are grown for their large yields, tough skins which guarantee their ability to travel well before they finally reach the shops, and their regular size.

The harvesting, transporting and packaging of vegetables often take their toll and the vegetables we purchase might not be as fresh as they should be. To gain the maximum nutritional value, you should eat a vegetable on the same day as it is picked, but obviously this is impractical unless you happen to grow your own or have a friend or neighbour who does so.

Another reason for growing your own vegetables is the widespread use of chemical sprays and fertilisers in their cultivation. Food can only be as good as the soil in which it is grown and vegetables produced in healthy soil with organic matter and natural compost are superior in quality and goodness to those that have been chemically sprayed, and even waxed in some instances.

Vegetables provide a rich source of nutrients in our diet: starch, protein, minerals and vitamins. There is a growing demand for organically grown garden produce and they can now be purchased in most health food stores, although they may be more expensive than the cheaper, mass-produced varieties which often lack the texture and flavour of the former. As many people are beginning to realise, they are a pleasure to eat as well as being 'good for you'. For many years they were regarded solely as a filler or as an accompaniment to meat or fish, often badly cooked and disliked. In fact, some people *never* ate vegetables at all, although Beau Brummel, the nineteenth century dandy, did admit that he 'once ate a pea'! Since the 1960s and the re-emergence of interest in foreign foods and traditional country cooking, vegetables have been championed by chefs, cookery writers and the new breed of 'foodies'. You don't have to be a vegetarian to enjoy the delights of vegetables — just adopt an experimental approach and have fun cooking them in new ways for, with their enormous range of colours, textures and flavours, they are the most versatile food of all.

Buying vegetables

Vegetables should always look and smell fresh and have a bright, wholesome appearance. They should be firm and crisp, not dry and soft with wilted, curling leaves. Never buy anything that looks calloused, faded and smells strongly or unpleasantly. The best places to shop are stores and market stalls where you can handle the produce yourself and assess their quality and freshness. It is difficult to make an informed choice if the vegetables are sealed inside polythene bags and plastic wrappings which conceal their true condition and cause condensation and 'sweating'. Always remove the vegetables from this horrendous packaging when you get them home and store in a cool, dry place.

Never be afraid of dirt, especially if you are buying fresh organically grown produce. Although it may sometimes hide a multitude of blemishes, it will not detract from the flavour and sweetness of the vegetables inside. In fact, the vegetables are more likely to be freshly picked than are prewashed and prepared clean ones. However, excessive dirt and mud on potatoes and root vegetables contribute to the overall weight and you may well end up paying for 50g/2oz or so of mud!

Although they can now be enjoyed all the year round thanks to modern cultivation under glass and better transportation, it is still best to buy vegetables that are in season in the area in which you live if you insist on freshness. Obviously, the more exotic items, such as avocados, are rarely local and have to be imported, unless you live in California or some other hot spot. The golden rule is to opt for freshness wherever possible and not a chemically induced appearance.

Cooking vegetables

As long ago as 1747, the celebrated Hannah Glasse wrote in *The Art of Cookery Made Plain and Easy* that 'most people spoil garden things by overboiling them. All things that are green should have a little crispness, for if they are overboil'd they neither have any sweetness or beauty.' It is a pity that more cooks have not taken heed of this excellent advice as overcooking is death to most vegetables and this often accounts for their unpopularity as far as vegetable-haters are concerned.

Vegetables should always be eaten as crisp and as tender as possible. They should have some 'bite' and freshness rather than be served up as a mushy mess. Achieving this is not difficult — it is a matter of timing and intuition rather than skill. Valuable nutrients, vitamins and minerals are easily lost if vegetables are over-cooked so aim to preserve as much flavour and food value as possible by rescuing them from the pan before they are destroyed.

Prepare vegetables at the last possible moment to minimise loss of vitamin C through oxidation, and *never* add bicarbonate of soda/baking soda to the cooking water. Although this is supposed to retain the greenness of the vegetables it detracts from their own intrinsic fresh flavour and reduces the vitamin C content. If they are cooked correctly, vegetables will stay fresh and green-looking anyway. Boiling in the minimum of water with the pan uncovered will help keep their bright green colour. Steaming above boiling water is a good way of cooking delicate vegetables, such as broccoli and cauliflower florets, and also ensures the minimum of vitamin and vegetable juice loss. Several vegetables can be cooked simultaneously if you have a multi-storeyed steamer, thus saving energy and space on top of the stove.

A plate of crudités with ailloli

The most delicious crudités we have ever eaten were in Paris. A large wicker basket arrived full of whole raw vegetables — vivid red, green and yellow bell peppers, tender heads of chicory/endive, scarlet tomatoes, crisp radishes, fennel and celery, cool green cucumbers, Chinese leaves, tiny button mushrooms, tender young carrots, large snowy cauliflowers and young pea pods. We helped ourselves to what we wanted, slicing off pieces of this and that and dipping them into the sauces provided — ailloli and a green herb mayonnaise. Served in this way as a first course or with a selection of hard and creamy cheeses as a light lunch, crudités make a colourful and healthy meal. The wicker basket is a novel idea but you may prefer to prepare the vegetables for your guests. Although it is best to do this at the last possible moment, just before serving the meal, it can be done a few hours in advance as most vegetables will keep fresh and crisp in iced water in the refrigerator. The quantities used will depend on how many people you are feeding and whether the dish is to be the main course. You will need:

carrots, peeled and thinly sliced
bell peppers, seeded and cut in thin strips
small tomatoes, washed and quartered
sticks of celery, cut in strips
radishes, cut in roses and kept in iced water until they open
    out like flowers
chicory/endive, separated into leaves
fennel bulb, cut in chunks
cucumber, cut in strips
button mushrooms
cauliflower, divided into florets
young pea pods, topped and tailed
courgettes/zucchini, cut in thin strips
spring onions/shallots

Prepare the vegetables and arrange on an attractive large serving plate, with bowls of ailloli (see recipe on page 173) and green mayonnaise (see recipe on page 173) in the centre. Other sauces and dips for crudités include guacamole (see recipe on page 127) and cacik (see recipe for chilled yoghurt and cucumber soup on page 78).

Aubergine caviare

This is not real caviare, of course, but a delicious, smoky flavoured aubergine/ eggplant purée, which is sometimes known as 'poor man's caviare' in the countries of the eastern Mediterranean from whence it comes. Serve it as a dip with slices of pitta bread and crudités, or as a *mezze* dish — the little tasters and dips served with drinks before a meal or as snacks throughout the day in the Middle East. A *mezze* table might include hummus, dolmades, salads, olives, nuts and goat's cheese as well as aubergine caviare.

2 large aubergines/eggplants
1 clove garlic, crushed
30ml/2 tablespoons olive oil
juice of 1 small lemon
salt and pepper
1.25ml/¼ teaspoon ground cumin
15ml/1 tablespoon chopped parsley
1 black olive

Place the aubergines/eggplants under a hot grill/broiler, turning occasionally until soft and the skins start to darken and burn. Remove and peel them, discarding any charred skin. Purée the pulp in a blender, processor or mortar, with the garlic, oil and lemon juice until the caviare is smooth and creamy. Season to taste and stir in the cumin. Pour into a serving dish. Sprinkle with parsley and decorate with a single black olive. Chill until required.

Baked avocado

You have probably eaten cold avocado many times but have you ever tried it hot? Filled with a delicately flavoured crabmeat and shrimp sauce and baked in the oven until golden-brown, avocado makes an unusual and filling first course. Allow half an avocado per person unless you are ravenously hungry.

2 ripe avocados
juice of ½ lemon
175g/6oz/¾ cup cooked or canned crabmeat
50g/2oz peeled, cooked shrimps
45ml/3 tablespoons grated Swiss cheese
5ml/1 teaspoon mild curry powder
15ml/1 tablespoon double/heavy cream (optional)
salt and pepper
squeeze lemon juice
15ml/1 tablespoon grated Parmesan cheese
Béchamel sauce:
25g/1oz/2 tablespoons butter
25g/1oz/3 tablespoons flour
300ml/½ pint/1¼ cups milk
pinch ground nutmeg

Make the béchamel sauce in the usual way and flavour with the nutmeg. Leave it to cool so that it becomes really thick. Halve and stone the avocados and sprinkle with lemon juice to prevent them browning. Scoop out a little of the flesh and dice. Reheat the sauce, stirring in the crabmeat and shrimps, grated cheese, curry powder, cream, seasoning and lemon juice. Gently add the avocado cubes.

Divide the mixture between the 4 avocado halves. Scatter over the Parmesan and bake in a preheated oven at 190°C, 375°F, gas 5 for 12-15 minutes. Place under a hot grill for 2-3 minutes until golden and bubbling and serve immediately.

Serves 4

Vegetable terrine

Light and colourful layered vegetable terrines and pâtés are among the best features of the Nouvelle Cuisine. If you have a food processor or powerful blender, they are easy to make and assemble and never fail to look impressive. They are the ideal way to start a summer lunch or dinner party, especially when served with a fresh puréed tomato sauce or a delicately flavoured green mayonnaise. Although the quantity of cream given here may sound a lot, the terrine feeds 6-8 people and therefore individual consumption is small. You can vary the vegetables used according to what is in season and even try colouring the mousseline a pale gold with saffron, a pale pink with tomato purée, or green with chopped spinach or watercress. Choose vegetables of contrasting colours and experiment with different patterns of coloured layers, using this recipe as a basis.

350g/12oz chicken breasts, skinned and boned
1 carrot
10 string beans
2 heads of broccoli
30ml/2 tablespoons peas
1 egg white
300ml/½ pint/1¼ cups double/heavy cream
chopped fresh herbs or chopped, blanched watercress
    (optional)
salt and pepper

Process or blend the chicken breasts to a smooth purée. Refrigerate in the processor bowl or blender goblet for at least 30 minutes until thoroughly chilled.

Meanwhile, prepare the vegetables. Peel and cut the carrot into thin julienne strips lengthways. Top and tail the beans and cut each in half, and divide the broccoli heads into small florets. Parboil the vegetables separately until tender but still firm. Refresh them in iced water and drain.

Whip the egg white lightly and add to the chilled chicken purée with the cream. Process until thoroughly blended to make a chicken mousseline, and season lightly. If wished, add a little chopped watercress or chopped herbs to the mousseline for a green-flecked appearance.

Butter a long, rectangular terrine and spread a thin layer of mousseline across the base. Then arrange the vegetables and mousseline in alternate layers, finishing with a layer of mousseline. Cover the terrine with a sheet of buttered foil and stand in a water-bath. Bake in a preheated oven for 30 minutes at 180°C, 350°F, gas 4 until firm and set.

Allow to cool and chill overnight before turning out. Gently run the point of a knife around the sides of the terrine and invert onto a serving dish. Serve sliced surrounded by a fresh tomato sauce or with green mayonnaise (see recipes on pages 171 and 173).

Serves 6-8

Guacamole

The main ingredient of this delicately spiced, pale green sauce is avocado, a native of central, tropical America and much favoured by the Aztecs. Guacamole is served throughout Mexico as a sauce with tacos — crisply fried tortillas rolled around a filling of meat and beans (see recipe on page 15). However, guacamole also makes a delicious first course to a meal or an appetizing dip, served with vegetable crudités, potato crisps and savoury biscuits. It is particularly popular on the west coast of the United States where it is eaten as a dip with drinks or cocktails before dinner. Quick and simple to make, it can be mixed with a fork or puréed to a smooth consistency in a blender or food processor.

2 ripe avocados
juice of ½ lemon
½ onion, chopped
1 clove garlic, crushed
¼ green pepper, chopped
2 tomatoes, skinned and chopped
5 coriander seeds
2 dried chillis, seeds removed and chopped
30ml/2 tablespoons plain yoghurt
salt and pepper
2.5ml/½ teaspoon sugar

Peel and stone the avocados and remove the flesh. Mash

well with the other ingredients until you have a smooth, creamy purée. Serve immediately with carrot, celery and red and green pepper cut into sticks, cauliflower florets, button mushrooms, spring onions, radishes and crisps or biscuits.

The addition of lemon juice should prevent the avocado from browning and thus it may be made a few hours in advance, if wished, sealed with plastic film and chilled until required.

Makes 300ml/½pint/1¼ cups

Vegetable soups

French onion soup gratinée

Onion soup is eaten in many regions of France, but especially so in the area around Lyons. There are many insipid commercially produced soups that claim to be the real thing, but onion soup should never be thin or watery with soggy bread and stringy cheese floating in it. In this delicious recipe, the onions have a sweet, melting quality and the soup is flavoured with wine and port and topped with crisp slices of French bread and golden, bubbling cheese.

450g/1lb onions, thinly sliced
30ml/2 tablespoons oil
15g/½oz/1 tablespoon butter
10ml/2 teaspoons sugar
30ml/2 tablespoons flour
900ml/1½ pints/3¾ cups beef stock
150ml/¼ pint/⅝ cup white wine
salt and pepper
pinch ground nutmeg
50ml/2floz/¼ cup tawny port (or 30ml/2 tablespoons cognac)
Croûtons:
8 slices French bread
olive oil for brushing
50g/2oz/½ cup grated Gruyère or Emmenthal/Swiss cheese

Gently sauté the onions in the oil and butter with the sugar. Cover the pan and leave them over low heat for at least 30 minutes until they are tender and golden and 'melting'. Stir in the flour and cook for 2 minutes. Add the stock, wine and seasoning and simmer gently for 30 minutes.

Add the port and simmer for a further 10-15 minutes. Meanwhile, make the croûtons. Put the French bread on a baking tray and bake in a preheated oven at 180°C, 350°F, gas 4 for 10-15 minutes until crisp and golden-brown. Brush the toasted bread with oil.

Pour the soup into a heated tureen or individual serving bowls and place the croûtons on top. Sprinkle with grated cheese and place in a hot oven or under the grill/broiler until bubbling and golden.
Serves 4

Green pepper soup

Green peppers make a surprisingly good, delicately coloured soup, which freezes well. For a smooth finish, a white sauce is stirred into the liquidised pepper soup. As peppers are relatively cheap and their availability is not governed by the seasons, this soup can be enjoyed all the year round.

3 green peppers, deseeded and chopped
1 large onion, chopped
15g/½oz/1 tablespoon margarine
550ml/1 pint/2½ cups chicken stock
salt and pepper
good pinch basil or oregano
chopped parsley and croûtons to garnish
For the sauce:
15g/½oz/1 tablespoon margarine
15g/½oz/2 tablespoons flour
300ml/½ pint/1¼ cups milk
good pinch ground nutmeg

Sauté the chopped pepper and onion in the margarine over gentle heat until soft. Add the chicken stock, seasoning and herbs and simmer for 15-20 minutes. Liquidise in a blender or food processor and return the soup to the pan.

Make a roux with the margarine and flour and cook gently for 2-3 minutes. Add the milk gradually, beating until you have a smooth sauce. Bring to the boil, stirring well until thickened and smooth. Season with nutmeg.

Stir the sauce into the soup and heat through gently. Check the seasoning and serve sprinkled with chopped parsley and fried bread croûtons.

Serves 4

Opposite: a Mexican party spread of crisp tacos filled with guacamole and chilli beef fillings in the foreground (see page 15) and a dip of creamy guacamole (see page 127) served with a wide range of colourful vegetable crudités for dipping. Small crispbreads, savoury biscuits and potato crisps are also suitable

Minestrone

You can add almost any vegetables to this hearty Italian soup, which can be served with crusty bread as a main course. The Genovese version adds pesto sauce just before serving for an interesting variation. Pesto sauce can be bought ready-made in jars in many Italian delicatessens but it is even better if you make it yourself (see recipe on page 51).

45ml/3 tablespoons olive oil
15g/½oz/1 tablespoon margarine
2 slices belly pork, roughly cubed
2 chicken joints, skinned
3 onions, chopped
2 leeks, chopped
1 stick celery, chopped
2 cloves garlic, crushed
3 carrots, chopped
1 parsnip, chopped
½ fennel bulb, chopped
½ green pepper, chopped
1 courgette/zucchini, sliced
450g/1lb/2 cups canned tomatoes
15ml/1 tablespoon tomato paste
15ml/1 tablespoon sugar
1.5litres/2½ pints/6 cups chicken stock
150ml/¼ pint/⅝ cup red wine
15ml/1 tablespoon dried basil
salt and pepper
1 rind from a Parmesan cheese (optional)
2 potatoes, peeled and diced
100g/4oz pasta shapes
50g/2oz/⅓ cup grated Parmesan

Heat the oil and margarine in a large saucepan and gently fry the pork and chicken until browned. Remove and put aside while you sauté the vegetables until tender. Add the canned tomatoes, tomato paste, sugar and stock.

Bring to the boil, reduce the heat to a simmer and replace the chicken and pork in the pan with the red wine, herbs, seasoning and Parmesan rind. This is worth adding if you can buy one or find an old rind lurking in your refrigerator as it improves the overall flavour of the soup.

Cover the pan and simmer for 1½ hours. Then add the potato and pasta shapes (bows or shells are attractive). Simmer for a further 30 minutes, adding more stock or wine if necessary. Serve hot with grated Parmesan cheese or pesto sauce.

Serves 6

Watercress soup

This refreshing, delicately flavoured soup can be served hot or chilled and is one of the best soups of all. It is thickened with potatoes, puréed, and served with cheese straws or fried bread croûtons.

1 large onion, chopped
2 large potatoes, peeled and diced
15g/½oz/1 tablespoon butter
175g/6oz watercress
1.1 litres/2 pints/5 cups chicken stock
salt and pepper
45ml/3 tablespoons cream
10ml/2 teaspoons lemon juice
watercress sprigs to garnish

Sauté the onion and potato gently in the butter until soft. Add the watercress and cook gently for a few minutes until it turns bright green and becomes tender. Add the chicken stock and bring to the boil. Simmer for 20 minutes and then purée or liquidise.

Return the soup to the pan and season to taste. Stir in the nutmeg and cream and heat through gently. Add the lemon juice and serve garnished with watercress sprigs.

If you wish to serve the soup chilled, then do not add the cream after liquidising the soup. Instead, leave it to go cold, chill well and stir in the cream immediately before serving.

Serves 4-5

Sorrel soup

Sorrel is a popular herb in France, and widely used for flavouring soups, sauces, omelettes and salads. In Britain and America it is not so familiar although it is easy to grow and often on sale in good greengrocers and vegetable markets throughout the summer months. When cooked it has a sharp lemony flavour, which is surprisingly refreshing. In this recipe, the sorrel leaves are sautéed in bacon fat in the manner of the great French chefs Carême and Escoffier.

50g/2oz/¼ cup bacon fat (or lard/shortening)
1 onion, finely chopped
450g/1lb sorrel
1.1 litres/2 pints/5 cups chicken stock
salt and pepper
pinch of grated nutmeg
2 egg yolks
75ml/3floz/⅜ cup single/light cream

Heat the bacon fat and sauté the onion until soft and

translucent. Trim the sorrel, removing the hard stems and washing the leaves well. Shred it and add to the pan. Cook gently over low heat until the leaves go soft and bright green. Add the chicken stock and seasonings and bring to the boil. Cover the pan and simmer gently for about 15 minutes.

Purée or liquidise the soup and return to the pan. Beat together the egg yolks and cream and stir in a little warm soup. Add this liaison to the soup in the pan and heat gently, stirring all the time until the soup thickens. Take care that it does not boil or it will curdle. Check the seasoning and serve hot or chilled.
Serves 4

Zuppa di funghi

This is the best recipe for mushroom soup that we know. It is thickened, not with flour, potato or a liaison of egg yolks and cream, but with a slice of bread — nothing could be simpler or more delicious. It is equally good served piping hot or chilled.

15g/½oz/1 tablespoon margarine
1 onion, chopped
1 clove garlic, crushed
275g/10oz open or field mushrooms, finely chopped
900ml/1½ pints/3½ cups chicken stock
1 slice white bread, 2.5cm/1in thick
salt and pepper
45ml/3 tablespoons double/heavy or soured cream
15ml/1 tablespoon chopped parsley

Heat the margarine in a large pan and sauté the onion and garlic until soft and translucent. Add the chopped mushrooms and stir over gentle heat until soft. Pour in the chicken stock and crumble in the bread. Season and cover the pan. Simmer gently for about 20 minutes.

Liquidise the soup in a blender or food processor and return to the pan. Stir in the cream and heat gently until it is very hot. Pour into serving dishes or a tureen, sprinkle with chopped parsley and serve. Alternatively, leave to cool and chill in the refrigerator.
Serves 4

Beetroot and ginger soup

This lovely clear red soup is a cheap and attractive way to start a dinner. Serve with a swirl of soured cream and chopped chives with little puff pastry *vatrushki*

in the traditional Russian manner.

300g/11oz raw beetroot, thinly sliced
225g/8oz white cabbage, shredded
1 clove garlic, grushed
small blade of mace
25g/1oz root ginger, grated
salt and pepper ·
750ml/1¼ pints/3 cups boiling water
15ml/1 tablespoon lemon juice
150ml/¼ pint/⅝ cup soured cream
chopped chives

Layer the beetroot and cabbage up in an ovenproof dish with the garlic, mace, ginger and seasoning. Pour in the boiling water, cover and cook in a preheated oven at 170°C, 325°F, gas 3 for 2-2½ hours until the vegetables are tender and the liquid is deep red in colour. Strain the soup into a tureen, add the lemon juice and serve topped with the soured cream and chives.
Serves 4

Nutty parsnip soup

The combination of parsnips, walnuts and a mild curry powder make this soup slightly sweet and spicy. It is an excellent, cheap soup for winter evenings and can be eaten with crusty granary bread and cheese as a supper snack.

450g/1lb parsnips
1 onion
15g/½oz/1 tablespoon margarine
5ml/1 teaspoon mild curry powder
675ml/1½ pints/3¾ cups beef or game stock
45ml/3 tablespoons finely chopped walnuts
5ml/1 teaspoon soft brown sugar
salt and pepper
300ml/½ pint/1¼ cups milk
chopped parsley or croûtons to garnish

Peel and dice the parsnips and chop the onions. Sauté them gently in the fat over low heat until softened and tender. Stir in the curry powder and cook for 2-3 minutes. Add the stock, walnuts, seasoning and sugar and bring to the boil. Reduce the heat to a simmer, cover the pan and cook gently for 15 minutes until the vegetables are tender.

Liquidise the soup and return to the pan. Add the milk, heat through gently, and serve garnished with chopped parsley or fried bread croûtons.
Serves 4-5

Spicy carrot and parsnip soup

This beautiful golden soup makes a warming first course or a filling supper, garnished with crisply fried bacon and chives. Serve it with crusty granary bread or herb croûtons (see recipe on page 169).

250g/9oz parsnips, chopped
450g/1lb carrots, chopped
1 large leek, sliced
1 onion, chopped
1 clove garlic, crushed
30ml/2 tablespoons oil
1.2litres/2 pints/5 cups chicken stock
150ml/¼ pint/⅝ cup milk
2.5ml/½ teaspoon turmeric
2.5ml/½ teaspoon nutmeg
salt and pepper
15ml/1 tablespoon soft brown sugar
squeeze lemon juice
4 rashers smoked streaky bacon
chopped chives

Sauté the chopped vegetables and garlic in the oil until soft. Add the chicken stock, bring to the boil, then reduce the heat to a simmer for 20 - 30 minutes.

Liquidise or sieve the soup until thick and smooth. Reheat in a saucepan with the milk, spices, seasoning, sugar and lemon juice to taste. Grill the bacon until crisp and serve crumbled over the soup in a serving dish or tureen with the chopped chives.

Makes 1.5litres/2½ pints/6 cups

Salads

Potato and dill salad

Serve this potato salad barely warm with cold meat, grilled fish or smoked sausages. New potatoes lend it a special sweetness but you can use old potatoes instead.

350g/12oz new potatoes
100ml/4floz/½ cup plain yoghurt (or mixed with soured cream)
4 rashers streaky bacon
15ml/1 tablespoon dried or fresh dill
salt and pepper
squeeze of lemon juice
chopped chives to garnish

Wash the potatoes and boil them in their skins until tender but still firm. Drain and cool a little before cutting into chunks. Mix in a bowl with the yoghurt (and soured cream if wished).

Grill/broil the bacon rashers until crisp and browned and crumble them over the potato salad. Mix in the dill, seasoning and lemon juice. Sprinkle with chopped chives and serve warm.

Serves 3-4

Caesar salad

This salad is widely eaten in the United States as a first course before the main dish is served. You should use crisp cos lettuce and a really fruity olive oil to obtain the right texture and flavour. Some people fry the bread croûtons in olive oil and garlic, but this increases the calorie content of the salad unnecessarily, so we have toasted the croûtons before tossing them in the salad dressing.

1 large cos lettuce
10 anchovy fillets, roughly chopped
6 slices French bread
1 egg
juice of 1 lemon
salt and pepper
50ml/2floz/¼ cup olive oil
dash Worcestershire sauce
1 clove garlic, crushed
50g/2oz/⅓ cup grated Parmesan

Wash and dry the cos lettuce and break up into small pieces. Place in a salad bowl with the anchovies. Remove the crusts from the bread and cut the bread into small dice. Arrange on a baking tray and bake in a preheated oven at 170°C, 325°F, gas 3 for 15 minutes until crisp and golden-brown.

Pop the egg into boiling water for 1 minute. Break the shell and add the coddled egg to the lemon juice, seasoning, olive oil, Worcestershire sauce and crushed garlic. Beat well until the dressing is thoroughly mixed. Add the toasted croûtons to the salad and toss well in the dressing. Sprinkle on plenty of freshly ground black pepper and sprinkle with freshly grated Parmesan cheese. Toss again and serve.

Serves 4

Opposite: a colourful assortment of vegetable soups which are suitable for every occasion. Reading clockwise from the top: minestrone (see page 130), watercress soup (see page 130), beetroot and ginger soup (see page 131) and spicy carrot and parsnip soup (see this page). All vegetable soups may be garnished with herb croûtons (see page 169)

Spinach and Roquefort salad

Although spinach salads were enjoyed widely in Tudor times they went out of fashion for three centuries. However, they are now reappearing on the menus of restaurants in the United States and Europe and have become a feature of the *nouvelle cuisine*, served with slices of hard-boiled egg or sliced *foie gras*. Our salad is simpler although you can add sliced or chopped egg if you wish. Raw spinach is rich in iron, calcium and vitamin C and so well worth eating from a health point of view. Crisp and delicious, it bears little resemblance to the soggy green mess which many people could not bear to eat in their schooldays. In winter, you can even serve the salad warm for an unusual variation. Just chop and fry the bacon and mix into the salad. Add the oil and 15ml/1tablespoon vinegar to the pan juices and when hot, toss the salad quickly in this dressing.

450/1lb young spinach leaves
100g/4oz button mushrooms, sliced
5 rashers smoked streaky bacon
50g/2oz Roquefort (or other blue cheese), crumbled
Dressing:
45ml/3 tablespoons olive oil
juice of 1 lemon
5ml/1 teaspoon sugar
salt and pepper

Wash the spinach and remove the tough stalks. Place in a salad bowl with the sliced mushrooms. Grill the bacon until crisp. Cool and crumble over the salad. Sprinkle with the crumbled Roquefort. Mix the dressing and gently toss the salad. Serve as a first course or with grilled fish.
Serves 4

Cucumber chartreuse

This savoury green jelly ring always goes down well at parties, and because it is essentially a buffet-type dish we have given quantities for about 12 people. It is a stunning centrepiece for a party-style table. An equally attractive and delicious jellied beetroot ring can be made using the same method. Just substitute raspberry jelly tablets for lime, red wine vinegar for cider vinegar, and 450g/1lb diced, cooked beetroot for cucumber. Prepare in the same way and fill the centre with a mixture of whipped soured cream and horseradish sauce. Both recipes were devised by a Dutch friend of ours — Anna Le Cornu.

275g/10oz lime jelly/jello tablets
hot water
300ml/½ pint/1¼ cups cider vinegar
15ml/1 tablespoon caster/superfine sugar
few drops of green vegetable colouring
450g/1lb cucumber, peeled and diced
small cherry tomatoes to garnish

Separate the lime jelly tablets into cubes and place in a large measuring jug. Pour in hot water to the 900ml/1½ pint/3½cup mark. Stir gently until the jelly cubes dissolve. Add the vinegar, sugar and food colouring and leave to cool until the mixture has the consistency of unbeaten egg white.

Fold in the diced cucumber and when it is evenly suspended throughout the jelly, pour the mixture into a 1.8 litre/3 pint/7½ cup ring jelly mould. Leave in a cool place until set. Turn the jelly out onto an attractive serving plate and fill the centre with cherry tomatoes.
Serves 12

Californian avocado salad

This, our favourite salad, is always served by our Californian friends. They were given the recipe by film star Laurence Harvey's chef and made their own additions and variations to create a really unusual salad which can be served as a first course or with quiches, cold meat and fish. Any crisp lettuce is suitable — the American romaine and red leafed lettuces are ideal, but Webbs, cos or curly endive are equally good. Always prepare the salad and toss it in the dressing *immediately* before serving to enjoy it at its best, or it will go limp and soggy.

1 crisp lettuce (romaine, iceberg, Webbs, cos etc)
1 carrot
1 red pepper
1 green pepper
1 stick of celery
1 courgette/zucchini
2 tomatoes
50g/2oz button mushrooms (optional)
2 rashers grilled crispy bacon
salt and freshly ground black pepper
1 avocado
100ml/4floz/½ cup French dressing
1-2 cloves garlic, crushed

Wash all the vegetables and salad stuff thoroughly and dry in a salad spinner or on absorbent kitchen paper. Discard the outer leaves of the lettuce and shred the remaining leaves coarsely into a large salad bowl. Peel and top and tail the carrot, and, using a potato peeler or coarse grater, grate the carrot into the bowl with the lettuce. Seed and dice the peppers, chop the celery and cut the tomatoes into small pieces. Mix with the other salad stuff in the bowl. Top and tail the courgette/ zucchini and peel off thin strips of skin to get a striped green and white effect outside. Slice thinly and horizontally into the salad bowl. Slice the mushrooms thinly and crumble the crisp grilled bacon rashers. Mix with the rest of the salad.

Add a little salt and plenty of freshly ground black pepper. Halve and stone the avocado and scoop out the flesh into a dish. Mix well with a fork and gradually mix in the French dressing and crushed garlic until you have a pale green puréed sauce. Toss the salad in the avocado dressing and serve immediately. For a more tangy flavour, add a little lemon juice.

Serves 4

Watercress and orange salad

This refreshing, fruity salad makes a colourful accompaniment to cold fish and meats or a vegetable quiche. The faintly bitter watercress sets off the sweetness of the orange.

2 bunches watercress
2 large oranges
2 spring onions, chopped
few black olives
30ml/2 tablespoons flaked almonds
chopped chives
Dressing:
45ml/3 tablespoons olive oil
juice 1 orange
salt and pepper

Wash the watercress and remove any thick, woody stalks. Arrange on a flat serving dish. Remove the peel and the rind from the oranges and slice thinly horizontally. Arrange the orange slices overlapping each other in a ring on top of the watercress with the spring onion and olives in the centre.

Mix and season the dressing and pour over the salad. Sprinkle with flaked almonds and chopped chives.
Serves 4

Red cabbage coleslaw

You can make a colourful, unusual coleslaw by substituting red for white cabbage. The whole chopping and grating operation can be performed very simply and quickly if you have an electric food processor. Otherwise, you will have to persevere by hand.

225g/8oz red cabbage, finely shredded
3 sticks of celery, chopped
1 small onion, finely chopped
1 carrot, grated
2 dessert apples, peeled, cored and diced
50g/2oz/½ cup chopped walnuts
30ml/2 tablespoons chopped parsley
Dressing:
50ml/2floz/¼ cup mayonnaise
50ml/2floz/¼ cup natural yoghurt
salt and pepper
juice of ½ lemon
1 clove garlic, crushed (optional)

Mix the prepared vegetables, apple and nuts together in a large bowl. Mix the dressing ingredients until well blended and toss the coleslaw. Sprinkle with chopped parsley and serve. This will keep well for several days in an airtight container in the refrigerator.

Serves 4

Chicory and hazelnut salad

Chicory is the perfect vegetable for crunchy winter salads. You can mix it with nuts, diced cheese, cubed cooked potato, hard-boiled egg, left-over Christmas poultry or smoked sausage in a creamy mayonnaise — delicious! Try this lighter, more refreshing mixture of chicory, nuts and orange in a yoghurt-based dressing.

2 heads of chicory/Belgian endive
50g/2oz button mushrooms, sliced
25g/1oz/⅓ cup roughly chopped hazelnuts
1 orange
chopped chives
Dressing:
juice of 1 lemon
75ml/3floz/⅜ cup natural yoghurt
salt and pepper
30ml/2 tablespoons finely ground hazelnuts

Cut off the base of the chicory, and separate and wash the leaves. Drain well and mix with the mushrooms and hazelnuts in a salad bowl or serving dish.

Make the dressing and pour over the chicory salad. Top with overlapping slices of orange (peel and pith removed) and scatter with chopped chives.
Serves 4

Hot vegetable dishes

Chicory au gratin

You have probably eaten raw chicory many times in salads but have you ever thought of cooking it? Chicory heads, wrapped in thin slices of ham and served in a bubbling cheese sauce, make a warming supper dish or first course. Known as chicory in Britain, as *endive* in France and as Belgian endive in the United States, chicory has a slightly bitter flavour which marries well with creamy sauces. You can substitute young leeks for chicory in this dish.

8 heads of chicory
juice of ½ lemon
10ml/2 teaspoons sugar
8 thin slices of ham
25g/1oz/2 tablespoons butter
25g/1oz/3 tablespoons flour
300ml/½pint/1¼cups milk (fresh or skimmed)
5ml/1 teaspoon Dijon mustard
salt and pepper
good pinch of ground nutmeg
100g/4oz/1 cup grated Gruyère/Swiss cheese
45ml/3 tablespoons fresh wholemeal breadcrumbs

Pop the chicory into boiling water with the lemon juice and sugar for about 10 minutes. Drain and set aside.

Make a white sauce: melt the butter in a pan, stir in the flour and cook for 3 minutes. Beat in the milk, a little at a time, over a gentle heat, and bring to the boil, stirring all the time to prevent lumps forming. When the sauce is thick, glossy and smooth, reduce the heat to a bare simmer and stir in the mustard, seasoning and nutmeg. Add most of the cheese, reserving a little for the top of the dish. Cook for a few minutes.

Make sure that each chicory is thoroughly dry (or it will make the sauce watery) and wrap in a slice of ham. Arrange in a buttered gratin dish and pour over the sauce. Sprinkle with the reserved cheese and breadcrumbs and bake in a preheated oven at 200°C, 400°F, gas 6 for 25 minutes until golden and bubbling. Serve immediately.

Serves 4.

Melanzane alla parmigiana

Layers of aubergine/eggplant, tomato sauce and Mozzarella cheese go into this appetising baked dish from Naples in southern Italy. It makes a delicious supper dish or a tasty first course if you are planning an Italian meal. Although it is eaten throughout Italy, nowhere does it taste better than eaten in a backstreet Neapolitan *ristorante* or *rosticceria*. However, using good quality Mozzarella cheese (not the many imitations that exist but the real cheese dripping with buttermilk.

1 aubergine/eggplant, thinly sliced
salt
30ml/2 tablespoons flour
45ml/3 tablespoons olive oil
175g/6oz Mozzarella cheese, thinly sliced
45ml/3 tablespoons Parmesan cheese, grated
1 small egg, beaten
Tomato sauce:
30ml/2 tablespoons olive oil
1 onion, chopped
450g/1lb canned tomatoes
15ml/1 tablespoon tomato paste
5ml/1 teaspoon sugar
30ml/2 tablespoons Marsala
2.5ml/½ teaspoon basil or oregano
salt and pepper
30ml/2 tablespoons pine nuts

Sprinkle the aubergine/eggplant slices with plenty of salt and leave them for about an hour to drain off excess moisture. Rinse and dry them and dust with flour. Fry them in the oil over medium to high heat until crisp and well-browned. Drain and keep warm.

Meanwhile, make the tomato sauce: sauté the onion in the oil, and add the tomatoes, tomato paste, sugar, Marsala, herbs and seasoning. Bring to the boil and reduce the heat to a simmer. Add the pine nuts and cook gently for 20-30 minutes until the sauce is thick.

Place a layer of aubergine/eggplant across the base of a buttered ovenproof dish, then a layer of tomato sauce and a layer of thinly sliced Mozzarella. Brush with beaten egg and sprinkle lightly with Parmesan. Continue building up the layers in this way until all the sauce, cheese and aubergine slices are used up. Finish with a layer of aubergine/eggplant, sprinkle with the remaining Parmesan and dot the top with a little butter.

Bake in a preheated oven at 190°C, 375°F, gas 5 for about 30-40 minutes until golden-brown, crisp and bubbling. Allow to cool a little before eating.

Opposite: crisp salads reading clockwise: American mozzarella salad (see page 74), watercress and orange salad (see page 135), Caesar salad (see page 132) and spinach and Roquefort salad (see page 134)

Carrots in orange juice

The major nutritional reason for eating carrots is their high vitamin A content. Cooked simply and flavoured with orange juice, they make a delicious accompaniment to most meat and chicken dishes. Use young tender carrots which are sweeter than the older, woody roots if you can get hold of them.

1kg/2lb carrots
15g/½oz/1 tablespoon butter
30ml/2 tablespoons flour
22.5ml/1½ tablespoons single/light cream or yoghurt
30ml/2 tablespoons chopped parsley
pinch of ground nutmeg
freshly ground black pepper
juice of ½ orange

Peel or scrape the carrots and slice thinly (this is quickly and neatly done in a food processor if you have one). Place them in a small pan and cover with salted water. Cook until tender but not mushy.

Blend the butter and flour together to make a *beurre manié* and add the cream, parsley and nutmeg. Drain the carrots, reserving 100ml/4floz/½ cup water, and add the reserved cooking liquid to the cream mixture. Place in a pan and bring to the boil, add the cooked carrots and orange juice and turn out onto a serving dish. Season with freshly ground black pepper. Scatter a little chopped parsley over the top and serve.
Serves 4

Carrot purée

Puréed vegetable dishes are among the most welcome features of the new style of cookery. Carrot purée is probably the most beautiful and flavoursome of all and goes well with grilled meat and fish, kebabs and many roasts and pies.

450g/1lb carrots
5ml/1 teaspoon brown sugar
15g/½oz/1 tablespoon margarine
30ml/2 tablespoons single/light cream or yoghurt
salt and pepper
good pinch nutmeg
chopped parsley (optional)

Peel or scrape the carrots and slice thinly. Cook in salted water with the brown sugar until tender, and drain. Place the carrots with the remaining ingredients in a blender or food processor and reduce to a smooth purée. Alternatively, sieve the carrots and mix in the other ingredients. Reheat until hot and serve, sprinkled with parsley if wished. The carrot purée can be made ahead of the meal and reheated at the last minute, or frozen until needed.
Serves 4

Baby marrows in lemon sauce

This is an economical, slimming recipe which you can make with young marrows or courgettes/zucchini. It is simple and quick to prepare and makes a tasty snack meal or accompaniment to a main course. If you do not have Swiss Gruyère cheese, use Cheddar or any hard cheese.

450g/1lb baby marrows
juice of ½ lemon
100ml/4floz/½ cup water
salt and pepper
15g/½oz/2 tablespoons grated Gruyère/Swiss cheese
Sauce:
22.5ml/1½ tablespoons cornflour/cornstarch
75ml/3floz/⅜ cup milk
15g/½oz/2 tablespoons grated Gruyère/Swiss cheese
salt and black pepper

Peel the marrows and remove the pulpy centres. Cut into large dice and place in a pan with the lemon juice, water and seasoning. Simmer for 6-8 minutes until tender but firm. Drain the marrows, reserving the cooking liquor.

Blend the cornflour with 15ml/1 tablespoon of the milk. Add the remaining milk and stir gently over a low heat until the sauce thickens. Beat in the marrow cooking liquor and season to taste. Add more lemon juice if wished for a more tangy flavour. Stir in the cheese. Pour over the cooked marrows, sprinkle the remaining cheese on top and flash under a hot grill until golden-brown and bubbling. Serve hot.
Serves 2

Tian de courgettes

This delicious vegetable gratin takes its name from the shallow dish in which it is baked. *Tians* are a speciality of Provence in southern France. They are made with many vegetables, including onions, aubergines and courgettes/zucchini. We have chosen this recipe because of its fine flavour and attractive appearance — overlapping layers like fish scales of creamy-green courgettes and red tomatoes peeping through a golden breadcrumb and cheese crust.

450g/1lb courgettes/zucchini
salt
30ml/2 tablespoons olive oil
2 onions, thinly sliced
½ red pepper, seeded and sliced in rings
½ green pepper, seeded and sliced in rings
1 clove garlic, crushed
450g/1lb tomatoes, thinly sliced
5ml/1 teaspoon sugar
2.5ml/½ teaspoon each basil and oregano
salt and pepper
olive oil to trickle over the tian
45ml/3 tablespoons fresh breadcrumbs
45ml/3 tablespoons grated Parmesan cheese

Wash and dry the courgettes/zucchini, and slice them thinly. Sprinkle with plenty of salt and leave for 30 minutes to drain them of excess moisture. Rinse in fresh water, drain and dry pat.

Heat the oil in a heavy pan and sauté the onion, pepper and garlic until soft and slightly browned. Sprinkle the tomatoes with the sugar. Butter a shallow gratin or *tian* dish and cover the base with the onion and pepper sautéed mixture. Arrange the sliced courgettes/zucchini and the tomato slices in overlapping layers across the dish widthways (a row of courgettes, a row of tomatoes, a row of courgettes etc) until all the mixture is used up. Sprinkle generously with herbs and season well. Dribble over a little olive oil and bake in a preheated oven at 180°C, 350°F, gas 4. After 30 minutes, remove the dish from the oven and sprinkle with breadcrumbs and cheese. Trickle a little more oil over the top and replace in the oven for another 15-20 minutes until the top is crisp and golden-brown. Serve hot or cold.

Serves 4

Cider-baked onions

Perhaps the best way to enjoy onions is to bake them whole and serve with a roast joint. Baked in cider, they are very sweet and tender and a beautiful golden colour.

4 large onions
good pinch of salt
400ml/14floz/1¾ cups medium-sweet cider

Peel and wash the onions and place in a saucepan. Cover with salted water, and boil for 45 minutes. Drain.

Place the onions in a large ovenproof dish. Pour in the cider and cover the dish with foil or a lid. Bake in a preheated oven at 180°C, 350°F, gas 4 for 1½ hours. Then remove the cover and cook for a further 15 minutes. Drain and serve. Any remaining cider and onion juices can be used to flavour the gravy or sauce that is to be served with the meat.

Serves 4

Savoy onion tart

Savoury cheese custard tarts are very popular throughout France and particularly delicious when hot, puffed-up and golden-brown. This onion tart, flavoured with white wine and Gruyère/Swiss cheese, hails from the mountainous *département* of Haute-Savoie. It makes a light supper dish or an appetising first course.

4 onions, thinly sliced in rings
30ml/2 tablespoons margarine
5ml/1 teaspoon sugar
pinch of salt
freshly ground black pepper
100ml/4floz/½ cup white wine
3 eggs, beaten
50ml/2floz/¼ cup single/light cream
100ml/4floz/½ cup milk
30ml/2 tablespoons grated Gruyère/Swiss cheese
pinch grated nutmeg
For the pastry case:
225g/8oz/2 cups wholewheat flour
100g/4oz/½ cup margarine
pinch of cinnamon
30ml/2 tablespoons grated Gruyère/Swiss cheese
pinch of salt
45ml/3 tablespoons water

Make the shortcrust pastry in the usual way and place the dough in a polythene bag in the refrigerator or a cool place for 30 minutes to rest, before rolling out to line a 20cm/8in flan case.

Sauté the onion rings gently in the fat over very low heat in a covered pan until they soften and start to 'melt'. Keep an eye on the pan to make sure the onions don't brown or stick to the base. Stir in the sugar, seasoning and wine and remove from the heat.

Whisk the egg, cream and milk until creamy and add the cheese and nutmeg. Stir into the onion mixture and pour into the prepared pastry flan case. Bake in a preheated oven at 190°C, 375°, gas 5 until the filling is well-risen, set and golden-brown. Serve hot or cold.

Serves 4

Fried potato skins

This dish of crisp-fried potato skins with a soured cream and chives dip is popular as a first course in the United States. It is easy to make and a good way of using up the skins from baked jacket potatoes. If you are baking potatoes specially for this dish, do not waste the soft floury potato inside. Purée it for future use.

6 large potatoes
oil for shallow-frying
150ml/¼ pint/⅝ cup thick soured cream
150ml/¼ pint/⅝ cup thick natural yoghurt
salt and pepper
chopped chives to garnish

Wash and scrub the potatoes thoroughly and cut out any blemishes. Pierce each potato with a skewer or fork 2 or 3 times and bake in a preheated oven at 200°C, 400°F, gas 6 for about 1¼-1½ hours, or until the potato skins are crisp and the insides are soft and floury. Cool thoroughly.

   Cut each potato in half and scoop out most of the pulp. Shallow-fry the potato skins in hot oil until crisp and golden-brown around the edges. Drain and pat dry with absorbent kitchen paper. Serve immediately with a bowl of mixed soured cream and yoghurt sprinkled with plenty of chopped chives.

Serves 4

Pumpkin au gratin

Huge golden, yellow and orange pumpkins are one of the culinary delights of autumn, and we always look forward to their appearance in the shops and markets in September. Popular in France, the United States and Latin America, pumpkin is a much under-rated vegetable in Great Britain, which is a pity because it has a subtly delicate flavour and makes excellent soups, sweet pies and savoury dishes. It can also be used to thicken meat and vegetable stews — no need for flour if you add plenty of cubed pumpkin. This recipe comes from south-western France and makes a tasty supper dish on chilly autumn evenings.

1kg/2lb pumpkin
1 onion, chopped
1 clove garlic, crushed
4 rashers smoked streaky bacon, chopped
30ml/2 tablespoons oil
450g/1lb tomatoes, skinned or chopped (or canned)
225g/8oz sweetcorn kernels (fresh or canned)

50ml/2 floz/¼ cup red wine
salt and pepper
5ml/1 teaspoon sugar
good pinch each of ground nutmeg and cinnamon
45ml/3 tablespoons fresh wholemeal breadcrumbs
45ml/3 tablespoons grated Parmesan
butter or oil

Cut the pumpkin into thin slices, discarding the outer peel, pulp and seeds. Boil in salted water until tender and drain. Put aside to cool.

   Sauté the chopped onion, garlic and bacon in the oil until soft and cooked. Add the tomatoes, corn kernels, wine, seasoning and sugar. Bring to the boil, then reduce the heat and simmer until the mixture is reduced and thickened.

   Butter a shallow gratin dish and arrange a layer of cooked pumpkin in the bottom. Sprinkle with spices and cover with layers of the tomato mixture and then the remaining pumpkin. Scatter the breadcrumbs and Parmesan over the top and dot with butter or dribble over some oil. Bake in a preheated oven at 180°C, 350°F, gas 4 for 35 - 40 minutes until it is cooked, bubbling and golden. Serve hot with a green salad.

Serves 4

Red cabbage casserole

Red cabbage is delicious when casseroled with apples in the German manner and served with game, Toulouse or German sausages, or beef. Magnificently coloured and faintly spicy, it is a warming winter dish. The cabbage should never be cooked to a mush as many people mistakenly do — it should be tender but still firm and slightly crisp.

550g/1¼lb red cabbage
25g/1oz/2 tablespoons butter
1 large onion, chopped
2 cooking apples, peeled, cored and sliced
pinch each of ground cinnamon, allspice and nutmeg
salt and pepper
30ml/2 tablespoons brown sugar
100ml/4 floz/½ cup red wine
15ml/1 tablespoon red wine vinegar

Remove and discard the outer leaves of the cabbage and cut out the central hard stalk. Shred, wash and drain the cabbage leaves. Heat the butter in a flameproof casserole dish, add the shredded cabbage, onion and apple and cook gently for 5 minutes until the onion is tender. Add the remaining ingredients and cover.

Bake in a preheated oven at 190°C, 375°F, gas 5 for about 1 hour until the cabbage is tender. It will turn the most beautiful rich, red Burgundy colour.
Serves 4

Cider-baked parsnips

Parsnips are a much under-rated root vegetable these days but are incomparable in the vegetable world for their natural sweetness and distinctive flavour. In the Middle Ages they were regarded as an aphrodisiac and thus were widely eaten.

4 parsnips
550ml/1 pint/2½ cups salted water
300ml/½ pint/1¼ cups medium-sweet cider

Trim and peel the parsnips and cut each into 4 pieces lengthways. Place them in a pan with the salted water and bring to the boil. Boil for 15 minutes and drain.

Transfer the parsnips to an ovenproof dish, cover with cider and bake for about 1 hour until tender and golden. Serve with roast meat or poultry.
Serves 4-6

Parsnip puffs

If you sometimes get bored with boiled or roast parsnips then try this recipe for parsnip puffs, crisp and golden on the outside and sweet and soft inside. Serve them with grilled fish or chicken. Vary the flavour and texture by adding chopped walnuts or almonds.

450g/1lb parsnips
50g/2oz/1 cup fresh wholemeal breadcrumbs
juice of ½ orange
15ml/1 tablespoon sherry
1 egg yolk
salt and pepper
good pinch of ground nutmeg
2 egg whites, beaten stiffly
30ml/2 tablespoons oil

Peel the parsnips and cut each into 4 pieces. Cook in boiling salted water until soft. Drain and then mash or process to a smooth purée. Mix in the breadcrumbs, orange juice, sherry, egg yolk and seasoning. Fold in the beaten egg white gently and form the mixture into small flat cakes, about 5cm/2in in diameter.

Heat the oil in a frying pan/skillet and fry the parsnip puffs until golden-brown. Serve immediately.
serves 4

Vegetable pie

Vegetable pie makes an economical and tasty family meal. We have chosen vegetables for their contrasting textures and colours, but you can vary the filling.
Pastry:
100g/4oz/½ cup margarine
50ml/2floz/¼ cup water
225g/8oz/2¼ cups wholemeal flour
15ml/1 tablespoon grated Parmesan cheese
2.5ml/½ teaspoon dry mustard
Filling:
1 small onion, chopped
1 clove garlic, crushed
2 small carrots, diced
1 parsnip, diced
1 leek, finely shredded
2 tomatoes, skinned and sliced
½ red pepper, seeded and diced
½ green pepper, seeded and diced
2 courgettes/zucchini, thinly sliced
50g/2oz button mushrooms, thinly sliced
1.25ml/¼ teaspoon basil and thyme
2.5ml/½ teaspoon chopped parsley
2 large eggs
150ml/¼ pint/⅝ cup milk
salt and pepper
50g/2oz/½ cup grated Gruyère/Swiss cheese
beaten egg to glaze

Make the pastry: place the fat and water in a mixing bowl with 15ml/1 tablespoon of the flour. Mix well and then gradually blend in the remaining flour, cheese and mustard to form a soft dough. Knead on a lightly floured board and then rest in the refrigerator for 15 minutes. Roll out half the dough to line a 20cm/8in flan case. Prick the base with a fork, fill with paper and baking beans and bake 'blind' in a preheated oven at 200°C, 400°F, gas 6 for 10 minutes. Remove the beans and paper and bake for a further 5 minutes until the pastry is dry. Remove and cool.

Fill the pie with the prepared vegetables and herbs. Beat the eggs and milk together with the seasoning and pour into the pie. Sprinkle with grated cheese and cover with the remaining dough. Seal the edges and brush with beaten egg. Decorate with pastry leaves made from the trimmings and make a small hole in the centre at the top. Bake in a preheated oven at 200°C, 400°F, gas 6 for 5 minutes, and then reduce the temperature to 180°C, 350°F, gas 4 for a further 50 minutes, until cooked and golden-brown.

Serves 4-5

Fruit

We can enjoy a wide range of fresh fruit all the year round now thanks to better and quicker transportation. Citrus fruits and many exotic, tropical fruits, such as bananas, pineapples and mangoes, are available most months of the year, although there are literally hundreds of fruits which never arrive in the shops, especially those from hot climates that do not travel successfully. However, one of the delights of a natural, healthy diet is eating the new fruits as they come into season – the first strawberries of summer, blackberries in the autumn, colourful, glowing tangerines at Christmas-time, and gooseberries in the late spring. Summer, of course, is the highlight of the year for all fruit-lovers for this is when the fruit stalls and window displays are a blaze of colour with exciting fruits of all flavours and textures – blushing golden-pink peaches and nectarines, bunches of ripe cherries, greengages, black and red currants, velvety plums and damsons.

Despite this abundance of fruit and its relative cheapness, most people eat very little of it, often preferring stodgy, fattening cakes and puddings to a fresh fruit snack or dessert. In Britain alone, the average person eats only 675g/1½lb of fruit per week. Yet fresh fruit is slimming, healthy, a good source of vitamins and one of the most delicious ways of ending a meal, either on its own or with cheese. It is so versatile that it can be baked, stewed, puréed, poached, made into fresh fruit salads, pie fillings, sorbets, mousses and soufflés.

Orchard fruits

Orchard fruits, or top fruit, refers to the tree fruits – apples, pears, peaches, apricots, nectarines, plums, greengages, damsons and cherries. Many of these fruits, particularly the softer stone/pit fruits, such as plums, and peaches, do not keep well once picked and should be eaten within a few days of purchase. There are many varieties, especially in the case of apples, and they are all suitable for eating or cooking, as well as preserving in jams, jellies and chutneys.

Soft fruits and berry fruits

Most soft fruits are seasonal, appearing only in the summer, although strawberries are imported and on sale at a high price at other times of the year in specialist shops. These imported fruits often lack the sweetness and flavour of home–grown seasonal fruit and may be watery in texture. Most soft fruits are best consumed on the day of purchase and should be picked over carefully before cooking or serving for damaged or mouldy berries. This is particularly true in the case of juicy raspberries and strawberries which often become mushy.

Citrus fruits

Citrus fruits are available throughout the year and are grown around the Mediterranean, and in the warm climates of South Africa, Israel and California. They include oranges, limes, lemons, grapefruit, tangerines, satsumas, clementines, kumquats and uglis, a cross between a grapefruit and a tangerine. They store well kept in a cool place and are rich in vitamin C. Eat them peeled and segmented or squeezed for their juice, or cook with them. They can be used to flavour both sweet and savoury dishes. Always wash them thoroughly if you are using the rind, as this is sometimes waxed and dyed to improve their appearance.

Exotic fruits

These are the colourful fruits from the tropics, many of which were unheard of until the discovery of the Americas at the end of the fifteenth century. Bananas, pineapples and melons are now available in most fruiterers and supermarkets, as are papayas, mangoes, passion fruit, dates and kiwi fruit. Other fruit to watch out for are persimmons, pomegranates and figs, which have been eaten since ancient times.

Dried fruits

The best of these are dried in the traditional way in the natural warmth of the sun. This way of preserving fruit has been practised since ancient times when the biblical King David demanded raisins instead of taxes. Although many fruits, including apples, bananas, pears and peaches, are now available in a dried form, the oldest dried fruits were Mediterranean crops of figs, dates and grapes. There is more concentrated natural goodness in dried than in fresh fruits, as they are rich in minerals (iron, calcium, phosphorus and potassium) and in the A and B group vitamins, particularly niacin and sometimes thiamine and riboflavin. They are high in protein and fibre and this gives them a gentle laxative effect. Always buy unsprayed dried fruits in reputable health food stores. Many are now dipped in potassium carbonate solution or sprayed with mineral oil or liquid paraffin to prevent the fruit sticking together and to give a glossy, luscious appearance. If the dried fruits are not guaranteed sun-dried, oil-free and unsprayed, wash them in hot water and dry before using.

Dried apricots were first cultivated in China and later spread to the Middle East where they are a favourite ingredient in dried fruit salads, meat tagines and savoury stuffings for meat and poultry. The wild ones from Afghanistan have the best flavour although they look darker and more withered than other varieties. They contain more protein than other dried fruits and are rich in iron, calcium, and B vitamins.

Currants are the dried tiny Corinth grapes which were first grown in Greece. They are small, hard and black and used mostly in baking fruit cakes and puddings, but are also good in pilaffs and rice stuffings. They are a good source of minerals and vitamins A1 and B1.

Dates were first cultivated in the river valley civilisations around the Tigris and Euphrates rivers about 5000BC. They have more natural sugar than other dried fruits and are rich in protein, minerals and vitamins.

Prunes are dried plums of which the large, moist Californian varieties are probably the best. They can be added to many fish and chicken dishes, North African tagines and stuffings, desserts and cheesecakes.

Raisins were advocated by the Greek physician Hippocrates as a preventive measure against fever and jaundice. Nowadays, raisins, the dried fruit of the muscat grape vine, are mixed into muesli, cakes, breads, stuffings and rice pilaffs.

Sultanas are the fruit of the seedless sultana grape vine, hence their name of seedless raisins in the United States. Sweeter than currants and raisins, they are also used in baking and are high in minerals and vitamin A.

Choosing and storing fruits

Always choose firm, undamaged fruit and avoid any with bruising, blemishes or soft patches. All fruit should look healthy with shining skin, and the best way to buy is to handle it yourself first. This is now possible in many supermarkets and self-serve greengrocers where you can pick out your own, but it is frowned upon at market stalls and many fruit shops where you are asked not to touch and the goods are often produced from behind the counter or the back of the shop and whisked away into a bag before you even see it. Some fruit is almost invisible in its mesh netting or polythene wrappings and it is impossible to detect any blemishes and judge its quality accurately. And then there are the fruits, particularly citrus fruits, that look perfectly good and appetising on the outside but are dry and lacking in flavour when you peel them. Citrus fruits should always feel heavy in your hand and have an oily, fresh-looking skin without any dry patches or wrinkles.

It is often a good idea to buy fruit slightly under-ripe and allow it to ripen at home. This takes 2-3 days at most and then you can eat it at its best. When there is a glut of fruit on the market, some may be sold off cheaply in large boxes and it is more economical to buy in bulk. Make it into jams and preserves or split the cost with a friend or neighbour to use it up. If you have your own apple or pear trees, the fruit can be puréed or sliced and frozen, or stored in an airy frost-free attic or garage, wrapped individually in newspaper and spaced out in slatted wooden trays or boxes.

Preparing fruits

Always thoroughly wash and dry fruits, with the exception of some soft fruits, before eating or cooking, as many are sprayed with insecticides. This will not be necessary if you grow your own organically. Raspberries and blackberries may lose their velvety bloom and downy texture if washed, but they should always be picked over like other soft fruit berries (strawberries, loganberries, blueberries and red and black currants) for any mouldy berries. Remove any leaves, stalks, stems or prickles before cooking or serving. Some fruit, such as apples and bananas, discolour easily and must be sprinkled with lemon juice to retain the fresh white colouring, before adding to tarts and salads.

Apricot soup

This delicious, delicately flavoured and coloured fruit soup can be eaten hot or cold at any time of the year, topped with a swirl of yoghurt or soured cream, and toasted almonds. Fruit soups are very popular in the Balkans — Hungary, Greece and Rumania. They are refreshing if served chilled on a hot summer's day, and warming in winter. Any white cooking wine will do although a Riesling or a Hungarian medium-dry Tokay will produce the best and most authentic result.

100g/4oz/¾ cup dried apricots
150ml/¼ pint/⅝ cup white wine
pinch each of ground allspice and cinnamon
550ml/1 pint/2½ cups water
15ml/1 tablespoon honey
salt and pepper
1 egg yolk, beaten
150ml/¼ pint/⅝ cup natural yoghurt or soured cream
30ml/2 tablespoons toasted flaked almonds

Soak the apricots for about 3 hours. Stew them in the wine and spices for about 1½ hours over a low heat until soft. Strain into a clean pan and add the water, honey and seasoning. Bring to the boil and then sieve or liquidise the soup.

Replace in the pan and gently stir in the beaten egg yolk over very low heat. On no account allow the soup to boil or it will curdle. When the soup thickens stir in the yoghurt. Serve warm or chilled topped with a swirl of soured cream or yoghurt and sprinkled generously with toasted almonds.

Serves 4

Savoury stuffed peaches

Peaches can be halved and sandwiched together with a savoury filling to make an unusual first course. In the summer months when there is a glut of cheap peaches on the market, one is continually looking for new ways of serving them and this is particularly good.

4 large peaches
150g/5oz lean, cooked ham
25g/1oz/2 tablespoons margarine
pinch of paprika
freshly ground black pepper
30ml/2 tablespoons natural yoghurt
5ml/1 teaspoon sherry
15ml/1 tablespoon chopped parsley

Wash and dry the peaches, split them in half and remove the stones/pits. Scoop out a *little* of the flesh to make a hollow cavity for the filling.

Purée or liquidise the ham, margarine, seasoning, yoghurt and sherry until thick and smooth. Mix in the reserved peach flesh and chopped parsley. Season to taste — you will most probably find that it is sufficiently salty without adding more. Pipe the purée, using a star nozzle, into the peaches and sandwich the peach halves together. Serve on a bed of lettuce leaves.

Serves 4

Grapefruit and avocado salad

This summer salad is light and refreshing on a hot day. You can add cooked shellfish (lobster, crab or prawns) if you wish to make it more filling and wholesome but it makes an adequate first course on its own.

2 Texas pink grapefruits
3 oranges
5ml/1 teaspoon sugar
bunch watercress or 2 heads of chicory
15ml/1 tablespoon chopped chives
Dressing:
1 avocado, halved and stoned
juice of ½ lemon
30ml/2 tablespoons chopped onion
2.5ml/½ teaspoon Dijon mustard
salt and pepper
pinch cayenne pepper
15ml/1 tablespoon natural yoghurt or mayonnaise

Peel the grapefruits and oranges, removing all the white pith and separate into segments, discarding the segment skins. Sprinkle with sugar and leave in a cool place (do not chill in the refrigerator).

Make the dressing: place all the ingredients in a blender or food processor and blend until smooth and creamy. Cover and chill for at least 30 minutes but not more than 1 hour or the dressing may start to brown.

Arrange the fruit segments on a bed of watercress or chicory leaves, top with the dressing and sprinkle with chopped chives, or you can divide the salad between individual serving dishes.

Serves 4

Opposite: some mouth-watering fruit desserts, reading clockwise: caramel oranges from Italy (see page 152), khoshaf, a Middle Eastern dried fruit salad (see page 154), a healthy fresh fruit salad (see page 155) and softly whipped apple snow (see page 146). They are all fresh and light — the perfect way to finish a meal

Baked apples with blackberries

Soft, fluffy baked apples are a delicious way of using up a surplus of Bramley cooking apples in the autumn. We have used blackberries, another autumn fruit, to stuff the apples, but you can try such combinations as chopped dates and nuts and honey, or just dark brown sugar, cinnamon and raisins. Blackberries are fun to harvest in country lanes and hedgerows, but never pick any that grow along the verges of busy roads as they may have a high lead content. To make dumplings, just peel the apples, fill in the same way and wrap up in shortcrust or puff pastry, making a small hole in the top through which the steam can escape.

4 large cooking/green apples
60ml/4 tablespoons soft brown sugar
60ml/4 tablespoons blackberries
60ml/4 tablespoons dark rum
25g/1oz/2 tablespoons butter

Core the apples and make a slit around the middle of each apple horizontally. This will allow the apple to puff up attractively in the oven. Place the apples in a baking dish and fill the centre of each with the sugar and blackberries. Pour a tablespoon of rum over each apple and top with a knob of butter.

Bake in a preheated oven at 200°C, 400°F, gas 6 for about 30 minutes. Serve with cream or fruit yoghurt or some fresh blackberry purée.

Serves 4

Apple snow

Fresh and light, this fruity dessert is a good way to round off a rich, filling meal. You can make it an attractive pale green colour if you wish by adding a few drops of green vegetable food colouring. Don't waste the yolks when you separate the eggs for this recipe. Instead, put them aside to make a gougère with a delicious seafood or vegetable filling (see recipe on page 75).

675g/1½lb cooking apples
good piece of lemon rind
45ml/3 tablespoons water
15ml/1 tablespoon Calvados
3 egg whites
100g/4oz/½ cup caster sugar
15ml/1 tablespoon nibbed almonds

Peel, core and slice the cooking apples. Cook gently over a very low heat with the lemon rind, water and Calvados until soft and pulpy. Remove the lemon rind, and liquidise or sieve the apple mixture when cool.

Whip the egg whites until stiff with the sugar and stir gently into the apple purée. Place in a serving dish, top with almonds and chill before serving.
Serves 4

Dorset apple cake

Moist, spicy apple cakes are the speciality of the English county of Dorset and are eaten spread with butter at tea-time. This version has a crunchy nut topping.

175g/6oz/¾ cup margarine
150g/5oz/⅔ cup soft brown Muscovado sugar
3 eggs
15ml/1 tablespoon honey
25g/1oz/⅓ cup bran
50g/2oz/½ cup chopped walnuts
2.5ml/½ teaspoon each of ground cinnamon and cloves
75g/3oz/½ cup raisins
225g/8oz grated apple
175g/6oz/1¾ cups wholemeal flour
2.5ml/½ teaspoon bicarbonate of soda/baking soda
7.5ml/1½ teaspoons cream of tartar
Topping:
50g/2oz/½ cup chopped nuts
30ml/2 tablespoons Demerara or soft brown sugar

Beat the margarine and sugar together until soft and creamy. Beat in the eggs, a little at a time, and then add the honey, bran, nuts, spices, raisins and grated apple. Gently fold in the flour, bicarbonate of soda and the cream of tartar.

Pour into a greased and lined 1kg/2lb bread tin and scatter over the topping mixture. Bake in a preheated oven at 180°C, 350°F, gas 4 for 15 minutes and then reduce the temperature to 170°C, 325°F, gas 3 for a further 1¼ hours. Serve warm with butter.

Baked apple in rum

Small, sweet dessert apples are essential in this simple pudding, which is quickly prepared and cooked. Despite its simplicity, it makes a sophisticated dessert and tastes delicious served with yoghurt. Remember that apple discolours quickly once peeled, so sprinkle slices with a little lemon juice to retain their whiteness.

675g/1½lb dessert apples (preferably Cox's orange pippins)
75ml/5 tablespoons dark Jamaica rum
30ml/2 tablespoons soft brown sugar

Peel and quarter the apples, remove the cores and slice thinly. Arrange them in overlapping concentric circles in a well-buttered ovenproof dish and pour in the rum. Sprinkle with sugar and bake in a preheated oven at 180°C, 350°F, gas 4 for 20 minutes, until tender. Serve with yoghurt.

Serves 4

Spicy apple pie

This is a very special apple pie, heavily spiced and flavoured with Calvados and enclosed in a crunchy nut pastry. It is delicious eaten hot or cold with cream, custard or fruit-flavoured yoghurt.

3 cooking/green apples
juice of ½ lemon
2.5ml/½ teaspoon each of ground cinnamon and nutmeg
3 cloves
30ml/2 tablespoons soft brown sugar
15ml/1 tablespoon Calvados (or brandy)
15ml/1 tablespoon milk
caster/superfine sugar for dusting
Pastry:
175g/6oz/1½ cups wholemeal flour
50g/2oz/⅓ cup ground almonds
100g/4oz/½ cup margarine
15ml/1 tablespoon soft brown sugar
45ml/3 tablespoons chopped hazelnuts
45ml/3 tablespoons cold water

Make the pastry: place the flour and ground almonds in a mixing bowl and rub in the fat. Add the sugar and nuts and mix in the water to form a pliable dough. Knead until smooth.

Divide the dough in two and roll out on a lightly floured board. Line a buttered pie dish with half of the dough. Peel, core and slice the apples and arrange in the pie dish. Sprinkle with the lemon juice and spices (sticking the cloves into pieces of apple), the sugar and Calvados. Damp the pastry edge and cover with the remaining dough. Trim and seal the edges and make a small hole in the top. Brush with a little milk and dust with caster sugar.

Bake in a preheated oven at 200°C, 400°F, gas 6 for 15 minutes and then lower the temperature to 180°C, 350°F, gas 4 for a further 20 minutes. Serve hot or cold.

Serves 4-5

Apple spice cake

This moist, spicy cake has an attractive crunchy nut topping. However, it has a limited shelf life and should be wrapped in foil and stored in an airtight container, and eaten within a few days of baking.

450g/1lb cooking/green apples
50ml/2floz/¼ cup sweet cider
juice of ½ lemon
175g/6oz/¾ cup margarine
175g/6oz/¾ cup soft brown sugar
1 egg, beaten
1.25ml/¼ teaspoon ground cloves
*2.5ml/½ teaspoon each of ground ginger, nutmeg
  and mace*
5ml/1 teaspoon ground cinnamon
5ml/1 teaspoon bicarbonate of soda/baking soda
350g/12oz/3¼ cups wholemeal flour
50g/2oz chopped stem ginger
50g/2oz/⅓ cup raisins
100g/4oz/1 cup chopped walnuts
175g/6oz/1 cup chopped dates
45ml/3 tablespoons apple juice or cider
Topping:
15ml/1 tablespoon Demerara or soft brown sugar
25g/1oz/¼ cup chopped nuts
2.5ml/½ teaspoon ground cinnamon
30ml/2 tablespoons desiccated coconut

Peel, core and slice the apples. Put in a pan with the cider and lemon juice and cook over gentle heat until soft. Cool and put aside. Cream the butter and sugar until soft and fluffy and gradually beat in the egg. Mix the spices and bicarbonate of soda/baking soda with the flour and fold into the cake mixture. Stir in the remaining ingredients. The mixture should be of a soft dropping consistency.

Pour into a greased and lined large cake tin and scatter the mixed topping ingredients over the top. Bake in a preheated oven at 170°C, 325°F, gas 3 for about 1¼ hours until the cake is cooked

Apricot fool

You can make this delicious dish all the year round even when apricots are out of season, for this fool is made with dried apricots. It is simplicity itself and brings a flavour of summer into the cold winter months.

100g/4oz/¾ cup dried apricots
juice of ½ lemon
15ml/1 tablespoon honey
100ml/4floz/½ cup whipped cream
40g/1½oz/¼ cup toasted almonds

Soak the apricots overnight. Simmer them over gentle

heat in a little water until tender. Strain and liquidise or pureé. When cool, stir in the lemon juice and fold in the whipped cream. Decorate with the toasted almonds. Serve chilled.

Serves 4

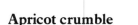

Apricot crumble

The beauty of this pudding is that it can be made all the year round as the apricots are dried, not fresh. In the summer, of course, you can substitute fresh, stewed apricots. It is simple to make and always appreciated.

225g/8oz/1½ cups dried apricots
15ml/1 tablespoon brandy or apricot brandy
50g/2oz/½ cup chopped walnuts
50g/2oz/¼ cup soft brown sugar
Topping:
50g/2oz/¼ cup margarine
100g/4oz/1⅛ cups wholemeal flour
50g/2oz/¼ cup soft brown sugar

Soak the apricots overnight and drain, reserving 15ml/ 1 tablespoon of the juice. Place the apricots, the reserved juice and brandy in a buttered ovenproof dish. Sprinkle with the nuts and sugar.

Make the crumble topping: rub the margarine into the flour and then stir in the sugar. Spread the crumble mixture over the apricots and smooth the top. Bake in a preheated oven at 180°C, 350°F, gas 4 for 40-45 minutes until cooked and golden-brown.

Serves 4

Banana bread

The addition of yoghurt makes thus fruity teabread especially moist. It is a great way of using up over-ripe bananas which you might otherwise throw away.

75g/3oz/⅜ cup margarine
150g/5oz/⅝ cup soft brown sugar
2 large ripe bananas, mashed
150ml/¼ pint/⅝ cup natural yoghurt
1 egg, beaten
200g/7oz/2 cups wholemeal flour
pinch of salt
7.5ml/1½ teaspoons bicarbonate of soda/baking soda
15ml/1 tablespoon chopped nuts

Cream the fat and sugar, then gradually mix in the banana, yoghurt and beaten egg. Fold in the flour, salt and bicarbonate of soda. Beat the mixture well.

Spoon into a well-greased baking tin and scatter the nuts over the top. Bake in a preheated oven at 180°C, 350°F, gas 4 for about 1 hour. Allow to cool and serve sliced and buttered.

Summer pudding

One of the joys of late summer is a brilliantly coloured summer pudding to celebrate the arrival of the first blackcurrants. This classic English pudding has been eaten for at least 300 years and was even served to invalids in the eighteenth century. You can use a mixture of soft fruits according to what is readily available although blackcurrants are the most important ingredient, giving the dish its distinctive colour and flavour. Try mixing them with black cherries, red-currants, blackberries, raspberries, blueberries and even strawberries.

450g/1lb mixed blackcurrants and other soft fruits
150g/5oz/⅝ cup soft brown sugar
15ml/1 tablespoon crème de cassis
8 slices of one-day-old white bread, 5mm/¼in thick

Put the mixed fruit and sugar in a saucepan and leave overnight (this helps to extract the juices from the fruit). Next day, bring to the boil and then reduce the heat and simmer for about 3 minutes. Allow to cool and add the cassis.

Remove the crusts from the bread. Place one slice of bread in the base of a 900ml/1½ pint/3½ cup pudding basin. Cut the other slices to fit around the sides of the basin, filling the gaps with small bread pieces. Pour in half of the fruit mixture and cover with a slice of bread. Press down securely and make sure that there are no gaps. Press a small plate or saucer down on top and weight it with a heavy tin or a metal weight. Leave in the refrigerator for at least one day before serving.

To turn out the pudding, run the point of a thin knife carefully around the edge of the pudding to loosen it from the basin. Cover with a serving plate and invert the pudding quickly. Remove the basin and serve in small slices with fresh cream or yoghurt. You can pour more crème de cassis over the top if wished to cover any stray white patches.

Serves 4 - 5

Opposite: a traditional Christmas spread, reading
clockwise: Christmas pudding (see page 155), mincemeat
pies (see page 155), florentines (see page 20) and a
jug of warm mulled wine (see page 169)

Blackcurrant sorbet

Water ices were invented by the Chinese, and the technology of making ices was brought to the Levant by Arab traders and then on to Europe by Italian merchants in the seventeenth century. In fact, our word 'sorbet' evolved from the Arab work *shariba*, meaning a cold drink. Deliciously cool and elegant, blackcurrant sorbet is enhanced by the addition of crème de cassis. You can pour a little of the liqueur over the sorbet when you serve it.

225g/8oz blackcurrants
100ml/4floz/½ cup water
15ml/1 tablespoon crème de cassis
50g/2oz/¼ cup soft brown sugar
5ml/1 teaspoon lemon juice

Purée or sieve the blackcurrants. Boil the water, crème de cassis and sugar to make a thick syrup. Cool and add the blackcurrant purée and strain. Stir in the lemon juice and pour into an ice-tray or sorbetière.

Freeze in the freezing compartment of a refrigerator or in a freezer. If you are using an ice tray, then stir the sorbet every 30 minutes or so to ensure that it freezes evenly. The sorbet should be frozen and ready to eat after 4-5 hours. Serve in tall glasses as a refreshing end to a meal. The sorbet does not keep indefinitely so eat within 2 days.

Serves 3-4

Tart citron

A bitter-sweet lemon tart is a good way to end a meal and can be quickly prepared if you have a food processor or mixer. It is less rich and fattening than most other puddings and a little goes a long way.

Pâte sucrée:
225g/8oz/2¼ cups wholemeal flour
pinch of salt
175g/6oz/¾ cup margarine
2 egg yolks
50g/2oz/¼ cup soft brown sugar
Filling:
grated rind and juice of 3 lemons
75g/3oz/⅓ cup soft brown sugar
2 eggs and 1 egg white
75ml/3floz/⅓ cup double/heavy cream
100g/4oz/1 cup ground almonds
good pinch of cinnamon
Topping:
1 lemon, thinly sliced

1 orange, thinly sliced
100g/4oz/½ cup brown sugar

Make the pâte sucrée: if you have a food processor, process the sifted flour, salt and margarine for 15 seconds, add the yolks and sugar and process for about 10 seconds. Knead into a ball and chill in the refrigerator for at least 30 minutes.

Alternatively, sift the flour onto a pastry board, make a well in the centre, add the salt and softened margarine, sugar and egg yolks and mix with your hand, drawing the flour, a little at a time, into the centre until you have a smooth dough.

Beat together the filling ingredients until thick and smooth. Line a 25cm/10in flan ring with the pastry and pour in the filling. Bake in a preheated oven at 190°C, 375°F, gas 5 for 30 minutes until set and golden. Cool.

Heat the lemon and orange slices in a little water over low heat for about 10 minutes until tender. Remove and drain, keeping about 75ml/3floz/⅜ cup of the liquid. Add the brown sugar and stir over gentle heat until dissolved. Bring to the boil, add the lemon and orange slices and cook rapidly until they are well-coated with thick syrup. Remove and arrange in a border around the top of the tart (lemon, orange, lemon, orange and so on). Leave to cool and serve.

Serves 6-8

Lemon mousse

One of the lightest and most refreshing desserts of all is a pale, fluffy lemon mousse. Serve it after a rich main course or at the end of a light summer lunch. For a delicious variation, try making a lime mousse, substituting 2 limes instead of lemons.

25g/1oz/4 tablespoons gelatine
150ml/¼ pint/⅝ cup boiling water
4 eggs, separated
100g/4oz/½ cup caster/superfine sugar
juice and grated rind of 2 lemons

Sprinkle the gelatine onto the boiling water and leave to dissolve. Stir well when it cools. Whisk the egg yolks and sugar until light and fluffy. Add the grated lemon rind and juice. Slowly mix in the cooled gelatine mixture and leave in a cool place while you whisk the egg whites until they stand in stiff peaks.

When the lemon mixture starts to gel, gently fold in the egg whites with a metal spoon. Divide the mixture between individual serving dishes or tall glasses and leave to set. Decorate with chopped nuts, citron peel or lemon slices.

Serves 4

Sussex pond pudding

This traditional English pudding is deliciously light in its thin suet crust. The tangy filling flows out to form a 'pond' around the pudding when it is cut. A Seville orange is essential because its flavour is more bitter than that of a sweet orange. This pudding probably evolved in the early eighteenth century when Seville oranges were very popular and not used solely for making marmalade as they are nowadays. If you cannot obtain Seville oranges, then lemons or even limes make a good substitute. You can also add mixed dried fruits.

225g/8oz/2¼ cups wholemeal flour
100g/4oz/1 cup shredded suet
pinch of salt
20ml/4 teaspoons baking powder
150ml/¼ pint/⅝ cup water
Filling:
150g/5oz/⅝ cup butter, cut in small pieces
150g/5oz/⅝ cup granulated or brown sugar
1 small Seville orange (or lemon), well-washed
good pinch of ground nutmeg

Make the suet pastry: mix the flour, suet and salt with the baking powder. Gradually add the water to form a soft dough. Knead lightly and roll out to a large circle, keeping a little pastry aside with which to make the lid. Line a buttered 900ml/1½ pint/3½ cup pudding basin with the dough, allowing it to overlap the rim at the top.

Place half the butter inside the pudding with half the sugar. Prick the orange all over and place it on top of the butter. Sprinkle in a pinch of nutmeg and then fill with the remaining butter and sugar. Cover with the dough lid and dampen and seal the edges of the pudding.

Butter a piece of foil and fold over the centre to form a pleat (this will allow the pudding to expand during cooking). Cover the basin loosely with the foil and then a pudding cloth (or tea towel) and tie it securely around the rim with string, folding the corners of the cloth up over the string and the top of the pudding. Tie them to form a handle with which to lift the pudding out of the pan.

Lower the pudding into a large pan of boiling water which should reach half-way up the sides of the basin.

Cover with a lid and steam for 4 hours, adding more boiling water whenever the level starts to drop.

Remove from the pan and take off the cloth and foil covers. The pastry should be a rich-golden colour. Gently slide a long, thin knife around the sides of the pudding, place a plate on top and invert the pudding onto it. Lift the basin off carefully and serve immediately.

Serves 4

Lime pound cake

This fresh-tasting, lightly textured cake is steeped in a sharp, lime syrup flavoured with gin before serving. It is quick and simple to make in a food processor or an electric mixer and is easily whisked up for a family tea. Pound cake is an old American favourite and was traditionally made with a 'pound' each of butter, sugar and flour. This version, which we discovered on a trip to the United States, is less rich and absolutely delicious. You can use white or wholemeal flour.

175g/6oz/¾ cup margarine
175g/6oz/¾ cup soft brown sugar
grated rind of 2 limes
4 eggs
225g/8oz/2¼ cups plain white or wholemeal flour
5ml/1 teaspoon baking powder
2.5ml/½ teaspoon salt
45ml/3 tablespoons lime juice
Topping:
juice of 2 limes
100g/4oz/½ cup soft brown sugar
15ml/1 tablespoon gin
small piece of candied citron peel

Cream the margarine and sugar with the grated lime rind. Beat in the eggs and then the sifted flour, baking powder and salt. Finally stir in the lime juice.

Line a rectangular cake tin with baking or greaseproof paper and pour in the cake mixture. Place low down in a preheated oven at 180°C, 350°F, gas 4 and bake for about 1¼ hours until the cake has risen and is cooked right through. Insert a long skewer to test it — it is ready when it comes out clean.

Remove the paper wrapping from the cake and stand on a deep plate. Heat the lime juice, sugar and gin over low heat until the sugar has dissolved. Bring to the boil, reduce the heat and cook for a few minutes until the syrup starts to thicken. Make some holes with a skewer in the top of the cake and pour over the hot syrup. Spoon any syrup that collects in the plate over the top and sides of the cake. Decorate with the citron peel and leave to cool.

Orange sorbet

The new *sorbetières* on the market can produce wonderfully smooth, soft fruit sorbets but they are an extravagant toy for most people. However, excellent results can be obtained with a freezer or the ice-box in a refrigerator. Contrary to what you may have been told, sorbets do not have a long freezing life and should be eaten within 36 hours if they are to be enjoyed at their best. You can serve the sorbet as a dessert, spooned into the scooped-out shells of oranges, or as a refresher between courses.

400ml/14floz/1¾ cups orange juice
juice of 1 lemon
50g/2oz/¼ cup caster/superfine sugar

Place the orange and lemon juice in a pan and add the sugar. Stir over low heat until the sugar is thoroughly dissolved. Pour the mixture into a freezing tray and freeze for 30 minutes or so — it should be frozen around the edges but still soft in the centre. Break it up with a fork *or* beat with an electric beater *or* process in a food processor until it is really smooth. Return to the freezer until ready to serve. If you are using the fork method, it will be necessary to repeat this breaking-up process 5 times with 30 minute intervals between each.

Serves 4

Caramel oranges

This popular Italian recipe makes a light and refreshing end to a meal but try to watch your calories by resisting the temptation to serve it with cream.

4 large oranges
175g/6oz/¾ cup soft brown sugar
200ml/7floz/⅞ cup water
15ml/1 tablespoon kirsch

Carefully cut away all the peel and white pith from the oranges. Use a potato peeler to pare the peel from one orange and cut into thin, matchstick strips. Boil these strips for 5 minutes in water, then drain and put aside. Slice the oranges horizontally and secure each sliced orange with a cocktail stick/toothpick.

Make the syrup by dissolving the sugar in half the water over a low heat, stirring. Boil the sugar syrup until it starts to turn a deep golden colour. Remove

from the heat and, standing well back from the pan, add the remaining water, the kirsch and strips of peel. Stir over a gentle heat to dissolve any caramel lumps, and then pour the syrup over the oranges. Leave to cool, chill well and serve.

Serves 4

Stuffed peaches with walnuts

Peaches stuffed with sweet macaroon fillings are a feature of Italian desserts. They make a nice fresh way to finish a summer meal. Use large, fairly ripe peaches for the best results.

4 large, ripe peaches
40g/1½oz/⅜ cup walnuts
100g/4oz macaroons or ratifia biscuits
1 egg yolk
15ml/1 tablespoon brandy
pinch salt
15ml/1 tablespoon yoghurt
100ml/4floz/½ cup sieved sweetened raspberries

Wash the peaches gently and pat dry with absorbent kitchen paper. Cut each in half and remove the stone/pit. Carefully hollow out a little of the flesh in each to enlarge the cavity and set aside for the filling.

Grind the walnuts and macaroons almost to a powder in a blender or food processor and mix with the egg yolk, reserved peach flesh, brandy, salt and, lastly, the yoghurt. The mixture should have the consistency of a fairly stiff paste. Divide it between the peach halves and sandwich them together so that a little filling is just visible around the centre of each. Serve on a bed of Melba sauce. Just sieve 100g/4oz fresh raspberries and sweeten to taste.

Serves 4

Ginger and pear upside-down cake

This delicious cake has a sticky nut topping and is strictly for ginger lovers. If you like ginger, it is well worth investing in a small jar of preserved stem ginger in syrup. It can be added to cakes, jams and puddings. Preserved ginger in honey is also very good.

Topping:
50g/2oz/¼ cup margarine
75g/3oz/⅜ cup Demerara sugar
22.5ml/1½ tablepoons ginger syrup
25g/1oz/¼ cup chopped nuts
grated rind and juice of ½ lemon

5 dessert pears
30ml/2 tablespoons chopped glacé cherries
Cake:
100g/4oz/½ cup margarine
100g/4oz/½ cup soft brown sugar
2 eggs
100g/4oz/1⅛ cups wholemeal flour
5ml/1 teaspoon baking powder
25g/1oz/¼ cup ground almonds
50g/2oz/½ cup chopped hazelnuts
30ml/2 tablespoons ginger syrup
5 pieces preserved stem ginger, chopped

Make the topping: melt the margarine and add the sugar, stirring until dissolved. Add the ginger syrup and boil until thickened and syrupy. Add the nuts and lemon rind.

Peel, core and slice the pears and sprinkle with the lemon juice. Pour the syrup into a well-greased 20cm/8in square baking tin and arrange the pears neatly on top. Scatter the chopped cherries around the pears (chopped mixed candied peel may be used in place of cherries).

Make the cake by creaming the margarine and sugar and beating in the eggs. Stir in the flour, baking powder and ground almonds, and then add the chopped nuts, syrup and ginger. Pour into the tin over the pears and bake in a preheated oven at 190°C, 375°F, gas 5. After 10 minutes reduce the heat to 180°C, 350°F, gas 4 and bake for a further 45 minutes.

It is a good idea to cover the cake with aluminium baking foil for the first 45 minutes to prevent it browning and then remove the foil about 10 minutes before the end. Allow to cool a little and carefully turn out the cake with the sticky pear-side uppermost onto a serving dish. Cut into squares and serve.

Serves 6

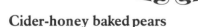

Cider-honey baked pears

You can use dessert or cooking pears in this recipe as long as they are hard; if they are too soft, they will disintegrate when cooked. This is a traditional country dish from the orchard and cider-producing areas of England. In the West Country it was served with lashings of thick, clotted cream but it still tastes good topped with fruit-flavoured yoghurt.

6 hard pears
3 thin strips lemon peel
2.5cm/1in cinnamon stick
300ml/½ pint/1¼ cups medium sweet cider
75ml/3floz/⅜ cup water

30ml/2 tablespoons honey
30ml/2 tablespoons chopped mixed nuts

Peel the pears, leaving the stems intact, and flatten their bases so that they will 'stand up' in an ovenproof dish without toppling over. Add the lemon peel and cinnamon. Pour over the cider and water, and trickle the honey over the top.

Bake at 170°C, 325°F, gas 3 for about 1¼ hours until the pears are tender but still firm. When the pears are cool, remove from the dish and reheat the syrup to boiling point. Boil for about 5 minutes until it is reduced and thick, and pour over the pears. Decorate with chopped nuts and serve.

Serves 6

Peephole pear tart

This pear tart derives its name from the central hole cut in the top of the pastry crust through which cream or yoghurt is poured immediately before serving. It is a lovely dessert to make when the new season's pears are coming into the shops in the autumn.

3 large dessert pears (Williams for preference)
30ml/2 tablespoons thin honey
pinch of ground cloves
25g/1oz/¼ cup chopped walnuts
caster/superfine or soft brown sugar for dusting
Pastry:
150g/5oz/⅔ cup margarine
100g/4oz/½ cup soft brown sugar
225g/8oz/2¼ cups wholemeal flour
pinch of salt
5ml/1 teaspoon ground cinnamon
25g/1oz/¼ cup chopped walnuts
1 egg, beaten

Make the pastry: cream the margarine and sugar until soft and fluffy. Mix in the flour, salt, cinnamon and nuts, and blend in the beaten egg to form a stiff paste. Chill in the refrigerator for at least 30 minutes before rolling out.

Roll out two-thirds of the paste and use to line a 20cm/8in flan case. Peel, halve and core the pears and arrange them, widest end outermost, in a circle inside the flan case. Brush with honey and sprinkle with nuts and ground cloves. Roll out the remaining pastry and cut a circle, 5cm/2in in diameter, out of the centre. Cover the flan with this and seal the edges securely. Brush with a little water and dust with sugar. Bake in a preheated oven at 200°C, 400°F, gas 6 for 10 minutes and then lower the oven temperature to 180°C 350°F, gas 4 for a further 30 minutes. Pour some cream or yoghurt through the peephole, and serve warm or cold.

Serves 5-6

Pears in muscatel with rum sauce

Here is a delicious dessert which is low in calories and full of flavour. The rum sauce lifts the pears from being a fairly humble dish to a refreshingly different way to end a meal.

4 large dessert pears (Williams for preference)
1 large orange
150ml/¼ pint/⅝ cup orange juice
150ml/¼ pint/⅝ cup Muscatel wine
50g/2oz/¼ cup soft brown sugar
Rum sauce:
3 eggs
50g/2oz/¼ cup soft brown sugar
150ml/¼ pint/⅝ cup reserved cooking liquor from pears
50ml/2floz/¼ cup rum

Peel the pears with a potato peeler and level off the base of each one. Leave the stalk intact. Peel the oranges thinly with a potato peeler and cut the peel into very thin julienne strips. Place the pears upright in a pan with the orange rind, juice and wine and bring to the boil. Cover the pan, reduce the heat to a bare simmer and cook gently for 15 minutes. Remove the pears and strain off 150ml/¼ pint/⅝ cup of the cooking liquor to make the rum sauce.

Stir the sugar into the remaining liquor, dissolve over low heat and then boil steadily until it becomes syrupy. Pour the syrup over the pears and chill well. The strips of peel make an attractive garnish.

Make the rum sauce: whisk the eggs and sugar until almost white in a basin or the top of a double-boiler away from the heat. Whisk in the reserved pear liquor and place the basin over a pan of boiling water. It must be suspended above the water, *not* sitting in it, or the eggs may scramble. Continue to whisk above the boiling water until the mixture thickens and will hold a trail from the whisk. Whisk in the rum, remove from the heat and stand the basin in a bowl of cold water to cool it as quickly as possible. Chill in the refrigerator

Serves 4

Khoshaf

This dried fruit salad, sweetened with honey and flavoured with cinnamon, is widely eaten throughout the Middle Eastern countries. You can use a selection of dried fruits: apricots, figs, pears, peaches, prunes, apple rings and raisins.

450g/1lb/3 cups mixed dried fruit
50g/2oz/⅓ cup blanched almonds
45ml/3 tablespoons clear honey
grated rind and juice of ½ lemon
2.5cm/1in cinnamon stick
15ml/1 tablespoon blossom water (optional)
25g/1oz/¼ cup pistachio nuts

Cover the dried fruit with water and soak overnight. Place the fruit in its juice in an ovenproof dish with the almonds, honey, lemon rind and juice, cinnamon stick and blossom water (optional). Bring to the boil and then remove the pan from the heat, cover with a lid and place in a preheated oven at 170°C, 325°F, gas 3 for about 1 hour.

Add the pistachio nuts and cook for a further 30 minutes. Remove the cinnamon stick and serve the khoshaf hot or cold on its own or with thick yoghurt.

Serves 4

Fruit and yoghurt brulée

When you get bored with fruit salad, try this healthy alternative: just marinate the fruit in rum or brandy, top it with chilled yoghurt, sprinkle with sugar, flash under a hot grill, and hey presto you have a delicious fruit brulée with a thin, crisp caramel covering. You can use almost any fruit — pears, apples bananas, grapes and oranges in winter; and strawberries, peaches, apricots and raspberries in summer.

450g/1lb prepared fruit (chopped pineapple, diced apple,
  peaches, apricots, pears, sliced banana, orange segments,
  strawberries, raspberries etc)
30ml/2 tablespoons soft brown sugar
45ml/3 tablespoons rum or brandy or orange liqueur
100ml/4floz/½ cup apricot yoghurt
brown or caster/superfine sugar for dusting

Place the prepared fruit in a shallow ovenproof dish and fill it to within 2.5cm/1in of the rim. Sprinkle with brown sugar and your favourite spirit or liqueur. Spread thickly with yoghurt and chill well in the refrigerator or even in the freezer.

Dust lightly with sugar and flash the dish under a very hot preheated grill/broiler until the sugar caramelises. Rotate the dish if necessary to obtain an even, crisp caramel layer. Cool thoroughly and chill before serving.

Serves 2-3

Fresh fruit salad

You can make a refreshing, low-calorie fruit salad with almost any fruit, depending on which fruits are in season and readily available. Thus soft berry fruits, such as strawberries and raspberries, tend to predominate in summer fruit salads, whereas bananas, apples, pears and grapes are popular ingredients in winter versions. Aim for contrasting flavours, colours and textures. If you are preparing the dessert for a special occasion, try to include some more unusual, exotic fruits, such as sliced kiwi fruits, chunks of mango or papaya, and peeled lychees.

various fresh fruits: bananas, sliced; grapes, halved and pipped/seeded; apples, cored and cubed; pineapple chunks; oranges, peeled and segmented; kiwi fruit, peeled and sliced; apricots, stoned/pitted and quartered; cherries, stoned/pitted; strawberries; raspberries
lemon juice to keep apple and banana white
honey to sweeten
orange juice to pour over the salad
liqueur for flavouring (optional)

Prepare the fresh fruits and place in an attractive serving bowl. Sprinkle the fruits that discolour easily like bananas and apples with lemon juice to keep them white. Stir the honey into the orange juice and pour over the salad. This is more healthy and less sweet than making a traditional sugar syrup. Add a few drops of your favourite liqueur if liked. Kirsch and most orange liqueurs will lift the fruit salad out of the ordinary.

Christmas puddings

A really good traditional Christmas pudding should be rich, moist and so dark that it is almost black. How you serve it is a matter of personal taste — with brandy butter and cream, or flaming in brandy if you go in for showmanship. This is a really old-fashioned recipe which has been in our family for at least 100 years and never fails to please. The quantities given are enough to make 2 puddings but if you do not intend to eat them straight away, they will keep well for several months before the final boiling in a cool, dry place.

225g/8oz/1⅓ cups raisins
225g/8oz/1⅓ cups sultanas/seedless raisins
225g/8oz/1⅓ cups currants
100g/4oz/1 cup mixed chopped candied peel
225g/8oz/1 cup Barbados or soft brown sugar
15ml/1 tablespoon mixed spice
15ml/1 tablespoon ground nutmeg

2.5ml/½ teaspoon salt
225g/8oz/4 cups fresh breadcrumbs
175g/6oz/1½ cups plain flour
225g/8oz/2 cups shredded suet
50g/2oz/⅓ cup chopped blanched almonds
100g/4oz grated cooking/green apple
grated rind and juice of 1 lemon
4 eggs, beaten
300ml/½ pint/1¼ cups stout, Guinness or any strong brown ale

Mix all the dry ingredients together in a large mixing bowl and don't forget to have a wish as you do so! Gradually add the beaten egg and stout until the mixture is thoroughly blended. Divide it between 2 well greased, large pudding basins and cover with some greased baking paper and a pudding cloth. Secure with string around the rim to hold the cloth in place. Aluminium foil can be used if the puddings are to be cooked and eaten straight away but if you intend to keep them a few weeks or even months before cooking, it is not suitable.

To cook the puddings, place in a large pan of fast-boiling water which reaches halfway up the sides of the basins. Boil for at least 10 hours and cool. Store in a cool, dry place until the appointed day and then boil in the same manner for a further 4 hours.

Serves 6

Mincemeat pie filling

Mincemeat is a reminder of those grand mediaeval dishes liberally flavoured with wine and spices and bursting with exotic dried fruits. It has become the traditional filling for pies at Christmas.

225g/8oz/1⅓ cups raisins
225g/8oz cooking/green apples, finely chopped
225g/8oz/2 cups candied peel
225g/8oz/1⅓ cups currants
225g/8oz/2 cups shredded suet
225g/8oz/1 cup soft brown sugar
2.5ml/½ teaspoon salt
good pinch of mixed spice
100ml/4floz/½ cup port wine or brandy or rum

Mix all the ingredients together and pour into sterilised jars and seal, topping up the jars with a little more brandy or port wine if wished. Store until needed and use for filling pies and tarts with a sugar paste crust (for recipe see page 169). Bake the pies in a preheated oven at 200°C, 400°F, gas 6 until golden (20-30 minutes) and dust with icing/confectioner's sugar.

Fruit and vegetables can be preserved as jams, jellies, chutneys, pickles and liqueurs and may be kept for months if stored in a cool, dry place. In the past, every country house had a store cupboard or even a special stillroom full of preserves to add spice and flavour to the monotonous winter diet when fresh vegetables and fruit were scarce. Home-made preserves are easy and inexpensive to make and are always rewarding. Make them when fruit and vegetables are abundant and cheap or when you have surplus produce from your own garden. Some can even be made with free foods from the hedgerows — blackberries, sloes, blueberries (in North America) and elderberries. The preserving method you choose will be determined by the nature, quality and ripeness of the fruit or vegetables.

Jams and jellies
Jams, often known as jellies in the United States, are made with whole fruit or fruit pulp which is boiled with sugar until the pectin and acid in the fruit react with the sugar to produce a set. Jellies are bright and clear and made with the strained juice of the cooked fruit pulp boiled up with sugar until the mixture sets.

Home-made jams and jellies always taste so much better than commercial brands and have been eaten spread on bread, in cakes or puddings, or made into sweet sauces and tart fillings since the nineteenth century. Use fresh, slightly under-ripe fruit (over-ripe fruit has a low pectin content) and cut out any damaged or bruised parts. Always wash it thoroughly. Hull strawberries or top and tail berries such as currants and gooseberries. Apricots, plums, damsons and other stone/pit fruit may be left whole if wished, or the inner kernel of the stone added to the jam to give it a pleasant almond flavour.

To obtain a good set, pectin, acid and sugar must be present in the right quantities. All fruit contains natural pectin and acid but in varying amounts so it may be necessary to add extra acid in the form of lemon juice, citric or tartaric acid, or even commercial pectin extract to fruits with a low pectin content. Fruits that are high in pectin include apples, currants (black and red), citrus fruits, cranberries, damsons, gooseberries and quinces. Fruits with a medium setting quality include raspberries, greengages, plums and apricots, whereas low-set fruits are strawberries, cherries, blackberries, figs and rhubarb.

The preserving agent in jams and jellies is sugar. As it has a hardening effect on fruit, it should always be added to thoroughly softened fruit and completely dissolved in the mixture before boiling, or it may re-crystallise later in the bottled jam. It should always be added in the correct quantity as too little will shorten the shelf-life of the jam.

Cook the jam in a large heavy aluminium or stainless steel pan or a special preserving pan with a pouring lip. Boil hard to obtain a good set. You can use a sugar thermometer or a simple saucer test to ascertain when the jam has reached setting point. Jam usually sets at 105°C, 220°F when the sugar concentration is about 65 per cent. If you haven't got a sugar thermometer (and even if you have, it is just as well to do this test as a double check), when the jam starts to look thick and syrupy, drop a teaspoonful of the boiling jam onto a cold saucer and leave to cool (you can pop it into the refrigerator to speed it up). When it starts to solidify, gently push the surface with your finger. It is ready if it wrinkles. If set, remove the jam from the heat and skim any scum off the surface before bottling. If it is still syrupy and runny, continue boiling for a few more minutes and then retest in the same way.

You can bottle most jams within 2-3 minutes of removing them from the heat, but those with large berries such as strawberries should be left to cool before bottling so that the fruit is dispersed evenly throughout the jam and does not rise to the surface. Jars must be sterilised and warmed before filling. Place them upside-down in the oven at 130°C, 250°F, gas ½ for 20 minutes, and then pour in the hot jam, carefully wiping away any spills with a damp cloth. A good way to fill them is to dip a jug into the pan of hot jam and pour it into the jars. Place a waxed disc, waxed side down, on top of the jam and cover the jar with a cellophane cover, moistened with water and placed damp side uppermost and secured with an elastic band for a really airtight fit. Label and store when cool in a dry, dark cupboard.

Jellies are made in the same way as jams except that the cooked fruit is placed in a jelly bag and the fruit juice drained through the muslin into the preserving pan below. The fruit juice alone is boiled up with the sugar to make a clear jelly. Test for the setting point and bottle in the same way as for jams.

Marmalades are made with bitter citrus fruit(Seville oranges, lemons, limes or grapefruit) according to the jelly method. The pectin is contained in the pips/seeds and these are placed in a muslin bag immersed in the cooking marmalade before adding the sugar. Thinly or thickly cut peel is added to the clear jelly. Marmalades are sometimes flavoured with honey, ginger or whisky. The name is derived from the Portuguese word *marmela* for quince, as the earliest marmalades were made with quinces, not citrus fruits. Citrus fruit marmalade was made popular by the Keiller family in Scotland in the eighteenth century and later by a Mrs Cooper of Oxford in the nineteenth century who made it as a breakfast spread for Oxford undergraduates.

Chutneys and pickles

These are savoury preserves and relishes made with vegetables and fruit flavoured with spices, vinegar and sugar. They are essentially oriental, chutneys being derived from the piquant Hindustani relish *chatni*, or 'chutnee' as it came to be called. Although a similar preserve of dried fruits, vegetables, spices and honey was known in mediaeval France, the first chutneys were brought back to Britain by the East India Company at the end of the seventeenth century. They are now widely eaten with cold meats and cheese and as an accompaniment to curries.

Chutneys are one of the easiest ways of preserving fruit and vegetables and they keep well, their flavour improving and mellowing as the months go by. Unlike jams, which demand good-quality fruit, chutney can be made with over-ripe produce, although any damaged parts should be removed. Sugar is the sweetening preserving agent (along with vinegar) and brown sugar gives a rich, dark colour and good flavour. Malt vinegar should be used in preference to lighter wine vinegars which are less flavoursome. Spices may be used whole and bruised and tied in a muslin bag immersed in the cooking chutney, or freshly ground.

It is important to cook chutney slowly for several hours over low heat until the full flavours develop and the mixture thickens. Give the chutney an occasional stir once it starts to thicken. Pour into warm sterilised jars and cover with special vinegar-proof paper or soft muslin dipped in melted paraffin wax. Screw on the metal caps which have been immersed for a few minutes in boiling water and thoroughly dried, or cover with plastic covers. Greaseproof paper and cellophane jampot covers are not suitable as they allow evaporation to take place. Label the jars and leave to cool before storing in a really dry, dark, cool cupboard for at least 2-3 months before opening and consuming. They improve with age.

Fruit liqueurs, preserves and ratafias

You can make delicious fruit liqueurs and ratafias by infusing alcohol with fruit and sweetening it with sugar. Liqueurs used to be common in the nineteenth century, together with cordials, and are still popular in some wine-growing country districts of France. In fact, they used to be drunk as a medicine or digestive.

They are the easiest of all preserves to make, requiring no special skills — just a good palate and a love of food.

Liqueurs have been made for centuries, flavoured with fruit, herbs, spices, honey, chocolate, coffee beans, seeds, nuts and flowers. Many are still closely guarded secrets, such as Chartreuse which is made by French Carthusian monks. Their recipients are sworn to lifelong secrecy regarding their magic formula and ingredients. Liqueurs may be served as a warming winter drink, as a digestive with coffee after dinner, or may be used as a flavouring in savoury dishes, cakes and desserts. Fruit preserved in spirits or liqueurs may be eaten on its own as a dessert, with cream or yoghurt, as a topping for ice-cream and sorbets, or as a filling for pies and gâteaux.

You can make liqueurs at home with brandy, rum, gin, whisky and vodka. As a rough guide, quantities are usually in the ratio of two-thirds spirit to one-third sugar added to the fruit. Use the cheapest supermarket brands of spirits and the rough *eau-de-vie de marc* cooking brandy. The results will be just as good as using best quality three star cognac. The fruit should be in good condition, ripe and undamaged. Prick it all over to allow the juices to flavour the spirit and the spirit, in turn, to impregnate the fruit. Stones/pits can be left in the fruit or may be cracked and the white inner kernels added to the liqueur to give it a faintly almond taste. Bruised, blanched almonds are added to many liqueurs, especially sloe gin, for added flavour.

Make the liqueur in a wide-necked jar or a demi-john if you are preparing large quantities. Cork it securely and leave for 2-3 months, shaking from time to time to dissolve the sugar. Most liqueurs take on a lovely colour from the fruit as they mature. Strain liqueurs to be drunk through muslin or cheesecloth at least twice to remove any sediment and fruit before bottling. We like to bottle liqueurs in old unwashed brandy, port or sherry bottles as this also adds flavour. Label the bottles and leave as long as possible before drinking as all liqueurs mellow and improve with age. The flavour may be quite harsh if drunk too soon after bottling. Some can be put down for years without any ill effects. They may even get forgotten at the back of a dark cupboard and when discovered, sometimes years later, will give a lot of pleasure.

Some liqueurs, such as cherry brandy, can be drunk without straining the fruit. Spoon the cherries in their delicious liquid over sorbets and ice-creams or add to fruit salads. Many liqueurs, such as those made with oranges, prunes and apricots, can be topped up with fresh fruit and brandy as the level starts to drop.

Chutneys and pickles

Apple and ginger chutney

This chutney is a good way of coping with a glut of windfall apples — it is best to use cooking apples or sharp dessert apples. A spicy, fruity chutney, it goes well with most hot curries.

450g/1lb onions, chopped
3 cloves garlic, crushed
300ml/½ pint/1¼ cups water
2.5kg/5lb apples, peeled, cored and sliced
900ml/1½ pints/3½ cups white wine vinegar
7g/¼oz root ginger
10 peppercorns
6 dried chillis
350g/12oz/2 cups raisins
5ml/1 teaspoon salt
5ml/1 teaspoon mustard seeds
10ml/2 teaspoons ground ginger
5ml/1 teaspoon paprika
50g/2oz preserved stem ginger, chopped
1kg/2lb/4 cups soft brown sugar

Simmer the onion and garlic in the water until tender. Add the apple and 300ml/½pint/1¼ cups of the wine vinegar. Crush and bruise the root ginger and place in a muslin bag with the peppercorns and chillis. Add to the pan. Cook the apple mixture to a pulp.

Add the remaining vinegar and all of the other ingredients. Stir over a low heat until all of the sugar dissolves, and then bring to the boil and boil briskly until reduced and thickened. Remove the muslin bag and bottle in the usual way.

Makes 3.5kg/7lb chutney

Green tomato chutney

If you have a surplus of home-grown tomatoes, this chutney is an excellent way of using up any green ones. It improves with age and ideally should not be eaten for at least 3 to 4 months after bottling.

450g/1lb onions, chopped
450g/1lb cooking apples, peeled, cored and chopped
2kg/4lb green tomatoes, well washed and chopped
550ml/1 pint/2½ cups white wine vinegar
15g/½oz root ginger
2.5ml/½ teaspoon dry mustard
25g/1oz pickling spice
225g/8oz/1⅓ cups raisins

400g/14oz/1¾ cups soft brown sugar
5ml/1 teaspoon salt

Place the chopped onion, apple and tomato in a preserving pan with half the quantity of vinegar. Crush and bruise the root ginger and tie in a muslin bag with the mustard and pickling spice. Place in the pan and cook until tender.

Add the remaining vinegar and other ingredients and stir over a gentle heat until the sugar dissolves. Boil rapidly until the sauce thickens and is much reduced. Remove the muslin bag and bottle in the usual way.

Makes approximately 3kg/6lb chutney

Orange pickle

This tangy orange pickle goes especially well with ham and pork dishes, or even with cold duck and goose. It should be stored for at least one month before opening to enjoy it at its best.

6 large oranges
5ml/1 teaspoon salt
450g/1lb/2 cups soft brown sugar
30ml/2 tablespoons honey
200ml/6floz/¾ cup white wine vinegar
100ml/4floz/½ cup water
4-5 whole cardamoms
freshly ground black pepper
2.5ml/½ teaspoon grated root ginger
few mustard seeds
2.5ml/½ teaspoon each of ground cinnamon and cloves
5-6 whole allspice berries, crushed

Place the oranges and salt in a pan and cover with hot water. Bring to the boil, then reduce the heat and simmer for about 1 hour until tender. Strain and cool.

Place the remaining ingredients in a pan and stir over low heat until the sugar dissolves. Bring to the boil and simmer for 10 minutes. Remove from the heat and cool. Strain the syrup into another pan.

Slice the oranges thinly, removing any pips, and add to the syrup. Bring to the boil, then simmer gently for 20 minutes, stirring frequently. Remove from the heat, cool for 5 minutes and then bottle in the usual way.

Makes 2 pots of pickle

Mint chutney

The tangy, aromatic flavour of fresh garden mint makes

this chutney quite irresistible. It is the ideal partner for cold lamb or cheese and biscuits.

1kg/2lb cooking apples
450g/1lb onions, chopped
3 cloves garlic, crushed
½ red pepper, deseeded and chopped
½ green pepper, deseeded and chopped
50g/2oz root ginger
8 peppercorns
550ml/1pint/2½ cups red wine vinegar
300ml/½ pint/1¼ cups cider vinegar
450g/1lb/2 cups soft brown sugar
7.5ml/1½ teaspoons coriander seeds
8 whole allspice berries
15ml/1 tablespoon salt
100g/4oz fresh mint, chopped

Peel, core and slice the apples and place in a heavy preserving pan with the onion, garlic and peppers. Crush the root ginger and tie in a muslin bag with the peppercorns. Add to the pan and cover with the vinegars. Bring to the boil and simmer for about 25 minutes until tender.

Add the sugar, spices and salt and heat through gently, stirring until the sugar is completely dissolved. Then boil the chutney slowly until it is thick (about 1 hour). Remove from the heat and add the chopped mint. Bottle in the usual way.

Makes 1.5kg/3lb chutney

Peach chutney

This spicy chutney is excellent served with curries. It is very expensive to make your own mango chutney, the traditional accompaniment to curry, but peaches make a good alternative. Make it in the summer when peaches are plentiful — it keeps well and will last for several months before opening.

10 large peaches
450g/1lb onions, chopped
50g/2oz/⅓ cup chopped dates
50g/2oz/⅓ cup chopped dried banana
225g/8oz/1⅓ cups raisins
15g/½oz root ginger
7.5ml/1½ teaspoons salt
15ml/1 tablespoon mustard seeds
15ml/1 tablespoon ground ginger
grated rind and juice of 2 lemons
450ml/16floz/2 cups white wine vinegar

500g/1lb2oz/2¼ cups Demerara sugar
freshly ground black pepper

Wash and stone/pit the peaches and slice thinly. Place in a preserving pan with the onion, dates, banana and raisins and just cover with water. Simmer until tender. Crush and bruise the root ginger and add to the pan tied in a muslin bag.

Add the remaining ingredients, stirring well until the sugar dissolves over a gentle heat. Bring to the boil and continue boiling until the chutney is thick and reduced in volume. Remove the muslin bag containing the ginger and bottle and seal in the usual way.

Makes 2.5kg/5lb chutney

Red tomato chutney

Make this chutney when tomatoes are cheap at the end of the summer. It is easy to make at home and much more economical than buying commercially bottled jars. It is delicious with cold meats, pies and cheese.

2.5kg/5lb red tomatoes, skinned and chopped
150g/5oz onions, chopped
2 cloves garlic, crushed
25g/1oz pickling spice tied in muslin
900ml/1½ pints/3½ cups malt vinegar
10ml/2 teaspoons paprika
pinch of cayenne pepper
5ml/1 teaspoon mustard seeds
5ml/1 teaspoon ground allspice
5ml/1 teaspoon salt
450g/1lb/2 cups Demerara sugar
275g/10oz/1⅔ cups raisins

Place the tomatoes, onion, garlic and the bag of pickling spice in a preserving pan. Cook over low heat until tender. Add half the quantity of vinegar and all the spices and seasoning. Simmer until thick.

Add the remaining vinegar, sugar and raisins and stir over low heat until the sugar dissolves. Continue cooking until the chutney is thick. Remove the muslin bag and bottle in the usual way.

Makes approximately 3kg/6lb chutney

Apple ginger pie filling

This spicy mixture makes a lovely pie filling or can be added to stewed fruit, apple pies and crumbles as an additional flavouring. Bottled and sealed correctly, it will keep for several months. An alternative spice to ginger is cinnamon: make in the same way but substitute a 5cm/ 2in cinnamon stick, 5ml/1 teaspoon ground cinnamon, and a good pinch each of ground allspice and cloves.

2kg/4lb/8 cups soft brown sugar
1.8 litres/3 pints/7½ cups water
2kg/4lb cooking apples
2.5cm/1in cinnamon stick
25g/1oz/2 tablespoons ground ginger
25g/1oz/¼ cup chopped preserved stem ginger

Dissolve the sugar in the water, stirring all the time over a gentle heat and then bring to the boil. Boil hard until you have a thick sugar syrup.

Peel, core and thinly slice the apples and add to the sugar syrup with the cinnamon. Boil until the apples are soft and transparent and then add the ground ginger. Boil for 5 minutes and lastly stir in the stem ginger. Bottle and store in the usual way.

Spicy pear chutney

This dark red chutney is an excellent way of using up hard cooking pears or windfalls in the autumn. It complements all cold cooked meats. You can reduce or increase the amount of chilli powder according to how hot you like your chutney.

25g/1oz root ginger
12 cloves
5ml/1 teaspoon whole allspice berries
1.5kg/3lb pears, peeled, cored and sliced
450g/1lb cooking apples, peeled, cored and sliced
400g/14oz onions, chopped
400g/14oz/2⅔ cups raisins
1 clove garlic, crushed
400g/14oz green tomatoes, chopped
1.1litres/2 pints/5 cups white wine vinegar
5ml/1 teaspoon salt
2.5ml/½ teaspoon ground nutmeg
5ml/1 teaspoon chilli powder
675g/1½lb/3 cups soft brown sugar

Crush and bruise the root ginger and tie in a muslin bag with the cloves and allspice. Place in a preserving pan with all the ingredients except the sugar. Simmer for about 1½ hours until tender.

Add the sugar and stir over low heat until it dissolves. Bring to the boil, then simmer until the chutney thickens and reduces. Remove the muslin bag and bottle in the usual manner.

Makes approximately 4.5kg/9lb chutney.

Greengage relish

Greengages may sound like an unusual fruit to make into chutney but they do in fact make a delicious relish, especially if served with cheese and biscuits or cold meats.

1kg/2lb greengages
450g/1lb apples
450g/1lb onions, chopped
1 clove garlic, crushed
5g/¼oz root ginger, crushed
4 chillis
12 peppercorns
350g/12oz/2 cups raisins
225g/8oz/1 cup soft brown sugar
30ml/2 tablespoons honey
10ml/2 teaspoons ground ginger
5ml/1 teaspoon ground allspice
1.25ml/¼ teaspoon ground cloves
5ml/1 teaspoon dry mustard
5ml/1 teaspoon turmeric
15ml/1 tablespoon mustard seeds
salt and pepper
550ml/1 pint/2½ cups white wine vinegar

Wash and stone/pit the greengages. Peel, core and slice the apples. Place in a preserving pan with the onion and garlic and cover with water. Place the root ginger, chillis and peppercorns in a muslin bag and add to the pan. Cook gently until tender.

Add the remaining ingredients and cook over a gentle heat, stirring until all the sugar is completely dissolved. Boil the relish until reduced and thickened. Remove the bag and bottle in the usual way.

A colourful array of home-made liqueurs and preserves:
1 Cherry brandy
2 Quince vodka
3 Blackcurrant rum
4 Chestnuts in brandy
5 Pears in brandy
6 Orange liqueur
7 Sloe gin
8 Rumpot
9 Damson gin
10 Pineapple ratafia
11 Raspberries in sherry
12 Figs in brandy

Spiced orange slices

These preserved spicy slices of orange are delicious with ham or cold duck — a more sophisticated accompaniment for a special occasion than chutney or relish. They go particularly well with the left-over festive remains of the Christmas goose or turkey. The quantities given below will fill one large jar — double up to make 2 or 3 jars of the preserve, but a little goes a long way.

3 large seedless oranges
150ml/¼ pint/⅝ cup white wine vinegar
225g/8oz/1 cup granulated sugar
4 whole cloves
5ml/1 teaspoon whole allspice berries
2.5cm/1in stick of cinnamon
10ml/2 teaspoons brandy

Wash the oranges and cut them horizontally into 5mm/¼in thick slices. Place them in a pan and cover with water. Bring to the boil, reduce the heat to a gentle simmer and cook, covered, for about 1½ hours until they are tender.

Carefully remove the oranges with a slotted spoon and throw away the cooking liquid. Heat the vinegar, sugar and spices, stirring until all the sugar dissolves. Bring to the boil and add the orange slices. Add a little water if there is not enough liquid to cover the orange slices. Simmer for 30 minutes, remove the oranges and place in a warmed bottling jar.

Return the pan to the heat, add the brandy and boil hard until the syrup has reduced a little. Pour into the jar over the orange slices and seal in the usual way. Do not open and eat for at least a month.

Pumpkin chutney

Pumpkin may seem an unusual ingredient for a chutney, but, to our minds, this is the most delicious of all. A beautiful dark, golden-brown colour and full of succulent, tender chunks of pumpkin, this spicy chutney is marvellous served with hot curries. You can even stir a little into the curry sauce. You can use canned rather than fresh tomatoes in this recipe, if wished.

450g/1lb onions, chopped
1kg/2lb red tomatoes, skinned and chopped
1.1litres/2 pints/5 cups cider or white wine vinegar
3kg/6lb pumpkin flesh, cut in chunks
150g/5oz/¾ cup raisins
15ml/1 tablespoon salt
20ml/4 teaspoons ground ginger
10ml/2 teaspoons ground black pepper

10ml/2 teaspoons ground allspice
2 cloves garlic, crushed
5ml/1 teaspoon ground mace
2.5ml/½teaspoon ground cloves
1kg/2lb/4 cups soft brown sugar

Put the chopped onion and tomato in a preserving pan with half the quantity of vinegar. Cook gently for about 20 minutes until tender. Add the remaining vinegar and other ingredients and cook gently over low heat, stirring until the sugar dissolves.

Bring to the boil and boil rapidly until the chutney thickens and reduces. The pumpkin chunks should be tender but not mushy. Bottle in the usual manner.

Makes approximately 4kg/8lb chutney

Jams and jellies

Greengage jam

You may be surprised to learn that greengages make a delicious dark pink jam which is superb with buttered toast or muffins. You can crush a few stones/pits and add a little kernel for a faintly bitter almond flavour.

1kg/2lb greengages
225ml/8floz/1 cup water
1kg/2lb/4 cups soft brown sugar

Stone/pit the greengages and place in a preserving pan with the water. Simmer until the liquid is reduced and the fruit tender.

Add the sugar and stir well until dissolved. Bring to the boil and boil briskly for 10-15 minutes until setting point is reached. Skim the jam, pour into warmed jars and seal in the usual manner.

Makes 2kg/4lb jam

Apricot and almond jam

In this jam, the sweetness of the apricots is offset by the lemony flavour and crunchy texture of the nuts. It is a beautiful golden colour but does not keep as well as some jams after being opened. Keep in the refrigerator to prolong its life after opening.

1.5kg/3lb fresh apricots
300ml/½ pint/1¼ cups water
grated rind and juice of 1 lemon
1.5kg/3lb/6 cups soft brown sugar
40g/1½oz/¼ cup split almonds

Wash and stone/pit the apricots. Place in a preserving pan and cover with water. Stew gently until the fruit is tender. Add the lemon and sugar and stir over a gentle heat until thoroughly dissolved. Add the nuts. Bring to the boil and boil hard until the jam reaches setting point (about 110°C, 225°F). Skim the top and bottle in the usual way.

Makes about 2.5kg/5lb jam

Damson jam

In our opinion, damsons make the best jam of all — firm textured, fruity and an intensely deep purple in colour. Do not remove the stones/pits from the damsons before cooking — these add to the flavour. You can skim off some when they rise to the surface while the jam is cooking.

1.5kg/3lb damsons
550ml/1pint/2½ cups water
2kg/4lb/8 cups soft brown sugar

Wash the damsons, remove the stalks and place in a preserving pan with the water and simmer until tender (approximately 45 minutes).

Add the sugar and stir over a gentle heat until dissolved. Bring to the boil and boil rapidly until the jam reaches setting point. Remove the stones as they rise to the surface with a slotted spoon. Pour into warmed jars and seal in the usual way.

Makes 2.5kg/5lb jam

Quince jelly

The scented exotic quince originated in Asia and makes an exquisite bright pink jelly to serve with ham, pork, duck or game, or just to spread on bread and butter. Quinces are becoming rare and are stocked only by good greengrocers in the autumn. If you have an old house, you may be fortunate enough to have quince trees in your garden. The fruit should be cooked when it turns golden and ripe.

2kg/4lb quinces
5ml/1 teaspoon whole allspice berries
2.3litres/4 pints/10 cups water
15g/½oz powdered citric acid
sugar (see below)

Cut up the quinces roughly and place in a pan with the allspice and water. Bring to the boil and simmer for about 50 minutes until the fruit is tender. Strain through a jelly bag or double folded muslin cloth. The easiest way to do this is to hang the bag up above a large pan or bowl and leave it to drip for several hours or overnight.

Measure the liquid and bring to the boil. Remove from the heat and add the citric acid and sugar. Allow 450g/1lb/2 cups sugar to every 550ml/1 pint/2½ cups of juice. Stir over a gentle heat until the sugar dissolves. Bring to a rapid boil and then boil hard until the jelly reaches setting point (this takes about 15 minutes). Bottle in the usual way.

Makes approximately 1kg/2lb jelly

Lemon curd

Delicious for spreading on bread and toast or for filling tarts and sandwiching sponge cakes, lemon curd has a shelf life of only 6-8 weeks and should be stored in the refrigerator or a cool place after opening. You can make orange or lime curd in the same way using 3 oranges or 3 limes.

100g/4oz/½ cup butter
225g/8oz/1 cup caster/superfine sugar
grated rind and juice of 3 lemons
3 eggs

Melt the butter in the top of a double-boiler or in a basin suspended over a pan of hot water. Stir in the sugar, lemon rind and juice. Beat the eggs and strain through a sieve into the lemon mixture. Cook over gentle heat, stirring well until the lemon curd thickens. Pour into hot sterilised jars and seal in the usual way.

Makes approximately 450g/1lb lemon curd

Marrow and ginger jam

If you have the good fortune to live in the country and grow your own marrows in the garden, then this makes a very inexpensive jam. Marrow has a low pectin/acid content and thus some lemon juice is essential to get a good set. Rhubarb is another fruit which marries well with ginger and makes an excellent jam.

1.5kg/3lb marrow
15g/½oz root ginger
400ml/14floz/1¾ cups water
550g/1lb 4oz/2½ cups soft brown sugar
grated rind and juice of 1 lemon
100g/4oz preserved or crystallised ginger, chopped

Peel the marrow and remove the seeds. Cut into small chunks (the prepared marrow should weigh about 1.2kg/2½lb) and place in a preserving pan. Crush and bruise the root ginger, tie in a muslin bag and add with the water to the pan. Cook until tender.

Add the sugar and stir until dissolved. Next add the lemon rind and juice and the preserved ginger. Bring to the boil and boil hard for about 15 minutes until the jam reaches setting point. Remove the muslin bag, skim the jam and spoon into warmed jars. Seal in the usual way.

Makes 2kg/4lb jam

Plum and apple jam

Plums and apples, the fruits of late summer and early autumn, make an unusual and rewarding jam. Never be afraid to experiment with mixing fruits in new combinations — mixed fruits often make the best jams and preserves of all.

675g/1½lb plums
675g/1½lb apples
450ml/16floz/2 cups water
5ml/1 teaspoon ground cinnamon
1.5kg/3lb/6 cups soft brown sugar

Place the plums, stalks removed, in a preserving pan. Peel, core and slice the apples and add to the pan. Cover with the water and simmer gently until just tender.

Add the cinnamon and sugar and stir over a gentle heat until the sugar is completely dissolved. Bring to the boil and boil rapidly until the jam reaches setting point. Skim off any stones/pits that rise to the surface and cool slightly before pouring into hot jars and bottling in the usual way.

Makes 2.5kg/5lb jam

Strawberry preserve

This is one of the great summer preserves — full of juicy whole fruit. It is a jam that should be allowed to cool a little before bottling to prevent all the strawberries from floating to the tops of the jars.

2kg/4lb ripe strawberries
juice of 2 lemons
1.5kg/3lb sugar

Hull the strawberries and wipe them gently with kitchen paper. Place in a preserving pan with the lemon juice and cook gently over a low heat for about 15-20 minutes, stirring gently, until the fruit mixture reduces and the

juices run out.

Add the sugar and stir until it dissolves, taking care not to break up the fruit too much. Bring to the boil and boil until the jam reaches setting point. Remove the scum from the top of the jam and leave to cool for about 30 minutes until a skin forms on the surface of the jam. This will ensure that the fruit is evenly distributed throughout the jam when bottled. Stir well and bottle in hot jars in the usual way.

Makes approximately 3kg/6lb jam

Thick-cut orange marmalade

Breakfast marmalades are easy to make when Seville oranges are in the shops. They taste better than the commercial brands and keep well if stored in a dry, dark place such as a cool, ventilated cupboard or larder.

1.5kg/3lb Seville oranges
1 lemon
2.8 litres/5 pints/12½ cups water
3kg/6lb/12 cups preserving sugar
15g/½oz/1 tablespoon margarine

Wash the oranges and lemon in boiling water to remove the wax with which they are sprayed. Although this wax makes them last longer it also hardens the peel. Cut each orange in half, squeeze out the juice into a large pan. Cut the peel into shreds, place in the pan with the water. Tie all the orange pips/seeds in a piece of muslin and add to the pan. Leave for 24 hours.

The following day, bring to the boil, and then simmer for about 2 hours or until the peel is soft. Remove the bag of pips/seeds, cool and squeeze out any juice and pectin (this is the setting agent of the marmalade). Add the sugar and stir well over low heat until it dissolves. Bring to the boil and add the margarine to cut down on the scum that forms on the surface of the liquid. Boil hard. When the marmalade reaches setting point (104°C, 220°F), remove the pan from the heat and let it stand for 15-20 minutes. Skim off any scum.

Pour the marmalade into warmed, sterilised jars and seal and cover in the usual way.

Makes approximately 5kg/10lb marmalade

Home-made jams, pickles and chutneys are all good ways of preserving fruit and vegetables. Most will keep for several months if bottled and stored in a cool, dark place

Liqueurs and preserves

Blackcurrant rum

Blackcurrants steeped in rum with sugar make a delicious liqueur. It is made in many country districts of Great Britain and in Denmark where it is known as *solbaerrom*. The method is the same as for sloe gin.

450g/1lb/4 cups blackcurrants
900ml/1½ pints/3½ cups dark rum
350g/12oz/1½ cups sugar
6 blanched almonds

Prick or crush the blackcurrants after removing any stalks and leaves. Put them in a wide-necked jar with the rum, sugar and bruised almonds. Leave in a cool place for 2-3 months, shaking the jar occasionally. Strain through muslin to extract the fruit and all the sediment, and bottle. Leave the blackcurrant rum for 5-6 months before drinking.

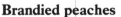

Brandied peaches

Perhaps the most delicious preserves of all are fruits in brandy or other spirits. They make a delicious dessert on cold winter days and may be added to pies and fruit salads or served with home-made ice-creams and sorbets. Never use a good brandy for preserving fruit — the cheaper French *marc* or supermarket brands are quite adequate. Although the initial cost may seem prohibitive, a little of this preserve goes a long way and keeps on the kitchen shelf for months and months. Make it in the summer when peaches are at their most abundant and cheap. To make one jar you need the following:

6 medium-sized peaches
400ml/14floz/1¾ cups water
300g/11oz/1⅜ cups sugar
2.5cm/1in stick cinnamon
150ml/¼ pint/⅝ cup brandy (approx. measure)

Wash the peaches and prick each several times with a fork. Place the water and half the quantity of sugar in a saucepan and bring slowly to the boil, stirring with a wooden spoon until the sugar has completely dissolved. Add the peaches and cinnamon and simmer gently for 6 - 7 minutes, turning the peaches occasionally. Then remove the peaches with a slotted spoon and put them aside to cool.

Add the remaining sugar to the pan and stir over a gentle heat until dissolved. Bring to the boil and continue boiling until you have a thick syrup (110°C on a sugar thermometer). Allow to cool.

Measure out an equal quantity of brandy and mix with the sugar syrup. Place the peaches in a large bottling jar and pour in the liquid. Seal and store in a cool place. The peaches are best if kept for 2 or 3 months before eating. Make them in the late summer to eat at Christmas.

Rumpot

A rumpot is a great standby in your kitchen for serving unexpected guests, dressing up ice-cream, filling special pies or flan-cases and gâteaux, or as an accompaniment to mousses and fools. You can use nearly any good-quality fruit except bananas, apples, pears and citrus fruits. Use a heavy stone or earthenware jar but a thick glass jar is more attractive so that you can view the colourful layers of fruit within. You can start making your rumpot at the beginning of the summer and add seasonal fruits to it as they come into the shops or you harvest them in your garden. By the autumn, it should be full and then you can leave it for three months or so to eat at Christmas. If the pot has no top, you can purchase a large cork at most stores and chemists which sell wine-making equipment.

Mixed fruit: strawberries, raspberries, blueberries, grapes,
*   melon (cut in cubes), greengages, plums, apricots,*
*   peaches, cherries, nectarines etc.*
Sugar: the same weight as the fruit
Rum: enough dark rum to cover the fruit

Wipe the fruit with a soft cloth to remove any dust or dirt. Do not wash it. Weigh out an equal quantity of sugar. Arrange the fruit in contrasting coloured layers in an earthenware or glass jar. Put the sugar and rum in a pan and stir over low heat until completely dissolved. Allow to cool and pour over the fruit, adding more rum if necessary.

Seal the jar with a cork, lid or stopper and add more fruit whenever you like and top up with more rum and sugar until the jar is full. Store for 2-3 months before eating. You can always replace any eaten fruit with more fruit and rum as the level in the rumpot drops.

Chestnuts in brandy

This is a luxurious way of preserving chestnuts when they are plentiful in the autumn. We collect the windfalls and make them into stuffings or roast them on the open fire, but we always save a few to make this splendid preserve. Seeped in brandy syrup, chestnuts can be used to uplift humble ice-cream or a fruit salad.

225g/8oz chestnuts in their shells
225g/8oz/1 cup sugar
300ml/½ pint/1¼ cups water
60ml/4 tablespoons brandy

Wash and dry the chestnuts and make a slit with a sharp knife in the pointed end of each one. Place the chestnuts in a pan and cover with water. Bring to the boil and cook steadily for 3 minutes. Remove from the heat, drain and peel off the shells and the inner skin. Place the peeled nuts in a pan of fresh water and bring to the boil. Simmer gently until cooked and tender but not over-soft and floury. Leave them to cool.

Make the syrup: dissolve the sugar in the water over low heat and then boil rapidly until reduced and thick. Remove from the heat, add the brandy and leave to cool. Pour over the chestnuts and bottle.

Damson gin

You can make a lovely pink liqueur with summer damsons using gin and sugar or even kirsch. It makes a warming winter drink. Remember when making these fruit liqueurs that they should always be stored in a cool, dry place away from direct heat and sunshine.

175g/6oz damsons
100g/4oz/½ cup sugar
450ml/16floz/2 cups gin
2 drops almond essence

Wash and dry the damsons and remove the stones/pits. Place in a wide-necked jar with the sugar, gin and almond essence. Seal and leave in a cool place for 3 months, shaking often. Strain and bottle in the usual way and drink after 2 months.

Pineapple ratafia

The advantage of this liqueur is that it can be made at any time of the year, unlike those ratafias made with seasonal fruits. Use cheap cooking brandy or the French *eau-de-vie de marc*, not quality brandy.

1 large pineapple
300ml/½ pint/1¼ cups brandy
225g/8oz/1 cup sugar

Slice the pineapple thinly, removing the thick, outer peel. Place the slices in a wide-necked jar or cut into chunks and place in a small jar. Add the sugar and cover with the brandy. Leave for 2-3 months before bottling and drinking.

You do not have to bottle the liqueur. You can use the pineapple in its lovely syrup as an extravagant topping for ice-cream or as a filling for special gâteaux.

Quince vodka

Quinces are less common then they used to be, but you can still buy them in the autumn to make quince jelly and pies or, more unusual and equally delicious, quince vodka. This tastes suprisingly good even a few weeks after it is made, but it is best to leave it for several months for a really smooth, mellow flavour.

4 quinces
350ml/12floz/1½ cups vodka
100g/4oz/½ cup sugar
pinch each of ground cinnamon and mace

Gently rub the grey fluff off the quinces and chop them finely, including the central core. Place in a bottling jar with the vodka, sugar and spices and seal. Leave in a cool, dark place for at least 3 months, shaking occasionally. Strain and bottle in the usual way and drink after 2-3 months.

Sloe gin

The best and most warming fruit liqueur of all, sloe gin should be made in the autumn after the first frosts. Sloes are the small, hard fruit of the blackthorn. These black berries with a bluish tinge can be harvested in the hedgerows but you must take care as the sloes nestle among sharp thorns. To make sloe vodka, just substitute the same quantity of vodka for gin.

450g/1lb/4 cups sloes
900ml/1½ pints/3½ cups gin
275g/10oz/1¼ cups sugar
8 blanched almonds

Prick the sloes all over with a sharp needle and discard any stalks and leaves. Place them in a large jar or bottle with the gin and sugar. Bruise the almonds and add to the jar. Seal or cork the jar and leave for 3 months, shaking occasionally to dissolve the sugar. As the weeks go by, the gin will gradually turn beautifully pink.

After a couple of months, taste the sloe gin and add

more sugar if necessary. This is a matter of personal taste. A good way to sweeten the liqueur is to dissolve the sugar over low heat in a little gin and then add to the liqueur. Strain the sloe gin twice through muslin before bottling. Although the gin can be drunk straight away, its flavour improves with keeping and it is a good idea to put a bottle down for the following year or even longer if you can bear it. Do not throw the sloes away after straining the gin — they can be mixed with chopped nuts and melted chocolate to make delicious petit-fours. Pour into a shallow tin, leave to harden and cut into squares.

Pears in brandy

Another spirited preserve, but this recipe uses hard pears and a smaller quantity of brandy. If you have a glut of cooking pears from your garden in the autumn, this is a good way to use them up and enables you to enjoy them throughout the year.

1.3kg/2½lb hard pears
grated rind and juice of 1½ lemons
1kg/2lb/4 cups soft brown sugar
4 cloves
2.5cm/1in stick of cinnamon
45ml/3 tablespoons brandy

Peel and core the pears and cut into quarters. Place a layer of pears in an ovenproof dish and scatter over some of the lemon rind and sugar. Continue layering in this way until all the pears are used up. Sprinkle the remaining sugar and the lemon juice over the top. Leave overnight in a cool place.

The next day, add the cloves and cinnamon stick and place in a preheated oven at 140°C, 275°F, gas 1 for 2-3 hours until tender and golden. Cool.

Place the pears in warm bottling jars. Add the brandy to the cooking juice and pour over the pears. Seal and store in a cool place.

Orange liqueur

Served at the end of a good dinner or mixed with soda water or sparkling white wine as a light aperitif, orange liqueur is a delicious drink. It can also be used in cooking to flavour fruit salads, soufflés, mousses and cakes, and every time you peel an orange, you can top up the level in the liqueur bottle with some more peel. Again, use a cheap brandy and some large juicy oranges.

You can add a little fruity white wine to the liqueur to make it go further.

1kg/2lb large juicy oranges
1 litre/1¾ pints/4¼ cups brandy
450g/1lb/2 cups caster/superfine sugar
1 cinnamon stick

Peel the oranges with a potato peeler and cut the peel into thin julienne strips. Squeeze the oranges and mix the juice with the brandy and sugar. Add the strips of rind and the cinnamon stick and pour into a large bottling jar and seal. Leave for 2-3 months, shaking occasionally, before drinking. If the liqueur is very cloudy, strain it through muslin into clean bottles and cork them. Store in a dry, cool place.

Cherry brandy

Home-made cherry brandy tastes delicious and you can eat the fruit floating in it as well as the liqueur. Use the slightly sour Morello cherries if you can get hold of some. Cherry brandy is one of the liqueurs that improves enormously with age, and if you can bear to leave it for several years you will be well rewarded by its exquisite flavour and smoothness. However, for the more impatient among us, it can be drunk after 6 months, although it will keep for up to 20 years or more. The quantities of cherries and brandy will depend on your own purse and weakness for the drink, so find a wide-necked bottling jar and fill it with:

cherries, stalks trimmed and pricked all over
sugar to come halfway up the jar
brandy to cover the fruit

Cork or seal the jar and store in a dry, cool, dark place for at least 6 months before drinking. Shake the jar gently once a week to dissolve the sugar. In time, the liqueur will acquire a mellowness and a slight flavour of almonds. Drink the liqueur and use the cherries as a special topping for ice-cream.

Tip: You can make other delicious liqueurs and fruit preserves in the same way as outlined above. Here are some unusual ideas for you to try at home:
1 Raspberries bottled with sugar in brandy or sherry.
2 Figs bottled in a syrup of brandy and honey.
3 Apricots bottled in a brandy sugar syrup.
4 Plums or damsons in brandy sweetened with sugar and flavoured with bruised, blanched almonds.

Basic Recipes

Basic wholemeal shortcrust pastry

Use this basic pastry for pies, flans and quiches. You can mix it by hand or in a food processor. Ensure that the fat is soft and not too hard by removing it from the refrigerator several hours before using it.

225g/8oz/2¼ cups wholemeal flour
pinch of salt
100g/4oz/½ cup margarine
45-60ml/3-4 tablespoons cold water

Sift the flour and salt into a large bowl. Cut the margarine into small pieces and rub into the flour until the mixture resembles fine breadcrumbs. Mix in the cold water with a rounded or palette knife until the mixture binds to form a soft dough. Knead gently until smooth on a lightly floured board and then rest in the refrigerator for 10 minutes before rolling out and using.

Makes 225g/8oz pastry

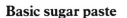

Basic sugar paste

This sweet pastry is ideal for making sweet pies and flans. It is easily made in a food mixer or processor. Always rest and chill the dough in the refrigerator before rolling out and using. It is best to soften the margarine or warm the processor bowl before starting. The pastry can be made in advance in large batches and frozen until required.

150g/5oz/⅝ cup margarine
50g/2oz/¼ cup superfine/caster or soft brown sugar
1 large egg
pinch of salt
225g/8oz/2¼ cups plain flour

Cream the margarine and sugar until soft and fluffy. Add the egg and salt and blend well. Add the flour and process again until the dough forms a smooth ball which leaves the side of the bowl clean. Chill in the refrigerator before using.

Makes 225g/8oz sugar paste

Herb croûtons

Serve these crisp green croûtons with soup as an attractive garnish. They go well with smooth, puréed vegetable soups.

30ml/2 tablespoons chopped fresh parsley
10ml/2 teaspoons chopped fresh thyme

1 clove garlic
75g/3oz/6 tablespoons margarine
salt and pepper
2 thick slices of bread, crusts removed

Place the chopped herbs, garlic and margarine in an electric blender and liquidise until smooth. Season with salt and pepper and heat the mixture in a frying pan over gentle heat. Cut the bread into 1.25mm/¼ inch dice and add to the pan. Fry in the herb mixture until green and crisp. Drain and use as a garnish for soup.

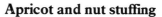

Apricot and nut stuffing

You can use this stuffing mixture for poultry or lamb. Instead of using fresh breadcrumbs, you can use 50g/2oz/¼ cup long-grain brown rice cooked in boiling salted water for 15 minutes. Mix with the other ingredients as described in the method below.

100g/4oz/2 cups fresh breadcrumbs
15ml/1 tablespoon chopped parsley
2.5ml/½ teaspoon each of thyme and oregano
5ml/1 teaspoon lemon balm (optional)
grated rind and juice of 1 lemon
100g/4oz/¾ cup dried apricots, soaked overnight and chopped
50g/2oz/½ cup chopped walnuts or pine nuts
salt and pepper
good pinch each of ground nutmeg and mace
15ml/1 tablespoon oil
1 egg, beaten

Mix all the ingredients together in a large bowl until well-blended. If the stuffing seems too dry, add a little hot water or more beaten egg to bind it. Fill the cavity of a chicken or a boned leg of lamb with the stuffing and roast in the usual way. Or you can bake the stuffing separately in a well-greased ovenproof dish at 190°C, 375°F, gas 5 for about 1 hour until golden-brown and crisp on top. Serve with a roast bird or joint.

Makes approximately 225g/8oz/2 cups stuffing

Mulled wine

This makes a warming drink on winter evenings and always goes down well at parties and Christmas-time. This amount makes 6-8 glasses, so increase the quantities if you are having a party. Serve in strong, heat-resistant glasses as the hot liquid may crack ordinary glasses.

1 bottle claret
3 cloves
1 cinnamon stick
good pinch of grated nutmeg
1 lemon, thinly sliced
1 orange, thinly sliced
50g/2oz/¼ cup soft brown sugar
300ml/½ pint/1¼ cups water
50ml/2 floz/¼ cup port wine or brandy (optional)

Put all the ingredients in a pan and place over low heat, stirring gently until the sugar has dissolved. Heat through very gently until the mulled wine almost reaches boiling point, but do not allow to boil. Simmer for 10-15 minutes and remove the cinnamon stick and cloves before serving.

Serves 6-8

Apricot glaze

This is used to brush over hot open apple and pear tarts or to give Danish pastries their glossy golden finish. It can be made in larger quantities if wished and stored in the freezer or refrigerator until required.

450g/1lb apricot jam or jelly
75ml/5 tablespoons water
lemon juice to taste

Place the jam and water in a heavy pan and stir gently over low heat until the jam dissolves. Boil gently and quickly until the glaze is clear and smooth and add a little lemon juice. Brush the warm glaze over tarts or Danish pastries.

Sauces and stocks

Basic chicken stock

Home-made stock always gives a dish a better flavour than a stock made with bouillon cubes and boiling water, so it is well worth knowing how to make it. Use the carcase of a chicken, turkey or even game birds, and freeze what you don't need straight away in handy 300ml/½ pint/1¼ cup or 550ml/1 pint/2½ cup containers for future use.

450g/1lb chicken bones and any skin
1.1 litres/2 pints/5 cups water
1 whole onion, skinned
1 whole carrot, peeled

Wash the bones or carcase and place in a large pan with the water. Bring to the boil and skim off any fat on the surface. Add the vegetables and simmer gently for 2 hours. Strain and use.

Makes 1.1 litres/2 pints/5 cups stock

Basic beef stock

This stock is made with beef bones which can be obtained from your butcher. Use it in soups, stews and casseroled dishes.

1kg/2lb beef bones
2.1 litres/4 pints/10 cups water
1 onion, peeled
1 carrot, peeled

Wash the bones and trim away any excess fat. Place in a large saucepan with the water and bring to the boil. Reduce the heat to a simmer, add the whole onion and carrot and half-cover the pan. Simmer gently for 3-4 hours. Strain and use, or cool and freeze until required.

Makes 2.1 litres/4 pints/10 cups stock

Court-bouillon

Fish can be poached in a court-bouillon if it is to be served either hot or cold. This is a good way of cooking salmon. Add 300ml/½ pint/1¼ cups white wine for a really special stock.

1 onion, sliced
1 carrot, sliced
1 stick celery, sliced
2 litres/3 pints/7¼ cups water
1 bay leaf
sprig of parsley and thyme
6 peppercorns
fish trimmings (optional)

Place the onion, carrot, celery and water in a large saucepan with the bay leaf. Tie the herbs and peppercorns in a small piece of muslin cloth to make a *bouquet garni* and add to the pan with the fish trimmings and white wine (optional). Bring to the boil, cover with a lid and then simmer for at least 30 minutes. Strain and use for poaching fish or as a stock for fish soups and sauces. If covered, the court-bouillon will stay fresh in the ref-rigerator for up to 3 days. You can reduce the stock for making sauces by boiling hard after straining it.

Makes 2 litres/3 pints/7¼ cups court-bouillon

Basic béchamel sauce

This is the most basic white sauce of all. It should always be smooth and glossy and can be used as a coating sauce for meat and vegetables, a binding sauce, a pouring sauce or as the basis of some savoury dishes such as hot soufflés.

Coating sauce:
300ml/½ pint/1¼ cups milk
½ onion, studded with 1 clove
25g/1oz/2 tablespoons margarine
25g/1oz/3 tablespoons flour

Thick binding sauce:
150ml/¼ pint/⅝ cup milk
¼ onion, studded with 1 clove
25g/1oz/2 tablespoons margarine
25g/1oz/3 tablespoons flour

Pouring sauce:
550ml/1 pint/2½ cups milk
1 onion, studded with 1 clove
25g/1oz/2 tablespoons margarine
25g/1oz/3 tablespoons flour

All 3 versions of this basic sauce are made using the same method. Place the milk and clove-studded onion in a pan and bring to the boil. Quickly reduce the heat and simmer gently for 5 minutes. Remove from the heat, cover the pan and leave for 15 minutes until the milk is infused. Strain and set aside to make the sauce.

Melt the margarine in a clean pan and stir in the flour to make the *roux*. Cook for 1 minute over gentle heat and then gradually beat in the strained warm milk until the sauce is smooth, thick and glossy. When the sauce starts to bubble, reduce the heat and simmer gently for 5 minutes. Season and use as required.

Basic velouté sauce

This is made in the same way as a béchamel sauce but using stock instead of milk. It can be mixed with a little cream and chopped vegetables, fish or meat as a filling for vol-au-vents, or blended with fortified wines to make a tasty sauce.

50g/2oz/¼ cup margarine
50g/2oz/6 tablespoons flour
550ml/1 pint/2½ cups chicken stock
salt and pepper

Melt the margarine and stir in the flour. Cook for 1-2 minutes over gentle heat. Gradually beat in the boiling stock until the sauce is thick and smooth. Season to

taste and add a squeeze of lemon juice if wished.
Makes 550ml/1 pint/2½ cups sauce

Barbecue sauce

This tangy tomato sauce can be served with kebabs, grilled/broiled meat, sausages and spare ribs. It is quickly and easily made and small quantities can be frozen for future use.

1 onion, finely chopped
1 clove garlic, chopped
25g/1oz/2 tablespoons margarine
450g/1lb canned tomatoes
15ml/1 tablespoon wine vinegar
15ml/1 tablespoon brown sugar
1.25ml/¼ teaspoon cayenne pepper
5ml/1 teaspoon made mustard
1 thick slice of lemon
30ml/2 tablespoons Worcestershire sauce
60ml/4 tablespoons tomato ketchup
15ml/1 tablespoon tomato paste
salt and pepper

Sauté the onion and garlic in the margarine until tender. add the canned tomatoes, vinegar, sugar, cayenne, mustard and slice of lemon. Bring to the boil and cook vigorously for about 15 minutes until the sauce reduces and thickens. Stir in the remaining ingredients and continue cooking for another 5 minutes, or until the sauce is thick with a tangy flavour. Remove the lemon slice, adjust the seasoning and serve.

Makes approximately 300ml/½ pint/1¼ cups sauce

Fresh tomato sauce

Serve this sauce with vegetable terrine or cold fish. It is very refreshing and can be made in seconds in a blender or food processor. It is flavoured with fresh herbs and sautéed shallots.

450g/1lb tomatoes, skinned and chopped
100g/4oz shallots or onions, chopped
30ml/2 tablespoons olive oil
few leaves fresh basil or 5ml/1 teaspoon dried basil
5ml/1 teaspoon oregano
5ml/1 teaspoon caster/superfine sugar
salt and pepper
juice of ½ lemon

Place the skinned tomatoes in a blender or processor

and process until well-puréed. Sauté the shallots in the olive oil until soft and add the tomato purée with the herbs, sugar, seasoning and lemon juice. Process for a few seconds and serve chilled.

Makes 300ml/½ pint/1¼ cups sauce

Avocado sauce

This delicious, quick sauce goes well with fish and chicken kebabs, cold shellfish and many salads.

1 large, ripe avocado
juice of 1 lemon
150ml/¼ pint/⅝ cup natural yoghurt
salt and pepper
chopped chives and parsley

Peel and stone the avocado and scoop out the flesh. Mash with the lemon juice and yoghurt, and check the seasoning. Sprinkle with chopped fresh herbs and serve immediately.

Mushroom sauce

This sharp, creamy sauce is based on an old Russian recipe and goes well with lamb and chicken dishes or can be used as a filling for vol-au-vents.

225g/½lb large (preferably field) mushrooms
1 onion
15g/½oz/1 tablespoon margarine
salt and pepper
150ml/¼pint/⅝ cup soured cream
few drops mushroom ketchup (optional)
2.5ml/½ teaspoon chopped fresh or dried dill

Chop the mushrooms and onion and sauté in the margarine over low heat for 10-15 minutes until soft. If a lot of juice runs out of the mushrooms, turn the heat up high for 2-3 minutes until it evaporates.

Season and gently stir in the soured cream, a little at a time. Add a few drops of mushroom ketchup, if wished, and the dill. Pour into a sauce boat, sprinkle with more dill and serve.

Orange sauce

This sweet orange sauce can be served with many desserts, especially hot soufflés and baked or puréed fruit. It is simple to make and, if kept in a screw-top jar, can be stored in the refrigerator for several days. For a more bitter-sweet sauce, use less sugar.

2 oranges
300ml/½ pint/1¼ cups water
225g/8oz/1 cup sugar
5ml/1 teaspoon arrowroot

Wash the oranges and peel thinly with a potato peeler. Place the peel and water in a pan and heat until it *almost* boils. Remove from the heat, cover and let it stand for 10 minutes.

Mix the sugar and arrowroot together in a basin and strain the orange water over the top, discarding the peel. Stir well and heat to boiling point, stirring all the time until the sauce thickens. Boil for 1 minute, remove from the heat and add the squeezed juice of the 2 oranges. Cool and serve.

Makes 300ml/½ pint/1¼ cups sauce

Salad dressings

Yoghurt salad dressing

A lemony yoghurt dressing complements the fresh crispness of many salads and can be mixed in seconds. It is healthier and more slimming than mayonnaise and oily French dressings.

150ml/¼ pint/⅝ cup natural yoghurt
salt and pepper
juice of ½ small lemon
30ml/2 tablespoons chopped chives

Mix the yoghurt, seasoning, lemon juice and chives together and decorate with more chives if wished. You can add chopped spring onions/shallots, crushed garlic or a pinch of mustard powder to vary the flavour.

Makes 150ml/¼ pint/⅝ cup dressing

Blue cheese salad dressing

The best cheese to use in this dressing is Roquefort. It crumbles easily and has a delicious slightly salty flavour. However, creamy blue cheeses, such as Gorgonzola, are also suitable. Serve with green or spinach salads.

100ml/4floz/½ cup natural yoghurt
75g/3oz Roquefort or other blue cheese, crumbled
15ml/1 tablespoon soured cream
squeeze of lemon juice
freshly ground black pepper
chopped chives to garnish

Mix all the ingredients together until thick, smooth

and creamy with a fork, or blend in a liquidiser. Toss the salad of your choice in the dressing and sprinkle with chopped chives.

Makes 150ml/¼ pint/⅝ cup dressing

Basic mayonnaise

To make a perfect mayonnaise, all the ingredients should be at room temperature before beginning. It is no good using eggs straight from the refrigerator or olive oil so cold that it has congealed. Remember to add the oil very slowly indeed, initially in drops, and only when the sauce starts to thicken in a thin, steady trickle. If it is added too quickly, the mayonnaise may well curdle. However, it can be saved by breaking another egg yolk into a clean bowl and then slowly adding the curdled mayonnaise, beating all the time until the sauce 'takes' and thickens. The mayonnaise can be made by hand with a hand-held or an electric whisk, or in a blender or food processor.

2 egg yolks
2.5ml/½ teaspoon salt
2.5ml/½ teaspoon dry mustard
freshly ground black pepper
15ml/1 tablespoon white wine vinegar
300ml/½ pint/1¼ cups olive or salad oil
15ml/1 tablespoon hot water
squeeze of lemon juice (optional)

Whisk the egg yolks, salt, mustard, pepper and vinegar together until thoroughly blended. Add the oil, drop by drop, whisking all the time until the sauce starts to thicken. Then add the oil more quickly in a thin, steady trickle, whisking well until all the oil is incorporated. Stir in the hot water to stop the mayonnaise separating and a squeeze of lemon juice if wished.

Makes 300ml/½ pint/1¼ cups mayonnaise

Ailloli

This provençal garlic mayonnaise is traditionally served with cold fish or bouillabaisse. You can vary the amount of garlic, depending on personal taste and the sensitive noses of your family and friends! Ailloli may also be served with a dish of *crudités* (raw vegetables) or as a sauce for new potatoes and hard-boiled eggs.

6 cloves garlic
2 egg yolks

good pinch salt
300ml/½ pint/1¼ cups olive oil
5ml/1 teaspoon lemon juice
freshly ground black pepper

Crush the cloves of garlic in a mortar until pulpy. Mix in the egg yolks and salt with a wooden spoon and stir well. Gradually add the olive oil, beating all the time. Add it drop by drop initially until the mayonnaise starts to thicken and becomes creamy, and then in a steady trickle, beating until it is used up and the sauce is really thick. Add the lemon juice and some freshly ground black pepper. Check the seasoning and serve. The ailloli should be really thick, smooth and golden with a distinctive garlic flavour. You can make it in a blender goblet or food processor if you prefer.

Makes 300ml/½ pint/1¼ cups ailloli

Green mayonnaise

You can make this mayonnaise in your electric blender or food processor. As long as you bear a few simple rules in mind, making mayonnaise in this way is very easy. Never use eggs straight from the refrigerator or oil that is too warm or has congealed with cold. Make sure that eggs and oil are at room temperature. Use white wine, tarragon or cider vinegar in preference to malt which has a harsher, more overpowering flavour. Lastly, if having taken all these precautions the mayonnaise still curdles, then simply start all over again and beat the curdled mayonnaise into a fresh egg yolk. Serve this mayonnaise with salads and fish or vegetable terrines.

2 egg yolks
15ml/1 tablespoon white wine vinegar
pinch of dry mustard
salt and pepper
225ml/8floz/1 cup olive oil
30ml/2 tablespoons lemon juice
45ml/3 tablespoons chopped fresh herbs (chives, parsley, basil, tarragon or chervil)

Put the egg yolks, vinegar, mustard and seasoning into the blender or food processor and blend them together. With the machine still operating, pour in the oil in a slow, steady, thin trickle. Process until the mayonnaise becomes thick and creamy. Add the lemon juice and chopped herbs, blend for a few seconds until the mayonnaise is a delicate, pale green and then switch off the power. Transfer to a serving dish and serve.

Makes 300ml/½pint/1¼ cups mayonnaise

Index